THE ROUGH GUIDE TO

DORSET, HAMPSHI[...] & THE ISLE OF WI[...]

written and researched by
Matthew Hancock and Amanda Tomlin

roughguides.com

E58
E2
E167
Pro-Teign
DREAM CHASER

Contents

OPPOSITE LYME REGIS HARBOUR **PREVIOUS PAGE** PILSDON PEN, DORSET

Introduction to Dorset, Hampshire and the Isle of Wight

Dorset, Hampshire and the Isle of Wight may be relatively small but they pack in a diverse array of riches, including fantastic coastline, stunning unspoilt countryside and some beautiful places to stay. Within a couple of hours' drive of London, you can be cycling in two of England's finest national parks, discovering the country's only UNESCO Natural Heritage Site, exploring its original capital city and its largest island, or hiking along Britain's longest footpath. And that's before you've even sampled the excellent local restaurants or laid your towel on some of the country's finest beaches.

The verdant, well-to-do county of Hampshire is commutable from the capital, and provides a comfortable lifestyle for many, much as it did when Jane Austen lived here. Its biggest draws are the **New Forest** and the **sailing** resorts of the Solent. It's also home to two of England's greatest ports: **Southampton**, today with a burgeoning nightlife and great shopping, and the traditional powerhouse of the navy, **Portsmouth**, with its iconic Spinnaker Tower and historic dockyards.

Separated geographically from Hampshire some seven thousand years ago, the **Isle of Wight** – the smallest county in England, at least when the tide is in – lies only a few miles offshore, but has an altogether different atmosphere. Much of the island has retained a feel of the 1950s, with no motorways, little development, few large-scale buildings and a distinctly laidback lifestyle. It has long been popular for its small seaside resorts and bracing walks, not to mention its unusual geology, most evident in the rock stacks of the **Needles**, the countless fossils found on its coastline and the striped cliffs of **Alum Bay**. The island also hosts some of the country's best **festivals** – including the famous Cowes sailing week, the Isle of Wight music festival, which pulls in the biggest names in rock and pop, and the more independent Bestival.

ABOVE STUDLAND BAY

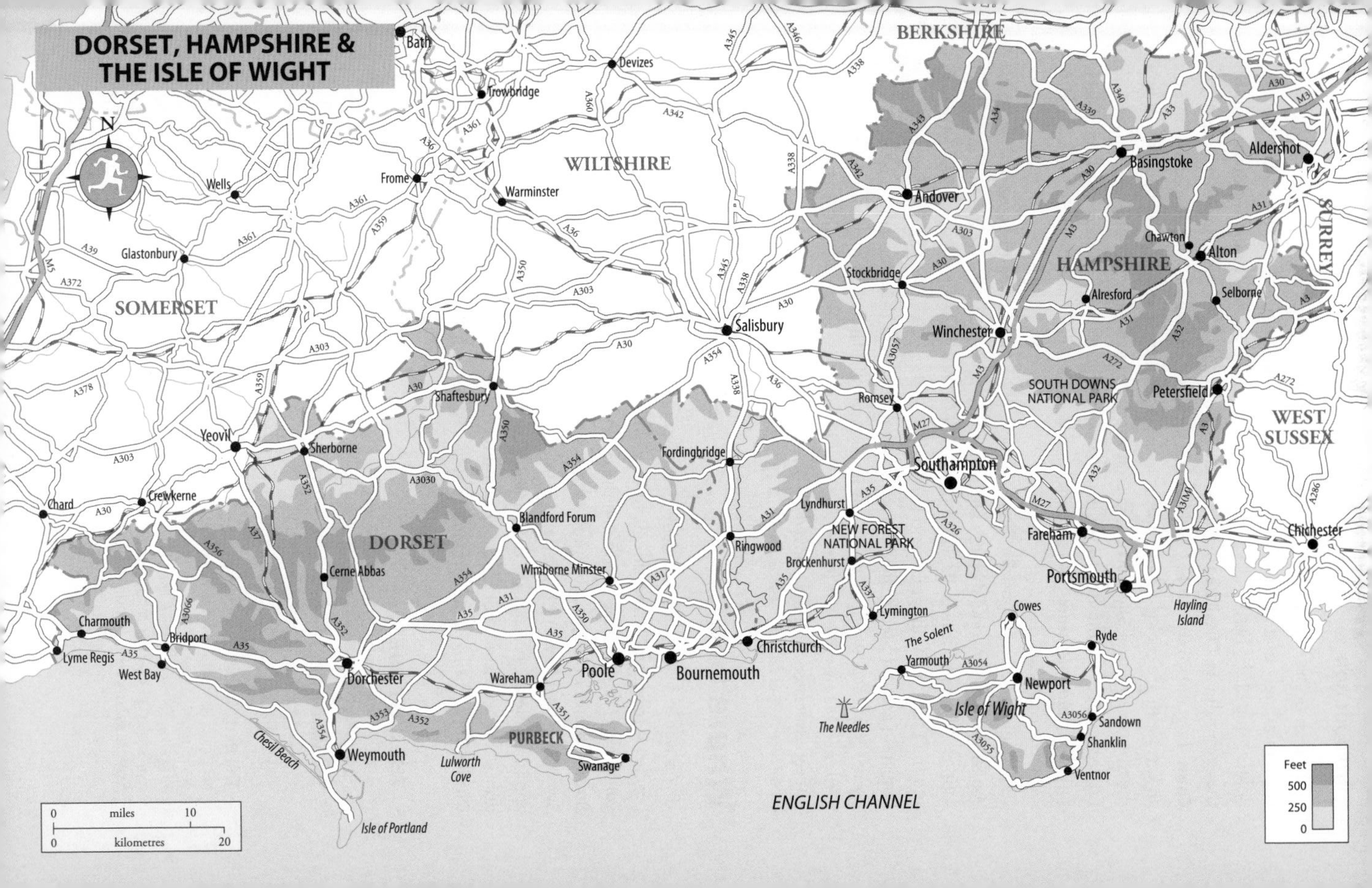

DORSET, HAMPSHIRE & THE ISLE OF WIGHT
N
BERKSHIRE
SURREY
WILTSHIRE
SOMERSET
HAMPSHIRE
WEST SUSSEX
DORSET
PURBECK
SOUTH DOWNS NATIONAL PARK
NEW FOREST NATIONAL PARK
Isle of Wight
ENGLISH CHANNEL
The Solent
The Needles
Hayling Island
Chesil Beach
Lulworth Cove
Isle of Portland
Bath
Devizes
Trowbridge
Frome
Warminster
Wells
Glastonbury
Salisbury
Yeovil
Sherborne
Shaftesbury
Chard
Crewkerne
Blandford Forum
Cerne Abbas
Wimborne Minster
Charmouth
Lyme Regis
Bridport
West Bay
Dorchester
Weymouth
Wareham
Poole
Bournemouth
Swanage
Christchurch
Fordingbridge
Ringwood
Lyndhurst
Brockenhurst
Lymington
Yarmouth
Cowes
Newport
Ryde
Sandown
Shanklin
Ventnor
Southampton
Romsey
Stockbridge
Andover
Winchester
Basingstoke
Aldershot
Chawton
Alton
Alresford
Selborne
Petersfield
Fareham
Portsmouth
Chichester
Feet
500
250
0
miles
kilometres
10
20

The west of the island overlooks **Dorset**, that much further from the capital and correspondingly more rural and unspoilt. Most visitors flock to its coastline, which boasts some of the best beaches in the UK – from the extensive sands of **Bournemouth** to the extraordinary **Chesil Beach** off the Isle of Portland. It also embraces the **Jurassic Coast**, England's only UNESCO Natural Heritage Site, whose varied coastline exposes an extraordinary geological mixture of rock stacks, arches and coves. Inland, you'll find the historic towns of **Sherborne** and **Shaftesbury** as well as pretty, quintessentially English villages surrounded by rolling downs, heathlands and deep river valleys. This is superb terrain for nature lovers, cyclists and walkers, and is usually fairly uncrowded even when the coasts are heaving.

The region's strategic position between the capital and the coast has made it home to countless famous people throughout the ages, from the legendary King Arthur (whose supposed Round Table is displayed in Winchester) to Sir Walter Raleigh in Sherborne, and the Duke of Wellington, who lived in Hampshire's Stratfield Saye. Some of England's greatest literary figures are also associated with the area – you can visit the former residences of Charles Dickens in Portsmouth; Jane Austen, who spent much of her life in Hampshire; T.E. Lawrence, who lived in Dorset; and Thomas Hardy, who is forever associated with his beloved "Wessex".

Where to go

If you want a seaside holiday, there are plenty of options: the **Isle of Wight** has a variety of beaches – from pebble and shingle to fine sand – and wherever you go on the island, you're never far from the sea. For all the facilities of a large resort, look no further than **Bournemouth** or **Weymouth**, both with fantastic, sandy town beaches. Smaller in scale, **Swanage**, **West Bay** and **Lyme Regis** exude plenty of traditional, bucket-and-spade appeal, while the beaches around **Shell Bay** are hard to beat, backed by miles of sand dunes and heathland. For a quieter swimming spot, try the wonderful pebble beach at **Durdle Door**, the bay at **Chapman's Pool** (accessible only by boat or on foot) or the

THE BEST PUBS

From beachside inns to thatched rural gastropubs, the region boasts plenty of alluring spots for a swift pint. Here are our favourites.

The Mayfly Near Stockbridge (Hampshire). Delicious food, fine beers and an idyllic garden next to the clear-flowing River Test. See p.202

The Red Shoot (New Forest). Tasty local produce, its own microbrewery and fine walks nearby. See p.179

Ship Inn (New Forest). A bustling gastropub overlooking Lymington harbour. See p.188

Spyglass Inn Ventnor (Isle of Wight). Great location right on the seafront, a lively atmosphere and huge portions of delicious food. See p.268

The Square and Compass Worth Matravers (Dorset). Simply the best pub in Dorset, straight out of a Hardy novel. See p.79

The Dancing Man Brewery Southampton (Hampshire). Enjoy fine home-brewed beers and good food at this atmospheric microbrewery in Southampton's medieval Wool House. See p.227

OPPOSITE FROM TOP GOLD HILL, SHAFTESBURY; PORTSMOUTH WITH SPINNAKER TOWER

sand-and-shingle beaches of **Highcliffe** and **Hengistbury Head**, backed by sandstone cliffs. The coasts are also rich in wildlife, with a sea-horse reserve in **Studland**, puffins nesting on the cliffs at **Durlston**, Britain's largest colony of mute swans at **Abbotsbury**, and the rare red squirrel thriving on the Isle of Wight and **Brownsea Island**.

History fans will find much to explore, too: this area was historic Wessex, where England's first kings – including, perhaps, King Arthur – made their home. Formerly England's capital, **Winchester** offers a fascinating insight into the country's past, while the region's mighty castles include **Corfe Castle**, **Sherborne** and **Carisbrooke** on the Isle of Wight. There's also **Maiden Castle** near Dorchester, a superb example of an Iron Age defensive settlement, while **Cerne Abbas**'s chalk giant dates back at least to Roman times. Maritime history is richly evident in **Southampton** and **Portsmouth**, home to the *Mary Rose* and Nelson's HMS *Victory*.

Contemporary seafarers are spoilt for choice, too, with major sailing centres at **Lymington**, **Cowes**, **Poole Harbour** and **Portland**, site of the 2012 Olympic sailing events. Other watersports, such as windsurfing, kayaking and kitesurfing, are all on offer along the coast. For the less sporty, there are some fantastic museums and family attractions, including the **National Motor Museum** at Beaulieu, **Bovington Tank Museum**, and the fairground rides at **Blackgang Chine** on the Isle of Wight.

For many people, however, it is the rural beauty and timeless quality of the countryside, in particular its two national parks – the New Forest and the South Downs – that make these regions so special. Hikers should look no further than the **South West Coast Path**, Britain's longest footpath, which starts at Poole and follows the Dorset coast to Lyme Regis. And there are fantastic walks inland, including superb river rambles along the **Itchen**, upriver from **Buckler's Hard**, north along the **Test**, and throughout the **New Forest** and the Isle of Wight, both crisscrossed with cycleways and footpaths.

When to go

The region has a relatively **mild climate**, with a south-facing, sheltered coastline and few extremes of weather. The **summer** is the obvious time to head for the coastal resorts, though you'll be hard pushed to find space to lay your towel on a hot day during the school holidays. This is peak time on the roads and for accommodation prices too: other busy times are Easter, Christmas, New Year and the school half-terms, and it is also sensible to avoid travelling on Friday evenings, when people flock down for the weekend. The very best times to visit are May and June, when the countryside is at its most lush, the evenings long and the weather often superb. **Spring** is perfect for exploring the New Forest, when its woodlands and heaths are peppered with ponies and their foals, while **autumn** sees an explosion of spectacular colours, as well as pigs roaming wild in search of acorns.

Winter, too, has its attractions: it's hard to beat holing up in a country pub in front of a log fire after a long walk on a crisp, sunny winter's day. The flipside is that when it rains, many of the region's best footpaths become virtually impassable or treacherously slippery. Some of the seaside resorts and more remote attractions and accommodation options may also close in low season. This, however, gives a certain desolate appeal to some of the coastal towns such as Lyme Regis and Swanage, with the additional advantage of quieter roads and easier parking.

Author picks

Our authors have explored every corner of the region over the last few years and share their favourite experiences here.

Eco retreats No need to worry about your carbon footprint at Bournemouth's eco-friendly *Green House Hotel* (p.47), while the superbly located *Pig on the Beach* (p.72) serves up plenty of locally foraged and home-reared produce. For luxury and comfort with a low environmental impact, the treehouse and shepherd's huts at the Isle of Wight's *Into the Woods* (p.252) have a real wow factor, or there's low-carbon camping at *Eweleaze Farm* near Weymouth (p.115).

Hidden coastal spots You can't beat a crab pasty at Steephill Cove (p.266) on the Isle of Wight, a hidden gem of a fishing hamlet. For seclusion even in the height of summer though, try Chapman's Pool (p.79), which you can only reach on foot.

Favourite walk Though barely outside the suburbs of Bournemouth, it's hard to beat a brisk walk over Hengistbury Head (p.46), with its memorable views over Christchurch harbour.

Wild swimming Head to the remote Dancing Ledge (p.77), a rocky ledge off the Purbecks, to experience wild swimming at its best.

Picnic spot The New Forest has endless spots for a picnic, but we love Ober Water (p.165), with its ancient trees, cooling stream and lots of rope swings to dangle from.

Top restaurant For sumptuous, innovative cocktails and top-quality cuisine, search out *The Larderhouse* in the Bournemouth suburb of Southbourne (p.49), our favourite dining spot.

Best views There's a dazzling urban landscape visible from Spinnaker Tower (p.234), but you'll see the best of rural Dorset from the Hardy Monument (p.96) and get views of amazing coastal scenery from Swyre Head (p.81).

Our author recommendations don't end here. We've flagged up our favourite places – a perfectly sited hotel, an atmospheric café, a special restaurant – throughout the guide, highlighted with the ★ symbol.

FROM TOP DANCING LEDGE; SHADY PICNIC SPOT IN THE NEW FOREST; THE VIEW FROM SPINNAKER TOWER

16

things not to miss

It's not possible to see everything Dorset, Hampshire and the Isle of Wight have to offer on a short trip. What follows is a selective taste of the region's highlights: quaint pubs, majestic castles, fun activities and intriguing architecture. All highlights are colour-coded by chapter and have a page reference to take you straight into the Guide, where you can find out more.

1

1 DURDLE DOOR
Page 81
Swim under this iconic limestone arch from the adjacent pebble beach.

2 PADDLE BOARDING, POOLE HARBOUR
Page 59
The world's second-largest natural harbour is perfect for water sports, including kitesurfing, paddleboarding, windsurfing and kayaking.

3 HIGHCLERE CASTLE
Page 185
Experience the opulence of the real house behind *Downton Abbey*.

4 NEW FOREST PONIES
Page 164
Watch the ponies fearlessly wandering down village streets – but be sure to guard your picnic.

5
6
7
8

9

5 CYCLE THE SOUTH DOWNS WAY

Page 201

Its hills may be high and challenging, but you can't beat the views from one of the UK's best long-distance cycle paths.

6 HMS VICTORY

Page 235

Explore Nelson's flagship to get an insight into the harsh realities of naval life during the Battle of Trafalgar.

7 WINCHESTER CATHEDRAL

Page 197

This historic treasure-trove shelters everything from the ancient tombs of King Cnut and William Rufus to contemporary sculpture by Antony Gormley.

8 CORFE CASTLE

Page 68

This dramatic hilltop ruin has far-reaching views, and you can often spot the Swanage steam train puffing along in the valley below.

9 WALK THE SOUTH WEST COAST PATH

Page 66

You can tackle the entire Dorset stretch of Britain's longest footpath, or simply walk some easy sections in a day.

10 LYMINGTON

Page 186

Hang out with the yachtie set along the pretty harbourfront in prosperous Lymington.

10

11

11 WALK TO TYNEHAM VILLAGE

Page 80

Lovely walks and countryside surround this abandoned village, which has been left to crumble since the 1940s.

12 BOURNEMOUTH BEACH

Page 39

Chill out on south England's ultimate resort beach – a fabulous seven-mile stretch of sand.

13 THE NEEDLES

Page 273

These dramatic chalk stacks off the Isle of Wight can be seen from the picturesque eastern side of the island.

14 A PINT AT THE SQUARE AND COMPASS, WORTH MATRAVERS

Page 79

Grab a pie and pint at Britain's best pub – it's quirky and cosy inside, with fantastic coastal views from the garden, though you may have to share your seat with a chicken.

15 ABBOTSBURY CYGNET HATCHING

Page 122

Visit the swannery in May or June, and you'll be surrounded by fluffy cygnets.

16 FESTIVALS ON THE ISLE OF WIGHT

Page 254

The island's eponymous music festival is one of the country's best, while Bestival (pictured) is an end-of-summer fancy dress spectacle.

12

13
14
BEER GARDEN
15
16

Itineraries

The following itineraries will allow you to sample the best the regions have to offer, from bike rides across the Purbecks to walking through the New Forest, and from Charles Dickens' birthplace to the inspiration behind Enid Blyton's *Famous Five* stories.

A WEEKEND IN THE NEW FOREST

Here's how to get the most out of this wonderfully diverse national park, famed for its roaming ponies.

FRIDAY

Beaulieu This pristine village has donkeys on its green and the National Motor Museum in Beaulieu House, with attractions for all ages. **See p.168**

Dinner Splash out at *The Terrace*, the New Forest's only Michelin-starred restaurant. **See p.169**

SATURDAY

Rent a bike Visit the pretty village of Burley in the heart of the forest and rent a bike for the day. **See p.176**

Lunch Enjoy a generous lunch at *The Cider Pantry* – and of course a pint of home-made cider from their own orchards. **See p.176**

Bolderwood Cycle through ancient forest to Bolderwood, where a deer-feeding station lures out the woodland animals most days. **See p.175**

Dinner Have a delicious meal at family-friendly *The Pig*, which specializes in forest produce. **See p.167**

SUNDAY

Fritham Take a walk around this pretty village in the less-visited north of the forest. **See p.180**

Lunch The beautifully positioned *Royal Oak* in Fritham has an enormous garden and serves sumptuous local produce. **See p.180**

THE GREAT OUTDOORS

You can enjoy plenty of activities over the course of a week – all while experiencing some of England's least spoilt countryside and best coastal landscapes.

❶ **Rib Ride, Mudeford** Forget your hairstyle and blast out on a high-speed boat from Mudeford Quay to the Needles on the Isle of Wight. **See p.183**

❷ **New Forest Water Park** Have fun and try to avoid a Total Wipeout at the UK's first floating inflatable obstacle course, on a lake outside Ringwood. **See p.156**

❸ **Go Ape, Moors Valley Country Park** This is designed to test your agility and climbing skills as you tackle a rope course strung over a series of trees. **See p.156**

❹ **Zip Wire, Bournemouth** It may be short, but the world's first pier-to-shore zip wire is a pretty exhilarating ride. **See p.39**

❺ **Cycle the Purbecks** Experience beautiful country lanes and paths on this superb back route from Wareham to the Sandbanks peninsula. **See p.71**

❻ **South West Coast Path** Walk a section of the stunning long-distance coast path that crosses the region. **See p.66**

ABOVE FROM LEFT CHESIL BEACH; GO APE, MOORS VALLEY COUNTRY PARK; PRAWNS AT THE MASTER BUILDERS, BUCKLER'S HARD

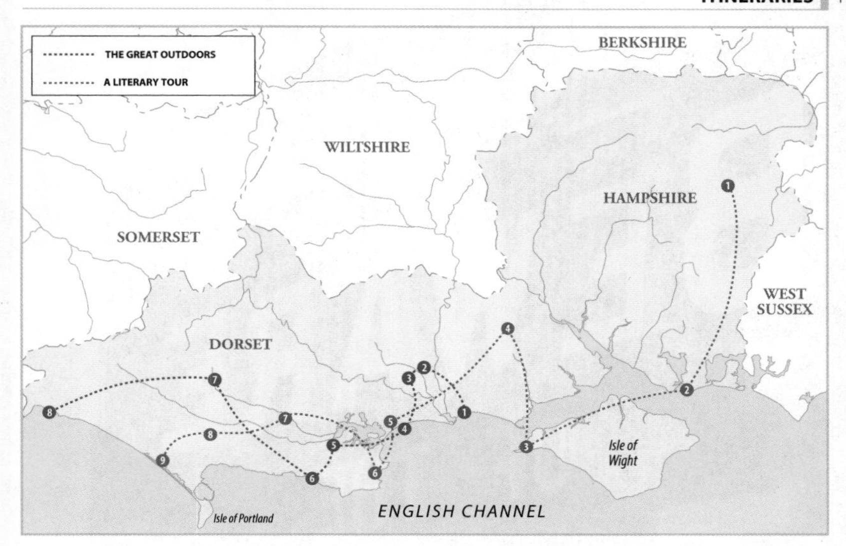

❼ **Badger Watch, Dorset** You won't come closer than this to cute live badgers in the wild. **See p.100**

❽ **Fossil Tours, Charmouth** Penetrate the secrets of the Jurassic Coast by taking a fossil tour on this craggy beach. **See p.133**

A LITERARY TOUR

Share the landscapes and buildings that have inspired some of Britain's greatest writers by following this week-long itinerary.

❶ **Jane Austen, Chawton** Visit the great writer's home and the village that's little changed from when she lived here in the nineteenth century. **See p.207**

❷ **Charles Dickens, Portsmouth** Though most associated with London, you can visit the home where Dickens was born in Portsmouth, where he set parts of *Nicholas Nickleby*. **See p.236**

❸ **Alfred, Lord Tennyson, Tennyson Down** It's easy to see why this clifftop walk was so popular with the Victorian poet whose monument now stands at the down's summit. **See p.271**

❹ **Sir Arthur Conan Doyle, Minstead** Sherlock Holmes's creator worked as a GP in Portsmouth and you can visit his unassuming grave in the pretty churchyard of Minstead. **See p.175**

❺ **Mary and Percy Bysshe Shelley, Bournemouth** The author of *Frankenstein* is buried in St Peter's Church alongside the heart of her famous poet husband. **See p.43**

❻ **Enid Blyton, Swanage** The children's author spent her holidays in the Purbecks, which she turned into the exciting locations for her *Famous Five* novels. **See p.70**

❼ **T.E. Lawrence, Clouds Hill** This "hut in a wood" was the retreat for Lawrence of Arabia, who died in a motorcycle accident nearby. **See p.83**

❽ **Thomas Hardy, Dorchester** You can see where the great writer lived at Max Gate in Dorchester, or visit the altogether humbler Hardy's Cottage nearby, to see where he was born. **See p.92 & p.97**

❾ **Ian McEwan, Chesil Beach** Walk up the endless pebbles on Chesil Beach to see the place that inspired one of England's greatest contemporary writers, whose famous novel takes the same name. **See p.120**

SIGN AT CORFE CASTLE STATION, SWANAGE TO NORDEN STEAM RAILWAY

Basics

Getting there

Most people approach the region by car along the M3 and M27 motorways, or by train – there are direct lines from London's Waterloo station as well as from Bristol, Birmingham and stations in the north. There are also regular National Express coaches from London's Victoria station and most other major cities. Ferry links run to Weymouth, Poole and Portsmouth from France, Spain and the Channel Islands. The region has two international airports, at Bournemouth and Southampton, with flights from many European countries. Most of Hampshire and East Dorset is only one to two hours' travelling time from London, though add a good hour to reach the far corners of western Dorset. Any visit to the Isle of Wight, of course, involves a ferry trip.

By car

It's a quick and easy drive along the **M3** and **M27** from London to Southampton or along the **A3** to Portsmouth (both around 90min). Coming from the north, there are good connections using the A34/M3/M27 corridor. Just beyond Southampton, the motorways end – Dorset and the Isle of Wight have no motorways at all – and it's another thirty minutes or so along the **A31** and **A388** to Bournemouth and Poole. Heading further west, things slow down beyond Ringwood when the A31 becomes one lane each way and bottlenecks form around Wimborne throughout the summer from lunchtime on a Friday (heading south) and mid-afternoon on a Sunday (heading north). The **A35** from Poole to Lyme Regis is better, having sporadic sections of dual carriageway, though traffic jams often build up around the Dorchester bypass.

By train

Most **trains** into the region are run by South West Trains from London Waterloo (Ⓦ southwesttrains .co.uk). In addition, CrossCountry (Ⓦ crosscountry trains.co.uk) runs long-distance trains from the Midlands and the north, while First Great Western (Ⓦ firstgreatwestern.co.uk) runs services from Bristol to Southampton and Portsmouth, and Southern Railway (Ⓦ southernrailway.com) serves the south coast between Southampton, Portsmouth and Brighton.

The **Waterloo-to-Weymouth** line serves all the major towns in East Dorset and Hampshire, including Basingstoke (45min), Winchester (1hr), Southampton (1hr 20min), Brockenhurst for the New Forest (1hr 30min), Bournemouth (1hr 50min), Poole (2hr 10min), Dorchester (2hr 45min) and Weymouth (3hr), with trains running approximately every thirty minutes to an hour. Trains to Portsmouth (1hr 40min) run on a separate line **via Guildford** every thirty minutes. The far north and west of Dorset is served by trains **via Salisbury** every two hours to Gillingham (2hr) for Shaftesbury, Sherborne (2hr 10min), and Axminster (2hr 45min) for Lyme Regis and Bridport. For details of fares and specific routes, see Ⓦ nationalrail.co.uk.

There are no specific rail passes that cover Dorset and Hampshire, but if you plan to visit the region several times by train, it may be worth getting a **Network Railcard** which gives you a third off the price for up to four adults travelling together and sixty percent off for up to four children: the pass costs £30 for a year and can only be used on off-peak trains (see Ⓦ railcard.co.uk /network for details).

By coach

Regular National Express **coaches** (Ⓦ national express.com) from London Victoria serve the main towns in the area, including Winchester, Portsmouth, Southampton, Ringwood, Bournemouth, Dorchester and Weymouth. There are also less regular services from Gatwick and Heathrow airports and other regional towns in the UK. **Fares** tend to be lower than on the train, especially if you can book in advance and be flexible about when you travel, though journey times are almost always longer than on the train.

By ferry

Two major **ports**, Portsmouth and Poole, are served by **ferries from France**, and Portsmouth also has links **from Spain**. Weymouth currently has no direct scheduled international services, though at the time of going to press, High Speed Ferries was planning to start one. A fourth port, Southampton – the largest of them all – has no cross-Channel ferries, only boats to the Isle of Wight and huge ocean liner cruise ships.

Portsmouth can be reached from several ports in France: **from Caen**, Brittany Ferries has 2–3 services daily (6–7 hours), including a longer overnight boat; **from St Malo** it has one daily service (9hr), returning overnight; **from Cherbourg** it runs one to two daily fast catamarans (3hr); while Condor Ferries has one sailing a week from Cherbourg (5hr). **From Le Havre**, Brittany Ferries runs a daily economy service (4hr) returning overnight (8hr). From Spain, Brittany Ferries sails twice a week **from Bilbao** (24hr or 32hr) and three times a week **from Santander** (20hr).

Poole is served by one daily ferry **from Cherbourg** on Brittany Ferries (4hr 30min), while Condor Ferries runs daily ferries (summer only) **from St Malo** via the Channel Islands (approx 6hr). **Fares** vary enormously according to the season, the day, the time, the route and the type of boat: check with the ferry companies for details.

FERRY CONTACTS

Brittany Ferries T 03301 597000, W brittany-ferries.co.uk
Condor Ferries T 01202 207216, W condorferries.co.uk
High Speed Ferries W highspeedferries.com

By plane

Both Bournemouth and Southampton airports have regular scheduled flights throughout the year from many towns and cities in Western Europe. Ryanair (W ryanair.com) is the main budget airline to serve **Bournemouth airport**, with flights from Spain, Portugal and Malta. Other airlines that fly to Bournemouth are Thomson (W thomson.co.uk), with a range of holiday destinations in Spain, Greece and Turkey, and easyJet (W easyjet.com) from Geneva (winter only).

Flybe (W flybe.com) is the main budget airline serving **Southampton airport**, with flights from France, Holland, Spain, Germany, Switzerland and Italy, as well as from several regional cities in England, Scotland and Ireland.

Getting to the Isle of Wight

Three **ferry companies** serve the Isle of Wight (see p.246) on four different routes. **Wightlink** runs the Lymington to Yarmouth car ferry, a high-speed catamaran from Portsmouth to Ryde (foot passengers only), and a car ferry from Portsmouth to Fishbourne. **Red Funnel** runs a high-speed catamaran for foot passengers from Southampton to West Cowes and a car ferry from Southampton to East Cowes, while **Hovertravel** runs a hovercraft from Southsea in Portsmouth to Ryde for foot passengers only.

ISLE OF WIGHT FERRY CONTACTS

Hovertravel T 01983 717700, W hovertravel.co.uk
Red Funnel T 02380 019192, W redfunnel.co.uk
Wightlink T 03339 997333, W wightlink.co.uk

Getting around

The most practical way of getting around the region is by car, though congestion in some towns and on the main routes to and from the coast can be a problem. Train or coach is feasible if you are travelling to one of the main towns, but if you want to explore the rural areas, a car or bicycle is pretty much essential. Travelling around the Isle of Wight is doable without a car as the island has a reasonable public transport network and plenty of cycle routes. The Traveline website (W traveline.org.uk) gives timetables and routes for all public transport, directing you to the relevant company for your journey.

By train

Dorset, in particular, is poorly served by trains, as during the Industrial Revolution three of the most powerful landowning families clubbed together to prevent train lines from crossing their land. The result is one main line along the coast, one skirting the northern edge of the county, and one minor route towards the western edge of the county between Dorchester and Yeovil, continuing on to Bristol; trains run every couple of hours or so (contact First Great Western for details; W firstgreatwestern.co.uk).

Hampshire is better served: as well as the main-line trains (see p.19), some smaller branch lines are also operated by South West Trains, such as the Brockenhurst to Lymington line, which runs along a jetty to connect with the Isle of Wight ferry. The south coast line connects Brighton with the main line at Eastleigh, near Southampton, and runs to Fareham, Portsmouth Harbour, Southsea and Havant.

The **Isle of Wight** has one main train route, the Island Line (W islandlinetrains.co.uk), which runs from Ryde Pier Head to Shanklin (see p.249). If you plan to use the train several times during your visit, it may be worth buying a season ticket: a weekly season ticket giving unlimited travel on the line costs £19.

In addition, the region has three independent **steam train** lines: the Watercress Line between

Alton and Alresford (see p.206); the Swanage Railway to Norden (see p.68); and the Isle of Wight Steam Railway, which runs from Wootton to connect with the Island Line at Smallbrook Junction (see p.256). All three run through picturesque countryside, and tend to have seasonal services only.

By bus

While National Express provides coach links between the main towns in the area and major UK cities (see p.19), there are also several smaller regional bus companies. **Wilts and Dorset** (Ⓦ wdbus.co.uk) is the main company in East Dorset: based in Bournemouth, it serves Poole, Christchurch, Ringwood, Fordingbridge, Wimborne, Blandford Forum and the Purbecks. West Dorset is served mainly by **First Bus** (Ⓦ firstgroup.com), with services around Dorchester, Weymouth, Portland, Bridport and Lyme Regis, as well as the area around Portsmouth and Southampton. **Bluestar** (Ⓦ bluestarbus.co.uk) runs buses in the south Hampshire region, with services to Southampton, Romsey, Winchester, Totton, Hythe and Lymington. Buses on the Isle of Wight (see p.249) are run by **Southern Vectis** (Ⓦ islandbuses.info).

In several towns, there are guided **bus tours** of the surrounding countryside, which can be a useful way of seeing all the attractions in the area if you are short of time. Most will pick up from your hotel and they can usually be booked through the local tourist offices. A good example is the Bournemouth-based Discover Dorset (Ⓦ discoverdorset.co.uk), which collects from hotels and language schools around Bournemouth, and runs half-day tours (£20) to the Jurassic Coast and Stonehenge, as well as a full-day Purbeck and Lulworth tour (£35).

By car

Most people **drive** around the region, with main routes to and from the coast suffering from congestion in the summer, particularly on Friday afternoons heading south and on Sunday afternoons heading north (see p.19). Bottlenecks also form around the coastal towns of Swanage, Bournemouth, Poole, Weymouth and Bridport, as well as inland around Dorchester, Wareham and Lyndhurst in the New Forest. The queues for the Studland ferry can also be horrendous on sunny weekends. Once you are off the main roads, however, the tiny rural country lanes can be a pleasure to drive down, particularly in the northern section of the New Forest, central Hampshire and northern Dorset.

Parking is not particularly problematic, except in peak summer holiday season: most of the big towns have ample car parks or on-street pay-and-display machines. Most towns charge around £1 per hour for parking.

By bicycle

Cycling (see p.28) in the region is a pleasure once you are off the main roads. Good areas to travel around by bike are the New Forest, the Purbecks, north Dorset, central Hampshire and the Isle of Wight. Most towns have bike rental outlets; we have listed many in the Guide.

On foot

With stunning coastal routes, plus plenty of inland footpaths and bridleways through beautiful rural scenery, the region is a joy to walk in. Following the **South West Coast Path** is the most popular way to explore the coast, with reasonable transport links and

TOP DRIVES

Here are our six favourite scenic drives around the region:

Studland to Corfe Castle Head up past the golf course for Poole Bay vistas and down until the amazing ruins of Corfe Castle come into view. See p.70

Cerne Abbas to Milton Abbas Take the narrow back roads to enjoy Dorset scenery little changed from Hardy's "Wessex". See p.99

Burton Bradstock to Abbotsbury This fantastic road passes high above the coast, with stupendous views of the Fleet Lagoon. See p.122

Shaftesbury to Tollard Royal Full of loops, twists and turns, the B3081 winds through the beautiful woods and hills of Cranborne Chase. See p.151

Rhinefield to Bolderwood A classic New Forest drive through ancient woodland. See p.167

St Catherine's Point to Freshwater Hugging the clifftop, this road takes in the best coastal scenery along the unspoilt south of the Isle of Wight. See p.269

good accommodation options en route; the website Ⓦ southwestcoastpath.com provides detailed maps and route descriptions for the entire route and suggestions for shorter walks. The unofficial **South Downs Way** website Ⓦ southdownsway.co.uk provides similar information for the region's second long-distance footpath, including useful transport advice for accessing sections of the path (see p.201).

Accommodation

A quiet revolution has taken place in the quality of English seaside accommodation over the past decade. Most south-coast resorts now have at least one boutique-style B&B or guesthouse, but more importantly their advent has led to a serious improvement in the quality of all accommodation. While you will still find a few swirly carpeted, chintzy B&Bs, the vast majority have really upped their game, and even simple B&Bs now tend to provide clean rooms, modern light decor, comfy beds and decent-quality breakfasts, so you shouldn't find it too difficult to get reasonably priced accommodation of a good standard.

Hotels, guesthouses and B&Bs

There's a big overlap between small **hotels**, **guesthouses** and **B&Bs**, all of which can offer a wide variety of accommodation and facilities. A farmhouse or manor house B&B in the country, for example, may have a pool, grand dining room and large grounds, while a town hotel may be more basic with fewer facilities; most places now also offer free wi-fi. **Prices** are not always an accurate guide either to the quality of the accommodation – in high season a fairly simple place on the coast will charge a lot more than somewhere more comfortable and luxurious inland. As very few places in this Guide are more than an hour's drive from the coast, you're often better off opting for a delightful country B&B, and driving to the seaside. Out of high season, however, it's always worth negotiating a good rate.

Country inns and gastropubs

Inland Dorset and Hampshire have some lovely **country inns** and **gastropubs** with rooms. Often in the middle of nowhere, these places tend to have highly regarded restaurants specializing in local, seasonal food with a few rooms upstairs. They vary tremendously in terms of how luxurious they are – some have iPod docks and all mod cons, others are simpler and more rustic in style – but the ambience is usually friendly, with the emphasis on a good meal and a comfortable room to stay the night.

Hostels

There are only seven YHA **hostels** in the area covered in this Guide – two on the Isle of Wight, one in the New Forest, and the other four along the Dorset coast. They vary from lively seaside townhouses, such as at Swanage, to basic, rural, walkers' shelters, such as Litton Cheney. You don't have to be a member to stay at a YHA hostel, though the annual membership of £15 per person will reduce your nightly rate by about £3; for details, contact Ⓣ 01629 592700, Ⓦ yha.org.uk.

In the larger coastal towns, such as Bournemouth, Southampton, Portsmouth and Weymouth, you'll also find some **independent hostels**. These usually provide basic-quality dorm-bed accommodation from around £15 a night. In rural areas, **walkers' barns** provide simple, hostel-style dorm-bed accommodation, usually on farms or campsites, for around £10 a night.

Camping

There is no shortage of **campsites** in the region, many in the most spectacular locations, and in the summer camping can be one of the best ways to visit the region.

ACCOMMODATION PRICES

The prices we quote for hotels, guesthouses and B&Bs in this Guide refer to the cheapest available double/twin room in high season (usually August for most of the region), including breakfast, unless otherwise stated. For hostels we give the price of a bed in a shared dorm, plus the price of a double, if there are any. For campsites, we quote the price of a two-man tent, pitched yourself; if a campsite uses a different pricing system (eg per person), we make this clear.

BEST PLACES TO STAY

There are some great places to stay in the region – here are some of the more unusual ones.

Mudeford beach huts No power, no running water, barely room to swing a cat, but you can't beat a night out on the sandspit in one of the best-located beach huts in the UK. See p.46

East Shilvinghampton Farm Comfy beds, soft duvets, running water – yet you're sleeping in a field. Wake up to gorgeous rural views and the sounds of chicken, geese, goats and sheep. See p.121

Lighthouse cottages, Durlston Stay on a remote clifftop below a working lighthouse. See p.76

Clavell Tower, Kimmeridge Spend a night in this Victorian tower perched on the cliffs with great views. See p.80

Summer Lodge, Evershot In the heart of Hardy's "Wessex", you can stay in this lovely, luxurious country house, part of which was designed by Hardy himself. See p.135

Alexandra Hotel, Lyme Regis Unbeatable views, excellent food and friendly staff at this fantastic clifftop hotel, looking out over the harbour, the beach, the Cobb and along the coast. See p.132

Xoron, Bembridge This converted World War II gunboat, moored in Bembridge harbour on the Isle of Wight, makes a cosy and atmospheric B&B. See p.262

The **New Forest campsites** are an experience in themselves (see box, p.178), with ponies peering into your tent in the morning and vast tracts of traffic-free tracks to cycle down safely. Head along the coastal path, and you can't fail to notice that some of the most **dramatic clifftop locations** are home to campsites. While this may be disappointing for walkers, it's great for campers, and if you're staying at one, the views from your tent can be stunning. In addition, there is a series of **farm campsites** in idyllic rural locations where children can collect the eggs for breakfast, and enjoy the atmosphere of a working farm. For those who prefer more comfort, several places have yurt camping, while glamping specialists Featherdown Farms (W featherdown.co.uk) have five sites in the region, a couple in rural Hampshire – one in the New Forest, one in rural Dorset, and one by the Fleet Lagoon, all with comfortable, ready-erected tents on working farms.

Several companies in the region rent out **campervans** for touring the area, including Isle of Wight Campers (T 01983 642143, W isleofwightcampers.co.uk), which rents out traditional VW campervans, and Kamperhire (T 01489 715621, W kamperhire.co.uk), which has more modern models and is based just outside Southampton.

Self-catering

There's an enormous array of **self-catering accommodation** available in the region, from converted lighthouses on clifftops to remote, rural farmhouses, to high-tech architect-designed homes. There are also many cottages on working farms that vary from simple cottages to luxurious barn conversions with a pool and all mod cons. Prices range from about £200 a week in low season to well over £1000 in high season, depending on the size, facilities and location.

The companies below all rent out properties in the region; for private rentals, tourist boards and small ads can help.

SELF-CATERING ACCOMMODATION

Dorset Coastal Cottages T 08009 804070, W **dorsetcoastalcottages.com.** Has a huge array of cottages of all shapes and sizes, some in rural Dorset, others right by the coast.

Dorset Cottage Holidays T 01929 481647, W **dhcottages.co.uk.** Specializes in cottages in Purbeck, but also some further afield in Weymouth, Poole and Wimborne.

Farm and Cottage Holidays T 01237 459888, W **holidaycottages.co.uk.** A wide range of accommodation throughout the region, from barn conversions to modern bungalows.

Farmstay UK T 02476 696909, W **farmstayuk.co.uk.** Provides a variety of accommodation on working farms in the region, some organic.

Halcyon Holiday Cottages T 07515 881329, W **halcyonholidaycottages.co.uk.** For larger groups, Halcyon has several properties in the New Forest that sleep up to 38.

Isle of Wight Farm and Country Holidays W **wightfarmholidays.co.uk.** A good selection of cottage and barn conversions around the Isle of Wight.

Island Cottage Holidays T 01929 481555, W **islandcottageholidays.com.** Rents out some more unusual properties on the Isle of Wight and in the Purbecks, including the Indian Summer House, built by Queen Victoria on the Osborne House estate.

Landmark Trust T 01628 825925, W **landmarktrust.org.uk.** Hugely popular accommodation in historic buildings around the country; we list the region's best ones in the Guide.

National Trust Cottages 03448 002070, nationaltrustcottages.co.uk. Lovely properties on prime National Trust land, including the only holiday houses on Brownsea Island and some former coastguard's cottages on the Needles in the Isle of Wight.
New Forest Cottages 01590 679655, newforestcottages.co.uk. An enormous variety of places to rent in all regions of the New Forest, from traditional thatched cottages to modern family homes.
Rural Retreats 01386 898277, ruralretreats.co.uk. Has several cottages in the area including converted former lighthouses in stunning locations, such as St Katherine's Point on the Isle of Wight and Anvil Point near Swanage.

Food and drink

At the forefront of the local, seasonal food movement, Dorset, Hampshire and the Isle of Wight have no shortage of decent places to eat and drink. The region's restaurants harbour several Michelin-starred chefs, though you're just as well off choosing one of the smaller independent restaurants and cafés that specialize in simple dishes made from local ingredients. Probably the best way to experience the region's specialities is to head to one of many farm shops, delis or farmers' markets and pick up some delicious local produce for a picnic.

Restaurants

There is a scattering of well-known chefs with **restaurants** in the region. Mark Hix has his *Oyster and Fish House* in Lyme Regis (see p.133); TV chef Rick Stein has two restaurants in the area, one in Winchester and one at Sandbanks (rickstein.com); and, of course, Hugh Fearnley-Whittingstall's *River Cottage* is on the Devon/Dorset border, near Lyme Regis (see p.128), with a second branch in Winchester (see p.201).

There are also some very well-regarded local establishments, whose chefs are less well known but who produce food of an equally high standard, often at much lower prices. Along the coast, fish is the mainstay and several places serve reasonably priced, locally caught **fish and seafood** in great coastal locations. Some of the best are: the *Hive Beach Café*, right on the beach in Burton Bradstock (see p.129); the *Crab House Café* in Portland (see p.116) for oysters from the Fleet Lagoon; *The Pig on the Beach* at Studland (see p.72) for local fish and foraged herbs and vegetables; *West Beach* in Bournemouth (see p.49) for great sea views and fresh fish; *Pebble Beach* on the clifftop at Barton-on-Sea (see p.185); and *The Crab Shed* on the Isle of Wight, for tasty home-made crab pasties served warm on the beach (see p.268).

Inland, too, many restaurants and gastropubs make use of **local wild produce**, such as venison, game, rabbit and mushroom. Some good places to try are: *Thompson's* on the Isle of Wight (see p.256), run by one of Britain's youngest Michelin-starred chefs, Robert Thompson; *La Fosse* in Cranborne (see p.256) for local meat and game; and *The Pig* in the New Forest (see p.167), which uses its own home-grown fruit, veg, herbs and eggs.

Regional specialities

A predominantly rural area, Dorset, Hampshire and the Isle of Wight enjoy plenty of **locally grown** fruit, vegetables and herbs, as well as organic and free-range farms selling pork, chicken, beef and lamb. Game is also widely available, as is **wild produce** such as nettles, wild garlic, mushrooms and, of course, fish and seafood.

An increasing number of artisan products, such as cheeses and bread, ice cream, chutney, pickles and jams, are made in the area. The best-known **bakery** is the *Famous Hedgehog Bakery* (see p.152), outside Wimborne, whose organic breads and pastries are renowned. There's also the *Town Mill Bakery*, which makes organic bread, pizzas and pastries in the centre of Lyme Regis (see p.133), with another branch in Poundbury.

The best-known local **cheese** is the Dorset Blue Vinney, a delicious Stilton-like cheese that is made throughout the county. Denhay Cheddar is made at Denhay Farm near Bridport, while Woolsery goat's cheese comes from Up Sydling near Dorchester. Lyburn Farm in Hamptworth in the New Forest makes a range of delicious cheeses, including a garlic and nettle cheese and a full-flavoured Old Winchester; you can sample them at various pubs in the area, such as the *Royal Oak* in Fritham (see p.179), or buy them from their farm shop (Mon–Fri 8am–4.30pm) or local farmers' markets.

There are several highly regarded companies whose **ice creams** – made using local milk, cream and other ingredients – can be found in the region. New Forest ice creams, based in Totton, near Southampton, is the largest, while Purbeck ice creams, based in Kingston, near Wareham, produces some unusual flavours, such as chilli and liquorice. Barford

Farmhouse, just outside Wimborne, makes sorbet from locally grown blueberries: it has its own shop and a pretty ice-cream garden (Easter–Oct Wed–Sun & bank hol Mon 11.30am–5.30pm; July & Aug also Tues; Ⓦ barford-icecream.co.uk). Minghella produces the best-known ice cream on the Isle of Wight (see box, p.259).

The best place to sample local regional produce is at a **farmers' market**. Most small towns in the region have one at least once a month, with Winchester hosting the country's largest farmers' market every other Sunday. For dates and details of farmers' markets in Hampshire and Dorset, check Ⓦ hampshirefarmersmarkets.co.uk, and Ⓦ visit-dorset.com/food-and-drink/local-produce-and-markets. On the Isle of Wight, markets are held every Friday morning in Newport and every Saturday morning in Ryde; see Ⓦ islandfarmersmarket.co.uk.

Drink

Some of the best **pubs** in the country are in Dorset, Hampshire and the Isle of Wight (see box, p.6), from welcoming, rural places with cosy bars, low beams and open fires to vast, bustling pubs whose crowds spill out onto the seashore on a sunny afternoon. Many serve a good range of local ales – some even have their own on-site breweries – as well as food of all descriptions, varying from home-made pies and local cheese ploughman's to Thai curries and full-blown Michelin-standard restaurant meals. Most pubs will open late morning and close before midnight, with restricted hours on Sundays; we give details in the Guide. Food service hours in rural and coastal pubs, in particular, can vary from day to day – kitchens may close if the pub's not busy, or the weather is poor – so it's always worth checking the kitchen opening times on the pub's website, on Facebook or by phone.

Local beer

There are three main local long-established **breweries** in the region, all brewing their own individual award-winning beers and ales. **Ringwood Brewery** produces a variety of different beers in Ringwood, ranging from the light, summery ale, Boondoggle, to the strongest offering, Old Thumper. **Hall and Woodhouse**, based in Blandford Forum, brews a huge range of ales, including the gingery Blandford Fly and the floral-flavoured bitter, Tanglefoot. Look out, too, for beers brewed by **Palmers** in Bridport, such as the light Dorset Gold and the darker full-strength Tally Ho. The three breweries above all offer tours and tasting sessions.

There are also some smaller, newer independent breweries worth looking out for, such as the **Dorset Piddle Brewery** (Ⓦ piddlebrewery.co.uk) in Piddlehinton, producer of the light, fruity Jimmy Riddle and the stronger Silent Slasher; the **Dorset Brewing Company** (Ⓦ dbcales.com) in Weymouth – check out their lager-type Chesil or the Durdle Door bitter; the **Bournemouth Brewing Co** (Ⓦ bournemouthbrewery.co.uk), with its flagship Wessex Wobble bitter; and the **Itchen Valley Brewery** (Ⓦ itchenvalley.com) in New Alresford, which produces a fine Winchester ale. On the Isle of Wight, the local breweries to look out for are Goddards (Ⓦ goddards-brewery.co.uk) in Ryde, with its award-winning Fuggle-Dee-Dum, and Yates (Ⓦ yates-brewery.co.uk) in Ventnor. Several pubs in the region have their own **microbreweries** attached, including the *Bankes Arms* in Studland (see p.69) and the *Flowerpots Inn* in Cheriton (see p.203), both well worth a visit.

Wines and spirits

With their mild climates, Dorset, Hampshire and the Isle of Wight now have several **vineyards** producing wines and sparkling wines of a reasonable quality. While they still have a long way to go to compete with the more traditional wine-producing countries – particularly on price, as many are more expensive than the French equivalent – they are improving rapidly. Several of the vineyards also provide bed and breakfast accommodation and tours: some worth looking out for are **Adgestone** (Ⓦ adgestonevineyard.co.uk) and **Rosemary** vineyards (Ⓦ rosemaryvineyard.co.uk) on the Isle of Wight, **Setley Ridge** (Ⓦ setleyridge.co.uk) in the New Forest, and the **Wickham Vineyard** (Ⓦ wickhamvineyard.com) in Shedfield, between Southampton and Portsmouth.

Dorset is also the birthplace of a couple of new spirits that have gained a good reputation among mixologists at some of London's trendiest bars and restaurants: **Conker Gin** (Ⓦ conkerspirit.co.uk) is made in the backstreets of Southbourne, a suburb of Bournemouth, with an appealing mix of botanicals including elderberries, samphire and local gorse flowers; while the highly regarded **Black Cow vodka** (Ⓦ blackcow.co.uk) is the world's only milk-based vodka, made from milk produced by cows on a farm deep in the Dorset countryside, inland from Bridport.

Festivals

There are plenty of events and festivals in the region throughout the year – ranging from Southampton's Asian Mela to the British Beach Polo championships. In July and August, in particular, every small town and resort has its own festival or carnival – we've picked out some of the best, listed below; the region also hosts several great music festivals (see opposite).

MARCH/APRIL

Lambing weekend Kingston Maurward (usually the first two weekends in March) **Ⓦ kmc.ac.uk.** Pretty much the closest you can get to a sheep giving birth – you can also help to bottle-feed the young lambs.

Giant Easter Egg Hunt Lulworth Castle, East Lulworth (late March to mid-April) **Ⓦ lulworth.com.** Go home with plenty of free eggs – if you can find them hidden around the grounds of the castle first.

MAY

International Beach Kite Festival Weymouth (early May). Huge festival of kites on the beach, culminating in impressive fireworks.

The Lyme Regis Fossil Festival Charmouth and Lyme Regis (early May). Talks and fossil hunts on the famous Jurassic Coast, together with performance artists and family entertainment.

Walk the Wight Isle of Wight (early May) **Ⓦ isleofwightwalkingfestival.co.uk.** The UK's largest walking festival, including a cross-island trek for those who like a challenge.

Christchurch Food Festival (mid-May) **Ⓦ christchurchfoodfest .co.uk.** Stalls and restaurants celebrating international flavours – cookery demonstrations from celebrity chefs, tastings and special menus.

Beaulieu Truckmania Beaulieu (end of May) **Ⓦ beaulieu.co.uk.** Monster trucks, truck agility courses and tank displays from the army in the fine grounds of Beaulieu.

Dorchester Festival (late May/early June) **Ⓦ dorchesterarts.org .uk/dorchester-festival.** An innovative biennial festival (takes place on odd years) with theatre and music and performances at the Corn Exchange, plus free events in the town's Borough Gardens.

Dorset Art Weeks (end of May/early June) **Ⓦ dorsetartweeks .co.uk.** Biennial event in which over 300 artists across the county open up their studios to the public.

JUNE

Bournemouth Wheels Festival (early June) **Ⓦ bournemouth wheels.co.uk.** Racing cars, quad bikes, monster trucks, supercars, stunt shows, BMX displays and military vehicles take over the seafront and clifftop from the town centre along to Southbourne in this vast, noisy festival.

Old Gaffers Festival Yarmouth, Isle of Wight (early June) **Ⓦ yarmoutholdgaffersfestival.co.uk.** Named after the gaff sailing boats that come from all round the country to participate in three days of events and entertainment round Yarmouth. Held biennially, in odd years.

World Stinging Nettle-Eating Competition The Bottle Inn, Marshwood, Dorset (mid-June) **Ⓦ bottle-inn.net.** Annual competition to see who can eat the longest stinging nettles, helped along by the pub's fine selection of ales.

Bournemouth Food Festival (mid-June) **Ⓦ bournemouth foodanddrink.co.uk.** Street food stalls, cookery demonstrations, cocktail competitions, a farmers' market and live music in Bournemouth town centre.

Bridport Food Festival (mid-June) **Ⓦ bridportfoodfestival.co.uk.** Local suppliers and producers display their wares round town at stalls, cafés and restaurants, with cookery demos and cake competitions.

Portsmouth Festivities (end of June) **Ⓦ portsmouthfestivities .co.uk.** The town holds ten days of music, shows, films and special events around the city.

Tankfest Bovington, Dorset (end of June) **Ⓦ tankmuseum.org.** The world's biggest display of live tank action, featuring the Tank Museum's working beasts, with mock battles and plenty of gunfire.

Round the Island Race Isle of Wight (late June/early July) **Ⓦ www.roundtheisland.org.uk.** The world's top sailors take part in this challenging round-the-island race to and from Cowes.

JULY

British Beach Polo Championships Sandbanks, Poole (early July) **Ⓦ sandpolo.com.** Two days of beachside competition featuring the top names in this exclusive sport – followed by a giant beach party with top-name DJs.

Gold Hill Fair Shaftesbury (early July) **Ⓦ facebook.com /Goldhillfair.** Food stalls and live entertainment around the famous "Hovis" hill.

Winchester Hat Fair (early July) **Ⓦ hatfair.co.uk.** The longest-running street arts festival in the UK, with fun and innovative acts from around the world performing throughout town.

Bourne Free Pride (mid-July) **Ⓦ bournefree.co.uk.** Parades, live shows and street parties celebrating the LGBT community.

Farnborough Air Show (mid-July) **Ⓦ farnborough.com.** Biennial air spectacular, with planes of all sorts zooming overhead.

Southampton Mela (mid-July) **Ⓦ southamptonmela.com.** Vibrant festival celebrating the town's Asian community with dance, music and arts.

Wareham Carnival (late July) **Ⓦ www.wareham-carnival.org.uk.** A weekend of live music and various events round town.

New Forest Show New Park, Brockenhurst (end of July) **Ⓦ newforest show.co.uk.** Giant agricultural show displaying the best of the New Forest's livestock along with equestrian shows, stunts and pig races.

Sandown Carnival (end of July) **Ⓦ sandowncarnival.com.** Lively parades, events and fireworks at the Isle of Wight's principal south-coast resort.

The Great Dorset Chilli Festival St Giles House, Wimborne-St-Giles (last weekend in July) **Ⓦ greatdorsetchillifestival.co.uk.** A celebration of the chilli with cooking demos, music, tastings and, of course, a chilli-eating competition.

Swanage Carnival and Regatta (end of July/early Aug) **Ⓦ swanagecarnival.com.** Various events in and around the seaside resort, including parades and firework displays.

AUGUST

Cowes Week Cowes, Isle of Wight (first/second week in Aug) **Ⓦ aam cowesweek.co.uk.** One of the world's largest sailing events. See p.252.

Garlic Festival Newchurch, Isle of Wight (mid-Aug) **garlic-festival.co.uk.** Celebration not only of garlic but also arts and crafts from the island, together with live music, food stalls, beer tents and more.

Bournemouth Air Festival (mid- to late Aug) **bournemouthair.co.uk.** The Red Arrows are usually the highlight of this spectacular flying display over three days along the length of the seafront.

Great Dorest Steamfair Tarrant Hinton, Blandford Forum (late Aug) **gdsf.co.uk.** Huge and lively show celebrating steam engines of all sorts – the largest of its kind in the world – together with stalls and entertainment.

SEPTEMBER

Southampton Boat Show (mid-Sept) **southamptonboatshow.com.** Giant exhibition of the latest boats available to aspiring sailors, Roman Abramovichs and the like.

The Isle of Wight Cycling Festival (mid-Sept) **sunseaandcycling.com.** Various trails for people of all ages and abilities – including the Hills Killer mountain bike challenge.

Cheese Festival Sturminster Newton (mid-Sept) **cheesefestival.co.uk.** Sample some of the finest local cheeses. Also cheese-making demonstrations and children's entertainment. See p.148.

International Charity Classic Car Show Newport/Ryde, Isle of Wight (mid-Sept) **visitisleofwight.co.uk.** Classic and retro cars and bikes descend over a weekend.

Wessex Heavy Horse Show and Country Fayre Shaftesbury (last weekend of Sept) **wessexheavyhorsesociety.org.uk.** Rare breeds of horse together with ferret racing, bird displays and traditional entertainment.

OCTOBER

Pumpkin Competition and Beer Festival *Square and Compass*, Worth Matravers (early Oct) **squareandcompasspub.co.uk.** An extraordinary assembly of giant pumpkins vies for attention with fantastic local ales at this classic Dorset pub.

Purbeck Film Festival Isle of Purbeck (last 2 weeks in Oct) **therex.co.uk.** The UK's largest rural film festival with screenings in village halls and historic buildings such as Corfe Castle: includes the popular Screen Bites where films are shown with the relevant food.

Exbury Ghost Train (late Oct) **exbury.co.uk.** A special ghoulish train ride is laid on in the lead-up to Halloween, along with other events in Exbury Gardens in the New Forest.

NOVEMBER

Bonfire Night (around Nov 5). Various displays are held throughout the region – some of the best are at the Beaulieu National Motor Museum, Fort Nelson near Portsmouth and Stanpit in Christchurch.

DECEMBER

Winchester Christmas Festival (all month) **visitwinchester.co.uk.** Inner Close, Winchester. Wooden stalls and an ice rink transform the area into a winter wonderland round Winchester's cathedral in the run-up to Christmas.

Music festivals

For a relatively small area, a huge selection of **music festivals** takes place over the summer season. As well as the big-hitters – The Isle of Wight Festival, Bestival and Camp Bestival – there's a wide range of smaller, independent festivals. They may not attract the really big names, but often provide excellent bands, a more chilled-out vibe and a lower ticket price.

MAY

Mayfest Winchester (late May). A day of music in pubs and squares around the town, including folk, jazz, blues, ceilidhs and children's entertainment.

JUNE

Wimborne Folk Festival (second weekend in June) **wimbornefolk.co.uk.** A weekend of live folk.

Isle of Wight Festival Seaclose Park, Newport (mid-June) **isleofwightfestival.com.** The biggest and best-known festival, attracting major bands: from Bruce Springsteen to Busted, from Tinie Tempah to Iggy Pop, it's an eclectic mix of talent. See p.254.

JULY

Blissfields Bradley Farm, Alresford (early July) **blissfields.co.uk.** Small, intimate festival with comfy yurts featuring big names such as Sam Smith and Dizzee Rascal as well as up-and-coming bands and DJs, fuelled by local food and drink.

Swanage Jazz Festival (early July) **swanagejazz.org.** Various big and up-and-coming traditional jazz, blues and contemporary jazz performers around town.

Larmer Tree Larmer Tree Gardens, Dorset/Wiltshire borders (mid-July) **larmertreefestival.co.uk.** Family-orientated festival with storytelling, art installations and plenty of music – the likes of Tom Jones, Jools Holland and Jamie Cullen are regulars.

Camp Bestival Lulworth Castle, East Lulworth (end of July) **campbestival.net.** Provides good music, good food and drink and plenty of family-friendly entertainment – including jousting sessions and comedians – in a lovely setting.

AUGUST

Summer Gathering Gaunts House, Dorset (mid-Aug) **gauntshouse.com.** Hippy-ish festival with plenty of yoga and t'ai chi together with music, dance and entertainment.

SEPTEMBER

Bestival Robin Hill Country Park, Isle of Wight (early Sept) **bestival.net.** Alternative music festival hosted by Radio 1 DJ Rob da Bank, featuring acts such as The Cure, Rizzle Kicks, Stevie Wonder and Elbow.

End of the Road Larmer Tree Gardens, Dorset/Wiltshire borders (early Sept) **endoftheroadfestival.com.** Celebrates the end of the festival season with a relaxed, easygoing atmosphere, and always interesting line-up of folk, alternative and indie, all in the magical setting of Larmer Tree Gardens.

Sports and outdoor activities

The big draw in this region is the coast, which offers tremendous opportunities for swimmers, sailors and watersports enthusiasts, though the rural inland areas also offer great walking and cycling. The region's rivers, too, provide excellent fishing, particularly in Hampshire. Spectator sports are plentiful, and range from one of the world's most famous sailing events to watching cricket at its birthplace.

Walking

All three counties boast superb **walking** terrain, across rolling downs, through river valleys and along a dramatic coastline, and though there are no mountains to tackle, there are plenty of challenging hills and extremely steep sections of coastline. The whole of the **Isle of Wight** is well equipped for walkers, as is **Purbeck** in Dorset and the **New Forest** in Hampshire. Two long-distance paths cross the region: the famous **South West Coast Path** (see p.66), which begins at Poole Harbour, and the **South Downs Way**, which starts in Winchester (see p.201).

We've highlighted the best local walks throughout the Guide. These aim to provide a cross section of the region's varied landscapes. Most of these routes are straightforward to follow and can be enjoyed easily in a day or less, but even for short hikes you need to be properly equipped with an OS map (see p.32). Even with a map, always follow local advice and listen out for local weather reports – British weather is notoriously variable and conditions on some of the coastal paths in particular can be hazardous. Along with the walks in this book, we list some of the best walking guidebooks (see p.286). Local tourist offices are also excellent resources: as well as having walk leaflets, sometimes for a small fee, many offices organize regular guided walks that are perfect for inexperienced walkers or those who want on-the-ground information. See Ⓦvisit-dorset.com/things-to-do/activities/walking, Ⓦhants.gov.uk/guidedwalks.htm and Ⓦislandbreaks.co.uk/things-to-do/activities/walking for details.

Cycling

With several well-signed cycle routes, the Isle of Wight and the New Forest are particularly geared up for **cyclists**. The latter has several bike rental outlets and even a bus to take cyclists to the start of routes (see p.164). But there are plenty of other cycling possibilities and you're never very far from one of the numbered routes that make up Britain's **National Cycle Network**, 10,000 miles of signed cycle route, a third on traffic-free paths (including disused railways and canal towpaths), the rest mainly on country roads. All the routes are detailed on the Sustrans website (Ⓦsustrans.org.uk), a charitable trust devoted to the development of environmentally sustainable transport.

Most local tourist offices and good bookshops stock a range of **cycling guides** (see p.286) with maps and detailed route descriptions. You can also get maps and guidance from Sustrans and from Cycling UK (Ⓦcyclinguk.org) or organize a trip through a **cycling holiday operator** (see p.30).

Watersports

With hundreds of miles of coastline and inland waterways, the whole region offers excellent water-sports opportunities. Conditions for **sailing** around the Isle of Wight and the Solent are renowned, the waters celebrated for their double tides and challenging conditions. Not surprisingly, the area has spawned some of the globe's best sailors, many of whom return to take part in the **Cowes Week** sailing regatta on the Isle of Wight, one of the most famous sailing events in the world (see p.252). The UK Sailing

TOP FIVE WALKS

Studland to Swanage (Dorset). This clifftop trail offers fantastic views over Old Harry Rocks. See p.70

Langton Matravers to Worth Matravers (Dorset). A bracing coastal walk taking in archetypal Purbeck scenery. See p.78

Fritham to Frogham New Forest walk (Hampshire). A good walk along a ridge and through a range of New Forest scenery, from open heath to ancient woodlands. See p.180

Beaulieu to Buckler's Hard (New Forest). This tranquil riverside walk joins two of the region's traditional villages. See p.169

Tennyson Down (Isle of Wight). No wonder Tennyson was inspired: far-reaching views, towering cliffs and the Needles vie for your attention. See p.271

Academy (☎ 01983 294941, 🌐 uksa.org) in Cowes is England's finest instruction centre for windsurfing, dinghy sailing, kayaking and kitesurfing and offers non-residential and residential courses. **Weymouth** and **Portland**, too, have excellent watersports facilities, so much so that they hosted the sailing events for the 2012 Olympics.

But though offshore conditions are not for the faint-hearted – the English Channel being the busiest shipping lane anywhere, crisscrossed by container ships as well as giant cross-Channel ferries – there are also plenty of opportunities for less experienced sailors and other watersports enthusiasts. The shallow waters of **Poole Harbour** are excellent for beginner-level windsurfers, kayakers and kitesurfers, who can use the dedicated areas away from commercial craft. **Christchurch Harbour** is also extremely shallow and good for beginner sailors and for watersports – it has hosted international youth windsurfing competitions. Equipment rental is available from most major resorts, with prices for windsurf rental starting at around £15 per hour and kayaks around £10 per hour, while tuition for watersports starts at around £25 per hour.

Surfing has long been popular along the south coast of the Isle of Wight and around Bournemouth, in particular at the suburb of Boscombe (see p.43). Despite the failure of Europe's first artificial surf reef here, you can still surf along this stretch of coast when conditions are right, and it's a good place for beginners to try their hand. There are a couple of surf schools/rental shops here, plus some expensive "surf pods" (glorified beach huts) that you can rent by the week (🌐 bournemouthbeachhuts.co.uk). Bournemouth Surf School (🌐 bournemouthsurfschool.co.uk) offers surf and paddle-board lessons starting at around £35 (for 2hr sessions), plus surfboard rental from around £5 per hour and paddleboards for around £10 per hour.

EQUIPMENT RENTAL AND LESSONS

H2O 91 Salterns Rd, Poole ☎ 01202 733744, 🌐 **h2o-sports.co.uk.** Various watersports lessons and equipment rental in Poole Harbour.

Harbour Challenge Outdoor Education Centre Keysworth Rd, Hamworthy, Poole, BH16 5AS ☎ 01202 772436, 🌐 **harbourchallenge.co.uk.** Sailing, kayaking and watersports instruction for children and adults in Poole Harbour.

Paracademy Victoria Square, Portland, DT5 1AL ☎ 01305 824797, 🌐 **paracademyextreme.co.uk.** Kitesurfing and power-kiting lessons and equipment rental in Portland Harbour.

Studland Sea School Middle Beach, Studland, BH19 3AP ☎ 01929 450430, 🌐 **studlandseaschool.co.uk.** Based on Middle Beach, the highly recommended Studland Sea School rents out kayaks, gives lessons and runs excellent guided kayak tours round Old Harry Rocks, through cliff arches and sea caves. Also runs kayak/snorkelling, fishing, coasteering and foraging trips.

Wight Water 5 Rew Close, Ventnor, PO38 1BH ☎ 01983 866269, 🌐 **wightwaters.com.** Watersports training and equipment rental on the Isle of Wight.

Diving and rock climbing

The area is known for its excellent **diving**, especially around Lulworth and Portland where there are several dive schools (see p.119). Along with clear water, the chief appeal is a series of old wrecks that are easily accessible from the shoreline. See 🌐 ukdiving.co.uk for further information. The Isle of Portland is also something of a magnet for rock climbers, with about nine hundred climbing routes around its craggy shoreline, long sculpted by years of quarrying which has led to steep climbs with few overhangs. Note, however, that certain parts of the coast are off-limits during nesting seasons for some sea birds – always obey the signs or check with the local tourist office on 🌐 visitweymouth.co.uk. Purbeck, too, has some challenging climbs, most on sea cliffs, many with overhangs: Dancing Ledge and Winspit quarries near Worth Matravers (see p.77) are particularly popular.

Fishing

There are many first-rate fishing rivers in the region, but none better than the **Avon**, **Itchen** and **Test**, all in Hampshire. These are rated three of the top **fly-fishing rivers** in the country thanks to the chalky substrata. Alkaline water filters up through the chalk, creating clear river water with a consistent year-round temperature. This is perfect for plant and marine life, with salmon, grayling and trout in particular flourishing along with freshwater shrimp. The fish are well supplied with native stoneflies, caddis flies and other insects, which all makes for excellent fly-fishing conditions. Note, however, that most of the rivers are carefully managed so fishermen will need to find out about obtaining local permits.

Sea fishing is also popular in the area and Bournemouth beach is often lined with fishermen landing sea bass. Most of the main resorts' harbours, such as Mudeford, Swanage, West Bay, Lymington and Lyme Regis, also offer fishing trips, usually to catch mackerel.

Spectator sports

You can catch top-quality **cricket** throughout the region. The small town of Hambledon in Hampshire is regarded as the birthplace of modern cricket (see box, p.242), but by now the whole county of **Hampshire** is the cricket powerhouse. The club is based at the modern Ageas Bowl (perhaps better known by its traditional name of the Rose Bowl), Botley Road, Southampton (T 02380 472002, W ageasbowl.com), where you can also see occasional test matches. The county cricket season runs from around May to September, though for the full English cricketing experience, you may prefer to seek out a local match at a village green.

Football is, of course, England's national sport, and in recent years South Coast teams have been flourishing. **Southampton** have had FA Cup success, reaching the final in 2003 and famously winning it in 1976, and have played for several years in the Premiership at the modern St Mary's Stadium (T 02381 780780, W www.saintsfc.co.uk). However, the real success story is the meteoric rise of **Bournemouth AFC** from Division Two to the Premiership within six years under manager Eddie Howe: at 31, Howe was the league's youngest manager when he took over the team in 2009. Bournemouth's Vitality Stadium – still known to its fans as Dean Court – in King's Park (T 03445 761910, W afcb.co.uk) is currently the smallest in the Premiership, so tickets are pretty hard to come by. Despite winning the FA Cup as recently as 2008, the fortunes of **Portsmouth**, who play at the atmospheric but ageing Fratton Park (T 02392 731204, W portsmouthfc.co.uk), plummeted after bankruptcy, leaving them loitering in the lower leagues.

Activity holiday operators

Most operators offering **activity holidays** are likely to have two types of trip: escorted (or guide-led) and self-guided, the latter usually slightly cheaper. On all holidays you can expect luggage transfer each night, pre-booked accommodation, detailed route instructions, a packed lunch and backup support. Some companies offer budget versions of their holidays, staying in hostels or B&Bs, as well as hotel packages.

BOATING AND SAILING

Classic Sailing T 01872 580022, W classic-sailing.co.uk. Hands-on sailing holidays on traditional wooden boats and tall ships, departing from Southampton and Portsmouth.

CYCLE TOUR OPERATORS

Country Lanes T 01590 622627, W countrylanes.co.uk. Cycle day-trips, mainly in the New Forest and the Isle of Wight, including bike rental, a pub or picnic lunch or a cream tea.

WALKING

Contours Walking Holidays T 01629 821900, W contours.co.uk. Short breaks or longer walking holidays and self-guided hikes on the Isle of Wight, along the South Downs Way and on the South West Coast Path.

The Discerning Traveller T 01743 792622, W discerningtraveller.co.uk. Self-guided graded walking holidays in Dorset, based in B&Bs and guesthouses.

Footscape T 01935 817618, W footscape.co.uk. Dorset-based walking company offering a range of self-guided or guided walks around the Jurassic Coast and rural Dorset, from two nights to a week or more.

HF Holidays T 03454 708558, W hfholidays.co.uk. Guided week-long and weekend walking holidays on the Isle of Wight and Purbeck.

Hidden Britain Tours T 01256 814222, W hiddenbritaintours.co.uk. Gentle and low-key guided day walks in and around the New Forest, plus guided tours of Highclere Castle (home of Downton Abbey) and Jane Austen's Chawton.

GENERAL ACTIVITY

YHA T 0800 0191700, W yha.org.uk. Huge range of good-value hostel-based activity weekends and holidays, from walking, climbing and biking to surfing, kayaking and caving.

Travel essentials

Costs

The south of England is one of the priciest parts of the country, due to its relative affluence and proximity to the capital. Even if you're camping or hostelling, using public transport, buying picnic lunches and eating in pubs and cafés, your minimum expenditure will be around £50–60 per person per day. Couples staying in B&Bs, eating at unpretentious restaurants and visiting a fair number of tourist attractions are looking at £60–100 per person per day, while if you're renting a car, staying in hotels and eating well, budget for at least £120. This last figure, of course, won't even cover your accommodation if you're staying in stylish or grand country-house hotels.

Many of the region's **historic attractions** – from castles to stately homes – are owned and/or operated by the **National Trust** (T 03448 001895, W nationaltrust.org.uk) whose properties are denoted in the Guide with "NT". Most of the other historic sites are operated by **English Heritage** (T 03703 331181, W www.english-heritage.org.uk), whose properties are labelled with "EH". Both organizations charge entry fees for some of their sites, though many others are free. If you plan to visit more than half a dozen places owned by either, it's worth considering an annual membership (NT £63; EH £52), which allows unlimited entry to each organization's respective properties – and you can join on your first visit to any attraction.

There are also many **stately homes** that remain privately owned, in the hands of the landed gentry, who tend to charge £10–15 for admission to edited highlights of their domain. Other old buildings are owned by local authorities, which generally have lower admission charges or allow free access.

Municipal art galleries and museums across the region often have free admission, while private museums and other collections usually charge for entrance, but rarely more than £10. **Cathedrals** and some of the larger churches charge admission – of around £7 – but most ask for voluntary donations.

The admission charges given in the Guide are the full adult rate, unless otherwise stated. **Concessionary rates** for senior citizens (over 60), under-26s and children (generally from 5 to 17) apply almost everywhere, from fee-paying attractions to public transport, and typically give around fifty percent discount; you'll need official identification as proof of age. The unemployed and full-time students are often entitled to discounts too, and under-5s are rarely charged.

Crime and personal safety

Covering a largely rural area, Dorset, Hampshire and the Isle of Wight are relatively crime-free and visitors will feel pretty safe in all but a few small inner-city areas of the larger cities, such as Portsmouth and Southampton.

The **emergency numbers** for the Police, Fire Brigade, Ambulance and Coastguard are ⓣ 999 or ⓣ 112.

Health

Citizens of Commonwealth countries that have reciprocal healthcare arrangements with the UK – for example, Australia and New Zealand – are entitled to free medical treatment within the UK's National Health Service (NHS), which includes the vast majority of hospitals and doctors. The same applies to citizens of EU and EEA countries, on production of their **European Health Insurance Card** (EHIC) or, in extremis, their passport or national identity card – though it's advisable to check this on ⓦ ehic.org.uk before travelling, given the results of the UK's 2016 referendum on EU membership. If you don't fall into either of these categories, you will be charged for all medical services, so insurance is strongly advised.

Minor complaints and injuries can be dealt with at a **doctor's (GP's) surgery**, or by calling NHS Direct ⓣ 111 for free 24-hour medical advice by phone. For complaints that require immediate attention, you can turn up at the 24-hour casualty (A&E) department of the local **hospital**. In an **emergency**, call an ambulance on ⓣ 999 or ⓣ 112.

MAIN HOSPITALS

Basingstoke and North Hampshire Hospital Aldermaston Rd, Basingstoke, RG24 9NA ⓣ 01256 473202, ⓦ hampshirehospitals.nhs.uk

Dorset County Hospital Williams Ave, Dorchester, DT1 2JY ⓣ 01305 251150, ⓦ dchft.nhs.uk

Poole Hospital Longfleet Rd, Poole, BH15 2JB ⓣ 01202 665511, ⓦ poole.nhs.uk

Queen Alexandra Hospital Southwick Hill Rd, Cosham, Portsmouth, PO6 3LY ⓣ 02392 286000, ⓦ www.porthosp.nhs.uk

Royal Bournemouth Hospital Castle Lane East, BH7 7DW ⓣ 01202 303626, ⓦ rbch.nhs.uk

Royal Hampshire Hospital Romsey Rd, Winchester, SO22 5DG ⓣ 01962 863535, ⓦ hampshirehospitals.nhs.uk

St Mary's Hospital Parkhurst Rd, Newport, Isle of Wight, PO30 5TG ⓣ 01983 524081, ⓦ iow.nhs.uk

Southampton General Hospital Tremona Rd, Southampton, SO16 6YD ⓣ 02380 777222, ⓦ suht.nhs.uk

LGBT travellers

Most of the region's **LGBT** action is in the big cities – Bournemouth, Portsmouth and Southampton – leaving the rest of the area with a somewhat limited, low-key scene. LGBT listings and news can be found at PinkNews (ⓦ pinknews.co.uk) and Gay Times (ⓦ gaytimes.co.uk). For information and links, go to ⓦ gaybritain.co.uk and ⓦ gaytravel.co.uk.

Mail

Virtually all **post offices** are open Monday to Friday from 9am to 5.30pm, and on Saturdays from 9am to 12.30 or 1pm, with smaller branches closing on Wednesday afternoons too. In major cities main offices stay open all day Saturday, while in small and rural communities you'll find sub-post offices operating out of general stores, though post office facilities are only available during the hours above even if the shop itself is open for longer.

Stamps are on sale at post offices, newsagents and other shops advertising them. The **Royal Mail** website (W royalmail.com) details postal services and current postage costs, and can help you find individual post offices.

Maps

The most detailed **maps** of the area are produced by Ordnance Survey (OS), whose maps are vital if you intend to do any walking in the region. Their 1:50,000 (pink) Landranger series shows enough detail to be useful for most walkers and cyclists, and there's more detail still in the full-colour 1:25,000 (orange) Explorer series. There are three areas in this Guide covered by the Explorer series: OL29 covers the Isle of Wight; OL22 covers Bournemouth, Southampton and the New Forest; and OL15 covers Purbeck and South Dorset. Of the Landranger maps, 195 covers Bournemouth and Purbeck; 119 covers Portsmouth and East Hampshire; 132 covers Winchester and around; 144 covers Basingstoke and North Hampshire; 118 covers Shaftesbury and Blandford Forum; and 117 covers West Dorset.

The **National Cycle Network** of cross-country routes along country lanes and traffic-free paths is covered by a series of excellent waterproof maps (1:100,000) published by Sustrans (W sustrans.org.uk): the OS Tour 7 covers Hampshire, including the New Forest and the Isle of Wight.

Otherwise, for general route-finding the most useful resources are the **road atlases** produced by AA, RAC, Geographers' A–Z and Collins, among others, at a scale of around 1:250,000.

Money

Britain's currency is the **pound sterling** (£), divided into 100 pence (p). Coins come in denominations of 1p, 2p, 5p, 10p, 20p, 50p, £1 and £2. Notes are in denominations of £5, £10, £20 and £50. Scottish and Northern Irish banknotes are legal tender throughout Britain, though some traders may be unwilling to accept them.

Every sizeable town and village has a branch of at least one of the main high-street **banks** with an ATM. **Credit and debit cards** can be used widely either in ATMs or over the counter. MasterCard and Visa are accepted in most hotels, shops and restaurants in Britain, American Express and Diners Club less so. Plastic is less useful in rural areas, and smaller establishments such as B&Bs will often accept cash or cheques only.

Opening hours and public holidays

General **business hours** are Monday to Saturday 9am to 5.30 or 6pm, although the **supermarket** chains tend to stay open until 8 or 9pm from Monday to Saturday, with larger ones staying open round the clock. Most major stores and supermarkets **open on Sundays**, too, usually from 11am or noon to 4pm, though some provincial towns still retain an **early-closing day** (usually Wed) when most shops close at 1pm. **Banks** are usually open Monday to Friday 9am–4/5pm, with some branches also open Saturday mornings.

Banks, businesses and most shops close on **public holidays**, though large supermarkets, small corner shops and many tourist attractions don't. However, nearly all museums, galleries and other attractions are closed on Christmas Day and New Year's Day, with many also closed on Boxing Day (Dec 26).

Phones

There are few remaining public **phone boxes** in the region: those that do still exist usually take debit and credit cards (minimum charge £1.20) and coins (minimum charge 60p). Most people, however, rely

PUBLIC HOLIDAYS

Britain's public holidays, also known as bank holidays, are:

January 1
Good Friday
Easter Monday
First Monday in May
Last Monday in May
Last Monday in August
December 25
December 26

Note that if January 1, December 25 or December 26 falls on a Saturday or Sunday, the next weekday becomes a public holiday.

on the **mobile phone** network, which has decent coverage in all the major towns and cities and most of the countryside. There are occasional blind spots, and coverage can be patchy in rural and hilly areas, but generally you should have few problems: note, however, that in some coastal areas of the Purbecks, your phone may ping to a French network, which obviously has a stronger signal than the British one.

Time

Greenwich Mean Time (GMT) is used from late October to late March, when the clocks go forward an hour for British Summer Time (BST). GMT is five hours ahead of the US Eastern Standard Time and ten hours behind Australian Eastern Standard Time.

Tipping

Although there are no fixed rules for **tipping**, a ten to fifteen percent tip is anticipated by restaurant waiters. Some restaurants levy a "discretionary" or "optional" **service charge** of 10 or 12.5 percent. If they've done this, it should be clearly stated on the menu and on the bill. However, you are not obliged to pay the charge, and certainly not if the food or service wasn't what you expected. Cafés and bars may also leave a jar at the bar for small tips. The only other occasions when you'll be expected to tip are in taxis, and in upmarket hotels where porters, bellboys and table waiters expect and usually get a pound or two.

Tourist information

Many towns in the region have cut back on their **tourist offices** in recent years, though the main resorts still have fully staffed offices, while smaller towns may well have seasonal kiosks, staffed by volunteers, and with fairly erratic opening hours; full details are in the Guide. Most offices can provide information about accommodation, local attractions and facilities such as boat trips and bike rental, and many also sell or give away maps of local walking routes. The official national website, Ⓦvisitengland.com, has coverage of Dorset, Hampshire and the Isle of Wight, and the area has a number of useful regional websites too.

USEFUL TOURIST WEBSITES

Ⓦ **islandbreaks.co.uk** Ferry crossings, accommodation, festivals and activities on the Isle of Wight.

Ⓦ **thenewforest.co.uk** Campsites, activities and maps in the New Forest.

Ⓦ **visit-dorset.com** Provides information on accommodation, attractions, markets and events in the county.

Ⓦ **visit-hampshire.co.uk** Farmers' markets, shopping, events and activities in the county.

Ⓦ **visitsoutheastengland.com** Tourism South East official website that covers Hampshire, including the New Forest, and the Isle of Wight.

Travellers with disabilities

In many ways, the UK is ahead of the field in terms of facilities for travellers with disabilities. Train stations and airports are generally accessible, and many buses have easy-access boarding ramps. The number of accessible hotels and restaurants is also growing, and reserved parking bays are available almost everywhere. For further information see Ⓦtourismforall.org.uk or Ⓦaccessibleguide.co.uk.

Travelling with children

The region covered in this Guide is particularly suited to **holidaying with children**, with safe, sandy beaches, lovely campsites, traffic-free cycle routes, farms to visit, castles to clamber around and plenty of wet-weather attractions. Older children, too, are well catered for, with watersports such as sailing, surfing and windsurfing available all along the coast, while the larger resorts, such as Bournemouth, Weymouth and Southampton, provide good clubbing opportunities for older teens. There are also, of course, great festivals – the Isle of Wight and Bestival are excellent for teenagers, while Camp Bestival and the Larmer Tree are aimed at younger kids.

Most **pubs and restaurants** nowadays welcome families: some have specific family rooms or beer gardens, others are happy seeing children eat in the bar/dining area. Many **B&Bs and hotels** have family rooms, though some won't accept children under a certain age (usually 12); where this is the case, we have detailed it in the Guide. There's also no shortage of good-quality self-catering accommodation in the region (see p.23), which is often the most practical way to holiday with children.

Under-5s generally travel free on public transport and get in free to attractions; 5- to 16-year-olds are usually entitled to **concessionary rates** of up to half the adult price. Note that at attractions aimed specifically at children, such as theme parks and adventure farms, the children's rate is usually only a pound or so cheaper than the adults' rate.

149

Bournemouth and Poole

HENGISTBURY HEAD

Bournemouth and Poole

Long famed for its mild climate and immaculate sandy beaches, Bournemouth is one of Britain's most famous seaside resorts. In contrast to neighbouring Poole, which dates from the thirteenth century, Bournemouth is a relatively new town, founded around two hundred years ago and originally the playground of wealthy Victorians such as Gladstone, Edward VII and his mistress, Lillie Langtry, and Charles Stewart Rolls (of Rolls-Royce fame). Its beautiful setting – soft sandstone cliffs above golden sands – has inspired writers such as Robert Louis Stevenson and J.R.R. Tolkien.

Since World War II, **Bournemouth** has expanded to become Dorset's largest town, with its current population standing at over 160,000. Fortunately, only on a hot day in high summer does the **beach** get truly packed, and the town has enough shops, gardens and sights – including a tethered balloon, an oceanarium and the fascinating **Russell-Cotes Museum** – to occupy visitors and residents alike.

To the east of Bournemouth is the beautiful **Hengistbury Head** nature reserve, while the town's western suburbs now merge with neighbouring Poole to form a coastal conurbation of around a third of a million people. **Poole** has a very different feel, however, set inside an almost landlocked, giant natural harbour dotted with islands, including the idyllic **Brownsea Island**. The ancient port's long history of trade and boat building is still evident along its quay, where inns and fishermen's cottages overlook the comings and goings of fishing boats, yachts and pleasure cruisers.

Bournemouth

With seven miles of clean, sandy beach, a lively pedestrianized town centre and pleasant gardens, **Bournemouth** has plenty for families, while its nightlife attracts clubbers from all over the country. Once known largely for its retirement homes, the town now has a much younger, more vibrant air, abetted by its university and language schools, while weekenders down for stag and hen nights give the town centre a raucous atmosphere in summer. By day, however, its quaint cliff railways, pier and plethora of well-tended public gardens lend Bournemouth an undeniably genteel feel, while its sands form the best town **beach** on the south coast, with the quirky **Russell-Cotes Museum** on the clifftop above, overlooking the sea.

Bournemouth's **Central Square** divides the **Central and Lower Gardens**: this neatly paved plaza is the fulcrum for the town's largely pedestrianized shopping streets, which house a humdrum selection of chain shops. To the west is the suburb of **Westbourne**, where a couple of Victorian arcades house some upmarket shops, while the eastern cliff leads to the suburb of **Boscombe**, traditionally a rather run-down area, but now experiencing a resurgence following the construction of Europe's first artificial surf reef. Beyond Boscombe, the residential suburb of **Southbourne** leads to the end of Bournemouth's beach at the dramatic **Hengistbury Head**.

Marconi in Bournemouth p.39
Bournemouth by the book p.42
Percy Bysshe and Mary Shelley p.43
Beach living p.46
Bournemouth events and festivals p.48
Poole Harbour p.54

THE RUSSELL-COTES MUSEUM

Highlights

❶ **Bournemouth beach** Relax on the seven-mile stretch of sandy, south-facing shore that runs from Bournemouth to the Sandbanks peninsula in Poole. **See p.39**

❷ **The Russell-Cotes Museum** Check out the eclectic collection of Victoriana at this beautiful clifftop museum. **See p.40**

❸ **Walking on Hengistbury Head** Head out for a breezy hike over this isolated spit of land that seems a world away from the bustling town below. From the top, take in views over Christchurch harbour, the pretty painted Mudeford beach huts, the Isle of Wight and across to the Purbecks. **See p.46**

❹ **Cocktails at Urban Reef** Hang out at Boscombe's *Urban Reef* for a coffee, a cocktail or a meal and watch the surfers, kayakers and paddle-boarders gliding along the waters. **See p.50**

❺ **Boat trip to Brownsea Island** Take a boat trip out to this idyllic island in the middle of Poole Harbour – once there, you can follow nature trails through the woods, spotting red squirrels en route, or simply picnic among the peacocks and chickens which roam wild. **See p.56**

HIGHLIGHTS ARE MARKED ON THE MAP ON P.38

1

Brief history

Bournemouth was just open **heathland** until, some two hundred years ago in 1811, **Captain Lewis Tregonwell** built a holiday home on the site of what is now the *Royal Exeter Hotel*. A retired army officer, who had spent much of his career guarding this wild stretch of coast from invasion and smugglers, Tregonwell built a series of holiday villas, and planted hundreds of pine trees and a garden walkway to the beach known as **Invalids' Walk**, which was expanded in the 1860s to become today's Pleasure Gardens.

During the nineteenth century Bournemouth developed as a resort for the wealthy, and, because of its mild climate, it became popular with invalids. The roll call of famous **Victorians** who visited the resort for their health included Robert Louis Stevenson, Charles Darwin and Benjamin Disraeli, who came here for his gout on the recommendation of Queen Victoria. This royal approval, combined with the town's healthy reputation, sealed Bournemouth's status, and by the 1890s it was attracting such visitors as the Empress of Austria, Empress Eugenie of France and the King of the Belgians.

Wealthy landowner **Sir George Tapps-Gervis** was keen to develop Bournemouth into a resort to rival Brighton and Weymouth, so had Westover Villas, Westover Gardens and the *Bath Hotel* built in 1837, and under his guidance other hotels began to appear and grand villas started to line the clifftop. Bournemouth's **pier** was built in 1880, and the arrival of the **railway** in 1900 further boosted the town's popularity as a seaside resort.

Bournemouth's **population** grew dramatically too, from 692 in 1851 to 59,000 by 1900, and by the 1920s it had become a major resort, with facilities such as cliff lifts to take

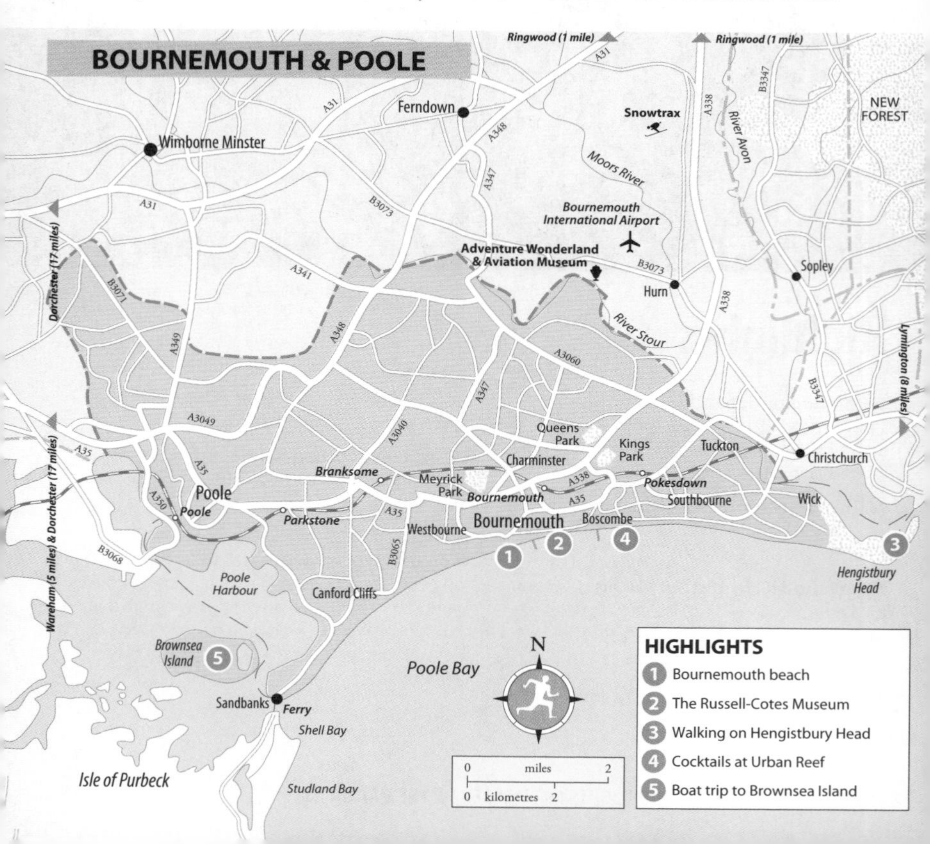

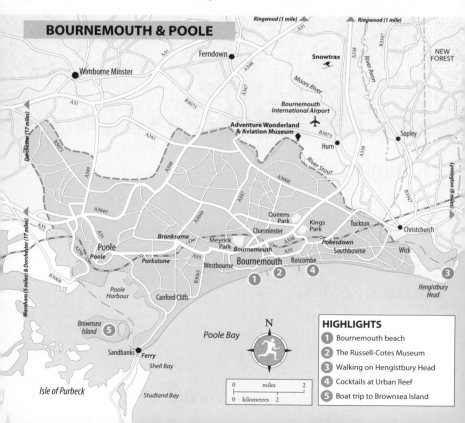

MARCONI IN BOURNEMOUTH

Bournemouth played a key part in the fledgling communication industry when **Guglielmo Marconi** (1874–1937) constructed a 30m-high radio mast at the *Madeira Hotel* on Bournemouth's West Cliff, in order to carry out experiments with radio transmission. In January 1898, the full impact of Marconi's work was realized. Close to death, the ailing former prime minister William Gladstone had gone to Bournemouth for his health, followed by the country's newspaper reporters. When a heavy snowstorm knocked out all the telegraph lines between London and Bournemouth, Marconi stepped in to relay news of Gladstone's rapid decline back to London by wireless, via a mast that he had set up at the *Needles Hotel* in Alum Bay, on the Isle of Wight (see p.272), four and a half miles away. This proved invaluable publicity for Marconi and his work, and on June 3, 1898, the world's **first commercial radio message** was sent from the *Needles Hotel* to the *Maderia Hotel*. Marconi later moved his experiments to the *Haven Hotel* in Sandbanks, Poole, which became a field headquarters for his company for 28 years and from where he succeeded in transmitting radio messages to and from passing shipping.

people to the beach, electric trams and buses, a theatre and a resident symphony orchestra. It continued to thrive until the postwar period, but by the 1970s suffered the same fate as most British seaside resorts as cheap air travel lured holiday-makers abroad. In the twenty-first century, however, the success of Bournemouth's university and language schools has attracted a laidback student/surfer crowd, while the credit crunch brought Bournemouth's core visitors, families, back to the town, after decades of holidaying abroad.

The beach

Bournemouth's golden sands are the obvious magnet for most visitors. Come on a hot day in the school holidays and the town-centre **beach** is inevitably heaving – it is best to head west towards Westbourne (see p.43) or east to Southbourne (see p.45) to escape the crowds. Bournemouth's pedestrianized promenade runs all the way to Hengistbury Head to the east and Sandbanks to the west – you can cycle the whole seven miles, outside July and August, when cycling is restricted to before 10am and after 6pm. There's also a seasonal toy train (Easter–Oct daily 1–2 hourly), which trundles from the pier east to Boscombe or Southbourne and west to Westbourne.

The pier

The beach spreads either side of Bournemouth's Victorian **pier**, itself stuffed with the usual arcades and amusements. Built in 1880, then extended in 1894 and 1909 to more than 300m long, the pier was used as a landing stage for steamers travelling along the south coast – more than 10,000 people landed on it one bank holiday in 1901. Today, boat trips still run in summer to Swanage, Poole, Sandbanks and the Isle of Wight, as well as high-speed, high-adrenaline excursions along the coast (see p.47). At the end of the pier stands the **Pier Theatre**, designed in 1960 by Elisabeth Scott, architect of Stratford's pioneering Royal Shakespeare Theatre and one of only two women to feature in the UK passport; the theatre closed in 2013, and today houses an indoor activity centre. The pier is also home to the world's first pier-to-shore **zip-wire**, a quick but exhilarating ride with dual wires so you can race down with a friend (April–Sept £18; Oct–March £15; Ⓦ rockreef.co.uk/pier).

Oceanarium

Pier Approach, West Beach, BH2 5AA • Daily 10am–5pm; low season may close at 4pm; peak season may stay open till 6pm • £11.95, under-16s £7.95; advance online £9.50, under-16s £6.50 • Ⓣ 01202 311993, Ⓦ oceanarium.co.uk

Just west of the pier on the seafront, the **Oceanarium** houses an impressive collection of sea creatures from around the world, including brightly coloured angelfish and corals, terrapins, stingrays and giant turtles, in themed areas, such as the Great Barrier Reef, Africa and the Ganges and the very dark Deep-sea Abyss. The highlight is walking along a tunnel through a huge tank, with sharks and stingrays passing over you as they swim. There's also a pair of crocodiles, a family of lively otters and some very friendly penguins to watch, as well as various talks and feeding sessions throughout the day.

Russell-Cotes Museum

Russell-Cotes Rd, East Cliff, BH1 3AA • Tues–Sun & bank hol Mon 10am–5pm • £6, under-16s £4 • ⓣ 01202 451858, ⓦ russellcotes.com

In attractive landscaped gardens with spectacular sea views, the **Russell-Cotes Museum** is one of the south coast's most unusual museums. Displaying the artworks and east Asian

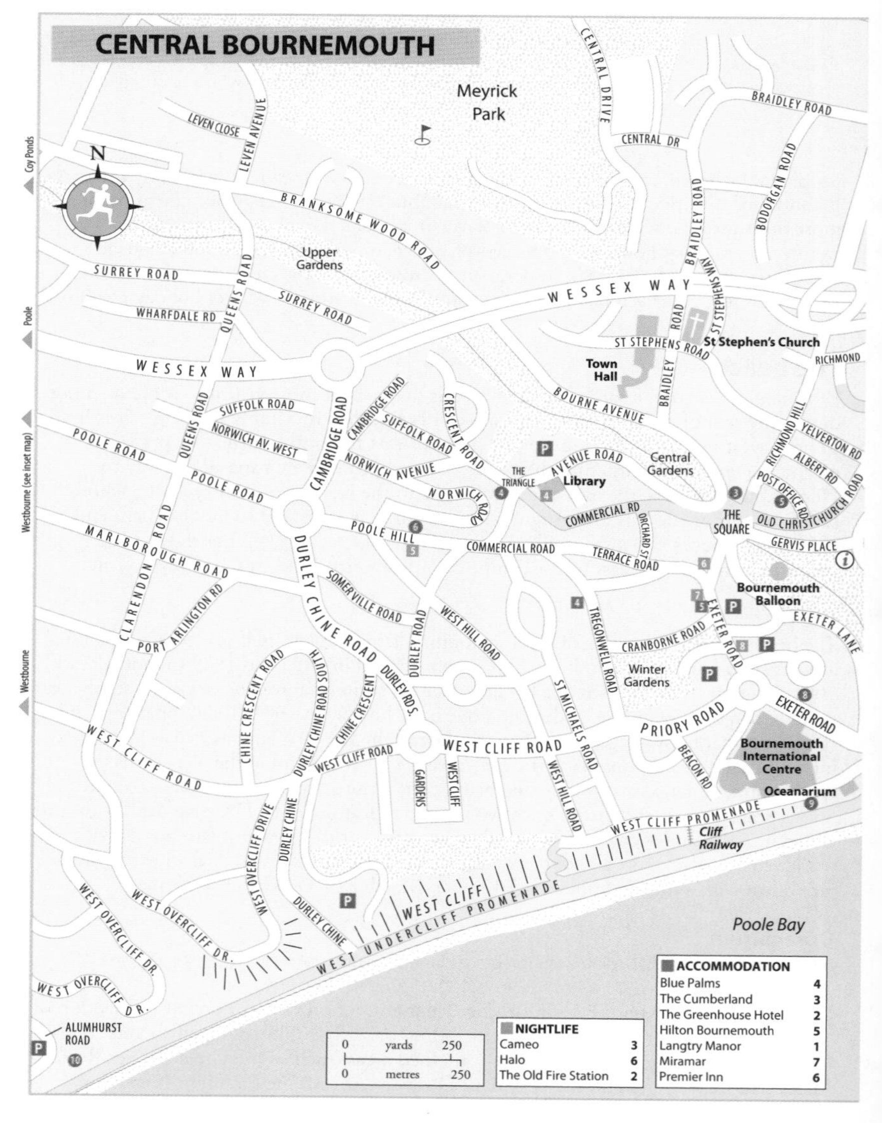

crafts collected by the wealthy Russell-Cotes family in the nineteenth century, the ornately decorated mansion and its eclectic collection was bequeathed to Bournemouth in 1922 after the death of Sir Merton Russell-Cotes, one of Bournemouth's most influential mayors, who also set up the town's first library and the seafront promenade. The clifftop museum houses a treasure-trove of Victorian artefacts, furniture and art from the family's travels in Russia, Japan and elsewhere, including Siamese swords and Italian paintings, such as Rossetti's *Venus Verticordia* (1864). Look out, too, for curios such as a table belonging to Napoleon and the axe that supposedly beheaded Mary, Queen of Scots. The museum also houses England's most important collection of

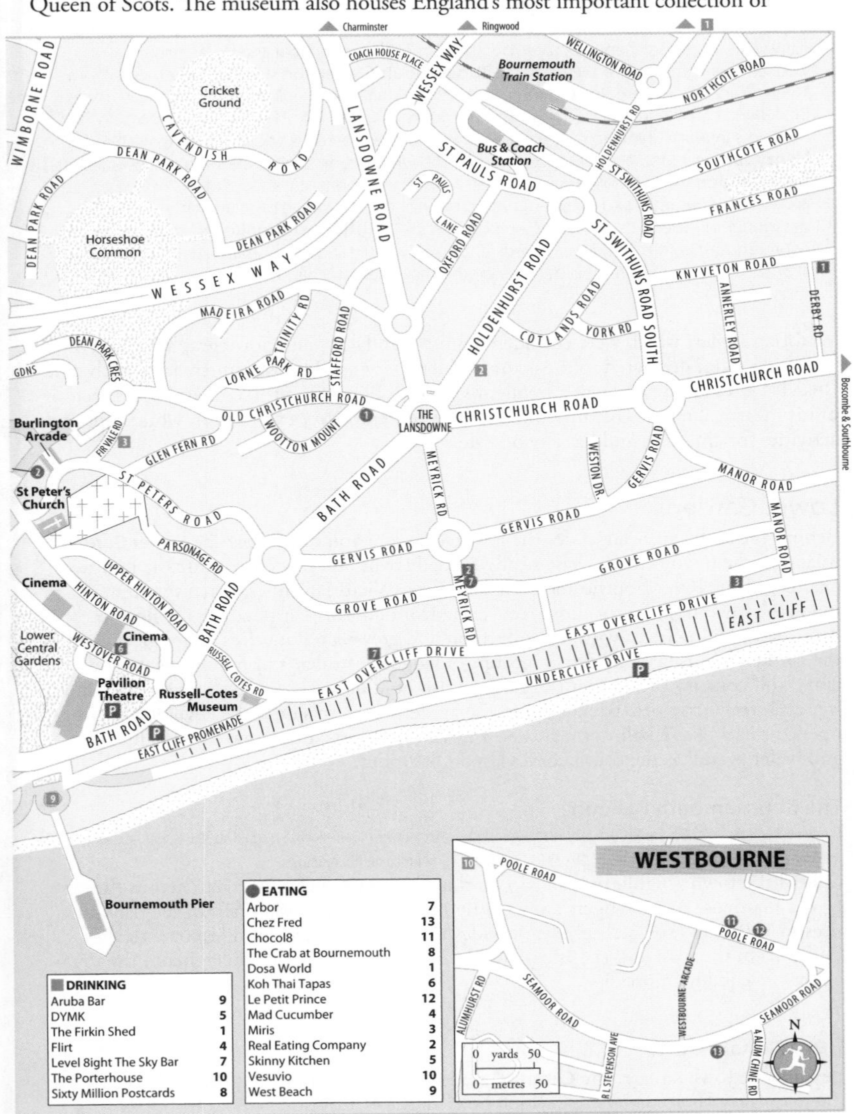

BOURNEMOUTH BY THE BOOK

Bournemouth has been the home of and inspiration for some of Europe's greatest and most imaginative writers. **Thomas Hardy** (see box, p.97) called Bournemouth "Sandbourne" in his books, describing it as "a fashionable watering place… like a fairy place suddenly created by the stroke of a wand": the pier is described in *The Hand of Ethelberta*, while Tess kills Alec in a fictional Bournemouth boarding house in *Tess of the D'Urbervilles*. **Mary Shelley**, author of *Frankenstein*, is buried in St Peter's Church along with the heart of her husband, **Percy Bysshe** (see box opposite), and her parents, William Godwin and feminist **Mary Wollstonecraft**.

In 1876–77, French Symbolist poet **Paul Verlaine** taught French at a Westcliff school after being released from prison for shooting fellow poet and teenage lover Rimbaud. **Oscar Wilde**'s early years were also spent teaching at a Bournemouth prep school and he later spent weekends at the *Royal Bath Hotel*. A frail **Robert Louis Stevenson** was in Bournemouth from 1884–87, initially undergoing treatment with a partly hallucinogenic drug – which may have influenced his writing of *The Strange Case Of Dr Jekyll And Mr Hyde*. He also wrote *Kidnapped* at his house in Alum Chine Road (a plaque marks the spot where his house stood), while his friend, **Henry James**, based his 1893 short story, *The Middle Years*, on Boscombe spa after several visits. **J.R.R. Tolkien** took his holidays for 30 years in the same room of the *Hotel Miramar* (see p.47), and in the 1960s retired to Bournemouth to be near the sea, which inspired some of the descriptions in *The Lord of the Rings*. He died here in 1973. **Rupert Brooke** also took holidays in Bournemouth before World War I, predicting – sadly, with hindsight – that "I shall expire vulgarly at Bournemouth, and they will bury me on the shore near the bandstand."

Victorian nudes, which were considered quite scandalous and pornographic at the time. There is a room dedicated to the actor Sir Henry Irving, who was much admired by the Russell-Cotes family and was a frequent visitor to Bournemouth, containing a selection of his theatrical relics. The museum also puts on temporary exhibitions, workshops and activities for children, and has a good café.

Lower Gardens

Behind the seafront, head under the low flyover and you can follow the **Lower Gardens** inland to the town centre. These neatly tended lawns and flowerbeds line the narrow channel of the River Bourne and were laid out in Victorian times, when the fresh sea air made the town popular for those recovering from illness. War poet Rupert Brooke described walking here "with other decrepit and grey-haired invalids", though these days the gardens are usually filled with groups of language students or families playing on the crazy-golf courses. In summer the gardens also hold outdoor concerts, workshops and free children's activities. Backing onto the gardens' eastern side is the **Pavilion Theatre**, opened in 1929 as a ballroom, and now hosting concerts, big-name comedians, theatre and ballet as well as the south coast's largest ballroom.

The Bournemouth Balloon

The Lower Gardens, BH1 2AQ • Easter–Oct daily 10am–8pm; Oct–Easter Mon–Fri 11am–5pm, Sat & Sun 10.30am–6pm: all flights weather dependent • £12.50, under-14s £7.50 • ⓣ 01202 558877, ⓦ bournemouthballoon.com

One of the town's highlights is a trip on the **Bournemouth Balloon** tethered in the Lower Gardens. As passengers sway gently in the hanging basket below, the balloon rises to 150m and, on a clear day, provides views up to nineteen miles, over to the Purbecks in the west and the Isle of Wight in the east. At night, the lights of the town below are equally impressive.

Central Gardens

Beyond the town square, the **Central Gardens** pass in front of the **town hall**, formerly the luxurious *Mont Dore Hotel*, which housed one of England's first telephones – its number was 3. In front stands Bournemouth's **war memorial**, erected in 1921 and flanked by two stone lions. The gardens then follow the Bourne stream north on its route through the Upper Gardens and onto Coy Pond Gardens. It's a pleasant two-mile urban walk along the stream, through gardens that get progressively less formal and landscaped the further north you walk.

St Peter's and St Stephen's churches

East of Bournemouth square, on Hinton Road, **St Peter's Church** graveyard is the final resting place of Mary Shelley, author of *Frankenstein* (see box below). The Grade I-listed church, built in 1879, was where Britain's prime minister William Gladstone took his last communion in 1898. The nearby **St Stephen's Church** on St Stephen's Road is of more interest architecturally, however: built by master Victorian church builder J.L. Pearson, it had an Italian-style campanile added in 1907, and has a beautifully vaulted interior.

Westcliff and Westbourne

Bournemouth's beach becomes progressively less busy as you head towards its affluent western suburbs. Here, the sandstone cliffs are interspersed with narrow gulleys known as **chines**, originally cut by streams but now mostly neat grass-banked approach roads or footpaths. Many of the town's hotels (see p.47) are strung out along and inland from the clifftop along these stretches. At **Westcliff**, you can access the clifftop via one of Bournemouth's ancient funicular railways. Robert Louis Stevenson (see box opposite), author of *Treasure Island*, set up home above the lovely beach at neighbouring **Alum Chine**, backed by exotic gardens and where one of the leafiest chines makes a fine walk up to Westbourne. History could have altered its course here – a young Winston Churchill fell off one of the bridges on this walk and nearly died. While it boasts few specific sights, **Westbourne** has some of Bournemouth's most upmarket, fashionable shops and restaurants gathered in and around a fine Victorian arcade.

Boscombe

Set below craggy cliffs, just under two miles east of Bournemouth pier, **Boscombe** has a laidback youthful vibe, an excellent beach and its own pier: originally built in 1889, the pier today is a simple walkway from which to admire the sea. When Boscombe was built, it was considered the smartest of Bournemouth's suburbs – possibly due to its spa and theatre – in contrast to today, when it has a more alternative feel.

The seafront

East of the pier lies the former **surf reef**, built in 2009 with sand-filled geotextile bags dumped offshore to create regular breakers. Unfortunately, it has never really worked properly, and it is now not used for surfing, though it is hoped that the underwater

PERCY BYSSHE AND MARY SHELLEY

Bournemouth and Boscombe have long been pilgrimage sites for fans of **Mary Shelley**, author of *Frankenstein*, and her husband, the poet **Percy Bysshe Shelley**. Mary Shelley's son, Sir Percy, bought Boscombe Manor in 1849 in the hope that Bournemouth's sea air would help his ailing mother, but she was to die two years later. Mary is buried in Bournemouth's St Peter's Church (see above), close to the heart of Percy Bysshe. In typically ghoulish Victorian fashion, Sir Percy then exhumed Mary's parents from a cemetery in London, so that the remains of William Godwin and Mary Wollstonecraft – author of *A Vindication of the Rights of Woman* – could rest with their daughter in Bournemouth.

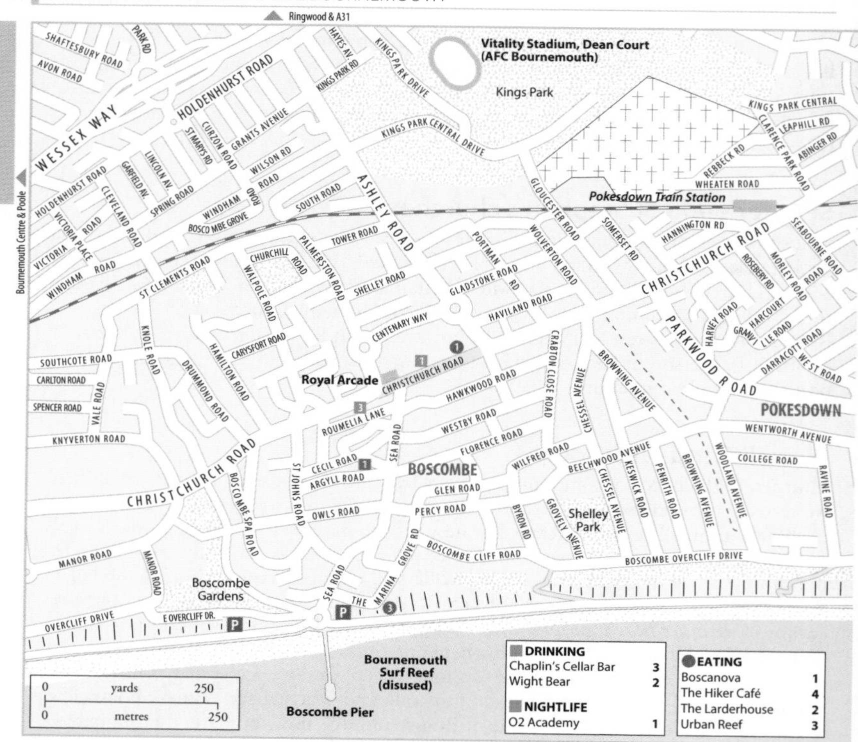

structure will attract new marine life and divers. Despite its lack of success, the reef spearheaded a major improvement in Boscombe's fortunes as part of a redevelopment plan that included a revamped plaza and the renovation of leafy Boscombe Gardens, which run up a wooded chine past children's play areas, cycle paths and a crazy-golf course – a toy train runs from here in summer to save the uphill hike. The formerly run-down seafront has received a face-lift too, with a revamp by Wayne Hemingway of the original 1950s beach into trendy **surf pods**.

On the opposite side of the chine are further neatly tended clifftop gardens, which extend as far as **Shelley Park**. This was all originally part of the Shelley estate, whose Boscombe Lodge – now converted into flats – sits in the northern edges of the park (see box, p.43).

The town centre

Boscombe was originally known for its spa water, which bubbled up from the foot of its cliffs, attracting health-conscious visitors from the 1870s. By the 1890s, it was considered an upmarket resort, with a smart shopping arcade and its own theatre on the high street. After World War II, Boscombe's fortunes dipped and it became synonymous with bedsit-land, drugs and petty crime. Around a mile inland, its pedestrianized high street is lively enough by day, with a good range of shops and cafés, but remains slightly seedy after dark. The renovated **Royal Arcade** is splendid, however, and the former Grand Theatre – now the **O2 Academy** (see p.52) – is the fashionable place to go at night, hosting big-name gigs and club nights, while several new bars and restaurants have opened nearby.

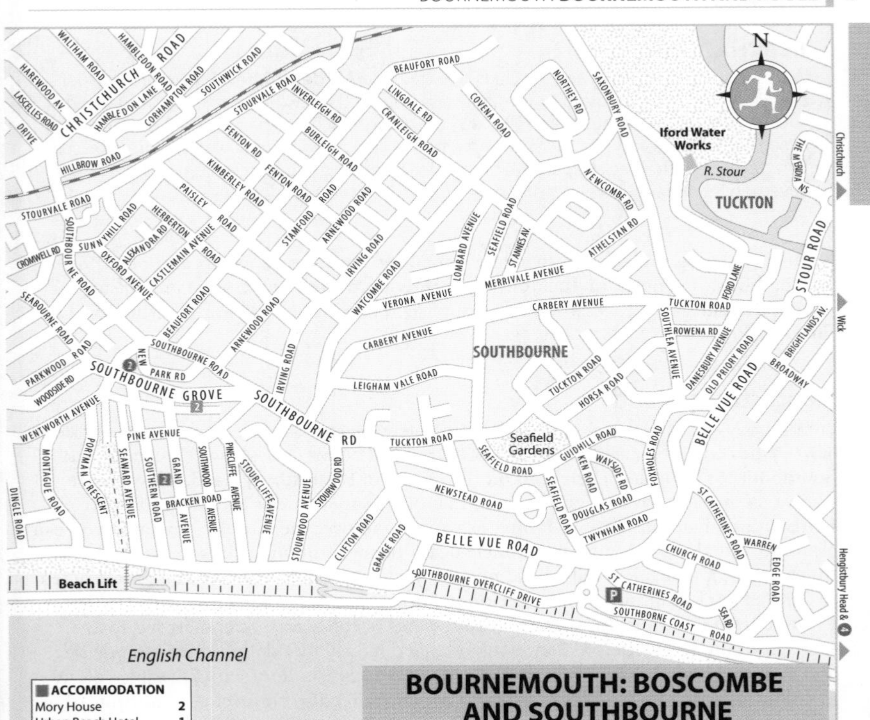

Southbourne

East of Boscombe the beach runs below sandstone cliffs to neighbouring **Southbourne**. This stretch tends to be relatively quiet even in summer, since access down the cliff is steep, but it catches the last of the day's sun, and the views towards the Isle of Wight are superb. Southbourne's Victorian pier was dismantled in 1900, but Southbourne High Street has seen a resurgence in the last few years with the opening of some decent new pubs, cafés and restaurants.

The suburb's main claim to fame is as the site of Britain's first ever fatal plane crash in 1910, which killed pioneer pilot Charles Stewart Rolls. The man behind Rolls-Royce took part in one of England's first ever air shows on the flat grassland above Southbourne beach, crashing his plane while attempting to land.

Apart from the beach and Hengistbury Head, the best local walks are along the River Stour, which divides this part of Bournemouth from neighbouring Christchurch.

Wick

A riverside path leads south from the bridge at **Tuckton** through parkland to the attractive hamlet of **Wick**; regular boats (Easter–Oct; Ⓦbournemouthboating.co.uk) run from the *Tuckton Tea Gardens* to Christchurch and Hengistbury Head, while in Wick itself there is a small passenger ferry over the river to Christchurch (see p.181). Beyond Wick lies a nature reserve known as **Wick Fields**; once a rubbish tip, this area now consists of verdant wetlands and grassy meadows, some of it grazed by cattle and with fine views back over Christchurch Priory. A path continues out to Hengistbury Head,

BEACH LIVING

With a stupendous outlook and a secluded position, the **Mudeford beach huts** are some of the few huts in Britain that allow overnight stays (Feb–Oct). They don't come cheap – indeed, you won't get much change from £200,000 if you plan on buying one, making them about as expensive per square foot as Sandbanks (see p.55) – and they have very basic facilities. You can rent the huts for the week (£800–1500), or just for a weekend in the off season: look out for adverts in the hut windows or on the notice board at the café.

popular with dog walkers and twitchers who often spot herons, egrets and other wading birds. Just north of Tuckton, the former **Iford Waterworks** is where Tolstoy's novels, then illegal in Russia, were first published by Count Vladimir Chertkov and his Free Age Press.

Hengistbury Head

visithengistburyhead.co.uk • Approach road daily 7am–10pm • **Land train** Daily except Christmas day • £1.80 single • **Ferry from Mudeford Quay** Every 15min: Easter–Oct daily; Nov–March Sat & Sun (weather permitting) • £1.50 single • 07968 334441, mudefordferry.co.uk

Southbourne's bungalows peter out on the fringes of **Hengistbury Head**, a low nature reserve set around a 37m-high headland that offers superb views over the coast and Christchurch harbour. Various footpaths run up and over the scrubby headland; you can also walk out along the sand-and-shingle beach below crumbling cliffs, or round the inner harbour, which is usually bustling with yachts or windsurfers. Cycling is restricted to a paved track running through deciduous woods parallel to the inner harbour.

A **land train** also runs this route, out to the end of the head, which narrows to a sandspit known as **Mudeford Sandbank**. Flanked largely by tidal mudflats on one side and a sandy beach on the other, this spit has one café-restaurant and a sizeable colony of colourful beach huts (see box above). Regular ferries also connect the sandspit to Mudeford Quay, on the other side of the harbour (see p.183), while less frequent boat trips run here from Tuckton (see p.45) and Christchurch (see p.181).

The land train leaves and arrives by *The Hiker Café* (see p.49), just by the main car park. Alongside this are fenced-off **double dykes**, a pair of defensive ditches built in 1 BC to protect a port which once traded with Europe – various coins and amphorae have been found on this spot. Evidence of Iron Age settlements has also been found on the Head, which until the last century was a flourishing centre for smugglers. For a time, the Head was owned by Gordon Selfridge (of shopping fame), and only World War I prevented his plan to build a giant castle on the top. For further information about the history and wildlife of the headland, the **Visitor Centre** (see opposite) is worth a browse, with exhibits, a wildlife garden, and webcams trained on the herons' nests in spring.

ARRIVAL AND DEPARTURE — BOURNEMOUTH

By plane Bournemouth's international airport (bournemouthairport.com) is a short drive northeast of the centre at Hurn, just off the A338. An airport shuttle bus runs to and from the town centre hourly (6.40am–6.30pm; 20–30min; £8 return); taxis to the centre cost around £16.

By train The train station is on Holdenhurst Rd, about a mile inland, by the main Wessex Way bypass. Frequent buses connect the station to the seafront and town centre, or it's a 15–20min walk.

Destinations Brockenhurst (3–4 hourly; 15–30min); Dorchester (1–2 hourly; 45min); London Waterloo (2–3 hourly; 1hr 50min–2hr 30min); Poole (2–3 hourly; 10min); Southampton (4–5 hourly; 30–50min); Weymouth (2 hourly; 50min–1hr); Winchester (4 hourly; 50min–1hr).

By bus The bus station is next to the train station, just off the main Wessex Way on Holdenhurst Rd, and is served by long-distance buses operated by National Express. Bournemouth's suburbs are well connected by local buses (see opposite).

Destinations London (hourly; 2hr 30min); Southampton (10 daily; 55min–1hr); Weymouth (5 daily; 1hr 20min–1hr 30min); Winchester (3 daily; 1hr 40min).

By car Strung out over a series of hills and dips, central Bournemouth can be confusing for drivers, with its one-way systems and pedestrianized areas: your best bet is to head for the seafront, where you'll find plenty of pay-and-display car parks, and walk from there along the gardens into the centre.

GETTING AROUND

By bus Local services are run by Yellow Buses (01202 636110, bybus.co.uk), with single fares starting from £1.60, or £4 for all-day travel, and More Bus, with day tickets for £4.10 (01202 338420, morebus.co.uk). More Bus also runs services to other local towns, such as Salisbury, Ringwood, Verwood, Wimborne and Lymington.

By taxi Taxi ranks at the station; along Westover Rd; and outside the BIC (see p.52). Fares from the station to anywhere within the town are around £5. Try United Taxis (01202 556677, 556677.com).

By bike You can rent bikes from On Yer Bike, 88 Charminster Rd (£12/day, £15/week; 01202 315855, onyerbike.co.uk). Alternatively, Front Bike Hire has a kiosk on the seafront, just east of the pier (Feb–Oct, but can deliver bikes the rest of the year; £5/hr, £15/day; 01202 373280, front-bike-hire.co.uk).

INFORMATION AND TOURS

Tourist office Centrally located on Pier Approach (April–June, Sept & Oct daily 10am–5pm; July & Aug Mon–Sat 9am–6pm, Sun 9am–5pm; Nov–March daily 10am–4pm; 01202 451734, bournemouth.co.uk). Can book accommodation.

Visitor Centre Hengistbury Head (daily: Easter–Oct 10am–5pm; Nov–Easter 10am–4pm; 01202 451618, visithengistburyhead.co.uk).

Boat trips Dorset Belle Cruises (01202 724910, dorsetcruises.co.uk) runs speedboat rides and cruises from Bournemouth Pier to Poole, Swanage, and along the coast.

Bus tours Discover Dorset (01202 557007, discoverdorset.co.uk) runs minibus tours (half-day £20; full-day £35) to nearby places such as Stonehenge, Bath and the Jurassic Coast, picking up from hotels and language schools throughout Bournemouth and Poole.

ACCOMMODATION

CENTRAL BOURNEMOUTH

Blue Palms 26 Tregonwell Rd, Westcliff, BH2 5NS 01202 554986, bluepalmshotel.com; map pp.40–41. A small but welcoming hotel in a tranquil backstreet, with well-kept, good-sized rooms. The owners are helpful and there's a comfortable communal living area and a small garden. **£90**

The Cumberland East Overcliff Drive, BH1 3AF 01202 290722, cumberlandbournemouth.co.uk; map pp.40–41. This sumptuous Art Deco building is right on the seafront, and has its own substantial outdoor pool with decking in the front garden. It also has a leisure club and stylish bar. Rooms are more standard, though bag one with a sea view and you won't be disappointed. **£135**

★**The Greenhouse Hotel** 4 Grove Rd, BH1 3AX 01202 498900, thegreenhousehotel.co.uk; map pp.40–41. Boutique-style, eco-friendly hotel in an attractive Victorian villa well placed for both the beaches and the town centre. The hotel has been well renovated, with stylish rooms that come with incredibly comfortable beds and organic linen and duvets, plus an excellent restaurant (see p.48). The hotel takes environmental issues very seriously, while not compromising on luxury or comfort, and the staff are friendly. **£140**

Hilton Bournemouth Terrace Rd, BH2 5EL 01202 804775, hilton.com/bournemouth; map pp.40–41. Newly opened, modern hotel in the centre of town with all the usual luxuries – a spa and health club, pool, good restaurant and cocktail bar (see p.50). The smart rooms are spacious with stylish decor and large windows – many have great views over the town, and some have a private balcony. **£160**

Langtry Manor 26 Derby Rd, East Cliff, BH1 3QB 01202 553887, langtrymanor.co.uk; map pp.40–41. Not particularly handy for the seafront, but a highly atmospheric former hideaway of Edward VII, who had the place built for his mistress Lillie Langtry in 1877. Standard doubles are spacious and well equipped, and if you feel like splashing out, you can stay in the king's grand former bedroom (£265). It also hosts theme nights, including Murder Mystery weekends, and Edwardian banquets on Saturdays in its restaurant. **£90**

Miramar East Overcliff Drive, BH1 3AL 01202 556581, miramar-bournemouth.com; map pp.40–41. Built as a diplomat's home with its own attractive gardens on the clifftop, this pleasant hotel has a friendly atmosphere and good-sized rooms. It's worth paying £15 extra for a sea view or, even better, a sea-facing balcony (£37.50 extra). **£150**

Premier Inn Westover Rd, BH1 2BZ 0870 423 6462, premierinn.com; map pp.40–41. In a lovely 1930s Art Deco building where the cover of a Beatles album (*With the Beatles*) was shot, this may be a chain hotel but it's very central and offers good-value accommodation. All rooms, including those for families, are the same price, so request one with sea views; off-season rates can be as low as £39. **£118**

BOSCOMBE AND SOUTHBOURNE

★**Mory House** 31 Grand Ave, Southbourne, BH6 3SY 01202 433553, moryhouse.co.uk; map pp.44–45. A friendly family-run guesthouse on a leafy tree-lined road, a few minutes' walk from the sea. The spotlessly clean rooms in this Edwardian house are all light and airy and decorated in a contemporary style, and the breakfasts are great. **£85**

BOURNEMOUTH EVENTS AND FESTIVALS

Classic Cars on The Prom April–Sept, Sun 4–6.30pm Ⓦ classiccarsontheprom.com. Classic cars from 1915 to the early 1980s gather along the seafront from the pier stretching up Westcliff most summer Sundays.

Bournemouth Wheels Early June Ⓦ bournemouthwheels.co.uk. A celebration of all things vehicular, from monster trucks, quad-bike races, stunt bikes, supercars and military vehicles to bmx and skating displays; much of the clifftop and seafront is cordoned off for this event.

Bourne Free Early July Ⓦ bournefree.co.uk. Bournemouth's annual LGBT celebration, with a parade, live music, drag acts and open-air films centred around the bandstand and The Triangle.

Friday Night Fireworks Fri in Aug, 10pm (varies by year). Free firework display from the pier.

Candlelight Nights Aug, Wed from 8pm. Children gather from dusk in the Lower Gardens to light more than 15,000 candles.

Bournemouth Air Festival Aug Ⓦ bournemouthair.co.uk. Hugely popular event with spectacular fly-pasts and stunts over the seafront by planes old and new, including the Red Arrows.

Bournemouth Arts by the Sea Festival Oct Ⓦ artsbournemouth.org.uk. A week of arts events around the town, usually involving pyrotechnics in the Lower Gardens, outdoor theatre, light displays and the Vintage mobile cinema.

Christmas Market Nov–Dec. Traditional wooden chalets fill Bournemouth Square, selling crafts and food.

Urban Beach Hotel 23 Argyll Rd, Boscombe, BH5 1EB Ⓣ 01202 301509, Ⓦ urbanbeachhotel.co.uk; map pp.44–45. A short (but steep) walk from Boscombe beach, this old Victorian townhouse has been given a boutique makeover. There is a variety of rooms, the least expensive with shower cubicles, but all are en-suite and stylish with designer furniture, comfy beds and DVDs. The downstairs bar-restaurant and terrace are also recommended. **£100**

EATING

Bournemouth's restaurant scene has improved in recent years, and there is now a decent choice of places to eat. Many of the town centre's cheap and cheerful restaurants and cafés are along the **Old Christchurch Road**, while **Charminster Road** has a good range of restaurants, with cuisines including Lebanese, Thai, Persian, Turkish, Spanish and Japanese.

THE TOWN CENTRE AND BEACH

★**Arbor** 4 Grove Rd, BH1 3AX Ⓣ 01202 498900, Ⓦ arbor-restaurant.co.uk; map pp.40–41. Seasonal, local ingredients beautifully served and presented at this stylish restaurant, in the eco-friendly *Greenhouse Hotel* (see p.47) in the centre of Bournemouth. Try main courses such as venison loin with suet pudding, or the chef's seafood plate, created from fresh local fish and seafood: there's a good-value three-course lunch and early evening menu too (£20). Daily 12.30–2pm & 5–10pm.

The Crab at Bournemouth Park Central Hotel, Exeter Rd, BH2 5AJ Ⓣ 01202 203601, Ⓦ crabatbournemouth.com; map pp.40–41. Light and airy restaurant that specializes in fish and seafood, such as Dorset rock oysters (six for £12), a half lobster (£23) or the trio of market fish (£20) made with the day's fresh catch. The pre-theatre set menu is good value, with three courses for £22, or two courses for £18. Mon–Thurs noon–2.30pm & 5.30–9.30pm, Fri & Sat noon–2.30pm & 5.30–10pm, Sun noon–2.30pm & 5.30–9.30pm.

Dosa World 280 Old Christchurch Rd, BH1 1PH Ⓣ 01202 318535, Ⓦ dosaworldbournemouth.co.uk; map pp.40–41. Basic café/restaurant serving excellent-value authentic South Indian dosas and other specialities, such as idli (a sort of mini doughnut made with lentils and rice and served with chutney and sambar). The huge, lacy dosa pancakes are stuffed with mildly spiced potato and vegetables or chicken tikka, and come with a selection of home-made chutneys and sauces (£4–7). Other dishes such as aubergine curry and mutton curry are delicious too, but can be on the spicy side for some. It's all very reasonably priced, and you can eat a full meal for around £12 a head. Mon–Fri noon–3pm & 6–10.30pm, Sat & Sun noon–10.30pm.

Koh Thai Tapas Daimler House, 38–40 Poole Hill, BH2 5PS Ⓣ 01202 294723, Ⓦ koh-thai.co.uk; map pp.40–41. Lively restaurant with stylish Thai decor – all dark wood furniture, comfy sofas and fresh orchids. The food is beautifully presented and can be ordered in tapas size or full portions. The delicious vegetable tempura (£5.50) followed by a tapas-sized veggie panang curry (£7) is easily big enough and won't break the bank. The cocktails are great too, and service is friendly and polite. Mon 5.30–10pm, Tues–Sun 12.30–3pm & 5.30–10pm.

Mad Cucumber 7 The Triangle, BH2 5RY ⓣ01202 236407, ⓦmadcucumber.com; map pp.40–41. You don't have to be vegan to enjoy the laidback vibe and tasty food at Bournemouth's only vegan lounge, with dishes such as mushroom stroganoff, or chickpea patties with salad and rice (main courses £6–8). The baked goods are fantastic too, including carrot cake, coconut cake and chocolate brownies. There's a good selection of games and books to browse, plus comfy sofas to hole up on, and performance art and open-mic evenings too. Mon noon–6pm, Tues, Thurs & Fri noon–9pm, Sat 10am–9pm, Sun 10am–6pm, open later in summer; check website.

Miris 53 Bourne Ave, BH2 6DW ⓣ07588 065360, ⓦmirisrestaurant.com; map pp.40–41. Family-run restaurant right in the centre of town serving large portions of (mostly meaty) Central European dishes, such as beef stroganoff and chicken or pork schnitzel (mains £10–15). The puddings are good and the lunch menu is great value at £12 for three courses. Tues–Sat noon–10pm, Sun noon–5pm.

Real Eating Company 2 Yelverton Rd, BH1 1DF ⓣ01202 291072, ⓦreal-eating.co.uk; map pp.40–41. Light, airy café with comfy seating, wooden floors and a full-size bay window. Just off the main shopping drag, it's a good spot for a quick lunch, with freshly made sandwiches and hot meals such as frittata (£7) and macaroni cheese, as well as tasty all-day breakfasts such as scrambled eggs, avocado and spinach on toast (£7.25). Mon–Sat 8am–6pm, Sun 9am–5pm.

Skinny Kitchen 14 Post Office Rd, BH1 1BA ⓣ01202 801238, ⓦskinnykitchen.co; map pp.40–41. Friendly café/restaurant where the menu shows the fat, calorie and protein levels of all the meals, which you can customize to suit your needs. Dishes include "skinny" pizzas (around £10), waffles, pancakes and steak, as well as courgette noodle dishes (£12) and great salad bowls, plus juices, shakes and protein drinks. Daily 11am–11pm.

Vesuvio Seafront, Alum Chine, BH4 8AN ⓣ01202 759100, ⓦvesuvio.co.uk; map pp.40–41. Bright and airy beachside restaurant, serving a range of generous pizzas, pasta and Italian main dishes. There's a pizza oven, a children's playground at the back and a lovely terrace overlooking the sea at the front. Expect to queue for a table in high season. Daily 10am–10pm.

West Beach Pier Approach, Westcliff, BH2 5AA ⓣ01202 587785, ⓦwest-beach.co.uk; map pp.40–41. This award-winning seafood restaurant has a prime position on the beach, with decking out on the promenade. It's smart and stylish, and you can watch the chefs at work in the open kitchen, or admire the sea views through huge floor-to-ceiling windows. Fish and seafood dishes – half a Poole Bay lobster with garlic and herb butter, chips and salad for £18.50 – feature strongly on the menu, as well as locally caught daily specials. Daily 9am–10pm; closed Mon evenings in winter.

WESTBOURNE

Chez Fred 8–10 Seamoor Rd, BH4 9AN ⓣ01202 761023, ⓦchezfred.co.uk; map pp.40–41. Top-quality fish and chips at this sit-down restaurant and takeaway, which regularly wins awards and is popular with locals and visiting celebs – hence the queues at peak times. Mon–Sat 11.30am–2pm & 4.30–9pm, Sun 4.30–8.30pm.

Chocol8 52 Poole Rd, BH4 9DZ ⓣ01202 766000, ⓦchocol8.co.uk; map pp.40–41. Entertaining café and chocolate shop with lavish, over-the-top decor, Louis V chairs, and shelves full of luxurious chocolates and cakes shaped like handbags or shoes. Sink back in the comfy chairs with a coffee or delicious hot chocolate, accompanied by Baileys or tiramisu truffles. Mon–Sat 9am–6pm.

★**Le Petit Prince** 48 Poole Rd, BH4 9DZ ⓣ01202 989874, ⓦlepetitprince.co.uk; map pp.40–41. Lovely French bakery and patisserie with a few tables on the street in front, selling great French cakes, bread, pastries and macarons, all made on the premises. Breakfast is baguette and jam or croissants (filled with ham and cheese, £3.50). For lunch, they do great toasted sandwiches with salad (around £5)– the Magic Bean toastie with butter beans, spinach and hummus is delicious, as is the Petit Prince toastie with bacon and avocado – or home-made quiche of the day. Mon–Sat 8.30am–5pm, Sun 9am–3pm.

BOSCOMBE AND SOUTHBOURNE

★**Boscanova** 650 Christchurch Rd, Boscombe Pedestrian Precinct, BH1 4BP ⓣ01202 395596, ⓦthecaffeinehustler.com; map pp.44–45. Boscombe's most bohemian café, with plenty of bare brick, works of art and a very good-value Mediterranean-influenced menu. The food is all freshly cooked and the meze (£9) is superb, as are the all-day breakfasts (in vegan, veggie and meat versions), soups, pancakes and fresh juices. Mon–Fri 8am–4pm, Sat 8am–5pm, Sun 9am–4pm.

The Hiker Café Hengistbury Head, Broadway, BH6 4EN ⓣ01202 428552, ⓦhikercafe.co.uk; map pp.44–45. Bright and airy café with outdoor tables by the land train departure point. The staff are efficient and friendly, and the food is all fresh and very good value, with hearty and filling breakfasts, grills, soups, sandwiches and cakes – the bacon-and-egg baps, made with free-range eggs, are huge (£4.50). Daily: summer 9am–5/5.30pm; summer school hols 8.30/9am–7pm; spring and autumn 9am–5pm; winter 9am–4.30pm.

★**The Larderhouse** Southbourne Grove, Southbourne, BH6 3QZ ⓣ01202 424687, ⓦthelarderhouse.co.uk; map pp.44–45. This excellent restaurant with a wood-fired oven and covered garden at the back is run by the world's best bartender, who took the top prize in the 2014 World Class bartending competition for his innovative and entertaining cocktails. The food is very tasty and freshly made with a Spanish/British vibe – baked eggs with chorizo and manchego or wood-fired roasted ham hock, for example (£8.50), but the drinks are just as important here. Enjoy the great wine list, or head upstairs to the Library (Wed–Sun), an atmospheric lounge bar where you can sample some of his fantastic concoctions such as the award-winning Copper Colours (£9), made with garlic-infused vodka, brandy, clementine oil and absinthe. Kitchen Mon–Thurs 11am–9pm, Fri & Sat 11am–10pm, Sun noon–10pm; open later for drinks.

★**Urban Reef** The Overstrand, Undercliff Drive, Boscombe, BH5 1BN ⓣ01202 443960, ⓦurbanreef.com; map pp.44–45. Lively, Art Deco-style restaurant/bar/café in a fabulous position on the seafront. It has great views from all three floors, and a large terrace for drinks at the front. The food is good – local and seasonal – and reasonably priced, ranging from pancakes with berries and maple syrup (£5) for breakfast, through tapas-style bar snacks such as octopus, steak tartare and Dorset crab pâté (£4.75 a plate), to steaks (£20), pumpkin ravioli (£11) and daily fish specials for dinner. Daily 9am–10pm.

DRINKING

Bournemouth's pub scene has improved in recent years, with the advent of microbreweries such as the Bournemouth Brewing Company (ⓦbournemouthbrewery.co.uk) and the Brewhouse and Kitchen chain (ⓦbrewhouseandkitchen.com) opening branches in Poole, Bournemouth and Southbourne, and there are also more than enough bars and clubs in the town centre to keep a vibrant nightlife pulsing until the small hours. The area around The Triangle is the hub of Bournemouth's gay life, with several long-standing bars and clubs: for further info and listings, check ⓦgaybournemouth.net.

Aruba Bar Pier Approach, BH2 5AA ⓣ01202 554211, ⓦaruba-bournemouth.co.uk; map pp.40–41. This Caribbean-themed bar with soaring ceilings, palm trees and resident parrot is recommended principally for its location above Bournemouth pier, with fantastic views along the beach and an outdoor terrace with comfy swing seats. By day, it's a chilled place to hang out, sip a mojito (£7) and watch the surfers below, while at night it turns into party city, with DJs and dancing. Mon–Thurs & Sun 9am–midnight, Fri & Sat 9am–3am.

Chaplin's Cellar Bar 529 Old Christchurch Rd, Boscombe, BH1 4AG ⓣ01202 251953, ⓦchaplins-bar.co.uk; map pp.44–45. Real ales, home-cooked locally sourced food at reasonable prices, friendly staff and quirky decor are all on offer at this atmospheric bar and music venue. Downstairs is where daily live music, comedy, cinema, open-mic or poetry evenings take place, while upstairs is more chilled, with comfy sofas, tables and a book exchange. The garden is a delight, with several terraces and a covered outdoor seating area. Mon & Tues 11.30am–1am, Wed & Thurs 11.30am–2am, Fri & Sat 11.30am–2.30am, Sun noon–1am.

DYMK 31 Poole Hill, BH2 5PW ⓣ01202 318566, ⓦdymk-bar.com; map pp.40–41. Good-value cocktails and drinks at this friendly gay bar. Hosts nightly events including drag acts, karaoke and cabaret. Daily 4pm–1am.

The Firkin Shed 279 Holdenhurst Rd, BH8 8BZ ⓣ01202 302340; map pp.40–41. Cosy local micropub with a fine selection of real ales and ciders – it may not look much from the outside, but inside it's all reclaimed wooden furniture, old piano and friendly vibe. No mobile phones, live music now and again and chatting to your neighbour is encouraged. Tues & Wed 4–11pm, Thurs–Sat noon–11pm, Sun noon–9pm.

Flirt 21 The Triangle, BH2 5RG ⓣ01202 553999, ⓦflirtcafebar.com; map pp.40–41. Friendly café-bar with quirky decor – a row of airline seats and Barbie and Ken dolls hanging from the ceiling – but also laidback comfy sofas, a giant screen and tables outside on The Triangle. It's a popular hang-out for gay and straight people alike, and the menu features sandwiches (£5–7), salads, tortillas, waffles (£4.50–6.50) and ice-cream sundaes (£7). Daily 9am–11pm.

Level 8ight The Sky Bar Terrace Rd, BH2 5EL, ⓣ01202 200188, ⓦlevel8skybar.com; map pp.40–41. Enjoy fantastic views through floor-to-ceiling windows or from the eighth-floor balcony at Bournemouth's highest cocktail bar, in the swanky *Hilton* hotel (see p.47), while sipping innovative cocktails. Many are made with local ingredients – try the delicious samphire and gin-based sea lavender martini, or the Bournemouth Sour, which packs a punch with the local Conker gin, elderberries and gorse flowers. Daily 11am–midnight.

The Porterhouse 113 Poole Rd, Westbourne, BH4 9BG ⓣ01202 768586, ⓦtheporterhouse.com; map pp.40–41. A small, friendly local pub with a good selection of local draught ales and ciders and plenty of board games. Mon–Thurs 11am–11pm, Fri & Sat 11am–midnight, Sun noon–11pm.

★**Sixty Million Postcards** 19–21 Exeter Rd, BH2 5AF ⓣ01202 292697, ⓦsixtymillionpostcards.com; map pp.40–41. One of Bournemouth's best bars, attracting an unpretentious but trendy student crowd. It's a chilled place to hang out – grab a booth and one of their tasty burgers (veggie or meat) and settle down to a game of Scrabble or a chat. Offers a good range of beers, a fine mojito, and DJ sets and live music. Mon–Thurs & Sun noon–late, Fri & Sat noon–2am.

CLOCKWISE FROM TOP LEFT HENGISTBURY HEAD (P.46); *URBAN REEF*, BOSCOMBE; THE BOAT TO BROWNSEA ISLAND (P.56) >

1

Wight Bear 65 Southbourne Grove, Southbourne, BH6 3QU ☎01202 433733, ⓦbearbeerfamily.co.uk; map pp.44–45. Friendly, lively, buzzing little micropub, where mobile phones are banned and dogs are welcome – there's no bar, staff come round and take your order from a blackboard of interesting craft ales and ciders. They also serve the local Conker gin, coffees and a few tasty, locally made nibbles, such as Scotch eggs and pork pies. Mon 4–11pm, Tues–Sat noon–11pm, Sun noon– 10.30pm.

NIGHTLIFE

Cameo Firvale Rd, BH1 2JA ☎01202 900071, ⓦcameonightclub.co.uk/bournemouth; map pp.40–41. Bournemouth's largest nightclub is a glitzy affair, with private booths and four different dance floors/bars all rocking a different vibe. Also runs mixologist masterclasses where you can learn how to make cocktails – and drink them too. Tues 10pm–4am, Thurs 9pm–2am, Fri & Sat 9pm–4am.

Halo Exeter Rd, BH2 5AQ ☎01202 552562, ⓦhalobournemouth.com; map pp.40–41. Inside a converted church, this lively club has everything you need for a good evening out – stiltwalkers, laser shows, fire-dancers – plus DJ sets, live music and club nights from the likes of Basement Jaxx, Danny Howard and Richy Ahmed. Daily 8pm–6am.

★**02 Academy** 570 Christchurch Rd, Boscombe, BH1 4BH ☎01202 399922, ⓦacademymusicgroup.com/o2academybournemouth; pp.44–45. Inside Boscombe's former opera house, the 02 is now home to live music, club nights with visiting DJs such as Annie Mac, and themed events like retro roller discos. Also hosts live acts such as Jess Glynne, Simple Minds, a variety of tribute bands and the latest X-Factor stars.

The Old Fire Station 36 Holdenhurst Rd, BH8 8AD ☎01202 963889, ⓦoldfirestation.co.uk; map pp.40–41. DJs, club nights, and one of the country's longest-running student nights, Lollipop, take place in this popular venue in a converted fire station. Also hosts live acts now and again – Ed Sheeran, David Guetta and Pendulum have all played here.

ENTERTAINMENT

Cinemas The Odeon, 35–43 Westover Rd, BH1 2BZ; ABC, 27–28 Westover Rd, both on ☎0871 224 4007, ⓦodeon.co.uk. Both centrally located, showing the latest big-name films.

Bournemouth International Centre (BIC) Exeter Rd, BH2 5BH ☎01202 456400, ⓦbic.co.uk. Just west of the pier is the brown brick building of the town's largest venue for big-name concerts, events and political party conferences: in winter, it also has a popular indoor ice rink.

Pavilion Theatre Westover Rd, BH1 2BU ☎01202 456400, ⓦbournemouthpavilion.co.uk. Smaller concerts, comedians and plays can be seen in the Pavilion Theatre.

Football Bournemouth FC – originally called Bournemouth and Boscombe Athletic – play at Dean Court (the Vitality Stadium), in King's Park, Boscombe. Their astonishing rise within just six years from the bottom of League Two to the Premier League in 2015 is one of football's success stories. Since their promotion, tickets are hard to come by, but if you can get hold of them you'll see some of England's top teams playing at the country's smallest Premier League stadium (for fixtures and tickets, see ⓦafcb.co.uk).

DIRECTORY

Hospital Royal Bournemouth Hospital, Castle Lane East ☎01202 303626, ⓦrbch.nhs.uk.

Watersports Sorted Surf Shop, 42 Sea Rd, Boscombe, BH5 1BQ (☎01202 399099, ⓦsortedsurfshop.co.uk), rents out equipment and runs courses and lessons for a variety of watersports, including surfing, kayaking, paddle-boarding, kitesurfing and windsurfing.

Poole

Arranged around the second-largest natural harbour in the world (after Sydney), **POOLE** is best approached by sea, when its magnificent position overlooking the wooded slopes of **Brownsea Island** can really be appreciated. The town has a reputation for being a millionaire's playground, largely because of the phenomenal prices of properties on the **Sandbanks peninsula**. Its luxurious reputation is reinforced by the fleet of Sunseeker pleasure boats that frequent the marina – they are built in a shipyard opposite the town quay and feature in several James Bond films. Poole's outskirts consist largely of unglamorous 1970s tower blocks, shopping complexes and bypasses, though the atmospheric **old town** behind Poole Quay is where the town's charm

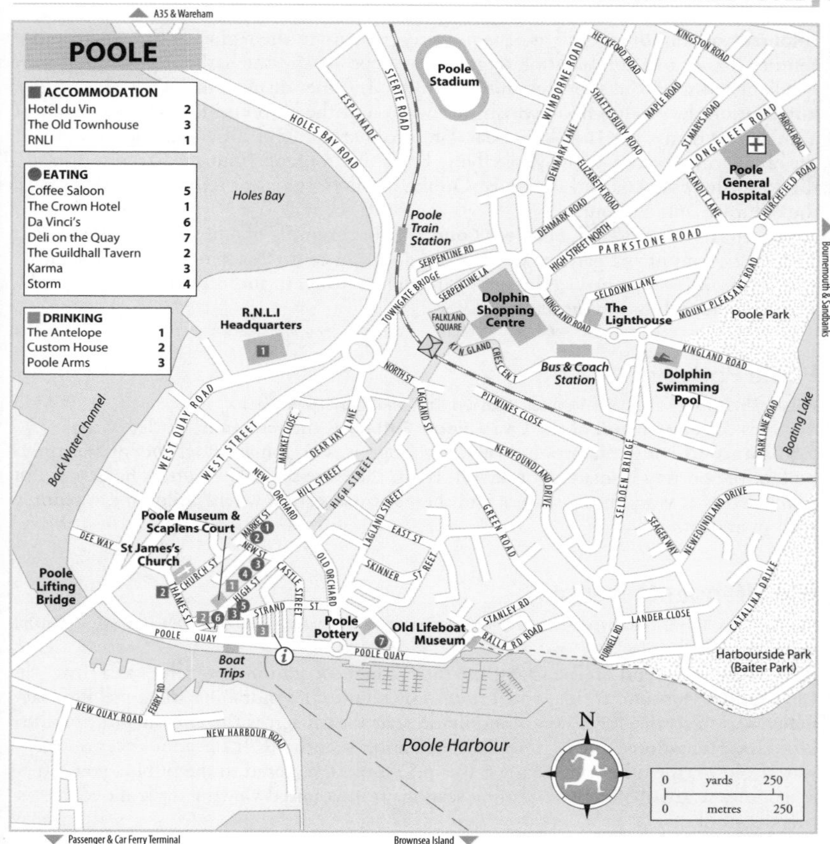

becomes evident. Developed in the thirteenth century, this ancient and historic port area was successively colonized by pirates, fishermen and timber traders and still contains over a hundred historic buildings.

Today, **The Quay** is home to an atmospheric strip of pubs, cafés and bars overlooking fishing boats, pleasure cruisers and the giant cross-Channel ferries that rumble out from the headland opposite. In summer, the central area is closed off to traffic and hosts events, including Thursday-night concerts, firework displays and Tuesday-night motorbike meets. Various kiosks sell tickets for **boat trips** up and down the coast, upriver to Wareham and to Brownsea Island (see p.57).

Poole Museum

4 High St, BH15 1BW • **Poole Museum** April–Oct Mon–Sat 10am–5pm, Sun noon–5pm; Nov–March Tues–Sat 10am–4pm, Sun noon–4pm • **Scaplens Court** Aug Mon–Sat 10am–4.30pm, Sun noon–4.30pm • **Scaplens Court Garden** May–Sept daily 1–4pm in good weather • Free • Ⓦ poolemuseum.co.uk

At the bottom of Old High Street, **Poole Museum** traces Poole's development over the centuries, in a building that successfully combines a contemporary glass entrance with an eighteenth-century warehouse, and the medieval town cellars behind, which house the local history centre. The third floor has an excellent display of local ceramics, with plenty of examples of the highly regarded Poole Pottery, from early samples to brightly coloured contemporary designs. The industry grew up in the region in the nineteenth century thanks to a combination of good clay deposits and the harbour providing excellent transport links for the finished products. Other displays include an Iron Age longboat on the ground floor, which was dug out of the harbour in 1964; carved out of a single tree trunk, the 10m-long boat dates from around 300 BC. Look out, too, for the fascinating footage of the Poole flying boats that took off from the harbour during the 1940s for east Asia and Australia. On the top floor is a great terrace with views over the old town and harbour.

Adjacent to the museum, **Scaplens Court** is a fine example of a medieval house, with a Tudor herb and physic garden. Used as an education centre for school groups for most of the year, it is only open to the public in August, when it puts on demonstrations of domestic life, exhibitions and events.

Poole Pottery

The Quay, BH15 1HJ • Mon–Sat 9am–5.30pm, Sun 10.30am–4.30pm • Free • ⓦ poolepottery.co.uk

Towards the eastern end of the Quay, **Poole Pottery** is the remaining outlet of the town's once-thriving ceramics industry. Although it is no longer independent and the bulk of the pottery is made in Stoke-on-Trent, there are still a few potters here; you can watch artists at work in the studio, and there's also a section where children can paint their own pots.

Old Lifeboat Museum

Fisherman's Dock, BH15 1RA • Run by volunteers, so opening hours erratic, but aims for April–early Dec daily 10am–4pm • Free • ⓣ 01202 666046, ⓦ poolelifeboats.org.uk

At the far eastern end of The Quay, the former lifeboat station now serves as a tiny **Old Lifeboat Museum**. Inside, you'll find some nautical memorabilia and a real lifeboat which was in service for 23 years and made several runs across the Channel during the Dunkirk evacuations. The current lifeboat station is at the RNLI headquarters on the waterfront on the other side of town (see p.57); though closed to the public, you can sometimes watch the lifeboat training sessions from a raised viewing deck above the practice pool.

POOLE HARBOUR

Formed during the last Ice Age, **Poole Harbour** is the second-largest natural harbour in the world after Sydney. Its surrounding heath and wetlands contain eighteen designated Sites of Special Scientific Interest, and most of the coastline is remarkably unspoilt, despite the sprawl of Poole and the well-hidden oil-pumping station at Brands Bay. It is also extremely shallow, with an average depth of just 50cm, making it ideal for a range of sea- and birdlife. The same conditions also make it great for **watersports**; kite- and windsurfing, wake-boarding, paddle-boarding, kayaking, sailing and power-boating can all be done through The Water Sports Academy in Sandbanks (see p.59). Cross-Channel ferries use a specially dredged, 7.5m-deep channel to negotiate the harbour, though patrols frequently have to rescue smaller boats caught by the deceptive tidal shallows. In all, the harbour consists of sixty miles of coastline, and shelters eight islands – mostly uninhabited – of which Brownsea Island is the largest.

The harbour has long been a busy waterway – the discovery of an Iron Age longboat here, now housed in Poole Museum (see p.53), shows that there was water traffic as far back as 300 BC. During the 1940s it also doubled as an airstrip, becoming the UK base for both military and commercial **flying boats**. Run by BOAC, they took off from the harbour to carry mail and passengers to the colonies, even travelling as far as Australia.

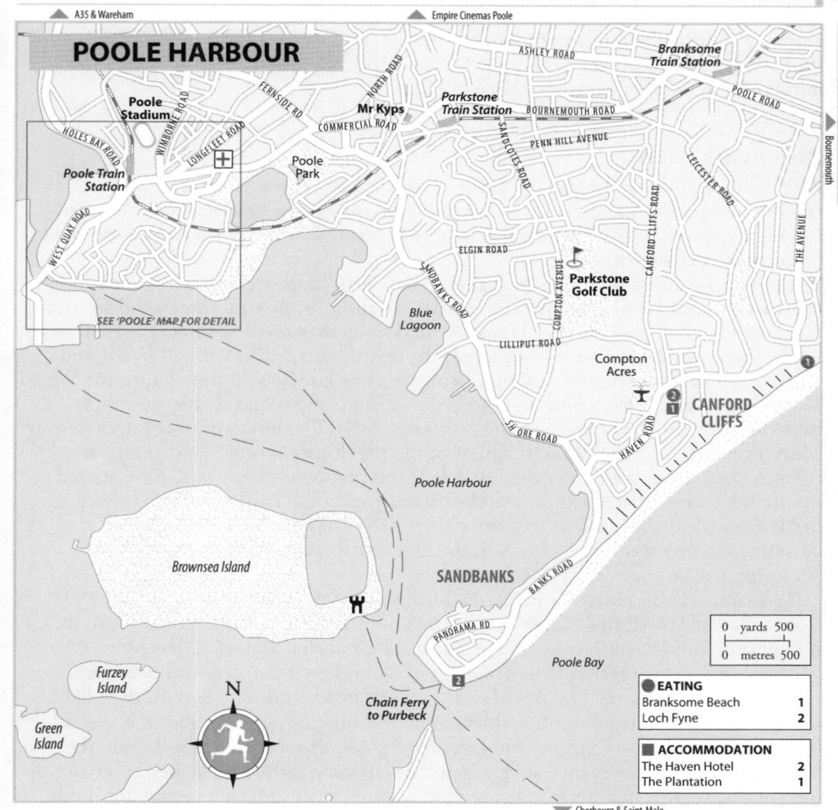

Poole Park

thearkpoolepark.co.uk

From Poole Quay, there's a pleasant waterfront walk via the broad **Harbourside Park**, aka Baiter, then further north to the more interesting **Poole Park**, an attractive space gathered round a substantial boating lake. As well as a large children's playground, there are tennis courts, a small ice rink, an indoor soft play area and a mini-train that trundles round a leafy duck pond daily.

Sandbanks and the beaches

The enviable position of **Sandbanks** – the flat, curved sandspit that protects Poole Harbour from the sea – has propelled house prices on this narrow peninsula to some of the highest in the world. Many of the properties back onto the soft sand **beach** (winner of a European Blue Flag for cleanliness and water quality more times than any other UK beach), while others, such as that of football manager Harry Redknapp, boast private moorings directly on the harbour. Most people, however, come for the beach and the **watersports** – the shallow harbour makes it excellent for learning windsurfing and kitesurfing (see p.59).

At the far end of the peninsula, a **chain ferry** (daily every 20min 7am–11pm, return 7.10am–11.10pm; £1 single; £4.10 with a car; sandbanksferry.co.uk) crosses the entrance of Poole Harbour to the superb beaches at the eastern end of the Isle of Purbeck (see p.71); the short ride is great fun, especially when giant cross-Channel ferries pass by in the surprisingly deep channel.

Brownsea Island

Mid-Feb to mid-March Sat & Sun 10am–4pm; mid-March to Oct daily 10am–5pm • £7, children £3.50; NT • Ⓦ nationaltrust.org.uk/brownsea-island • Ferries run every 30min (hourly mid-Feb to mid-March) from Poole Quay (20–40min; £10.50 return) or from near the chain ferry on the Sandbanks peninsula (30min; £6.50 return) • Ⓦ brownseaislandferries.com & Ⓦ greensladepleasureboats.co.uk

The ferry trip across the harbour makes a wonderful approach to the beautiful **Brownsea Island**, known for its red squirrels, wading birds and other wildlife. You can spot many of these species along themed trails that reveal a surprisingly diverse landscape – much of it heavily wooded, though there are also areas of heath and marsh, and narrow, shingly beaches. Brownsea was largely self-sufficient until World War I – it is said that incomers could only work on the island if they could play a musical instrument to entertain the residents. In 1927, the island was purchased by Mary Bonham Christie, who let much of the previously farmed land revert to natural heathland. When she died in 1961, the National Trust took over, backed by the John Lewis Partnership, which still maintains the castle. There has been a **castle** (closed to the public) here since the reign of Henry VIII, though the current structure was largely built in the eighteenth century and remodelled in Victorian times.

The island is also known for being the birthplace of the **Scout movement**. In 1907, Robert Baden-Powell took 22 working-class boys from Poole and Bournemouth to set up camp on the south coast of the island, an event that kicked off the now widespread Scouting movement. Though only John Lewis partners and employees can stay at the castle, the National Trust rents out two seaside cottages on the island (Ⓦ nationaltrustholidays.org.uk), while scouts and other groups can stay at a specially designated campsite – a magnet for scouts and guides from around the world. The National Trust lays on **events**, such as guided walks and nature trails, but otherwise the only public facilities are a harbourside shop, visitor centre and **café-restaurant**. Look out, too, for the fabulous summer Shakespeare performances at the **Open Air Theatre** (Ⓦ brownsea-theatre.co.uk).

Compton Acres

164 Canford Cliffs Rd, BH13 7ES • Daily: Easter–Oct 10am–6pm; Nov–March 10am–4pm • £7.95 • Ⓣ 01202 700778, Ⓦ comptonacres.co.uk • Bus #50 from Bournemouth & #52 from Poole

One of Dorset's most famous gardens lies on the outskirts of Canford Cliffs at **Compton Acres**, signposted off the A35 Poole road, towards Bournemouth. Spectacularly sited over ten acres on steep slopes above Poole Harbour, the gardens were laid out in the 1920s by a wealthy entrepreneur. They are divided into seven garden areas, each with a different theme, including a formal Italian garden and an elegantly understated Japanese Garden, whose meandering streams crossed by stone steps and wooden bridges make it a peaceful place to wander. There are also a couple of cafés/tearooms, a garden centre, a shop and a children's play area.

ARRIVAL AND DEPARTURE — POOLE

By train The station is north of the town centre on Serpentine Rd. It's about a 15min walk down the High St to Poole Quay.

Destinations Bournemouth (every 20min; 10min); London (2–3 hourly; 2hr 10min); Weymouth (2 hourly; 40–50min).

By bus Buses pull up in front of the Dolphin Centre. Local services are run by More Bus (Ⓣ 01202 338420, Ⓦ morebus.co.uk) and Yellow Buses (Ⓣ 01202 636110, Ⓦ bybus.co.uk). There are regular National Express services (11 daily; 3hr 5min–4hr) to London.

GETTING AROUND

By taxi Try Poole Taxis (T 01202 377020, W taxispoole.co.uk) or PRC Streamline Taxis (T 01202 373737, W prcstreamline.co.uk).

By bike The Water Sports Academy, Banks Rd, Sandbanks (T 01202 708283, W thewatersportsacademy.com), rents out mountain bikes for £20/day, or £12.50/half a day.

INFORMATION AND TOURS

Tourist office In Poole Museum, 4 High St (April–June, Sept & Oct daily 10am–5pm; July & Aug daily 10am–6pm; Nov–March Mon–Sat 10am–4pm, Sun noon–4pm; T 01202 262600, W pooletourism.com).

Boat trips Numerous boats leave from Poole Quay on trips round the harbour, to Swanage, out to Old Harry Rocks and upriver to Wareham. Companies include Brownsea Island Ferries (T 01929 462383, W brownseaislandferries.com), Greenslade Pleasure Boats (T 01202 669955, W greensladepleasureboats.co.uk) and Dorset Belle Cruises (T 01202 724910, W dorsetcruises.co.uk).

ACCOMMODATION

IN TOWN

Hotel du Vin Thames St, BH15 1JN T 01202 785570, W hotelduvin.com/locations/poole; map p.53. Inside a fine old mansion with a double staircase, this lovely hotel is well located in the old town near the Quay. The rooms, all plush and beautifully decorated, range from simple and stylish to large open-plan suites with a luxurious two-person bath and private terrace. The restaurant is good too, and there's a superb wine cellar, and a very cosy bar – great in winter, with its own log fire – as well as a lovely summer terrace. **£165**

RNLI West Quay Rd, BH15 1HZ T 0870 833 2000, W rnli.org/college; map p.53. The RNLI national headquarters is a modern, light and airy building, right on the waterfront, that doubles as a good-value hotel. Originally built for lifeboat crews on training courses, the rooms are all of a decent size, spotlessly clean and with views over Poole Harbour. There's a pleasant café and restaurant downstairs with a waterside terrace, and the staff are very friendly. **£105**

The Old Townhouse 7 High St, BH15 1AB T 01202 670950, W theoldtownhouse.co.uk; map p.53. Attractive little Victorian-style B&B in a great location opposite the museum, with a wood-panelled tearoom/breakfast room on the ground floor. The decor in the four rooms may be rather traditional, but they are spotless and comfortable – one has its own terrace – and the owners go out of their way to be helpful. **£95**

POOLE HARBOUR

The Haven Hotel Sandbanks, BH13 7QL T 01202 707333, W fjbhotels.co.uk/haven-hotel; map p.55. At the far end of the peninsula overlooking the chain ferry and Studland beach, this four-star hotel is in a great location, with a good restaurant, a spa, indoor and outdoor pools and the usual luxury facilities. It's worth paying extra for a sea-view room. **£165**

The Plantation 53 Cliff Drive, BH13 7JF T 01202 701531, W the-plantation.co.uk; map p.55. Colonial-style gastropub, with a comfy bar area and a spacious conservatory restaurant, which extends into a pleasant garden where, in summer, you can relax in cosy canvas shelters. The rooms are light and airy with stylish decor and all mod cons. **£140**

EATING

IN TOWN

Coffee Saloon 2 Grand Parade, Old High St, BH15 1AD W coffeesaloon.com; map p.53. Cosy little coffee shop with beer barrels for tables and wooden benches and stools to sit on. The coffee is good, and sourdough toasties, with fillings such as sausage and barbecue sauce or meatballs and cheese, are great (£4). Mon–Sat 8am–4pm, Sun 10am–4pm.

The Crown Hotel 23 Market St, BH15 1NB, T 01202672137, W thecrownhotelpoole.com; map p.53. Old-style pub with a piano and wood-burner and a secluded courtyard. It serves excellent food, such as New Forest mushrooms (£7) or scallops with lentils (£9.50), followed by the likes of roast shank of Dorset lamb (£17) or fish pie (£9.50). However, it's the mussels that are the speciality, cooked in a choice of sauces such as cider, apple and bacon, or tomato, thyme and chilli, as well as the classic *marinière* (£11 with bread; £13 with chips). Mon & Tues 4–11pm, Wed & Thurs noon–11pm, Fri & Sat noon–midnight, Sun noon–8pm.

Da Vinci's 7 The Quay, BH15 1HJ T 01202 667528, W da-vincis.co.uk; map p.53. Set in an old warehouse on Poole Quay, this is an old-fashioned Italian restaurant with friendly service and harbour views. The menu features inexpensive pizza and pasta, as well as pricier traditional dishes, such as vitello Milanese (£17), and daily fish specials. Mon–Fri noon–2pm & 5.30–10pm, Sat & Sun noon–10.30pm.

Deli on the Quay Unit 17 Dolphin Quays, The Quay, BH15 1HH T 01202 660022, W delionthequay.com; map p.53. Bright, light harbourfront café-deli with floor-to-ceiling shelves stacked with delicious preserves, wines and the like. The café is a great breakfast or lunch stop, serving fresh croissants, excellent coffee, pies, quiches and a good selection of sandwiches. Summer Mon & Wed–Fri 8.30am–5pm, Tues 8.30am–8.30pm, Sat & Sun 9am–5pm; winter Mon–Fri 8.30am–4pm, Sat & Sun 9am–4pm.

★**The Guildhall Tavern** 15 Market St, BH15 1NB, ⓦguildhalltavern.co.uk; map p.53. Fantastic French seafood restaurant with marine-themed decor and a small patio at the back, serving local fish and shellfish as well as traditional French dishes such as snails in garlic butter (six for £7) and boeuf bourguignon (£18). There's a very reasonable lunchtime set menu (two courses for £16 or three for £19.50) or splash out on the *fruits de mer*, such as crab, lobster, oysters and scallops. Tues–Thurs 11.30am–3.30pm & 6–9.30pm, Fri & Sat 11.30am–3.30pm & 5.30–10pm.

Karma 22 High St, BH15 1BP ⓣ01202 670181, ⓦkarma-mediterranean.co.uk; map p.53. Atmospheric dining room with quirky decor, bare brick arches and wooden tables. The food is Mediterranean/Middle Eastern cuisine; the tasty meze include aubergine dip, spinach and feta filo pastries and falafel (starter platter to share £13), and there are mains such as hearty grills (chicken or lamb kebab and rice), moussaka and kleftiko (£13–16). Tues–Thurs 5.30–9.30pm, Fri & Sat 5.30–10.30pm.

Storm 16 High St, BH15 1BP ⓣ01202 6749970, ⓦstormfish.co.uk; map p.53. The owner of this long-established restaurant catches his own fish and grows his own vegetables, or uses local suppliers – unsurprisingly, fish and seafood are the specialities. The menu changes daily according to what is available, but expect delicious dishes like Goan fish curry (£18.50) or local crab and prawn risotto (£20). Mon–Fri 6pm–late, Sat 5.30pm–late.

POOLE HARBOUR

Branksome Beach Branksome Chine, BH13 6LP ⓣ01202 767235, ⓦbranksomebeach.co.uk; map p.55. In a 1930s Art Deco building that used to house a swimming pool, this restaurant is right on the beach, with a great outdoor terrace. The menu is predominantly Modern British, with main courses (£13–20) such as local grilled plaice or roast breast of guinea fowl. Service can sometimes be a bit shaky, but the views are fab. April–Sept Mon–Wed 10am–5pm, Thurs & Fri 10am–10pm, Sat 9.30am–10pm, Sun 9.30am–5pm; Oct–March Mon–Fri 10am–5pm, Sat & Sun 9.30am–5pm.

Loch Fyne 47 Haven Rd, BH13 7LH ⓣ01202 609000, ⓦlochfyneseafoodandgrill.co.uk; map p.55. A light, airy colonial-style building with a bustling atmosphere. It serves excellent fresh fish, including more unusual dishes such as roast cod Malabar curry (£13.50), as well as the classic shellfish platters. Look out too for the good-value lunch set menus (two courses for £11). Mon–Thurs 7.30am–10.30pm, Fri 7.30am–11pm, Sat 8am–11pm, Sun 8am–10.30pm.

DRINKING

The Antelope 8 High St, BH15 1BP ⓣ01202 672029; map p.53. Cheerful five-hundred-year-old pub set round an internal courtyard, with cosy brick walls and flagstone floors. Its serves cheap and cheerful pub grub, such as sausage and mash or burgers (£9), and there's regular live music (usually tribute bands) and quiz nights: it also offers B&B in upstairs rooms. Daily 11am–10pm.

Custom House The Quay, BH15 1HP ⓣ01202 676767, ⓦcustomhouse.co.uk; map p.53. Complete with double staircase outside, the historic Georgian Customs house has a great outdoor terrace overlooking the harbour – it's a fantastic spot to catch the last of the day's sun with a cool glass of wine. Inside, there's a lively bar with several small alcoves, plus live music in the summer. It also has a good-value bar menu, with steaks and mussels the specialities, and a fine-dining restaurant upstairs. Tues–Sat 10am–11pm, Sun 10am–8pm.

Poole Arms 19 The Quay, BH15 1HJ ⓣ01202 673450, ⓦpoolearms.co.uk; map p.53. Completely covered with green tiles, this wonderfully atmospheric historic pub is reassuringly old-fashioned, with prints of old Poole on the walls, draught beers and a decent pub menu featuring fish specials. Mon–Sat 11am–11pm, Sun noon–11pm.

ENTERTAINMENT

For information on restaurants, theatres, clubs and festivals, pick up *Do More Dorset* magazine, free from bars, clubs and restaurants, or check out its website ⓦdomoremag.com.

Empire Cinema Tower Park, BH12 4NY ⓣ0871 4714714, ⓦempirecinemas.co.uk. Multiplex cinema in the Tower Park complex on the bypass into town.

Mr Kyps 8a Parr St, Ashley Cross, Lower Parkstone, BH14 0JY ⓣ01202 748945, ⓦmrkyps.net. Poole's premier live music venue, with a stream of mostly tribute bands but the occasional big-name band or up-and-coming star, including the likes of The Cuban Brothers, Ban Manners and Geno Washington.

The Lighthouse 21 Kingland Rd, BH15 1UG ⓣ01202 280000, ⓦlighthousepoole.co.uk. Southern England's largest art centre has an excellent calendar of live music, theatre, films, dance, art exhibitions and children's shows; also shows art-house films.

DIRECTORY

Hospital Poole Hospital, Longfleet Rd, BH15 2JB (Ⓣ 01202 665511, Ⓦ poole.nhs.uk).

Waterpark Splashdown (Ⓣ 01202 716123, Ⓦ splashdownpoole.co.uk) at Tower Park on the Poole bypass, BH12 4NY, has waterslides, rapids and flumes, both indoors and outdoors, plus splash pools and jacuzzis.

Watersports The Water Sports Academy, Banks Rd, Sandbanks, BH13 7PS (Ⓣ 01202 708283, Ⓦ thewatersportsacademy.com), rents out equipment and provides training for all sorts of watersports, including kayaking, sailing, windsurfing, wakeboarding and waterskiing.

The Isle of Purbeck

THE STEAM TRAIN AT CORFE CASTLE

The Isle of Purbeck

Though the Isle of Purbeck is far from being an island, its geographical inaccessibility makes it feel like one, especially if you approach it by ferry from Poole. It also has the timeless quality of an island, with Wareham and the amazing ruins of Corfe Castle rooted in past centuries, and only Swanage having anything approaching resort status. Its coast is remarkably unspoilt, in no small part thanks to large sections being owned by the Ministry of Defence – as demonstrated by the fascinating ruined village of Tyneham, which remains as it was when it was requisitioned by the military in the 1940s. Cliffs and inaccessible coves make this stretch of the South West Coast Path truly spectacular, especially round Lulworth Cove, and the iconic Durdle Door. Its other coves, such as Kimmeridge, Worbarrow Bay and Chapman's Pool, have their own allure, though beach lovers should head for the Studland peninsula and the glorious sands of Shell Bay.

Though only quite small – about fifteen miles by ten miles – Purbeck has a lot to see and do. As well as its truly great outdoors, there are also plenty of wet-weather attractions like Monkey World rescue centre, T.E. Lawrence's home at Clouds Hill and the Tank Museum at Bovington, all accessible from workaday **Wool**. The **Swanage–Norden steam train** is a fun, if pricey, way of getting around, but the best way to explore the area is by walking or cycling its wonderful footpaths and countryside. Most people drive, however, as local buses are fairly limited, which means that it can get very busy on summer weekends, particularly around the traffic bottlenecks of **Corfe Castle** and **Wareham**.

Wareham and around

Gateway to the Isle of Purbeck if you arrive by road or train, **WAREHAM** is a small, pretty town with a bustling Thursday market, which makes a good base for exploring the surrounding countryside, with the **Arne Nature Reserve** a great spot for local walks and birdwatching. There are plenty of attractions nearby that will appeal to children, such as an excellent local farm park, **Farmer Palmer's**, and the **Margaret Green Animal Sanctuary**.

The best approach is from the south across the River Frome, from where you get a good view of the town's skyline, little changed since medieval times. Indeed, the grid pattern of its streets indicates its Saxon origins, and much of the old town is still ringed by the old town walls (or the grassy mounds that remain), which formed defensive ramparts from the tenth century. The tourist office (see p.66) has leaflets detailing a walk round the town. There are also delightful walks in either direction following the **River Frome** – cross the bridge south of the town to pick up the path going east.

DURDLE DOOR

Highlights

❶ **Corfe Castle** Set in the heart of Dorset's loveliest countryside next to the village of the same name, these fairy-tale ruins rise spectacularly to form one of England's most impressive castles. **See p.68**

❷ **Shell Bay** Soft, extensive sands stretch around this lovely bay, making it the perfect beach destination. **See p.70**

❸ **Kayaking round Old Harry Rocks** Take an exciting kayak tour from Studland's beautiful Middle Beach around dramatic chalk stacks, through cliff arches and into sea caves. **See p.71**

❹ **Swanage to Norden railway** Hop on a steam train for a gentle chug from the lively coastal resort of Swanage through beautiful rolling countryside past the ruins of Corfe Castle. **See p.75**

❺ **Tyneham** In a remote Dorset valley, this ruined village was forcibly evacuated in World War II and has remained eerily empty ever since, though its schoolhouse and church are maintained as they were in wartime. **See p.80**

❻ **Durdle Door** Dorset's iconic geographical landform is one of the highlights of the Jurassic Coast and sits on a lovely shingle beach. **See p.81**

HIGHLIGHTS ARE MARKED ON THE MAP ON P.64

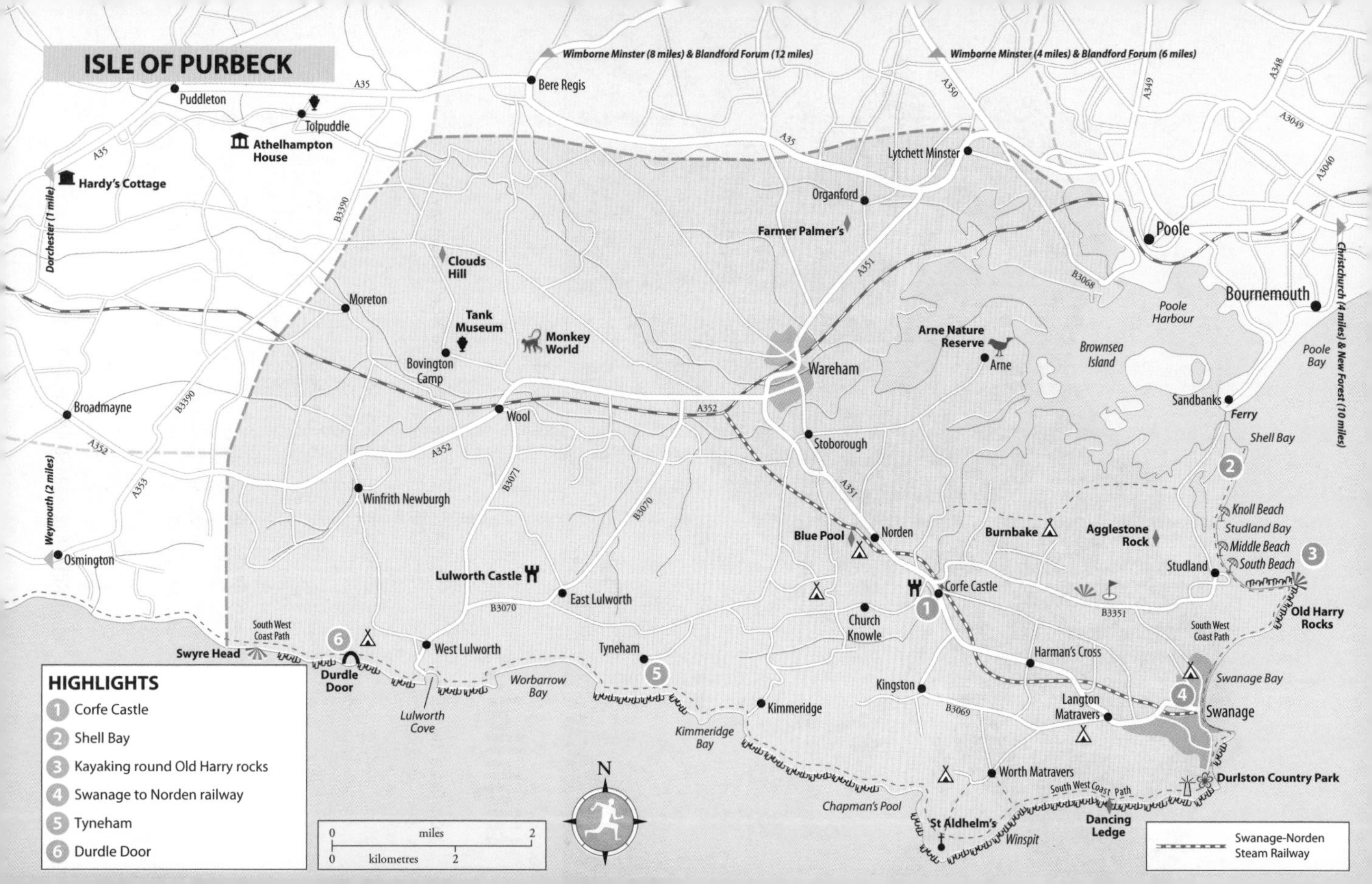
ISLE OF PURBECK
Wimborne Minster (8 miles) & Blandford Forum (12 miles)
Wimborne Minster (4 miles) & Blandford Forum (6 miles)
Christchurch (4 miles) & New Forest (10 miles)
Dorchester (1 mile)
Weymouth (2 miles)
Puddleton
Tolpuddle
Athelhampton House
Hardy's Cottage
Bere Regis
Lytchett Minster
Organford
Farmer Palmer's
Poole
Bournemouth
Poole Harbour
Poole Bay
Brownsea Island
Arne Nature Reserve
Arne
Sandbanks
Ferry
Shell Bay
Clouds Hill
Moreton
Tank Museum
Monkey World
Bovington Camp
Wareham
Broadmayne
Wool
Stoborough
Winfrith Newburgh
Osmington
Lulworth Castle
East Lulworth
Blue Pool
Norden
Burnbake
Agglestone Rock
Knoll Beach
Studland Bay
Middle Beach
South Beach
Studland
Corfe Castle
Church Knowle
Old Harry Rocks
South West Coast Path
Swyre Head
Durdle Door
West Lulworth
Lulworth Cove
Worbarrow Bay
Tyneham
Kimmeridge
Kimmeridge Bay
Kingston
Harman's Cross
Langton Matravers
Swanage
Swanage Bay
Worth Matravers
Chapman's Pool
St Aldhelm's
Winspit
Dancing Ledge
Durlston Country Park
A35
A350
A349
A348
A3049
A3040
A351
A352
A353
B3390
B3068
B3071
B3070
B3351
B3069
HIGHLIGHTS
1 Corfe Castle
2 Shell Bay
3 Kayaking round Old Harry rocks
4 Swanage to Norden railway
5 Tyneham
6 Durdle Door
0 miles 2
0 kilometres 2
N
Swanage-Norden Steam Railway

St Martin-on-the-Wall

North St, BH20 4AG • Opening hours erratic; phone ⓣ 01929 550905 to check, or pick up key from AF Joy in North St

At the north end of town, **St Martin-on-the-Wall** is one of the most complete Saxon churches in Dorset and parts of it date back to 1030. It holds a faded twelfth-century mural of St Martin offering his cloak to a beggar. The church's most striking feature, however, is a romantic effigy of T.E. Lawrence in Arab dress, carved by Eric Kennington, the official World War II artist. It was destined for Salisbury Cathedral, but was rejected by the dean there who disapproved of Lawrence's sexual proclivities.

Wareham Town Museum

3 East St, BH20 4NS • Easter–Oct Mon–Sat 10am–4pm • Free • ⓣ 01929 553448, ⓦ greenacre.info/WTM

The small **museum** next to Wareham's town hall romps through the town's history, with displays of pottery and the famous local geology. Of most interest is the T.E. Lawrence memorabilia, a good place to whet your appetite before visiting nearby Clouds Hill (see p.83) where he lived.

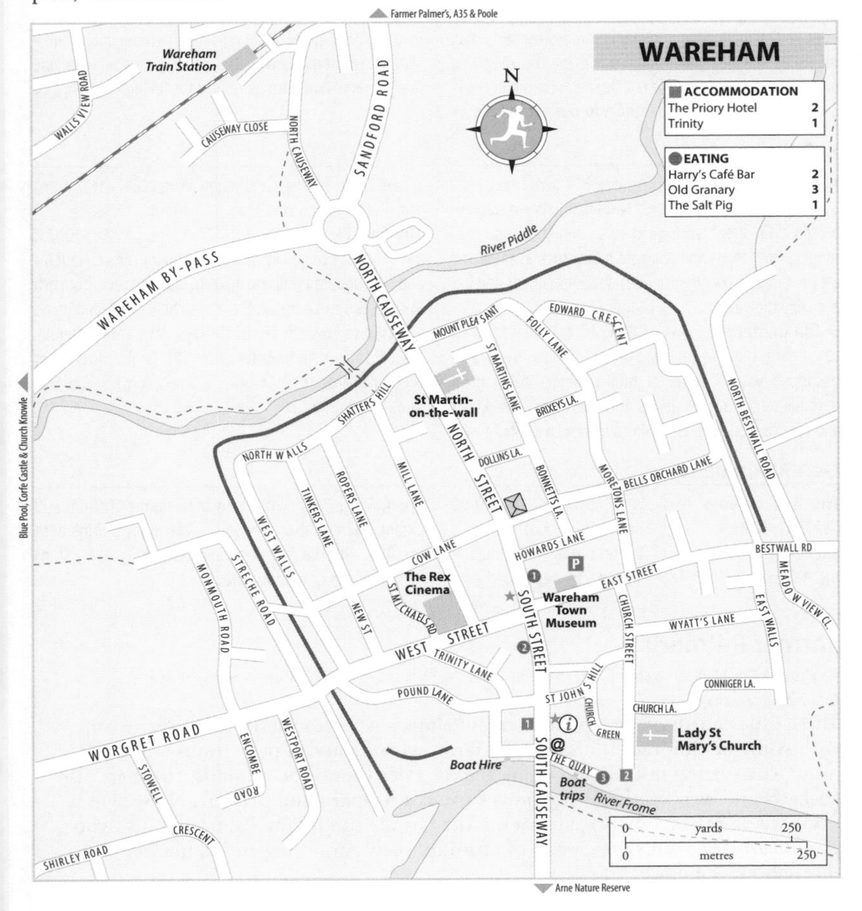

ARRIVAL AND DEPARTURE — WAREHAM

By train Wareham is on the main London to Weymouth train line (every 30min–1hr; around 2hr 40min from London). The station is around a 15min walk north of town.

By bus Wareham is served by National Express coaches from London (1 daily; 4hr 20min) and Poole (2 daily; 15–20min), and by bus #40 from Poole, Corfe Castle and Swanage (daily, 1 hourly).

INFORMATION AND ACTIVITIES

Tourist office In Wareham Library on South St (Mon 10am–5pm, Tues 9.30am–6.30pm, Wed–Fri 9.30am–5pm, Sat 9am–5pm; 01929 552740, visit-dorset .com).

Boat rental You can rent canoes, motor boats and kayaks from the quay to go up the River Frome, from around £10 per hour (01929 550688, warehamboathire.co.uk).

Boat trips You can take a boat trip up here from Poole when tidal conditions allow (dorsetcruises.co.uk). From £15 return.

ACCOMMODATION

The Priory Hotel Church Green, BH20 4ND 01929 551666, theprioryhotel.co.uk. This luxury hotel is housed in a former priory (as the name suggests) dating back over 500 years. Rooms range from old-style luxurious ones in the main house through to more contemporary rooms in the old boathouses down by the river. The rather formal restaurant offers a three-course menu (£48), as well as a cheaper lunch, and you can eat outside on the terrace in fine weather. Minimum two-night stay at weekends. **£220**

Trinity 32 South St, BH20 4LU 01929 556689, trinitybnb.co.uk. Close to the river, this homely B&B in a Grade II-listed building has charming rooms in a sixteenth-century townhouse, some en suite, with one family room. Minimum two-night stay in high season. **£70**

EATING

Harry's Café Bar 20 South St, BH20 4LT 01929 551818, harrysbars.co.uk. Fashionable bar-restaurant on the main street, with good-value breakfasts and food ranging from tapas and wraps to mains such as steak and ale pie (around £6–9). Also does delicious coffees and has a small patio garden. Daily 10am–11pm.

★ **Old Granary** The Quay, BH20 4LP 01929 552010, theoldgranarywareham.co.uk. Stylishly renovated gastropub with a series of bright rooms and a great riverside terrace on two levels. It serves decent breakfasts and teas, as well as classy main courses such as plaice with capers, burgers, salads and veggie dishes (£11–16). Mon–Sat 11am–11pm, Sun 11am–10.30pm.

The Salt Pig 6 North St, BH20 4AF 01929 550673, thesaltpig.co.uk. Attractive and buzzy café, restaurant and farm shop specializing in fresh, local produce, from fish to cheeses and ice cream. The menu changes depending on what's in season, but expect the likes of venison casserole, sea bass fillets and lobster (£14–28). It also does great sharing boards (£18). Mon–Fri 8am–7pm, Sat & Sun 8am–10pm.

ENTERTAINMENT

The Rex Cinema 14 West St, BH20 4JX 01929 552778, therex.co.uk. Film buffs should definitely drop by The Rex, one of Dorset's oldest cinemas – the hall was built in 1889, and it has been used as a cinema since 1927, with many of its original fittings still extant. There is also a bar so you can enjoy a drink with the film, and the *Five and Dime* café (daily 8am–5pm) for breakfasts or light lunches.

Farmer Palmer's

Wareham Rd, Organford, BH16 6EU • Daily: Feb, March, Nov & Dec 10am–4pm; April–Oct 10am–5.30pm • £8.75 • farmerpalmers.co.uk

Three miles north of Wareham, **Farmer Palmer's** is a great destination for anyone with younger children. It's a working farm, where you can pet various animals, watch cows being milked and enjoy tractor rides round the grounds; there are also go-karts and wet-weather attractions such as a haybarn and play area, as well as a café serving reasonably priced snacks. The farm is run by the Palmer family, who give informative talks on aspects of farming, such as milking and lamb-feeding, throughout the day.

A ROUND WALK FROM CORFE CASTLE TO THE BLUE POOL

This lovely five-mile round walk takes in a mixture of hills, ancient woodland and heathland, with a small section on road. Start on the **Purbeck Way**, a signed footpath just north of the junction between the A351 to Wareham and the minor road to Church Knowle. This section is fairly steep, skirting some old clay pits. The path then descends to pass the west edge of **Norden Farm campsite** (see p.69) – take the gate at the far end of the camping field which passes into the ancient woods of Norden Plantation. Bear left and follow this path (signed East Creech). After around 25 minutes the path meets a minor road – bear sharp right, staying on the path, which cuts off a corner of the road itself. You eventually rejoin this road for the last 100m or so before the signed turning right to the **Blue Pool** (see below). To return, take the track sharp right out of the Blue Pool exit, which skirts its perimeter fence before crossing the broad Norden Heath. Follow the signs back to Norden Farm from where you can return to Corfe Castle (see p.68) the way you came.

Blue Pool

Furzebrook, BH20 5AR • March–Nov daily 9am–dusk • £6 • ⓦ bluepooltearooms.co.uk

Around three miles southwest of Wareham lies the **Blue Pool**, a clay pit whose waters are famed for their remarkable colours, varying from bright green to blue – or grey if you catch it on a dull day. It's rather overpriced, but the tearooms (from 10am) and surrounding woodlands are a peaceful place to spend an hour or so and the grounds include a great playground for kids. There's also a small museum detailing the history of clay mining in the area. Continue on the road beyond to end up over a steep ridge – this makes a dramatic alternative approach to Corfe Castle (see p.68).

Church Knowle

CHURCH KNOWLE is a typical, tiny Purbeck village, enveloped by lovely walking countryside. It's also home to the **Margaret Green Animal Rescue** (daily 10am–4pm; free; ⓦ margaretgreenanimalrescue.org.uk), where you can wander around the attractive grounds and view the animals that have been rescued and are waiting to be re-homed. They usually have lots of domestic animals – from cats to gerbils and guinea pigs – as well as larger animals, such as horses, goats and sheep.

ACCOMMODATION AND EATING — CHURCH KNOWLE

East Creech Farm East Creech, BH20 5AP ⓣ 01929 480519, ⓦ eastcreechfarm.co.uk. This lovely rural campsite, just over a mile from Church Knowle, has a good children's play area and great views of Poole Harbour. It also lets out a cottage in a converted barn (sleeps four, £685/week). Daily bread and milk are available from the farm and there is a small summer tearoom. Only open April–Oct. £12

New Inn Tyneham Rd, BH20 5NQ ⓣ 01929 480357, ⓦ newinn-churchknowle.co.uk. Originally a sixteenth-century farm, this cosy pub with an inglenook fireplace has retained a traditional feel. Very popular at weekends, it serves good, hearty pub food – steak and ale pie, scampi, roast of the day (mains £12–15) – inside or out in a beer garden. Mon–Sat 11am–3pm & 6–11pm, Sun noon–3pm & 6–11pm.

Arne Nature Reserve

Arne, BH20 5BJ • Free access • ⓦ rspb.org.uk/arne

Around five miles southeast of Wareham, **Arne Nature Reserve** encompasses idyllic woodland and tidal mudflats next to Poole Harbour and Long Island, with an information post by the car park detailing the latest sightings. There are several marked trails around the reserve and along its shingle beaches, where you can spot rare wading birds as well as deer. **Arne** itself is a pretty little hamlet with a beautiful thirteenth-century church of St Nicholas. The rest of the village was largely evacuated in World War II, when the area was used as a decoy site – flares and smoke were sent up from here to lure bombers away from an explosives factory across the bay at Holton Heath.

Corfe Castle

Dominated by the castle that gives it its name, the village of **CORFE CASTLE** is very pretty, its low cottages built with soft Purbeck stone (see box, p.77). There are also some fine **walks** around Corfe; to the east, for instance, you can pick up the Purbeck Way, which eventually joins the coastal path between Swanage and Studland (both around seven miles from Corfe). Alternatively, head west up West Hill opposite the castle, where you can join a great ridge walk which cuts down to the attractive neighbouring village of Church Knowle (see p.67), a three- to four-mile round walk.

Corfe Castle

The Square, BH20 5EZ • Daily: March & mid-Oct to mid-Nov 10am–5pm; April to mid-Oct 10am–6pm; mid-Nov to Feb 10am–4pm • £9, children £4.50; NT • ⓦ nationaltrust.org.uk/corfe-castle

The first sighting of the towering ruins of **Corfe Castle** never fails to impress, particularly if you approach from Church Knowle – the castle's hilltop position makes it look impregnable. The castle defends virtually the only gap in a ridge of low, steep hills that stretch for fourteen miles, all the way from Ballard Down on the coast near Swanage to Worbarrow Bay.

The castle was first built in the eleventh century by William the Conqueror and expanded in the thirteen century by King John, who used it as both a prison and a royal residence. Later monarchs were less taken with it, however, and Queen Elizabeth I sold it to her chancellor before it passed into the hands of Sir John Bankes, Attorney General to Charles I. As a Royalist stronghold, the castle withstood a Cromwellian siege for six weeks, and was gallantly defended by Lady Bankes. It fell only after one of her own men, Colonel Pitman, eventually betrayed the castle to the Roundheads, who set about demolishing much of the structure with gunpowder. Apparently the victorious Roundheads were so impressed by Lady Bankes's courage that they allowed her to take the keys to the castle with her when she was turfed out – they can still be seen in the library at the Bankes's subsequent home, Kingston Lacy (see p.144). You can still clamber round its towers and ramparts, which command superb views over the surrounding countryside and the Norden to Swanage steam railway (see box opposite). Look out, too, for screenings of films in the castle grounds during the summer, as part of the Purbeck Film Festival (ⓦ filmfreeway.com/festival/PurbeckFilmFestival), England's largest rural film festival.

Town museum and Model Village

Museum 1 West St, BH20 5HA • Daily 10am–5pm • Free • **Model village** The Square, BH20 5EZ; April–Oct Mon–Thurs, Sat & Sun 10am–5pm; Nov–March Mon–Wed, Sat & Sun 10am–4pm • £3.95, under-16s £2.75 • ⓦ corfecastlemodelvillage.co.uk

It's worth a quick peer inside the town **museum**, housed inside England's smallest town hall: it contains historical artefacts and photographs of Corfe Castle in days gone by. Young children will enjoy the **Model Village** opposite, a mini reproduction of the village of Corfe Castle – there's even a miniature model of the model village. It's a

CORFE CASTLE RIDGE

Corfe Castle sits in a gap in a natural **ridge**, with paths up onto the ridge from either side of the castle. To walk east, head downhill from the village and turn right into Sandy Hill Lane. After five minutes, you'll see a track off to your left, which gradually climbs the ridge with ever better views the higher you go. You can follow the ridge upwards to a mast at the top. To head west, take the track to the side of the *National Trust Tearooms* which leads down the west side of the castle. Turn left and cross the road and you'll pick up a footpath, which crosses the **Corfe River** and heads left up the opposite ridge. Again there are fantastic views. You can continue along the ridge all the way to Tyneham (see p.80), a walk of around two hours.

ENID BLYTON

The Isle of Purbeck was the favourite holiday destination for **Enid Blyton** in the 1930s. She mostly stayed in Swanage, swimming each morning around both piers with her husband, who later owned the local golf club. Purbeck's heathlands and castles were the inspiration for many of her *Famous Five* children's stories, while most of the Famous Five's holidays begin on the steam train (see box, p.75). Blyton turned Corfe Castle into "Kirrin Castle" for her children's adventures, and Brownsea Island, then privately owned by an eccentric recluse, is the mysterious Whispering Island in her *Five Have a Mystery to Solve*. For more on Blyton, visit the **Ginger Pop shop** in the Square in Corfe Castle (Easter–Oct Mon–Thurs, Sat & Sun 10.30am–5pm; Easter hols daily 10.30am–5pm; W gingerpop. co.uk). There are Blyton-themed souvenirs for sale – including the infamous golliwogs – alongside *Famous Five* books and, of course, ginger beer.

quirky place in attractive gardens, with an enchanted fairy garden, and a selection of giant outdoor games.

ARRIVAL AND DEPARTURE — CORFE CASTLE

By train Corfe Castle station, on Station Road, is part of the Norden to Swanage Steam Railway (see box, p.75).

By bus Bus #40 runs hourly every day from Swanage and Wareham (around 15min) and Poole (1hr), stopping on East Street in Corfe Castle.

By car There is limited parking on the minuscule central square and drivers are advised to head to the signed car parks to the south of the village or either side of the castle.

ACCOMMODATION

Bankes Arms Hotel 23 East St, BH20 5ED T 01929 480206, W bankesarmshotel.co.uk. Comfortable accommodation with a range of newly refurbished en-suite rooms, above a sixteenth-century inn on the main East St. The inn has its own garden and good-value bar food, as well as a restaurant serving dishes such as crab linguine and roast pheasant. **£130**

Mortons House East St, BH20 5EE T 01929 480988, W mortonshouse.co.uk. If your budget allows, first choice in Corfe Castle has to be *Mortons House*. A sixteenth-century manor house with a beautiful walled garden and log fires, this award-winning small hotel has snug rooms, some with four-poster beds and stone fireplaces. The restaurant offers reasonably priced fish, meat and game from around £18. **£160**

Norden Farm Norden, BH20 5DS T 01929 480098, W nordenfarm.com. Tucked into a tranquil valley about a mile north of Corfe Castle, this working farm has extensive fields for tents and caravans, good facilities, its own shop and a menagerie of animals. March–Oct. There's also a small cottage (sleeps 4) and a larger Georgian house (sleeps 14) on site. **£13**

EATING

The Greyhound The Square, BH20 5EZ T 01929 480205, W greyhoundcorfe.co.uk. One of England's oldest coaching inns, the high-profile and very popular pub has a pleasant garden out the back with fine views of the castle. You can enjoy good-quality pub grub, such as pulled pork sandwiches or fish and chips (around £9–14), as well as more elaborate dishes such as scallop and langoustine risotto (£16). It also hosts regular live music and various food and beer festivals throughout the year. Food served Mon–Sat noon–9pm, Sun noon–8pm.

Model Village Courtyard Café The Square, BH20 5EZ T 01929 481234. There is free entry to the Model Village café, with tables set out in an attractive sunny courtyard. As well as tea and cakes it serves inexpensive lunches using herbs and salad from its own garden. Daily 10am–5pm; stays open later in July & Aug.

National Trust Tearooms The Square, BH20 5EZ T 01929 480332. By the entrance to the castle, the *National Trust Tearooms* has a lovely garden and serves light lunches and afternoon teas, with a fine selection of home-made cakes. Daily: March & Oct 10am–5pm; Nov–Feb 10am–4pm; April–Sept 10am–5.30pm.

Studland and around

Pretty **STUDLAND** is a well-to-do village spread out above a lovely stretch of coast. From the bottom of the hill below the *Bankes Arms* pub, a footpath leads down to Studland's small but appealing **South Beach**. After years of unsuccessful attempts to defend the beach from natural coastal erosion, the National Trust has finally accepted the inevitable and abandoned its coastal defence plans here. The whole lot will probably soon disappear – so make the most of the narrow sandy strip backed by beach huts while you can. The sea shelves gently here so swimming is generally safe, though occasional seaweed deposits can leave a pungent aroma in the summer.

Old Harry Rocks

South of Studland village, just beyond the path down to the beach is the start of the coastal path to **Old Harry Rocks**. It's around a twenty-minute walk to this dizzy and spectacular landform – a series of chalk stacks rising sheer out of the sea, some tunnelled with arches and caves. You can walk right up to the cliff edge – take great care as this section is unfenced. Indeed, until the late eighteenth century, you could walk right onto Old Harry itself before erosion led to its current position. Eventually it will face the same fate as so-called Old Harry's Wife – a sad chalk stump alongside that collapsed in 1896.

The **coastal path** continues west from here all the way to Swanage – a lovely walk of around an hour over soaring cliffs, the coast path eventually dropping steeply down to join the eastern end of Swanage's sandy beach. Alternatively, you can walk to the top of the hill above Old Harry Rocks and then turn right to skirt back to Studland over Ballard Down.

Agglestone Rock

From the village of Studland, a signed path leads up to **Agglestone Rock**, part of the Godlingston Heath National Nature Reserve. This peculiar sandstone ball looks like it has been dropped on the open heathland from outer space – there are various legends as to how it got here, including that it was thrown by the devil in an attempt to knock down the "skittles" of Old Harry. The scientific explanation is that it is an eroded pedestal rock that has fallen on its side. It's a steep walk from the village to the rock – an easier approach is to drive along the road through Studland, then take the right-hand fork signed to Corfe Castle, which leads along the top of a ridge with dramatic views back over Poole Harbour. Before you reach the golf club, once owned by Enid Blyton and her husband (see box, p.69), you'll see a signed path leading off the road down to Agglestone Rock.

Shell Bay

Heading north from Studland, the road passes along a narrow isthmus of land, most of it forming the Studland Heath Nature Reserve, which faces Poole Harbour on one side and the sea on the other. It's a lovely walk along the coast from Studland's narrow **South Beach**, through **Middle Beach**, and the lively **Knoll Beach**, with its watersports

THE SOUTH WEST COAST PATH

The **South West Coast Path**, Britain's longest footpath, begins its 630-mile coastal route from Shell Bay to Minehead in Somerset via Land's End. Conceived in the 1940s, the path was fully opened in the 1970s, much of it thanks to the National Trust, through whose land many miles of the route pass. Check Ⓦ explorethesouthwestcoastpath.co.uk for detailed descriptions of sections of the walk, or consult the South West Coast Path Association (Ⓦ southwestcoastpath .org.uk) for estimated timings and recommend fitness levels for each stage. We describe sections of the walk in the chapter below, but before you set off, always check local weather conditions as footpaths can be steep and slippery, and get a copy of the OS map OL15 (Purbeck and South Dorset).

A CYCLE FROM SHELL BAY TO WAREHAM

This one- to two-hour cycle ride takes in some of the best scenery of the Purbecks – but skirting Poole Harbour, it avoids the killer hills of the coast. The route is well signed but it helps if you have a good map such as OS map OL15.

Start at the Purbecks side of the **chain ferry from Poole** (about a thirty-minute bike ride from Poole train station) and cycle up the approach road for around a mile, towards Studland. At the second bend in the road you will see a wooden sign pointing to the right, signed **Norden/Ower**. Take this gravel track and follow the wooden signs through farmland until you pick up a tarmac road (heading left), which passes through tranquil forest. Continue on this road for about 1.5 miles until you reach a T-junction. Continue straight on here along a sand and gravel track, which follows the route of a **Victorian tramway** once used to carry clay from the clay pits to local potteries. You pass through beautiful rolling countryside before bearing left along a gravel track. Turn right where the track joins a road near **Bushey farm**, then follow the road (signed Norden) where it bears to the right. The road continues into forestry land where you follow signs to Hartland Moor, crossing a couple of roads as you pass through the suitably spooky woods of **Wytch Heath** before passing into open farmland, crossing an ancient bridge at **Shorford**. Pass through a couple of gates and you join a minor road just before **Hartland Moor**. Turn right onto this road, a narrow and undulating country lane. Bear left to the small village of **Ridge** (do not take the right-hand fork to Arne), from where you can wend through the village to your right until you reach the riverside walk opposite Wareham. Turn left here and cycle up the river for half a mile, past flashy moored yachts, and you will then be able to cross the bridge into Wareham. From here, you can take the train back to Poole (departures every 30min–1hr).

facilities and naturist section, which leads into **Shell Bay**, a magnificent stretch of icing-sugar sand. This whole stretch of coast is backed by a remarkable heathland ecosystem that's home to all six British species of reptile – adders are quite common, so be careful – and it's also the only place in the UK to have breeding populations of both the native species of **sea horse**. They breed in the offshore seagrass meadows, and boats are currently discouraged from anchoring off South Beach, in order to protect their population. The beach gets packed in summer, though the central stretch – a bit of a walk from any of the car parks – is quieter. At the top end of the beach is a chain **ferry** (see p.55) connecting the Isle of Purbeck with Sandbanks in Poole, though in summer and at busy weekends there are queues of over an hour to get across.

ARRIVAL AND ACTIVITIES — STUDLAND AND AROUND

By bus Bus #50 from Bournemouth Square to Swanage runs hourly, via Sandbanks ferry: it make several stops at the turnings to the main beaches and as it passes through the village.

By car There are pricey National Trust car parks by the ferry, at Middle Beach and Knoll Beach, and beside the *Bankes Arms* for South Beach.

Kayaking Studland Sea School, Middle Beach (T 01929 450430, W studlandseaschool.co.uk). Take one of their excellent guided kayak tours round Old Harry Rocks, through cliff arches and sea caves; the company also offers coasteering, snorkelling and fishing off kayaks.

ACCOMMODATION AND EATING

The Bankes Arms Manor Rd, Studland, BH19 3AU T 01929 450225, W bankesarms.com. Wonderful old pub, once a haven for smugglers, which serves a great range of real ales from local independent breweries. It also has its own on-site microbrewery, the Isle of Purbeck Brewery. The food is inconsistent and it gets very busy in summer, but frankly you can forgive anything for the joy of sitting in the substantial garden with fantastic bay views, or in the Purbeck stone interior, where log fires roar. Attractive rooms are available above the pub too; bag a room at the front if you can, for those gorgeous views. En-suites cost £10 extra, and there's a two-night minimum stay at weekends. Daily 11am–11pm. **£90**

★ **Burnbake** Rempstone, BH20 5JH T 01929 480570, W burnbake.com. The lovely rural campsite *Burnbake* has rope swings in the woods and a small shop, as well as some wooden lodges to rent (sleeping 4–6 people). To get there, take the right-hand fork to Corfe Castle beyond Studland village, and it's signed to the right off the road. Easter–Sept only. **£15**

STUDLAND AT WAR

One of England's most important World War II relics is on the coast path between South and Middle Beach. During the war, the whole of the Studland peninsula was evacuated so that the bay could be used as a rehearsal ground for the Normandy D-Day Landings. A 27m-long bunker, known as **Fort Henry**, was built by Canadian troops in 1943, with concrete walls almost 1m thick, and a 24m recessed observation slit from where the troops' activities in the bay below could be viewed in safety. Winston Churchill, King George VI and generals Eisenhower and Montgomery all sheltered in this pillbox, watching the rehearsals and discussing tactics for the forthcoming invasion of France. In April 1944, six amphibious tanks sank in the bay during rough weather, with the loss of six lives: this tragic accident, however, had a positive result in that it was then realized that the tanks were not seaworthy in rough conditions and should drive into shallow water, thus ensuring the success of the landings in June. You can go inside the bunker and peer through the observation slit, or clamber on the remains of the protective dragon's teeth and pillboxes on the beach below.

Joe's Café South Beach, BH19 3AN ⓣ07931 325243. In a small wooden shed on the beach, this laidback café serves fairtrade coffee and superb simple lunches such as couscous and Greek salads, as well as organic soup and sandwiches (about £5). Easter–Sept daily 10am–dusk; Oct–Easter Sat & Sun 10am–dusk.

★Pig on the Beach Studland Bay, BH19 3AU ⓣ01929 450288, ⓦthepighotel.com/on-the-beach. An eighteenth-century manor house in a fantastic location with lovely gardens leading down to the sea: renovated in *The Pig's* signature shabby-chic style, it has very comfortable rooms – some have sea views, all have luxurious showers and Nespresso machines – or you can stay in a converted shepherd's hut in the grounds. The restaurant is great too, specializing in locally caught or foraged ingredients, plus herbs and veg grown in the cottage garden; it's very popular so booking is recommended. Hours vary. **£170**

Swanage and around

SWANAGE, Purbeck's only real resort, is idyllically set in a natural sandy bay surrounded by green rolling hills. It grew up as a port for the local quarrying trade, but thrived with the arrival of the railway, which turned it into a popular Victorian seaside town. There are some great **walks** in the surrounding countryside: head north along the beach and you'll see steps up the cliff which join the **coastal path to Studland** via Ballard Down (see p.70), and south from the town the path continues along the coast through **Durlston Country Park**.

Swanage has plenty of fine Victorian townhouses, though its most ornate structure is the Town Hall; its facade was designed by Christopher Wren but dismantled and moved here after its original London home, Mercers Hall in Cheapside, was demolished. Though the old town is pleasant enough, Swanage's real appeal lies in its **beach** – a fantastic swathe of soft sand that stretches from the centre east under Ballard Down – as you'd expect, it gets progressively quieter as you head away from town, especially the eastern stretches below high cliffs. In summer the eastern section has areas where you can rent pedaloes and jet skis and there are also a couple of seasonal beach café kiosks. Peak season sees large crowds and traditional Punch and Judy shows on the beach, but for much of the year the town has a decidedly laidback and sleepy feel.

ARRIVAL AND INFORMATION — SWANAGE

By train The station is the southern terminus of the Swanage Steam Railway, which runs as far as Norden, just north of Corfe Castle (see box, p.75). This line is currently being extended to Wareham, where passenger services will connect with mainline routes to London.

By bus Swanage is served by bus #40 from Poole via Wareham and Corfe Castle (daily, 1 hourly; 1hr 10min), and bus #50 from Bournemouth station via the chain ferry and

FROM TOP THE SQUARE AND COMPASS, WORTH MATRAVERS (P.79); PUNCH & JUDY SHOW ON SWANAGE BEACH >

PUNCH & JUDY
SWANAGE
SHOWS DAILY
12:30 2.30 4.00
Adults & Children
£1 00
FROM
MID JULY

Studland (daily, 1 hourly; 1hr 10min). They both pull in outside the train station.

By boat In season (usually Easter–Oct, weather dependent) boat trips arrive at the town pier from Bournemouth and Poole; check website for timetables (citycruisespoole.com and dorsetcruises.co.uk).

Tourist office By the beach at The White House, Shore Rd, BH19 1LB (Easter–Oct daily 10am–5pm; Nov–Easter closed Sun; 01929 422885, swanage.gov.uk). This can give details of local accommodation and summer events, including the Swanage Carnival (swanagecarnival.com) in late July.

ACCOMMODATION

Bella Vista 14 Burlington Rd, BH19 1LS 01202 761186, bellavista-swanage.co.uk. Formerly a B&B, this is now a holiday let that can sleep sixteen. There are fantastic views from most of the bedrooms and a great garden that overlooks the beach. Free parking. One-week minimum stay. £307

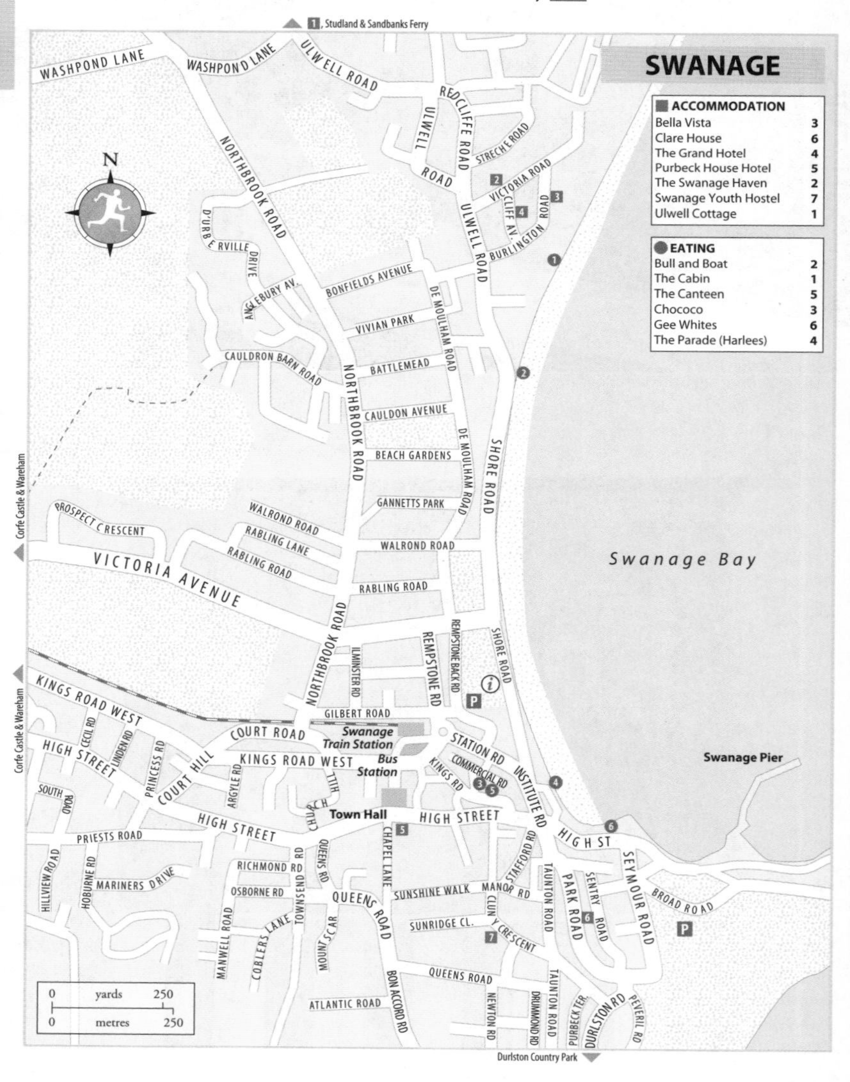

NORDEN TO SWANAGE STEAM RAILWAY

Corfe is the first main stop on the atmospheric **Norden to Swanage steam railway** (April–Oct daily; Nov–March Sat, Sun & school hols; Norden to Swanage single ticket £7, children £5; return ticket £12.50, children £7.60; all-day ticket £20, children £13; ⓦ swanagerailway.co.uk). The line dates from 1885, though British Rail closed it down in 1972 and took up all the track. Since 1975, it has been run by volunteers, who have gradually replaced the track, re-opened the line, and maintained the old station buildings. It's a lovely route, chuffing mostly through fields and woods with stops at the tiny stations of **Harman's Cross** and **Herston Halt**. The full run from **Norden**, just under a mile north of Corfe, to **Swanage** takes just forty minutes. Services run roughly hourly from 10am till 5pm, but check the website for a full timetable: they also run special events, including Santa Specials and Thomas the Tank Engine days. Volunteers have now cleared the tracks as far as Wareham, where it joins the main line to London, and in April 2009 the first passenger service from Waterloo to Swanage since 1972 ran along the whole line. A trial scheduled service from Swanage to the main line at Wareham is due to start in 2017, with the ultimate aim of connecting with the London service within another couple of years.

Clare House 1 Park Rd, BH19 2AA ⓣ 01929 422855, ⓦ clare-house.com. A Grade II-listed Victorian townhouse which once housed an indoor market, in a central location on the western side of town. The rooms are spacious and the owners friendly; two nights minimum in high season. **£115**

The Grand Hotel Burlington Rd, BH19 1LU ⓣ 01929 423353, ⓦ grandhotelswanage.co.uk. Dating from 1898, this classic Victorian seaside hotel has lovely grounds leading down to the beach, and great views from the public rooms. The bedrooms have been updated with wi-fi and TVs and there's a restaurant, an indoor pool, a jacuzzi and a health club. **£160**

Purbeck House Hotel 91 High St, BH19 2LZ ⓣ 01929 422872, ⓦ purbeckhousehotel.co.uk. Once the private home of George Burt, who also owned Durlston Castle (see p.76), this amazing Victorian pile is quite a sight, with soaring ceilings, dark wood and acres of floral wallpaper, not to mention the original bellrings for servants (including ones for the Dressing Room and Ladies' Room). There's a bar, a formal dining room and substantial grounds that include a modern annexe, though rooms in both buildings have contemporary facilities. **£140**

The Swanage Haven 3 Victoria Rd, BH19 1LY ⓣ 01929 423088, ⓦ swanagehaven.com. Billing itself as a boutique guesthouse, this pleasant B&B is in a good location, with comfortable rooms (though some are quite small) with all mod cons, including its own bar, restaurant and spa. The breakfasts include home-baked breads and the decked garden has a great outdoor hot tub. No children; two-night minimum stay for most of the year. **£95**

Swanage Youth Hostel 20 Cluny Crescent, BH19 2BS ⓣ 0845 3719346, ⓦ yha.org.uk/hostel/swanage. In the quiet top part of town, this official hostel has comfortable dorms, doubles and family rooms (from £70) in an appealing Victorian villa. Dorms **£21.50**, doubles **£50**

Ulwell Cottage Ulwell Rd, BH19 3DG ⓣ 01929 422823, ⓦ ulwellcottagepark.co.uk. This well-equipped campsite and holiday park about a mile out of Swanage on the Studland road has an indoor pool, children's play area, shop, restaurant and bar. **£13.50**

EATING

Bull and Boat 2 Ulwell Rd, BH19 1LH ⓣ 01929 422222, ⓦ bullandboat.co.uk. In an enviable position facing the beach, with outdoor tables on a narrow terrace, this is a lovely spot for a coffee or drink. Food and service is a bit hit and miss; the menu features sizeable steaks (£22), burgers (£13) and the like, as well as salads and baguettes (£7–9). Daily 9.30am–11pm.

The Cabin Burlington Rd, below the Grand Hotel, BH19 1LU ⓦ facebook.com/TheCabinSwanage. This is a great little beach café with tables set on a series of terraces spilling down to the seafront. It serves breakfasts, soups, toasties (£4) and sandwiches, (£3–5), plus tasty seafood such as crab burger (£5.50), crab salad (£12.50) and tempura prawns (£8.50). Opening hours weather dependent; check online. Café is open when flags fly outside.

The Canteen 10–12 Kings Rd East, BH19 1ES ⓣ 01929 426066, ⓦ thecanteenswanage.co.uk. This friendly restaurant with parquet flooring and Moroccan cushions has a youthful vibe and serves a good range of dishes such as hummus focaccia (£6), crab linguine (£14) and roast hake fillets (£15). Thurs–Sat 11.30am–2.30pm, Sun noon–9pm.

Chococo Commercial Rd, BH19 1DF ⓣ 01929 422748, ⓦ chococo.co.uk. Tucked away in an alley behind Station Rd, the wonderful *Chococo* sells its own chocolates made with local ingredients, such as cream, lavender and honey: you can choose your own selection (£7 for 100 grams). The dark chocolate chilli truffles are heaven; you can watch them being made in the shop window opposite, or have a go yourself during workshops. Also serves coffee, tea, cakes and ice creams. Mon–Sat 10am–5pm, Sun 11am–4pm.

Gee Whites The Old Stone Quay, 1 The High St, BH19 2LN ⓣ 01929 425720. Fashionable seafood bar with little wooden tables and a roof terrace near the quay serving local lobster, crabs and mussels. The menu changes daily according to what's been caught, but on a summer's evening it's a great spot to enjoy zingingly fresh fish and seafood (most £6.50–9.50), washed down with a glass of ice-cold cava; it also serves a variety of pizzas (£8.50–12.50). April & May daily noon–4pm; June–Oct noon–9pm; Nov–March Sat & Sun only, weather permitting.

The Parade (Harlees) 1 The Parade, BH19 1DA ⓣ 01929 422362. Good-quality fish-and-chip restaurant with a few indoor tables and an upstairs dining room (April–Sept only). As well as the usual battered cod and haddock, it serves fine locally caught fish such as red mullet and trout, and you can eat well for around a tenner. Daily 11.30am–2.45pm & 4–8.30pm.

2

Durlston Country Park

Lighthouse Rd, BH19 4JL • **Visitor centre** Daily April–Oct 10am–5pm; Nov–March 10am–4pm • Free • Car park April–Oct £5/day; Nov–March Mon–Fri £2/day, Sat & Sun £3/day • ⓣ 01929 424443, ⓦ durlston.co.uk

About a mile out of Swanage, on the main coastal path, lies **Durlston Country Park**, set in 280 acres of coastal woodland and crisscrossed with clifftop paths. It is a great place for a picnic or for wind-blown walks – giant turtles and a resident school of dolphins can sometimes be spotted from the cliffs, which also shelter sea birds such as a puffin colony. You can find out about the local wildlife and organized events at the park's visitor centre inside **Durlston Castle**, a Victorian folly built by wealthy local George Burt, which also contains a shop and the smart *Seventhwave* café-restaurant (see below). George Burt also built the Great Globe that sits south of the castle, a huge carved globe made from Portland limestone. From here, the cliff path below skirts round to the entrance to the **Tilly Whim Caves**. These were once limestone quarries – named after a quarryman, Tilly, and a basic crane called a whim – and later became a popular visitor attraction, but you only have to look at the ominous cracks around the entrance to see why they were closed.

A further ten minutes along the coast path brings you to **Anvil Point Lighthouse**, opened in 1881 by Neville Chamberlain's father, then Minister of Transport. Beyond the lighthouse, the coastal path continues beyond the park towards Dancing Ledge and Worth Matravers (see opposite).

ARRIVAL AND INFORMATION — DURLSTON COUNTRY PARK

By bus Bus #5 runs from Swanage (late May to Sept daily 10am–4.30pm, every 30min; 15min).

ACCOMMODATION AND EATING

Rowena/Veronica Cottages Anvil Point Lighthouse, BH19 4JL ⓦ ruralretreats.co.uk. Perched on the clifftop, these two pretty whitewashed cottages (both sleeping five) huddle below a lighthouse with stupendous views out to sea. On a summer's day, they are delightful, though they may be a little remote for some in winter – it's a good two miles to the nearest shops and surrounded by very steep cliffs. Two nights minimum. **£500**

★**Seventhwave** Lighthouse Rd, BH19 2JL ⓣ 01929 421111, ⓦ 7eventhwave.com. This stylish restaurant inside Durlston Castle has stunning views over the coast. It serves breakfasts, tapas-style snacks (from £5), fresh fish and other mains (pork loin, risotto etc) for £10–12. Mon–Fri 9.30am–4pm, Sat & Sun 9.30am–4.30pm.

The South Purbeck Coast

Part of the World Heritage Jurassic Coast, the segment of the Dorset coast that runs from Swanage to Lulworth is truly spectacular, although most of it traces along steep cliffs, which means access to the sea is somewhat limited. Here, the idyllic villages of **Langton** and **Worth Matravers** are both good bases for some great coastal walks. The western stretches between **Kimmeridge** and **Lulworth**, known as the Ranges, are owned by the Ministry of Defence, and are often closed to the public during military

PURBECK STONE

Purbeck stone gives the warm, greyish tint to the local villages of Swanage, Worth Matravers, Kingston and Corfe Castle, while **Purbeck marble** – actually a limestone that can be polished to look like marble – has also been used extensively for slab flooring in many of England's cathedrals. The stone has been quarried since Roman times, much of it along the coast so that the heavy stones could be carried away by boat. Like Portland (see p.117), the town of Swanage largely grew up round the quarrying trade, with the miners working in metre-high galleries that plummeted steeply down, following the natural dip in the rock that was sandwiched between ridges of clay. The clay was removed from above and below, after which the stone could be carted out in blocks – an extremely hazardous occupation. Today, open-cast quarrying continues in Purbeck, though many of the quarries have closed: you can visit or see the disused quarries around **Tilly Whim Caves**, **Dancing Ledge** and **Winspit**, which supplied the stone for Lulworth and Durlston castles. These days the disused mines are home to several species of bats – but keep clear of the entrances, which can be dangerously unstable.

exercises, when through-roads are also barred. These usually take place during the week – rarely at weekends or during holidays – and there are plenty of signs on all the approach roads to warn of this, as well as red flags flying over the area. The upside of MOD-ownership is that the entire vicinity is remarkably unspoilt, with no modern development. Many rare species of flora and fauna thrive here, while several of the villages were evacuated during World War II and have remained empty ever since, notably the ghost village of **Tyneham**.

Langton Matravers and Dancing Ledge

Some two miles out of Swanage and just inland from the South West Coast Path (see box, p.70), the small village of **LANGTON MATRAVERS** is a pleasing medley of Purbeck stone houses. From the car park at Langton House, or from the path alongside *Tom's Field Campsite* (see below), there's a lovely 1.5-mile walk over the downs to the coast and **Dancing Ledge**, a low rock ledge washed over by the sea at high tide, which Victorian quarrymen blasted into a natural bathing pool for local school children to swim in. It remains a popular bathing spot, though be warned that reaching it involves a fairly steep scramble down rocks. The cliffs around are also popular with climbers.

ACCOMMODATION AND EATING — LANGTON MATRAVERS

King's Arms 27 High St, BH19 3HA ⓣ 01929 422979. This traditional pub on the high street attracts a healthy mix of locals and tourists from the nearby campsites. There's real ale on tap, a small beer garden and moderately priced good-quality pub food. Daily noon–11pm.

★**Tom's Field Campsite** Tom's Field Rd, BH19 3HN ⓣ 01929 427110, ⓦ tomsfieldcamping.co.uk. The well-run *Tom's Field Campsite*, just north of Langton Matravers, has pitches in a series of enclosures on a grassy slope. The campsite has its own shop, as well as a kitchen serving breakfast in the summer, but only takes reservations for stays of five nights or more – for shorter stays, especially on sunny weekends, you'll need to arrive early to be sure of getting a pitch. It also lets out bunks (£13) in a converted Nissen hut – *The Walker's Barn* – or you can rent a converted pigsty called *The Stone Room* (£30), which sleeps two. **£16**

Worth Matravers

A couple of miles up the coast from Langton Matravers, **WORTH MATRAVERS** is the quintessential Purbeck village, complete with a picturesque church, duck pond and dazzling views over the surrounding downs, which are best enjoyed from one of England's finest pubs, the *Square and Compass* (see p.79). This doubles as a **museum**,

A ROUND WALK FROM LANGTON TO WORTH MATRAVERS

Langton Matravers is the starting point of a great three-hour **walk** to Worth Matravers via the coast and back again inland. Start at the footpath on the Langton side of *Tom's Field Campsite*, from where you head uphill through fields. You will soon cross the route back (on the Priest's Way), but continue straight on across more fields before a steep slope takes you down towards the coast. It's a short detour to Dancing Ledge (see p.77) or you can continue west along the coastal path. This stretch, above high cliffs, is relatively flat all the way to the inlet of Seacombe, above ledges cut into the cliffs by quarrymen. Take the path up Seacombe Bottom (signed Worth Matravers), a fairly steep climb up a delightful valley. To return, head out of Worth Matravers on the road towards Langton Matravers, and after 200m you will pick up a path signed Swanage, off to the right. This soon joins the dirt path of the Priest's Way. It's about one and a half miles back on this, past a couple of working quarries, before you pick up the path you started on above *Tom's Field*.

housing a fine collection of local fossils; it also puts on various exhibitions throughout the year, including one for local sculptors, and in autumn there's a pumpkin festival, when the garden is laid out with pumpkins the size of tables.

St Nicholas Church

St Nicholas Church is one of the oldest churches in Dorset and is the final resting place of **Benjamin Jesty**, the first recorded person to use a vaccination against smallpox, some twenty years before Edward Jenner. Jesty was a farmer who noticed that those people who had caught the milder disease of cowpox and recovered from it were usually immune to the more serious smallpox. In 1774, during a bad outbreak of smallpox, Jesty took his pregnant wife and two young sons and deliberately infected them with cowpox from an infected cow's udder. The sons suffered a mild case of cowpox, but stayed free of the more serious smallpox. Jesty's wife recovered from a bad fever and lived another fifty years. Although Jesty was scorned for his actions, he carried on his pioneering work after the family moved to Worth Matravers in 1797. The medical establishment never accepted his work, although the inscription on his gravestone reads that Jesty was "the first person (known) that introduced the Cow Pox by inoculation".

Winspit

One of the best walks from Worth Matravers takes the signed footpath from Worth's little pond down to **Winspit**. It's about a mile and a half down a steep valley path to the coast where you'll find a series of eerie former quarries and ruined quarrymen's homes – the quarry caves look incredibly unstable, though there are no fences and most people happily wander around them. You can then continue along the coast path east towards Langton Matravers, or southwest for another mile and a half to St Aldheim's head.

St Aldheim's Head

Accessible by a very rough road – so best to walk from Worth Matravers along the well-signed route via Weston Farm (around a further two miles) – is the wild headland of **St Aldheim's**, with dramatic views from its clifftop. The head was used as a major radar station during the last war, remnants of which can still be seen just east of a tiny lifeguard station (there's usually someone there to show you around it). Take a look, too, inside the ancient **St Aldheim's Chapel**. Possibly Norman in origin, legend has it that it was built as a warning to other sailors by a father, whose son drowned in a storm in 1140.

ARRIVAL AND DEPARTURE — WORTH MATRAVERS

By bus The #44 runs to and from Swanage via Kingston (Mon–Fri 2 daily; 25min), stopping near the *Square and Compass*.

ACCOMMODATION AND EATING

★Square and Compass BH19 3LF ⓣ01929 439229, ⓦsquareandcompasspub.co.uk. The best pub in Dorset – some say in the country – this has been serving drink since 1776, and still seems straight out of a Thomas Hardy novel: the bar is a tiny hatch, the interior is a winter fug of log fires, walkers, children and dogs (and the occasional live band or performer). Outside you may have to move the odd chicken to sit on a motley collection of stone seats and wooden benches. Regularly winning CAMRA awards for its local ales and ciders, the only food it serves is two home-made pies or pasties – one meat, one veggie, both delicious. Mon–Thurs noon–3pm & 6–11pm, Fri–Sun noon–11pm.

Weston Farm Campsite BH19 3LS ⓣ07974 565420, ⓦworthcamping.co.uk. This working dairy farm opens up thirteen acres of fields during the summer holidays. Facilities are simple – there's a shower block and catering van – but the location is superb and there's usually plenty of space. Per person £7

Worth Matravers Tea and Supper Room BH19 3LQ ⓣ01929 439368, ⓦworthmatraverstearoom.co.uk. A lovely vintage-style tearoom, with a cosy wood-burner inside and a pretty garden out back. It serves light lunches and tasty cakes all day, as well as the indulgent Chocolate Cream Tea – chocolate scones, clotted cream and chocolate sauce and a rich cup of hot chocolate (£7). There are also more substantial lunches, such as wild venison burger (£12.50), and the tasty evening meals include Lyme Bay hake (£18.50). Opening hours vary each month; check website for times.

2

Chapman's Pool

From just beyond the church in Worth Matravers, you can pick up a fine walk to **Chapman's Pool** (two miles), with a fairly steep final descent to a semicircular bay. The beach is a mixture of mud and gravel, but as it can only be reached on foot or by boat, it is especially popular in summer with walkers and yachties.

Kingston

Two miles northwest of Worth Matravers is another attractive stone village at **KINGSTON**, whose hilltop position commands superb views down towards Corfe Castle. There are some great walks from here too, either south to the coast at Chapman's Pool (two miles), or on the Purbeck Way down to Corfe Castle – take the path that leaves from the eastern edge of the village or pick up the well-signed path off the B3069, around a mile east of Kingston.

EATING — KINGSTON

The Scott Arms West St, BH20 5LH ⓣ01929 480270, ⓦthescottarms.com. An old inn with a warren of cosy rooms at the front and a large, modern-looking back room that doubles as its restaurant. But the biggest draw is its garden, which commands a stupendous view over Corfe Castle in the valley below, a scene that can have changed little in five hundred years. The food is substantial, varied and good value (around £12 for mains), while in summer the Jerk Shak sets up in the garden selling fantastic Caribbean food. Daily 11am–11pm.

Kimmeridge

Five miles by road east of Kingston lies a lovely Dorset cove, **Kimmeridge Bay**. It's part of the Smedmore Estate, so you have to pay to park your car here, but the small quarry car park a ten-minute walk above the bay is free. The beach here is not particularly appealing, an almost-black mixture of limestone ridges and fossil-rich clay, so rich in oil that you can literally set fire to it. BP has exploited this area, which happens to be the largest onshore oil field in the country, though it's so well landscaped you'd hardly believe it; evidence is a nodding donkey that's been extracting oil from the ground since the 1950s.

Despite the oil, the row of fishermen's cottages and idyllic location make the bay well worth a visit. It forms part of the **Purbeck Marine Wildlife Reserve**, and you can find details of a marked snorkelling trail (May–Sept; bring your own equipment) at the small marine centre (April–Sept Tues–Sun & bank hols 10.30am–5pm; Oct–March

Sun noon–4pm) at the east end of the bay – the limestone ridges that jut out to sea make the area particularly rich in marine life; dolphins, Portuguese man-of-war, spider crabs and brittlefish have all been spotted around here.

Clavell Tower

Sitting on the hillside to the east of Kimmeridge Bay, the **Clavell Tower** was built in 1830 as an observatory and folly by a local reverend – 25m from its current position. In 2007/8 the structure was moved inland as it was getting perilously close to the eroding cliff edge. The tower was visited often by Thomas Hardy, and also inspired the P.D. James novel, *The Black Tower*.

ACCOMMODATION AND EATING — KIMMERIDGE

Clavell Tower BH20 5PF ☎ 01628 825925, landmarktrust.org.uk. Just off the South West Coast Path, this historic tower makes for a romantic holiday stay with amazing views. The circular rooms are on four floors with the bedroom surrounded by a 360-degree balcony. Sleeps two. Minimum stay four nights. £454

Clavell's Café and Farm Shop BH20 5PE ☎ 01929 480701, clavellscafe.co.uk. On the road into Kimmeridge, this attractive café dishes up high-quality local produce such as Dorset crab and pea risotto (£13), plus Sunday roasts and Thursday evening fish and chips; it also serves breakfasts, sandwiches and traditional cream teas. On Friday and Saturday evenings it's more of a restaurant, with dishes such as monkfish and prawn kebab and local lobster thermidor: booking recommended for evening meals. March–Oct Mon–Wed & Sun 10am–5pm, Thurs–Sat 10am–5pm & 7–9pm; Nov–April daily 10am–5pm.

Tyneham

Open most weekends and at other times except when the ranges are closed by the army: check tynehamopc.org.uk or ☎ 01929 404819 for closing dates

Five miles by road east of Kimmeridge, nestled in a remote valley reached via the army ranges, **Tyneham** was a thriving rural community until it was taken over by the army during World War II. The entire population was evacuated, thinking that they would come back after the war, but they were never allowed to return. Most of the village is now in ruins, but you can wander around and get a good idea of what life would have been like in prewar rural Dorset. Some of the buildings, such as the church, have been restored and maintained in their original condition: the school room (10am–4pm) is still laid out as it would have been in the 1940s, with desks, samples of work and textbooks, a teacher's blackboard and little coat hooks with the children's names.

Tyneham also marks the starting point of a great **two-hour round walk** via Flower's Barrow, which embraces superb coastal views from the top of a ridge, part of the South West Coast Path and an Iron Age hillfort. Start at the track that leads uphill behind Tyneham's church. This heads to the top of the ridge; by a communications mast, turn left and follow the track towards the coast for fifteen minutes. As it begins to go downhill, take the clear grassy track on the left – the views over the coast and inland over the ranges and to Lulworth Castle from the top here are absolutely stunning. Within ten minutes you will reach **Flower's Barrow**, an Iron Age fort in a distinctive concave dip with awesome views over the coast. The fort – probably a protective gateway for coastal routes north – was built by the Durotriges tribe, who also built Maiden Castle. From the fort, join the coastal path east, which heads down a very steep grassy hill to Worbarrow Bay – this is a fifteen-minute walk. From the beach, it's a mile back to Tyneham up a wooded valley, home to various wildlife including badgers and bats.

Worbarrow Bay

Worbarrow Bay is a crescent-shaped sand-and-shingle beach overlooked by the distinctive hillock of Worbarrow, which you can climb up. It's not the nicest beach on this stretch, but is good for beachcombing and to admire the remarkably blue water thanks to its chalky substrata. Like Tyneham, there was once a thriving community here, though the fishermen were also moved out during the war and little is left. To get here, take the signed track from Tyneham (about a mile).

Lulworth and around

The quaint thatch-and-stone village of **WEST LULWORTH** forms a prelude to **Lulworth Cove**, a highly picturesque, almost circular bay surrounded by tall cliffs. Sadly, the diminutive and highly picturesque former fishing village at the head of the cove is now dwarfed by a giant car park and its attendant tourist facilities, including the **Lulworth Heritage Centre** (daily: March–Oct 10am–6pm; Nov–Feb 10am–4pm; free, Ⓦlulworth.com) which details the local geology. And it is the geology that pulls in hundreds of school parties as well as tourists. If you can, come out of season when the cove's magic returns and the surrounding coastal paths are quieter. Immediately west of the cove, **Stair Hole** is a roofless sea cave riddled with arches that will eventually crumble to form another cove. Stair Hole is also famous for the so-called Lulworth Crumple – a perfect cross section of folds in the rock.

Durdle Door

Accessible only by foot, it takes a little effort to see Dorset's other iconic site – the limestone arch of **Durdle Door** – but it is worth it. Most people take the uphill route, which starts from the car park at Lulworth Cove, but you can avoid the steep climb by walking from the *Durdle Door Holiday Park*, on the road to East Chaldon from West Lulworth. The arch itself sits at the end of a long shingle beach (which can be accessed via steep steps), a lovely place for catching the sun's rays and swimming in fresh, clear water. There are other steps to a bay just east of Durdle Door, St Oswald's Bay, with another shingle beach and offshore rocks that you can swim out to.

Swyre Head

Most visitors go no further along the coast path than the steps above Durdle Door, but it is well worth pushing west for at least another twenty minutes. This will take you to the top of the immensely steep slope of **Swyre Head**, a clifftop hill above a smaller rock arch, Bat's Hole. From the top the views back along the coast are stunning. You can return on the coast path, or cut up the wonderfully named Scratchy Bottom round a conservation area, returning to Lulworth Cove via the Newlands campsite.

Lulworth Castle

East Lulworth, BH20 5QS • Mon–Fri & Sun: Easter–Oct 10.30am–5pm; Nov & Dec 10.30am–4pm • £5, car park £3 • Ⓣ01929 400352, Ⓦlulworth.com/castle-park

Set in extensive grounds, the impressive **Lulworth Castle** was built in the sixteenth century by Viscount Bindon to entertain royal hunting parties. The castle has been altered over the centuries and much of the present ornate interior dates from rebuilding work after a fire in 1929. The grounds (free except for car park) include a small children's animal farm complete with alpacas, pygmy goats and pot-bellied pigs. The castle also lays on various events, foremost of which is **Camp Bestival**, a three-day music festival with an emphasis on family entertainment: details on Ⓦcampbestival.net.

ARRIVAL AND DEPARTURE — LULWORTH

By bus The #104 runs from Wool to Lulworth Cove (Mon–Sat 1–2 daily; 25min), then on to Wareham (50min).

By car Drivers get funnelled into the giant car park (£3/2hr) by Lulworth Cove, though if you don't mind a short if steep walk, you can usually park up in West Lulworth around the church.

ACCOMMODATION

Bishops Main Rd, Lulworth Cove Ⓣ01929 400552, Ⓦbishopscottage.co.uk. Traditional hotel in prime position near the bottom of the road to the cove. There are three small budget rooms in the attic, while the comfortable first-floor rooms are huge with views out to the hills (£170), and there's also an outdoor pool. **£80**

Durdle Door Holiday Park Lulworth Cove, BH20 5PU 01929 400200, lulworth.com/durdle-door-holiday-park. You can't beat the location of this campsite up on the cliffs above Durdle Door – there are fabulous views from the touring field, while tents can be pitched in a more sheltered wooded field. It's a 20min walk across fields to Lulworth Cove and there's also a shop and café/bar on site. Closed Nov–Feb. **£33**

Limestone Hotel Main Rd, West Lulworth, BH20 5RL 01929 400252, limestonehotel.co.uk. Attractive country house set back from the main road above West Lulworth, with a bar/restaurant with open fires and friendly staff. The rooms are smart and comfortable – the standard ones don't have views, but it's worth paying extra for The Lookout or The Writers Room, both of which look out over the village and countryside, and there are two dog-friendly ground-floor rooms too; minimum two nights stay in summer. **£115**

Lulworth Cove Inn Main Rd, Lulworth Cove 01929 400333, lulworth-coveinn.co.uk. With a great location right on the main street leading down to the cove and overlooking the duck pond, this is the first choice in Lulworth itself, especially if you can bag one of the front rooms that come with their own cove-view terraces (£20 extra). There's also a pub downstairs (see below). **£100**

Lulworth Cove Youth Hostel School Lane, West Lulworth, BH20 5SA 0870 3719331, yha.org.uk/hostel/lulworth-cove. West Lulworth has a very basic YHA hostel in a lovely rural location, a stone's throw from the Dorset Coast Path. Sporadic opening in winter. Dorms **£18.50**

EATING

Boat Shed Café Main Rd, Lulworth Cove 01929 400810. Simple café in great location right on the cove with outside seats and friendly service. It serves good-value sandwiches (from £3), which can come with a bowl of home-made soup (£6.50), plus larger dishes such as a fresh mackerel baguette and salad (£10) or beef chilli (£7). Daily 10am–4pm.

Castle Inn Main Rd, West Lulworth, BH20 5RN 01929 400311, thecastleinn-lulworthcove.co.uk. This sixteenth-century thatched pub has a lovely terraced garden, a good range of local real ales and a selection of traditional pub games – plus en-suite rooms upstairs (£95). The bar meals consist of high-quality pub grub, with dishes such as home-made steak-and-ale pie and beef bourguignon. It's also very dog-friendly. Daily noon–10pm.

Lulworth Cove Inn Main Rd, Lulworth Cove 01929 400333, lulworth-coveinn.co.uk. Pub offering local Blandford ales, real fires, a pleasant garden and standard pub grub, with rooms upstairs (see above). Daily 11am–11pm; food served noon–9pm.

The Weld Arms East Lulworth, BH20 5QQ 01929 400211, weldarms.co.uk. This great thatched pub dates back to the seventeenth century with log fires inside and a big beer garden backing onto fields. The seasonal menu includes staples such as fish and chips (£12.50), as well as more unusual choices such as pumpkin and hazelnut linguine (£11.50). Mon–Sat noon–11pm, Sun noon–10pm.

Wool and around

There is little of interest in workaday **WOOL**, whose main claim to fame is being the residence of the D'Urbervilles in Hardy's *Tess of the D'Urbervilles*. However, you may well pass through it, as it is on the main rail line and gives easy access to a number of local attractions.

Monkey World

Longthorns, BH20 6HH • Daily: Sept–June 10am–5pm; July–Aug 10am–6pm • £11.75, children £8.50 • 01929 462537, monkeyworld.co.uk

Around a mile and a half north of Wool, **Monkey World** is a well-run primate sanctuary in 65 acres of attractive Purbeck countryside, home to 240 animals, including the largest collection of chimps outside Africa. Most of the animals have been rescued from laboratories, zoos or circuses around the world and include gibbons, orang-utans, macaques and woolly monkeys, along with an array of very cute smaller beasts such as lemurs, squirrel monkeys and marmosets. All the enclosures have loads of swings, ropes, trees and ladders for the monkeys to play on, and at the end of the park there's a great adventure play area for children, with similar rope ladders and climbing frames. You can watch the animals being fed at various stages in the day.

The Tank Museum

Bovington, BH20 6JG • Daily 10am–5pm • £13 annual pass for unlimited entry • ⓣ 01929 405096, ⓦ tankmuseum.org

Near the rather bleak Bovington Camp army barracks lies the impressive **Tank Museum**, which contains the world's biggest collection of tanks and is one of the most important collections of military vehicles in the world, from the earliest armoured vehicles to the latest models available to the British army. You can scramble around inside them, practise driving them in simulators, learn about various military operations, and see a re-creation of life in the trenches in the eerie and hard-hitting World War I experience. You can also see the Sherman M4 tank, star of the 2014 Brad Pitt film *Fury*, parts of which were shot here at the museum. Dramatic displays of the tanks in action are also held during the school holidays in the outdoor tank arena; check the website for other events.

Clouds Hill

King George V Rd, Bovington, near Wareham, BH20 7NQ • Mid-March to Oct Tues–Sun and bank hols 11am–5pm or dusk • £5.50; NT • ⓣ 01929 405616, ⓦ nationaltrust.org.uk/clouds-hill

After being stationed at nearby Bovington, Thomas Edward Lawrence, aka Lawrence of Arabia (1888–1935), spent his retirement at **Clouds Hill**. It was his sanctuary from the fame that he achieved after writing *Seven Pillars of Wisdom*, a classic account of his campaigns in World War I to unite Arab forces against the Ottoman Turks. Despite having no electricity, kitchen or bathroom, the basic cottage – Lawrence called it "a hut in a wood" – played host to the likes of George Bernard Shaw, Siegfried Sassoon and Lady Nancy Astor: today, the atmospheric cottage is peppered with photos of Lawrence's life, and still has no electric light or heating. Lawrence was also a motorbike fan, and it was on his bike on the road from Bovington that he died – it was officially recorded as an accident, though many believe it was suicide. There is a pleasant three-mile round walk from the cottage to a hilltop picnic spot.

ARRIVAL AND DEPARTURE — WOOL AND AROUND

By train Wool station, on Station Rd, is on the main London to Weymouth rail line with regular services via Southampton (daily, 1–2 hourly; 1hr 15min), Bournemouth (30min) and Poole (20min).

Central Dorset

THOMAS HARDY'S COTTAGE, HIGHER BOCKHAMPTON

Central Dorset

The most rural, traditional part of the county, bucolic central Dorset was the region that inspired Thomas Hardy, who used many of its ancient sites in his evocative novels of Victorian England. Hardy's birthplace can be visited at the tiny village of Higher Bockhampton, as can his later home in Dorchester where he spent most of his life. This country town is steeped in history; it's home to a Roman villa, the ancient Maumbury Rings and the even older hillfort of Maiden Castle. The area is dotted with grand country mansions, too, including Athelhampton House and Kingston Maurward, both surrounded by elaborate grounds. A little north you come to the idyllic village of Cerne Abbas, best known for its mysterious chalk figure carved into a hillside and as a wonderful area for walks, while further north another historic town, Sherborne, is the ancient capital of Wessex and home to a magnificent abbey and two castles.

There are limited bus services in this rural area, and it's a pleasure to drive along the pretty country lanes, so travelling by car is best. It's also ideal cycling and walking country, peppered with country pubs and thatched villages. But be aware, there are some steep hills and valleys.

Dorchester

DORCHESTER, Dorset's county town, is forever associated with local author **Thomas Hardy**, who called it "Casterbridge" in his novels. The settlement, however, predates Hardy by thousands of years, and if you explore its backstreets, you'll quickly discover its ancient and distinctive character. Stone Age relics can still be seen at Maumbury Rings, and dotted around are the remains of Roman walls and a villa, while the names of several of its pubs and cafés hark back to the time of Judge Jeffreys' "Bloody Assizes" and to the local Tolpuddle Martyrs. For most visitors, however, this is essentially **Thomas Hardy**'s town: he spent much of his life in **Max Gate**, to the southeast of town; his statue now stands on High West Street; and there is a re-creation of his study in the **Dorset County Museum**. The modern centre has a pleasant core of mostly seventeenth-century and Georgian buildings, with some grand Victorian additions, notably the mock medieval keep, now the **Military Museum**. There are also an unusually large number of museums for a town this size, including some surprising re-creations of history at the **Tutankhamun Exhibition** and the **Terracotta Warriors Museum**, as well as the family-oriented **Teddy Bear** and **Dinosaur museums**. The new **Brewery Square** complex on the site of the Old Eldridge Pope brewery, opposite the market place (home of the weekly **market**, Wed 6.30am–3pm), has breathed live into a formerly run-down part of town by Dorchester South station. Designed by the Conran practice,

Hardy's Wessex p.92
A round walk from the Hardy Monument p.94
Hardy times p.97
Sir Walter Raleigh p.103

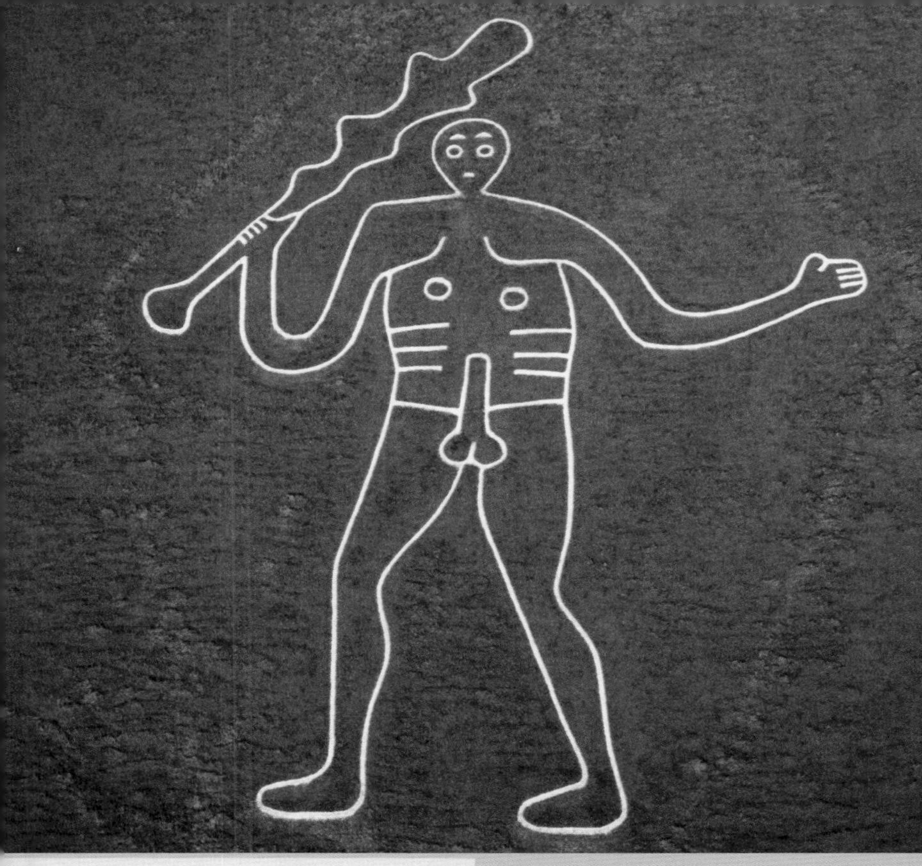

THE CERNE ABBAS GIANT

Highlights

❶ **Maiden Castle** One of Europe's greatest hillforts, partly dating back to the Stone Age, and an atmospheric spot for a windswept wander. **See p.94**

❷ **Kingston Maurward** The manor and gardens of what is now an agricultural college represent the best of rural English opulence, plus there's no end of fluffy animals to pet. **See p.96**

❸ **Stinsford** A traditional Dorset village, whose church is the final resting place of two literary giants: Thomas Hardy and the poet Cecil Day-Lewis. **See p.96**

❹ **Hardy's Cottage** Little changed since Hardy's day, this tiny, picturesque thatched cottage is an atmospheric rural vision, and the approach to it is via a lovely wooded walk, too. **See p.97**

❺ **Cerne Abbas** Dorset's most visited site, the Cerne Abbas Giant stands proud on his hillside, while the village of Cerne Abbas below is also a delight. **See p.99**

❻ **Badger watching** Spend a magical evening watching badgers – and their cubs if you're lucky – foraging and playing in the wild in the Piddle Valley. **See p.100**

❼ **Sherborne New Castle** Once the home of Sir Walter Raleigh, with fantastic lakeside walks. **See p.104**

HIGHLIGHTS ARE MARKED ON THE MAP ON P.88

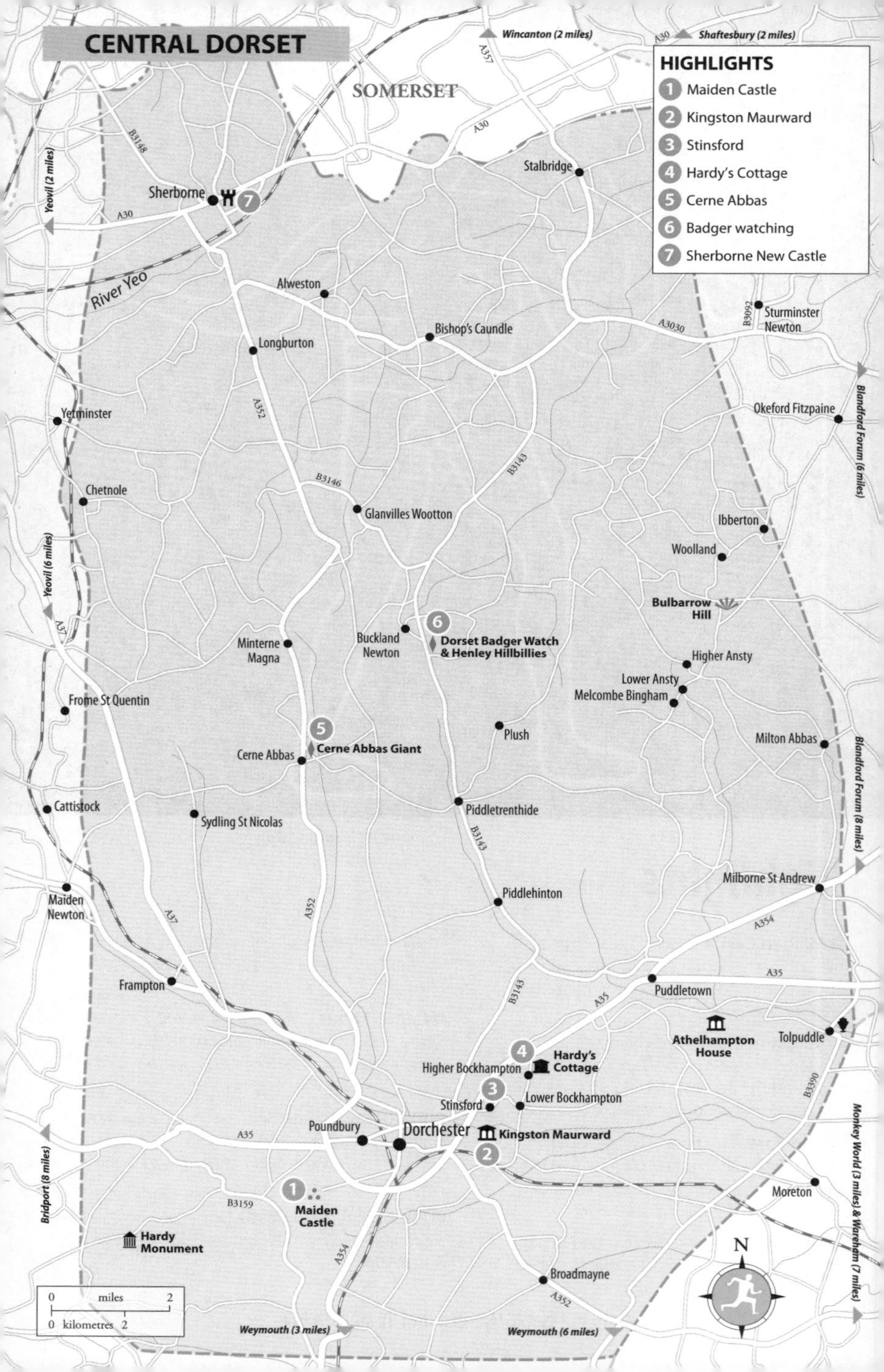

CENTRAL DORSET
HIGHLIGHTS
1 Maiden Castle
2 Kingston Maurward
3 Stinsford
4 Hardy's Cottage
5 Cerne Abbas
6 Badger watching
7 Sherborne New Castle
SOMERSET
Wincanton (2 miles)
Shaftesbury (2 miles)
Yeovil (2 miles)
Yeovil (6 miles)
Blandford Forum (6 miles)
Blandford Forum (8 miles)
Bridport (8 miles)
Weymouth (3 miles)
Weymouth (6 miles)
Monkey World (3 miles) & Wareham (7 miles)
Sherborne
Stalbridge
River Yeo
Alweston
Bishop's Caundle
Longburton
Sturminster Newton
Okeford Fitzpaine
Yetminster
Chetnole
Glanvilles Wootton
Ibberton
Woolland
Bulbarrow Hill
Buckland Newton
Dorset Badger Watch & Henley Hillbillies
Minterne Magna
Higher Ansty
Lower Ansty
Melcombe Bingham
Frome St Quentin
Cerne Abbas
Cerne Abbas Giant
Plush
Milton Abbas
Cattistock
Sydling St Nicolas
Piddletrenthide
Maiden Newton
Piddlehinton
Milborne St Andrew
Frampton
Puddletown
Athelhampton House
Tolpuddle
Hardy's Cottage
Higher Bockhampton
Lower Bockhampton
Stinsford
Poundbury
Dorchester
Kingston Maurward
Moreton
Maiden Castle
Hardy Monument
Broadmayne
A30
A357
B3148
A352
B3146
B3143
A3030
B3092
A37
A354
A35
B3390
B3159
N
0 miles 2
0 kilometres 2

the listed brewery buildings have been converted into shops, restaurants, cafés, a cinema and housing, based round a square with fountains (and an ice rink in winter). The next stage of the development will include a hotel, health spa and The Maltings arts centre with a theatre, art gallery and studio space.

Brief history

The **Maumbury Rings**, to the south of the town, are evidence that this was an important site in Stone Age times (around 2500 BC), though they were later adapted by the Romans, who held vast gladiatorial contests here. In around 60 AD, the Romans established a settlement called Durnovaria that, by the second century AD, was large and important enough to have its own aqueduct, public baths and forum. Remnants of their stay are apparent in the form of the **Roman Town House** (see p.90) and the old Roman Wall at the end of Princes Street, though most of these were replaced in the eighteenth century by tree-lined avenues called "Walks" (Bowling Alley Walk, West Walk and Colliton Walk). After the Romans left, Dorchester became a provincial agricultural town known for its wool and breweries. In the Middle Ages it held three weekly markets, and entertainment, including bear-baiting, took place at the Maumbury Rings. Much of the town was destroyed in a series of fires in the seventeenth century (resulting in a ban on thatched cottages in 1776). Around this time, Dorchester became associated with the notorious **Judge Jeffreys**, who, after the ill-fated rebellion of the Duke of Monmouth against James II, held his "Bloody Assizes" on Cornhill in 1685. A total of 292 men were sentenced to death, though most got away with a flogging and transportation to the West Indies, while 74 were

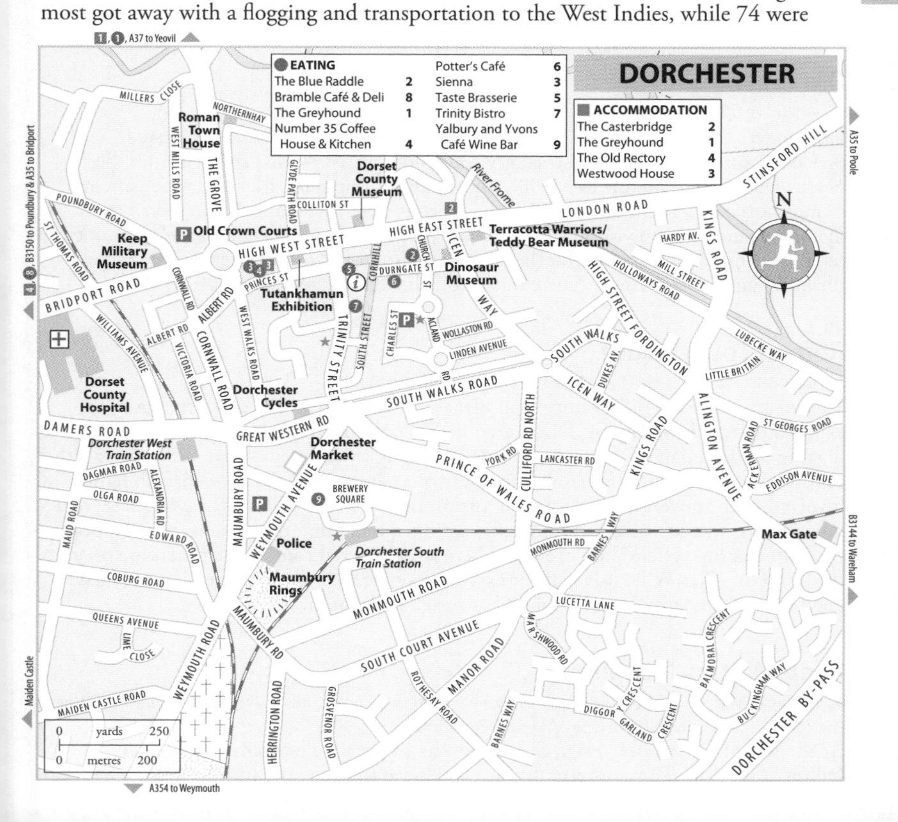

hung, drawn and quartered, their heads stuck on pikes throughout Dorset and Somerset. Some were executed at Maumbury Rings – used then for public hangings.

Throughout the nineteenth century, Dorchester flourished as a **market town** – it was at this time that the **Tolpuddle Martyrs** (see p.98) were tried in Dorchester for attempting to improve workers' rights. The railway arrived in 1847, in a flurry of great social change. This was the Dorchester that Thomas Hardy regularly visited from his home at nearby Higher Bockhampton before he moved here in 1885. Today, the town remains a thriving market town with a population of around 20,000, swelled by the modern extension of **Poundbury** to the east (see p.92).

Dorset County Museum

High West St, DT1 1XA • Mon–Sat: April–Oct 10am–5pm; Nov–March 10am–4pm • £7 • ⓦ dorsetcountymuseum.org

The best place to learn about Dorchester's history is the impressive **Dorset County Museum**. Founded in 1846 to record the county's social and environmental history, the Victorian building, complete with balconied galleries, is quite a sight. Inside, there is a rich hotchpotch of archeological and geological displays tracing Celtic and Roman history, including a section on Maiden Castle; some fine paintings, including works by Thomas Gainsborough; and some evocative historical photos of the region. There's also a Jurassic Coast gallery explaining the history of the local coastline, with the help of animated flying dinosaurs, as well as fossils and treasures found along its 95-mile length. Pride of place goes to the re-creation of Thomas Hardy's study, where his pens are inscribed with the names of the books he wrote with them.

Old Crown Courts

58–60 High West St, DT1 1UZ

Dorchester's **Old Crown Courts** were built in 1796, though an older court existed previously on the site. It was in this very courtroom, in 1834, that six men from the nearby village of Tolpuddle (see p.98), known as the Tolpuddle Martyrs, were sentenced to transportation. The room in which the Martyrs were tried has been preserved as a memorial, and you can visit it, sit behind the judge's desk and bang his gavel or ponder their fate from the juror's bench. The courts are currently closed for refurbishment and the building of a new visitor centre/museum, which is due to open in 2017.

Roman Town House

Colliton Park, DT1 1UZ • Open access • Free • ⓦ dorsetforyou.com/roman-town-house

Tucked away behind the County Hall is the only example in the country of a fully exposed **Roman Town House**. Discovered in 1937 almost by chance (while workers were digging the foundations for a new council building), the remains date from the fourth century and were almost certainly the home of an important Romano-British family involved in the governing council of Durnovaria. It's a fine villa with a well-preserved mosaic floor: the mosaics and some of the rooms, including the remains of a hypocaust (Roman heating system), are protected beneath a covered roof, while others are open to the elements. Picture boards make it easy to imagine the villa in its heyday, giving a good idea of how the Romans would have used each room.

Keep Military Museum

Corner of Barrack Rd and Bridport Rd, DT1 1RN • April–Sept Mon–Sat 10am–5pm; Oct–March Tues–Fri 10am–4.30pm; Feb & Oct half-terms Mon–Sat 10am–4.30pm • £6.50, children £2.50 • ⓦ keepmilitarymuseum.org

At the top of Dorchester High Street rise the impressive battlements of **Keep Military Museum**. Though resembling a medieval fortress, the building is a Victorian replica built in 1879, and traces the fortunes of the Dorset and Devonshire regiments over three hundred years, showcasing uniforms and weapons. You can also see one of the cells beneath the fortress, which has been reconstructed to give an idea of what life was like in a military prison. While the military history is of fairly specialist interest, most people will find the highlight a trip up the narrow spiral staircase to the battlements, from where you get sweeping views over the town and surrounding countryside.

Tutankhamun Exhibition

High West St, DT1 1UW • Daily: April–Sept 10am–5pm; Oct–March 10am–4pm • £9, children £7 • Ⓦ tutankhamun-exhibition.co.uk

It seems rather incongruous to have a reconstruction of Tutankhamun's tomb in a converted church in Dorset, but the **Tutankhamun Exhibition** is just that, and will be of interest to those who enjoy Egyptology. It houses many of the re-created artefacts from the British Museum's original exhibition on Egypt's most celebrated pharaoh, with a replica of his tomb as it would have been on its discovery in 1922, copies of his treasures and a model of the mummy itself.

Terracotta Warriors Museum and Teddy Bear Museum

High East St, DT1 1JU • Daily: April–Sept 10am–5pm; Oct–March 10am–4pm • Each museum £6, children £4 • Ⓦ terracottawarriors.co.uk; Ⓦ teddybearmuseum.co.uk

Another of Dorchester's seemingly incongruous museums, but actually quite interesting and certainly worth a browse on a wet day, is the **Terracotta Warriors Museum**. Impressive replicas of the warriors line up alongside interactive displays on the history of why they were made, certainly enough to whet your appetite to see the real things in China.

Upstairs in the same building, the **Teddy Bear Museum**, with its collection of bears throughout the ages, will certainly appeal to younger children. A series of rooms is furnished in traditional style, each "manned" by some cute bears, including a few human-sized ones plus celebrity bears such as Paddington and Rupert. You can also see copies of the original books and magazines in which the bears first appeared.

Dinosaur Museum

Icen Way, DT1 1EW • Daily: April–Sept 10am–5pm; Oct–March 10am–4pm • £7, children £6 • Ⓦ thedinosaurmuseum.com

Paleontologists, children and anyone else with an interest in the terrible lizards will enjoy the **Dinosaur Museum**, with its interactive displays, giant models and hands-on activities on dinosaur-related themes. As well as genuine fossils found in the region and further afield, there's a fine life-sized model of a T-Rex, plus exhibits that re-create what the dinosaurs would have felt and sounded like. It's all very hands-on – touching the exhibits is encouraged – and full of fascinating dinosaur facts.

Maumbury Rings

Around ten minutes south of town, near the Dorchester South train station, a series of grassy ridges marks the **Maumbury Rings**, where many of Dorchester's less savoury historical events were carried out – including gladiator fights, bear-baiting and public executions (see p.280). In the first century AD, the Romans converted the Neolithic site here into one of the largest amphitheatres in the country by removing earth from the centre of the rings and using it to make a bank round the edge. The Rings were further re-modelled in 1642–43 to become an artillery fort, built to protect Dorchester's southern edge during the English Civil War. Today, the site is used as a skate park, and hosts the odd band, play and firework display.

Max Gate

Arlington Ave, DT1 2AB • Mid-March to Oct Wed–Sun 11am–5pm • £7; NT • nationaltrust.org.uk/max-gate

Anyone who has also been to Hardy's Cottage (see p.97), where Thomas Hardy was born, will realize how much the author's social standing had improved by the time he moved to **Max Gate** in 1885. Hardy helped design this rather austere house, which was much smaller when he first moved in, but after the success of *Jude the Obscure* he enlarged it to almost double its original size. Hardy lived here until his death in 1928, and it was here that he wrote *Tess of the D'Urbervilles*, *Jude the Obscure* and *The Mayor of Casterbridge*.

Poundbury

Welded onto the western suburbs of Dorchester is Prince Charles' "eco-community" of **Poundbury**, part of the Duchy of Cornwall's estate. Begun in 1993, and not due to be completed until around 2025, the town was designed as a traditional community, mostly modelled on country cottages and Georgian houses, built in a series of wending streets, squares and crescents. The result, however, is a sprawling, suburban enclave that dominates the rural landscape, particularly when viewed from its western approach. It's a place that divides opinions – the central Butter Cross square is undoubtedly pretty and the lack of street furniture is refreshing, but whilst some of the architecture is interesting, much of it is pastiche lining oddly wide and soulless streets. It is around fifteen minutes' walk west of town; the Dorchester tourist office sells a map of it, which may come in handy as there are virtually no signposts.

ARRIVAL AND DEPARTURE — DORCHESTER

By train Dorchester has two train stations, Dorchester West and Dorchester South, though in fact they are both pretty central and under a 10min walk apart.

Destinations Dorchester South: Bournemouth (1–2 hourly; 40–45min); London (1–2 hourly; 2hr 40min); Weymouth (3–4 hourly; 10–15min). Dorchester West: Bath (8 daily; 1hr 50min–2hr); Bristol (8 daily; 2hr 20min–2hr 30min); Weymouth (10 daily; 15min).

By bus Local buses to and from Dorchester are run by Damory Coaches (damory.co.uk) and First Wessex, Dorset & South Somerset (firstgroup.com). Most stop along Trinity Street and at Dorchester South station, with regular services to and from Poundbury, Weymouth, Bridport, Portland and Lyme Regis. National Express

HARDY'S WESSEX

Thomas Hardy set many of his novels in "Wessex", an ancient name for an area that embraced much of southwest England, and in particular in "South Wessex", which is modern-day Dorset. Hardy used fictional names for his towns, such as "Sandbourne" and "Casterbridge", which, although they have changed hugely since his day, still obviously refer to Bournemouth and Dorchester respectively. Some rural communities that Hardy described are little changed today: Beaminster, for example, is easily recognized as Hardy's "Emminster" in *Tess of the D'Urbervilles*, which ends in "Wintoncester" prison – based on Winchester. The riverside setting of Sturminster Newton, where Hardy also lived, is called "Stourcastle" in *The Return of the Native*. Below is a list of some of Hardy's better-known fictional names and the real-life places they represent:

Abbot's-Cernel Cerne Abbas
Abbotsea Abbotsbury
Anglebury Wareham
Budmouth Weymouth
Chaseborough Cranborne
Evershead Evershot
Havenpool Poole
Kingsbere Bere Regis
Knollsea Swanage
Lulwind Cove Lulworth Cove
Marlott Marnhull
Mellstock Stinsford and Higher & Lower Bockhampton
Port Bredy Bridport
Shaston Shaftesbury
Isle of Slingers Isle of Portland
Solentsea Southsea
Stoke Barehill Basingstoke
Street of Wells Fortuneswell

coaches also stop at Dorchester South station with services to Bournemouth (4 daily; 1hr–1hr 40min), London (1 daily; 4hr) and Weymouth (4 daily; 20–25min).

By car There are plenty of short- and long-stay car parks around the centre.

GETTING AROUND AND INFORMATION

Tourist office 11 Antelope Walk, DT1 1BE (Mon–Sat: April–Oct 9am–5pm; Nov–March 9am–4pm; ⓣ01305 267992, ⓦvisit-dorset.com/about-the-area/areas-to-visit/west-dorset). It has some useful free leaflets detailing various historical walks around town, such as the Thomas Hardy walk and the Roman Town walk, which vary from 30 to 90min.

Bike rental Dorchester Cycles, 31 Great Western Rd (£12/day; ⓣ01305 268787, ⓦdorchestercycles.co.uk).

ACCOMMODATION

IN TOWN

The Casterbridge 49 High East St, DT1 1HU ⓣ01305 264043, ⓦthecasterbridge.co.uk. Friendly hotel in a Georgian building on the main through-road with a relaxing communal lounge and small courtyard garden. The rooms are homely and comfortable, if a little dated in style. **£85**

Westwood House 29 High West St, DT1 1UP ⓣ01305 268018, ⓦwestwoodhouse.co.uk. Comfortable Georgian townhouse on the busy High St, with seven well-furnished rooms, including a good-sized family suite on the third floor. Service is friendly and efficient and the breakfasts are recommended. You can't park outside, but there's a reasonably priced car park nearby. **£95**

OUT OF TOWN

The Greyhound Sydling St Nicholas, DT2 9PD ⓣ01300 341303, ⓦdorsetgreyhound.co.uk. A traditional pub with cosy rooms, in a pretty thatched village eight miles north of Dorchester. The rooms are in a separate annexe across the car park from the pub (see p.94), with a rack of wellies to borrow for country walks. **£90**

The Old Rectory Winterbourne Steepleton, DT2 9LG ⓣ01305 889468, ⓦtheoldrectorybandb.co.uk. In a lovely former rectory dating from 1850 in the tiny, pretty village of Winterbourne Steepleton, four miles west of Dorchester, this B&B has four comfortable en-suite rooms, one with a four-poster, and attractive well-kept gardens. **£90**

EATING

The new **Brewery Square** complex is home to a good selection of chain restaurants, including *Carluccio's*, *Côte Brasserie*, *Wagamama*, *Zizzi*, *Nando's* and *Pizza Express*, several of which have outdoor tables on the square. For more independent, local restaurants and cafés, the **town centre** is a better bet.

IN TOWN

The Blue Raddle 9 Church St, DT1 1JN ⓣ01305 267762, ⓦblueraddle.co.uk. Real ales, plenty of character, and the odd live folk band make this friendly local pub a great place for a quiet pint or a hearty meal of decent home-made food, made from local, seasonal ingredients (mains £9–11.50). Cash only; dogs welcome. Mon 6.30–11pm, Tues–Sat 11.30am–3pm & 6.30–11pm, Sun noon–3pm & 7–10.30pm.

Number 35 Coffee House & Kitchen 35 High West St, DT1 1UP ⓣ01305 549269, ⓦcoffeehouseandkitchen.com. Friendly little café that takes its coffee very seriously, with regular guest brews. The beautiful bay-windowed front room is tiny, but there's also a cosy room at the back with comfy sofas and books. They serve sandwiches (£3) and quiches (£4) for lunch, and tasty Saturday brunches like kedgeree (£8) and pancakes (£4–7). Mon–Thurs 7.30am–3pm, Fri 7.30am–3pm & 4–9pm, Sat 8.30am–3pm.

Potter's Café 19 Durngate St, DT1 1JP ⓣ01305 260312. Very appealing bistro/café with a roaring log fire in winter and a small garden at the back. Serves a range of inexpensive sandwiches, quiche, salads and soup (mushroom and courgette is tasty), as well as more substantial dishes such as tempura red mullet with sweet potato chips (£10). Mon–Sat 9.30am–4pm, Sun 10am–4pm.

Sienna 36 High West St, DT1 1UP ⓣ01305 250022, ⓦsiennadorchester.co.uk. Former Masterchef contestant Marcus Wilcox is the chef at this upmarket restaurant which specializes in locally sourced Modern British cuisine, with innovative dishes such as crab with pineapple, coconut, squid ink and cashews (£8) or roast chicken with truffle and asparagus (£16.50). It's tiny, so reservations recommended. Tues–Sat noon–2pm & 7–9pm.

Taste Brasserie Trinity St, DT1 1UB ⓣ01305 257776, ⓦtastebrasserie.co.uk. Lively and reliable café, with a few tables outside on the street, serving good-value lunches made from local ingredients. They do sandwiches (£6–7) and fish, meat or vegetable sharing platters (£11.50), plus hearty hot dishes such as Portland crab linguine (£11). Mon–Fri 8.30am–4pm, Sat 9am–5pm.

Trinity Bistro Trinity St, DT1 1TT ⓣ01305 757428. Tucked down a side alley, this quirky, laidback little restaurant with an open kitchen is worth seeking out for its excellent fish and seafood dishes with a Caribbean twist, plus specials such as goat curry and spicy jerk fish; mains £13–20. Cash only. Wed–Sat noon–3pm & 7–10pm.

Yalbury and Yvons Café Wine Bar Dukes Auction House, Brewery Square, DT1 1GA ⓣ01305 260185, ⓦycscafe.com. Tucked away by Dorchester South station, this friendly café serves tasty sandwiches with local fillings (£4–5), a great Dorset cheeseboard (£7.50), and a good selection of vegetable frittatas and quiches (£4–4.50). Portions are large and come with a flowerpot of delicious home-made rosemary and garlic bread. There's also a fine array of French patisserie on offer and the hot chocolate, made from a mixture of chocolates which you melt into hot milk and whisk yourself, is to die for. Mon–Sat 7.30am–4.30pm, Sun 9am–3pm.

3

OUT OF TOWN

Bramble Café & Deli The Pediment, 17 Buttermarket, Poundbury, DT1 3AZ ⓣ01305 259826, ⓦbramblecafedeli.com. Run by 2009 Masterchef winner Matt Follas, this cosy café with tables outside on the square serves tasty brunch dishes such as bubble and squeak with eggs and bacon (£5), excellent sandwiches and ciabattas (£5–7.50), plus heartier hot dishes (£6–8) like beetroot and kale spelt risotto. On Fri & Sat evenings, Follas cooks a short menu of good-value seasonal dishes, such as rabbit cooked in red wine (£13). Mon–Thurs 8.30am–4.30pm, Fri & Sat 8.30am–4.30pm & 6.30–8.30pm.

The Greyhound Sydling St Nicholas, DT2 9PD ⓣ01300 341303, ⓦdorsetgreyhound.co.uk. Reasonably priced pub meals, such as home-made beef and wild boar burger (£13), are served in the cosy bar with an open fireplace, and a comfortable conservatory opens onto a small garden. Rooms available (see p.93). Mon–Sat 11am–3pm & 5.30–11pm, Sun noon–10pm.

Around Dorchester

Though Hardy would struggle to recognize many aspects of modern-day Dorchester, much of the surrounding countryside is little changed, and the area is well worth exploring. Nearby is **Maiden Castle**, one of Europe's greatest Iron Age hillforts and a must-see. Hardy's birthplace can be visited in **Higher Bockhampton**, while the nearby village of **Tolpuddle**, famed for its trade union martyrs, is highly attractive in its own right. There are also some grand estates at **Athelhampton House** and **Kingston Maurwood**, the latter with superb grounds and adjacent to pretty **Stinsford**, where Hardy's heart lies buried in the church graveyard.

Maiden Castle

Only just over a mile southeast of Dorchester, and approached through residential suburbs, the spectacular hillfort of **Maiden Castle** nevertheless whisks you back thousands of years. It's a fairly steep – but lovely – climb up grassy paths to the top, where you begin to get an idea of the scale of the defences. The site, which covers a total area of 47 acres, is made up of concentric earthen ramparts enclosing a grassy plateau the size of fifty football pitches. This was once home to several hundred of the Durotriges tribe who would have been protected by the vast ramparts – some rising to 6m in height – topped by wooden fences and staggered gates to hinder enemy attacks.

A ROUND WALK FROM THE HARDY MONUMENT

There are several great walks around the Hardy Monument. One of the most dramatic is a four-mile round walk. It begins just east of the Hardy Monument: to find the start, walk down the road towards Martinstown for 200m, until you see a wooden signpost to Bincombe and the **Jubilee Trail**. Follow the Binscombe path along a ridge, then take the signed Jubilee Trail to the south. This crosses several fields (usually full of lambs in spring), passing a ruined farm which featured in John Schlesinger's classic 1967 film version of *Far from the Madding Crowd*, starring Alan Bates and Julie Christie. The signed path then dips into a narrow valley called **Hell Bottom**. At the foot of the valley, just before the footpath joins a road, pick up the path to the left which heads uphill through more fields to rejoin the main South West Coast Path. Turn left and you'll pick up the ridgeway that you started on.

FROM TOP ATHELHAMPTON HOUSE (P.98); MAIDEN CASTLE >

The Durotriges built all this in around 450 BC on the site of an even older Stone Age settlement dating back to around 3000 BC. There is evidence that the Stone Age dwellers built a defensive ditch of 545m in length; they also left various burial mounds. The site was finally conquered by the Romans in 43 AD, when the residents were either killed or moved out to what was to become Dorchester. In the fourth century, the Romans built a temple here (its foundations survive), but shortly afterwards the site was abandoned. Today it is grazed by sheep, but there are various footpaths around the ramparts; there is nothing to stop you finding one with a good view for a picnic.

Hardy Monument

DT2 9HY • April–Sept Wed–Sun 11am–4pm Free; NT • Ⓦ nationaltrust.org.uk/hardy-monument

Visible from miles around on an exposed hilltop near Portesham, the **Hardy Monument** is not dedicated to the well-known author, but to his distant relative, Vice Admiral Thomas Masterman Hardy of "Kiss me, Hardy" fame. The 21m-high monument commemorates Hardy, who served aboard Nelson's ship HMS *Victory* (see p.235) during the Battle of Trafalgar in 1805. Built of Portland stone, the monument has a steep, spiral staircase inside with 120 steps to the top: the views from here are stunning – as far as Devon and the Isle of Wight on a clear day. If you are not up to the climb, or the monument is closed, you can walk around its base, which gives pretty good views too, over to Lyme Bay in the south and Bulbarrow Hill in the north.

Kingston Maurward

DT2 8PY • Daily 10am–5.30pm; closed for a couple of weeks over Christmas • £6.50, children £4.50 • Ⓣ 01305 215003, Ⓦ kmc.ac.uk

The **Kingston Maurward** estate, two miles northeast of Dorchester, is made up of a classic Palladian house, built in 1720, and its attractive gardens. The estate is now used by an agricultural college, so the house is not open to the public, but the grounds and animal park, which are also used for teaching purposes, are fine attractions. The grounds encompass various types of garden, from the "Capability" Brown-style rolling lawns leading down to a lake and a temple, to the more formal Arts and Crafts-style series of Edwardian garden rooms, and a tranquil Japanese garden. The animal park is great for children, being home to pigs, ducks, chickens, ponies, goats, guinea pigs, donkeys and emus, many of which can be cuddled and fed. There are regular keeper talks about the animals' welfare, an entertaining children's play area and sometimes tractor rides round the estate. Highlight of the year at Kingston Maurward is the series of **lambing weekends** – the dates vary according to the weather, but they usually take place over two or three weekends in March – where you can get up close to the lambing pens and watch the lambs being born. There are always informative staff on hand to answer questions, and you can even bottle-feed the lambs.

Stinsford

Just behind the walls of the Kingston Maurward estate, **St Michael's Church** in **Stinsford** (Hardy's "Mellstock" in *Under the Greenwood Tree*) is an attractive little country church dating from the early thirteenth century. For such a small building – its average congregation is thirty – it has a surprisingly large number of eminent residents: buried in its churchyard are Thomas Hardy's heart, his two wives, his parents, his brother and two sisters, his grandparents, aunt, uncle and cousin, as well as the poet laureate Cecil Day-Lewis, father of the actor Daniel Day-Lewis. Hardy was baptized here, after which he attended, then taught at, the Sunday school. Although Hardy wanted to be buried at Stinsford, it was decided that he should be honoured with a place in Poet's Corner in Westminster Abbey. On January 16, 1928, his ashes were buried in Westminster Abbey at the same time as his heart was buried here in the grave of his first wife, Emma, where

HARDY TIMES

Thomas Hardy (1840–1928) was born in the village of Higher Bockhampton, just outside Dorchester, the oldest of four children. He spent much of his childhood exploring the countryside that was to have such a great influence on his books – some of the most charming of his descriptions of the village he was born and grew up in can be found in *Under the Greenwood Tree* (see p.285). A keen reader, he studied Latin, Greek and French, played the violin and helped his father, a stonemason and builder, with various building projects. Aged 16, he was apprenticed to an architect in Dorchester, later moving to London in 1862 to work with architect Arthur Blomfield. Though successful, Hardy never felt comfortable in London and returned to Dorset with ambitions to be a writer.

He married **Emma Lavinia Gifford** in 1874, shortly after he had begun to make money from his novels *Under the Greenwood Tree* (1872), *A Pair of Blue Eyes* (1873, based on his courtship of his wife) and *Far from the Madding Crowd* (1874). The last was successful enough for him to give up his work as an architect and write full time. The Hardys moved briefly to Sturminster Newton, where he wrote *The Return of the Native* (1878). In 1885, Hardy designed his own "cottage", Max Gate in Dorchester, where he wrote some of his finest works: *The Mayor of Casterbridge* (1876), *The Woodlanders* (1887), *Tess of the D'Urbervilles* (1891) and *Jude the Obscure* (1895). The latter two books were seen as extremely risqué, with *Tess of the D'Urbervilles* based on a true-life murder, and the "explicit" *Jude the Obscure* dealing with issues such as illegitimacy, fratricide and suicide. The controversy placed a great strain on his wife, and they soon became estranged, though Hardy was greatly depressed by her sudden death in 1912. They had no children. Hardy then turned to writing poetry, his greatest love, though his poems were never as successful as his novels.

In 1914 he married his secretary, **Florence Emily Dugdale** (1879–1937), who was nearly 40 years his junior. Hardy died at his home Max Gate in Dorchester on January 11, 1928; his remains lie in Poet's Corner in Westminster Abbey, though his heart was removed and lies in the church at Stinsford (see p.96), alongside his wives Emma and Florence.

they were later joined by his second wife, Florence. Inside the church you can see the Norman font where Hardy was baptized, and the beautiful stained-glass memorial window, designed by Douglas Strachen in 1930, and dedicated to Hardy: it features the colours of Egdon Heath, and the storm and tempest from Hardy's favourite Bible lesson – 1 Kings, chapter 19 – which is read here on June 1 each year to celebrate the author's birthday.

Hardy's Cottage, Higher Bockhampton

Higher Bockhampton, DT2 8QJ • Cottage Mid-March to Oct Wed–Sun plus bank hol Mon 11am–5pm • £7 • Visitor centre daily 10am–4pm • Free • ⓣ 01305 262366, ⓦ nationaltrust.org.uk/hardys-cottage

The attractive hamlet of **HIGHER BOCKHAMPTON**, three miles northeast of Dorchester, is known for one thing: **Hardy's Cottage**, where the famous author was born and lived until the age of 34, with his two sisters and brother. A lovely path winds from the car park through the ancient woodland of Thorncombe Woods to the cottage – a fitting approach that gives a sense of the rural isolation that Hardy writes about so frequently. The cottage is a simple cob and thatch affair, built in 1800 by Hardy's grandfather and surrounded by a small, pretty garden. It is little altered since the author's days, and has been simply furnished. Downstairs, the parlour is the main room – a larger version of it features as the parlour where the villagers dance in *Under the Greenwood Tree* – while next door is the tiny office where Hardy's father and grandfather did their accounts. Upstairs are three bedrooms, the first belonging to Hardy's two sisters, the second to his parents, and the third to Hardy himself, which he later shared with his younger brother Henry; it was here that he wrote *Under the Greenwood Tree* and much of *Far from the Madding Crowd*. From his window, he could gaze out at the Hardy Monument, commemorating his distant relative (see p.96), though today the view is obscured by trees. A new **visitor centre** by the car park has information on life in Hardy's times, activities for children, details on walking trails around the woods, a bird's nest cam, and a café with outside tables looking onto the woods.

ACCOMMODATION AND EATING **HIGHER BOCKHAMPTON**

Greenwood Grange DT2 8QH 01305 268874, greenwoodgrange.co.uk. A small lane leads from Hardy's cottage through the hamlet back to the car park, where you'll find *Greenwood Grange*, sixteen beautifully furnished self-catering cottages (sleeping 2–12) in converted barns and farm outbuildings, some built by Thomas Hardy's father. The stylish complex aims to be eco-friendly, with an organic vegetable garden, and also has an indoor pool, plus lovely gardens with a trampoline, and tennis courts. One-week minimum stay. **£154**

Yalbury Cottage Lower Bockhampton, DT2 8PZ 01305 262382, yalburycottage.com. In a tiny hamlet a mile south of Higher Bockhampton, this 350-year-old thatched cottage has been extended to house a well-kept B&B and a highly regarded restaurant. The comfortable rooms have views over the neighbouring fields, or onto the pretty gardens, dotted with tables and chairs for alfresco drinks in the summer. The restaurant is small and popular – the three-course menu features dishes such as local snails, Lyme Regis scallops and Dorset seabass (£37.50) – so advance booking is essential. Tues–Sat 7–9pm, Sun 12.30–2pm. **£120**

Athelhampton House

Athelhampton, DT2 7LG • March–Oct Good Friday, Mon–Thurs & Sun 10.30am–5pm; Nov–Feb Sun 10.30am–dusk • £13; £11.70 online • athelhampton.co.uk

Five miles east of Dorchester, **Athelhampton House** is a striking fifteenth-century manor house, surrounded by attractive walled gardens dotted with fountains and interesting topiary pyramids. Thomas Hardy's father, a builder, was involved in the restoration of the house in the nineteenth century, while Hardy himself set his story, *The Waiting Supper*, here and painted a fine watercolour of the house. The rooms inside are furnished with suitable grandeur and finery, many housing interesting antiques. The Tudor Oak Hall, built by Sir William Martyn in 1485, is the most impressive room, with its hammer-beam ceiling, original fireplace and oriel window. Outside, the gardens (laid out in 1891) are worth exploring, and there's a lovely riverside walk tracing the banks of the River Piddle. There's also a decent café in the former coach house.

Tolpuddle

Some eight miles east of Dorchester, just off the A35, is the pretty little village of **Tolpuddle**, of interest principally because of the **Tolpuddle Martyrs**. In 1834, six villagers – George and James Loveless, Thomas and John Standfield, John Brine and James Hammett – were sentenced to transportation for forming the Friendly Society of Agricultural Labourers, in order to petition for a small wage increase on the grounds that their families were starving. The men spent three years in Australia's penal colonies before being pardoned following a public outcry – and the Tolpuddle Martyrs passed into history as founders of the trade union movement. Six memorial cottages were built in 1934 to commemorate the centenary of the martyrs' conviction, and the middle one has been turned into a little **museum** (April–Oct Tues–Sat 10am–5pm, Sun 11am–5pm; Nov–March Thurs–Sat 10am–4pm, Sun 11am–4pm; free; tolpuddlemartyrs.org.uk), which charts the story of the men, from their tough rural lives before their conviction, to the horrors of transportation in a convict ship and the harsh conditions of the Australian penal colonies. Only one of the martyrs, James Hammett, remained in Tolpuddle after their pardon: he worked as a builder's labourer on his return and died in the village aged 80 in 1891. He is buried in the graveyard of the twelfth-century church of St John the Evangelist, in front of which the Martyrs' Tree still stands, where the Friendly Society meetings often took place.

North of Dorchester

Lord's Day bells from Bingham's Melcombe, Iwerne Minster, Shroton, Plush,
Down the grass between the beeches, mellow in the evening hush,
Gloved the hands that hold the hymn-book, which this morning milked the cow –
While Tranter Reuben, Gordon Selfridge, Edna Best and Thomas Hardy lie in Mellstock Churchyard now.'

Extract from John Betjeman's poem "Dorset"

Betjeman's words apply to the whole of central Dorset, but are at their most apt in the countryside north of Dorchester – a rolling rural idyll scattered with thatched villages. Designated an Area of Outstanding Natural Beauty, it's crisscrossed with footpaths, and it's a pleasure just to take a meandering drive down the winding country lanes that wend their way through farmland and valleys, passing villages with improbable names such as Plush, Droop and Melbury Bubb, as well as those of the **Piddle Valley**. However, most visitors head straight for two main sights of interest, the **Cerne Abbas Giant** and the historic abbey and gardens of **Milton Abbas**.

3

Cerne Abbas

Nestled into a deep valley six miles north of Dorchester, **CERNE ABBAS** is one of the most historic and prettiest villages in Dorset. It is also the most visited site in the county, principally because of the famous **chalk giant** that stands on a hillside just outside the village. The picturesque high street boasts some fine old pubs and an attractive church, though its most historic site is the former **Abbey**, founded in 987 and later visited by various royals including King John and Henry III: today, its remains are privately owned (£1 donation in box outside). You approach it up Abbey Street, once the heart of the medieval town with its row of ancient cottages. Many of the monastic visitors stayed in the **Guest House**, dating from 1470, which is the first building you come to as you enter the site. Beyond here is a small exhibition area in the Abbey Porch, once the entrance to the Abbey Hall.

Cross the churchyard opposite the abbey and you'll see **St Augustine's Well** – actually more of a spring – where St Augustine is said to have offered shepherds beer or water. When they opted for the latter, St Augustine rewarded them with a brewery.

The Cerne Abbas Giant

The best place to see the **giant** is to follow signs to the car park and viewpoint on the hillside opposite. Here you can gaze upon the 55m-high man carved out of chalk in all his priapic glory, flourishing a club over a disproportionately small head. No one knows when it was carved, but it dates back to at least Roman times and is almost certainly a fertility symbol – it was long believed that childless women could bear children after lying on his crotch.

You can walk right up to and around the giant, though the carving is now fenced off to avoid erosion and, in fact, you can barely make it out from close up. A better option is to follow the well-signed **Giant's Walk**, a one-hour-thirty-minute trail round and over the Giant's hill, returning via a ridge across fields, with great views back across the valley.

ARRIVAL AND DEPARTURE — CERNE ABBAS

By bus There are buses to Cerne Abbas (Mon–Sat 4–6 daily) from Dorchester and Sherborne.

ACCOMMODATION AND EATING

Abbots 7 Long St, DT2 7JF ⓣ 01300 341349, ⓦ abbotsbedandbreakfast.co.uk. Comfy beds and light, bright decor feature in the five decent rooms (four are en suite) above an excellent teashop with a pretty tea garden, right on the High St. It's child- and dog-friendly – there's one family room – and the breakfasts are good. **£85**

New Inn 14 Long St, DT2 7JF ⊕01300 341274, ⊕thenewinncerneabbas.co.uk. Recently refurbished sixteenth-century former coaching inn with cosy wood-burners inside and a lovely garden. The menu features dishes such as monkfish tail with couscous (£16) and fish stew (£14) along with bar food such as steak in ciabatta (around £7.50). There are four comfortable bedrooms above the pub, with wood beams and low ceilings, as well as eight more contemporary rooms in the stable block behind, opening onto the courtyard. Daily noon–2pm & 7–9pm. **£95**

The Piddle Valley

The **Piddle Valley** wends its way north from **Puddletown** through a series of picturesque villages and archetypal Dorset countryside – all rolling hills and fields, dotted with pheasants and lambs in spring. The river, more of a stream at its higher end, runs alongside the B3143 up to **Buckland Newton** at the head of the valley, via the pretty thatched villages of **Piddlehinton** and **Piddletrenthide**. From the latter, a small lane leads steeply uphill then down again into the next valley and the tiny village of **Plush**, little more than a cluster of houses and a pub. The whole region is crisscrossed with farm tracks and paths – taking pretty much any one of them will result in a pleasant rural walk, and you should aim to end up at one of the valley's great local pubs.

Badger Watch Dorset

Old Henley Farm, Buckland Newton, DT2 7BL • Badger-watching season April–Oct; viewing sessions 6.30pm–midnight, advance booking essential • Adults £15, under-16s £12 • ⊕01300 345293, ⊕badgerwatchdorset.co.uk

Budding naturalists will enjoy watching wild badgers forage and play at close quarters, at **Badger Watch Dorset**. There are four badger setts, housing up to twenty badgers in total, dug into a wooded bank, with two heated, lit hides from where you can view the animals. The badgers tend to forage before dusk and you can stay until midnight, when the lights are turned out. The animals are wild, so there is no guarantee when, or even if, they will arrive, but if you are patient and quiet, you are highly likely to see some activity. The badgers are fed with peanuts, and have become used to the lights, and they tend to arrive one at a time nervously padding down the bank, starting at any noise, then gradually becoming more confident as they feed. If you visit in June or July you may well see cubs playing too; other wildlife that you can spot here includes bats, owls, rabbits, foxes, hares and pheasants.

The farm also has various daytime **activities** such as quad-biking, hovercraft racing, archery and clay-pigeon shooting: check ⊕henleyhillbillies.co.uk.

ACCOMMODATION AND EATING — THE PIDDLE VALLEY

Brace of Pheasants Plush, DT2 7RQ ⊕01300 348357, ⊕braceofpheasants.co.uk. This sixteenth-century, thatched pub tucked away in the tiny village of Plush is a real get-away-from-it-all spot. Inside it's cosy, if slightly shabby, with a roaring fire and a restaurant serving well-cooked local food, such as Dorset wild boar sausages (£13) and venison steaks (£19). There are four comfortable rooms above the pub as well as some more spacious ones in the old skittle alley in the garden: all have been refurbished and are nicely decorated. Daily noon–3pm & 7–11pm; winter closed Sun evening & Mon. **£115**

Piddle Inn Piddletrenthide, DT2 7QF ⊕01300 348468, ⊕piddleinn.co.uk. Friendly village pub with an open fire inside and the River Piddle running alongside its back terrace. The menu features decent pub staples – try the home-made pies (£10) or gourmet burgers (£10) – plus baguettes (£7.50), ideally washed down with one of their real ales. There are three comfortable rooms upstairs, two with views over the river. Daily noon–11.30pm. **£75**

★**The Thimble Inn** 14 High St, Piddlehinton, DT2 7TD ⊕01300 348270, ⊕thimbleinn.co.uk. The staff are friendly at this cosy thatched pub with flagstone floors, comfy armchairs by the wood-burner and window seats, plus a pretty stream running through the back garden. The food is tasty and includes good-sized baguettes, such as roast pork and apple sauce with chips (£7.50), or chicken and leek pie and a selection of burgers (around £12.50). Mon–Fri 11.30am–3pm & 5.30–11pm, Sat 11.30am–11pm, Sun 11.30am–10.30pm.

Milton Abbas

From Cerne Abbas, it's a wonderful cross-country drive along winding lanes, which cross the Piddle Valley, to the village of **MILTON ABBAS**, nine miles east. Built in 1780 by architect Sir William Chambers, Milton Abbas was England's first planned village, and is comprised of sturdy thatched houses on either side of a wide road, and lawns in front. It's easy to see how the village, so regimented in style, differs from others nearby with their winding lanes and higgledy-piggledy cottages of varying ages. Today it's an extremely pretty place, made up of a row of cottages, almshouses, a church and the thatched *Hambro Arms* pub (see below).

Milton Abbey

DT11 0BZ • Abbey usually daily 10am–5pm

A mile south of the village is **Milton Abbey**, founded in 938 by King Athelstan: it burned down after being hit by lightning in 1309 and the present Abbey Church was started soon after. The choir and transept were built by the end of the fourteenth century though the nave was never finished, leaving the church looking rather incomplete. A sizeable town grew up around the abbey, with more than a hundred houses, a grammar school and many taverns. After the Dissolution of the Monasteries, the estate was sold off to a succession of families, until in 1752 it was bought by John Damer, who knocked down the old monastic buildings and built the present mansion on their site: it was arranged around a quadrangle, making it particularly suitable for its current use as a school. He also had the impressive grounds landscaped by "Capability" Brown.

Once the house and gardens had developed into a grandiose estate, Damer, now Lord Milton, decided that the squalor of the nearby town was lowering the tone of the place and, with the high-handedness typical of many eighteenth-century landlords, had the town destroyed and rebuilt a mile away up the hill – out of sight and earshot of the manor. The church and gardens are now owned by a public school, but they will usually permit visitors to have a look around the abbey. You can walk from the abbey along a footpath known as the Monk's Path, which leads to the bottom of the village.

3

ARRIVAL AND DEPARTURE — MILTON ABBAS

By bus Buses run to Milton Abbas from Dorchester (Mon–Fri 3 daily; 55min–1hr) and Blandford Forum (Mon–Fri 1 daily; 15min).

ACCOMMODATION AND EATING

Fox Inn Ansty, DT2 7PN ⓣ01258 880328, ⓦfoxinnansty.co.uk. Three miles northwest of Milton Abbas, the *Fox Inn* is a good option for food and lodging. A 200-year-old pub that was formerly a family home, it has peaceful, comfortable rooms, a lovely garden and a cosy bar serving local real ales. The food is reasonably priced, with local game a speciality – try the pan-fried rabbit with potato rosti (£14). Mon–Sat 11am–11pm, Sun noon–11pm. **£80**

Hambro Arms The Street, DT11 0BP ⓣ01258 880233, ⓦhambroarms.com. With low beams, a log fire and comfy sofas, the thatched *Hambro Arms* serves local ales and good pub grub, plus some more unusual dishes such as quail Scotch egg (£6.50) and roast sea trout (£16.50). It also has a few good-value rooms, which are comfortable, clean and recently refurbished. Tues–Fri noon–2.30pm & 6.30–9pm, Sat noon–3pm & 6.30–9pm, Sun noon–7.30pm. **£86**

Bulbarrow Hill

North of Milton Abbas, narrow wooded lanes wend to an elongated chalk ridge known as the Dorset Downs. At 274m (899ft), the highest point of the ridge is **Bulbarrow Hill**, around a mile south of the pretty little village of **Woolland**. The views from the top are stunning – on a clear day you can see as far as Shaftesbury and sometimes even Glastonbury. The hill is named for its ancient barrows, or burial grounds, and also marks the site of **Rawlsbury Camp**, an Iron Age hillfort. Like the nearby Hambledon

Hill (see p.148), this is a delightfully unspoilt spot with distinctive rings of earth embankments, now grazed by sheep.

The road alongside Rawlsbury Camp forms part of the Wessex Ridgeway, a 137-mile long-distance path that runs from Lyme Regis to Marlborough in Wiltshire. This section is popular with paragliders and has some great walks, as well as wonderful views to the north over some of Dorset's least spoilt countryside, a relatively flat rural landscape of farms and picturesque villages such as Okeford Fitzpaine.

Sherborne

In the far northwest corner of Dorset, ten miles north of Cerne Abbas, the pretty town of **SHERBORNE** was once the capital of Wessex, its church having cathedral status until Old Sarum usurped the bishopric in 1075. Its golden days are behind it, but with an exclusive public school and handsome architecture, it retains a sense of both affluence and importance, not to mention oodles of history that makes it a must-visit in anyone's Dorset itinerary. The town boasts two "castles", both associated with Sir Walter Raleigh (see box opposite) and both around fifteen minutes' walk from the centre, while the attractive **Cheap Street** (pedestrianized noon–4pm Mon–Sat) runs through the heart of town, and is worth browsing for its interesting antique and quirky gift shops.

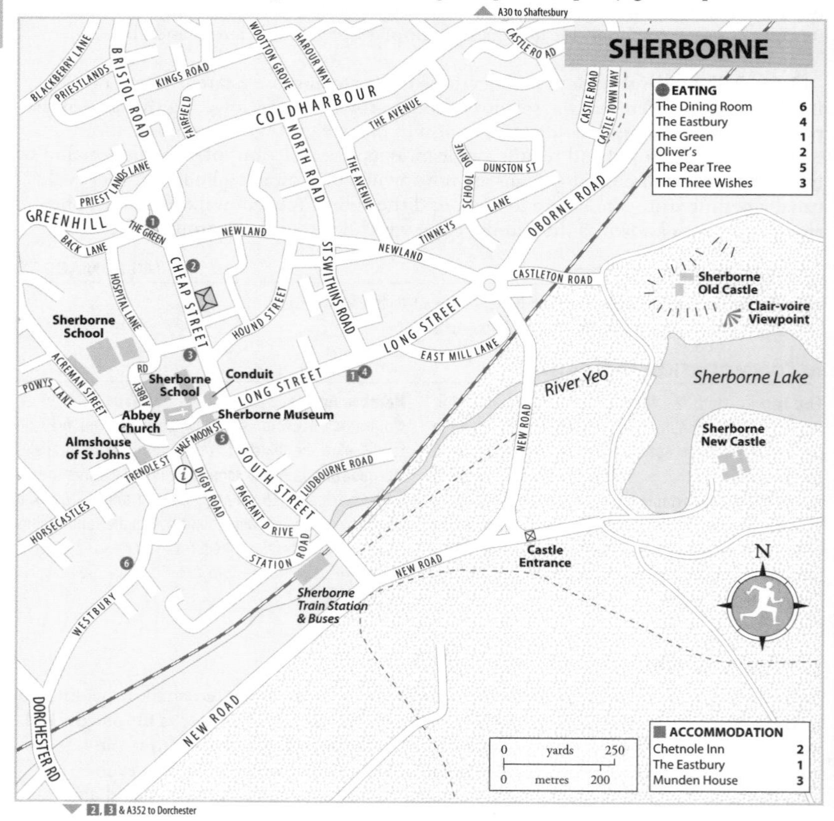

Abbey Church

Abbey Close, ST9 3LQ • **Church** Daily: April–Oct 8am–6pm; Nov–March 8am–4pm • Tours usually April–Sept Tues 10.30am & Fri 2.30pm, but phone in advance to check • Free, but donation welcome • T 01935 812452, W sherborneabbey.com • **Almshouse** May–Sept Wed, Thurs & Sat 2–4pm • £2 • W stjohnshouse.org

Sherborne's former historical glory is best embodied by the magnificent **Abbey Church**, which was founded in 705, later becoming a Benedictine abbey. Most of its extant parts date from a rebuilding in the fifteenth century, and it is one of the best examples of Perpendicular architecture in Britain, particularly noted for its outstanding **fan vaulting**. Indeed, Simon Jenkins in his *England's Thousand Best Churches* goes so far as to say, "I would pit Sherborne's roof against any contemporary work of the Italian Renaissance".

The church also has a famously weighty peal of eight bells, the heaviest in the world, led by "Great Tom", a tenor bell presented to the abbey by Cardinal Wolsey. Among the Abbey Church's many tombs are those of Alfred the Great's two brothers, Ethelred and Ethelbert, and the Elizabethan poet Thomas Wyatt, all located in the northeast corner. The **almshouse of St John's** on the opposite side of the Abbey Close was built in 1437 and is a rare example of a medieval hospital. Visitors can look round the medieval chapel and antechapel, though the building is still used for respite care, while another wing provides accommodation for Sherborne's well-known public **school**, one of the most expensive in the country: founded in 1550, it has appeared in various films, including *Goodbye Mr Chips* (1969).

Sherborne Museum

Church Lane, DT9 3BP • Feb–Easter Tues & Thurs 10.30am–12.30pm; Easter to mid-Dec Tues–Sat 10.30am–4.30pm & fourth Sun of the month 10am–1pm • Free • W sherbornemuseum.co.uk

Sherborne Museum, near the abbey, has an eclectic collection of memorabilia to do with the town, including a model of the Old Castle before it was ruined, a mummified cat, and exhibits of Edwardian underwear. The fully furnished Sherborne Doll's House may well appeal to small children, and there are also photos of parts of the fifteenth-century *Sherborne Missal*, a richly illuminated tome weighing nearly fifty pounds, now housed in the British Library. Just outside the museum is a fine old relic, the **conduit**: this arched former washhouse was moved here after the dissolution of the monastery in 1539, and has since been used as the town's water supply and, later, as a police station and a bank.

SIR WALTER RALEIGH

Famed for his explorations of the New World – he helped the English colonize Virginia in the 1580s and is often credited with introducing potatoes and tobacco to the UK – **Sir Walter Raleigh** was one of the Elizabethan era's most flamboyant and controversial figures. A writer, poet and explorer, he became a favourite of Queen Elizabeth I, helping put down rebellions in Ireland and (allegedly) laying down cloaks over puddles for her. He blotted his copybook in 1591, however, when he secretly married one of the royal ladies-in-waiting without the queen's permission, and both were sent packing to the Tower of London for their sins. When they were released, they retired to the **New Castle** in Sherborne in 1594. The gardens still contain Raleigh's Seat, where he liked to smoke his newly discovered tobacco. It is said a passing servant was so surprised at this novel sight that he threw a jug of beer over him, believing that Raleigh was on fire. After Elizabeth's death, Raleigh was framed for a plot against the recently crowned King James, and sentenced to prison again in Winchester's Great Hall. His estate in Sherborne was forfeited to the king, who handed it to Sir John Digby in 1617; Raleigh was beheaded a year later, after he was accused of further machinations.

Sherborne Old Castle

Castletom, DT9 3SA • Daily: April–June, Sept & Oct 10am–5pm; July & Aug 10am–6pm • £4; EH • www.english-heritage.org.uk/visit/places/sherborne-old-castle

Queen Elizabeth I first leased, then gave, Sir Walter Raleigh the twelfth-century **Sherborne Old Castle**, but it seems that he despaired of feudal accommodation and built himself a more comfortably domesticated house in the adjacent deer park in 1594. The Old Castle was pulverized by Cromwellian cannon fire for the Digby family's (see below) obstinately Royalist leanings and now lies in ruins, with the southwest gatehouse being the most intact section. You can wander round the castle's old walls, or view it from the adjacent Sherborne New Castle.

Sherborne New Castle

New Rd, DT9 5NR • Easter–Oct Tues–Thurs, Sat, Sun, bank hol Mon & Easter Fri: castle 11am–5pm; gardens 10am–6pm • Castle & gardens £11, gardens only £6, under-16s free; EH • sherbornecastle.com

3

The Digby family acquired Raleigh's former house and have lived there ever since, remodelling the original structure to provide comforts for visitors like Prince William of Orange (who stayed in 1688), the poet Alexander Pope (1724) and George III (1753). You can still make out parts of the original Raleigh house in the Solarium, with its Tudor ceiling, and in the splendid kitchens, with the original ovens. It's also evident in the entrance hall, where there's also a pipe given to Raleigh by Native Americans (and subsequently damaged in the 1941 Blitz). Elsewhere, priceless furniture, ceramics and books are displayed in a whimsically Gothic interior, remodelled in the nineteenth century. Don't miss the fabulous painting of *Elizabeth I in Procession*, by Robert Peake the Elder; the ornate panelled Oak Room; the upstairs photos showing the house's use as a Red Cross hospital in World War I and as HQ for the D-Day landings in World War II; and the basement museum, housing archeological remains from the Old Castle. Outside there are alluring tearooms with tables on the lawn and lovely lakeside walks in grounds laid out by "Capability" Brown in 1753 – you can see over the Old Castle from the **Clair-Voire viewpoint**, signed from the gardens.

ARRIVAL AND INFORMATION — SHERBORNE

By train The station is in the south of the town, about a 5min walk from the centre, and is served by hourly trains between London (2hr 15min) and Exeter (1hr 10min).

By bus Buses pull in outside the train station, with regular services from Dorchester (6–7 daily; 1hr), Yeovil (6–7 daily; 20min) and Blandford Forum (2–3 daily; 1hr 25min).

Tourist office 3 Tilton Court, Digby Rd (Mon–Sat: Easter–Aug 9am–5pm; Sept–Nov 9.30am–4pm; Dec–Easter 10am–3pm; 01935 815341, visit-dorset.com/about-the-area/areas-to-visit/west-dorset).

ACCOMMODATION

IN TOWN

The Eastbury Long St, DT9 3BY 01935 813131, theeastburyhotel.co.uk. In a fine Georgian house, this is the smartest choice in town, with its own restaurant (see opposite), bar and lovely walled gardens complete with a croquet lawn. The front rooms are on the small side and it is worth paying extra for a superior room, which is spacious and boutique in feel, overlooking the gardens. **£150**

OUT OF TOWN

Chetnole Inn Chetnole, DT9 6NU 01935 872337, thechetnoleinn.co.uk. About seven miles southwest of Sherborne is this lovely traditional country pub with log fires, local ales and an attractive garden filled with waddling ducks. The comfortable rooms overlook the village church and are well decorated, with Egyptian cotton sheets and flatscreen TVs. The food is good quality too, and reasonably priced, with main courses such as slow braised pork belly for £13. **£95**

Munden House Alweston, DT9 5HU 01963 23150, mundenhouse.co.uk. Lovely thatched B&B in a small village, just a couple of miles southeast of Sherborne. The comfortable, well-decorated rooms offer fantastic views over the gardens and surrounding countryside. There are also three self-catering cottages (sleeping 2–4; from £125) in the grounds. **£105**

EATING

The Dining Room Westbury, DT9 3EH ⓣ01935 815154, ⓦthediningroomsherborne.com. Housed in an eighteenth-century former girls' school but with a smart contemporary interior, this fine-dining restaurant specializes in Modern British cooking. Dishes include local grilled mackerel (£15) and New Forest mushroom open lasagne (£12), sometimes with an interesting twist, such as the cinnamon-dusted Lyme Bay scallops (£9). Mon–Sat noon–2pm & 6.30–9.30pm, Sun noon–3pm.

The Eastbury Long St, DT9 3BY ⓣ01935 813131, ⓦtheeastburyhotel.co.uk. Upmarket hotel (see p.105) restaurant, serving excellent-quality seasonal food from local producers, including vegetables and herbs grown in their own garden. There are lovely views from the conservatory restaurant and the garden, where you can eat in summer. Main courses such as bass with crab and saffron tortellini cost around £19, or you can go the whole hog with the seven-course tasting menu (£55). Daily noon–2pm & 6.30–9pm.

★**The Green** 3 The Green, DT9 3HY ⓣ01935 813821, ⓦgreenrestaurant.co.uk. In a pretty Grade II-listed building, with a walled garden at the back, this fantastic restaurant serves interesting, innovative, skilful and (most importantly) delicious food. The chef combines inspiration from his Russian childhood with local ingredients to produce starters such as hay-smoked sea trout with keta caviar (£9) and mains like coal fish with caviar brandade and a lobster vinaigrette (£16), as well as interesting *zakuski* – a sort of Russian tapas. Tues–Sat noon–2.30pm & 6.30–9.30pm.

Oliver's 19 Cheap St, DT9 3PU ⓣ01935 815005, ⓦoliverscoffeehouse.co.uk. With long wooden benches laid out in a former butcher's, still adorned with the original tiles, this friendly café-deli serves great cakes and coffee, plus sandwiches, toasties and quiche, accompanied by oodles of atmosphere. Mon–Fri 9am–5pm, Sat 9.30am–5pm, Sun 10am–4pm.

The Pear Tree Half Moon St, DT9 3LN ⓣ01935 812828, ⓦpeartreedeli.co.uk. The place to come for a light lunch, this café-deli serves delicious soups, sumptuous salads and sandwiches (£4–5), as well as selling local produce to put together a fine picnic. Mon–Fri 9am–5pm, Sat 9am–6pm, Sun 10.30am–5pm.

The Three Wishes 78 Cheap St, DT9 3BJ ⓣ01935 817777, ⓦthethreewishes.co.uk. With a lovely walled garden at the back, this bistro serves tasty coffee and sandwiches (£6–7) as well as more hearty meals, such as Durdle Door beef with thyme dumplings (£11), or linguine with prawns and coconut milk (£10). Mon–Thurs 9.30am–5.30pm, Fri & Sat 9.30am–5pm, Sun 11am–3pm.

Western Dorset

THE VIEW TOWARDS GOLDEN CAP

Western Dorset

From the Regency resort of Weymouth, with its jutting peninsula of Portland, to the pretty town of Lyme Regis – so beloved of Jane Austen – the coastline of western Dorset is one of the most varied and dramatic in the country, combining history with stunning unspoilt beaches and cliffs. The eastern section is dominated by the eighteen-mile-long pebble bank of Chesil Beach, which ends near the picture-postcard village of Abbotsbury on the Fleet Lagoon, with its six-hundred-year-old swannery. From here, sandstone cliffs lead up to Golden Cap, the south coast's highest point, with the lively market town of Bridport just inland. The far western stretch around Charmouth and Lyme Regis is rich in fossils, and has thrown up some of the country's most important geological finds.

Inland, western Dorset is a bucolic idyll dotted with quaint villages like pretty **Evershot**, winding country lanes and unexpected hills with far-reaching views, such as **Pilsdon Pen**, site of an Iron Age hillfort. With only one main town, the modest **Beaminster**, and one in-road, the A35, the inland area is a joy to explore. It's also at the forefront of the local food renaissance – Hugh Fearnley-Whittingstall's *River Cottage* is nearby – and a visit to a thatched country pub serving seasonal food and real ales, followed by a walk along pretty much any country footpath, will rarely disappoint.

The coast is fairly easy to explore by public transport, with buses connecting the main towns and trains serving Weymouth and the region inland of Lyme Regis, though to reach the more out-of-the-way spots it's best to have a car.

Weymouth

An elegant and bustling town, **WEYMOUTH** has one of the best beaches in western Dorset and some fine Georgian buildings, though the town had long been a port before the Georgians popularized it as a resort. It's possible that a ship unloading a cargo here in 1348 first brought the Black Death to English shores, and it was from Weymouth that John Endicott sailed in 1628 to found Salem in Massachusetts. However, Weymouth's name is inextricably linked with "mad" King George III, who came here to recuperate in 1789. Part of his remedy was to take to the sea in a bathing machine while a band played "God Save the King". It's said he then drank the seawater and ate cuttlefish and earwigs for good measure. Amazingly, his physical – if not mental – health improved after the experience. A likeness of the monarch on horseback

LYME REGIS BEACH

Highlights

❶ **Abbotsbury Swannery** May to June is the time to visit, when you can stroll amid the squawking, fluffy cygnets – and can even watch the eggs hatching. **See p.122**

❷ **Lyme Regis** A pretty seaside town with excellent restaurants, cafés and shops, great coastal walks and a lovely beach. **See p.129**

❸ **Alexandra Hotel, Lyme Regis** You can't beat the location, or the service, at this lovely historic hotel, where you can wake up to stunning views over the gardens, the harbour, and along the coast. **See p.132**

❹ **Fossil tours at Charmouth Heritage Centre** Informative and fascinating tours, which prove incredibly satisfying when you come home with your pockets filled with fossils plucked on the beach. **See p.133**

❺ **Climb Golden Cap** It's a bracing, steep walk up the south coast's highest cliff with far-reaching coastal views. **See p.134**

❻ **Evershot** An unspoilt thatched village that remains pretty much as it was in Thomas Hardy's time. **See p.135**

HIGHLIGHTS ARE MARKED ON THE MAP ON PP.110–111

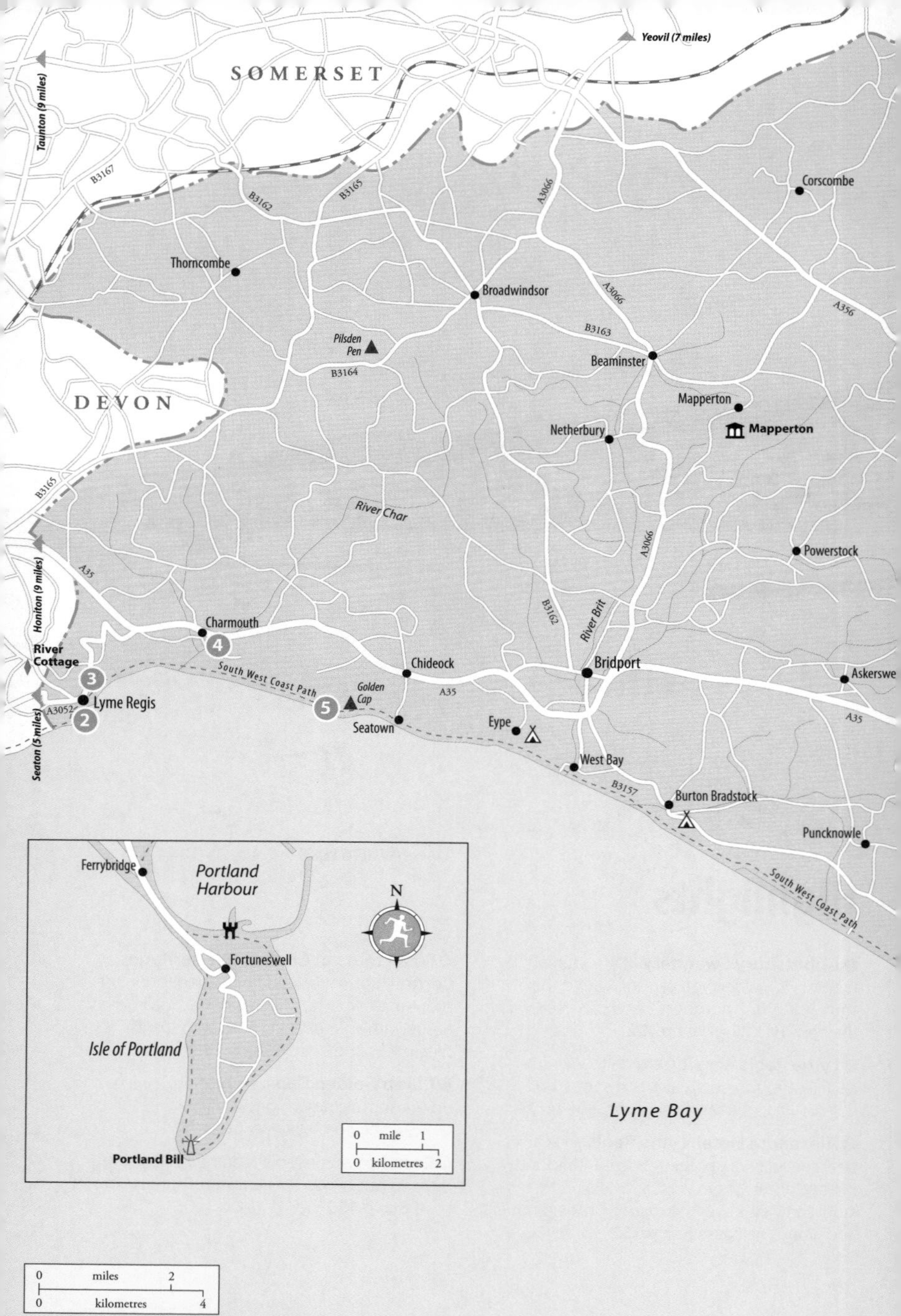

WESTERN DORSET

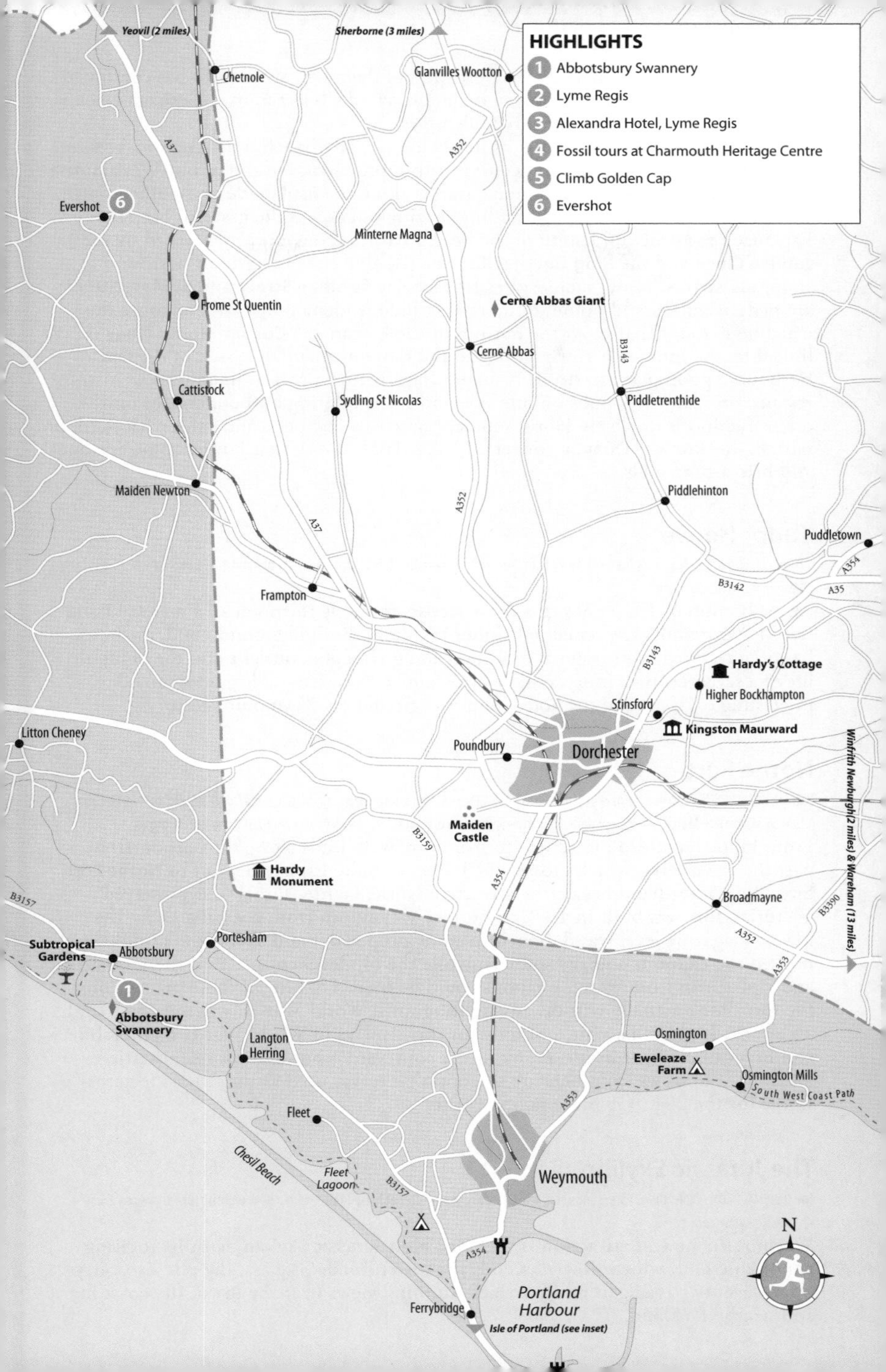

HIGHLIGHTS
1 Abbotsbury Swannery
2 Lyme Regis
3 Alexandra Hotel, Lyme Regis
4 Fossil tours at Charmouth Heritage Centre
5 Climb Golden Cap
6 Evershot
Yeovil (2 miles)
Sherborne (3 miles)
Chetnole
Glanvilles Wootton
A37
A352
Evershot
Minterne Magna
Frome St Quentin
Cerne Abbas Giant
Cerne Abbas
B3143
Cattistock
Sydling St Nicolas
Piddletrenthide
Maiden Newton
Piddlehinton
Puddletown
A354
B3142
A35
Frampton
Hardy's Cottage
Higher Bockhampton
Stinsford
Kingston Maurward
Litton Cheney
Poundbury
Dorchester
Winfrith Newburgh (2 miles) & Wareham (13 miles)
Maiden Castle
B3159
Hardy Monument
Broadmayne
B3390
B3157
Subtropical Gardens
Abbotsbury
Portesham
A353
Abbotsbury Swannery
Langton Herring
Osmington
Eweleaze Farm
Osmington Mills
South West Coast Path
Fleet
Chesil Beach
Fleet Lagoon
Weymouth
N
Portland Harbour
Ferrybridge
Isle of Portland (see inset)

is now carved into the chalk downs northwest of the town. Weymouth has continued to be a popular seaside resort ever since, and received a boost to its self-esteem when it hosted the sailing events at the 2012 Olympics.

Weymouth's main attraction is its lovely long, sandy **beach**, but it's also a pleasant town to explore. A few buildings survive from pre-Georgian times, but Weymouth's most imposing architectural heritage stands along the **Esplanade**, a dignified range of bow-fronted and porticoed buildings gazing out across the graceful bay. The Esplanade runs the full length of the beach, with the town centre marked by the **Jubilee Clock** and the **King George III statue**. Behind here is a grid of narrow shopping streets; some, such as the atmospheric **St Alban Street** and **St Mary Street**, are pedestrianized and home to interesting independent shops; others house the usual high-street chains. At the bottom of the Esplanade, **Custom House Quay** is linked by the moveable Town Bridge to the more intimate quayside of the **Old Harbour**, a good place to stroll. Its main drag, Trinity Road, is lined with restaurants, cafés and pubs on one side and boats offering **harbour cruises** on the other. Behind is the lively Hope Square, home to a few pubs and cafés with outdoor tables, plus **Brewers Quay**, a converted Victorian brewery that houses some antiques and bric-a-brac stalls.

Tudor House

3 Trinity St, DT4 8TW • May–Oct Tues–Fri 1–3.45pm, Sun 2–4pm; Nov, Dec & Feb–April first Sun of month 2–4pm • £4 • Ⓦ weymouthcivicsociety.org

At the bottom of Trinity Street is **Tudor House**, formerly the home of a merchant and one of Weymouth's few remaining Tudor buildings. Built in around 1600, the house has been restored to its original condition and gives a good insight into the domestic life of a seventeenth-century, middle-class family. Knowledgeable guides provide interesting tours around the house, and background on Weymouth's history.

Nothe Fort

Barrack Rd, DT4 8UF • Feb half-term & Oct half-term daily 11am–4.30pm; late Feb to late March, early Oct & late Oct to mid-Dec Sun 11am–4.30pm; late March to late Sept daily 10.30am–5.30pm • £8, under-16s £1 • Ⓣ 01305 766626, Ⓦ nothefort.org.uk

From Hope Square, a pleasant fifteen-minute walk leads along the harbourfront, past the town ferry, which crosses the harbour to the Esplanade, out to **Nothe Fort**. Sitting on a headland beside the attractive Nothe Gardens, this well-preserved Victorian fort was built in 1872 to protect Weymouth from coastal attack. The lowest magazine level was designed to store gunpowder and shells, the middle level housed the cannons and the soldiers, while the top level consisted of the ramparts and a platform from which weapons could be fired. Despite all these precautions, the fort didn't actually witness any fighting until World War II, when it came under air attack. It's worth a visit, not only for the displays of World War II memorabilia – children can clamber inside a tank in the courtyard – but also for its fantastic location. The views from here are so good that it was used as the main spectators' venue for the 2012 Olympic sailing events.

The Jurassic Skyline

The Quay, DT4 8DX • Daily, times vary: summer at least 11am–5pm; winter at least 11am–4pm, check website for variations • £6.50 • Ⓦ jurassicskyline.com

Weymouth's newest attraction is the 53m-high **Jurassic Skyline**, with its rotating panoramic pod, which slowly ascends the tower. Made of glass, the pod can carry up to seventy passengers and provides stunning views over the town, the coastline and nearby Portland.

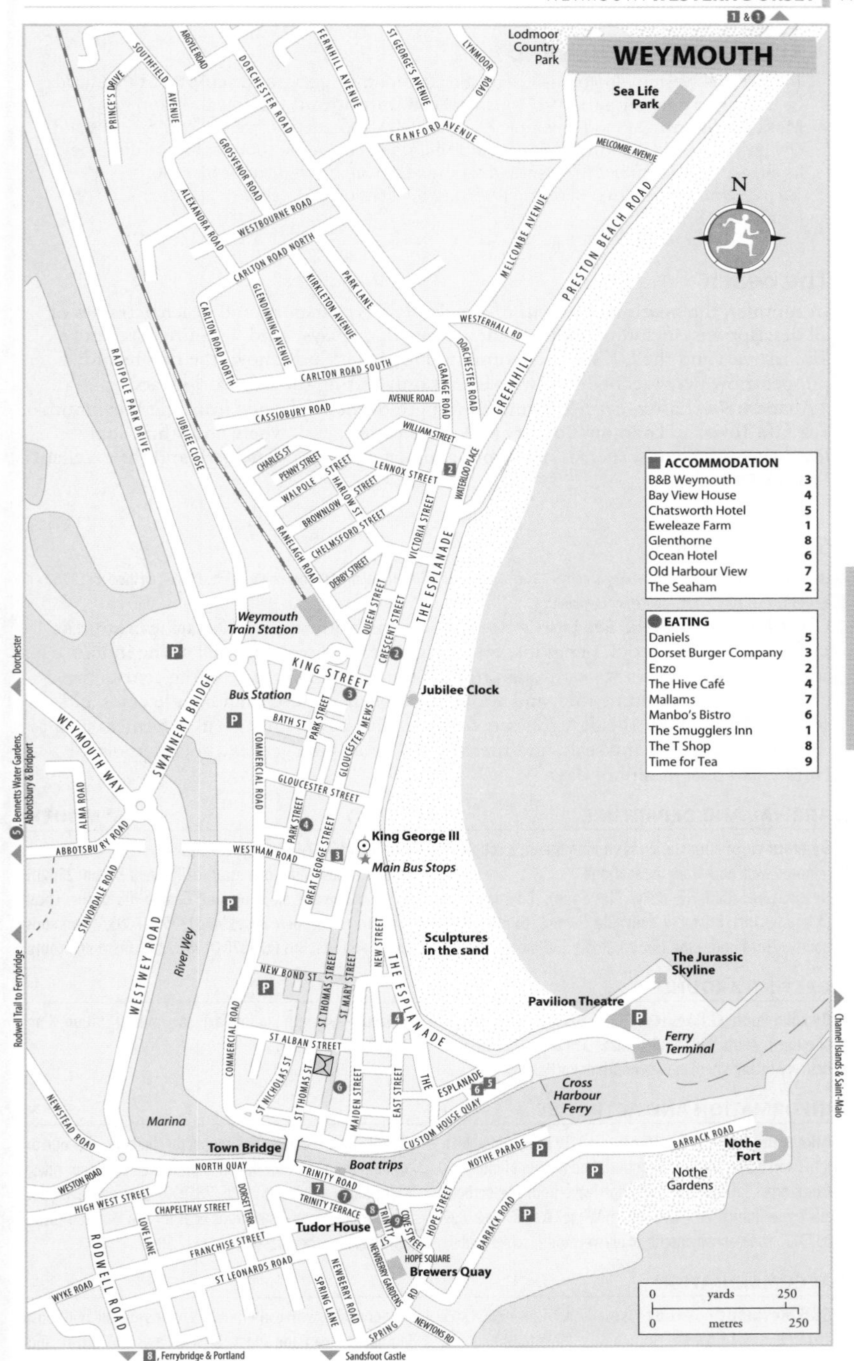
WEYMOUTH
Sea Life Park
Lodmoor Country Park
Weymouth Train Station
Bus Station
Jubilee Clock
King George III
Main Bus Stops
Sculptures in the sand
The Jurassic Skyline
Pavilion Theatre
Ferry Terminal
Cross Harbour Ferry
Town Bridge
Boat trips
Marina
River Wey
Tudor House
Brewers Quay
Nothe Fort
Nothe Gardens
ACCOMMODATION
B&B Weymouth 3
Bay View House 4
Chatsworth Hotel 5
Eweleaze Farm 1
Glenthorne 8
Ocean Hotel 6
Old Harbour View 7
The Seaham 2
EATING
Daniels 5
Dorset Burger Company 3
Enzo 2
The Hive Café 4
Mallams 7
Manbo's Bistro 6
The Smugglers Inn 1
The T Shop 8
Time for Tea 9
Dorchester
5, Bennetts Water Gardens, Abbotsbury & Bridport
Rodwell Trail to Ferrybridge
Channel Islands & Saint-Malo
8, Ferrybridge & Portland
Sandsfoot Castle
yards 250
metres 250
4

SCULPTURES IN THE SAND

Towards the western end of the beach, look out for the quirky **sand sculptures** that have been created here since the 1920s, first by **Fred Darrington**, and now by his grandson **Mark Anderson**. During the winter, Mark models sculptures for international festivals and clients, such as the Ministry of Sound and Selfridges, and in the summer he can often be found on Weymouth beach. Past sand sculptures made by Fred and Mark include Tutankhamun, a full-sized Mini and the Empire State Building: see Ⓦ sculpturesinsand.com for more examples.

The beach

In summer, the **beach** is the focus of activity, with watersports and beach activities of all descriptions, including donkey rides, firework displays, sand sculpting (see above), kite festivals and the UK's longest-running Punch and Judy show (the first recorded puppet show here was in 1881, with breaks only during the two world wars).

A **land train** (Easter–Sept; £3) runs the length of the Esplanade from the Weymouth Sea Life Tower to **Lodmoor Country Park** at its eastern end, where you'll find some low-key amusements, such as mini-golf, a model railway, a skate park and the excellent **Sea Life Park**.

Sea Life Park

Lodmoor Country Park, DT4 7SX • Daily: summer 10am–5/6pm; winter 11am–4pm • Advance online tickets £16.50; on the door £23.50 • Ⓣ 01305 761070, Ⓦ visitsealife.com/Weymouth

Great for wet days, the **Sea Life Centre** is home to a wide variety of marine creatures including sharks, turtles, penguins, otters, caymans and seals. As well as the indoor aquariums, one with a walk-through tunnel, there's a sea-horse breeding centre, the crocodile creek log flume ride, and a rock pool where children can handle crabs and starfish. Throughout the day, you can watch feeding times for various creatures, such as the otters, penguins and seals, and there are outdoor water-jets and splash pools for children to play in on hot days.

ARRIVAL AND DEPARTURE — WEYMOUTH

By train Weymouth station is on King Street, a couple of minutes' walk back from the seafront.

Destinations Bath (7 daily; 2hr 5min); Bournemouth (3 hourly; 1hr); Bristol (7 daily; 2hr 50min); London (1–2 hourly; 2hr 45min–3hr 15min); Poole (3 hourly; 45min); Southampton (1–2 hourly; 1hr 50min).

By bus Buses from Dorchester (daily every 20min; 25min) pull in at the bus stops by King George III's statue. Local buses are run by More Buses (Ⓣ 01305 827005, Ⓦ morebus.co.uk) and First Bus (Ⓣ 0870 0106 022, Ⓦ firstgroup.com).

GETTING AROUND

By bike Portland Bikes (Ⓣ 07523 37059, Ⓦ portlandbikehire.com), rents out adults' bikes (£12/day), with free delivery to anywhere in Weymouth or Portland.

By taxi Weymouth Station Taxis, Weymouth Station, King St (Ⓣ 01305 788888).

INFORMATION AND ACTIVITIES

Bike tours Portland Bike Hire (see p.120) runs guided bike tours and walks around Weymouth and further afield.

Boat trips Cruises and boat trips leave from the harbour alongside Trinity Rd; Weymouth White Water (Ⓣ 07899 892317, Ⓦ weareweymouth.co.uk/weymouth-white-water) offers high-speed RIB trips round the harbour and out to Portland (from £18 for 40min trip) as well as longer rides; White Motor Boats (Ⓣ 01305 785000, Ⓦ weareweymouth.co.uk/white-motor-boats) runs boat trips to Portland castle (£5) and along the Jurassic Coast (£12.50).

ACCOMMODATION

B&B Weymouth 68 The Esplanade, DT4 7AA Ⓣ 01305 761190, Ⓦ bb-weymouth.com. Weymouth's first boutique B&B, with contemporary rooms and all mod cons. Rooms are clean and spacious (sea views £10 extra), and there's a lovely lounge/bar with a sea view and tea, coffee and biscuits available all day. Breakfasts are organic and local where possible, and they lend bikes for free. **£90**

★**Bay View House** 35 The Esplanade, DT4 8DH ⓣ01305 782083, ⓦbayview-weymouth.co.uk. This friendly guesthouse is clean and well kept. All the rooms are comfortable, but the best value are those at the front with a bay window giving great views along the coast, at a bargain £65. The family rooms cost just a little more at £75, and there's also free wi-fi and private garage parking. **£60**

Chatsworth Hotel 14 The Esplanade, DT4 8EB ⓣ01305 785012, ⓦthechatsworth.co.uk. Lovely guesthouse in a great location. The furnishings are modern and all the rooms have either harbour or sea views. On fine days breakfast is served on the terrace. The hotel also does meals specializing in local fish caught daily by the friendly owner's brother. Minimum two-night stay in summer. **£110**

★**Eweleaze Farm** Osmington, DT3 6ED ⓣ01305 833690, ⓦeweleaze.co.uk. Just under five miles from Weymouth is this spectacular seasonal clifftop campsite. It has seven fields (some car-free) and fantastic sea views, plus solar-powered showers, an on-site farm shop – selling its own home-baked organic bread and local produce – and, to top it all, its own shingle beach. You can also stay in a couple of quirky cottages (4–6 people), including *The Lookout* on a clifftop (£850 a week). Aug only. Mon–Thurs & Sun **£16**, Fri & Sat **£32**

Glenthorne Castle Cove, 15 Old Castle Rd, DT4 8QB ⓣ01305 777281, ⓦglenthorne-holidays.co.uk. Three two-bedroom self-catering apartments attached to a Victorian rectory, in a prime position overlooking the sea. Some apartments have sea views, and all have access to lovely large gardens leading directly to Castle Cove beach, with a heated outdoor pool, table tennis and trampoline. One-week minimum stay in high season. **£121**

Ocean Hotel 15 The Esplanade, DT4 8EB ⓣ01305 782012, ⓦtheoceanweymouth.co.uk. The *Ocean Hotel* is in a great location with a bright breakfast terrace overlooking the harbour: all the rooms have views either over the sea at the front or over the harbour at the back. Also has family rooms and limited parking. **£80**

Old Harbour View 12 Trinity Rd, DT4 8TJ ⓣ01305 774633, ⓦoldharbourview.co.uk. Cosy guesthouse in a great location right on the harbour front. It has just two rooms in a Georgian townhouse, but it's worth asking for the one at the front with a harbour view. The owners are friendly, and the breakfasts feature local free-range eggs and smoked fish. Two-night minimum stay. **£98**

The Seaham 3 Waterloo Place, DT4 7NU ⓣ01305 782010, ⓦtheseahamweymouth.co.uk. Attractive Georgian terraced house at the quieter end of town. The rooms are comfortable and well furnished and some have sea views; breakfast includes a good choice of local free-range products with vegetarian options. Free parking. **£100**

4

EATING

Daniels 159 Abbotsbury Rd, DT4 0JX ⓣ01305 787720, ⓦdanielsfishandchips.co.uk. This award-winning fish-and-chip shop serves the freshest fish and tastiest chips in the area – a standard cod and chips will set you back £6. It also has good veggie options, such as pea fritters. It's about a mile out of the town centre and also has branches in the Littlemoor shopping centre, and in Fortuneswell on Portland. Mon 5–10pm, Tues–Sat noon–1.30pm & 5–10pm.

Dorset Burger Company 6 King St, DT4 7BH, ⓣ01305 780888, ⓦthedorsetburgercompany.co.uk. With its shabby-chic decor, this lively restaurant serves fantastic burgers made with chicken, beef or pork from Dorset farms – even the chillies in the searing Dorset Naga burger are local. Burgers cost £9–12, including chips and coleslaw, and the desserts are tasty too. Mon 6–9.30pm, Tues 5.30–9.30pm, Wed & Thurs 5.30–10pm, Fri 5.30–10.30pm, Sat noon–10.30pm, Sun noon–9.30pm.

Enzo 110 The Esplanade, DT2 7EA ⓣ01305 778666, ⓦenzo-ristorante.co.uk/enzo. Traditional Italian restaurant with clean, contemporary decor, tiled floors and modern furnishings; it's right on the seafront, but slightly away from the hubbub of the main drag. It serves authentic, freshly made pizzas (£8–10), a range of pasta dishes (£9–10) and daily local specials such as steaks (around £18). Excellent value and friendly service. Daily 12.30–2.30pm & 5.30–10.30pm.

★**The Hive Café** 20 Park St, DT4 7DQ ⓣ07867 898498, ⓦbit.ly/HiveCafeWeymouth. Great veggie and vegan café with friendly service, a little courtyard at the back, a cosy upstairs room with a wood-burner and live music on summer evenings. The food is fantastic – home-made quiche and filo pastries, falafel and a great-value meze with a pasty and a selection of salads for £6 – and portions are big. Tasty cakes are made with honey from their own hives, and the hot lemon, ginger and honey drink (£2) is delicious. Wed–Sun 11am–4pm; summer also Tues 11am–4pm, plus evenings for live music.

Mallams 5 Trinity Rd, DT4 8TJ ⓣ01305 776757, ⓦmallamsrestaurant.co.uk. In a great location overlooking the harbour – ask for a window seat – this cosy restaurant specializes in seasonal meat and game and local fish and seafood. Mains include hake with sag aloo, herb-crusted lamb and venison with butternut squash (£19–25). Service is good and the quality of the cooking high. Mon–Sat from 7pm.

Manbo's Bistro 46 St Mary St, DT4 8PU ⓣ01305 839839, ⓦmanbosbistro.com. Good-value fish, pasta and meat dishes, such as monkfish linguine (£14.50) and venison steak (£19), at this friendly family-run bistro.

THE RODWELL TRAIL AND SANDSFOOT CASTLE

Running from Abbotsbury Road, near the centre of Weymouth, to Ferrybridge, the **Rodwell Trail** is a leafy two-mile cycle- and walkway along the old **Great Western railway line**. Built in 1865 to carry passengers and Portland stone between Weymouth and Portland, the rail line later served the factory at Ferrybridge where torpedoes were invented by Robert Whitehead in 1891 and tested in the harbour; the factory at Ferrybridge continued to make the weapons up until 1993. The train line was closed in 1965 and the track taken up – in 2000, it was re-opened as a cycle- and walkway. The bottom end of the trail runs alongside the harbour, giving wonderful views of Portland and the coast: it is well signposted, but if you want a map, pick one up from Weymouth tourist office (see p.114).

The trail passes, about twenty minutes' walk from its end at Ferrybridge, the ruins of **Sandsfoot Castle** (free access) surrounded by fine gardens. It was one of a pair of sea defences built by Henry VIII – the other being Portland Castle opposite (see p.117) – who feared attack from the continent after his dissolution of the monasteries. It was built partly using stones from Bindon Abbey near Wool, which Henry had had dismantled. The castle was later occupied by parliamentary forces during the English Civil War and used as a mint, but coastal erosion has caused the structure to slowly collapse.

The dining area is narrow with an open kitchen at the back, and there are a few tables on the pedestrianized street in front. Mon 6–9pm, Tues–Thurs noon–2.30pm & 6–9pm, Fri noon–2.30pm & 6–9.30pm, Sat noon–3pm & 6–9.30pm.

The Smugglers Inn Osmington Mills, DT3 6HF ⓣ01305 833125, ⓦsmugglersinnosmingtonmills.co.uk. Location is all at this thatched thirteenth-century pub – in a small village a couple of hours' wander east on the South West Coast Path from Weymouth – which has a fine garden with great views over the coast. The food hits the spot, too, after a morning at the beach or a coastal stroll, with decent lunches like pulled pork subs (£8) and baguettes (£5–6), and a selection of real ales. Mon–Sat 11am–11pm, Sun noon–10.30pm.

The T Shop 11a Trinity St, DT4 8TW ⓣ01305 788052. Quaint little teashop with tables on the waterfront and harbour views. It serves light lunches such as organic soup, and delicious home-made cakes and sandwiches. As well as the traditional type of cream tea, it does a tasty savoury version with a pot of tea, a cheese scone, a chunk of cheese and chutney – good value at £4. Daily 10am–4.30pm.

Time for Tea 8 Cove St, DT4 8TR ⓣ01305 777500. A lovely tearoom-cum-brasserie, with tables outside on Hope Square. It serves delicious home-made cakes, plus classic French dishes: breakfast can be continental or a more substantial eggs florentine, while lunch features dishes such as croque monsieur (£6), a hearty tartiflette (£9) or *soupe de poissons*. Daily 9.30am–5pm, plus 7–9pm on the third Fri & Sat of the month.

Ferrybridge

A couple of miles south of Weymouth, the mainland "bridge" to Portland begins by the workaday town of **FERRYBRIDGE**. The area is particularly good for diving, thanks to rich marine life and various sunken wrecks, including the *Aeolian Sky*, a Greek freighter that sank twelve miles off Portland in 1979. Ferrybridge also marks the start of some fine local walks, such as the Rodwell Trail (see box above).

ACTIVITIES — FERRYBRIDGE

Boat trips The Fleet Observer (ⓣ01305 759692, ⓦthefleetobserver.co.uk) runs a boat on the Fleet Lagoon from the jetty by the *Ferry Bridge Inn* (£7/1hr trip).

EATING AND DRINKING

Crab House Café Ferrymans Way, Portland Rd, Wyke Regis, DT4 9YU ⓣ01305 788867, ⓦcrabhousecafe.co.uk. This upmarket beach shack by the Fleet Lagoon is renowned for its superb fish and seafood, including oysters from its own beds nearby. You can't guarantee what will be on the menu, as it varies according to what has been caught that day, but expect dishes such as herb-crusted pollock (around £16). There are tables outside overlooking Chesil Beach, and reservations are advised for the restaurant, though you may be lucky enough to squeeze into the café area. Wed & Thurs noon–2pm & 6–8.30pm, Fri & Sat noon–2.30pm & 6–9pm, Sun noon–3.30pm.

The Isle of Portland

A giant lump of largely treeless land jutting out from the sea and connected to the mainland by a narrow causeway, the **ISLE OF PORTLAND** is a strange place. Labelled the "Gibraltar of Wessex" by Thomas Hardy, it's best known for its hard white limestone, which has been quarried here for centuries (see box below), as testified by the ragged, broken cliffs around its shorelines and its various exposed quarries dotting the top. First impressions are not appealing – with an industrial port and a bleak prison, and towns as hard and unforgiving-looking as the rocks themselves – but head for the far side of the island and linger awhile and you may well acquire a taste for the strange landscape.

The largest settlement on Portland is **Fortuneswell**, immediately at the end of the causeway as you enter the island. Its western side merges with the appealing former fishing village of **Chiswell**, tucked behind the huge bank of stones that constitutes the southern end of Chesil Beach (see box, p.120). To the east is **Castletown** and the vast Portland Harbour, one of the world's deepest: a naval base since 1872, it was the hub of the sailing events in the 2012 Olympics.

Portland Castle

Liberty Rd, DT5 1AZ • Daily: April–June, Sept & Oct 10am–5pm; July & Aug 10am–6pm • £5; EH • T 03703 331181 • W www.english-heritage.org.uk/visit/places/portland-castle

Commissioned by Henry VIII in 1540 to protect the two-mile stretch of water between here and its sister castle at Sandsfoot (see box, p.116), known as Portland Roads, **Portland Castle** is remarkably well preserved. It was besieged during the Civil War, later used as a prison, then a private home, and finally a military base during World War II. The castle has an attractive garden and there are great views of the harbour from the ramparts, once the best-defended place in the country. It was a frequent target for German bombs during World War II, and you can still see sections of a Mulberry harbour, which was towed back here after use in the D-Day landings (see p.282).

Verne Citadel

Just beyond Portland Castle, behind the vast Ocean View development, a (signposted) path leads steeply up to the top of the island. This was once a cliff railway employed to transport Portland stone down to the harbour, and is now a precipitous but rewarding twenty- to thirty-minute walk up to the 150m summit of Verne Hill. The castle at the

PORTLAND'S QUARRIES AND THE DINOSAUR MUSEUM

Portland is dotted with **quarries**, many still working, and some of the world's finest buildings – including St Paul's Cathedral, the British Museum and the UN headquarters in New York – have been constructed from the distinctive **Portland stone**. It was also used for the 1800m breakwater that protects Portland Harbour – the largest artificial harbour in Britain – which was built by convicts in the mid-nineteenth century. Of very high quality, the stone is extremely hard and durable but with an even structure, so it can be cut in any direction without cracking. It was formed in the Jurassic Period, around 135 million years ago, when the Purbeck coast would have been a shallow, warm sea.

Plans have been approved to convert one of the disused quarries into a dinosaur-themed museum and visitor attraction, **Jurassica** (W jurassica.org). Due to open in 2021, the 35m-deep quarry will be transformed into a prehistoric world, re-creating coastal conditions of 150 million years ago, complete with animatronic dinosaurs. With support from David Attenborough, architect Renzo Piano and the founder of the Eden Project, Tim Smit, the ambitious project is forecast to cost around £80 million and attract some 600,000 visitors a year, so will be a huge boon to the economy of Portland – though the sudden death of its main visionary Michael Hanlon in early 2016 has left the project in some doubt.

A354 to Ferrybridge & Weymouth

THE ISLE OF PORTLAND

Portland Port
Sailing Academy
Portland Castle
CASTLETOWN
Balaclava Bay
Underwater Explores
PORTLAND BEACH ROAD
CASTLE ROAD
Chesil Beach
CASTLE RD
FORTUNESWELL
Verne Citadel
CHISWELL HIGH STREET
OSBORNE ROAD
Chesil Cove
CHISWELL
NEW ROAD
Portland Bike Hire
PRIORY ROAD
West Bay
Tout Quarry
WIDE STREET
EASTON LANE
GROVE ROAD
THE GROVE
Hallelujah Bay
REFORNE STREET
EASTON ST
EASTON
WAKEHAM
WESTON ROAD
WESTON
Portland Museum
Rufus Castle
Mutton Cove
Church of St Andrew
Church Ope Cove
WESTON STREET
SOUTHWELL ROAD
AVALANCHE ROAD
SOUTHWELL
Freshwater Bay
N
Wallsend Cove
PORTLAND BILL ROAD
Sandholes
0 yards 500
0 metres 500
Cave Hole
Portland Bill
Portland Bill Lighthouse
Pulpit Rock

ACCOMMODATION	
Church Ope Studio	3
Heights Hotel	2
Portland YHA	1

EATING	
The Boat that Rocks	1
Cove House Inn	3
The Jailhouse Café	2
Lobster Pot	5
New Inn Portland	4

4

top, **Verne Citadel**, was built in Victorian times as a fortress: convicts sentenced to hard labour carried out much of the construction work on the building, which is now a working prison – and has its own café run by offenders on day release (see p.120).

Tout Quarry

Open access • For workshops contact ⓣ 01305 826736, ⓦ learningstone.org

The main road through Portland leads steeply up on to the headland then splits, with the western fork heading past **Tout Quarry**. Opened in 1983, this huge, open-air sculpture park has animals, figures and shapes carved out of the quarried rock face. Sadly it's rather run-down and unkempt and many of the sculptures have been damaged; also, there's no signage, so you'll be lucky to find specific works, such as Antony Gormley's dramatic *Still Falling* figure. Despite this, it's worth wandering around seeing what you can find, and clambering up through the arches for fantastic views down the western edge of the island and along Chesil Beach.

Church Ope Cove

The eastern fork of the Isle of Portland's main road leads through the town of Easton towards the south of the island at the pretty hamlet of **Church Ope Cove**, where you'll find Portland's only beach and the **Portland Museum** (Easter–Oct Sat–Thurs 10.30am–4pm; check the website for sporadic opening times the rest of the year; £3.50; ⓦ portlandmuseum.co.uk), in two thatched seventeenth-century cottages with a pretty garden. Inside is an assorted collection of displays on all things related to Portland, including stone carvings, fossils and information on birth-control pioneer Marie Stopes, who lived in the Old Lighthouse on Portland and founded the museum. There's a lovely round walk (about 30min) from the museum down a steep path that leads to the pebbly beach: en route, you'll pass beneath an archway belonging to the Norman **Rufus Castle**, built for William II, who was known as Rufus because of his red hair. The island's oldest castle, and thought to be the earliest building to be constructed from Portland stone, it is privately owned and closed to the public. After visiting the beach – which is home to a collection of beach huts with strange rock gardens – backtrack a short way up the steps to where a path leads off to the left to the ruined **Church of St Andrew**, Portland's oldest surviving building. Thought to date from the twelfth century, the tumbledown church and overgrown graveyard make a great place to wander. From here a small path winds up through woods to join the main road and car park near the museum.

Portland Bill

South of Church Ope is a couple of miles of fairly bleak landscape that improves greatly at **Portland Bill**, the southern tip of the island. This blowy headland is a great place for scrambling over rocks, flying kites and enjoying windswept coastal walks. It's capped by a **lighthouse** which has guarded the promontory since the eighteenth century. You can take a guided tour up the 153 steps of the present one, which dates from 1906, for fabulous views (Easter–Oct daily 10am–5pm; Nov–Easter Mon–Wed, Sat & Sun 11am–3pm; closed first two weeks of Jan; £7). The ticket includes entry to

DIVING IN PORTLAND

The waters around Portland are home to some great **dive sites**, particularly because of the many wrecks from World War II that lie around the island. **Castletown** is the island's dive centre, with several outfitters offering dive trips, boat charters and equipment rental. For more information, check out the Underwater Explorers dive shop, Unit 1, Maritime Business Centre, Mereside, DT5 1F (daily 9am–5pm; ⓣ 01305 824555, ⓦ underwaterexplorers.co.uk).

4

CHESIL BEACH

An extraordinary geological tombolo, **Chesil Beach** is a 200m-wide, 15m-high bank of 100 million tonnes of pebbles that extends for eighteen miles. Its component stones gradually decrease in size from fist-like pebbles at Portland to "pea gravel" at Burton Bradstock in the west – during fog, fishermen can tell where they are by the size of the shingle. This sorting is caused by the powerful coastal currents, which make it one of the most dangerous beaches in Europe – churchyards in the local villages display plenty of evidence of wrecks and drownings, so swimming is not recommended. It is also slowly being pushed inland by the sea, by about 5m every hundred years or so.

Enclosing the **Fleet Lagoon**, where oyster beds have flourished since the eleventh century, Chesil is also popular with sea anglers, and its wild, uncommercialized atmosphere makes an appealing antidote to the south-coast resorts. But think carefully before walking down the beach – in *Notes from a Small Island*, Bill Bryson describes it as "the most boring walk I've ever had" as the pebbles "are nearly impossible to walk on since you sink to your ankle-tops with each step." Other authors, however, have been more inspired: Ian McEwan took various pebbles from the beach to gain inspiration for his award-winning *On Chesil Beach* – when this became known, the local council threatened to fine him £2000, as removing the pebbles is an offence. An apologetic McEwan duly returned them to their rightful place.

the adjacent visitor centre (same hours as lighthouse; £3; T 01305 821050, W trinityhouse.co.uk), which has interactive exhibits relating to the lighthouse, including a re-created sea journey in the "Into the Dark" zone.

4

ARRIVAL AND DEPARTURE — THE ISLE OF PORTLAND

By bus Bus #1 runs frequently between Weymouth and Portland (daily every 20–30min; 35min).

INFORMATION AND ACTIVITIES

Tourist information Brochures, public transport information and details of events can be obtained from the small Visitor Information Centre in the *Heights Hotel* (Yeates Rd, DT5 2EN; T 01305 821361, W visit-dorset.com).

Bike tours Portland Bike Hire (T 07523 37059, W portlandbikehire.com) runs guided bike tours and walks from their base in the Visitor Information Centre, and rents out bikes.

ACCOMMODATION

Church Ope Studio Church Ope, DT5 1JA T 01305 860428, W churchopestudio.com. This tiny, self-catering studio is the only place to stay in Church Ope, right on the coast path with lovely sea views. It's well furnished with a wood-burner, wet room and wi-fi and is dog-friendly. One-week minimum stay. **£54**

Heights Hotel Yeates Rd, DT5 2EN T 01305 821361, W heightshotel.com. Right at the top of the hill, this rather old-fashioned place has plain rooms, but it does have a heated outdoor pool and fabulous views over the coast. **£150**

Portland YHA Hardy House, Castletown, DT5 1AU T 0845 3719339, W yha.org.uk/hostel/portland. An Edwardian house that used to belong to the First Admiral of the Navy, this friendly youth hostel has a garden and barbecue area and fine views over Chesil Beach. It's in a good location for divers. Dorms **£22**

EATING

The Boat that Rocks Portland Marina, Osprey Quay, DT5 1DX T 01305 823000, W www.tbtr.co.uk. In a great location down by the harbour, with tables outside on the waterfront and a cocktail bar upstairs on the terrace, plus regular live bands. Service is friendly and the menu includes pizzas (£8–10), burgers, steaks and fresh fish. Daily 10am–10pm; Fri & Sat in summer bar stays open till 2am.

Cove House Inn 91 Chiswell, DT5 1AW T 01305 820895, W thecovehouseinn.co.uk. An atmospheric pub, tucked into the sea wall, with outside tables abutting the pebbly Chesil Beach: inside, it's cosy with a wood-burner and big windows that look out over the sea. The food is good, with pub staples such as steak-and-ale pie (£10), as well as a daily local fish menu, which could include mackerel, sea bass or a good portion of scallops with new potatoes and salad (£12). Mon–Sat 11am–11pm, Sun noon–10.30pm.

The Jailhouse Café The Verne, DT5 1EQ T 01305 825186, W jailhousecafe.co.uk. Despite the rather intimidating approach – it is in a prison, after all – this unusual café run by inmates serves up huge portions of great-value food, such as steak-and-kidney pie with chips or scampi and chips (main courses around £6), plus hearty baguettes (chicken or beef with coleslaw) for £4–5. It feels a bit institutional inside, but there are tables outside in the garden, where the views are stunning. The service is friendly, the coffee is good and the inmates get a chance to learn a trade and work. Daily 10am–3pm.

Lobster Pot Portland Bill, DT5 2JT 01305 820242, lobsterpotrestaurantportland.co.uk. This good-value place enjoys a great position right on the headland by the lighthouse, with outdoor tables on the clifftop. Head here for lunches, such as chicken escalopes (£9) or local crab sandwiches (£7.50), and tasty cream teas with home-made scones (£5.50). Mon–Fri 10am–4.30pm, Sat & Sun 9am–4.30pm.

New Inn Portland 35 Easton St, DT5 1BS 01305 821232, newinnportland.co.uk. Cosy pub with wood-burner serving local shellfish and seafood in dishes such as a tasty bouillabaisse (£18), or Portland crab pâté (£8) – Wednesday is *moules frites* night (£12), with mussels straight from the harbour. The garden has a pizza oven and a lively cocktail bar in summer (phone to check pizza nights). They also have five comfortable B&B rooms (£85). Mon–Thurs noon–10pm, Fri & Sat noon–11pm, Sun noon–6pm; closed Mon in winter.

The Fleet Lagoon

The largest tidal lagoon in Britain, the **Fleet Lagoon** is separated from the sea by the eighteen-mile-long Chesil Beach, creating a unique home for marine- and birdlife. Some 150 types of seaweed and sea grasses thrive in its waters, giving shelter and food to 25 species of fish, including sea bass and mullet. This in turn attracts thousands of birds throughout the year. Winter visitors include brent geese from Siberia and wigeon from Russia, while spring sees southern migrants from Africa including little terns and grey herons. Its most famous birds are the giant population of mute swans at Abbotsbury (see p.122). During the seventeenth century, there were attempts to drain the lagoon to create agricultural land; fortunately for today's wildlife, the system of dams and sluices that were built failed miserably, with salt water constantly percolating through the shingle. The plan was abandoned and the lagoon has been kept intact ever since. Long associated with smuggling, the lagoon was immortalized in the children's adventure story *Moonfleet* by J. Meade Falkner, which was set in the nineteenth century at *Moonfleet Manor* (see p.122). The lagoon also played an important role during World War II, when Barnes Wallis's bouncing bombs were tested here in September 1942, before being used against the Germans, as immortalized in the film *The Dam Busters*.

ACCOMMODATION AND EATING — THE FLEET LAGOON

★ **East Shilvinghampton Farm** Portesham, DT3 4HN 01420 80804, featherdown.co.uk. A lovely farm in a beautiful valley, a couple of miles inland from the lagoon. It has seven spacious, luxurious Featherdown Farm tents – ready-erected, with running water, a toilet, a wood-burning stove and comfortable beds – in an idyllic field that looks down the valley, with horses, goats and chickens in the paddock next door (3 nights' min stay; £560). There are also a couple of B&B rooms in the farmhouse plus a basic camping field (no facilities). Camping **£20**, doubles **£80**

The Elm Tree Inn Shop Lane, Langton Herring, DT3 4HU 01305 871257, theelmtreeinn.com. Traditional village pub, with wood-burner inside and tables outside in a pleasant garden. The food is good, with dishes such as ham, egg and chips, cottage pie and goat's cheese pie (all around £10) plus real ales – as well as local seafood

A WALK ALONG THE FLEET LAGOON

The pretty village of **Langton Herring** is worth exploring for its thatched cottages and narrow lanes, its cosy pub, and a tiny blacksmith's forge (Sun 11am–4pm; the-village-blacksmith.co.uk) where you can watch the blacksmith working on the hand-crafted metalwork. It offers access to one of the loveliest stretches of the Fleet Lagoon via a series of footpaths that radiate from the south and west of the village. A fine **one-hour round walk** is to take the footpath from the far west of the village, by Ivy Cottage. The path crosses fields before joining the Fleet Lagoon by **Rodden Hive**, a small inlet that's a haven for wading birds. You can then follow the South West Coast Path south and east until **Under Cross Plantation**, where the path climbs back to Langton Herring. For a shorter walk, cut back up to the village along the Coastguard's path, or extend the walk further along the lagoon to Gore Cove, before retracing your steps to the village.

specials. Mon & Tues 11am–2.30pm, Wed–Fri 11am–2.30pm & 6–10.30pm, Sat 11am–3pm & 6–11pm, Sun 11am–4pm & 6–10.30pm; longer hours in summer.

Moonfleet Manor Fleet, DT3 4ED ⊤01305 786948, ⓦmoonfleetmanorhotel.co.uk. Informal, child-friendly hotel in lovely grounds overlooking the Fleet Lagoon. There's a free crèche, a large, well-equipped games room and an indoor pool, plus tennis courts and a good restaurant. They have a range of comfortable family rooms (£325) and interconnecting rooms. **£235**

Abbotsbury

Eight miles west of Weymouth, the pretty village of **ABBOTSBURY** has a surprising number of attractions for such a small place. The Swannery is the highlight – it's unique, especially at hatching time – though all the sights are worth a visit, particularly if you have children. If you have time, it's worth buying tickets in advance online; the **Abbotsbury passport** ticket (adults £17, under-16s £14, cheaper in advance online; ⓦabbotsbury-tourism.co.uk) gives entry to all three sights.

The Swannery

New Barn Rd, DT3 4JG • Mid-March to Oct daily 10am–5pm • £12, under-16s £9 • ⊤01305 871858, ⓦabbotsbury-tourism.co.uk/swannery

First and foremost in Abbotsbury is the **Swannery**, established over six hundred years ago by Benedictine monks who built an abbey here in the 1040s and bred the swans for their lavish banquets. Ballerina Anna Pavlova visited here in 1920 to gain inspiration for her movements in *Swan Lake*, and scenes from the 2009 film *Harry Potter and the Half-Blood Prince* were filmed here. Today, the swannery is the only place in the world where you can get so close to a colony of nesting mute swans; you can walk around their nests, and along pretty paths through reed beds. Feeding time (twice daily, noon & 4pm) is spectacular, with up to 600 birds squabbling and flapping over the food. The best time to visit is when the cygnets hatch (May–June), when the whole site is studded with neat nests, cracking eggs and extremely fluffy cygnets. It can get very busy at this time, particularly during school holidays, though the swans themselves seem fairly oblivious to the crowds. A tractor trip runs from the entrance down to the nesting sites, and there is also a maze, where you can get lost in rows of twisted willows laid out in the shape of a swan.

Subtropical Gardens

Bullers Way, DT3 4LA • Daily: spring 10am–5/6pm; winter 10am–4pm • £12, under-16s £9 • ⊤01305 871387, ⓦabbotsbury-tourism.co.uk/gardens

With twenty acres of exotic and unusual plants, the large **Subtropical Gardens** sit in a sheltered wooded valley whose mild climate allows the non-native plants to thrive. Established in 1765 by the Countess of Ilchester as a kitchen garden, the grounds now house a mixture of formal and informal areas, with walled gardens, valley walks and coastal views. In spring, the magnolias and camellias are particularly impressive, followed by colourful rhododendrons and hydrangeas in the summer. Various events are held in the gardens throughout the year, such as floodlit evenings in the autumn and Shakespeare plays in the summer.

Children's Farm

Church St, DT3 4JJ • Mid-March to mid-Sept & Oct half-term daily 10am–5pm; mid-Sept to late Oct Sat & Sun 10am–5pm • £10.50, under-16s £9 • ⊤01305 871817, ⓦabbotsbury-tourism.co.uk/childrens_farm

Abbotsbury's **Children's Farm** is based in England's largest tithe barn, which was built by Benedictine monks in the 1390s. It has been fully restored and now holds a great children's soft-play area with slides and swings, as well as models of smugglers and

PORTLAND BILL (P.119) >

WEARS HILL

Halfway between Abbotsbury and Burton Bradstock, **Wears Hill** offers some of the best views of this beautiful stretch of coast. A path signed from the spectacular coast road takes you to a former Iron Age hill fort, which was also used as a beacon to alert local villagers of attack from the Spanish armada. It's a toughish ascent, but once on top, the Fleet Lagoon and the coast stretch out beneath you. The hill is on the South Dorset Ridgeway, part of the South West Coast Path: keen walkers can tackle the full seventeen-mile section from West Bexington to Osmington Mills.

villagers. Outside is an aviary plus straw bales to play on and tractors to ride, though, of course, the animals are the main attraction. There are ponies to groom, donkeys to pet, guinea pigs to cuddle, alpaca to stroke, goat-racing to watch, then children can bottle-feed the baby goats and take them for a walk on a lead.

St Catherine's Chapel

The fourteenth-century **St Catherine's Chapel** is a local landmark which sits on a hilltop and can be seen for miles around – it has even inspired a song by P.J. Harvey, *The Wind*. Built from local stone, it has immensely thick walls, which make it tiny inside despite its solid exterior appearance. There's a lovely ten-minute walk up to the chapel, starting from opposite the *Abbey House* car park: from here, the path leads steeply uphill to give fantastic views from the top.

ACCOMMODATION AND EATING — ABBOTSBURY

The Abbey House Church St, DT3 4JJ ⓣ 01305 871330, ⓦ theabbeyhouse.co.uk. On the site of the original abbey from which Abbotsbury took its name is this wonderfully located guesthouse, parts of which date from the fifteenth century. With over an acre of grounds and lovely views of the coast, the pretty gardens are the perfect spot to relax. The varied-sized rooms are traditionally decorated – a little pink and frilly, perhaps – but comfortable, with views over the gardens and the nearby tithe barn. **£90**

Abbotsbury Tea Rooms 26 Rodden Row, DT3 4JL ⓣ 01305 871757, ⓦ abbotsbury-tearooms.co.uk. Cosy tearooms with a lovely garden at the back, and friendly service. Lunches (£6–9) include tasty home-made soup, local crab sandwiches and cheese scones with Blue Vinny cheese and ham, while the cream tea and home-made cakes are delicious. Mon, Tues & Thurs–Sun 11am–5pm.

Bridport and around

Founded on land between the rivers Asker and Brit, **BRIDPORT** was mentioned in the Domesday Book of 1086 and was an important port before the rivers silted up in the early 1700s. Its fine buildings, however, mostly date from its days as a major rope-making centre – the pleasant old town of solid brick buildings has unusually wide streets, a hangover from when cords were stretched between the houses to be twisted and dyed (see box, p.126).

Arranged around a crossroads where North, South, East and West streets meet, Bridport has long been a lively market town. In the past, the streets had very distinct characters: East and West streets were home to the wealthy travellers and merchants, while South Street was populated by sailors and poor people. In the 1800s, the town had several inns – it is said that every other house on South Street sold beer.

Today, the town has a lively, slightly alternative feel, good cafés and restaurants and a vibrant twice-weekly **market** – it's best visited on a Wednesday or Saturday, when East, West and South streets fill with market stalls selling an assortment of local produce, arts and crafts, antiques, bric-a-brac and junk. With its beach just south of town at **West Bay**, Bridport also makes a good base for exploring a couple of nearby coastal villages, **Eype** and **Burton Bradstock**.

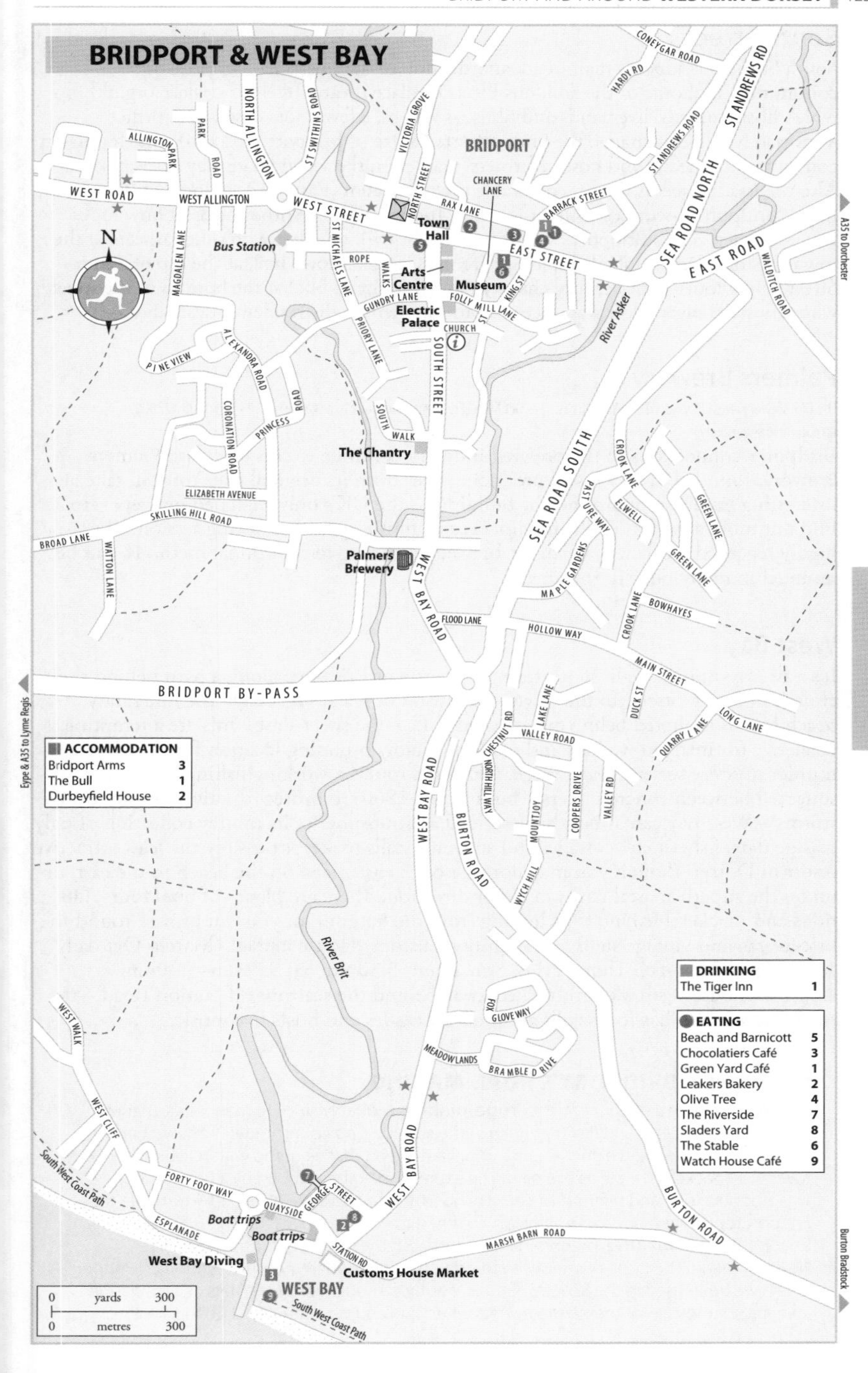
BRIDPORT & WEST BAY
BRIDPORT
Town Hall
Arts Centre
Museum
Electric Palace
Church
The Chantry
Palmers Brewery
Bus Station
Boat trips
Boat trips
West Bay Diving
Customs House Market
WEST BAY
River Asker
River Brit
South West Coast Path
South West Coast Path
A35 to Dorchester
Eype & A35 to Lyme Regis
Burton Bradstock
WEST ROAD
WEST ALLINGTON
WEST STREET
EAST STREET
EAST ROAD
SEA ROAD NORTH
SEA ROAD SOUTH
BRIDPORT BY-PASS
WEST BAY ROAD
BURTON ROAD
SOUTH STREET
NORTH STREET
NORTH ALLINGTON
ALLINGTON PARK
PARK ROAD
ST SWITHINS ROAD
VICTORIA GROVE
CHANCERY LANE
RAX LANE
BARRACK STREET
CONEYGAR ROAD
HARDY RD
ST ANDREWS ROAD
ST ANDREWS RD
WALDITCH ROAD
ST MICHAELS LANE
ROPE WALKS
GUNDRY LANE
FOLLY MILL LANE
KING ST
PRIORY LANE
SOUTH WALK
MAGDALEN LANE
PINE VIEW
ALEXANDRA ROAD
CORONATION ROAD
PRINCESS ROAD
ELIZABETH AVENUE
SKILLING HILL ROAD
BROAD LANE
WATTON LANE
FLOOD LANE
HOLLOW WAY
CROOK LANE
PASTURE WAY
ELWELL
GREEN LANE
GREEN LANE
MAPLE GARDENS
BOWHAYES
CROOK LANE
MAIN STREET
DUCK ST
LONG LANE
QUARRY LANE
LAKE LANE
CHESTNUT RD
VALLEY ROAD
NORTH HILL WAY
MOUNTJOY
COOPERS DRIVE
VALLEY RD
WYCH HILL
FOX GLOVE WAY
MEADOWLANDS
BRAMBLE DRIVE
WEST WALK
WEST CLIFF
FORTY FOOT WAY
ESPLANADE
QUAYSIDE
GEORGE STREET
STATION RD
MARSH BARN ROAD
ACCOMMODATION
Bridport Arms 3
The Bull 1
Durbeyfield House 2
DRINKING
The Tiger Inn 1
EATING
Beach and Barnicott 5
Chocolatiers Café 3
Green Yard Café 1
Leakers Bakery 2
Olive Tree 4
The Riverside 7
Sladers Yard 8
The Stable 6
Watch House Café 9
0 yards 300
0 metres 300
N

South Street

South Street is Bridport's main road, and the hub of the town's thriving artistic community: it's home to the fabulous Electric Palace theatre (ⓦelectricpalace.org.uk), which hosts comedy, live bands and films, as well as, a few doors down in a former Victorian Methodist chapel, the **Bridport Arts Centre** (ⓦbridport-arts.com), which puts on contemporary theatre and hosts a farmers' market on the second Saturday of every month. Also on South Street is the unremarkable **town museum** (Easter–Oct Mon–Sat 9am–5pm; free; ⓦbridportmuseum.co.uk), set in a fine Tudor building, with models of how ropes were stretched across Bridport's streets (see box below), together with other aspects of the town's history. Other notable buildings are the Georgian **town hall**, at the top of South Street, and a fourteenth-century **chantry** (closed to the public) at the bottom of the street, whose upstairs pigeon loft was once used to supplement the resident priest's diet.

Palmers Brewery

The Old Brewery, West Bay Rd, DT6 4JA • Tours Easter–Oct Mon–Fri 11am; 2hr (book in advance) • £10 • ⓣ01308 427500, ⓦpalmersbrewery.com

Bridport's connections to the brewing industry continue to this day, with **Palmers Brewery**, founded in 1794, still producing beer from its original site. You can take an interesting guided tour around the buildings – the UK's only thatched brewery – to find out more about the brewing process and finish up with a tasting session. The highly regarded local ales, which are brewed according to traditional methods, can be sampled in many pubs in the area.

West Bay

It's a twenty-minute walk south from the centre of Bridport, along a path behind the church in South Street, to the town's nearest bit of sea at **West Bay**. The fine sandy beach here is sheltered below majestic red cliffs – the sheer East Cliffs are a tempting challenge for intrepid walkers and made a suitably brooding location for the ITV murder mystery series, *Broadchurch*. Clustered round a working fishing harbour squeezed between concrete piers – built in the 1860s to protect the river estuary from storms – West Bay can at best be described as atmospheric. Its motley collection of ugly seaside flats, fishermen's cottages and souvenir stalls makes it possibly the least attractive resort in Dorset, though you may not care once ensconced on the beach to the east, or up on the superb coastal paths in either direction. There are plenty of **boat tours**, **RIB rides** and mackerel **fishing trips** leaving from the harbour, or you can browse round the bric-a-brac and vintage stalls at the quirky Customs House **market** (March–Oct daily 10am–5pm; Nov–Feb Thurs, Fri & Sun 10am–5.30pm, Sat 9.30am–5.30pm; ⓦcustomshousewestbay.com), tucked away behind the seafront off Station Road – the rambling site also has food stalls and bouncy castles and hosts live music.

IN THE NET: BRIDPORT'S ROPE-MAKING

Bridport has been a major centre for **rope-making** probably since Roman times, thanks to the top-quality hemp and flax that grew in the surrounding countryside. The town became famous for naval rope-making – Henry VII once decreed that all hemp within five miles of the town was for exclusive use of the navy. The expression "to be stabbed by a Bridport dagger" was a popular one and referred to being hanged, for nooses were also made using the tough Bridport rope. When naval rope-making switched to Portsmouth in the 1800s, Bridport swapped to **net-making**, predominantly kitting out the fishing fleets that set sail to Newfoundland. The trade continues to this day, though modern nets use synthetics; Bridport nets have been used in the Space Shuttle, for army camouflage, for the nets at Wimbledon and, most famously, for the Wembley nets when England won the World Cup in 1966.

ARRIVAL AND DEPARTURE

BRIDPORT AND AROUND

By bus Most buses stop on the main through-road or at the bus station on Tannery Road (firstgroup.com/ukbus/dorset).

Destinations Dorchester (hourly; 45min); Lyme Regis (hourly; 40min); West Bay (hourly; 15min); Weymouth (hourly; 1hr 25min).

INFORMATION AND ACTIVITIES

Tourist Information Centre Bridport Town Hall, Bucky Doo Square, South St, DT6 3LF (Mon–Sat: April–Oct 9am–5pm; Nov–March 10am–3pm; 01308 424901, westdorset.com).

Boat trips Available from West Bay for around £10 per person for a 1hr trip (westbayfishingtrips.co.uk or lymebayribcharter.co.uk).

West Bay Diving run diving trips to the local wrecks (westbaydiving.co.uk).

ACCOMMODATION

BRIDPORT

The Bull 34 East St, DT6 3LF 01308 422878, thebullhotel.co.uk. Friendly, boutique-style hotel in a former seventeenth-century coaching inn in the centre of town. The individually designed rooms are comfortable with all mod cons and Neal's Yard toiletries. The restaurant and bar are good, serving the likes of chicken breast with chorizo; mains £15–19. **£144**

WEST BAY

Bridport Arms DT6 4EN 01308 422994, bridportarms.co.uk. In a great location on the seafront, this unusual thatched pub has big rooms with big views, of the harbour or the sea. There's also a suite with jacuzzi (£20 extra). **£140**

Durbeyfield House DT6 4EL 01308 423307, durbeyfield.co.uk. Decent if simple rooms in an attractive Georgian townhouse a short walk to the harbour. Good views and friendly owners. **£80**

EATING

Bridport has a good selection of **restaurants** and **cafés**, many specializing in local produce. Look out, too, for the Bridport Food Festival in June (bridportfoodfestival.co.uk). In West Bay, the best-value food is from the colourful wooden huts along the harbour – they sell delicious fresh fish and chips.

BRIDPORT

Beach and Barnicott 6 South St, DT6 3NQ 01308 455688, beachandbarnicott.co.uk. Distinctive bar-restaurant in a Grade II-listed building, with four rooms on two floors, each decorated in a different style. The menu changes daily and uses local ingredients; expect dishes like sea trout with shrimp butter sauce (£14.50), or leg of duck with mustard mash (£15). Live music on Friday nights. Mon 10am–5pm, Tues–Thurs 10am–10pm, Fri 10am–2am, Sat 9.30am–2am.

Chocolatiers Café 47 East St, DT6 3JX 01308 458770. Lovely café selling delicious home-made Belgian chocolates to eat in or takeaway – try amaretto truffles, passion-fruit chocolates or chocolates shaped like a pint of Guinness or a high-heeled shoe. It also serves food such as sandwiches (from £4.50), chocolate chilli pots and cream teas (£4.75) – the coffee and cakes are great, and the drinking chocolate delicious, and both come with a small free chocolate mouse or frog. Mon–Sat 9.30am–5pm, Sun 11am–2.30pm.

Green Yard Café 4–6 Barrack St, DT6 3LY 01308 459466. Lovely family-run café, serving good-value veggie dishes made from local produce (£8–11): goat's cheese soufflé, lentil moussaka and bean tartlets, as well as a fish dish of the day. The soups are fresh and filling, as are the quiches, salads and sandwiches. Tues–Sat 9am–4pm.

★ **Leakers Bakery** 29 East St, DT6 3JX 01308 423296, leakersbakery.co.uk. The place to stock up for a picnic, with organic breads, pastries and cakes made in the on-site kitchen using local produce. Choose from cheese and cider cottage loaf, cheese, chilli and beer bread (all £1.20–3.30), or herb and feta muffins, while sweeter treats include ginger and date scones and delicious almond croissants. Mon–Fri 7am–5pm, Sat 6am–3pm.

Olive Tree 59 East St, DT6 3LB 01308 422882, olivetreerestaurant.net. Attractive, friendly and bustling Italian restaurant, serving a range of well-prepared pasta dishes, such as *linguini de la mare* (£11.50), and stone-baked pizzas (£10–12), as well as a range of meat and fish dishes (£16–20). Mon–Sat 11.30am–2pm & 6–9pm.

The Stable Behind The Bull, 34 East St, access via Chancery Lane, DT6 3LF 01308 426876, stablepizza.com. It has a barn-dance atmosphere and serves fantastic pizzas and pies, made with local ingredients – the West Country porker pizza is a tasty meat feast of local chorizo (£11.50) – that you can wash down with a variety of different ciders. Housed in *The Bull*'s former stables, on a summer's evening drinkers spill out into the courtyard outside. Daily noon–11pm.

WEST BAY

The Riverside DT6 4EZ 01308 422011, thefishrestaurant-westbay.co.uk. Reservations are recommended for this renowned restaurant which offers sumptuous fresh fish and seafood and fine views over the river. There is a daily

THE RIVER COTTAGE EFFECT

The area inland from Bridport and Lyme Regis has been an inspiration for the resurgence of interest in **local, seasonal food** in the UK. Chef **Hugh Fearnley-Whittingstall** moved here to the original **River Cottage** in 1998, bringing an infectious enthusiasm for self-sufficiency. He caught fish and seafood from West Bay, grew his own fruit and vegetables, promoted local artisan food producers, and raised his own animals. His campaign on poultry welfare highlighted the plight of intensively farmed chicken and led major supermarket chains to re-think their animal welfare policies, while he has also been very vocal in his support for sustainable fishing practices.

While Fearnley-Whittingstall still lives in Dorset, the **River Cottage headquarters** is now in a pretty little valley just into Devon, where it runs workshops on fishing, cooking with seasonal produce, bread-making, bee-keeping, growing vegetables, and foraging for food. It also hosts atmospheric, though pricey, events on Friday and Saturday evenings, plus Sunday lunch, where you are taken down to the farm on a tractor and trailer and sample a four-course meal of local seasonal produce (W rivercottage.net).

changing menu, but expect the likes of fillet of brill with crispy spinach and crab salad. Mains from around £18. Tues–Sat noon–2.30pm & 6.30–9pm, Sun noon–2.30pm.

Sladers Yard West Bay Rd, DT6 4EL T 01308 459511, W sladersyard.wordpress.com. This tastefully converted warehouse gallery showcases works by local artists and has a light and airy downstairs café, serving lovely cakes and good-value lunches made using local and organic ingredients where possible. The sharing meze with hummus, halloumi, falafel, olives and pitta bread is tasty (£9 for one person, £17 for two), and there are generous sandwiches (from £8). Daily 10am–5pm.

★**Watch House Café** DT6 4EL T 01308 459330, W watchhousecafe.co.uk. Nestled into a bank of shingle right on the beach, and with a fine outdoor terrace, this rightly popular café-restaurant is a must-visit. You can just have a coffee and cake or ice cream, but the real draw is the fresh fish and seafood, including a superb seafood broth (£12) and pan-fried scallops (£17). There is also a wood-fired oven which churns out good-sized pizzas (£10–14). Mon–Thurs & Sun 10am–3pm, Fri & Sat 10am–3pm & 6–8pm.

4

DRINKING

The Tiger Inn 14–16 Barrack St, DT6 3LY T 01308 427543, W tigerinnbridport.co.uk. Well known for its real ales, *The Tiger Inn* is a cosy pub with two bars in a lovely Grade II-listed former coaching inn. There's sports TV and a small beer garden. It also hosts a beer festival in late October. Mon–Thurs & Sun noon–11pm, Fri & Sat noon–midnight.

Eype

Just under two miles southwest of Bridport is the tiny, picturesque village of **EYPE**, whose name aptly means "steep place". It's accessed from the A35 by an incredibly narrow rollercoaster of a road that dips down through the village, finishing at a pretty pebble beach where you can join the South West Coast Path.

ACCOMMODATION — EYPE

Eype House Caravan Park DT6 6AL T 01308 424903, W eypehouse.co.uk. Lovely campsite sloping up the clifftop with great sea views, and just a short walk to the beach. It has caravans to rent (from £465/week), a wooden camping pod (from £48) and a great camping field for pitching your own. **£27**

Eype's Mouth Country Hotel DT6 6AL T 01308 423300, W eypesmouthhotel.co.uk. Comfortable rooms, many with views of the coast, at this friendly family-run hotel. There's a cosy bar and an outdoor terrace with splendid sea views and it's just a short walk down a steep lane to the beach. **£112.50**

Burton Bradstock

Around three miles southeast of Bridport, or a pleasant hour's walk along the South West Coast Path from West Bay, **BURTON BRADSTOCK** is regularly voted Dorset's best-kept village. It boasts a lovely stretch of cliff-backed pebble beach – though bathers should be aware of the strong currents here.

ACCOMMODATION AND EATING

BURTON BRADSTOCK

★Hive Beach Café Beach Rd, DT6 4RF ⓣ01308 897070, ⓦhivebeachcafe.co.uk. Top choice for food is this laidback café, overlooking the beach, which dishes up high-quality fresh seafood like Cornish sardines (£11), baked halibut (£17) and pan-fried scallops (£17.50), plus delicious cakes and coffee. Daily from 10am; closing times vary.

★Norburton Hall Shipton Lane, DT6 4NQ ⓣ01308 897007, ⓦnorburtonhall.com. The Edwardian *Norburton Hall* is a great place to stay, with five beautifully furnished, comfortable cottages (sleeping 2–8 people) to rent in converted outbuildings. The Hall's lovely rolling grounds and gardens are peaceful and the welcome here is warm. One-week minimum stay in high season. **£103**

Seaside Boarding House Cliff Rd ⓣ01308 897205, ⓦtheseasideboardinghouse.com. This stylish beachside bolthole was set up by the founding members of London's *Groucho Club*. Rooms are bright and contemporary, with bleached wood floors, and some have sea views to die for. There's a library and a top restaurant, with daily specials from £15. Daily 12.30–3pm & 6.30–10pm. **£180**

Lyme Regis and around

Dorset's most westerly town, **LYME REGIS** is also its most alluring, sheltering snugly between steep hills, just before the grey, fossil-filled cliffs lurch into Devon. Its intimate size and photogenic qualities make it a popular and congested spot in high summer, though the town still lives up to the classy impression created by its regal name; it was granted a royal charter by Edward I in 1284. It also has some upmarket literary associations – Jane Austen summered in a seafront cottage and set part of *Persuasion* in

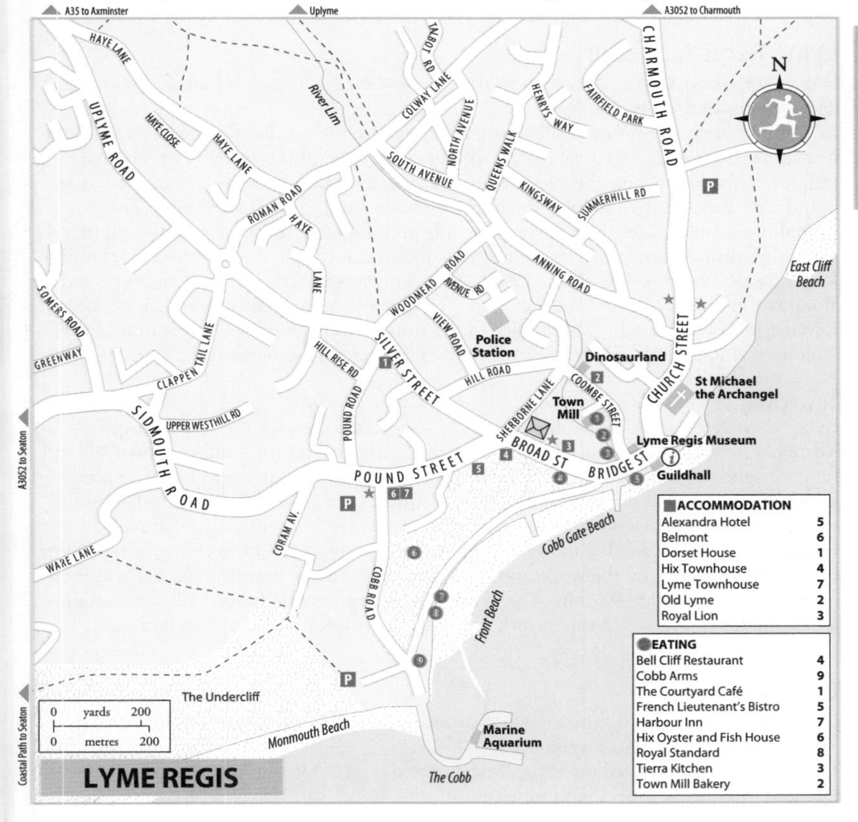

MARY ANNING AND THE ICHTHYOSAUR

The cliffs around Lyme are made up of a complex layer of limestone, greensand and unstable clay, a perfect medium for preserving fossils, which are exposed by frequent landslips. In 1811, after a fierce storm caused parts of the cliffs to collapse, 12-year-old **Mary Anning** discovered an almost complete dinosaur skeleton, a 9m **ichthyosaur** that's now displayed in London's Natural History Museum. A keen fossil-hunter, Anning was one of the first to recognize the significance of Lyme's fossils and sold them to curious visitors – her collecting is believed to have inspired the tongue-twister *She sells seashells on the seashore*. One of the town's most celebrated daughters, Anning is buried in the nearby fifteenth-century **church of St Michael the Archangel**, up Church Street. Hammering fossils out of the cliffs is frowned on by today's conservationists, however, and in any case is decidedly hazardous.

Lyme, while novelist John Fowles lived here until his death in 2005, and set his best-known book here. Austen's description of Lyme is still pretty accurate today: "the Cobb itself… with the very beautiful line of cliffs, stretching out to the east of the town, are what the stranger's eye will seek, and a very strange stranger it must be who does not see charms in the immediate environs of Lyme, to make him wish to know it better." The coast either side of Lyme is spectacular, with great walks heading west into Devon and east to the tiny hamlet of **Seatown**, via the towering **Golden Cap** and **Charmouth**, another favourite of Austen's.

Lyme Regis Museum

Bridge St, DT7 3QA • Easter–Oct Mon–Sat 10am–5pm, Sun 11am–5pm; Nov–Easter Wed–Sun 11am–4pm, daily in school hols £3.95, children free • ⓦ lymeregismuseum.co.uk

In a fine Victorian building overlooking the sea walls, the excellent **Lyme Regis Museum** provides a crash course in local history and geology. It was built in 1901 by Thomas Philpot, appropriately on the site of a fossil shop which kick-started the Jurassic Coast brand, and was, until 1826, also the home of Mary Anning (see box above). The museum not only traces the history of her life and the Jurassic Coast, but also plots Lyme's maritime history and its connections to famous people through time, including Jane Austen, William Pitt and Laurence Whistler, whose engraved glass can be viewed along with famous paintings of the town. You can also admire the office chair of the novelist John Fowles, who was curator of the museum for several years. From mid-2017, a modern zinc-and-glass Mary Anning Wing will include a geology gallery.

Town Mill

Mill Lane, off Coombe St, DT7 3PU • April–Sept daily 11am–4pm; Nov–Easter Sat & Sun 11am–4pm • Free • ⓦ townmill.org.uk

There has been a watermill on this site since the fourteenth century, and the **Town Mill** still functions today, grinding organic flour and producing enough hydroelectricity to power the complex as well as sell some back to the National Grid. You can visit the mill building, which is largely seventeenth century (though parts date from 1340), climbing steep, rickety ladders and watching the vast water wheel turn to power the grinding stones. More interesting, however, are the workshops that surround the mill, which include a pottery, a microbrewery, an award-winning cheesemonger and a great café (see p.132) – the artisans are happy for you to watch them work and will answer questions about their craft.

Dinosaurland

Coombe St, DT7 3PY • Feb half-term to Oct half-term daily 10am–5pm; Nov to mid-Feb opening hours vary, so call first to check • £5, under-17s £4 • ⓣ 01297 443541, ⓦ dinosaurland.co.uk

Housed in a Grade I-listed building, **Dinosaurland** is great for a rainy day, especially for families. This characterful museum, set inside a beautiful, galleried church dating from

1746, has a collection of fossils and models that romps through natural history using the hook of Mary Anning's famous ichthyosaur, found in the bay in 1811. Although the dinosaur skeletons are replicas, there are plenty of real fossilized ammonites and squid-like belemnites along with various contemporary beasties, including a 3.95m-long python skeleton, trays of butterflies and the remains of enormous crabs and lobsters.

The Cobb

Unlike many coastal towns, **Lyme Regis** has an interesting mix of architecture, from thatched cottages to ornate Victorian houses. While colour-washed cottages and elegant Regency villas line its seafront, Lyme's best-known feature is a briskly practical reminder of its commercial origins: **The Cobb**, a curving harbour wall first constructed in the thirteenth century. It has suffered many alterations since, most notably in the nineteenth century, when its massive boulders were clad in neat blocks of Portland stone.

Marine aquarium

The Cobb • March–Oct daily 10am–5pm; Jan & Feb Sat & Sun 10.30am–3pm, plus Feb half-term daily 10am–5pm • £6, under-16s £4.50; ten percent discount for online bookings • T 01297 444230, W lymeregismarineaquarium.co.uk

Set in a row of former fishermen's houses out on The Cobb is a **Marine aquarium** – expensive considering its size, but its display of local marine life is certainly fun and includes venomous weaver fish, sea scorpions, sea horses, pipe fish and an 80-year-old lobster. Children can hold some of the sea creatures and feed the mullet, and you can also see bits of old boat and planes recovered by fishermen, including the canopy of a Red Arrow that crashed in 1980.

The Undercliff

As you walk along Lyme's seafront and out towards The Cobb, look for the outlines of ammonites in the walls and paving stones. To the west of The Cobb lies the Undercliff, a fascinating jumble of overgrown landslips, now a nature reserve. An attractive path leads from behind the harbour up a steep flight of steps into the woodlands of the Undercliff, a jungle-like habitat riven with streams and valleys, and sudden open grassy areas affording dramatic sea views.

ARRIVAL AND INFORMATION — LYME REGIS

By train Lyme's nearest train station is in Axminster, five miles north, served by bus #X53 from Axminster to Weymouth via Lyme Regis.

Destinations Exeter (hourly; 45min); London (hourly; 2hr 45min); Salisbury (hourly; 1hr 15min).

By bus Most buses stop outside the post office on Broad Street.

Destinations Axminster (hourly; 25min); Bridport (hourly; 40min); Weymouth (7–9 daily; 1hr 30min).

By car Drivers will find the centre of town hard to park in, though there are plenty of car parks just uphill. The one on Pound St usually has enough space: from here, it's a steep 5min walk down into the town.

Tourist office Church St, DT7 3BS (March to mid-April Mon–Sat 10am–5am; mid-April to Oct Mon–Sat 10am–5am, Sun 10am–4pm; Nov–March Mon–Sat 10am–3pm; T 01297 442138, W lymeregis.org).

JOHN FOWLES AND THE FRENCH LIEUTENANT'S WOMAN

The iconic image of Meryl Streep standing on the Cobb staring moodily out to sea in **The French Lieutenant's Woman** is hard to avoid in Lyme. Shot here in 1981, the film was based on the 1969 book by **John Fowles**, who lived in Lyme from 1968 until his death in 2005, and wrote many of his best-known novels here, despite having an ambivalent relationship with the town. He was very involved with the community as curator of the town museum and an active chronicler of its historical society: however, he was a reclusive figure, whose *Journals* suggest a brooding darkness about the town and make clear that he found the place stifling and remote.

ACCOMMODATION

★**Alexandra Hotel** Pound St, DT7 3HZ ☎01297 442010, ⓦhotelalexandra.co.uk. Lyme's best hotel, this elegant eighteenth-century manor is set in large gardens with panoramic vistas. The rooms are all light and airy, beautifully decorated and often with stunning sea views. You can play croquet or take afternoon tea on the lawns, and there's a highly rated restaurant specializing in local food – you can even dine in privacy in the hotel's lookout tower. The friendly staff go out of their way to help and there are good facilities for children, including a playground, trampoline and family rooms. **£180**

Belmont 6a Pound St, DT7 3HZ ☎01628 825925, ⓦlandmarktrust.org.uk. Grade II-listed eighteenth-century villa, which has been owned by both Eleanor Coade (see box below) and, later, author John Fowles. Sleeps eight, and gets booked up well in advance. Four-day minimum stay. Four days **£660**

Dorset House Pound Rd, DT7 3HX ☎01297 442055, ⓦdorsethouselyme.com. A steep walk up at the top of the town, but with great views to compensate, this stylish B&B in a Regency villa has lovely rooms with a retro feel. The friendly owners are helpful, breakfasts are great and there's an honesty bar. **£105**

Hix Townhouse 1 Pound St, DT7 3HZ ☎01297 442499, ⓦhixrestaurants.co.uk/hix-townhouse. This boutique B&B has a variety of stylish contemporary rooms designed by owner and renowned chef Mark Hix, in a Grade II-listed Georgian townhouse. The best are on the top floor, with great sea views. A breakfast hamper is delivered to your room featuring delicious fresh produce. Two-night minimum stay at weekends. **£120**

Lyme Townhouse 8 Pound St, DT6 3HZ ☎01929 400252, ⓦlyme-townhouse.co.uk. Smart, clean B&B uphill from the main high street. The snug rooms are rather small, but all seven rooms are stylish, with nice touches such as coffee machines. Breakfasts are good. **£95**

Old Lyme 29 Coombe St, DT7 3PP ☎01297 442929, ⓦoldlymeguesthouse.co.uk. Central guesthouse right in the town centre, in a lovely 300-year-old stone former post office. There are six smallish but spruce bedrooms – all are en suite, or with a private bathroom. Free car park passes available. **£80**

Royal Lion Broad St, DT7 3QF ☎01297 445622, ⓦroyallionhotel.com. Welcoming seventeenth-century coaching inn on the main street, complete with uneven wooden floors, cosy lounges and a grand piano in the dining room. Bedrooms in the modern extension have sea-facing balconies, while the spacious family rooms in the extension have small patios. Older rooms in the main building overlook the high street. There's parking and a small pool. **£125**

4

EATING

Bell Cliff Restaurant 5–6 Broad St, DT7 3QD ☎01297 442459. A quaint seventeenth-century café-restaurant in a prime position at the foot of the high street, with a terrace overlooking the sea. It's a good place for well-priced breakfasts, lunches such as steak and kidney pie or gammon and pineapple (mains around £10), afternoon teas, coffees and cakes. Service is efficient and friendly and dogs are welcome. Daily 9am–4pm, later in summer.

Cobb Arms Marine Parade, DT7 3JF ☎01297 443242. Basic, local pub right on the harbour that serves the usual pub staples plus fresh fish at good prices from a daily specials menu, including scallops, mussels and crab. Dishes, such as John Dory with mushrooms, hake with sautéed potatoes or cod Benedict (£12–15), are simply prepared using locally caught fish. Daily 8am–midnight.

The Courtyard Café Town Mill, Mill Lane, DT7 3PU ☎01297 445757 ⓦcourtyardcafelyme.co.uk. Part of the mill complex, this pretty café has a cosy interior with plenty of outdoor tables in the courtyard. The menu covers cooked breakfasts (£8.50), sandwiches (from £7) and interesting lunch dishes such as cabbage fritters (£7.50), dressed crab (£7.50) and smoked mackerel tabbouleh (£9). Mon, Tues & Thurs–Sun 9.30am–4.30pm, Wed 10am–4pm; Nov–March closed Thurs.

ELEANOR COADE – BUSINESSWOMAN EXTRAORDINAIRE

Despite being little known today, **Eleanor Coade** (1733–1821) was one of Britain's most important businesswomen in the eighteenth century, and Lyme Regis's most eminent resident of the time. Coade's success came from perfecting the recipe and the manufacturing process for an incredibly durable artificial stone which could be sculpted into statues and ornate decorations for buildings. In 1769, Coade opened a factory in London where she mass produced "Coade Stone", and her designs became very popular with builders and architects of the time – Coade Stone went on to grace some of England's most important buildings, including Brighton's Royal Pavilion, Windsor Castle, the Royal Naval College in Greenwich and a statue of a lion on Westminster Bridge. Coade Stone is so hardwearing that plenty of examples of it can still be seen today, including on Coade's own house in Lyme Regis, **Belmont**; the beautiful villa was later owned by the author John Fowles (see box, p.131), who lived here 1968–2005. The house has been beautifully renovated and you can admire its facade from the top of Pound Street, or even stay here (see above).

French Lieutenant's Bistro 8–10 Bridge St, DT7 3QA ⓣ01297 442961, ⓦlymebarbistros.co.uk. A light, airy restaurant with a great terrace overlooking the sea, this serves tasty fish dishes such as monkfish curry and fresh brill (£15–19), as well as local lobster and crab salads. Mon–Wed & Sun 10am–6pm, Thurs–Sat 10am–9pm.

Harbour Inn 23 Marine Parade, DT7 3JF ⓣ01297 442299. Lively place serving good-value pub grub as well as more ambitious dishes, such as bouillabaise made with local fish, hake and gurnard (mains £14–18). Inside it's all wooden floors and pared-back decor, while outside there's a terrace facing the seafront, where drinkers spill out onto the promenade on summer evenings. Daily 11am–11pm.

Hix Oyster and Fish House Cobb Rd, DT7 3JP ⓣ01297 446910, ⓦhixrestaurants.co.uk/hix-oyster-fish-house. In a great location high above Lyme Regis beach, this friendly fish and seafood restaurant is owned by local boy turned celebrity chef Mark Hix. The building itself is lovely – plenty of wood and glass, with tables on the terrace and far-reaching views over the town and coast – and the food is fresh, well prepared and very tasty. Prices are quite reasonable, too, considering: choose a local seasonal dish such as hake with clams and you'll pay around £16 for a main course, or splash out on the Portland seabass for two (£45). April–Oct daily noon–10pm; Nov–March Tues–Sat noon–10pm, Sun noon–4pm.

Royal Standard 25 Marine Parade, DT7 3JF ⓣ01297 442637, ⓦtheroyalstandardlymeregis.co.uk. Beachside inn dating back 400 years, with a log fire inside and a great sea-facing beer garden that leads onto the beach outside. There are real ales on tap, brewed by Palmers in nearby Bridport, and decently priced pub grub as well as local grilled fish (from £11). Daily 10am–11pm.

Tierra Kitchen 1a Coombe St, DT7 3PY ⓣ01297 445189, ⓦtierrakitchen.co.uk. Overlooking the millstream, this is a bright vegetarian restaurant serving a range of tasty seasonal dishes such as parsnip and chickpea kofta and pastry filled with feta and tabbouleh (mains from £14). It also serves coffees, cakes and pastries. Wed–Sat noon–2.30pm & 6–9.15pm, Sun noon–2.30pm.

★**Town Mill Bakery** 2 Coombe St, DT7 3PY ⓣ01297 444754. A wonderful rustic-chic bakery/café selling a superb array of freshly baked breads to take away. Alternatively, sit on the low, communal benches to enjoy local and largely organic produce, including sublime breakfasts (local preserves, eggs and pastries), lunches (focaccia, soup and pizzas from £7) or afternoon tea, featuring a sublime layer cake. Daily 8.30am–4.30pm.

4

Charmouth and around

Three miles east of Lyme, set on a steep hillside, is the appealing town of **CHARMOUTH**, Jane Austen's favourite resort and another great place for finding fossils. The beach here is a mixture of sand and pebbles, with fossil hunters heading to the west of the beach beneath Europe's largest landslip sight – the coast here is very unstable and you should steer clear of the cliffs themselves. Practised eyes can easily find a plethora of fossilized belemnites loose on the beach.

Charmouth Heritage Coast Centre

Lower Sea Lane, DT6 6LL • **Heritage Centre** Easter–Oct daily 10.30am–4.30pm; Nov–Easter Thurs–Sun 10.30am–4.30pm • Free; donations welcome • **Tours** Year-round; check website for times; 2hr • £7.50, children £3 • ⓣ01297 560772, ⓦcharmouth.org/chcc

The **Charmouth Heritage Coast Centre** on the beach has an interesting display on the history and geology of the area's fossils, including a plaster cast of the complete fossilized skeleton of a scelidosaurus found here in 2000 – a dinosaur that has only been found in Charmouth. However, the main reason to visit is to do one of its excellent two-hour fossil-hunting tours, run by knowledgeable guides who can help even novice fossil hunters find them. Tours start with a talk at the visitor centre, then hammers and chisels are provided and you set off down the beach. The centre also runs rock-pooling tours for children and weekend-long fossil tours for serious geologists. There's a decent café too, serving sandwiches, cooked breakfasts and local Bridport pies.

ACCOMMODATION **CHARMOUTH AND AROUND**

The Abbots House The Street, DT6 6QF ⓣ01297 560339, ⓦabbotshouse.co.uk. Boutique B&B in a sixteenth-century house that has been completely renovated with stylish decor and furnishings. The four rooms all have freestanding baths and nice touches such as dressing gowns and home-made biscuits. No children. Two-night minimum stay. **£140**

Seadown Bridge Rd, DT6 6QS ⓣ01297 560154, ⓦseadownholidaypark.co.uk. Friendly, family-run campsite in a great location, alongside the River Char with direct access to the beach. The park is well maintained with lots of green fields in which to play games, or have a picnic or barbecue. There are caravans to rent (£555/week) plus plenty of space to pitch a tent. **£22**

★**White House Hotel** 2 Hillside, The Street, DT6 6PJ ⓣ01297 560411, ⓦwhitehousehotel.com. The lovely Regency *White House Hotel* is very well run, with a pretty terrace garden and comfortable rooms. The owners are friendly and efficient and the breakfasts are great, with eggs from their own chickens and locally made bread and jams. The award-winning restaurant uses local and seasonal ingredients (mains around £19), including herbs and vegetables from their own garden. **£140**

EATING

The Bank House The Street, DT6 6PU ⓣ01297 561600. Traditional café serving good-quality breakfasts and lunches with pleasant outside seating on Charmouth's main street. The cooked lunches are good value with dishes such as gammon and chips (£10) and a good variety of veggie options. Evening meals include seafood pasta (£12), mixed grills, fish and seafood dishes (£9–12). Winter Mon 11am–2.30pm, Fri & Sat 11am–2.30pm & 6–10pm, Sun 10.30am–3pm; summer also open Tues & Thurs 11am–2.30pm & 6–10pm.

Royal Oak The Street, Charmouth, DT6 6PE ⓣ01297 560277, ⓦroyaloakcharmouth.com. Good traditional pub serving Bridport ales and decent pub grub, such as luxury fish pie for £6. They have regular live music, including a monthly folk night. Mon–Fri noon–3pm & 6–11pm, Sat & Sun noon–11pm.

Golden Cap and Seatown

It's a lovely three-mile walk along the steep coastal path from Charmouth to the headland of **Golden Cap**, whose brilliant outcrop of auburn sandstone is crowned with gorse. It's the highest point on the south coast and the views are fantastic – as far as Dartmoor on a clear day. Before setting off, check with the Heritage Centre at Charmouth, as parts of the coastal path are closed periodically due to landslips. Alternatively, you can reach the Cap from **SEATOWN** (again check the path's condition before setting off), just under a mile from the A35 (turn off at Chideock). There's little to Seatown, save a pretty beach, some good walks and a great pub.

EATING GOLDEN CAP AND SEATOWN

Anchor Inn Seatown, DT6 6JU ⓣ01279 489215, ⓦtheanchorinnseatown.co.uk. Cosy pub with three small bars with wood-burners, plus fabulous sea views from the clifftop garden. The food features locally sourced and foraged ingredients with fish and seafood a speciality – expect specials such as a hot shellfish bowl with garlic (£20) or Lyme Bay scallops with belly of pork (£18). Nov–March Mon–Thurs 10am–3pm & 6–11pm, Fri 10am–11pm, Sat & Sun 9am–11pm; April–Oct Mon–Fri 10am–11pm, Sat & Sun 9am–11pm.

Beaminster and around

Five miles north of Bridport, **BEAMINSTER** (pronounced "Beminster") is a typical example of a traditional inland Dorset town – it was "Emminster" in *Tess of the D'Urbervilles*. There's little to see here today, though Hardy fans may want to seek out Beaminster Rectory on Clay Lane, off Hogshill Street, which was "Emminster Rectory" in *Tess*, where Angel Clare's parents lived. Much of the town centre is a conservation area, its most important buildings being the fine, honey-coloured **Church of St Mary** with an impressive 30m-high tower – where local men were hanged during the Bloody Assizes (see p.280) – and the fabulous Tudor **Parnham House**, just south of town and now privately owned.

Mapperton House

Beaminster, DT8 3NR • **Gardens** March–Oct Mon–Fri & Sun 11am–5pm • £9, under-15s free • **House tours** late March to Oct Mon–Thurs & Sun noon, 1pm, 2pm and 3pm; booking advised • £12, under-15s free (includes entry to gardens) • ⓣ01308 862645, ⓦmapperton.com

Three miles southeast of Beaminster off the B3163 lies **Mapperton House**. This Jacobean house – which has its own church – and its sumptuous gardens have featured in the film

THE JURASSIC COAST

A unique set of factors contributed to a 95-mile stretch of coast straddling Devon and Dorset being awarded UNESCO World Heritage status in 2001. Known as the **Jurassic Coast**, England's only Natural Heritage site was set up with the aim of safeguarding the amazing geological record displayed by the cliffs, coves and beaches along the coastline. It takes its name from Jurassic times, some 185 million years ago, when the south of England was covered by a warm sea called the Tethys Ocean.

The oldest rocks, in Devon, are some 250 million years old, the youngest being at Studland in Dorset. But each layer shows a snapshot of history and geology, recording a changing landscape that has at different times been desert, dinosaur-infested swamps and warm ocean. The Dorset section is richest for fossil hunters, particularly around Lyme Regis, where the coast is made up largely of unstable blue Lias (a Dorset corruption of "layers", referring to the layers of soft and hard rock) dating back to the Triassic period.

versions of *Tom Jones*, *Emma* and the 2015 version of *Far from the Madding Crowd*. The Italianate gardens are simply lovely, spreading out along a clefted dell and studded with fountains, fish ponds and statues of herons. They were landscaped in the 1920s (though the ponds date from the seventeenth century), with paths winding up to viewpoints over the coast. The house, enlarged in the 1670s, is home to the Earl and Countess of Sandwich, and has been restored to its original Tudor glory: its art collection includes paintings by Joshua Reynolds and Hogarth. There's also the excellent *Sawmill Café* (open to the public, April–Sept Mon–Fri & Sun 11am–5pm), which serves tasty lunches, cakes and cream teas.

4

Evershot

Seven miles east of Beaminster, through delightful Dorset countryside, the unspoilt village of **EVERSHOT** ("Evershead" in Hardy's *Tess of the D'Urbervilles*) has featured in many a film, such as the 1996 adaptation of Jane Austen's *Emma*. Set in the heart of a private estate complete with a 600-acre deer park, the village has a series of thatched cottages, a tiny shop and bakery, and a beautiful church with an unusual pointed clocktower.

ACCOMMODATION AND EATING — EVERSHOT

The Acorn Inn 28 Fore St, DT2 0JW ☎ 01935 83228, ⓦ acorn-inn.co.uk. "The Sow and Acorn" in Hardy's *Tess of the D'Urbervilles*, this atmospheric pub is all wooden beams, flagstones and log fires. The restaurant serves high-quality dishes using local ingredients (mains £15–20), while the bars have real ales and serve sandwiches made with bread from the village bakery (around £6). There's a skittle alley out back, plus ten comfortable bedrooms upstairs. Kitchen daily noon–2pm & 7–9pm; pub daily 8am–11.30pm. **£115**

★ **Summer Lodge** 9 Fore St, DT2 0JR ☎ 01935 482000, ⓦ summerlodgehotel.co.uk. If your budget can stretch to it, treat yourself to a stay at the lovely *Summer Lodge*. Set in a Grade II-listed Georgian mansion in superbly manicured grounds, it has a pool, a spa, luxurious rooms and attentive, friendly service. There are tennis courts and free bikes (and wellies) for guests. The west wing was designed by Thomas Hardy during his days as an architect – and the bar boasts an Armagnac dating back to Hardy's time. The award-winning restaurant (mains £25–30) is second to none and there's a highly rated wine cellar. Mon–Fri noon–1.45pm & 7–9pm, Sat & Sun 12.30–2pm & 7–9pm. **£325**

Pilsdon Pen

Five miles west of Beaminster, the Iron Age hillfort at **Pilsdon Pen** is one of Dorset's highest hills at 277m. Fourteen Iron Age roundhouses were found here during excavations in the 1960s. Wordsworth, who rented a house near here at the end of the eighteenth century, declared it the finest view in all England. The summit is best approached from the little car park (signposted) on Pilsdon Lane: from here, it's a steep but easy ten-minute climb. At the top, the defensive ridges are very obvious, while the views from the little triangulation point are stunning, across the Marshwood Vale to the sea.

East Dorset and the Avon Valley

THE VIEW FROM HAMBLEDON HILL

East Dorset and the Avon Valley

In general, the towns of east Dorset are highly picturesque and historic: the river Stour connects the small towns of Sturminster Newton and Wimborne Minster, famed for its ancient church, via Blandford Forum, with its splendid Georgian townscape. The River Avon passes through the attractive market town of Ringwood into some of England's least spoilt countryside. This is particularly true around Cranborne Chase – parts of which appear as almost a void on maps, with barely a road or town to be seen. Nearby lies the pretty town of Shaftesbury, best known for its steep, cobbled hill, now forever associated with sliced bread. Less feted but more historic hills include the impressive Hambledon Hill and Badbury Rings, both ancient Iron Age forts.

It pays to plan your trip round the area carefully, as many of the sights are not open every day or in the winter, but the region's walks and rural scenery are permanent attractions, as is the child-friendly **Moors Valley Country Park**. Highlights of the region include the rolling estate at **Kingston Lacy** and the walks around Fordingbridge in the **Avon Valley**, from where the River Avon begins its approach to the coast along the western edges of the New Forest National Park.

Wimborne Minster and around

On the banks of the Stour, a short drive north from the suburbs of Bournemouth, **WIMBORNE MINSTER** is a well-to-do market town best known for its great church, the **Minster of St Cuthberga**. The town's older buildings stand around the main square near the Minster, and most date from the late eighteenth or early nineteenth century. It's a tiny town, and pretty quiet – except on market days, when around four hundred stalls make up the south of England's largest covered **market** on Station Road about a mile from the centre (Fri 6.30am–2pm, Sat 7.30am–2pm & Sun 8am–2pm; ⓦwimbornemarket.co.uk).

Minster of St Cuthberga

High St, BH21 1EB • **Church** Jan & Feb Mon–Sat 9.30am–4pm, Sun 2.30–4pm; March–Dec Mon–Sat 9.30am–5.30pm, Sun 2.30–5.30pm • **Chained Library** April–Oct daily 10.30am–12.30pm & 2–4pm; Nov–March phone to check library hours • Free • ⓣ 01202 884753, ⓦ wimborneminster.org.uk

Built on the site of an eighth-century monastery, the **Minster of St Cuthberga** has two massive towers of mottled grey and tawny stone that dwarf the rest of the town. Previously, the church was even more imposing – its spire crashed down during morning service in 1602. What remains is basically Norman with a few later features, such as the Perpendicular west tower, which bears a figure dressed as a grenadier of the Napoleonic era, who strikes every quarter-hour with a hammer. Inside, the church is crowded with memorials and eye-catching details – look out for the orrery clock inside the west tower,

WIMBORNE MINSTER

Highlights

❶ **Minster of St Cuthberga** One of Dorset's finest churches, with its rare ancient chained library, in the heart of a pretty market town. **See p.138**

❷ **Kingston Lacy** Sumptuous seventeenth-century manor set in extensive grounds, with a world-class collection of Egyptian artefacts, plus paintings by the likes of Titian and Rubens. **See p.144**

❸ **Hambledon Hill** A former Iron Age fort, which makes for a great walk with superb, far-reaching views. **See p.148**

❹ **Gold Hill, Shaftesbury** This quintessential slice of England – all cobbles and thatched cottages – will be familiar from Ridley Scott's famous Hovis ad. **See p.149**

❺ **Cranborne Chase** Former royal hunting grounds – both King John and pop royalty Madonna have ridden here – and now one of England's least spoilt tracts of land. **See p.151**

❻ **Moors Valley Country Park** Swing through the treetops on the high-adrenaline Go Ape high-ropes adventure course, or whizz through the woods on a Segway. **See p.156**

HIGHLIGHTS ARE MARKED ON THE MAP ON PP.140–141

West Bourton
B3092
B3081
Gillingham
Gillingham
A350
Buckhorn Weston
Motcombe
B3081
B3092
A30
4
A350
Kington Magna
A30
Shaftesbury
Ludwell
East Stour
A30
B3092
Sherborne (7 miles)
B3081
CRANBORNE CHASE
Compton Abbas
Marnhull
Stalbridge
A350
B3091
Tollard Royal
5
B3092
Hinton St Mary
Larmer Tree Gardens
Iwerne Minster
Farnham
Sturminster Newton
A3030
Child Okeford
River Stour
Chettle
Tarrant Gunville
3
Hambledon Hill
Okeford Fitzpaine
Shillingstone
A357
A354
A350
Royal Signals Museum
Blandford Forum
Bulbarrow Hill
A354
Winterborne Stickland
Badbury Rings
Spetisbury
Milton Abbas
N
Winterborne Whitechurch
A31
Milborne St Andrew
Winterborne Kingston
A354
A31
A350
Puddletown
A35
Bere Regis
Dorchester (4 miles)

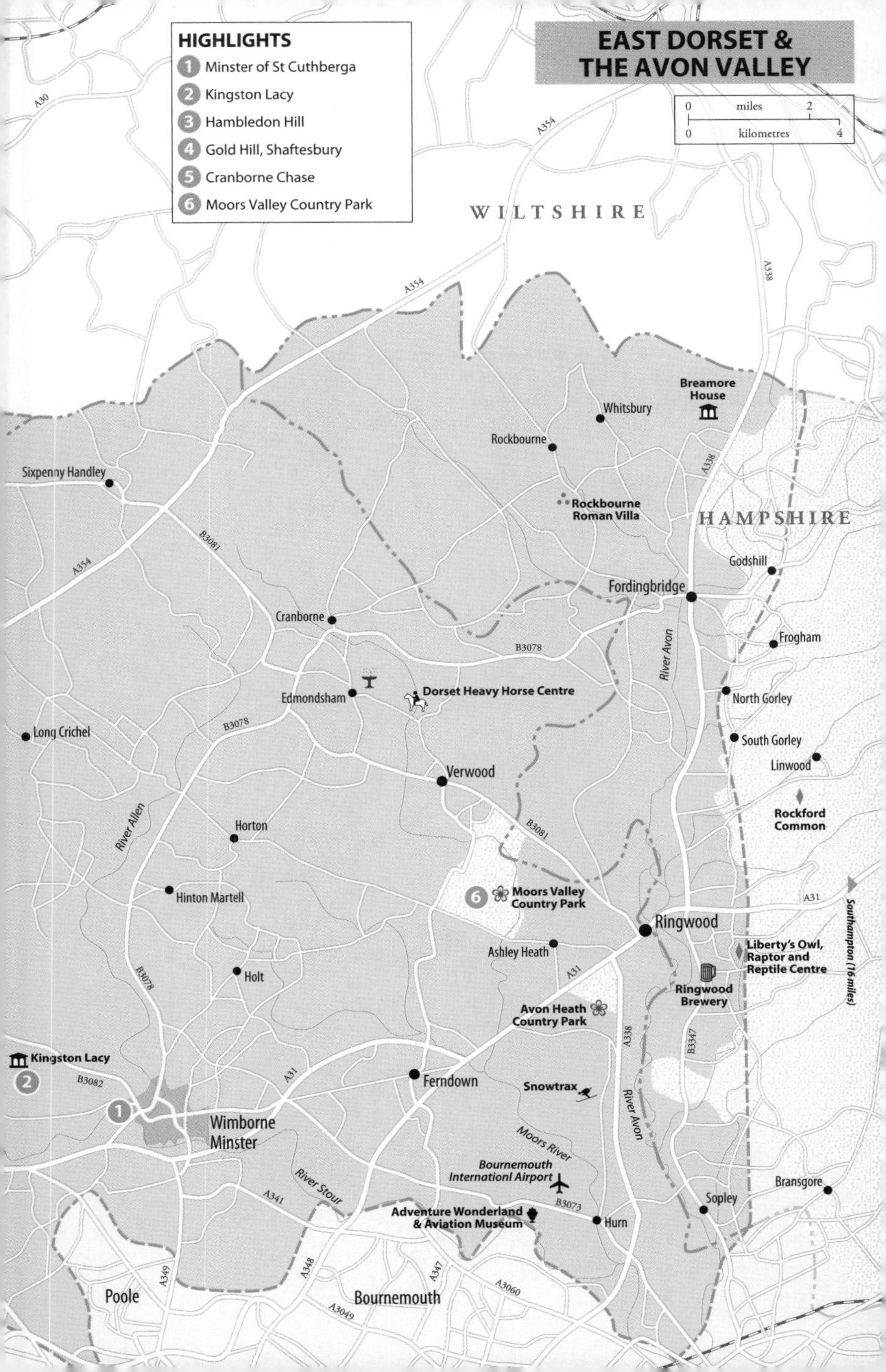
EAST DORSET & THE AVON VALLEY
HIGHLIGHTS
1 Minster of St Cuthberga
2 Kingston Lacy
3 Hambledon Hill
4 Gold Hill, Shaftesbury
5 Cranborne Chase
6 Moors Valley Country Park
0 miles 2
0 kilometres 4
WILTSHIRE
HAMPSHIRE
A30
A354
A338
B3081
B3078
B3082
A31
A341
A349
A348
A347
A3060
A3049
B3073
B3347
Breamore House
Whitsbury
Rockbourne
Rockbourne Roman Villa
Sixpenny Handley
Godshill
Fordingbridge
Cranborne
Frogham
Edmondsham
Dorset Heavy Horse Centre
North Gorley
South Gorley
Long Crichel
Linwood
Verwood
Rockford Common
River Allen
Horton
River Avon
Hinton Martell
Moors Valley Country Park
Southampton (16 miles)
Ringwood
Ashley Heath
Liberty's Owl, Raptor and Reptile Centre
Holt
Ringwood Brewery
Avon Heath Country Park
Kingston Lacy
Ferndown
Snowtrax
Wimborne Minster
Moors River
Bournemouth Internationl Airport
River Stour
Bransgore
Sopley
Adventure Wonderland & Aviation Museum
Hurn
Poole
Bournemouth

with the sun marking the hours and the moon marking the days of the month, and for the organ with trumpets pointing out towards the congregation instead of pipes.

Dating from 1686, the **Chained Library** above the choir vestry – and accessed via a narrow spiral staircase – is Wimborne's most prized possession. The country's second-largest chained library (and one of its oldest public libraries), it houses such treasures as a manuscript written on calfskin dating from 1343, and seventeenth-century accounts of how to make wine and catch elephants. The reason the books were chained, incidentally, was because it truly was a library and anyone could come and read the books – the chains were to prevent them being stolen.

Priest's House Museum

23–27 High St, BH21 1HR • Feb, March, Nov & Dec Mon–Sat 10am–3pm; April–Oct Mon–Sat 10am–4.30pm • £5.50 • priest-house.co.uk

The **Priest's House** on the High Street began life as lodgings for the clergy, then became a stationer's shop. Now it is a **museum** that gives a good insight into small-town life in the past, with several rooms furnished in the styles of different periods, such as a

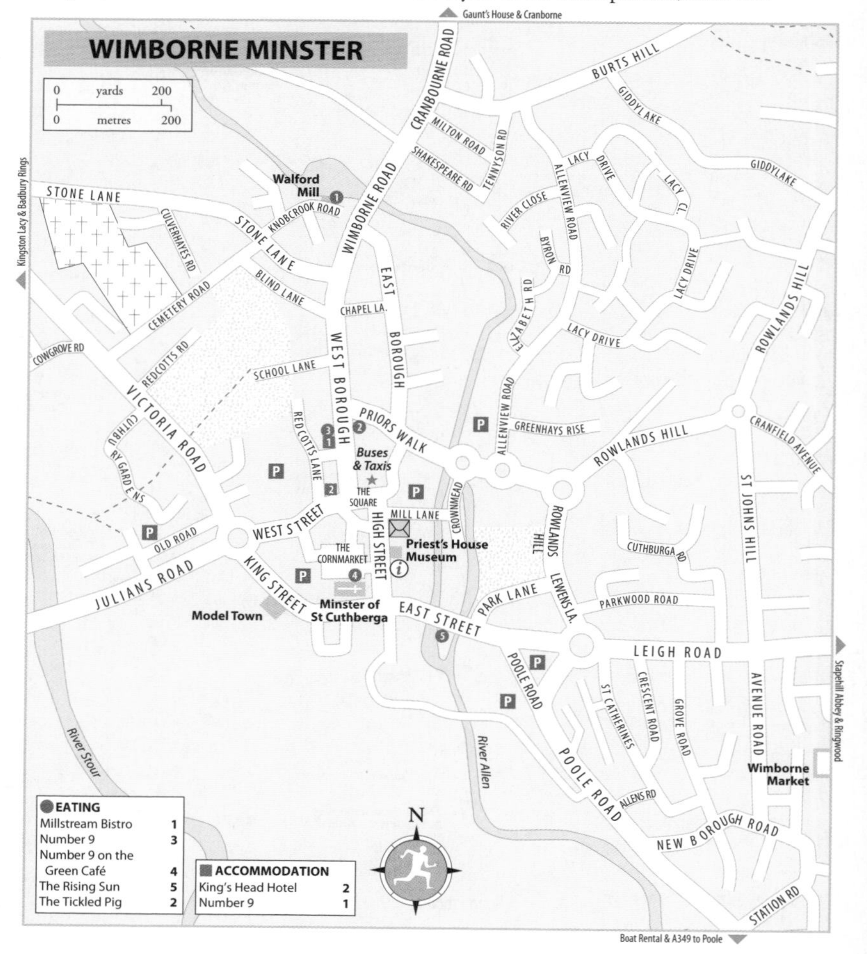

working Victorian kitchen and a Georgian parlour. There's also a walled garden at the rear, which is an excellent spot for afternoon tea in the summer.

Model Town

King St, BH21 1DY • Mid-March to Oct daily 10am–5pm • £6, under-18s £5 • wimborne-modeltown.com

Built in the 1950s, the quaint **Model Town** is a miniature replica of Wimborne as it was some sixty years ago, complete with traditional butcher's and baker's shops displaying tiny loaves of bread and life-like miniature pies in their windows. It's a snapshot of small-town England in the 1950s, with ringing telephone boxes, bobbies on bikes and a chiming church where a model couple are getting married. Children can run round peering into the windows, and there are also Wendy houses to play in and a working model railway.

ARRIVAL AND DEPARTURE — WIMBORNE MINSTER

By bus Wimborne is served by buses #3 and #4 from Poole (4–5 hourly; 30min) and bus #13 from Bournemouth (every 30min; 1hr). Both pull in at The Square.

By car Drivers should head for the central car park by the Minster.

INFORMATION AND ACTIVITIES

Tourist office 29 High St (Mon–Sat: April–Sept 10am–4.30pm; Oct–March 10am–4pm; 01202 886116).

Rowing boats Just south of the covered market, you can rent out rowing boats for a peaceful trip along the river south of town, for £12.50 per hour (11am–5pm: April–Sept Sat, Sun & hols; mid-July to Aug daily; hours are weather dependent, call 07568 342579 to check; dream-boats.org.uk).

ACCOMMODATION

King's Head Hotel The Square, BH21 1JG 01202 880101, thekingsheadhotel.com. Comfortable, good-value rooms with free wi-fi, in this pleasant eighteenth-century hotel right on the main square. The bar is relaxed with comfy sofas and a real fire, while the restaurant serves reasonably priced pub food, such as a range of steaks for £13–16. **£90**

Number 9 9 West Borough, BH21 1LT 01202 887557, number9wimborne.co.uk/accommodation. Three comfortable rooms above an excellent restaurant (see below), with organic bedding and Neal's Yard toiletries. **£110**

EATING

There are numerous **pubs** around Wimborne's main square, though they only really come to life at weekends when much of the surrounding rural community descends for a night out, or during the Wimborne Folk Festival in June (wimbornefolk.co.uk).

Millstream Bistro Walford Mill, Stone Lane, BH21 1NL 01202 841400, walfordmillcrafts.co.uk. Friendly café attached to the lovely gallery at Walford Mill where local arts and crafts are displayed (and for sale). The café has outdoor tables beside the millstream and serves tasty sandwiches, quiches, soups, plus more substantial meals such as wild mushroom lasagne (£10) and roasted cod (£12). Mon–Sat 10am–4pm, Sun 11am–4pm.

Number 9 9 West Borough, BH21 1LT 01202 887557, number9wimborne.co.uk/restaurant.html. A highly regarded restaurant with wooden floors and brick walls that serves locally sourced food with a modern twist, such as Dorset venison with dark chocolate and red wine sauce (£22). Rooms are available, too (see above). Tues–Sat noon–2.30pm & 6–9pm, Sun noon–2pm.

Number 9 on the Green Café 7 Cook Row, BH21 1LB 01202 887765, number9wimborne.co.uk/on-the-green.html. In an Elizabethan building with flagstone floors, opposite the minster, this cosy café on two floors serves home-made soup, sandwiches, quiches and tasty cakes made with organic, home-grown and local ingredients. Everything is around £6–9: try the Scotch egg or Wimborne pasty. Mon–Sat 9am–4.30pm, Sun 10am–4pm.

The Rising Sun 38 East St, BH21 1DX 01202 883464. Pleasant pub serving local Hall and Woodhouse ales with seats outside on the riverside terrace. Serves decent pub grub too, and puts on regular events such as Open Mic Wednesdays, where you can get a pie and a pint for £7. Mon–Thurs 11am–11pm, Fri & Sat 11am–midnight, Sun 11am–10pm.

The Tickled Pig 26 West Borough, BH21 1NF 01202 886778, thetickledpig.co.uk. Locally sourced seasonal ingredients, including veg grown in their own kitchen

5

garden, are skilfully made into interesting and beautifully presented dishes, such as hake with roasted cauliflower purée and clams (£18). There's seating in a small garden at the back and a deli counter at the front selling Dorset charcuterie and cheeses. Tues–Sat noon–3pm & 6pm–late.

Kingston Lacy

Wimborne Minster, BH21 4EA • **House** Daily: March–Oct 11am–5pm; Nov–Feb 11am–4pm • **Grounds** Daily: March–Oct 10am–4pm; Nov–Feb 10am–6pm • House & grounds £13.50, children £6.70; grounds only £8.60, children £4.30; NT • Ⓦ nationaltrust.org.uk/kingston-lacy

One of England's finest country houses, **Kingston Lacy** lies two miles northwest of Wimborne Minster, in parkland grazed by a herd of Red Devon cattle. Designed in the seventeenth century for the Bankes family, who were exiled from Corfe Castle (see p.69) after the Roundheads reduced it to rubble, the brick building was clad in grey stone during the nineteenth century by Sir Charles Barry, co-architect of the Houses of Parliament. William Bankes, then owner of the house, was a great traveller and collector, and the **Spanish Room**, lined with gilded leather and surmounted by a Venetian ceiling, is a superb scrapbook of his Grand Tour souvenirs. Kingston Lacy is also home to the largest private collection of Egyptian artefacts in the country, while its resident **pictures** are also outstanding, featuring works by Titian, Rubens, Velázquez and many other Old Masters. The house gets so swamped with visitors that timed tickets are issued at peak times, though you can then devote time to the extensive and attractive **gardens**, complete with woodland walks, a Japanese tea garden and a children's play area.

Badbury Rings

Like Hambledon Hill (see p.148) and Maiden Castle (see p.94), the **Badbury Rings**, four miles northwest of Wimbourne Minster, mark the site of an ancient Iron Age fort that was used from around 800 BC – though there are also Bronze Age barrows here (2200–800 BC). The defences – once capped by a wooden fort on the tree-topped hill – were dug into the chalk, leaving three raised ditches stretching to a height of 15m, though even these hardy fortifications were not enough to protect the inhabitants from the invading Romans, who successfully took it in around 43 AD. After the Roman occupation, a local monk, Gildas, narrated the tale of how later invaders were repelled by a brave warrior called Arthur – who may or may not have been the legendary King Arthur. Whatever the truth, it is a highly attractive and atmospheric spot, the countryside around remaining wild and remote despite once forming a hub of Roman roads that included Ackling Dyke, which ran from London to Dorchester and beyond.

Blandford Forum

A quiet market town (cynics say "Not only Bland by name…"), **BLANDFORD FORUM** does have sufficient sights to warrant a half-day detour from the nearby coast. Architecturally it is one of Dorset's most distinctive towns, being almost entirely Georgian, rebuilt in the eighteenth century after a fire destroyed the original town in 1731. Two local brothers – John and William Bastard (pronounced b'stard) – set about designing a harmonious townscape on the edges of the gently flowing River Stour, centred on the Town Hall and the **Church of St Peter and St Paul**. The church, completed in 1739, has impressive Ionic columns and box pews, though some of the current structure dates from the nineteenth century when the chancel was detached, wheeled out of the way and stuck on a new extension. Blandford's Latin-sounding name was actually a thirteenth-century translation of the old Saxon name *Cheping*, or **market**, which still forms the focal point of the town on Thursdays and Saturdays;

there are also farmers' markets on the second Friday of each month (details on Ⓦ blandfordforum-tc.gov.uk).

Fashion Museum

Lime Tree House, The Plocks, DT11 7AA • Mon & Thurs–Sat: April–Sept 10am–5pm; Oct, Nov & mid-Feb to March 10am–4pm • £5 • Ⓦ theblandfordfashionmuseum.com

The town's most interesting museum, the **Fashion Museum** is a collection of costumes displayed in a superb example of a Bastard Georgian townhouse. With more than five hundred items and accoutrements assembled by local woman Mrs Penny, the museum provides a fascinating take on the development of fashion from 1730 to the 1970s, including a room dedicated to accessories, featuring such delights as a silk parasol and mother-of-pearl fan. Exhibits include a display of Victorian wedding dresses, men's and women's hats and dresses by British designers such as Bruce Oldfield.

Town Museum

Beres Yard, DT11 7HQ • April–Oct Mon–Sat 10am–4pm • Free • Ⓦ blandfordtownmuseum.org

Opposite the Church of St Peter and St Paul in Beres Yard is the small **Town Museum**, charting four hundred years of Blandford's history. Inside is an eclectic jumble featuring everything from a Victorian pump organ to archeological remains, displays on the Bastard brothers and a diorama of the Blandford fire. There's a re-creation of a Victorian playroom with a nineteenth-century dolls' house modelled on a real Blandford house, plus a life-sized model of a railway platform from World War I as well as replicas of a forge and cobbler's shop.

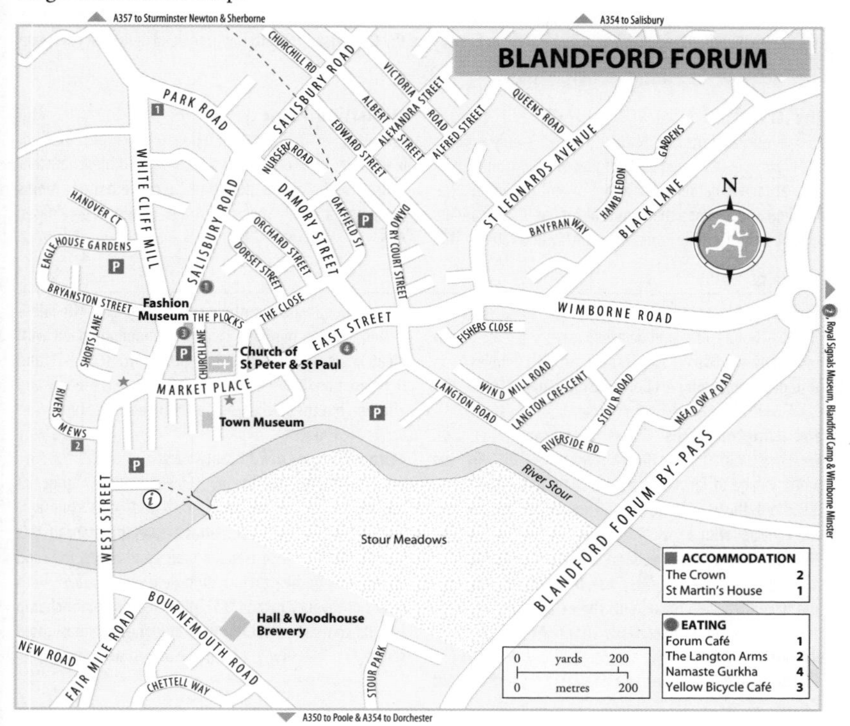

5

Hall & Woodhouse Brewery

Blandford St Mary, DT11 9LS • **Tours** Mon–Sat 10.30am; 2hr • £10 • T 01258 486004, W hall-woodhouse.co.uk

A ten-minute walk or short drive south of town at Blandford St Mary is the **Hall & Woodhouse Brewery**. This family-run brewery has been based in Blandford since 1899 and now produces the local Badger ales, one of the oldest trademarks on record, as well as pear and apple ciders. The tour shows you how the beer is brewed and involves a tasting session at the end.

Royal Signals Museum

Blandford Camp, DT11 8RH • Mid-Feb to Oct Mon–Fri 10am–5pm, Sat–Sun 10am–4pm; Nov to mid-Feb Mon–Fri 10am–5pm; closed over Christmas hols • £7.50, under-16s £5.50 • W royalsignalsmuseum.co.uk • As it is on a working army camp, over-15s must show a valid photo ID

A five-minute drive northeast of Blandford at Blandford Camp is the **Royal Signals Museum**, which traces the history of military signals and communications through the ages. Its chief attraction is one of the ENIGMA code machines and there are plenty of interactive displays, plus some armoured vehicles and military motorbikes.

ARRIVAL AND INFORMATION — BLANDFORD FORUM

By bus Blandford Forum is served by bus #183 from Dorchester (5 daily; 35min) and Weymouth (6 daily; 1hr) and the #X8 from Poole (hourly; 40min; W morebus.co.uk).

Tourist office Riverside House, West St (Mon–Sat: April–Sept 10am–4pm; Oct–March 10am–3pm; T 01258 454770), can give you details of local walks along the Stour, and B&Bs.

ACCOMMODATION

Finding a room is rarely a problem except during the Blandford Georgian Fayre, held every two years over the May bank holiday (W blandfordgeorgianfayre.co.uk), and the five days of the Great Dorset Steam Fair at the end of August (W steam-fair.co.uk).

The Crown West St, DT11 7AJ T 01258 456626, W crownhotelblandford.co.uk. The town's only hotel is *The Crown*, set in an elegant Georgian coaching inn with its own attractive gardens, bar and a decent restaurant. The building underwent a major refurbishment in 2016 and its spacious, comfortable rooms are stylishly decorated. **£160**

St Martin's House White Cliff, Mill St, DT11 7BP T 01258 451245, W stmartinshouse.co.uk. Best of Blandford's B&Bs is *St Martin's House*, in a former choristers' house, with period furniture, well-decorated rooms (including a family room; £90) and generous breakfasts. **£75**

EATING

Forum Café 34 Salisbury St, DT11 7RG T 01258 459104. Good coffee and delicious cakes – try the lemon and poppy-seed cake – in this small café that doubles as an antiques shop, selling Art Deco and other pieces. Mon–Sat 9am–5pm, Sun 10am–4pm.

The Langton Arms Tarrant Monkton, DT11 8RX T 01258 830225, W thelangtonarms.co.uk. In the pretty village of Tarrant Monkton, some five miles out of Blandford, this cosy thatched pub specializes in local beef and venison, with a variety of steaks on the menu (£21–26) plus home-made venison sausages (£13.50) and traditional pub staples. They use local game in season and bake their own bread, plus there's a large garden for outdoor eating in summer. Daily 10am–11pm.

Namaste Gurkha 11 East St, DT11 7DU T 01258 450769, W namastegurkha.co.uk. Cosy restaurant serving good-value, authentic and very tasty Nepalese dishes, such as momo – steamed dumplings filled with meat or vegetables (£5–6) – pork curries (£6–7) and Nepalese noodle dishes (£5–7). The service is friendly and efficient, but the spicing can be on the hot side. Tues–Sun 5.30–10.30pm.

Yellow Bicycle Café 30a Salisbury St T 01258 480356. Tasty sourdough flatbreads (£6.25) with a range of toppings – such as beetroot, carrot and goats' cheese or grilled halloumi and courgettes – are the stars at this Scandi-chic café with wooden tables and floors. The food is unusual and hearty, including delicious pancakes with sweet or savoury fillings (£5), plus creamy potato champ (similar to mashed potato) with bolognese or mushroom sauce (£7). Tues–Fri 9am–5pm, Sat 8.30am–5pm.

FROM TOP THE RIVERSIDE AT FORDINGBRIDGE (P.154); AVENUE OF BEECH TREES AT KINGSTON LACY (P.144) >

THE STURMINSTER NEWTON CHEESE FESTIVAL

Each September, usually over the second weekend, the sleepy town of Sturminster Newton bursts into life to honour cheese. The **festival** (ⓦcheesefestival.co.uk; £5), which started life in 2000 with a few stalls, has grown into a celebration of rural life, with three marquees full of local producers selling everything from bee boxes and crafts to cakes, fish and pies – and, of course, cheese. You can sample most of the wares, from local sausages, home-made breads and pastries to an astonishing variety of cheeses – look out for the pungent **Stickland goat**, and the deliciously creamy **Windswept cow**. Alternatively, you could simply sit on a hay bale in the field, listen to the band play and sip a pint of local cider.

Sturminster Newton and around

Surrounded by the beautiful, undulating countryside of the Blackmore Vale, **STURMINSTER NEWTON** is an attractive town on the River Stour, with a thatched market square. Thomas Hardy lived here when writing *The Return of the Native*, referring to the town as "Stourcastle" – his house, Riverside, is now a pair of private houses overlooking the river. The town is approached over a six-arched bridge on which a nineteenth-century plaque threatens anyone causing damage with transportation to Australia as a felon. The town makes a pleasant place for a brief stroll, especially during the Monday market (ⓦsturminsternewton-tc.gov.uk).

Sturminster Mill and Museum

DT10 2HW • **Mill** Mid-April to Sept Mon, Thurs, Sat & Sun 11am–5pm • £3, children £1 • ⓣ01747 854355 • **Museum** Jan–March Mon, Fri & Sat 10am–12.30pm; April–Dec Mon, Thurs & Fri 10am–3pm, Sat 10am–12.30pm • Free • ⓦsturminsternewton-museum.co.uk

The only sight of note in Sturminster is the seventeenth-century **Sturminster Mill**, just south of town on the A357, which is still working: people are always around to give you a quick guided tour, or you can wander at will watching the creaking mill machinery doing its job. From the mill, there are idyllic walks along the Stour, where you can often see otters. Other local walks are detailed in the leaflets available from the small town **museum** on Bath Road, which has some modest exhibits on the town's history.

Hambledon Hill

Four miles southeast of Sturminster lies the distinctive hillock of **Hambledon Hill**, an Iron Age fort, with terraced grassy flanks. Best approached from the small village of **Child Okeford** (follow signs to the village surgery from the village centre and you'll see a footpath signed off just past it to the right), it's only around twenty minutes to the top (184m), but it's a steep climb – up which General Wolfe used to train his troops before conquering Québec in the eighteenth century. In 1645, the slopes also witnessed a battle between Cromwell's New Model Army and some four thousand Dorset rebels, who were easily defeated as Cromwell trampled his way towards Sherborne. These days the hill is a far more peaceful nature reserve, protecting the Adonis blue butterfly that flourishes on the chalkland downs. It's a great spot for a picnic, with dazzling views across rolling fields.

Shaftesbury

Perched on top of a hill in the far north of Dorset, with steep gradients on three sides of town, many of **SHAFTESBURY**'s streets enjoy terrific views over the rolling countryside all around. Attracted by the favourable strategic position, it was the legendary King Alfred the Great who, in the ninth century, founded a sturdy, fortified town here, complete with a huge abbey. Little remains of either today, though parts of the former abbey walls form the edge of **Gold Hill**, the town's most famous sight, above which lies the grand **town hall**, built in 1827. Alongside, the fourteenth-century **St Peter's Church** is one of the few reminders of Shaftesbury's medieval grandeur, when it boasted a castle, twelve churches and four market crosses.

Gold Hill

Everything of note in Shaftesbury is within ten minutes' walk of the main High Street, though most visitors immediately seek out **Gold Hill**. This ridiculously pretty cobbled hill, lined with thatched cottages and leading up to sublime views from the top, was immortalized in a 1974 Hovis advertisement, directed by the then little-known Ridley Scott. Anyone familiar with the ad, showing a boy puffing with his bike up the steep cobbles, will instantly recognize the hill, though in fact it is surprisingly short.

Gold Hill Museum

Gold Hill, SP7 8JW • April–Oct daily 10.30am–4.30pm • Free • goldhillmuseum.org.uk

Right at the top of Gold Hill in a former doss house where entertainers and traders stayed during Shaftesbury's markets and fairs is the **Gold Hill Museum**. Inside, the seven rooms are devoted to aspects of the town's history, with displays including a wooden fire engine – Dorset's oldest – and a mummified cat. One room is devoted to domestic life, celebrating the Dorset button-making industry, for which the area was once

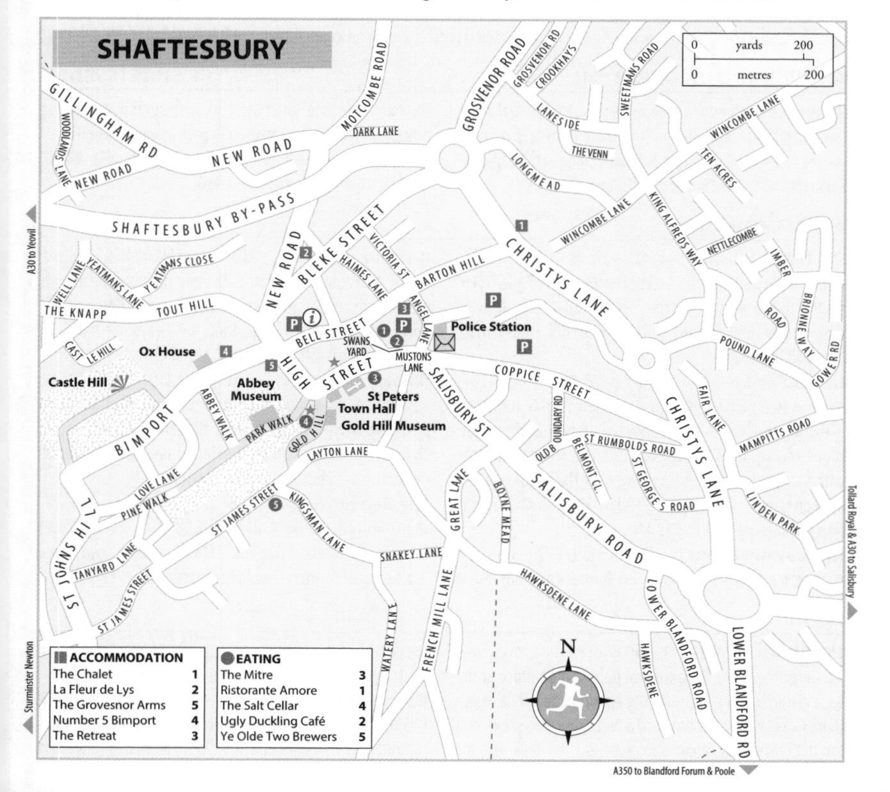

A WALK FROM GOLD HILL

There is a pleasant walk round Shaftesbury that starts by heading down **Gold Hill**. At the bottom, turn right and then right again, and climb either up through the park or further along up Tanyard and Laundry lanes. These take you up to **Park Walk**, laid out in the 1760s as a town promenade and commanding more splendid views. At the end of Park Walk, Love Lane marks the boundary of the original Saxon town. Heading a little north brings you to **Castle Hill**, a grassy viewpoint with more lovely views over the countryside to the north. Nearby, on Bimport, is the sixteenth-century Ox House, which featured as "Old Grove Place" in Hardy's *Jude the Obscure*.

renowned, with a collection of locally made buttons. However, the museum's real joy is its location, with fantastic views down Gold Hill from the pretty gardens.

Abbey Museum

Park Walk, SP7 8JW • Mid-March to Oct daily 10am–5pm • £3 • ⓦ shaftesburyabbey.org.uk

Pilgrims used to flock to Shaftesbury to pay homage to the bones of Edward the Martyr, brought to the **Abbey** in 978; only the footings of the abbey church survive, on Park Walk. The remains now form the **Abbey Museum**, which has displays detailing the history of the abbey – where King Cnut died – including statuary and illustrated manuscripts, and allows access to the scant abbey ruins around an attractive walled garden. Founded in 888 by Alfred the Great, the abbey was the first religious house in the country to be built solely for women, and Alfred's daughter Aethelgifu was the first abbess. Over the years it became one of the most powerful abbeys in England, with lands stretching as far as Purbeck in the south and Bradford-upon-Avon in the north, until it was dissolved by Henry VIII in 1539.

ARRIVAL AND INFORMATION — SHAFTESBURY

By bus Buses pull into the central High St, including the #X9 from Blandford Forum (Mon–Sat 4 daily; 45min; ⓦ damory.co.uk), and the #26/27 from Salisbury (Mon–Fri 3 daily, Sat 2 daily; 45min–1hr 15min; ⓦ salisburyreds.co.uk).

By car There is a large car park just behind the tourist office, though drivers can usually park along the High St.

Tourist office 8 Bell St (Mon–Sat 10am–4pm; ⓣ 01747 853514, ⓦ shaftesburydorset.com).

ACCOMMODATION

The Chalet Christy's Lane, SP7 8DL ⓣ 01747 853945, ⓦ thechalet.biz. About a 5min walk out of the town centre, this is a modern, comfortable B&B with all mod cons and helpful owners, though it is off a busy road. No credit cards. **£80**

La Fleur de Lys Bleke St, SP7 8AW ⓣ 01747 853717, ⓦ lafleurdelys.co.uk. Long-established, family-run hotel with a range of stylish rooms above a highly rated restaurant (three courses for £35). The rooms are comfortable, some with four-posters – the back rooms have the best views, the front ones are on a busy through-road. Minimum two nights over summer weekends. **£130**

The Grovesnor Arms The Commons ⓣ 01747 850580, ⓦ thegrosvenorarms.co.uk. This former coaching inn in the centre of town has had a successful makeover into a buzzy, boutique-style hotel. The rooms are stylish with comfy beds, coffee machines and flatscreen TVs, and the downstairs restaurant is good too, with a wood-fired pizza oven, plus local fish and meat dishes. **£125**

Number 5 Bimport 5 Bimport, SP7 8AT ⓣ 01747 228490, ⓦ fivebimport.co.uk. Small, friendly B&B in an attractive Georgian townhouse in the centre of Shaftesbury. There are just two rooms – the larger one opens onto the garden – so it's best to book in advance. **£110**

The Retreat 47 Bell St, SP7 8AE ⓣ 01747 850372, ⓦ the-retreat.co.uk. A friendly B&B with several large, comfortable rooms, including a family suite, on two floors in a Georgian former schoolhouse; good value. **£90**

EATING

The Mitre High St, SP7 8JE ⓣ 01747 853002, ⓦ youngs.co.uk/pubs/mitre. A traditional pub with a terrace at the back giving lovely views over the countryside, while inside there's a cosy dining room with a wood-burning stove. You can get reasonably priced pub grub, such as steak-and-ale pie (£12). Mon–Thurs 10.30am–11pm, Fri & Sat 10.30am–11.30pm, Sun noon–10.30pm.

Ristorante Amore 6 Mustons Lane, SP7 8AD ⓣ 01747 855566, ⓦ amoreshaftesbury.co.uk. An authentic Italian restaurant with a light and airy dining room in a converted chapel, complete with frescoes on the walls and ceiling. The service is friendly and the food tasty, with dishes such as roast chestnut arancini, gnocchi with gorgonzola and home-made pizzas (two courses £19; three courses £23). Tues–Sat noon–2pm & 6–10pm.

★**The Salt Cellar** Gold Hill, SP7 8JW ⓣ 01747 851838. Right at the top of the hill and with great views, with an attractive, pillar-lined interior and outdoor tables on the cobbles. The menu includes a good range of sandwiches and panini (around £5) plus home-made pies, such as salmon and potato or pork and apple (£5), and daily specials from around £8. Mon–Sat 9am–5pm.

Ugly Duckling Café Swans Yard, SP8 8JQ ⓣ 07772 327559. Friendly little local café tucked away in Swan's Yard with a couple of outdoor tables. Sells good-value, decent lunches (from around £5) such as toasties, baguettes, quiches, sausage rolls, and soup and bread. Cash only. Mon–Sat 9am–4pm, Sun 10am–4pm.

Ye Olde Two Brewers 24 St James St, SP7 8HE ⓣ 01747 854211, ⓦ 2brewers.co.uk. At the bottom of Gold Hill, this traditional pub has an attractive garden with good views, a skittle alley, a log fire, real ales and good pub food, such as Dorset venison burger (£14) and home-made faggots (£12.50). Tues–Sat noon–11pm, Sun noon–6pm.

Cranborne Chase

Designated as an Area of Outstanding Natural Beauty, **Cranborne Chase** became a royal hunting ground during the time of King John (1166–1216), which restricted its cultivation pretty much until the nineteenth century – it remains one of England's most unspoilt stretches of countryside. In 1714, the monarchs gave the land to the Pitt-Rivers family and today most of it is run by the Kingston Lacy estate. A chalk plateau, it stretches over 380 square miles into Wiltshire and is dotted with ancient hillforts and small villages, many with excellent pubs, as well as some superb gardens.

ARRIVAL AND GETTING AROUND — CRANBORNE CHASE

By bus The local buses are so sporadic as to be pretty useless as a means of visiting the area, with a few weekly services and the odd school bus serving the area: see ⓦ damory.co.uk if you are really determined. However, the most feasible way of exploring the region is by car or, if you're up to the steep hills, by bike.

Tollard Royal

The B3081 from Shaftesbury to **TOLLARD ROYAL**, seven miles southeast of Shaftesbury, is one of the most enjoyable roads in the region, winding up precipitous slopes, including the aptly named Zig-Zag Hill, with dazzling views over wooded valleys and pretty hamlets. The road passes through the neighbouring county of Wiltshire before returning to Dorset after a mile or two. Tollard Royal takes its name from the royal hunting lodge that was once here – King John is said to have had 22 in the area. It's still very popular with the hunting and shooting set, including film director Guy Ritchie (former husband of Madonna), who owns nearby **Ashcombe House Estate**, which was previously owned by the photographer Cecil Beaton.

ACCOMMODATION AND EATING — TOLLARD ROYAL

King John Inn SP5 5PS ⓣ 01725 516207, ⓦ kingjohninn.co.uk. A smart, friendly gastropub, which serves fine food using local, seasonal ingredients – look out for the more unusual dishes, such as asparagus and smoked eel risotto (£9) or haunch of venison (£18). The pub is rustic-chic with quarry tiles on the floor and an open fire, and has a great wine list. There are comfortable, stylish rooms above the pub and in a converted coach house across the yard, and a pleasant terraced garden at the back. Kitchen Mon–Sat noon–2.30pm & 7–9.30pm, Sun noon–3pm & 7–9pm; pub daily 11am–11pm. **£90**

Larmer Tree Gardens

Tollard Royal, SP5 5PT • Easter–June, first two weeks in Aug & last two weeks in Sept Sun–Thurs 11am–4.30pm, but check website as opening days vary • £4 • ⓦ larmertreegardens.co.uk

A mile or so from the village of Tollard Royal, the superb **Larmer Tree Gardens** were built as Victorian pleasure gardens by eminent archeologist General Augustus Pitt-Rivers with the aim of "educating" the local villagers and estate workers, and there are some of the finest private gardens in the country. They take their name from an old Wych Elm called the Larmer Tree, where King John would meet his entourage before his hunts. Nowadays there are lawns and walkways through idyllic gardens dotted with peacocks, picnic spots and shelters, together with a teahouse (Sun & bank hols only, 11am–4.30pm). Pitt-Rivers used the gardens for lavish entertainments including illuminated night-time dancing, which visitor Thomas Hardy called "quite the prettiest sight I ever saw". Fittingly, the gardens continue to host music festivals, with the laidback, child-friendly **Larmer Tree Festival** (Ⓦ larmertreefestival.co.uk) in July, and one of the last of the season, the chilled-out **End of the Road Festival**, in September (see p.27).

Farnham and Chettle

Part of the Pitt-Rivers' estate (see p.151), the pretty village of **FARNHAM** consists of an idyllic collection of cottages. A couple of miles southwest of Farnham, the delightful thatched village of **CHETTLE** is home to **Chettle House**, an attractive Queen Anne manor house, built in 1710 by Thomas Archer, whose trademark design can be clearly seen from the outside – all the corners are rounded. The house with its beautifully landscaped gardens was inhabited by the same family for over 150 years, but is not open to the public.

ACCOMMODATION AND EATING — FARNHAM AND CHETTLE

CHETTLE

Castleman Hotel DT11 8DB Ⓣ 01258 830096, Ⓦ castlemanhotel.co.uk. The largely Victorian *Castleman Hotel* is a quirky place – rather old-fashioned and slightly shabby, but in beautiful grounds, with unstuffy service. The spacious rooms have original features, and those at the back look out over the lovely gardens and verdant countryside. It has a highly regarded restaurant serving good-value meals based around local seasonal produce, such as roast partridge (£17). Mon–Sat 7–9pm, Sun noon–2pm & 7–9pm. **£100**

FARNHAM

Farnham Farmhouse DT11 8DG Ⓣ 01725 516254, Ⓦ farnhamfarmhouse.co.uk. A good-value, tranquil place with comfortable rooms in a large Victorian building on a working farm, surrounded by extensive farmland and its own orchard. It also has a heated outdoor pool, and there's an on-site therapy centre, in case you fancy a massage. **£80**

Museum Inn DT11 8DE Ⓣ 01725 516261, Ⓦ museuminn.co.uk. The fine, thatched *Museum Inn* takes its name from the museum Pitt-Rivers founded before its collection was moved to Oxford. Today it is a smart gastropub, serving top-notch local, seasonal and organic food, such as nettle risotto with wild mushrooms or venison carpaccio (mains from £13), plus a good selection of real ales. It also has some comfortable rooms. Kitchen Mon–Fri noon–2pm & 6–9pm, Sat noon–2.30pm & 6–9.30pm, Sun noon–3.30pm & 6–9pm; pub Mon–Sat noon–11pm, Sun noon–10.30pm. **£90**

FARM SHOPS

One of the joys of this rural area is to stock up and head off into the countryside for a picnic. Below are two farm shops where you can pick up some of the freshest local produce.

Famous Hedgehog Bakery Long Crichel, BH21 5JU Ⓣ 01258 830855, Ⓦ famoushedgehogbakery.co.uk. The charming village of Long Crichel, eight miles northeast of Blandford Forum, is home to one of the pioneers of Dorset's local seasonal food movement. The bakery here makes its own organic breads in a wood-fired oven, as well as delicious croissants, cakes and savoury pastries, many made with fruit, herbs and vegetables grown in the gardens next door. You can watch the bakers at work in the old stable block, or browse the shop for local cheeses and vegetables. Tues–Thurs 10am–4pm, Fri 9.30am–4pm, Sat 9am–noon.

Home Farm Tarrant Gunville, DT11 8JW Ⓣ 01258 830083, Ⓦ homefarmshop.co.uk. Seven miles northeast of Blandford Forum, the *Home Farm* café and shop is worth ferreting out for its diverse array of good-quality local produce, including meat, game and eggs from its own farm, local cheeses, vegetables, ice creams and home-made cakes. The tearoom has tables out in the yard, and sells its own delicious cakes, cream teas and light lunches (around £8–9). Tues–Sat 9am–5.30pm, Sun 10am–4pm.

Cranborne

There's not much to the pretty village of **CRANBORNE** (Thomas Hardy's "Chaseborough"), but it's a pleasant enough place with a stream running through it, a couple of pubs and some decent countryside walks. Much of this thriving village is owned by the Cranborne estate (Ⓦcranborne.co.uk), with Viscount Cranborne living in **Cranborne Manor** adjacent to the village. Although the house itself is closed to the public, there is limited access to its attractive landscaped gardens (March–Sept Wed 9.30am–4pm; £6).

ACCOMMODATION AND EATING — CRANBORNE

La Fosse London House, The Square, BH21 5PR Ⓣ01725 517604, Ⓦla-fosse.com. The highly regarded *La Fosse* serves real ales and good food using local ingredients. The menu changes according to what's in season – and they even provide a list of food miles, so you know it really is local – but you can expect dishes such as risotto with Wimborne snails or local venison (two-course menu £23; three-course menu £28.50). There are six stylish rooms upstairs, and a pretty patio at the back. Mon–Sat 7–9pm. **£90**

The Inn at Cranborne BH21 5PP Ⓣ01725 551249, Ⓦtheinnatcranborne.co.uk. Seventeenth-century village pub with a cosy interior – wooden beams, flagstone floors, wood-burners and so on. It serves local ales and has a good-value menu featuring dishes such as wild bream with clams (£15) and Dorset blue vinny risotto (£11). Mon 10.30am–10pm, Tues–Fri 10.30am–11pm, Sat 8.30am–11pm, Sun 8.30am–10pm.

Dorset Heavy Horse Centre

Edmondsham Rd, Verwood, BH21 5RJ • 10am–4pm: April–July & Sept Tues–Sun; Aug daily; Oct Thurs–Sun & half-term • £9.95, under-14s £9.45 • Ⓦdorset-heavy-horse-centre.co.uk

Just east of the village of Edmondsham is the **Dorset Heavy Horse Centre**, a child-friendly farm park offering wagon and pony rides, play areas and the chance to meet various breeds of horse, from giant shire horses to miniature ponies, as well as smaller animals such as pygmy goats and llamas. There is also a re-created blacksmith's, a petting area and café, and kids can help groom and feed the horses. It's a good-value day out, since the entrance fee includes a tractor ride and a horse-drawn wagon ride, and helps to fund the centre's rescue work.

Horton Tower

A couple of miles south of Edmondsham, **HORTON** is home to a good thatched pub, from which there's an hour-long signed round walk to the hexagonal, seven-storey **Horton Tower**, which dominates the landscape hereabouts. Resembling a truncated church spire, the tower was built in the eighteenth century by a local landowner so he could watch the hunts: at the time of its construction, it was the tallest non-religious structure in the country.

ACCOMMODATION AND EATING — HORTON

Drusilla's Inn BH21 7JH Ⓣ01258 840297 Ⓦdrusillasinn.co.uk. Pretty thatched pub with an inglenook fireplace, a pleasant garden and friendly service. It serves real ales and decent pub meals, made from local ingredients where possible, such as home-made pie and mash (£10). Daily 10am–11pm.

The Avon Valley

The **River Avon** runs pretty much due south along the western edges of the New Forest National Park. Although it is shadowed by the busy A338, it doesn't take much to escape the traffic, especially west of pretty **Fordingbridge** where there are some superb walks around the Roman villa at **Rockbourne** and along the Avon itself. To the south, the lively market town of **Ringwood** also has some fine local attractions in the form of two country parks, while at nearby **Hurn**, there's a theme park, dry-ski slope and aviation museum (see box, p.157) to keep the children entertained.

5

Fordingbridge

FORDINGBRIDGE has to contend with the busy A338, which skirts its flanks, as well as a fair amount of through traffic; sadly, this spoils an otherwise pleasant town on the willow-lined banks of the River Avon. There was a ford here at the time of the Domesday Book, superseded by a medieval seven-arched bridge that forms the focal point of the town today. There are some lovely walks up and down the river, including the **Avon Valley footpath**, which runs south to Christchurch in Dorset and north to Salisbury in Wiltshire, 34 miles in total.

Fordingbridge Museum

King's Yard • Easter–Oct Mon–Sat 11am–4pm • Free

Fordingbridge's only attraction is its small **museum**, which contains the usual local bits and bobs, such as a reproduction of an air-raid shelter, a Victorian dolls' house, and artefacts from the now-defunct cobbler's, ironmonger's and blacksmith's shops. It would be of limited interest were it not for the display upstairs on **Augustus John**, who lived in Fordingbridge from 1927 until his death in 1961 (see box below); the display includes a small collection of portraits of his various children and a self-portrait (1931).

ARRIVAL AND INFORMATION — FORDINGBRIDGE

By bus Bus #X3 runs from Fordingbridge (Mon–Sat 2 hourly, Sun 1 hourly) north to Salisbury (35min) and south to Ringwood (20min) and Bournemouth (1hr; W salisburyreds.co.uk).

Tourist office The tourist office is by the museum in King's Yard (April–Oct Mon–Fri 10am–4pm, Sat 10am–1pm; Nov–March Mon, Wed & Fri 10am–4pm; T 01425 654560).

EATING

The George Inn 14 Bridge St, SP6 1AH T 01425 652040, W georgeatfordingbridge.co.uk. The best place to eat in Fordingbridge, right by the bridge, with a lovely terrace overlooking the river. It's nice inside too, well decorated in a contemporary style with comfy sofas and cosy fireplaces: dishes include a fish sharing platter (£17) and *moules frites* (£13), plus more traditional pub dishes and a good range of daily specials. Mon–Sat 10am–11pm, Sun 11am–6pm.

AUGUSTUS JOHN IN FORDINGBRIDGE

An unlikely resident of a small and conservative country town, the flamboyant post-Impressionist artist **Augustus John** lived in Fryern Court in Fordingbridge, where he hosted wild parties attended by such guests as Hollywood film star Tallulah Bankhead, author T.E. Lawrence and the Bloomsbury Group. Britain's leading **portraitist** in the 1920s – he painted figures such as Churchill, Thomas Hardy and George Bernard Shaw – John's bohemian lifestyle did not sit very comfortably with local residents and he made no attempt to disguise his unconventional ways, delighting in upsetting the locals by riding bareback to the local pub, dressing flamboyantly and openly welcoming his many illegitimate offspring to the house. Indeed, John always patted every child he saw in the village on the head, as he said he couldn't be sure whether they were his or not. John had five legitimate children with his first wife Ida, and two with his mistress Dorelia, who lived with John and Ida in a *ménage à trois*, and whom he married after Ida's death. It was with Dorelia that he lived in Fordingbridge, though his many affairs continued, and up until his death in his eighties he continued to out-drink, out-party and out-flirt those half his age. After his death, the town was divided as to whether to celebrate John, or to play down the connection – eventually the celebrators won out and a statue of him was erected along the riverside by the bridge.

John's sister **Gwen** also lived in Fordingbridge at Burgate Cross for a couple of years. She too was an artist and studied under Whistler and Rodin, becoming the latter's mistress – but she was far more introverted than her younger brother and received much less acclaim than him during their lifetimes. Today, however, she is recognized as being the superior artist, a fact that Augustus John freely acknowledged.

Rockbourne Roman Villa

Rockbourne, SP3 3PG • April–Sept Thurs–Sun & bank hols 11am–4pm • £3.70, under-16s £2.50 • ⓦ hampshireculturaltrust.org.uk/rockbourne-roman-villa

Set in lush countryside around three miles northwest of Fordingbridge are the impressive remains of **Rockbourne Roman Villa**, once a large estate at the heart of substantial agricultural land. It was discovered by a farmer in the 1940s and was soon recognized as one of the most important villa complexes in the area. The information centre details what the villa would have been like in the fifth century AD and includes finds from excavations – such as coins and jewellery – and re-creations of the mosaics. The ruins themselves are sprinkled round the grassy fields and include a bathhouse, farm outbuildings, bedrooms and an impressive series of ceramic pipes for underfloor heating. Also worth a visit is the village of **ROCKBOURNE** itself, a mile further north, a picturesque row of thatched cottages and the starting point of a great walk (see box below).

Breamore House

Breamore, SP6 2DF • **House tours** 2–5pm (last tour 4pm): Easter weekend; April & Oct Tues & Sun; May–Sept Tues–Thurs, Sun & bank hols • **Museum** 1–5.30pm: Easter weekend; April & Oct Tues & Sun; May–Sept Tues–Thurs, Sun & bank hols • £9.50, under-16s £6 • ⓦ breamorehouse.com

A couple of miles east of Rockbourne, just off the main A338, **Breamore House** is a sumptuous Elizabethan manor built in 1583. Still used as a family home, the house is stuffed with ornate tapestries, ceramics, period furniture and paintings, including a rare James I carpet. Highlights include the giant Great Hall and the surprisingly spartan kitchens. There is also a small countryside **museum**, with a collection of agricultural tools and machinery including horse wagons, steam-powered farm machinery and some ancient tractors. Set in attractive grounds and parkland, the house, unsurprisingly, makes an appearance in various TV period dramas.

Ringwood

Despite being dominated by the busy A31, **RINGWOOD** remains a pleasant market town with an attractive pedestrianized centre, called The Furlong, and a good range of shops, cafés and facilities. The original settlement grew up along the river – the Domesday Book mentions a church and mill here – and in 1226 Henry III granted it the right to hold its own **market**, a lively affair which still takes place every Wednesday morning (ⓦ ringwood.gov.uk/town/market). It's also the transport hub for the region, though for most of its outlying attractions your own transport is useful.

A ROUND WALK FROM ROCKBOURNE TO WHITSBURY

This easy four-mile (1hr 30min) walk starts at the little car park by the village hall in **Rockbourne** (see above) and passes through farmland, lovely woods and a stud farm. From the car park, turn left onto the road and shortly right into Manor Farm, following the public footpath sign to the side of the farm itself. Keep left into a field and continue straight on, slightly uphill. You then exit the field through a gate into a lovely strip of dense beech woods, particularly beautiful in autumn. You should leave the woods after about fifteen minutes; then continue straight on past the famous Whitsbury stud farm, which trained, among others, the racehorse Red Rum. Turn right after the stud farm and continue down the road into **Whitsbury** (or you could take the signed path opposite, which trails round the back of Whitsbury via the church). The return from Whitsbury to Rockbourne starts from the road opposite the *Cartwheel Inn* (a great spot for lunch). Take the signed public footpath that skirts a few gardens before crossing fields, with lovely rolling views, on a track that wends back down to the water meadows just southeast of Rockbourne. The path is then signed right just before the stream, which takes you along the back of a few houses before heading back to the road near the village hall where you started.

Liberty's Owl, Raptor and Reptile Centre

Crow Lane, BH24 3EA • March, Oct & Feb half-term daily 10am–4pm; April–Sept daily 10am–5pm; Nov–Feb Sat & Sun 10am–4pm • £9, under-16s £6 • ⓦ libertyscentre.co.uk

Southeast of Ringwood, the **Liberty's Owl, Raptor and Reptile Centre** has an extensive collection of snakes, spiders, lizards, tortoises, owls, eagles, hawks and falcons. Also a rescue centre, it puts on daily flying displays of the birds of prey as well as creepy-crawly shows where children can get close to the snakes and spiders.

Ringwood Brewery

138 Christchurch Rd, BH24 3AP • **Shop** Mon–Sat 9.30am–5pm • **Tours** July & Aug Tues 3pm & 6.30pm, Thurs 3pm, Sat noon, 2pm & 4pm, Sun 12.30pm & 2.30pm; Sept Tues 3pm & 6.30pm, Sat noon, 2pm & 4pm, Sun 12.30pm & 2.30pm; Oct–June Tues 6.30pm, Sat noon, 2pm & 4pm, Sun 2.30pm; 1hr 30min; reservations essential • £8.50 • ⓣ 01425 471177, ⓦ ringwoodbrewery.co.uk

Since 1725 when the first brewery was set up to take advantage of the good-quality waters of the River Avon, Ringwood has been home to a lively brewing industry. Today, only one is left, the **Ringwood Brewery**, an independent family-run business that produces some of the best local ales. There's an on-site shop in the brewery yard where you can purchase some old Thumper or Boondoggle to take away, or you can find out more about the brewery's history and the production process – followed by a tasting, of course – on the brewery tour.

Ringwood Town and Country Experience

Salisbury Rd, Blashford, BH23 3PA • Daily 10am–4.30pm; closed Sat from Nov–Easter • £4.75, children £3.95 • ⓦ rtce.co.uk

Just outside Ringwood, off the A338 Salisbury Road, is the **Ringwood Town and Country Experience**, a motley collection of displays representing Olde England. There are re-creations of traditional shops, vintage cars and an old-fashioned railway station – educational for kids, though not so gripping for others.

Blashford Lakes

A series of flooded gravel pits that now form a nature reserve, **Blashford Lakes** lie a short drive north of Ringwood along the A338. It's a pleasant area for a stroll, with marked trails round the lakes from where you can spot various birds including egrets and kingfishers. Based at another lake further along the Ringwood Road (A338), the **New Forest Water Park** (ⓦ newforestwaterpark.co.uk) is home to a **watersports** centre, where you can do paddle-boarding, kayaking, wakeboarding and the like, or have a go on the new *Total Wipeout*-style course with a variety of inflatable obstacles on the lake (April–Sept only; £15/hr).

Moors Valley Country Park

Horton Rd, Ashley Heath, BH24 2ET • Daily: April & May 8am–6pm; June–Aug 8am–7pm; Sept–March 8am–5pm • **Restaurant and visitor centre** Daily 9am–4.30pm • Free • Parking £4–9 a day • ⓦ moors-valley.co.uk

Three miles west of Ringwood at Ashley Heath, **Moors Valley Country Park** is set in coniferous woodland with a large lawned central area encircling a lake. It's a great place to cycle or walk, with numerous trails, picnic spots and play areas as well as a treetop walkway trail, all free. In addition, you can pay to use the golf course, rent bikes, go on Segway tours, a high-ropes adventure course (book in advance on ⓦ goape.co.uk) and a narrow-gauge steam train, which skirts the lake and the excellent playgrounds.

ARRIVAL AND INFORMATION — RINGWOOD

By bus Ringwood is well served by the #X3 bus (2 hourly) to Fordingbridge (15min) Salisbury (45min) and Bournemouth (35min), and the #X6 to Poole (hourly; 1hr 20min). It is also on the fast National Express coach line (11 daily), which links it with Bournemouth (15–25min), Heathrow (2hr 5min–2hr 20min) and London (2hr 30min–3hr 30min). Buses pull in on the main square, The Furlong, where you'll find plenty of parking.

Tourist information Ringwood tourist office, The Furlong, Ringwood, BH24 1AZ (Mon–Thurs 9am–5pm, Fri 9am–4.45pm; ⓣ 01425 470896, ⓦ thenewforest.co.uk).

AVON VALLEY ACTIVITIES

Adventure Wonderland Merritown Lane, Hurn, BH23 6BA ⓦadventurewonderland.co.uk. With a series of low-key rides and play areas based loosely around the theme of Alice in Wonderland, the Adventure Wonderland theme park is best suited to under-12s. Full park £13.95, includes indoor play area. Full park early March, mid-Sept to mid-Oct & Dec Sat & Sun 10am–6pm; Feb half-term, mid-March to mid-Sept & autumn half-term daily 10am–6pm; indoor play area only Nov to mid-Feb daily 10am–6pm.

Aviation Museum Parley Lane, Hurn, BH23 6BA ⓦaviation-museum.co.uk. The Aviation Museum has a large collection of jet and propeller aircraft, including a Vulcan bomber, a helicopter and, oddly, a double-decker bus. You can clamber into them all, sit in the cockpit and driver's seat and play with the controls. It's right opposite the airport, so you get a good view of the planes taking off and landing, and you can even attempt to land your own plane at Bournemouth airport, or a selection of other airports around the world – on the flight simulator, of course. £6, under-17s £3. Daily: April–Oct 10am–5pm; Nov–March 10am–4pm.

Snowtrax Activity Centre Matchams Lane, Hurn, BH23 6AW ⓦsnowtrax.eu. The year-round Snowtrax Activity Centre has the country's widest dry-ski slope. You can rent skis and practise for £13.50 per hour, or take skiing lessons from around £26.50 per hour. They also offer rubber rings and sled descents (around £13/hr), and there's an "Alpine" bar and restaurant, plus a play area in the woods for younger children. Mon–Fri 10am–10pm, Sat 8.30am–10.30pm, Sun 9am–10pm.

ACCOMMODATION

Moortown Lodge 244 Christchurch Rd, BH24 3AS Ⓣ01425 471404, ⓦmoortownlodge.co.uk. Around a 10min walk from the centre of Ringwood, *Moortown Lodge* is a pleasant townhouse with comfortable, clean, smart rooms, including one with a four-poster. The best rooms are at the back; the front ones can be noisy. **£86**

EATING

Bakehouse 24 8–12 Lynes Lane, BH24 1BT Ⓣ01425 485170, ⓦbakehouse24.com. Friendly café where you can enjoy a coffee with delicious cakes, buns and pastries (£2–3) made in the on-site bakery – the chocolate and salted caramel tart is a particular favourite. They also run bread-making courses, or you can simply buy one of their tasty artisan loaves to take away (£2–3). Tues–Sat 8am–5pm, Sun 8am–1pm.

Boston Tea Party 15 The Furlong, BH24 1AT Ⓣ01425 479045, ⓦbostonteaparty.co.uk. Part of a small West Country chain, this busy café serves a wide range of all-day breakfasts, interesting brunch dishes such as sardines on toast with a poached egg (£7.50) plus salads, sandwiches and cakes, often home-made with local ingredients. You can eat at tables outside on the square or inside the former mill building. Mon–Sat 8am–6pm, Sun 9am–5pm.

Framptons 48–50 High St, BH24 1EG Ⓣ 01425 473114, ⓦframptonsbar.co.uk. Ringwood's liveliest café-bar, in a converted hardware shop with large windows and the original wooden cabinets on the walls, plus plenty of comfy sofas and a small garden at the back. It serves a good variety of breakfasts, while lunch includes sandwiches (£6.50–8.50) and pick 'n' mix sharing boards – there's also a tasty array of home-made cakes. In the evening, dishes such as *moules marinière*, steak and roast chicken are on offer (mains £12–15), or you can just come in for a cocktail. Children and dogs are welcome and there's live music on Sunday afternoons. Mon–Wed 8am–10pm, Thurs 8am–11pm, Fri 8am–11.30pm, Sat 8.30am–11.30pm, Sun 9.30am–7pm.

★Lantern Café Folly Farm Lane, BH24 2NN Ⓣ 01425 479926. A mile or so north of Ringwood, just off the A31, the superb *Lantern Café* is in a wonderful wooded location, with tables outside and a cosy wood-burner indoors. Run by the Lantern Community for people with learning disabilities, the light and airy café serves organic bread and pastries made at the on-site bakery, with tasty quiches, soups and a selection of salads made from home-grown organic vegetables. Veggie and vegan options are always available, and the daily specials, such as chickpea and aubergine curry with rice (£6.50), are delicious. Mon–Fri 8.30am–5pm, Sat 9am–3pm.

The Noisy Lobster 25 Market Place, BH24 1AN Ⓣ01425 474253, ⓦnoisylobster.co.uk. In a Grade II-listed building, but with a bright, contemporary interior, *The Noisy Lobster* specializes in local fish and seafood. The daily specials vary, while the menu usually features a generous dish of mussels, an excellent calamari starter plus local crab or lobster, as well as chunky burgers, steaks and veggie dishes (mains £10–18). There's a good-value Fizzy Friday special (fish and chips with a glass of prosecco for £14), and live music on Thursdays. Mon–Sat 11.30am–11pm.

The New Forest

CYCLING IN THE NEW FOREST

The New Forest

Covering about 220 square miles, the New Forest is one of the largest medieval forests in western Europe. It dates from 1079, when William the Conqueror requisitioned it as his hunting ground, and much of the forest is little changed since then, with some of its trees more than 400 years old. While parts of the forest consist of dense deciduous woods, most of it is open heathland, dotted with expanses of coniferous plantations. Made a National Park in 2005, this diverse landscape supports a flourishing wildlife such as rare butterflies, woodpeckers and deer, including the tiny sika deer, descendants of a pair that escaped from nearby Beaulieu in 1904. Its best-known animals are the New Forest ponies that roam at will, though they are officially owned by the Forest Commoners, whose rights to the forest date from Saxon times.

The ponies are just one of the attractions that have turned the area into one of southern England's main rural playgrounds, pulling in some eight million visitors annually. The liveliest and most accessible towns are **Lyndhurst** and **Brockenhurst**; the latter is on the main rail route and is the most agreeable town in the forest. Not so quaint but also on the rail route and close to some great unspoilt countryside is **Ashurst**, while smaller towns such as **Burley** – with its bizarre white witch connections – can also be rewarding. The northern stretches of the forest around **North Gorley** and **Fritham** are often overlooked by visitors but offer some of its finest walks, while the eastern stretches take in the beautiful **Exbury** gardens and the superb riverside **Buckler's Hard** and **Beaulieu**, which is famed for its abbey and must-see National Motor Museum.

The forest is also within reach of the shingle-and-sand beaches of **Highcliffe** and **Barton-on-Sea**, lying between the ancient town of **Christchurch** and the buzzy harbour of **Lymington**, where luxurious yachts ply the waters of a natural harbour alongside ferries to the Isle of Wight.

On summer weekends, the roads in the southern section of the forest can be very slow and busy. The best way, therefore, to experience the forest is by staying in a countryside B&B or camping in one of the official forest campsites; rough camping is not allowed. From all the campsites, there are plenty of cycle trails and footpaths that take you deep into the forest.

Brief history

The name New Forest is misleading, for much of this region's woodland was cleared for agriculture and settlement long before the Normans arrived, and its poor, sandy soils support only a meagre covering of heather and gorse in many areas. The forest was requisitioned by William the Conqueror in 1079 as a hunting ground, and the rights of

BEAULIEU HOUSE

Highlights

❶ **Brockenhurst** Rent a bike to explore the well-marked cycle routes near this idyllic New Forest town, complete with thatched cottages, a ford and great local walks. **See p.165**

❷ **The Pig** Sample fresh forest food at this boutique hotel's restaurant, with a menu featuring home-grown vegetables and foraged local produce. **See p.167**

❸ **National Motor Museum, Beaulieu House** Ride a monorail round the grounds of an ancient monastic estate, complete with a riverside walk at the idyllic village of Beaulieu. **See p.168**

❹ **Christchurch** England's largest parish church is the focal point of this ancient riverside town wedged between the Stour and Avon rivers. **See p.181**

❺ **Lymington** Rub shoulders with the yachting fraternity based in this historic harbour. **See p.186**

❻ **Hurst Castle** Take a boat out to this atmospheric coastal fort dating back to the time of Henry VIII. **See p.188**

HIGHLIGHTS ARE MARKED ON THE MAP ON PP.162–163

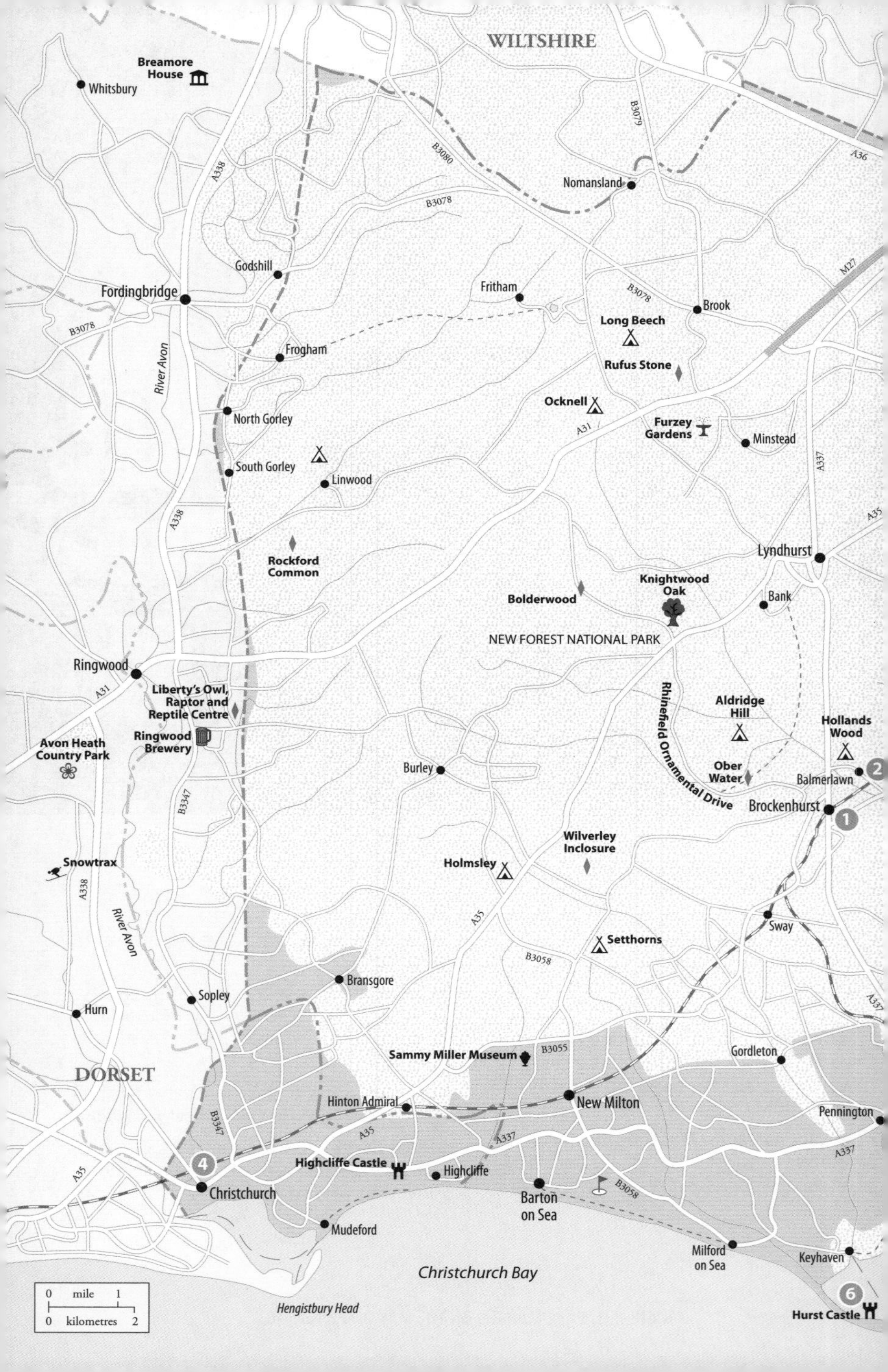
WILTSHIRE
Breamore House
Whitsbury
A338
B3080
B3079
A36
Nomansland
B3078
Godshill
Fordingbridge
Fritham
B3078
Brook
M27
B3078
Long Beech
Frogham
River Avon
Rufus Stone
Ocknell
North Gorley
A31
Furzey Gardens
Minstead
South Gorley
Linwood
A337
A338
A35
Rockford Common
Lyndhurst
Knightwood Oak
Bolderwood
Bank
NEW FOREST NATIONAL PARK
Ringwood
A31
Liberty's Owl, Raptor and Reptile Centre
Rhinefield Ornamental Drive
Aldridge Hill
Hollands Wood
Ringwood Brewery
Avon Heath Country Park
Ober Water
Burley
Balmerlawn
B3347
Brockenhurst
Wilverley Inclosure
Snowtrax
Holmsley
A338
River Avon
A35
Sway
Setthorns
B3058
Bransgore
Sopley
A337
Hurn
Gordleton
Sammy Miller Museum
B3055
DORSET
New Milton
Hinton Admiral
Pennington
B3347
A35
A337
A337
A35
Highcliffe Castle
Highcliffe
Christchurch
Barton on Sea
B3058
Mudeford
Milford on Sea
Keyhaven
Christchurch Bay
0 mile 1
0 kilometres 2
Hengistbury Head
Hurst Castle

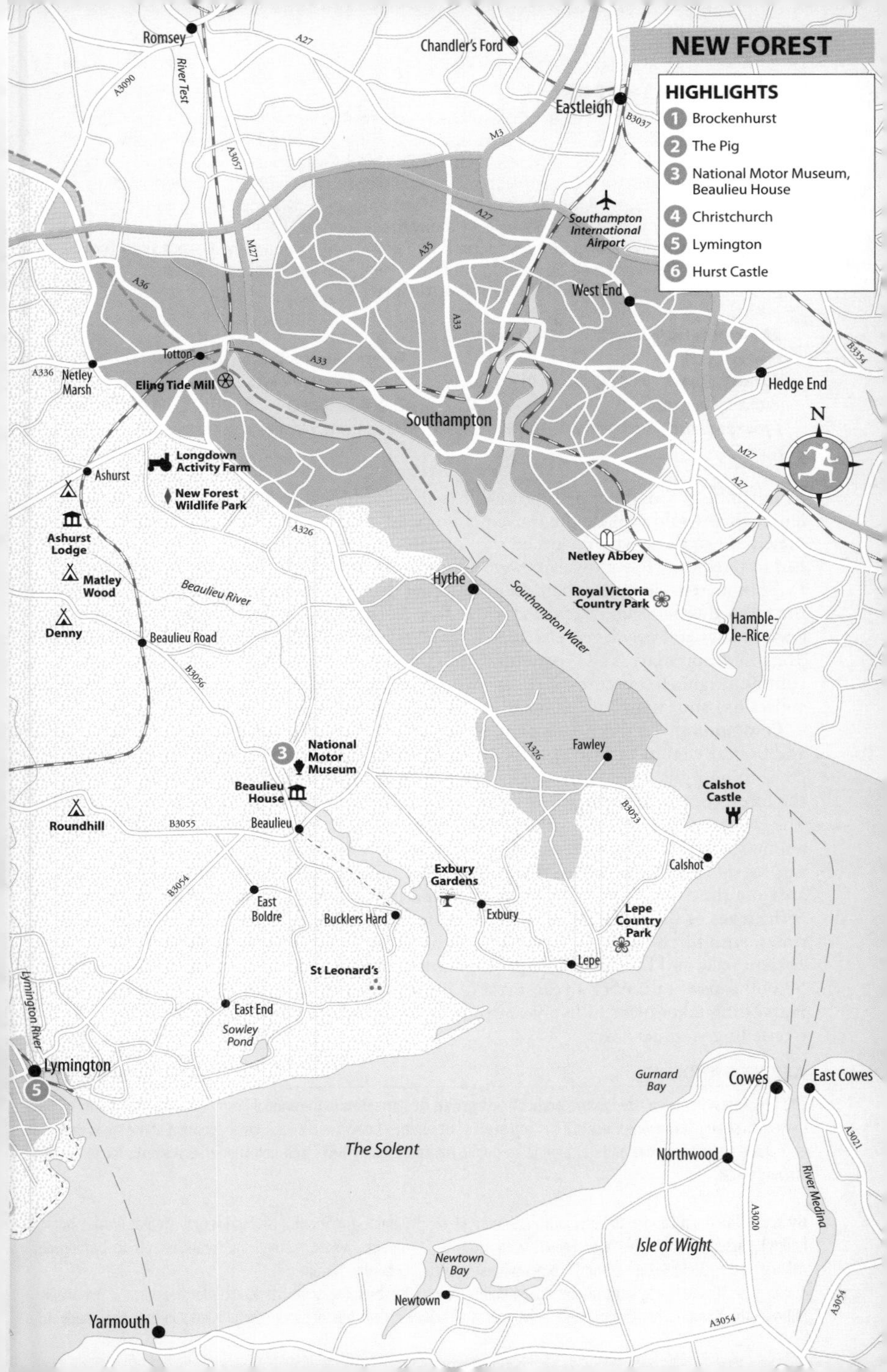
NEW FOREST
HIGHLIGHTS
1 Brockenhurst
2 The Pig
3 National Motor Museum, Beaulieu House
4 Christchurch
5 Lymington
6 Hurst Castle
Romsey
River Test
A27
A3090
Chandler's Ford
Eastleigh
B3037
M3
A3057
M271
A27
Southampton International Airport
A35
A36
A33
West End
Totton
A33
A336
Netley Marsh
Eling Tide Mill
Southampton
Hedge End
B3354
N
M27
A27
Longdown Activity Farm
Ashurst
New Forest Wildlife Park
Ashurst Lodge
A326
Netley Abbey
Matley Wood
Beaulieu River
Hythe
Southampton Water
Royal Victoria Country Park
Denny
Beaulieu Road
Hamble-le-Rice
B3056
Fawley
A326
National Motor Museum
Beaulieu House
Calshot Castle
Roundhill
B3055
Beaulieu
B3053
Calshot
B3054
Exbury Gardens
East Boldre
Exbury
Bucklers Hard
Lepe Country Park
Lepe
St Leonard's
Lymington River
East End
Sowley Pond
Lymington
Gurnard Bay
Cowes
East Cowes
The Solent
Northwood
A3021
A3020
River Medina
Isle of Wight
Newtown Bay
Newtown
Yarmouth
A3054
A3054

CYCLING IN THE FOREST

There are over a hundred miles of waymarked **cycle routes** in the forest – maps and routes are usually provided by bike rental companies, or you can download cycle routes from new-forest-national-park.com/new-forest-cycling.html. Cycle rental is typically £12–20 a day and most places also rent out tag-alongs, trailers, childseats and helmets. It is worth noting, however, that though there are numerous off-road routes, you will find cycling on the New Forest roads themselves less enjoyable. As many roads are narrow with little room for cars to pass, it's worth considering taking your bike on the hop-on, hop-off **New Forest Tour Bus** (maximum 4 bikes/bus: see opposite), so that you can cycle sections of the forest and bus the less interesting bits. The main **bike rental outlets** are:

AA Bike Hire Lyndhurst 02380 283349, aabikehirenewforest.co.uk
Country Lanes Brockenhurst 01590 622627, countrylanes.co.uk
Cyclexperience Brockenhurst 01590 624808, cyclex.co.uk
Forest Leisure Cycling Burley 01425 403584, forestleisurecycling.co.uk
Trax Bike Hire 01425 618562, bikehirenewforest.co.uk. Delivers to any location in the forest.

its inhabitants soon became subservient to those of his game. Forest laws prohibited fences that would impede the movement of wild animals, and terrible punishments were meted out to those who disturbed the animals – hands were lopped off and eyes put out. But in return the forest dwellers were allowed to graze their animals in the open forest. Later monarchs, less passionate about hunting than the Normans, gradually improved the forest dwellers' rights, and today the New Forest enjoys a unique patchwork of ancient laws and privileges, enveloped in an arcane vocabulary dating from feudal times. The forest boundary is the "perambulation", and owner-occupiers of forest land have common rights to obscure practices such as "turbary" (peat cutting), "estover" (firewood collecting) and "mast" or "pannage" (letting pigs forage for acorns and beechnuts).

"**Commoning**" has been a recognized way of life since the mid-sixteenth century and basically refers to living off the forest through "rights of common", largely the continuing right to graze livestock. There are still some three hundred commoners in the forest today, exercising their right to graze around six thousand ponies and cattle. The commoners are vital for the sustainability of the forest, as without the grazing animals much of the forest would be swamped by gorse and scrub. As a result, a trust was set up in 1992 to ensure that commoners could continue to afford to live in the area at a time when much of the forest property was being snapped up by outsiders.

The **trees** of the forest are now much more varied than they were in pre-Norman times, with birch, holly, yew, Scots pine and other conifers interspersed with the ancient oaks and beeches. Perhaps surprisingly, the Forestry Commission harvests some 50,000 tonnes of timber a year, most of it grown in fenced areas known as inclosures. Harvesting takes place in five-year cycles and care should be taken in areas where tree-felling is under way.

GETTING AROUND THE NEW FOREST

The New Forest has been rated as the world's finest **green destination** in the annual Responsible Tourism Awards. This may seem strange to anyone stuck in a traffic jam on a hot summer's day, but is an acknowledgement of the area's drive to encourage people to arrive and get around by public transport. Many B&Bs and hotels offer **discounts** for those not arriving by car.

By train The main London to Weymouth rail route (1–2 hourly) passes through the New Forest, with stops at Ashurst (1hr 35min–2hr 20min), Brockenhurst (1hr 40min–2hr 30min), Sway (1hr 40min–2hr 40min), New Milton (1hr 45min–2hr 45min), and Christchurch (1hr 50min–2hr 50min). Fast trains only stop at Brockenhurst, though, where a small line branches off to Lymington (2 hourly; 10min).

By bus The southern forest stretches have a reasonably efficient bus network. Useful routes include the hourly #6 from Southampton to Ashurst (35min), Lyndhurst (40min), Brockenhurst (55min) and Lymington (1hr 10min); and the coastal routes #X1 and #X2 (1–2 hourly) from Christchurch to Highcliffe (25min), Barton (1hr 10min), Milford (1hr 30min) and Lymington (1hr 45min). Both are run by Blue Star (T 01202 338421, W bluestarbus.co.uk). From July to mid-September, the open-top, hop-on hop-off New Forest Tour (NFT) buses (W thenewforesttour.info) run three circular routes around the Forest: the green route (7 daily) from Lyndhurst to Brockenhurst (15min), Lymington (30min), Beaulieu (50min) and Exbury (1hr 10min); the red route (6 daily) from Lyndhurst to Burley (20min), Ringwood (40min), Fordingbridge (55min) and Sandy Balls (1hr 5min), returning via Ashurst (1hr 40min); and the blue route (8 daily) from Brockenhurst to Burley (15min), New Milton (1hr), Barton (1hr 10min), Milford (1hr 30min) and Lymington (1hr 50min).

By car The speed limit through much of the New Forest is 40mph, and drivers should take particular care as ponies frequently graze at the side of – or even on – the roads, often with their foals.

By electric car Increasingly popular are the tiny, two-seater electric Twizy cars that are available to rent from several hotels in the forest as well as from Brockenhurst train station and Lymington (£29/half-day, £42/day; W hireatwizy.co.uk).

By bike The area is fully geared up for cycling, with plenty of off-road bike tracks: cycle rental companies have maps of the best ones (see box opposite).

On foot With 150 miles of car-free gravel tracks in the Forest, walking is superb – we list some of the best throughout this chapter. The Ordnance Survey Leisure Map 22 of the New Forest is best for exploring.

Brockenhurst and around

You'll frequently find New Forest ponies strolling down the high street of **BROCKENHURST**, the most attractive and liveliest town in the forest. Surrounded by idyllic heath and woodland and with a ford at one end – which usually attracts crowds of children when cars splash through – it is highly picturesque despite being spliced by the main London to Weymouth train line, making it upmarket commuter territory. The main street, Brookley Road, is where you'll find the bulk of shops, banks and places to eat and drink. There are no specific sights – most people come just to wander through the charming lanes lined with thatched cottages, soak up the traditional village atmosphere and stock up on picnic supplies. Brockenhurst is also within an easy cycle ride of three attractive forest campsites (see box, p.178).

Ober Water

One of the nicest picnic spots in the forest, **Ober Water** is a gently flowing stream running through a mixture of woodland and open grassland. It's an easy mile or so walk or cycle here from Brockenhurst, or you can park at a small car park opposite Aldridge Hill campsite. In summer, the stream is busy with kids playing on the rope swings dangling over the water from overhanging trees; in winter, when the campsite closes, the place is usually deserted. It also marks the starting point of some fine walks and bike rides – the best one to Bank (see box below).

ARRIVAL AND ACTIVITIES — BROCKENHURST

By train The train station is at the eastern edge of town with 1–2 hourly services from London (1hr 40min–2hr 30min), Southampton (15–20min), Bournemouth (25min) and Poole (40min). From the station, turn left and left

A CYCLE OR WALK FROM OBER WATER TO BANK

The four-mile track from **Ober Water** to **Bank** is one of the loveliest in the entire forest either on foot or by bike. From Ober Water, continue on the track which runs northeast, parallel to the stream. After half a mile you cross a bridge – another lovely spot for a picnic – before the track passes into the forest. Then follow the well-signed path (signed Lyndhurst) which wends its way slowly uphill through Forestry Commission land before emerging on a small country lane. Turn left here and you head downhill through the village of Bank, with its wonderful pub, the **Oak Inn** (see p.174).

again for Brookley road.

By bus Buses pull up alongside the train station. Brockenhurst is on the #6 route, and from July to mid-Sept there are regular NFT buses from Lymington and Lyndhurst (see p.165).

Cycling Brockenhurst is known for its cycling routes, and you can rent bikes from Cycle Experience right by the station (from £17/day; 01590 624808, cyclex.co.uk). They also give out maps of the best local routes.

ACCOMMODATION

Balmer Lawn Lyndhurst Rd, S042 7ZB 01590 623116, balmerlawnhotel.com. This giant Victorian pile was built as a hunting lodge; it was once visited by George V and still exudes (rather faded) colonial splendour. The rooms vary enormously, with some having been refurbished in a contemporary style, while others are more traditional. There are interconnecting rooms for families (£300), plus indoor and outdoor pools and a restaurant. **£100**

Careys Manor Lyndhurst Rd, S042 7RH 01590 623551, careysmanor.com. This Victorian country house and former home of Charles II's forester, John Carey, has a range of rooms, from traditional four-posters in the manor house to more contemporary ones with a terrace or balcony in the modern wing. It has a highly regarded Thai spa – though guests have to pay extra to use it – and three restaurants, the fine-dining *Cambium* restaurant, a less formal French brasserie, and the Thai *Zen Garden*. **£150**

Cottage Lodge Hotel Sway Rd, S042 7SH 01590 622296, cottagelodge.co.uk. A short walk from the main street, this excellent, small eco-friendly hotel is in a former forester's cottage, parts of which date from 1650. It has a variety of clean, comfortable rooms – some with four-poster beds made from local trees, some with private patios and one its own wood-burner. It's also home to the highly regarded *Fallen Tree Restaurant* (fallentreerestaurant.co.uk). **£90**

New Park Manor Lyndhurst Rd, S042 7QH 01590 623467, newparkmanorhotel.co.uk. A stylish,

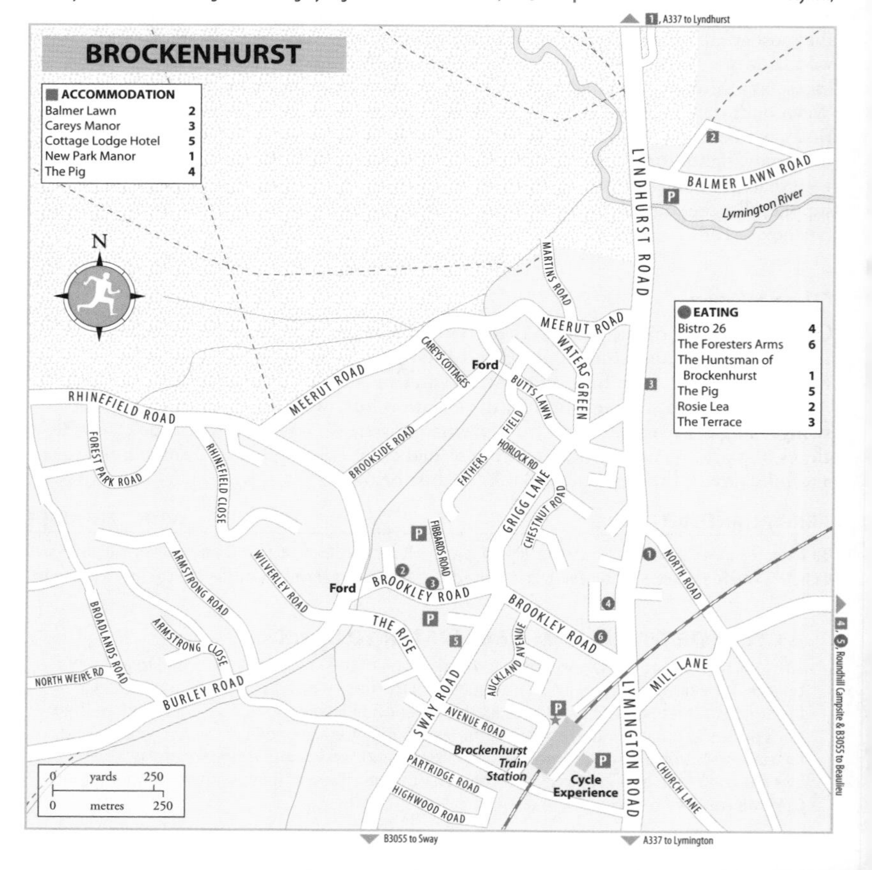

luxurious and family-friendly country-house hotel two miles north of Brockenhurst. The staff are helpful and there's a fantastic spa – with an outdoor hot tub where you can sip champagne while watching the deer in the neighbouring fields – as well as a restaurant specializing in local produce. It's a great choice if you're travelling with kids: there are plenty of rooms that sleep families (£235), as well as interconnecting rooms, and childcare in the hotel crêche is free. **£135**

★**The Pig** Beaulieu Rd, SO42 7QL ⓣ01590 622354, ⓦthepighotel.co.uk/brockenhurst. A couple of miles out of Brockenhurst, set in rural splendour, this sumptuous Georgian country house with its own tennis courts has boutique rooms in the main building, once a royal hunting lodge, plus spacious, contemporary rooms in the tastefully converted outbuildings. The smart but casual ethos – billed as "shabby chic" – is great for couples or families, with a games room and free use of wellies. You can eat your fab breakfast and other meals in the airy conservatory (see below). **£185**

EATING

Bistro 26 26 Lyndhurst Rd, SO42 7RL ⓣ01590 622459. Friendly local restaurant serving good-value bistro-style meals, such as River Test trout or Goan lamb curry (mains £13–17). The two-course lunch menu is a steal at £10. Daily noon–3pm & 6–10pm.

The Foresters Arms 10 Brookley Rd, SO42 7RR ⓣ01590 623397, ⓦforestersarms-brockenhurst.co.uk. Friendly, traditional pub with a few outdoor tables, right by the station. It serves good portions of reasonably priced classic pub food and is popular with students from the nearby college. Mon–Sat 11am–11.30pm, Sun 11.30am–11pm.

The Huntsman of Brockenhurst Lyndhurst Rd, SO42 7RH ⓣ01590 622225, ⓦthehuntsmanofbrockenhurst.com. A spacious, recently refurbished pub with several different bars and lounges and a pleasant garden and some smart en-suite rooms upstairs (£120). It serves up decent pub dishes, as well as steaks cooked on a charcoal grill (£17–27) and pizzas from a wood-fired pizza oven (£8–12.50). Mon–Thurs noon–11pm, Fri & Sat noon–midnight, Sun noon–10.30pm.

★**The Pig** Beaulieu Rd, SO42 7QL ⓣ01590 622354, ⓦthepighotel.co.uk/brockenhurst. Brockenhurst's best restaurant is in a fabulous country-house hotel (see above) where you dine in a lovely conservatory. All the ingredients are locally sourced with some from the hotel's own gardens or the surrounding forest – fish is smoked on site, eggs come from its own chickens – and the results are delicious. Try the home-smoked haddock salad, with poached egg and garden rocket (£13), or New Forest wood pigeon with locally foraged mushrooms (£14). Daily noon–2.15pm & 6.30–9.30pm.

Rosie Lea 6 Brookley Rd, SO42 7RBA ⓣ01590 622797. Lovely tearoom serving delicious home-made cakes and tasty sandwiches on vintage china. You can sit outside – they provide blankets and hot-water bottles when it's cold – or at one of the cosy tables inside; dogs welcome. Soup and a fluffy home-made cheese scone (£4.25) followed by a delicious cupcake hits the spot at lunchtime. They have a second, very pretty, branch, *Rosie Lea Kitchen*, serving similar food in the Setley Ridge Vineyard on Lymington Road, just outside Brockenhurst. Daily 9am–5pm.

The Terrace 58 Brookley Rd, SO42 7RA ⓣ01590 624625. Small café with a sunny terrace for breakfast, good for well-priced lunches such as home-made quiches, sandwiches or sausage and mash (all around £8), or just a drink – the smoothies are recommended. Daily 9am–5pm.

Rhinefield Ornamental Drive

The narrow and winding **Rhinefield Ornamental Drive** was once part of the Rhinefield House estate. The house was built in 1887, and exotic plants such as giant redwoods, azaleas and rhododendrons were planted on the surrounding land. Much of its former

A ROUND WALK NEAR BROCKENHURST

A fine hour's **round walk** along a disused railway track begins just out of town on the **road to Sway**, taking in open heathland and some dense woodland. By car, follow the road out of Brockenhurst that crosses the main rail line, then turn right. The road passes under a railway bridge – park on the right just afterwards, by a second raised railway line. The walk begins by passing under this line and goes along a wide track. When you reach a farm, turn left and follow the old dismantled railway line that once ran to Burley and Ringwood. After twenty minutes or so passing through rolling heathland, you'll cross a bridge over a path by an electricity substation. Take the track down to this lower path and go past the substation. The path leads into shady woodland. After 200m or so, take the first main path off to the right. This heads out of the woods and back across the heath, rejoining the track you started on by the farm.

grounds are now part of the New Forest and have walking trails through them. You can see the giant redwoods – including England's tallest, at 50m – on the marked Tall Trees trail, a mile-and-a-half walk from either Brock Hill or Blackwater car parks, which are near the bottom of the Ornamental Drive by Blackwater Arboretum, a small enclosure packed with various trees from around the world.

ACCOMMODATION **RHINEFIELD**

Rhinefield House Hotel SO42 7QB ⓣ01590 622922, ⓦhandpickedhotels.co.uk/rhinefieldhouse. Set in stunning grounds with its own small lake, indoor and outdoor pools and gastronomic restaurant, this sumptuous Victorian pile is unsurprisingly popular with honeymooners. There are some classic rooms in the main house, plus larger rooms in the more modern garden wing, many with views over the New Forest. **£170**

Beaulieu and around

Situated in the southeast corner of the New Forest, the village of **BEAULIEU** (pronounced "Bewley", and from the French meaning "Beautiful Place") is embraced by the extensive land of the Beaulieu estate. The village feels rooted in some distant England of the past: its quaint high street is lined with traditional shops and a minuscule primary school, while donkeys and New Forest ponies amble at will. But most visitors bypass the village to head to the main attraction of **Beaulieu House**, or to the nearby village of **Buckler's Hard**, also owned by the Beaulieu estate.

Beaulieu was the site of one of England's most influential monasteries, a Cistercian house founded in 1204 by King John – in remorse, it is said, for ordering a group of supplicating Cistercian monks to be trampled to death. Built using stone ferried from Caen in northern France and Quarr on the Isle of Wight, the **abbey** managed a self-sufficient estate of ten thousand acres, but was dismantled soon after the Dissolution. Its refectory now forms the parish church, which, like everything else in Beaulieu, has been subsumed by the Montagu family – the Montagus have owned a large chunk of the New Forest ever since one of Charles II's illegitimate progeny was made duke of the estate.

Beaulieu House and the National Motor Museum

Beaulieu, SO42 7ZN • Daily: June–Sept 10am–6pm; Oct–May 10am–5pm • £24, under-18s £12; advance online booking £19, under-18s £9 • ⓦbeaulieu.co.uk

Owned by the Montagus since 1538, **Beaulieu House** is a superbly arranged tourist complex, whose main draw, deservedly, is the **National Motor Museum**, which houses enough horsepower to make Jeremy Clarkson swoon. The collection was the brainchild of the third Lord Montagu who lived at Beaulieu until his death in 2015 and amassed some 250 cars and motorcycles including spindly antiques and recent classics, Formula 1 cars rubbing shoulders with land-speed racers, vintage Rolls-Royces, Ferraris and a Sinclair C5. Even if you're no petrolhead, you'll recognize many of the vehicles in the museum – Donald Campbell's record-breaking Bluebird, flying cars from Harry Potter and even Mr Bean's Mini, as well James Bond's Jaguar from *Die Another Day*. You can clamber on the London double-decker bus and nose around the re-created 1930s garage, while the entertaining ride-through display, "Wheels", takes you on a trip through the history of motoring. The upper floor features the motorcycle gallery, home to the largest collection of Ducati bikes outside Italy. Don't miss, too, the **World of Top Gear exhibition**, where some of the programme's more outlandish vehicles are on display – in the condition that the presenters left them – along with behind-the-scenes footage from the show.

An undersized **monorail** runs around the estate and through the Motor Museum; it's worth riding for a bird's-eye view of the cars, though it's an easy ten-minute walk from the museum through attractive gardens to the other sights. Formerly the abbey's gatehouse, the fourteenth-century **Palace House** is the unexceptional family home of the Montagus: its history is brought to life by guides dressed in Victorian clothing, who relate anecdotes about the Montagu-related memorabilia. Other draws on the estate include a **Secret Army exhibition** tracing how spies were trained here before being sent on missions in World War II, and the remains of the Cistercian **abbey**, whose undercroft houses an exhibition depicting medieval monastic life. Leave time, too, to explore the superb **gardens**, which spread alongside the river.

ARRIVAL AND DEPARTURE — BEAULIEU

By car There's a small pay-and-display car park in Beaulieu village, or you can try and find a spot along the high street.
By bus Regular NFT green route buses run from Brockenhurst or Lymington to Beaulieu's main street and outside the National Motor Museum from July to mid-Sept (see p.165).

ACCOMMODATION AND EATING

Montagu Arms Hotel SO42 7ZL ⊕01590 612324, ⓦmontaguarmshotel.co.uk. The best place to stay in the village is the *Montagu Arms Hotel*, housed in a seventeenth-century building with open fires and a lovely garden: all the rooms are smart and comfortable and some have four-poster beds. You can enjoy good-quality pub food at the on-site *Monty's Inn* (daily 11am–3pm & 6–11pm), or push the boat out for a meal at *The Terrace*, the New Forest's only Michelin-starred restaurant. The attractive dining room overlooks a pretty garden, where you can eat in the summer. The menu uses local, seasonal ingredients, some grown on the hotel grounds, and features the likes of Dorset Rose veal and South Coast sea bass. The three-course lunch menu is good value at £30, while the full tasting menu costs £90 a head. Tues 7–9.30pm, Wed–Sun noon–2.30pm & 7–9.30pm. **£160**

Steff's Kitchen High St, SO42 7YB ⊕01590 614951. Popular café attached to a garden centre, with tables out front on Beaulieu's pretty high street, plus plenty more in a flowery courtyard. Using local ingredients, it serves tasty sandwiches on artisan bread (£5–7), plus interesting toasties, such as Nutella and banana or Lymington crab and smoked local cheese. They also have weekly specials, all home-made, and a decent roast on Sundays. Daily: Nov–March 9am–4.30pm; April–Oct 9am–5pm.

Buckler's Hard

SO42 7XB • Daily: April–Sept 10am–5pm; Oct–March 10am–4.30pm • £6.50, under-18s £4.50; entrance fee includes all-day parking • ⓦbucklershard.co.uk

In an even more wonderful setting than Beaulieu is **BUCKLER'S HARD**, a couple of miles downstream on the River Beaulieu. A lovely two-mile **track** links Beaulieu and Buckler's Hard, passing through meadows and woods. A slightly longer but more enjoyable path runs alongside the river itself, taking you past the mudflats and oak woods, most part of the North Solent nature reserve. If you park in Beaulieu and walk along the river, you can wander freely throughout the village without paying the admission fee: you will need to buy a ticket, however, if you want to visit the museum.

Buckler's Hard doesn't look much like a shipyard now, but from Elizabethan times onwards dozens of men-of-war were assembled here from giant New Forest oaks. Several of Nelson's ships were launched here, to be towed carefully by rowing boats to Portsmouth. The largest house in this hamlet belonged to Henry Adams, the master shipbuilder responsible for most of the Trafalgar fleet; it's now an upmarket hotel and restaurant (see p.170). This contrasts with the simple Shipwrights Cottage nearby,

BOAT TRIPS FROM BUCKLER'S HARD

From Buckler's Hard, you can take a thirty-minute **boat trip** down one of the few private rivers in the country (Easter–Oct 8–9 daily; £5, under-18s £3), past oyster beds, flashy yachts and rural scenery. It's hard to believe that this peaceful, attractive section of river was requisitioned during World War II by the armed forces, and Mulberry harbours were constructed here, with secret agents trained in the remote riverside houses before being sent abroad for daring missions.

A ROUND CYCLE RIDE FROM EAST END TO BUCKLER'S HARD

This is an easy twelve-mile round cycle route which avoids the cost of parking at Buckler's Hard and takes in the gentle tamed countryside of this stretch of the New Forest, through ancient farmland and past well-heeled farmhouses. Park anywhere in the village of **East End**, around 4.5 miles from Buckler's Hard, and head out on the Lymington Road, past the *East End Arms* pub (see below). After a few hundred metres, turn left (signed Sowley), then turn right down **Tanner's Lane**. Though this is a cul-de-sac, it's a worthwhile detour to a small shingle beach with great views across to the Isle of Wight. Double back to Lymington Road and turn right towards **Sowley**, passing ancient oaks and a large fishing lake, Sowley Pond. After two miles or so, turn right on the road to Buckler's Hard, which is an easy 2.5 miles, via the impressive ruins of **St Leonard's** tithe barn. The return is the same way, but continue straight on at the Sowley turn-off, which is signed East End.

former home of Thomas Burlace, who worked on Nelson's favourite ship, the *Agamemnon*. At the top of the village, the **Maritime Museum** traces the history of the great ships and incorporates buildings preserved in their eighteenth-century form.

ACCOMMODATION AND EATING — BUCKLER'S HARD

Master Builders Hotel SO42 7XB ⊕0844 8153399, ⊕themasterbuilders.co.uk. Picturesque and peaceful, this wonderfully quirky hotel is in a sixteenth-century building with open fires and a superb location overlooking the river. The rooms are a mixed bunch: some have east Asian flourishes, others have a contemporary style, and some have views over the river. There's also the decent *Riverview* restaurant, and the *Yachtsman's Bar* – you can take your drink outside onto the lawns in nice weather. The bar menu has sandwiches, snacks, and mains such as New Forest sausage and mash (£10–14), while the restaurant menu is slightly pricier and more formal. Restaurant Mon–Sat noon–2.30pm & 7–9pm, Sun 12.30–3pm & 7–9pm; bar daily noon–9pm. **£145**

The East End Arms Lymington Rd, East End, SO41 5SY ⊕01590 626223, ⊕eastendarms.co.uk. This cosy pub – located at the start of an excellent round cycle ride to Buckler's Hard (see box above) – is owned by Dire Straits bassist, John Illsley. There's a bustling front bar serving cask ales, and a larger back lounge where you can enjoy excellent locally sourced grilled fish and meats (£13–17) while trying to identify the black-and-white photos of rock stars on the walls. There are five comfortable rooms upstairs. Mon–Thurs 1.30am–3pm & 6–11pm, Fri–Sat noon–11pm. **£110**

St Leonard's

Around three and a half miles southeast of Beaulieu, there's little nowadays to **St Leonard's** apart from the towering walls of a ruined tithe barn – once one of the largest in the country and partly dating back to the fourteenth century. There's also a later roofed barn, itself dating back to the sixteenth century, and both structures now stand in splendid isolation.

The eastern New Forest

The eastern extremities of the New Forest are relatively unvisited – mainly because of the looming eyesore of the Fawley oil refinery, whose smoke stacks dominate what would otherwise be pleasant countryside. This section of the forest is a strange mixture of industrial blight and thatched rural idyll, but is worth exploring for its colourful gardens at **Exbury** and the interesting riverside communities of **Calshot** and **Hythe** that abut the Solent.

Exbury Gardens

Exbury, SO45 1AZ • Daily mid-March to early Nov 10am–6pm • £11, under-15s £3.30 • ⊕exbury.co.uk

Three miles southeast of Beaulieu are **Exbury Gardens**, twenty miles of pathways wending through superb cultivated and semi-wild gardens abutting the Beaulieu River; a small steam train (£4.50 extra) trundles round much of the grounds. The gardens were the brainchild of Lionel Nathan de Rothschild, who in the 1920s set out to create one of the best woodland gardens in the UK. His banking family was immensely wealthy, but Lionel saw himself more as a gardener than a banker and bought the Exbury estate to indulge his passion. He dug ponds, laid irrigation pipes and planted the gardens with exotic species, only to die in 1942 before the gardens were completed. The Navy requisitioned the house; after the war, Lionel's son continued work on the gardens, and the family continues to develop it. Today you can wander round superb azalea and hydrangea walks, admire bog gardens and lawns, picnic by the river and visit the tearooms.

Calshot Castle

Easter–Sept daily 10.30am–4.30pm • £3.30, under-19s £2.30; EH • W www.english-heritage.org.uk/visit/places/calshot-castle

The sea turns into the river at the little village of **CALSHOT**, which has a pleasant shingle beach, though the scenery here is far more industrial. That doesn't prevent the beach huts here swapping hands for five-figure sums. The beach peters out at **Calshot Castle**, a diminutive round fort with a little moat built by Henry VIII – there are great views from its upper rooms over the estuary, packed with ferries, boats and lumbering container ships. Next to the castle is the giant, warehouse-like **Activities Centre** (T 02380 892077, W hants.gov.uk/calshot.htm), one of the largest outdoor activity centres in the country. As well as running a variety of watersports courses, there is also a dry-ski slope, a velodrome and climbing walls, plus a café-bar with good views.

Hythe

The small town of **HYTHE** sits opposite Southampton on the busy Southampton Water and was where Sir Christopher Cockerell first developed the hovercraft. Its other claim to fame is that it is the home of the world's oldest **pier train**, a fantastic contraption that dates back to 1922 and carries passengers down an extremely long pier to a ferry terminal for connections to Southampton. You can walk it in around ten minutes, but the train ride (Mon–Thurs 6.10am–8.40pm, Fri–Sat 7.10am–10.10pm, Sun 9.40am–5.40pm; every 30min; £1.60 single) is more fun, connecting with the **ferry** to Town Quay in Southampton (every 30min; 12min; £5.80 return). From Town Quay, a free shuttle bus takes passengers to WestQuay shopping centre (see p.224) and Southampton central station. There is not a lot else to Hythe, though a few Georgian buildings survive along the largely postwar high street and there is a lively Tuesday market. Also worth seeking out is the **marina** to the north of the pier, which has great views across the waters – especially impressive when the cruise liners sail into Southampton.

Ashurst and around

On the eastern edges of the New Forest, **ASHURST** can best be described as functional. It has a good range of shops, is right on the main rail line from Weymouth to London, has a fine campsite (see p.178) and makes a handy base for local walks and excellent children's attractions.

Longdown Activity Farm

Deerleap Lane, SO40 7EH • Mid-Feb to Sept & late Dec daily 10am–5pm; Oct daily 10am–4.30pm • £9, under-15s £8 • W longdownfarm.co.uk

Around a mile southeast of Ashurst, **Longdown Activity Farm** is great for younger children, with plenty of farm animals to admire and cuddle – so it's best to come in spring when there are lots of cute babies – and children can help feed the ducks, goats or calves, handle rabbits and guinea pigs, or collect eggs from the chickens. There are also tractor rides and go-karts and wet-weather activities including a ball park, a hay barn and trampolines.

New Forest Wildlife Park

Deerleap Lane, SO40 4UH • Daily: April–Oct 10am–5.30pm; Nov–March 10am–4.30pm or dusk • £10.95, under-17s £7.95 • Ⓦ newforestwildlifepark.co.uk

The **New Forest Wildlife Park** has a circular trail that takes you past and through various glass cages and enclosures, many containing animals that are (or were) native to the UK, such as dormice, pine martens, badgers, wild boar, foxes and wolves. Most prevalent are several species of owl – though they are kept in somewhat cramped conditions – and various species of playful otters: look for signs advertising feeding times. You can also wander through enclosures containing wallabies and deer, and there's a butterfly house (summer only), a decent café and pleasant picnic area.

Eling Tide Mill

Eling Lane, SO40 9HF • Ⓣ 02380 869575, Ⓦ elingtidemill.org.uk

Towards Totton on Eling Creek, at the head of Southampton Water, lies **Eling Tide Mill**, one of the few functioning tide mills left in England. You can watch the flour being milled in the same way as it has been for thousands of years, though the times it works depend on the tide; the mill is currently closed for refurbishment and should reopen in 2017 (check website for the latest news).

ARRIVAL AND DEPARTURE — ASHURST

By train There are 1–2 hourly services between Ashurst and London (1hr 35min–2hr 20min), Brockenhurst (10min), Southampton (15min), Bournemouth (35min) and Poole (50min). The station is on the edge of town; turn right when you exit and the centre is a couple of minutes' walk.

By bus Buses stop on the main road opposite the train station. Ashurst is on both the #6 bus route and, in summer, the red NFT circular route (see p.165).

ACCOMMODATION AND EATING

Hotel Terra Vina 174 Woodlands Rd, Netley Marsh, SO40 7GL Ⓣ 02380 293784, Ⓦ hotelterravina.co.uk. A mile and a half from Ashurst, the upmarket *Hotel Terra Vina* has comfortable boutique rooms, some with their

A ROUND WALK NEAR ASHURST

This two-hour **round walk** starts at the **Ashurst campsite** (see p.178) and, despite its proximity to the A35 and main rail line, takes in some surprisingly unspoilt heath and woods. Turn right at the access road to the campsite and walk across the field, parallel to the A35. After ten minutes you'll reach a quiet side road (to Ashurst Lodge). Turn left and follow the road through ancient woodland. After fifteen minutes, you'll reach the entrance to the lodge. Turn right before the entrance and follow the track that skirts a high wooden fence and bears left across open heath, where you'll often see plenty of ponies. Follow this path, with the fence to the left, and it soon crosses a clear-flowing stream. The path then climbs a low hill. At the top of the hill, the path divides a couple of times – keep right both times and the path heads towards Mapley woods, full of ancient oaks. The path then veers right, following the edge of the treeline. Within ten minutes, a track crosses the one you are on. Turn right here and head back across open heathland, parallel to the way you came. You'll cross back over the stream over a different bridge, keeping straight on when smaller paths cross the main one. You may see deer on this open stretch, before the path enters another fantastic wood full of ancient trees. Pick up a path through the woods shortly on the right. This follows the edge of the woods all the way back to the Ashurst Lodge road, which you cross to return the way you started, with the campsite ahead of you.

own terraces, in lovely wooded surroundings. It has stylish decor, an outdoor pool and a highly regarded restaurant with an impressive wine list, overseen by owner Gerard Basset, one of the world's top sommeliers. Daily noon–2.30pm & 7–9.30pm. **£165**

The New Forest Lyndhurst Rd, SO40 7AA 02380 292721, newforestashurst.co.uk. This substantial pub right by the station has a large restaurant area and garden with a children's play area overlooking rolling New Forest countryside. There's live music some weekends and an excellent Sunday carvery; at other times, filling mains start at around £11. Mon–Fri 11am–11pm, Sat 9am–11pm, Sun 11am–10.30pm.

Lyndhurst and around

An attractive New Forest town, **LYNDHURST** is sadly blighted by a choking one-way system that funnels much of the New Forest's traffic right down the high street – in high summer it's often largely stationary. The town's main sight is the brick **parish church**, St Michael's, worth a glance for its William Morris glass, a fresco by Lord Leighton and the grave of Mrs Reginald Hargreaves, better known as Alice Liddell – Lewis Carroll's model for Alice, who spent her life in Lyndhurst. Most people visit Lyndhurst, however, for practical reasons: it has a good selection of accommodation and restaurants as well as the **New Forest Centre** (daily 10am–5pm, last entry 4pm; £4; newforestcentre.org.uk), which houses a modest museum focusing on the history, wildlife and industries of the forest.

To escape the traffic, rent a bike (see box, p.164) and head out of town beyond the lovely viewpoint hillock of Bolton's Bench. Alternatively, head a mile south to the

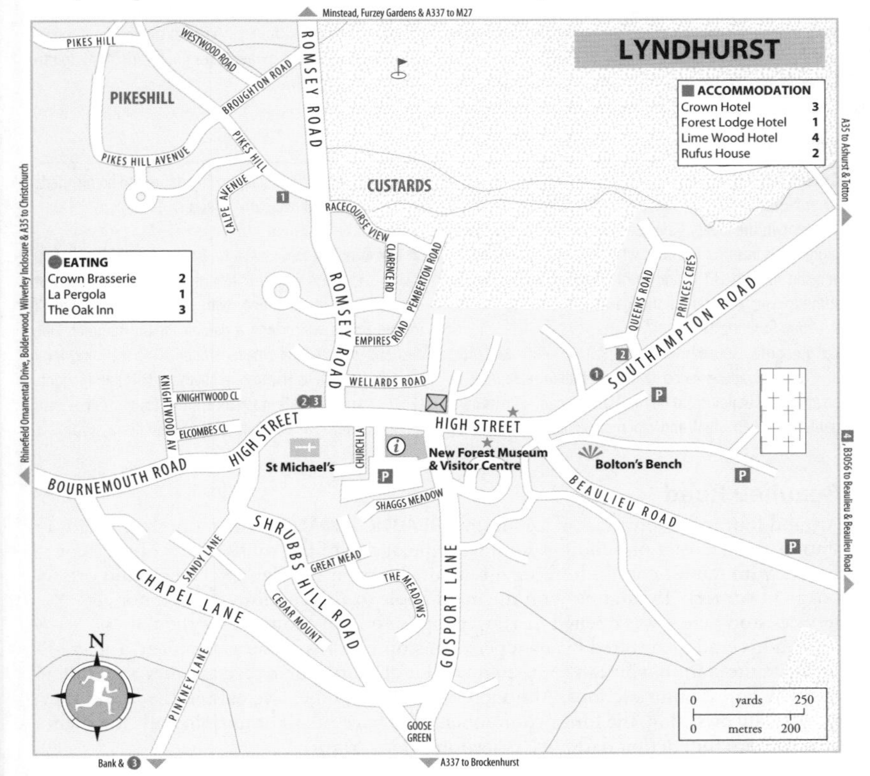

neighbouring village of **Bank**, a typically pretty New Forest village with some great surrounding walks and one of the forest's best pubs.

ARRIVAL AND INFORMATION — LYNDHURST

By bus Regular buses from Ashurst and Lymington pull in on the High St, as do the green and red NFT circular summer routes (see p.165).

Tourist information The tourist office is in the New Forest Centre, Main Car Park, off the High St (daily 10am–5pm; ⓣ 02380 282269, ⓦ newforestcentre.org.uk). It sells bus passes and maps, and lists events in the forest.

ACCOMMODATION

There's a decent choice of reasonably priced **accommodation**, most on the approach roads into town – with corresponding traffic noise. There are also two good campsites a short drive out of Lyndhurst at Denny and Mapley Wood (see box, p.178).

Crown Hotel High St, SO43 7NF ⓣ 02380 282922, ⓦ crownhotel-lyndhurst.co.uk. Traditional coaching inn dating from the 1600s, with a log fire and reasonably priced, comfortable rooms: make sure you ask for one at the back overlooking the gardens, as the front rooms can be noisy. There's also a good restaurant (see below). **£95**

Forest Lodge Hotel Pikes Hill, Romsey Rd, SO43 7AS ⓣ 02380 283677, ⓦ newforesthotels.co.uk/forest-lodge-hotel. Attractive Georgian building in a good location – a short walk from Lyndhurst High St but away from the main road, so there's less traffic noise. The rooms are comfortable and there's an indoor pool and sauna. **£170**

Lime Wood Hotel Beaulieu Rd, SO43 7FZ ⓣ 02380 287177, ⓦ limewoodhotel.co.uk. Set in its own substantial grounds around a mile from Lyndhurst, this luxury hotel combines contemporary design with a traditional country atmosphere. You can stay in plush rooms with free-standing baths, or in separate forest lodges in the grounds. Its two top-notch restaurants specialize in organic and local produce. **£275**

Rufus House Southampton Rd, SO43 7BR ⓣ 02380 282930, ⓦ rufushouse.co.uk. A couple of minutes out of town on the Ashurst road, opposite some fine New Forest countryside, this good-value place has plenty of character. Its tower room has a four-poster bed, though front rooms face a busy road. The owner takes good care of the rooms and guests. **£95**

EATING

Crown Brasserie High St, SO43 7NF ⓣ 02380 282922, ⓦ crownhotel-lyndhurst.co.uk. Attractive, informal brasserie in the *Crown Hotel* (see above), which uses local ingredients as far as possible, with main courses including venison haunch (£18) and roast monkfish tail (£16). In summer you can eat in the garden. Mon–Sat noon–9.15pm, Sun noon–9pm.

La Pergola Southampton Rd, SO43 7BQ ⓣ 02380 284184, ⓦ la-pergola.co.uk. Lively Italian restaurant in an attractive building out on the Ashurst road, with its own garden. Chicken, steak and veal main courses from around £15, tasty pasta and pizza from £9 and superb home-made desserts, as well as daily specials. Tues–Sun 11am–2.30pm & 6–10.30pm.

★ **The Oak Inn** Pinkney Lane, Bank, SO43 7FD ⓣ 02380 282350, ⓦ oakinnlyndhurst.co.uk. Lovely country pub just a mile south of Lyndhurst, with low wooden ceilings, a roaring fire in winter and a garden for the summer. Fine ales and decent food (mains around £14) featuring local ingredients such as Hampshire pheasant (£16) and faggots (£13)– it's best to book in advance. Mon–Fri 11.30am–3pm & 5.30–11pm, Sat 11.30am–11pm, Sun noon–10pm.

Beaulieu Road

Around four miles southeast of Lyndhurst, **BEAULIEU ROAD** is little more than a railway station and a cluster of buildings in the middle of one of the wildest parts of the New Forest, with fantastic walks heading off in any direction (though the low ground gets boggy in winter). The station – on the main Poole to London line, though not all services stop here – was opened in 1847 to appease Lord Montagu: as the railway crossed his land, he wanted his own personal stop near his home at Beaulieu. Today, opposite the station, you can see the **pony sales ground**, where several times a year there are New Forest pony auctions. Although most of the ponies live wild in the forest, they are actually owned by the forest commoners who have the right to train and ride them or sell them: for auction dates, see ⓦ newforestpony.com.

ACCOMMODATION AND EATING **BEAULIEU ROAD**

Beaulieu Hotel SO42 7YQ 02380 293344, newforesthotels.co.uk/beaulieu-hotel. The isolated position makes this pub and hotel a great place to hole up after a day's walking in the forest. It has comfortable and well-equipped family rooms with foldaway bunk beds (£180) as well as a decent pub food in the attached *Drift Inn*. Daily 11am–11pm. **£155**

Minstead

A couple of miles north of Lyndhurst, the pretty, one-shop, one-pub hamlet of **MINSTEAD** is an archetypal New Forest village with thatched cottages and a green. Its **church**, parts of which date from the thirteenth century, looks more like an extended cottage, and it is of interest for its unusual triple-decked pulpit as well as being the resting place of **Sir Arthur Conan Doyle**, creator of Sherlock Holmes. The church was initially reluctant to allow him to be buried here due to his fervent belief in spiritualism – a séance was held at his funeral at his request. Eventually, however, it was agreed that he could be buried at the far edge of the graveyard, where his grave is often decorated with mementoes, such as pipes, left by fans of the fictional detective.

Furzey Gardens

Minstead, SO43 7GL • **Gardens** Daily 10am–dusk • £8, under-17s £4.50: Nov to mid-Feb £3, under-17s £1 • **Gallery** Mid-Feb to Oct 10am–5pm • Free • furzey-gardens.org

A mile southeast of Minstead, the beautifully sprawling **Furzey Gardens** are at their most colourful in spring when the azaleas and rhododendrons are out. Children will enjoy climbing the tower and the treehouses and searching for the fairy doors that have been carved into trees around the gardens. There's also a café, art gallery and regular exhibitions of thatching, as well as a tiny thatched cottage, once home to a family with thirteen children, which has been restored to its original sixteenth-century condition.

Bolderwood

Six miles west of Lyndhurst, off the busy A35, a delightful narrow road winds to the ancient woodland around **Bolderwood**. The road is especially beautiful in autumn, when the colours are dazzling – there are various car parks along the route, perfect if you want to stop off and explore. One of the most popular is the Knightwood Oak car park where a short walk takes you to the venerable **Knightwood Oak**, one of the oldest trees in the forest which measures about 6.6m in circumference at shoulder height.

A WALK AROUND MINSTEAD

A lovely, bucolic **two-mile round walk** through native woods and over streams and fords starts from the **village green** in Minstead. From here, head up the lane to the church, then take the path that runs alongside its graveyard down through a wood of oaks, beeches and silver birch. At the bottom, there's a lane with a ford across a babbling stream: cross the lane and follow the signs to **Furzey Gardens**. This takes you along a quiet road; take the first turning on the left and continue through a further ford until the lane bears sharply left and you see two footpaths. Take the right-hand track and carry on along the path which runs alongside a field. Cross the stile and turn immediately right into the woods until you reach a stream; cross over the bridge and as the path climbs look for a yellow arrow on the right. Follow the arrowed path through more woodland and over a small stream, then continue along the path up through the woods, which brings you out in the Furzey Gardens car park. From the gardens it's a short walk back to the village: take the lane to the right, then turn right again round the bottom of the gardens. Continue along the lane until you see a stile on your left and a footpath sign. Follow this path across two fields until you reach a road, where you turn right, bringing you back to the village green.

At the top of the slope, Bolderwood itself is a large open area of grassland with an information hut. Three marked trails depart from behind the hut, the longest just two miles, a pleasant and easy walk through a mix of deciduous and coniferous woodland, over a stream and back. All three trails pass a deer-feeding centre. The resident deer population thrives in these parts and they aren't worried about coming right up to the edges of the fenced paddock where they are fed daily (at any time between 12.30pm and 2.30pm) except in winter during the rutting season.

Burley and around

Set in a dip and surrounded by dense woodland, **BURLEY** is as attractively located as any village in the forest, pulling in day-trippers galore. There is not a lot to the village apart from a few pleasant pubs and a series of shops that seem to be permanently set up for Halloween. This plethora of bizarre stores mostly specializes in witchcraft, many opening in the wake of A Coven of Witches, the first shop created by local self-proclaimed white witch, Sybil Leek, in the 1950s – shortly after England's witchcraft laws were repealed in 1951. Black-cloaked Leek, who was usually seen with a jackdaw on her shoulder, became a local celebrity, billing herself as high priestess of the white witches – who believed in being guided by the sun, moon and the stars in their bid to spread goodwill. Another local, Gerald Gardner from nearby Christchurch, took on the mantle of "Britain's chief witch" in 1954, after writing a book on Wicca (or modern witchcraft), called *Witchcraft Today*. His book inspired an increased interest in witchcraft and his version of the "old religion" throughout the country. Burley shopkeepers claim there are still white witches who follow Gardnerian Wicca in the forest today, mostly "Hedgewitches" – those who work alone rather than as part of a coven – and you'll find many of Burley's shops selling Hedgewitch spells.

New Forest Safari

Howard Close, BH24 4AJ • School summer hols and bank hol weekends daily noon–5pm • £3 • ⓦ newforestsafari.co.uk

The car park next to the *Queen's Head* in Burley marks the starting point of the **New Forest Safaris** – actually a thirty-minute tractor ride around the local deer park. They're great fun, getting you right up close to the resident red deer, which you can help feed.

ARRIVAL AND DEPARTURE — BURLEY

By bus Burley is served by the New Forest Tour buses (July to mid-Sept) on the circular red route from Lyndhurst and the blue route from Lymington (see p.165).

ACCOMMODATION AND EATING

Burley Manor 1 Ringwood Rd, BH24 4BS ⓣ 01425 403522, ⓦ burleymanor.com. This grandiose Victorian country mansion sits facing the deer park and has an oak-panelled dining room. The smart rooms have been recently refurbished; all are en suite, and some come with views over the gardens and deer park. **£150**

Burley Youth Hostel Cott Lane, BH24 4BB ⓣ 08453 719309, ⓦ yha.org.uk/hostel/new-forest. Simple hostel rooms in a large country house with a lovely garden. There are dorm rooms for between four and eight people plus family rooms (£95). They also have bell tents sleeping up to five (£120) and camping pods sleeping up to four (£115) in the garden. Dorms **£23**

★The Cider Pantry Pound Lane, BH24 4ED ⓣ 01425 403589, ⓦ newforestcider.co.uk/ciderpantry. Excellent café on a farm, with pigs, geese, an apple press and a shop selling its own cider. The café serves tasty, generously sized local dishes such as New Forest cider rarebit and cider sausage sandwiches (most £7–9), plus fantastic home-made cakes. Eat inside by the log fire or out in the garden. Daily 9am–4.30/5pm.

★White Buck Bisterne Close, BH24 4AT ⓣ 01425 402264, ⓦ whitebuckburley.co.uk. A short walk out of the village at Bisterne Close, this former country house has good food, such as local trout (£16), as well as a giant garden

HURST
CASTLE

for kids to run around in; it also has regular live music. Rooms consist of decent doubles of various sizes, with wooden floors and smart decor. Mon–Sat 11am–11pm, Sun 11am–10.30pm. £110

Wilverley Inclosure

Around three miles southeast of Burley, on the eastern side of the A31, lies **Wilverley Inclosure** – there are a few gravel laybys at the side of the road for parking. The New Forest has various inclosures (fenced areas for growing timber) and this is one of the densest, with impressively mature pines and deciduous trees. Various marked trails and cycle paths wend their way around the inclosure, though half the fun is getting lost in the thick, sloping interior, darkened by overhanging foliage even at midday. The surrounding area is also popular with local mushroomers, who often find rare edible species.

EATING — WILVERLEY INCLOSURE

Station House Station Rd, Holmsley, BH24 4HY T 01425 402468, W stationhouseholmsley.com. This bustling café is set in the former Holmsley railway station – you can still see the signals, and old tickets decorate the walls – just south of Wilverley Inclosure. It serves sizeable breakfasts, sandwiches and daily specials (£8–10), though it is best known for its superb home-made cakes and teas. Mon–Fri 10am–4pm, Sat & Sun 10am–5pm.

The northern New Forest

The forest is split into two parts by the busy A31, each with its own distinct geography and character. The **northern section** is sparsely populated and much less touristy, perhaps because it's less accessible, with no towns, few main roads and no train line. It is also less wooded than the southern stretches, with open heathland and rolling

FOREST CAMPSITES

In addition to several private sites, there are ten **campsites** in the forest run by **Camping in the Forest** (T 024 7642 3008, W campingintheforest.co.uk/england/new-forest). Some are very simple, with few or no facilities, so are suited to caravans and camper vans; others have full facilities for tents. The sites are particularly good for children, as they have open access to the forest, many have streams running through them, and ponies and donkeys wander freely. Most of the sites are low density to avoid the risk of fires, so there's plenty of space to run free. It's advisable to book beforehand to guarantee a pitch in high season, though some sites request a minimum stay of two nights. Unless otherwise stated, all the campsites are open from mid-March to late September, and you can expect to pay around £18–28 for a tent and two adults in high season.

Aldridge Hill Brockenhurst, SO42 7QD T 01590 623152. Beautiful site by the Blackwater stream, just a mile from Brockenhurst. Suitable for caravans and motorhomes, but has no toilet or shower facilities. Late May to early Sept.

Ashurst Lyndhurst Rd, SO40 7AR T 02380 292097. Large site, a 5min walk from Ashurst and the fine *New Forest* pub (see p.173). Full facilities for campers including a launderette, but no dogs allowed.

Denny and Matley Wood Beaulieu Rd, Lyndhurst, SO43 7FZ T 02380 293144. Simple woodland sites suitable for caravans and motorhomes, but with no toilet or shower facilities.

Hollands Wood Lyndhurst Rd, Brockenhurst, SO42 7QH T 01590 622967. Lovely wooded site, within easy cycling distance of Brockenhurst, with toilets, showers and a launderette.

Holmsley Forest Rd, Thorny Hill near Bransgore, BH23 7EQ T 01425 674502. Full facilities including children's play area and a shop. Mid-March to late Oct.

Ocknell and Longbeech Fritham, SO43 7HH T 02380 812740. Simple woodland and heathland sites. No toilets or hot water at Longbeech, and only toilets at Ocknell.

★ **Roundhill** Beaulieu Rd, near Brockenhurst, SO42 7QL T 01590 624344. Wonderful, spacious site with showers and toilets, and ponies galore.

Setthorns Wooton, New Milton, BH25 5WA T 01590 681020. Wooded site with no toilet or shower facilities. Open all year.

A ROUND WALK OR CYCLE ROUTE FROM FRITHAM

This 4.5-mile (approx 2hr) **round walk** is mostly on wide forestry tracks, and passes through a mixture of deciduous and coniferous forest and open heathland. It starts on the well-signed cycle route to Frogham by the forest car park at **Fritham**, just past the *Royal Oak* pub (see p.180). Take this path to Islands Thorn Inclosure – keep to the main path and ignore a branch off to the right. The route becomes more wooded, and after thirty minutes you'll reach a pretty stream with a bridge over it. Cross the bridge and bear left where the path divides. This climbs a low hill and after ten minutes you'll see a gate to the left, which leads into Amberwood Inclosure. Go through the gate, continuing on the path as it winds downhill slightly (ignore a track to the right). Some twenty minutes beyond the gate you can rest at an ornamental wooden bench dedicated to local conservationist Eric Ashby. The path then crosses a bridge and continues straight through double gates; around thirty minutes beyond the bench you exit the inclosure through a gate – bear left where the path divides just past the gate. This last section of around twenty minutes goes through the open Fritham Plain, dotted with ponies and gorse bushes, where parts of Kevin Costner's *Robin Hood: Prince of Thieves* was filmed in 1991.

countryside, which is great for walks or a picnic. There's a scattering of villages such as the picturesque **Fritham** and **South Gorley**, rural pubs and campsites, but its main appeal is simply exploring a landscape that's far less visited than the southern sections.

GETTING AROUND — NORTHERN NEW FOREST

By car You'll need a car to get around – public transport is virtually non-existent.

By bike You could explore by bike from the two towns just outside the forest, Ringwood (see p.155) or Fordingbridge (see p.154), which are on the red NFT circular bus route from the central forest (see p.165).

ACCOMMODATION AND EATING

High Corner Inn Linwood, BH24 3QY ⓣ01425 473973, ⓦhighcornerinn.co.uk. Tucked away down a bumpy gravel track in the middle of the forest, this pub is recommended for its location rather than its food, which is distinctly average. It's got a large garden and is great for a drink stop after a walk along some of the many nearby forest paths. Mon–Fri 11am–3pm & 6–11pm, Sat 11am–11pm, Sun 11am–10.30pm.

Red Shoot Camping Park Tom's Lane, Linwood, BH24 3QT ⓣ01425 473789, ⓦredshoot-campingpark.com. Right beside the *Red Shoot* pub and surrounded by beautiful forest, this private campsite has its own shop and play area for children – it's child-friendly, dog-friendly and well kept. March–Oct only, extra £8 charge per person. **£28**

★**Red Shoot Inn** Tom's Lane, Linwood, BH24 3QT ⓣ01425 475792, ⓦredshoot.co.uk. Cosy pub that brews its own ales and hosts a twice-yearly beer festival (usually April & Oct). It's very popular for weekend lunches, with decent pub grub such as beef stew with dumplings (£12) and a variety of sandwiches (£6.25). Mon–Fri 11am–3pm & 5.30–11pm, Sat 11am–11pm, Sun 11am–10.30pm.

South Gorley

Most drivers approach the northern section of the forest along the A338. A prettier route, however, is along the narrow road that runs north, parallel to the A338, via the diminutive village of **SOUTH GORLEY**, where **Hockey's Farm** (Mon–Sat 8am–6pm, Sun 9am–5pm ⓦhockeys-farm.co.uk) has a shop selling its own and other local produce, as well as a simple café and lots of animals to visit including donkeys, horses, alpacas and sheep. Right next door, **Avon Valley Nursery** has pick-your-own fruit and a seasonal toy steam train (weather permitting; phone for train schedule; ⓣ01425 652003, ⓦavonvalleynurseries.co.uk), which trundles round the farm's perimeter.

EATING — SOUTH GORLEY

Royal Oak Ringwood Rd, North Gorley, SP6 2PB ⓣ01425 652244, ⓦroyaloakgorley.com. One village north of South Gorley is this seventeenth-century thatched inn opposite a duck pond, with a pleasant beer garden outside and wood-burning stoves inside. Along with cask ales, there's a good range of decently priced pub food served daily (steaks, pan-fried liver and the like; £12–18), made using locally sourced ingredients. Mon noon–8pm, Tues–Thurs noon–10pm, Fri & Sat noon–11pm.

Rockford Common

A couple of miles south of South Gorley, **Rockford Common** is a popular spot for picnickers and families, who cluster round a small ford. Here you'll also find a huge sand quarry, where children run up and down the giant dune; there are plenty of rope swings strung up on the surrounding trees, and in summer the whole place is like a huge playground.

Fritham

The pretty Linwood road continues from Rockford Common through the northern part of the forest past rolling moorland – take the right-hand fork and you'll head back under the A31 to the southern section of the forest at Bolderwood (see p.175), while the left fork heads towards the spread-out village of **FRITHAM**, eight miles to the northeast. There are some great walks just beyond the wonderful *Royal Oak* pub (see below): the narrow road here continues for half a mile to an attractive reservoir with paths heading into the forest in all directions.

EATING — FRITHAM

★ **Royal Oak** SO43 7HJ ⓣ 02380 812606. This is one of the best – and smallest – pubs in the forest which serves a range of local cask ales. Inside, the three little rooms cram in open fires, wooden floorboards and assorted dogs, while the large garden overlooks rolling farmland. Best of all is the limited but top-notch lunch menu featuring local produce such as nettle and chilli cheeses, pork pies and summer crabs; main courses (£4.50–6) are served with great local chutneys. Cash only. July–Sept daily 11am–11pm; Oct–June Mon–Fri 11am–3pm & 5.30–11pm, Sat & Sun 11am–11pm.

The Foresters Arms Abbotswell Rd, Frogham, SP6 2JA ⓣ 01425 652294, ⓦ the.littlepubgroup.co.uk/the-foresters-arms. A pleasant garden, wood-burning stoves, bare brick walls and rustic-chic decor make this a great place to stop in for a quick pint after a walk – it's at the end of one of the forest's most appealing routes, from Fritham (see box below). Alternatively, stay for a sandwich (£6.50) or a full meal – hearty dishes such as coq au vin (£11.50) and steak and kidney pudding (£13) are on offer, made with local ingredients where possible. Mon–Thurs noon–10.30pm, Fri & Sat noon–11pm, Sun noon–10pm.

The Rufus Stone

The forest's most visited site, the **Rufus Stone**, stands southeast of Fritham, just off the A31, though you have to approach it by going north of the village and back via Brook. Erected in 1745, the stone marks the putative spot where the Conqueror's son and heir, **William II** – aka William Rufus, for his ruddy complexion – was killed by a crossbow bolt in 1100 during a hunting expedition. William was not at all popular in these parts, so the official story – that Sir Walter Tyrell's arrow bounced off a tree and hit the king by mistake – is hotly disputed. Tyrell allegedly escaped by having his horse shod

THE TRACK FROM FRITHAM TO FROGHAM

One of the New Forest's greatest walks or cycle rides is the eight-mile return route from **Fritham** west to the small village of **Frogham** along a spectacular ridge. The wide gravel trail is a dedicated cycle track but is also popular with walkers. Pick up the "Cycle route to Frogham" sign from next to Fritham's car park just past the *Royal Oak*. The track heads downhill through woodland – home to lots of deer and ponies – before a very steep climb up onto the ridge. The track then continues along the ridge, giving superb views over the rolling New Forest below. You then descend to eventually join a minor road – turn left and it is about a mile to the *Forester's Arms* in Frogham (see above).

with the horseshoes the wrong way round to confuse his trackers. The memorial you see today was erected in 1865 by the Victorians who encased the original stone in a protective layer of metal to deter vandals; it states "King William the Second, surnamed Rufus, being slain, as before related, was laid in a cart, belonging to one Purkis, and drawn from hence, to Winchester, and buried in the Cathedral Church, of that city". It's a tranquil spot despite its proximity to the main road.

Christchurch

Formerly called Twynham, meaning "between two rivers", **CHRISTCHURCH** is indeed shaped by its position, squeezed between the rivers Avon and Stour. Separated from Bournemouth's sprawl by the Stour, the town has a very different feel from its much larger western neighbour. Intimate and historic, it is at once likeable if generally sleepy – it has the highest percentage of retired people in the country. There is no beach here but its riverside location is lovely, and you can easily take a boat out to the nearest sandspit beach in high season, or from the suburb of Mudeford at the far side of Christchurch's large harbour.

Some of the town's prettiest streets are tucked behind the High Street – look out for the **ducking stool**, used to punish miscreants until the nineteenth century, though what you see today is a modern replica.

The Priory

Quay Rd, BH23 1BU • Mon–Sat 9.30am–5pm, Sun 2.15–5.30pm, subject to services • Church free, but donations welcome • **Tours** Daily 2.30pm & 6.30pm; 2hr • £10 • **Tower tours** Phone ahead for hours • £3 • ⓣ 01202 485804, ⓦ christchurchpriory.org

Christchurch's historic centre looks up to the enormous **Priory**, resembling a cathedral but actually England's longest parish church, parts of which date back to 1094. In the twelfth century, a legend developed about a miraculous beam which grew in length to fit the place it was intended for during the church's construction – a miracle only Christ could have performed – thus inspiring locals to change the town's name to Christchurch. The priory was added to over the centuries – look for the Lady Chapel, whose pendant vaulting is considered the earliest of its type in England. Henry VIII spared the priory during the Dissolution on condition that it was used as a parish church, which it has been ever since. There are free lunchtime recitals here most Thursdays, and it often hosts concerts by the BSO (Bournemouth Symphony Orchestra) among others. It's worth trying to take one of the **guided tours** that take place throughout the year, which visit parts of the church that are normally closed to the public, such as the crypt and the tower.

Norman Castle

Castle St, BH23 1DT • Daily 24hr • Free; EH • ⓦ www.english-heritage.org.uk/christchurch-castle-and-norman-house

Behind the Priory, next to the attractive riverside gardens, is the substantial ruin of a hilltop **Norman castle** – which offers great views over the old town – and a ruined house known the **Great Chamber**, built for the town bailiff. Dating from 1160, the house is all that's left of stone buildings built to defend the town and contains a rare Norman chimney.

The Quomps

Boats Easter–Oct roughly every 30min–1hr 30min • ⓣ 01202 429119, ⓦ bournemouthboating.co.uk

The riverside is an open area of grassland known as the **Quomps**, from where **boat trips** head upriver to Tuckton and out to the beach at Hengistbury Head (see p.46); the full trip from Tuckton to Hengistbury Head takes around forty minutes, and boat rental is also available.

6

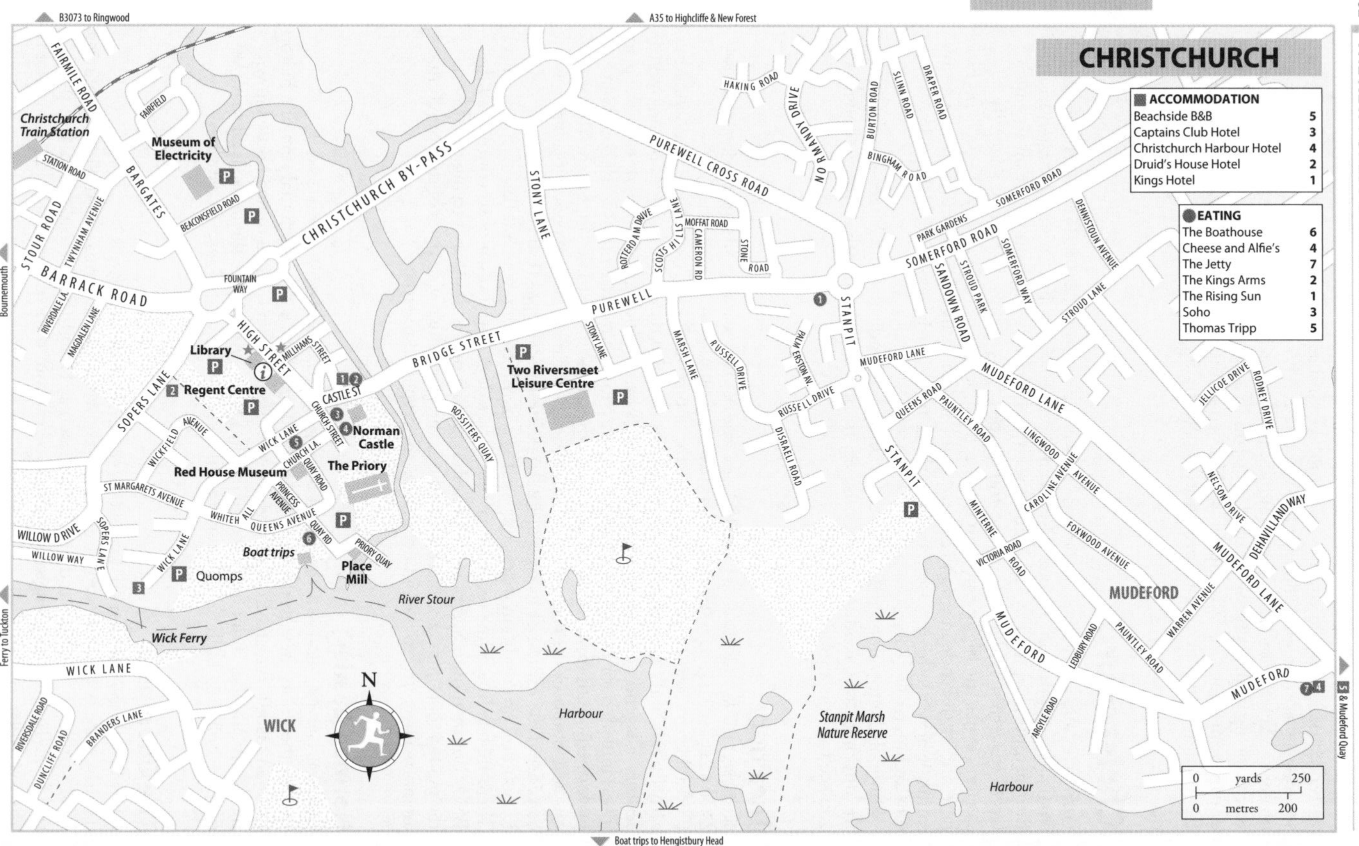

CHRISTCHURCH
ACCOMMODATION
Beachside B&B 5
Captains Club Hotel 3
Christchurch Harbour Hotel 4
Druid's House Hotel 2
Kings Hotel 1
EATING
The Boathouse 6
Cheese and Alfie's 4
The Jetty 7
The Kings Arms 2
The Rising Sun 1
Soho 3
Thomas Tripp 5
0 yards 250
0 metres 200
B3073 to Ringwood
A35 to Highcliffe & New Forest
Bournemouth
Ferry to Tuckton
Boat trips to Hengistbury Head
5 & Mudeford Quay
Christchurch Train Station
Museum of Electricity
Library
Regent Centre
Red House Museum
Norman Castle
The Priory
Two Riversmeet Leisure Centre
Boat trips
Place Mill
Quomps
River Stour
Wick Ferry
WICK
N
Harbour
Stanpit Marsh Nature Reserve
MUDEFORD

Also by the harbour you can visit the small water mill, **Place Mill** (April–Sept Tues–Sun & bank hols 11am–5.30pm; free), which is partly Saxon and was mentioned in the Domesday Book. Inside, you can clamber up the rickety ladders to see the workings of the mill, with the adjoining gallery hosting art exhibitions and a resident artist displaying local works.

Red House Museum

Quay Rd, BH23 1BU • Tues–Fri 10am–5pm, Sat 10am–4pm • Free • ⓦ hampshireculturaltrust.org.uk/red-house-museum-and-gardens

Just back from the Quay, **Red House Museum** is set in a Georgian former workhouse and now displays a fascinating mishmash of artefacts relating to local history, including some Arts and Crafts furniture. As well as detailing conditions in the original workhouse, there are archeological finds, traditional clothes from the eighteenth and nineteenth centuries, fossils and a lovely herb garden.

Christchurch Harbour and Stanpit Marshes

East of the town centre, Christchurch's suburbs wrap round the substantial **Christchurch Harbour**, whose shallow waters make it ideal for novice sailors and windsurfers. The best approach to the harbour is via the suburb of Mudeford, a mile or so east of the town centre. Here, a small car park gives access to **Stanpit Marshes**, whose tidal inlets were once notorious for tobacco smugglers. Today there is a fine half-hour harbourside walk through the marshes, which are usually full of ponies. Near the start of the walk is an information centre detailing local wildlife, which often includes rare wading birds.

Mudeford Quay

Once a fishing village, and still dotted with lobster cages, bustling harbourside **Mudeford Quay** is where ferries depart to Mudeford sandspit on Hengistbury Head (see p.46); the ferry company (ⓦ mudefordferry.co.uk) also offers boat rides, including turbo-charged rib rides to the Needles on the Isle of Wight (see p.273). Mudeford Quay is also a great spot for crabbers and the starting point of a seaside promenade that heads for around a mile east, alongside a sand-and-shingle beach to Highcliffe (see p.184).

ARRIVAL AND INFORMATION — CHRISTCHURCH

By train Christchurch is on the main Weymouth to London line; the station is about a mile north of the centre.

By bus Local buses from Bournemouth (every 10–15min; 30min) in the east, Lymington (1–2 hourly; 1hr 45min) in the west and Ringwood (2 daily; 1hr) in the north pull up at the bus stop outside Christchurch library, on the High St.

By car Every Monday, the high street is closed to traffic for the weekly market. There are plenty of pay-and-display car parks either side of the high street.

By ferry Ferries from Mudeford depart regularly for Hengistbury Head (every 15min: Easter–Oct daily; Nov–Easter Sat & Sun, weather permitting; check Facebook for hours). Singles £1.50; bikes £1.50; ⓦ mudefordferry.co.uk.

Tourist information Christchurch's tourist office is at 49 High St (Mon 9am–4.30pm, Tues–Sat 10am–4.30pm; ⓣ 01202 476816, ⓦ visit-dorset.com/about-the-area/areas-to-visit/christchurch), next to the Art Deco Regent Centre, which puts on shows and films. The tourist office can book coach tickets and sells tickets for the Regent Centre.

ACCOMMODATION

Beachside B&B 15 Southcliffe Rd, Friars Cliff, BH23 4EN ⓣ 01425 279660, ⓦ beachsidebreaks.co.uk. There are just three rooms (two en-suite and one with a private bathroom) in this clean, quiet and well-kept B&B, a few minutes' walk from Avon Beach. The friendly owner is helpful and welcoming and the breakfasts are good. **£90**

Captains Club Hotel Wick Lane, BH23 1HU ⓣ 01202 475111, ⓦ captainsclubhotel.com. Right by the river, the modern glass exterior resembles a car showroom – but things improve inside and there is a fine riverside terrace, bar, restaurant and spa. The contemporary rooms come with great river views. **£290**

Christchurch Harbour Hotel 95 Mudeford, BH23 3NT ⓣ 01202 483434, ⓦ christchurch-harbour-hotel.co.uk.

This is the top upmarket option, in lovely harbourside grounds with a good spa, pool, fantastic gardens and two good restaurants, including *The Jetty* (see below). The rooms are all smartly decorated with all mod cons, such as an iPod dock and power showers. The inland-facing rooms are less appealing, so treat yourself to one with a private terrace or overlooking the harbour. **£190**

Druid's House Hotel 26 Sopers Lane, BH23 1JE ⓣ01202 485615, ⓦdruid-house.co.uk. Well-regarded five-star guesthouse in a good location behind the high street, overlooking a park. Most rooms have terraces or balconies and all have iPod docks. **£125**

Kings Hotel 18 Castle St, BH23 1DT ⓣ01202 483434, ⓦthekings-christchurch.co.uk. Smart boutique-style hotel opposite the castle ruins with a good restaurant (see below) and a lively bar. The sixteen comfortable rooms vary in size and views, but all come with mod cons and White Company toiletries. **£175**

EATING

Christchurch has, in recent years, gained a reputation as a gastronomic town, with a good selection of top-class restaurants, regular **farmers' markets** and an **annual food festival** in May (ⓦchristchurchfoodfest.co.uk). After dark the town is generally sleepy, though the pubs can be lively.

The Boathouse 9 Quay Rd, BH23 1BU ⓣ01202 480033, ⓦboathouse.co.uk. A favourite of AFC Bournemouth's manager, Eddie Howe, this restaurant/bar overlooks the Quomps and the river and has a huge outdoor terrace. The food is somewhat pricey for the quality, but it's worth it for the lovely location. There's a decent range of breakfast choices, and the main menu includes dishes such as stone-baked pizzas (£10–12.50), *moules frites* (£15.50), fish pie (£13.50) and steaks (£22–25), plus a selection of fish specials. Daily 9am–10pm.

Cheese and Alfie's 10 Church St, BH23 1BW ⓣ01202 487000, ⓦcheeseandalfies.com. The quirky name sets the tone for this small, friendly café-restaurant which serves great breakfasts (the pan haggerty is a hearty mix of sautéed potatoes, ham, cheese and egg; £8), tasty brunches such as poached eggs, walnuts and field mushrooms on toast (£8), plus pasta, risotto, burgers and steaks in the evenings (mains £10–14). Good veggie selection. Mon & Tues 8.30am–5pm, Wed–Sat 8.30am–10pm, Sun 8.30am–4pm.

The Jetty 95 Mudeford, BH23 3NT ⓣ01202 483434, ⓦthejetty.co.uk. Attached to the *Christchurch Harbour Hotel* (see above), in a distinctive wooden restaurant with stunning views of Christchurch harbour, the area's top restaurant is overseen by chef Alex Aitken. The tasty dishes feature local fish and produce, such as the signature twice-cooked cheese soufflé (£8) and a fantastic Jetty cassoulet (£21). Mains £17–28. Mon–Sat noon–2.30pm & 6–10pm, Sun noon–8pm.

The Kings Arms 18 Castle St, BH23 1DT ⓣ01202 483434, ⓦthekings-christchurch.co.uk/dining. This stylish brasserie is overseen by *The Jetty*'s chef Alex Aitken, and the menu here features more affordable versions of his dishes. There's an emphasis on local produce, such as Mudeford crab on toast (£7.50) and Dorset lamb (£12.50). Most mains £15–21. Located in the *Kings Hotel* (see above). Mon–Sat noon–2.30pm & 6–9.30pm, Sun noon–3pm & 6–9pm.

★**The Rising Sun** 123 Purewell, BH23 1EJ ⓣ01202 486122, ⓦrisingpubs.com/rising_sun_christchurch.html. Excellent-quality MSG-free Thai food, much of it organic, served at a pleasant pub with a nice garden. Prices are reasonable (mains from £10), and the vegetable curries are particularly good. Mon–Sat noon–11pm, Sun noon–10.30pm.

Soho 7 Church St, BH23 1BW ⓣ01202 496140, ⓦsoholifestyle.co.uk. Comfortable café-restaurant serving a range of dishes, though it's the tasty pizzas (£7–12) cooked at the open kitchen that are the draw – the more unusual toppings include Thai beef or crispy duck with hoi sin sauce – along with a lovely outdoor terrace overlooking the castle. In the evenings, it is more of an upmarket bar serving cocktails (£7). Mon–Thurs 9am–11pm, Fri & Sat 9am–1pm, Sun 9am–10.30pm.

Thomas Tripp 10 Wick Lane, BH23 1HX ⓣ01202 490498, ⓦthomastripp.co.uk. Christchurch's liveliest pub defies the town's reputation for being full of retired people – a good-time, mixed crowd enjoys a great outdoor terrace, regular live music and DJ sessions. There's a decent menu of bar food, and in good weather an outdoor grill, *The Shack*, serves seafood and steaks. Mon–Sat 11am–midnight, Sun noon–midnight.

Highcliffe to Barton-on-Sea

The town of **Highcliffe**, three miles east of Christchurch, is unremarkable, though as its name suggests it sits on a high bluff above a fine stretch of shingle-and-sand beach, best accessed from the splendid Victorian pile of **Highcliffe Castle**. A similar landscape of bungalow-land extends east to **Barton-on-Sea**, another clifftop village above a shingle beach.

Highcliffe Castle

Rothesay Drive, BH23 4LE • **Grounds** Daily 7am–dusk • Free • **Castle** Feb–Dec 23 Mon–thurs & Sun 11am–5pm, Fri & Sat 11am–4.30pm • £3.50, under-16s free • **Tours** Tues & Thurs 2pm, Sun 11am; 1hr 15min • £5.95 • highcliffecastle.co.uk

It's something of a surprise to find, among the sprawl of bungalows that is **HIGHCLIFFE**, the towering splendour of **Highcliffe Castle**. Actually an ornate early Victorian mansion rather than a castle, it was built by Lord Stuart de Rothesay in the 1830s and is lavishly embellished with gargoyles and stained-glass windows salvaged from medieval buildings in France. You can look round the partially restored state rooms and galleries, while guided tours also take in the old kitchens and upper floors. Much of the castle's appeal, however, lies in the small but ornate grounds (complete with café), whose lawns boast fantastic views towards the Isle of Wight. Head west and you can join the coastal footpath which leads into a wooded nature reserve off Steamer Point and on to Mudeford Quay (see p.183), or you can take numerous paths south down the cliffs to the lovely **beach**.

6

Sammy Miller Museum

Bashley Cross Rd, BH25 5SZ • Mid-Feb to Nov daily 10am–4.30pm; Dec to mid-Feb Sat & Sun 10am–4.30pm • £7.50, children £3 • 01425 620 777, sammymiller.co.uk

Motorbike fans should seek out the **Sammy Miller Museum**, a few miles inland from Highcliffe at Bashley Cross Road, on the road to Sway. Named after the champion trials bike rider, who started the collection and is still very much involved with the museum, it houses a substantial collection of motorbikes including four hundred rare and classic racers, road bikes and sports bikes. Outside, children may prefer the grounds, where they can pet alpacas and various rabbits and guinea pigs; there is also a shop and tearooms.

Barton-on-Sea

Three miles up the coast from Highcliffe, **BARTON-ON-SEA** consists of a row of bungalows strung out facing the clifftop above a shingle beach. There's a broad grassy strip above the cliffs, great for kite flying or a picnic. A **coastal path** wends all the way from here past the neighbouring golf course to **Milford-on-Sea**, a bracing hour's walk high above the sea, though take care as the cliff is unstable.

ACCOMMODATION — HIGHCLIFFE TO BARTON-ON-SEA

Chewton Glen New Milton, BH25 6QS 01425 275341, chewtonglen.com. The most upmarket option in the area. Set in extensive manicured grounds leading down to the sea, it has a top-notch spa, its own golf course and tennis courts, indoor and outdoor pools and all the luxuries you would expect for the price, not to mention a renowned restaurant. **£325**

Waters Edge Guest House 10 Marine Drive West, Barton-on-Sea, BH25 7QH 01425 615485, watersedgeguesthouse.co.uk. Great location on the clifftop in Barton, good-value rooms and friendly, helpful owners, though the decor in the rooms is rather dated. It's definitely worth paying a bit extra (£110) for one of the sea-view rooms. **£95**

EATING

The Beachcomber Café Marine Drive East, Barton-on-Sea, BH25 7DZ 01425 611599, beachcomber-cafe.co.uk. Run by the same family for nearly thirty years, this refreshingly old-fashioned café sits right on the clifftop, with a lawned garden set out with benches offering superb views over the coast. It serves decent breakfasts until 11.30am, then a good-value lunch menu featuring sandwiches (£5), omelettes, tasty local kippers (£6), or larger dishes such as burgers, sausages and scampi and chips (mains £8–9). Jan–June & Sept–Dec daily 9am–6pm; July & Aug Mon–Fri 9am–6pm, Sat & Sun 9am–9pm.

Pebble Beach Marine Drive, Barton-on-Sea, BH25 7DZ 01425 627777, pebblebeach-uk.com. Highly rated restaurant which has great views over the Isle of Wight – best enjoyed from its broad terrace. It specializes in seafood and fish – the *plateau fruits de mer*, with crab, oysters and prawns, is £38 – though there are plenty of other options, such as chargrilled pork belly (£17) and asparagus crumble (£15). It also has a few comfortable rooms upstairs (£90). Mon–Fri 11am–2.30pm & 6–11pm, Sat 11am–3pm & 6–11pm, Sun 11am–3pm & 6–10.30pm.

Lymington and around

The best point of access for the Isle of Wight is **LYMINGTON**, whose estuary harbour is jam-packed with yachts as luxurious as the houses that radiate outwards in its leafy suburbs. It's a lively harbour town that makes a good base for exploring the local marshy coastline facing the Solent, and the nearby forest inland.

The old town around the quay is picture-postcard pretty, full of cobbled streets and handsome Georgian houses. Shipbuilding, using timber from the New Forest, helped the town flourish in the seventeenth and eighteenth centuries, boosted by smuggling – a warren of secret tunnels allegedly wends under the quay to the high street. These days it's the yachting fraternity that drives the town's economy, with two marinas at Yacht Haven and Berthton. The only real sights of note are the partly thirteenth-century church of **St Thomas the Apostle**, with a cupola-topped tower built in 1670, and the small but informative **St Barbe Museum** on New Street (Mon–Sat 10am–4pm; £6, under-16s £3; stbarbe-museum.org.uk), which traces the town's history and has a gallery for temporary exhibitions, all inside a former school: plans for renovation and enlargement of the museum mean that it will be closed until summer 2017. Otherwise

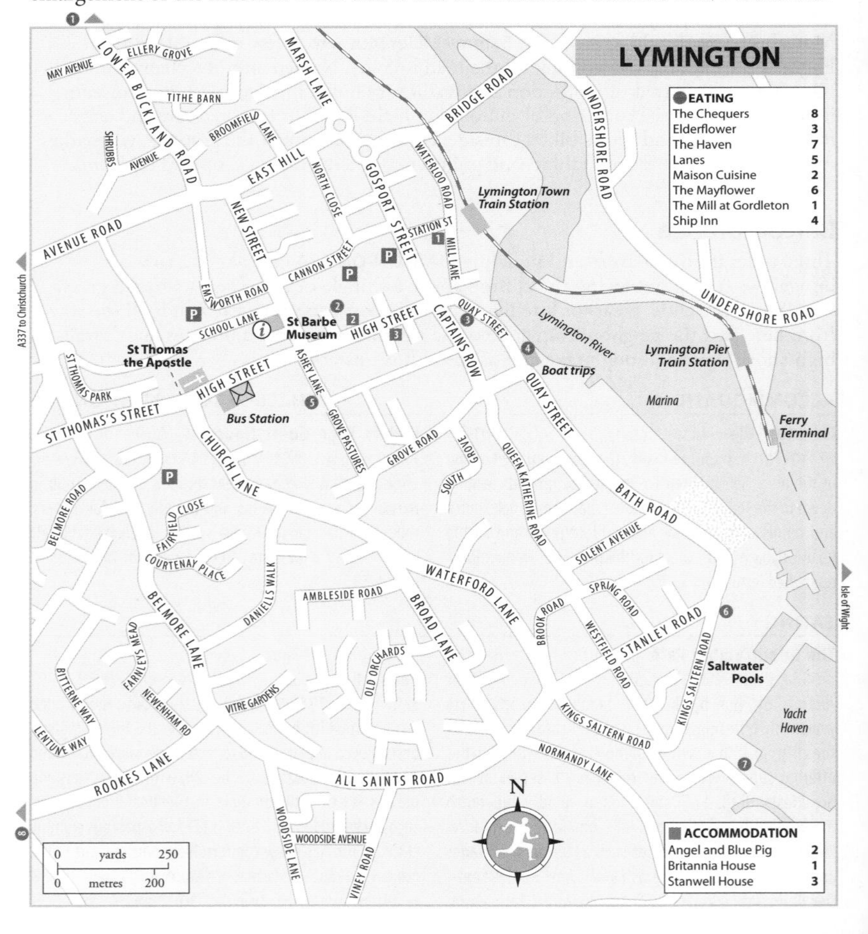

it's the boats' comings and goings and the town's fine array of shops that keep visitors busy. Summer **boat trips** run from the quay to the Needles on the Isle of Wight and around the Solent (Puffin Cruises T 07850 947618, W puffincruiseslymington.com).

Lymington Sea Water Baths

Bath Rd, SO41 3SE • May to mid-Sept daily 10am–6pm; check website for opening times the rest of the year • £2.50, under-14s £1.50 • W lymingtonseawaterbaths.org.uk

There are no beaches at Lymington, so locals use the giant **Lymington Sea Water Baths**, near the yacht club. Dating from 1833, they are the UK's oldest open-air seawater baths, though they now also feature an inflatable obstacle course, paddle-boards, kayaks and waterzorbing. Beyond here you can pick up the lovely coastal footpath to Keyhaven (see p.188), a two-and-a-half-mile route through the salt marshes and mudflats that are a haven for wading birds.

ARRIVAL AND INFORMATION — LYMINGTON AND AROUND

By train Lymington is on a branch line from Brockenhurst, where there are fast connections to London. Trains (2 hourly) call first at Lymington Town (10min), a short walk from the high street, and then run out to Lymington Pier (another minute or two) for connections to the Isle of Wight ferry.

By bus Lymington is on the #6, #X1 and #X2 routes (see p.165). Buses pull in outside the post office on the high street.

By ferry The Wightlink ferry crossing (T 03339 997333, W wightlink.co.uk) from Lymington to Yarmouth on the Isle of Wight is the fastest vehicle access to the island (40min) and is also one of the prettiest routes. Ferries leave daily approx hourly, 5.35am–10pm. Fares vary depending on the season and time of day, but expect to pay around £50–200 return for a car, or around £15 return for a foot passenger; look out for special offers on the website.

Tourist information The tourist office is currently at St Barbe Museum in New St (Mon–Sat 10am–4pm; T 01590 676969, W stbarbe-museum.org.uk). There are plans to refurbish the museum, at which time the tourist office will move to a temporary location elsewhere in the town; phone for details.

ACCOMMODATION

Angel and Blue Pig High St, SO41 9AP T 01590 672050, W angel-lymington.com. A pleasant pub with cosy lounges with open fires and a small garden. The stylish rooms are clean, comfortable and well refurbished, with some looking over the high street and others onto the patio at the back. **£125**

Britannia House Station St, SO41 3BA T 01590 672091, W britannia-house.com. An upmarket, friendly and central B&B, right by the train station. Some of the comfortable rooms are on the small side but there's also a larger apartment with a balcony (£120) and views over the harbour. All rooms have flatscreen TVs, and there's a fine sitting room commanding views over the yachts. **£90**

Stanwell House 14–15 High St, SO41 9AA T 01590 677123, W stanwellhousehotel.co.uk. The most upmarket choice in town, this handsome boutique-style hotel has an array of individually designed rooms – some of the more contemporary rooms open onto the garden, while others come with four-poster beds and Nespresso machines. Downstairs is a selection of well-regarded café-restaurants serving everything from fine dining to tapas to informal lunches in the conservatory. **£145**

EATING

The Chequers Ridgeway Lane, Lower Woodside, SO41 8AH T 01590 673415, W chequersinnlymington.com. About a mile southwest of Lymington tucked down a rural back lane, this ancient pub is a justifiably popular local haunt, especially at summer weekends when its walled garden and courtyard get packed with families enjoying its good-value pub food. There are great walks from here, too. Mon–Sat 11am–11pm, Sun noon–10.30pm.

Elderflower 4–5 Quay St, SO41 3AS T 01590 676908, W elderflowerrestaurant.co.uk. Excellent fine-dining restaurant serving innovative Modern British cuisine, with dishes such as jugged hare with lentils and roast turbot with nasturtium and lychee sauce (main £19–£25), as well as a nine-course tasting menu (£60). There are also two comfortable triple rooms above the restaurant (£90). Tues–Thurs noon–2.30pm & 6.30–9.30pm, Fri noon–2.30pm & 6.30–10pm, Sat 9.30am–2.30pm & 6.30–10pm, Sun 9.30am–2pm.

The Haven King Saltern Rd, SO41 3QD T 01590 679971, W havenrestaurant.co.uk. Wedged among the luxury yachts in Lymington harbour, this is not surprisingly a favoured haunt for the local sailing fraternity. The smart but laidback café-restaurant has a nautical-themed bar area, tables inside and a great raised terrace with views across the Solent. Fresh fish is the speciality, with dishes such as Mediterranean fish stew (£15), a half lobster and chips (£20), monkfish with curried mussel broth (£20) and fine cocktails – plus occasional live music. Daily 9am–midnight.

Lanes Ashley Lane, SO41 3RH ⓣ 01590 672777, ⓦ lanesoflymington.com. Set in an old chapel and former school, with some tables on an internal balcony, this bright and buzzy bar-restaurant serves locally sourced fish and meats (£17–23) including fresh sea bass and duck breast. Tues–Sat 11.30am–2pm & 6.30–9pm.

Maison Cuisine 8 Angel Courtyard, High St, ⓣ 01590 679269, ⓦ maisoncuisinelymington.co.uk. Nice deli and coffee shop with tables spilling out onto a little courtyard at the front serving croissants, soup, sandwiches, pies and quiches (£6–7) plus tasty salads – try the mackerel (£8.50). Mon–Fri 8.30am–4pm, Sat 9am–4pm.

The Mayflower Kings Saltern Rd, SO41 3QD ⓣ 01590 672160, ⓦ themayflowerlymington.co.uk. An attractive pub with plenty of space and a log fire inside, plus a lovely garden with tables overlooking the water. The good-value food comes in large portions, with a variety of burgers, fajitas and upmarket pub dishes (£10–13); there are barbecues outside in summer, too. Staff are friendly and it's great for kids and dogs. Mon–Wed 11am–11pm, Thurs & Fri 11am–midnight, Sat 10am–midnight, Sun 10am–10.30pm.

The Mill at Gordleton Silver St, Hordle, SO41 6DJ ⓣ 01590 682219, ⓦ themillatgordleton.co.uk. A pleasant restaurant and bar with smart, comfortable rooms (from £150), this 400-year-old watermill sits in its own beautifully landscaped gardens where ducks waddle freely. The menu features home-made and locally sourced produce such as Solent crab and cheddar soufflé (£11), or butternut squash risotto with Old Winchester cheese (£18). Grab a seat on the terrace overlooking the mill stream and you can't go wrong. Mon–Sat noon–2pm & 7–9pm, Sun noon–3pm & 6.30–8.30pm.

★Ship Inn The Quay, SO14 3AY ⓣ 01590 676903, ⓦ theshiplymington.co.uk. With a terrace facing the boats, this classy pub has an interior of bleached woods and chrome, which stylishly embraces the nautical theme. The menu is good value, and features dishes such as roast vegetable and olive tart, or prawn, crab and chorizo linguine (mains from £11). Mon–Thurs 11am–11pm, Fri–Sat 11am–midnight, Sun 11am–10.30pm.

Milford-on-Sea and Keyhaven

Set round a tranquil green, **MILFORD-ON-SEA** is the most attractive of the villages on this stretch, and has become something of a foodie destination with a surprising number of good restaurants for its size. Its harbour is at **KEYHAVEN**, just under a mile beyond the village, a picturesque spot popular with sailors; it has two sailing clubs and a pub, *The Gun*. The **ferry to Hurst Castle** leaves from here, and it's the starting point of a pleasant coastal walk across the salt marshes to Lymington (see p.186).

Hurst Castle

Easter–Sept daily 10.30am–5.30pm; Oct daily 10.30am–4pm; Nov–March Sat & Sun 10.30am–4pm • £4.80, children £3 • ⓦ hurstcastle.co.uk • **Ferry from Keyhaven** Easter–Oct daily 10am–5.30pm; every 20min • £6, children £3.50

Best reached by ferry from Keyhaven, or on foot along a mile-and-a-half-long shingle spit from Milford, **Hurst Castle** is spectacularly sited just under a mile from the Isle of Wight – there are great views from its various battlements and roofs. The castle was built by Henry VIII in 1544 as part of his coastal defences and was later used to imprison Charles I in 1648 before his execution. Much of the present structure was built during the Napoleonic Wars and in the 1870s, though its atmosphere derives from the fact that it has been largely untouched since soldiers were billeted here during World War II, when it was manned with gun batteries and searchlights. You can still see the cramped dorms where the soldiers slept and the small theatre where they put on plays. Temporary exhibitions are often held here and there's a small tearoom. Allow time, too, to explore the pretty shingle shoreline around the castle, and the tall lighthouse next door.

ACCOMMODATION — MILFORD-ON-SEA AND KEYHAVEN

The Bay Trees 8 High St, Milford-on-Sea, SO41 0QD ⓣ 01590 642186, ⓦ baytreebedandbreakfast.co.uk. Agreeable B&B in a seventeenth-century building that has variously been used as a shop, a bank and a poorhouse.

It has lovely gardens – the downstairs room opens directly onto them – as well as a four-poster upstairs, and the breakfasts are great. **£100**

The Marine B&B Hurst Rd, Milford-on-Sea, SO41 0PY ⓣ01590 644369, ⓦthemarinemos.co.uk. Modern building in Art Deco style right on the beach. The clean, comfortable rooms all have sea views and there's a large roof terrace above, with breakfast taken at the well-regarded on-site restaurant, *Blue Horizon*. **£150**

The Beach House Westover Hall Park Lane, Milford-on-Sea, SO41 0PT ⓣ01590 643044, ⓦbeachhousemilfordonsea.co.uk. This opulent, Grade II-listed Victorian mansion has a lovely garden that backs onto the clifftop. Its public rooms have lots of oak panelling, stained-glass windows and decorated ceilings, though the bedrooms are more contemporary, many with sea views. The restaurant also serves decent pub food. **£110**

EATING

The Gun Keyhaven, SO41 0TP ⓣ01590 642391. This attractive eighteenth-century pub has log fires, a nautically themed interior, a beer garden at the back and an impressive collection of 240 malt whiskies. It also has live music every other Thursday. However, the landlord is an acquired taste and the food can be rather hit-and-miss. Mon–Fri 11am–3pm & 6–11pm, Sat 11am–11pm, Sun noon–5pm; may stay open longer in summer.

La Perle 60 High St, Milford-on-Sea, SO41 0QD ⓣ01590 643557, ⓦlaperle.co.uk. The chef here trained under Raymond Blanc and specializes in French cuisine made with local seasonal ingredients. Dishes such as frogs' legs, Hampshire watercress soup (£7.50) and breast of local partridge (£18.50) are on the menu. Tues 6–9.30pm, Wed–Sat noon–2.30pm & 6–9.30pm, Sun noon–2.30pm.

Verveine 98 High St, Milford-on-Sea, SO41 0QE ⓣ01590 642176, ⓦverveine.co.uk. Top-quality restaurant that doubles as a fishmonger's – unsurprisingly seafood is the speciality, served in unusual and innovative dishes such as halibut with fizzy grapes or pressed octopus with mussels (mains £20–24). Alternatively, pick a fish from the daily catch menu and choose your garnish to go with it. The lunch menu is good value for cooking of this quality, at £21 for three courses. Tues–Sat noon–2pm & 6.30–10pm.

The Cave 2 Church Hill, Milford-on-Sea, SO41 0QH ⓣ01590 642195, ⓦthecavemos.co.uk. Great wine bar/bottle shop with chandeliers, plush decor and a fine selection of wines by the glass and beers, plus tasty tapas (from £4.40) and sharing platters of fish, cheese or seafood (£13). Tues–Sat noon–11pm, Sun noon–10pm.

Winchester and northern Hampshire

THE MAYFLY PUB AT TESTCOMBE, NEAR STOCKBRIDGE

Winchester and northern Hampshire

Northern Hampshire, its quintessentially English landscape encompassing wooded valleys and opulent farmland, is the ancient heart of the country, where Alfred the Great chose Winchester as his capital and where – allegedly – King Arthur set up his round table. Today, the city's main sight is its impressive cathedral, though it's also home to some more modern attractions such as the Science Centre and Planetarium and nearby Marwell Zoo. Just east of Winchester, the South Downs National Park embraces the Itchen Valley, whose clear-flowing rivers still feed the historic watercress beds that gave the name to the Watercress Line, a wonderful old steam train line connecting the town of Alton to pretty Alresford. An England of bygone days also survives at Selborne, where pioneering naturalist Gilbert White's house has been kept as a fascinating museum, though a more famous name from the past draws fans of Jane Austen to nearby Chawton, where the novelist spent much of her life.

Further north there are more historical attractions including the home of the Duke of Wellington at Stratfield Saye, the Roman remains at Silchester, the Stanley Spencer murals at the Sandham Memorial Chapel, and Highclere Castle, the real-life Downton Abbey of TV fame.

Winchester and around

A trip to **WINCHESTER**, Hampshire's county town, is a must – not only for the magnificent **cathedral**, chief relic of Winchester's medieval glory, but for the all-round well-preserved ambience of England's one-time capital. Indeed, with its lovely riverside walks, medieval remains – including the ruins of the original palace of the Bishops of Winchester, **Wolvesey** – and superb pubs and cafés, it warrants a day or two on any itinerary.

The town is fairly easy to find your way around. The largely pedestrianized **High Street** connects the Broadway in the east – where you'll find the bus station, tourist office and River Itchen – to the Great Hall in the west, from where it's a five-minute walk north to the train station. The main attractions lie just south of the High Street beyond the **Buttercross**, an impressive fifteenth-century monument dotted with figures representing, among others, the Blessed Virgin, St Swithun and Bishop William of Wykeham.

Brief history

Now a handsome market town, Winchester was once one of the mightiest settlements in England, and was originally capital of a Celtic tribe called the Belgares. When the Romans arrived they named it Venta Belgarum after the tribe, and for a time it became the fifth-largest town in Britain. The Saxons took over in the sixth century, changing its

JANE AUSTEN'S HOUSE, CHAWTON

Highlights

❶ **Winchester Cathedral** One of the most impressive and historic cathedrals in the country, containing the tombs of Jane Austen and some of England's earliest kings, plus some dazzling stained glass. **See p.197**

❷ **Wykeham Arms** Have a drink in this atmospheric pub in the heart of Winchester, with its warren of cosy rooms and open fireplaces. **See p.202**

❸ **Winchester Science Centre and Planetarium** Feel the forces and wonders of space at this futuristic planetarium. **See p.203**

❹ **Marwell Zoo** The extensive grounds of this zoo are as impressive as the beasts, which include rhinos, tigers and giraffes. **See p.203**

❺ **The Watercress Line** All aboard this great little steam train that chuffs through the heart of the region. **See p.206**

❻ **Chawton** You can visit Jane Austen's house in a village that has barely changed since the great author lived here. **See p.207**

❼ **Gilbert White's House** The former home of the original David Attenborough is surrounded by beautiful grounds. **See p.208**

HIGHLIGHTS ARE MARKED ON THE MAP ON PP.194–195

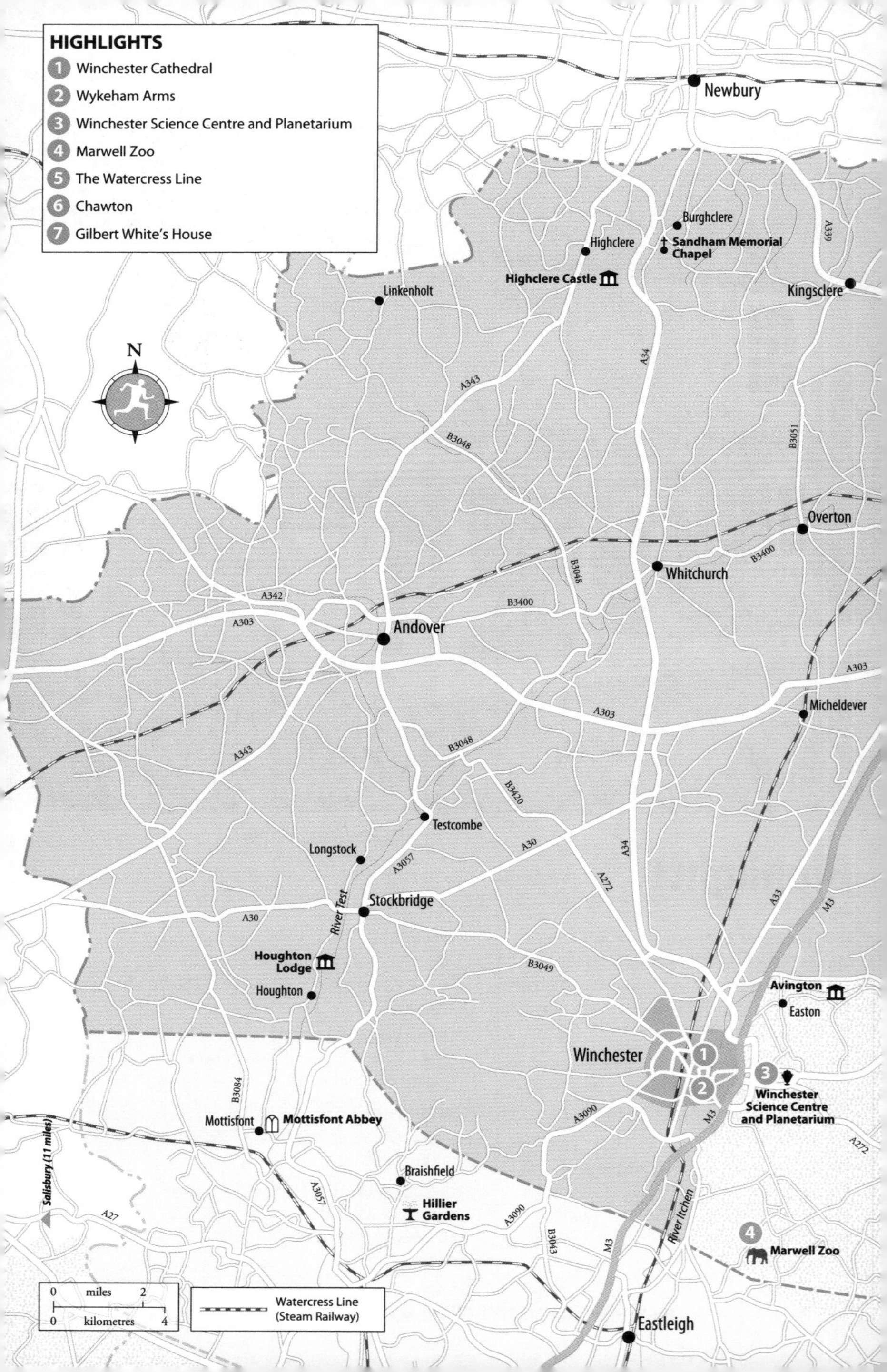
HIGHLIGHTS
1 Winchester Cathedral
2 Wykeham Arms
3 Winchester Science Centre and Planetarium
4 Marwell Zoo
5 The Watercress Line
6 Chawton
7 Gilbert White's House
Newbury
Burghclere
Highclere
Sandham Memorial Chapel
Highclere Castle
Kingsclere
Linkenholt
N
A339
A34
A343
B3048
B3051
Overton
B3400
Whitchurch
B3048
A342
B3400
A303
Andover
A303
Micheldever
A303
B3048
A343
B3420
Testcombe
Longstock
A30
A3057
A34
A272
A33
M3
Stockbridge
River Test
A30
Houghton Lodge
B3049
Houghton
Avington
Easton
Winchester
1
2
3
Winchester Science Centre and Planetarium
A272
B3084
A3090
M3
Mottisfont
Mottisfont Abbey
Salisbury (11 miles)
Braishfield
A3057
A27
Hillier Gardens
A3090
B3043
M3
River Itchen
4
Marwell Zoo
0 miles 2
0 kilometres 4
Watercress Line (Steam Railway)
Eastleigh

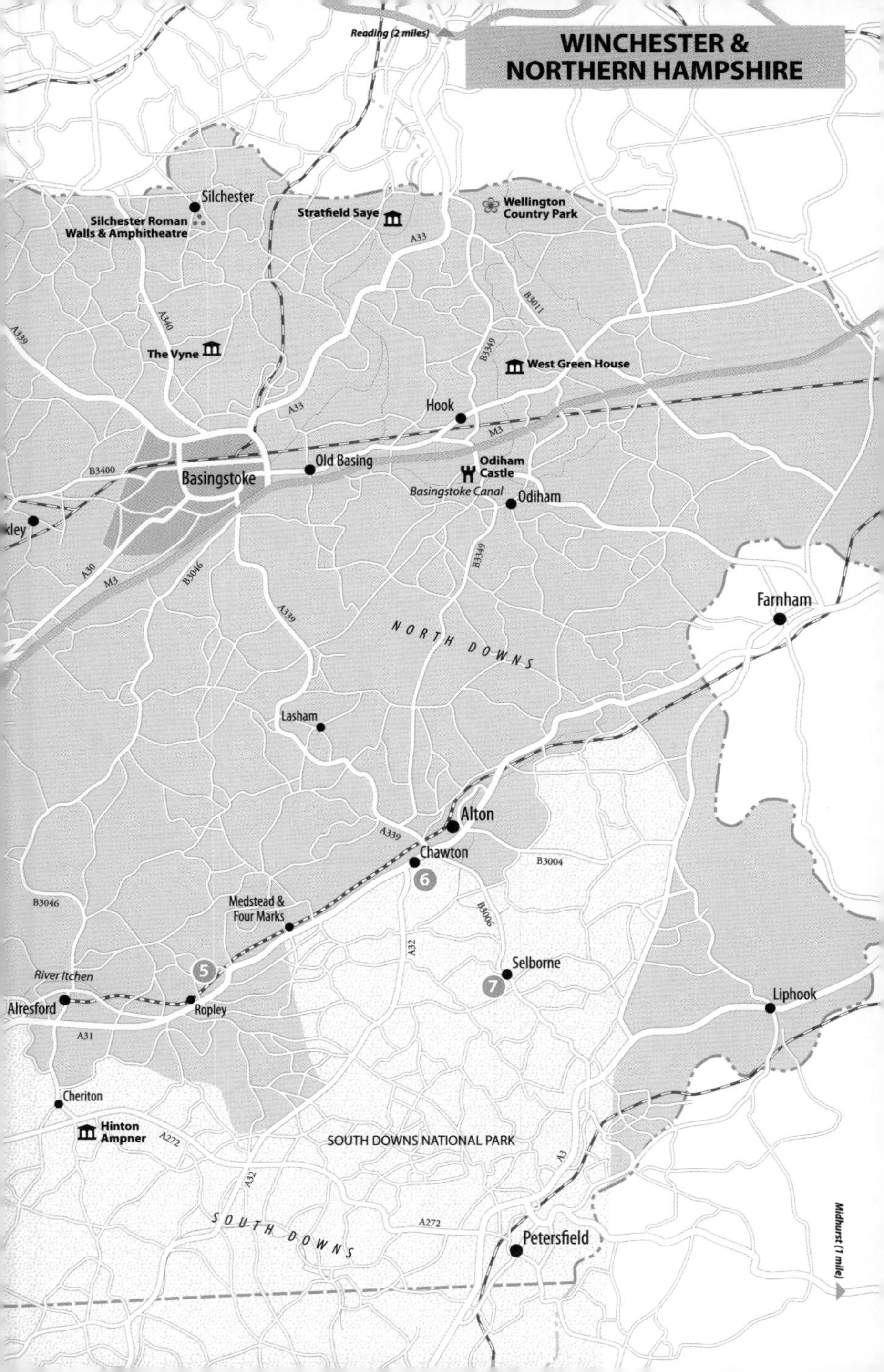
WINCHESTER & NORTHERN HAMPSHIRE
Reading (2 miles)
Silchester
Silchester Roman Walls & Amphitheatre
Stratfield Saye
Wellington Country Park
A33
B3011
A340
A339
The Vyne
B3349
West Green House
A33
Hook
M3
B3400
Basingstoke
Old Basing
Odiham Castle
Basingstoke Canal
Odiham
kley
A30
M3
B3046
B3349
A339
NORTH DOWNS
Farnham
Lasham
Alton
A339
Chawton
B3004
6
B3046
Medstead & Four Marks
B3006
A32
Selborne
5
River Itchen
7
Alresford
Ropley
Liphook
A31
Cheriton
Hinton Ampner
A272
SOUTH DOWNS NATIONAL PARK
A3
A32
SOUTH DOWNS
A272
Petersfield
Midhurst (1 mile)

name to Venta Caester – over the years this corrupted into Wintancaester and finally its present name. The Bishop of Wessex set up a cathedral here in around 676, but it was **Alfred the Great** who put Winchester on the map in the ninth century when he made it the capital of his Wessex kingdom. For the next couple of centuries Winchester ranked alongside London, its status affirmed by William the Conqueror's coronation in both cities and by his commissioning of the local monks to prepare the **Domesday Book.** A palace was erected in the tenth century, though this was rebuilt in grander style by William the Conqueror – the Normans also built a new cathedral in 1079, the **Hospital of St Cross** in 1136 and **Wolvesey Castle** as the bishop's residence. Winchester began to lose out to London in importance in the thirteenth century, though Bishop William of Wykeham, who was also England's Chancellor, founded Winchester College in 1382.

It wasn't until the English Civil War, when Cromwell took the city in 1645, that Winchester began its decline into provinciality. Cromwell later destroyed Winchester's

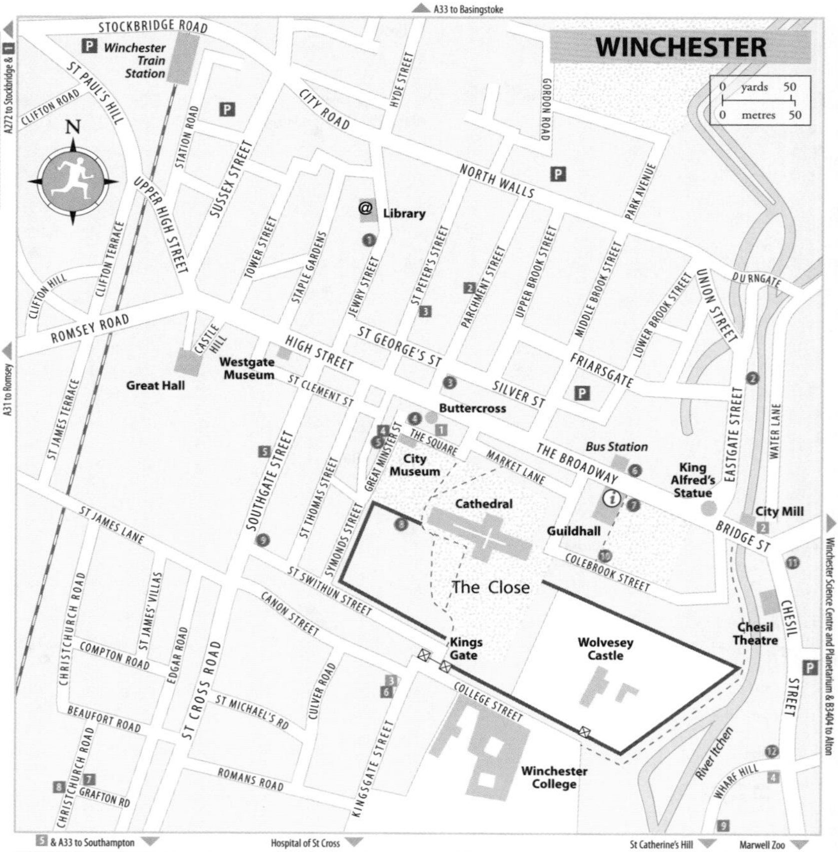

WINCHESTER

ACCOMMODATION

29 Christchurch Road	7
The Black Hole	9
Giffard House	8
Hannah's B&B	2
Hotel du Vin	5
Lainston Country House Hotel	1
The Old Vine	4
Winchester Royal Hotel	3
Wykeham Arms	6

EATING

The Black Rat	12
Brasserie Blanc	1
Café 1871	7
Café Monde	4
Cathedral Rectory	8
The Chesil Rectory	11
El Sabio	2
Forte Kitchen	3
The Green Man	9
The Old Vine	5
Palm Pan Asia	6
River Cottage Canteen	10

DRINKING

The Bell Inn	5
The Black Boy	4
Eclipse Inn	1
No. 5 Bridge Street	2
Wykeham Arms	3

castle – only sparing the Great Hall – to prevent it falling into Royalist hands. Much of today's Winchester was built in the seventeenth and eighteenth centuries; the resulting harmonious architecture is just one of the reasons why it has become such a popular, if expensive, commuter town, just an hour by train from London.

Winchester Cathedral

1 The Close, SO23 9LS • Mon–Sat 9.30am–5pm, Sun 12.30–3pm • £7.95 for unlimited visits within a year; includes free guided tour of cathedral, treasury and crypt • **Tower tours** Jan–May, Oct & Nov Wed 2.15pm, Sat 11.30am & 2.15pm; June–Sept Mon, Wed & Fri 2.15pm, Sat 11.30am & 2.15pm; 1hr 30min • £6 • ⓣ 01962 857200, ⓦ winchester-cathedral.org.uk

The first minster to be built in Winchester was raised by Cenwalh, the Saxon king of Wessex, in the mid-seventh century. Traces of this building have been unearthed near the present **cathedral**, itself begun in 1079 and completed some three hundred years later, producing a monument whose features range from early Norman to Perpendicular styles. The exterior is not its best attribute – squat and massive, the cathedral crouches solemnly over the tidy lawns of the Cathedral Close. It is only once inside that Winchester Cathedral's glories become apparent. Its 1000-plus years of history are evident at every turn – from the decorative tiled floors to the ornate ceilings, via the tombs of dignitaries and celebrities, fantastically carved altars and sumptuous stained-glass windows. Not only is this a revered church with the longest nave in England (170m), but also it is a veritable treasure chest of memorabilia and specially commissioned art, from medieval times up to the twenty-first century.

The interior

As you walk through the colossal cathedral entrance, light floods in from the giant **stained-glass window** in the east wall. During the English Civil War, horse-mounted soldiers rode thunderously into this giant space, plundering the church contents and smashing the stained glass. Under the reign of Charles II, the window was then pieced back together using whatever shards could be found. The result is an amazingly modern-looking mosaic – a head here, an angel there, but mostly a dazzling mishmash of colourful fragments.

The small upper-floor **treasury** can be accessed from this corner of the cathedral. It contains displays of priceless silver from local parish churches – though these constantly change, depending on what the churches can spare at the time.

Don't miss the superbly carved twelfth-century wooden christening **font**, or a peer into the Norman crypt – often flooded – where you can see **Antony Gormley**'s contemplative figure *Sound II*. The cathedral's original foundations were dug in marshy ground, and at the beginning of the last century a steadfast diver, William Walker, spent five years replacing the rotten timber foundations with concrete. The crypt still has shallow floods, but they are far less severe than in the past.

Other highlights include the **Fisherman's Chapel**, with ornate woodcarvings by contemporary artist Eugene Ball; and the **Lady Chapel**, in which every seat is imaginatively embellished with carved wooden animals. Look out, too, for the carved Norman font of black Tournai marble and the fourteenth-century misericords (the choir stalls are the oldest complete set in the country).

The tombs

The cathedral shelters various **tombs**, including those belonging to Jane Austen – close to the north wall a short way in from the main entrance – and several of the earliest kings of England. Many of the kings' remains were disinterred from the original Winchester Minster, which was demolished to make way for the new cathedral, and their bones placed in decorative tombs on top of the choir screen – including Cnut, William Rufus and King Cynegils (611–643). Look out, too, for the memorial **shrine to St Swithun**. Originally buried outside in the churchyard, his remains were later interred inside the cathedral where the "rain of heaven" could no longer fall on him, whereupon he took revenge and the heavens opened for forty days – hence the legend that if it rains on St Swithun's Day (July 15) it will continue for another forty. His exact burial place is unknown.

Great Hall

Castle Ave, SO23 8UJ • Daily except during occasional civic events 10am–5pm • Free, donation requested • T 01962 846476, W hants.gov.uk/greathall

The **Great Hall** is the vestigial remains of a thirteenth-century castle. The current hall was built in 1235 as part of a replacement for the crumbling original castle built by William the Conqueror and would have served as the royal dining room as well as a court and assembly hall for dignitaries. Most of this castle was destroyed by Cromwell during the English Civil War, though the hall was spared, being a useful assembly room – indeed, it was used as a court until 1974. It is now rated one of the best-preserved buildings of the genre in the country. Sir Walter Raleigh heard his death sentence here in 1603, though he wasn't finally dispatched until 1618, and Judge Jeffreys held one of his Bloody Assizes (see p.280) in the castle after Monmouth's rebellion in 1685. More recently, the wrought-steel gates, installed in 1983, commemorate the wedding of Prince Charles and Lady Diana. The main interest now, however, is a large, brightly painted disc slung on one wall like some curious antique dartboard. This is alleged to be **King Arthur's Round Table**, but the woodwork is probably fourteenth century, later repainted as a PR exercise for the Tudor dynasty – the portrait of Arthur at the top of the table bears an uncanny resemblance to Henry VIII. At the back of the hall is the attractive **Queen Eleanor's Garden**, a re-creation of a medieval herb garden named after the spouse of Henry III.

Westgate Museum

High St, SO23 9AP • Feb half-term to March Sat 10am–4pm, Sun noon–4pm; April–Oct Sat 10am–5pm, Sun noon–5pm • Free • T 01962 869864, W hampshireculturaltrust.org.uk/westgate-museum

It's hard to miss the distinctive **Westgate**, once one of the main gateways into the city. Now a titchy museum, this was used from the sixteenth to mid-eighteenth centuries as a debtors' prison, and you can still see the prisoners' scribbles on the walls along with an assorted collection of relics including medieval weights, measures and costumes. There are fine views across town from its roof, as well as activities for children, including the chance to try on some extremely heavy armour.

City Museum

The Square, SO23 9ES • April–Oct Mon–Sat 10am–5pm, Sun noon–5pm; Nov–March Tues–Sat 10am–4pm, Sun noon–4pm • Free • T 01962 863064, W hampshireculturaltrust.org.uk/winchester-city-museum

Set on three floors, the **City Museum** tells the story of Winchester using an imaginative medley of historical artefacts including re-created traditional shopfronts, some impressive Roman mosaics and displays of medieval coins and skeletons. There's a gift shop and usually special children's activities.

City Mill

Bridge St, SO23 0EJ • Mid-Feb to Oct daily 10am–5pm; Nov to mid-Feb daily 10am–4pm; closed over Christmas • £4.40; NT • T 01962 870057, W nationaltrust.org.uk/winchester-city-mill

At the east end of the Broadway, beyond the Guildhall and the august bronze statue of King Alfred, you come to the River Itchen and the eighteenth-century **City Mill**, where you can see restored mill machinery. The current building dates back to 1744, though there are records of a mill on this site in the Domesday Book. There's a video explaining the history of the building, attractive riverside gardens at the back and occasional demonstrations of flour milling. The highlight is the "Mill Race", where the water wheels are kept, and you can watch the powerful water rushing through the building. Over the bridge you can head up **St Giles' Hill**, a ten-minute climb – there are great views over the town from the top.

Wolvesey Castle

College St, SO23 9NB • April–Oct daily 10am–5pm • Free; EH • ⓦ www.english-heritage.org.uk/visit/places/wolvesey-castle-old-bishops-palace

Southeast of the cathedral, the remains of the Saxon walls bracket the ruins of the twelfth-century **Wolvesey Castle** – actually the palace for the Bishops of Winchester, who once wielded great clout over England's religious and political affairs. When it was built, it was one of the most important buildings in Winchester, encompassing its own stables, prison, chapel and gardens. The brainchild of Henry of Blois, who was Bishop of Winchester from 1129 to 1171, the palace slowly declined with the influence of the bishops and was largely demolished in 1786, when it was considered too old-fashioned. Nonetheless, the ruins remain highly impressive and still dwarf the current dwelling place of the Bishop of Winchester, a relatively modest house alongside it, built in 1680.

Winchester College and around

College St, SO23 9NA • **Tours** Mon, Wed, Fri & Sat 3–4 daily, Tues & Thurs 2–4 daily, Sun 1–2 daily • £7 • ⓣ 01962 621209, ⓦ winchestercollege.org

Winchester College is the oldest public school in England – established in 1382 by William of Wykeham for "poor scholars", it now educates few but the wealthy and privileged. The cloisters and chantry are open for **guided visits**, which include a look at the Gothic chapel and the red-brick school room, said to have been designed by Christopher Wren.

Jane Austen moved to the house at nearby **8 College St** (now privately owned) from Chawton in 1817, when she was already ill with Addison's Disease, and died there later the same year. The thirteenth-century **King's Gate**, at the top of College Street, is one of the city's original medieval gateways, housing the tiny St Swithun's Church.

The Hospital of St Cross

St Cross Rd, SO23 9SD • April–Oct Mon–Sat 9.30am–5pm, Sun 1–5pm; Nov–March Mon–Sat 10.30am–3.30pm • £4.50 • ⓣ 01962 851375, ⓦ stcrosshospital.co.uk

The Hospital of St Cross is the country's oldest continuing almshouse, caring for the Brothers of St Cross and the Order of Noble Poverty. Founded in 1132 as a hostel for the poor and extended in the fifteenth century, it even has its own surprisingly impressive twelfth-century church. You can still sample the Wayfarer's "dole" at the Porter's Lodge – a tiny portion of bread and beer – and stroll round the attractive Master's Garden.

A WALK ALONG THE ITCHEN TO ST CATHERINE'S HILL

The eastern fringes of Wolvesey Castle and Winchester College back onto the verdant plains of the River Itchen, whose cool, clear waters were historically irrigated to form idyllic water meadows – said to have inspired Keats' *Ode to Autumn*. It's around twenty minutes' walk south along the river to the foot of **St Catherine's Hill** and another twenty minutes to the top of this local wooded landmark that offers great views over the water meadows to the city below: a great place for a summer picnic.

ARRIVAL AND INFORMATION

WINCHESTER AND AROUND

By train Winchester train station is about a mile northwest of the cathedral, on Stockbridge Rd.

Destinations Bournemouth (2–3 hourly; 45–55min); London Waterloo (3–4 hourly; 1hr–1hr 15min); Portsmouth (hourly; 1hr); Southampton (4–5 hourly; 15–20min).

By bus If you arrive by bus, you'll find yourself at the Broadway bus station (T 08712 002233), opposite the tourist office.

Destinations Alton (Mon–Sat 8 daily; 25min); Alresford (Mon–Sat every 45min; 15–30min); London (9 daily; 1hr 50min–2hr 10min); Southampton (2 hourly; 50min).

By car Drivers should use the park and rides on the edge of the city or head for one of the well-signed central car parks, though note that the central area is mostly pedestrianized and has a somewhat confusing one-way system.

Tourist office Guildhall, High St, SO23 9GH (May–Sept Mon–Sat 10am–5pm, Sun & bank hols 11am–4pm; Oct–April Mon–Sat 10am–5pm; W visitwinchester.co.uk).

ACCOMMODATION

29 Christchurch Road 29 Christchurch Rd, SO23 9SU T 01962 868661, W bedbreakfastwinchester.co.uk. Reliable B&B in a charming Regency house located in a quiet residential part of town. The rooms are comfortable and the owner is friendly. No smoking. **£100**

The Black Hole Wharf Hill, SO23 9NP T 01962 807010, W theblackholebb.co.uk. A quirky B&B with an upstairs roof terrace that gives great views of the city – the ten rooms are not huge and are decorated in the style of a prison cell, but they are comfortable and well equipped with good bathrooms. **£100**

Giffard House 50 Christchurch Rd, SO23 9SU T 01962 852628, W giffardhotel.co.uk. Small hotel in an elegant Victorian building with high ceilings and a range of rooms – most of them are spacious and some overlook the attractive gardens. There is also a great patio bar and off-street parking. **£110**

Hannah's B&B 16a Parchment St, SO23 8AZ T 01962 840623, W hannahsbedandbreakfast.co.uk. Tucked away off Parchment St with a pretty patio in front, this smart boutique B&B run by the welcoming Hannah has three immaculate rooms, each decorated in an individual style. The rooms all have wooden floors, comfortable beds and large baths, plus all mod cons (including Netflix), and guests can make themselves at home in the lovely lounge with an open fireplace and grand piano. **£185**

★**Hotel du Vin** Southgate St, SO23 9EF T 01962 896329, W hotelduvin.com/winchester. The first of the classy *Hotel du Vin* chain, in a lovely Georgian townhouse that's been given a stylish makeover. With its plush rooms – including cottage-style options with their own private entrances and terraces – a lovely patio garden, chic bar and decent restaurant, it's a good choice, especially if you can bag one of their periodic special deals. **£150**

Lainston Country House Hotel Woodman Lane, Sparshot, SO21 2LT T 01962 776088, W lainstonhouse .com. Around ten minutes' drive from Winchester towards Stockbridge, this seventeenth-century mansion sits in 63 acres of grounds – it's luxurious and comfortable, with huge bedrooms and friendly staff. It has its own quality restaurant, specializing in local produce. **£175**

The Old Vine 8 Great Minster St, SO23 9HA T 01962 854616, W oldvinewinchester.com. An eighteenth-century inn in a great location overlooking the cathedral green. The lovely big rooms combine period features with modern designer decor – flatscreen TVs and Nespresso machines come in all rooms. There's a fine bar-restaurant below, too (see opposite), and a terrace in summer. **£130**

Winchester Royal Hotel St Peter's St, SO23 8BS T 01962 840840, W www.sjhotels.co.uk/hotels/winchester-royal -hotel. Very popular with wedding parties, rooms here are in a historic fifteenth-century building that has been a bishop's residence and a convent. The garden's lovely, though the atmosphere can be a tad fusty. Good low-season rates. **£130**

Wykeham Arms 75 Kingsgate St, SO23 9PE T 01962 853834, W wykehamarmswinchester.co.uk. Small but charming rooms, beamed and quirkily shaped, above an eighteenth-century pub (see p.202), or larger, more contemporary options (for the same price) in the annexe opposite. Minimum two-night weekend stays at busy times. **£120**

EATING

RESTAURANTS AND GASTROPUBS

The Black Rat 88 Chesil St, SO23 0HX T 01962 844465, W theblackrat.co.uk. This Michelin-starred restaurant serves up quality Modern British cuisine in a cosy former pub. Ingredients are locally sourced (some foraged, some grown in their own kitchen garden) with dishes such as game broth with faggots, or skate wing with cauliflower: expect to pay £40–45 a head. Reservations advised. Mon–Fri 7–9.15pm, Sat & Sun noon–2.15pm & 7–9.15pm.

Brasserie Blanc 19–20 Jewry St, SO23 8RZ T 01962 810870, W brasserieblanc.com. A smart but laidback French bistro bedecked with chandeliers, and set in a former butcher's. Try quality French dishes such as boeuf bourguignon (£16.50) or roast hake with saffron and seafood (£15.50); the all-day set menu (until 6.30pm) is a steal at £12.45 for three courses. Mon–Sat 8.30am–11pm, Sun 9.30am–10pm.

The Chesil Rectory 1 Chesil St, SO23 0HU T 01962 851555, W chesilrectory.co.uk. This cosy, wood-beamed fifteenth-century building serves excellent British cuisine with dishes such as Hampshire venison or sea bass with local mushrooms. Lunches and the early evening set menu are good value (three courses around £20), while at other times mains cost around £14–20. Mon–Sat noon–2.20pm & 6–9.30pm, Sun noon–3pm & 6–9pm.

El Sabio 60 Eastgate St, SO23 8DZ ⓣ 01962 820233, ⓦ elsabio.co.uk. Vibrant Spanish restaurant serving a fine range of tapas (most £6–7), along with great meat platters (£9 for two) and a tempting paella (around £28 for two), best downed with Spanish wines and beers. Mon–Wed 5–9pm, Thurs–Sat noon–2pm & 5–10pm, Sun noon–3.15pm & 6–9pm.

The Green Man 53 Southgate St, SO23 9EH ⓣ 01962 866809, ⓦ the.littlepubgroup.co.uk/the-green-man. Wooden floors, retro furnishings, quirky decor and comfy armchairs in this stylish gastropub that serves cask ales, tasty cocktails and local produce. Try dishes such as venison sausages with horseradish mash (£12.50) or the excellent local cheeseboard (£9 for three cheeses). Mon–Sat noon–11pm, Sun noon–10pm.

The Old Vine 8 Great Minster St, SO23 9HA ⓣ 01962 854616, ⓦ oldvinewinchester.com. Fashionable bar and bistro in a Grade II-listed building – you can also stay here (see opposite). A great place for a drink or a full meal, with good-value starters and main courses such as home-made Scotch eggs (£6), home-cured salmon (£7) and spicy pork goulash (£13); good veggie options too. Mon–Sat 11am–11pm, Sun noon–10.30pm.

Palm Pan Asia 166–167 High St, SO23 9BA ⓣ 01962 864040, ⓦ palmpanasia.co.uk. Stylish Asian restaurant in an attractive building serving a variety of tasty dishes, such as Malaysian chilli crab, Indonesian seafood stir-fry, Vietnamese spring rolls and a good selection of Thai dishes. Mains £10–24. Daily noon–2.30pm & 6–10.30pm.

★ **River Cottage Canteen** Abbey Mill, Abbey Mill Gardens, The Broadway, SO23 9GH ⓣ 01962 457747, ⓦ rivercottage.net/canteens/winchester. In a converted mill building, this is a great venue spread over several floors with outside seating by the millstream. The menu features local ingredients, such as South Coast hake (£17), and of course plenty of veggie options including New Forest mushrooms and local goats' cheese with polenta (£12.50). The cocktails are good, too. Mon & Sun 11am–5pm, Tues–Sat 11am–10.30pm.

CAFÉS

Café 1871 Guildhall, High St, SO23 9GH ⓣ 01962 840820, ⓦ www.guildhallwinchester.co.uk/eighteen71. Next to the tourist office, this relaxed and spacious café with tables outside on a small square does good-value sandwiches and self-service lunches (£4–8) as well as fresh croissants, pastries, coffees and teas. Mon–Sat 8am–5pm, Sun 10am–4.30pm.

Café Monde 22 The Square, SO23 9EX ⓣ 01962 877177. The outdoor tables of this bustling small café on a pedestrianized street get snapped up by people seeking a sunny spot for inexpensive breakfasts, lunches or tea and cakes. Mon–Sat 8am–6pm, Sun 9am–5pm.

Cathedral Refectory Inner Close, SO23 9LS ⓣ 01962 875258. Part of the cathedral visitors' centre, this glass-fronted self-service café does a good range of inexpensive snacks, soups, lunches (most around £5–8) and teas using local ingredients, plus home-baked cakes and biscuits. The big appeal is the outdoor tables in a tranquil garden. Daily: Jan–March 9.30am–4.30pm; April–Dec 9.30am–5pm.

★ **Forte Kitchen** 78 Parchment St, SO23 8AT ⓣ 01962 856840, ⓦ fortekitchen.co.uk. The best place in town for great lunches. There's a good selection of sandwiches plus more hearty mains such as smoked mackerel with spinach, poached eggs and sourdough (£9) or Hampshire beef burger (£10.50). The large upstairs dining room attracts a lively, arty clientele. Mon–Fri 8am–4pm, Sat 9am–5pm, Sun 9am–4pm.

DRINKING

The Bell Inn 83 Saint Cross Rd, SO23 9RE ⓣ 01962 865284. Right by St Cross Hospital, this historic pub serves a good selection of beers and well-priced pub food; it also has a walled garden full of old pub signs. Mon–Sat

THE SOUTH DOWNS NATIONAL PARK

The M3 motorway marks the westernmost boundary of the **South Downs National Park**, which embraces woodland, chalk uplands and several Areas of Outstanding Natural Beauty across Hampshire and Sussex. Created in 2010, and covering an area of 627 square miles, the park attracts more visitors than any of England's nine other national parks, and provides protection for the habitats of rare plants such as the musk orchid and wild thyme and birds like the nightjar and Dartford warbler, which were previously under threat from road and house building. Appropriately, the park includes the village of Selborne, where Gilbert White pioneered the study and protection of natural life in the area in 1789 (see p.208). Walkers can also enjoy the **South Downs Way**, a hundred-mile trail across the park from Winchester to Eastbourne. Full details are on ⓦ nationaltrail.co.uk/south-downs-way.

noon–11pm, Sun noon–10.30pm.

The Black Boy Wharf Hill, SO23 9NP ⊕01962 861754, ⊕theblackboypub.com. Fantastic old pub with log fires in winter, walls lined with books and low ceilings hung with old coins and miniature bottles. Good cask ales from local breweries are on draught and there's reasonable pub grub from a daily changing menu, as well as a small outdoor terrace. Mon–Thurs noon–11pm, Fri & Sat noon–midnight, Sun noon–10.30pm.

Eclipse Inn 25 The Square, SO23 9EX ⊕01962 865676, ⊕eclipseinnwinchester.co.uk. Opposite the cathedral, this attractive sixteenth-century inn has outside seating, perfect for catching the last of the day's sun. There's also decent, mid-priced pub food. Mon–Thurs & Sun 11am–11pm, Fri & Sat 11am–midnight.

No. 5 Bridge Street 5 Bridge St, SO23 0HN ⊕01962 863838, ⊕idealcollection.co.uk/no5bridgestreet. Calling itself a bar and kitchen with rooms (£120), this stylish spot, with an open kitchen and wooden floors, serves decent cocktails and a good menu of British dishes. Mon–Thurs 8am–11pm, Fri & Sat 8am–midnight, Sun 8am–10.30pm.

Wykeham Arms 75 Kingsgate St, SO23 9PE ⊕01962 853834, ⊕wykehamarmswinchester.co.uk. This eighteenth-century tavern is an atmospheric place, with a warren of cosy rooms, an open fireplace and a lively vibe. There's a small garden at the back, and it also has good food and rooms (see p.200). Daily 11am–11pm.

7

Stockbridge and around

Around eight miles west of Winchester, **STOCKBRIDGE**, literally meaning "bridge over the river", grew up at a crossing point over the River Test and a meeting place for two ancient roads – the east–west route between Winchester and Salisbury, and the north–south road along the Test Valley. Once a sizeable town used by Welsh sheep drovers as a stopping point on their way to markets further east – the thatched Drovers House still has a Welsh inscription on its walls – it's now little more than one street, laced with streams and dotted with a few pubs, hotels, antique shops and restaurants. Its main *raison d'être* today, however, as the fishing equipment shops along the high street testify, is **fishing** in the River Test, one of England's best chalk streams for fly-fishing. Salmon, trout and grayling can all be caught in the river and in the chalk streams that feed it.

Houghton Lodge

North Houghton, Stockbridge, SO20 6LQ • **Gardens** March–Oct daily 10am–5pm • £6.50, children £3 • **House** Visits by appointment only • £16, see website for booking and details • ⊕01264 810502, ⊕houghtonlodge.co.uk

A mile and a half south of Stockbridge, **Houghton Lodge** is a splendid and rare example of a late eighteenth-century *orné* (rural retreat), probably used originally as a fishing lodge for the local gentry. Built in the Natural Style, its thatched roof and rounded form are designed to blend in with the surrounding landscape, and it has been the backdrop for many TV and film productions, including the BBC's 1999 version of *David Copperfield*. However, it is the gardens that are the main attraction – they are a real delight, full of wild woodlands and ornate topiary with some lovely walks along the River Test, and a field of alpaca to visit. There is also an orchid house and a greenhouse, which is used as an art gallery, plus a pleasant tearoom.

ACCOMMODATION AND EATING — STOCKBRIDGE AND AROUND

Mayfly Testcombe, SO20 6AX ⊕01264 860283, ⊕themayfly.co.uk. With an idyllic garden alongside the clear-flowing River Test, the *Mayfly* pub, three miles north of Stockbridge in Testcombe, is a great spot for a drink or a decent meal with favourites such as lamb tagine, roast duck breast or sea bass with asparagus (around £11–13). It serves a good range of real ales and has a cosy interior, with wood-burners for the winter. Daily 10am–11pm.

Peat Spade Inn Longstock, SO20 6DR ⊕01264 810612, ⊕peatspadeinn.co.uk. The *Peat Spade Inn*, a couple of miles north of Stockbridge in Longstock, can organize fishing trips, guides, equipment and tuition, and has some great footpaths nearby for walkers. It has comfortable rooms and an excellent restaurant serving classic English dishes using local produce – including, of course, trout from the River Test (mains around £12–23). Daily noon–2.15pm & 6.30–9.15pm. **£145**

East of Winchester

East of Winchester, you can see rural Hampshire at its best, alongside family-friendly activities like the **Winchester Science Centre and Planetarium** and **Marwell Zoo**. Well-marked footpaths follow the **Itchen Valley** through pretty villages full of thatched cottages, while a series of attractive provincial towns and villages is worth a visit for their archetypal Englishness as well as for their literary connections. **Alton** and **Alresford** are linked by the **Watercress Line**, along which a restored steam train chugs through bucolic countryside. The village of **Chawton** makes the most of its famous former resident, Jane Austen, as does **Selborne**, with its lesser-known but equally influential son, Gilbert White.

Winchester Science Centre and Planetarium

Telegraph Way, SO21 1HX • Mon–Fri 10am–4pm, Sat, Sun & bank hols 10am–5pm • Museum £12, under-17s £8.40 • Planetarium prices vary according to the film shown • T 01962 863791, W winchestersciencecentre.org

A couple of miles east of Winchester at Morn Hill is the impressive **Winchester Science Centre**, a hands-on science and technology museum that's particularly interesting for children. The main hall has various devices that explain scientific processes – wind tunnels, cranes, sound waves, telescopes and locks among other things – while downstairs is more suitable for older children, with a flight simulator, machines that create vortexes and information on recycling. Of interest to people of any age is the UK's largest stand-alone **planetarium**, with several daily shows about space projected onto a vast domed ceiling, in which you really feel as if you are floating in space or moving about in a rocket. The centre also has its own shop and café.

Marwell Zoo

Colden Common, SO21 1JH • March–Oct usually daily 10am–5pm, in school hols and some weekends 10am–6pm; Nov–Feb daily 10am–4pm; check website for exact hours • April–Oct £19, under-17s £15; Nov–March £15, under-17s £11.50 • T 01962 777407, W marwell.org.uk

Deep in the countryside south of the Itchen Valley, seven miles from Winchester, the wonderful **Marwell Zoo** spreads over the grounds of the fourteenth-century Marwell Hall. It's home to tigers, leopards, rhinos, lemurs, gibbons, penguins and red pandas among others. The animals live in large enclosures over a 140-acre site, which is divided into various habitats such as the Australian Bush Walk – where you can get up close to wallabies and kookaburra – and Tropical World – with rainforest flora and fauna. On a sunny day, watching the zebras and giraffes wander through the spacious African Valley, you could almost be on a real safari. A free road train runs around the park and there are plenty of picnic spots.

Cheriton

Eight miles east of Winchester, the lovely village of **CHERITON** is an idyllic medley of thatched cottages clustered round its own green, with the wonderful *Flower Pots Inn* not far away. On a hilltop nearby lies a monument to the Civil War Battle of Cheriton, which took place near here on March 29, 1644. Some 20,000 soldiers took part in a battle to halt the Royalist advance, and the monument commemorates the many who died here.

ACCOMMODATION AND EATING — CHERITON

★ **Flower Pots Inn** Brandy Mount, SO24 0QQ T 01962 771318, W flowerpotscheriton.co.uk. A brewery, pub and B&B rolled into one, this lovely village inn brews its own beer in converted outbuildings in the back garden, producing ales such as the seasonal Elder Ale, made in summer with local elderflowers, or the altogether more powerful Flowerpots IPA. It also serves simple home-made food, such as hotpots and bacon and mushroom baps, and runs an annual beer festival in August. There are also four simple, en-suite B&B rooms. No credit or debit cards. Mon–Sat noon–2.30pm & 6–11pm, Sun noon–3pm & 7–10.30pm. £85

Hinton Ampner

Bramdean, SO24 0LA • **House** Mid-Feb to Dec daily 11am–4.30pm • **Gardens & estate** Daily 10am–5pm • £11.30, children £5.65; NT • 01962 771305, nationaltrust.org.uk/hinton-ampner

The estate of **Hinton Ampner**, with its lovely landscaped gardens and vast grounds, lies around nine miles east of Winchester. Built in 1793 as a hunting lodge, a traditional Georgian structure, it was re-modelled and enlarged in 1867 in mock-Tudor style and then rebuilt in the 1930s by Ralph Dutton, the last private owner of the estate, in neo-Georgian style with landscaped gardens to match. Dutton also bought all the land around the house, including a local village, in order to preserve the fine views. In 1960, a fire destroyed most of the house and its furnishings. Undaunted, he rebuilt his empire and collected more valuable antiques, including a fireplace from Marie Antoinette's palace in Saint-Cloud (now in the library), paintings by Pellegrini and an ornate Meissen clock. He also fitted a number of mod cons, such as an en-suite bathroom with a window specifically placed so that he could survey all he owned while sitting on his private lavatory. After he died in 1985 without heirs, the entire estate, including the local village, was bequeathed to the National Trust.

Avington Park

Avington, SO21 1DB • **House and gardens** Tours May–July & Sept Sun & bank hols 2.30pm, 3.30pm & 4.30pm; Aug Mon & Sun 2.30pm, 3.30pm & 4.30pm; 1hr • £8 • 01962 779260, avingtonpark.co.uk

The village of **AVINGTON**, about five miles northeast of Winchester, consists of little more than the Avington estate. The road through the village passes through **Avington Park** – you can pull up by a nature area with trails around a small lake, and an excellent view of **Avington House**. This may be all you get to see of the house, though, due to its limited opening hours. The park once belonged to Winchester Cathedral before passing into private hands at the time of Henry VIII. In the mid-seventeenth century the house was owned by one of Charles II's staff, who had the property enlarged to accommodate his boss and his mistress Nell Gwynne. King George IV also stayed here before it was sold to John Shelley – brother to the poet – in 1847. It is still privately owned, but the interior has all the attributes of a royal palace to this day, complete with soaring painted ceilings, giant mirrors and chandeliers.

Alresford

About seven miles northeast of Winchester, the attractive Georgian town of **ALRESFORD** (pronounced Allsford) grew up on the cotton and tanning trade, but is now recognized principally as the final stop on the Watercress Line (see box, p.206). Watercress has long grown wild in the chalky streams in these parts, but it was not until the advent of the railway that it became viable to grow it commercially, and Hampshire is still the main producer of watercress in England today.

The best way to explore the town is to walk the well-marked mile-long **Millennium Trail**, which takes you along the River Arle, a tributary of the Itchen. You may well see watercress growing wild here, and much of the marshy riverside is now a designated Site of Special Scientific Interest, home to otters and voles. The trail leads back via **Broad Street**, once the site of a major woollen market but today lined with the town's most handsome houses, shops and restaurants. May is a good time to visit Alresford, to coincide with the annual **Watercress Festival** (watercressfestival.org), an extravaganza of food markets and live entertainment.

ZONE
SALE

THE WATERCRESS LINE

The **Mid Hants steam railway**, better known as the **Watercress Line** (T 01962 733810, W watercressline.co.uk), chugs for ten miles through rolling Hampshire countryside between **Alton** and **Alresford**. Opened in 1865, the railway takes its name from the fresh watercress that it used to transport – initially all the way to Southampton. Nowadays the line is maintained by volunteers, and tickets (adults £16, under-17s £8, family ticket £40) allow you to travel up and down the line as often as you want in a day or to hop off at one of the two intermediary stations. There's not a lot to the first, **Medstead & Four Marks**, though it does lay claim to being the highest station in southern England, a surprising fact considering the apparently flat landscape. The second stop, **Ropley**, has a pleasant picnic area alongside the tracks, and steam buffs may wish to look round the workshed, where trains are repaired. They also lay on special family days and events – including a "Real ale train" (some Fri & Sat evenings) and Silver Service meals in the dining car (Sat evenings & Sun lunch) – check website for dates; reservations for dining are essential.

ARRIVAL AND DEPARTURE — ALRESFORD

By bus Although by far the most interesting way to arrive in Alresford is on the Watercress Line steam train (see box above), the #64 bus (daily, every 30min) also runs between Winchester (20min) and Alton (25min), stopping at The Green in Alresford.

Alton

Once famed for its cloth manufacturing, today **ALTON** is a pleasant enough town with a bustling shopping centre, though not much else to detain you apart from the fifteenth-century **Church of St Lawrence** with its Norman tower. Its main interest to visitors is as the starting point of the Watercress Line steam railway, which runs south to Alresford.

ARRIVAL AND DEPARTURE — ALTON

By bus In addition to the Watercress Line steam train (see box above), the #64 bus (daily, every 30min) runs from Winchester (20min) via Alresford (25min) to Alton, stopping on the High Street and at the railway station.

ACCOMMODATION

Manor Farm West Worldham, GU34 3BD T 01420 80804, W featherdown.co.uk. The splendid *Manor Farm*, where you sleep in well-equipped, ready-erected tents on a working farm, lies a couple of miles east of Alton; there's a wood-fired bread oven, hens for fresh eggs and a shop selling local produce. You can also opt for the luxury of your own private wood-fire-heated hot tub outside your tent. Tents sleep six. Four-day minimum stay. **£114**

Chawton

"Everybody is acquainted with Chawton and speaks of it as a remarkably pretty village" wrote Jane Austen to her sister Cassandra. Indeed, **CHAWTON** is still a pretty village, and one that has become a magnet for fans of the author, who lived here from 1809 to 1817 during the last and most prolific years of her life. Almost all her six books, including *Pride and Prejudice* and *Persuasion*, were written or revised here in **Jane Austen's House**, in the centre of the village.

Jane Austen's House

GU34 1SD • Jan to mid-Feb Sat & Sun 10.30am–4.30pm; mid-Feb to May & Sept–Dec daily 10.30am–4.30pm; June–Aug daily 10am–5pm • £8, under-17s £4 • T 01420 83262, W jane-austens-house-museum.org.uk

A relatively humble, plain red-brick building, **Jane Austen's House** is where the novelist wrote some of her greatest works. Here you can see extracts from Austen's original manuscripts, a lock of her hair, pieces of her jewellery and the desk at which she wrote her masterpieces – a small, simple table in the dining room. The house has been decorated and furnished as it would have been in Austen's time, with evocative details providing insights into her daily life, such as the tea chest in the dining room, whose key Jane kept because tea was so expensive that the servants kept stealing it. Upstairs is her sewing box and washing closet, as well as a beautiful patchwork bedspread made by Jane, her sister and her mother. You can also see two amber crosses given to the girls by their brother Charles – an event the author perhaps had in mind when she wrote of William Price presenting his sister Fanny with an amber cross in *Mansfield Park*. Outside, you can look around the cottage's bakehouse, which now houses the Austens' donkey carriage, while in the attractive gardens renovated outbuildings house a learning centre that shows a short film about the family and hosts various children's activities.

Chawton House

GU34 1SJ • Easter–Oct Mon–Fri 1.30–4.30pm, Sun & bank hols 11am–5pm • House & gardens £7, under-16s £3; gardens only £4, under-16s free • T 01420 541010, W chawtonhouse.org

A short walk from Jane Austen's house – past **St Nicholas Church**, which the author regularly attended and where her mother and sister are now buried – is **Chawton House**, which belonged to Jane's brother, Edward Austen Knight. He inherited the house from the childless Knight family and, needing space for his eleven children, moved here, allowing Jane, her mother and sister to live in the smaller Chawton cottage – though in fact Edward spent little time in the Great House, as it was known. It passed on to his children who did live here, and the house remained in the Austen family until 1987, when it was bought up in a sorry state of repair by American IT millionaire Sandy Lerner, who wanted a place to keep her historic manuscripts of female writers. It now contains the **Chawton House Library**, with an impressive collection of women's writing in English from 1600 to 1830.

ARRIVAL AND DEPARTURE — CHAWTON

By bus The #64 bus from Winchester (every 30min; 35min) stops at Chawton roundabout, a 10min walk from the village centre over a very busy dual carriageway, while the #37/38 runs from Petersfield to the village centre (Mon–Fri 7 daily; 45min).

AUSTEN'S POWERS

Jane Austen (1775–1817) lived through the French Revolution and Napoleonic Wars – a time of great change. And perhaps this is one reason why her tales of small-town society and the minutiae of middle-class life in the early nineteenth century struck such a chord with readers. Her novels, dealing with local gossip, rumour and social conventions, could be considered the reality TV of the day – a comfort in times of turmoil – and continue to fascinate readers today. Although she wrote only six novels, their influence has been far-reaching, with her plots re-used, adapted and satirized over the years, culminating in *Bridget Jones' Diary* as a modern take on *Pride and Prejudice*, at once parodying the novel while closely following its plotline.

Chawton, where Austen spent the last seven years of her short life, is a major draw for fans. Although she used fictional names for most of the towns in her novels, Chawton and its surrounding countryside fit many of her descriptions of places to this day. **Basingstoke**, then a small town, is probably the "Meryton" of *Pride and Prejudice*, while *Persuasion* is partly set in **Lyme Regis** (see p.129), where Austen liked to holiday. Jane and her sister Cassandra also attended regular dances and card evenings at **The Vyne** (see p.212), near Basingstoke, when her father was the vicar at nearby Steventon Church. Before Austen moved to Chawton, the family spent some time in **Southampton**, which also exploits its connections with the writer. The city's **Bargate** (see p.224) marks the start of the Jane Austen Heritage Trail, commemorating the fact that the novelist went to school there in 1783, while **Netley Abbey** (see p.231), just outside Southampton, is thought to be the inspiration for *Northanger Abbey*. Austen died in **Winchester**, and now lies in Winchester Cathedral (see p.197).

ACCOMMODATION AND EATING

Cassandra's Cup Winchester Rd, GU34 1BS ⓣ01420 83144, ⓦcassandrascup.co.uk. Opposite Jane Austen's House, *Cassandra's Cup* tearoom has a lovely terrace that catches the last of the day's sunshine. It serves good home-made cakes, tea and scones, plus toasted sandwiches and quiches, as well as daily lunch specials (£8–11) such as lasagne. It also has one B&B room to rent out next door. March–Oct Tues–Sun 10am–4.30pm; Nov–Feb Fri–Sun 10am–4pm. **£85**

The Greyfriar Winchester Rd, GU34 1SB ⓣ01420 83841, ⓦthegreyfriar.co.uk. This traditional village pub has a pleasant beer garden, and serves reasonably priced food made from locally sourced ingredients – including vegetables from the gardens at Chawton House. The main menu features pub staples such as steak and Guinness pie (£11), while specials may include seafood linguine (£13) or a Thai red curry (£12). It's child- and dog-friendly. Mon–Wed noon–10.30pm, Thurs–Sat noon–11pm, Sun noon–9pm.

Selborne

The attractive village of **SELBORNE**, some four miles southeast of Chawton, is best known as the home of the naturalist Gilbert White (1720–93), whose 1789 book *Natural History and Antiquities of Selborne* documented the flora and fauna that he saw around him, becoming the first detailed record of natural history. His observations and descriptions of the local wildlife led to a pioneering understanding of the interdependence of animals and plants in nature.

Gilbert White's House and Oates Museum

The Wakes, High St, GU34 3JH • Jan to mid-Feb Fri–Sun 10.30am–4.30pm; mid-Feb to March & Nov to mid-Dec Tues–Sun 10.30am–4.30pm; April, May, Sept & Oct Tues–Sun 10.30am–5.15pm; June–Aug daily 10.30am–5.15pm • £9.50, under-16s £4; gardens only £7.50 • ⓣ01420 511275, ⓦgilbertwhiteshouse.org.uk

You can see the original manuscript of White's book in the **Gilbert White House and Oates Museum** on Selborne High Street, where White lived for much of his life and carried out his painstaking documentation: it has been restored according to his descriptions, with some of his original furnishings. Downstairs, the kitchen has been re-created with eighteenth-century utensils, while the parlour has some replica costumes from the era. Upstairs is White's study and desk, and his bedroom, with the original bed-hangings.

The first floor of the house is principally given over to the **Oates Collection**, which is dedicated to the Oates family: like Gilbert White, Frank Oates was a pioneering natural historian, who studied wildlife in Africa, bringing back artefacts and specimens from his intrepid expeditions over there. However, it is his nephew, Captain Lawrence Oates, who is the family's most famous member – and most of the exhibition is devoted to him. Lawrence Oates bravely sacrificed his life during Captain Scott's ill-fated Antarctic expedition of 1911, uttering the famous words "I'm just going outside. I may be some time" as he stepped into a blizzard, aware that his ill health was slowing the progress of the expedition. Sadly, his death was in vain, as all the other team members also perished on their return journey from the South Pole. Despite the slightly tenuous connection with Gilbert White, the exhibition is fascinating. Viewing the original artefacts from the doomed polar expedition – including a sledge, wind suits and snowshoes – it may seem surprising that they managed to survive for so long with such poorly adapted equipment. There's also poignant footage from the actual expedition, with Scott, Oates and the other team members talking and joking on camera.

The gardens

Gilbert White was a keen horticulturist too, and the stunning **gardens** are much larger and grander – twenty acres – than you would expect from the size of the house. Having been restored to their eighteenth-century condition, they are divided into different sections by topiary hedges, including a kitchen garden, a herb garden and a wild garden, with a series of marked walks that take from fifteen to forty-five minutes. Partly cultivated

SELBORNE WALKS

A lovely hour's round walk starts in **Selborne's churchyard**, opposite Gilbert White's House, and mostly follows the valley of a small stream – keep the stream on your right and you can't go wrong. It starts off along the signed **Hanger's Way**, which heads downhill across a stream (a lovely picnic spot) and into Short Lythe woods, past large, fallen trees. Ten minutes into the walk you'll pass through two sets of gates into Long Lythe woods. After a further ten minutes, you'll exit the woods into a meadow with a clutch of small lakes – another fine picnic spot, though it can be muddy in wet weather. Go straight on between two of the lakes over a stile into more woodland. Leaving the woods, you cross a field, bearing left towards Priory Farm. Turn right through the farm onto a track, picking up a footpath signed to the right again. You are now returning in the direction you came. The path goes up through a field into lovely woodland, which wends back to join a narrow road, Hucker's Lane, uphill back to Selborne.

If you still have the energy, you can continue the walk up **Selborne Hill** via the aptly named Zigzag path, which White and his brother cut into the hillside. From the village car park, it's a further twenty minutes or so up through beech woods to the top of the hill, where there are fantastic views back over the village and surrounding countryside. Alternatively, for a round walk, head right before the Zigzag path, and up through the woods – then turn left, and loop back through the woods to the top of the Zigzag path, which will bring you steeply back down to the village car park (30–40min round walk).

but mostly lawned, the grounds are designed to make the most of various viewpoints, with an eighteenth-century "ha ha" – a wall set into the ground so as not to disturb the view. Back in the house, the small **café** has been furnished in eighteenth-century style and serves light lunches, teas and home-made cakes, as well as some traditional recipes including cinnamon or cheese and watercress scones.

EATING **SELBORNE**

Selborne Arms High St, GU34 3JR ⓣ01420 511247, ⓦselbornearms.co.uk. With its own beer garden, this traditional pub serves real ales and a fine Winchester cheese ploughman's (£7) along with full meals (from £11) such as local sausages and mash, or home-made shepherd's pie. Mon–Fri 11am–3pm & 6–11pm, Sat 11am–11pm, Sun noon–11pm.

North Hampshire

Compared to Hampshire's southern reaches, where the New Forest is the highlight, **north Hampshire** is of little interest to holiday-makers. Its main town is the rather dull, modern **Basingstoke**, which cannot compete with Hampshire's southerly capital city of Winchester in terms of history or aesthetics. This is commuter country, dotted with pretty, pricey stockbrokers' villages, surrounded by the gentle, rolling rural landscapes.

It's also home to a few grand country estates, whose impressive manor houses are a tangible reminder of the affluence and influence of the inhabitants hereabouts – not least the grand **Stratfield Saye**, and **Highclere Castle**, better known around the world as Downton Abbey. Also worth exploring are the historic ruins of **Basing House**, the aristocratic splendours of **The Vyne**, and the splendid Roman remains at **Silchester**, as well as the gardens at **West Green House** and **Wellington Country Park**.

Basingstoke

Even residents of **BASINGSTOKE** would admit that it is rarely on anyone's tourist itinerary. For most of its past it was little more than a small market town, until it was decided in the 1960s to make it an overspill town for London, with several major companies moving their headquarters this way. Today it's a large, relatively affluent town with a population of around 90,000, and good shopping facilities and transport links; being just off the M3 and only 45 minutes from London by train, it's also popular with commuters. In town there is only really one sight for visitors, the impressive Milestones museum, but there are plenty of – largely historic – attractions nearby.

Milestones museum

Leisure Park, Churchill Way, West Basingstoke, RG22 6PG • Tues–Fri & bank hols 10am–4.45pm, Sat & Sun 11am–4.45pm • £9.45, under-16s £5.75 • T 01256 477766, W hampshireculturaltrust.org.uk/milestones-museum

Housed inside a huge, modern aircraft-hangar-like building, the **Milestones museum** contains life-sized Victorian and 1930s street scenes that have been re-created, complete with shops, a village square and a pub. The staff are dressed in traditional costumes – children have the chance to dress up too – and you can wander along cobbled lanes into the buildings. Artefacts from the past, such as prewar washing machines and hoovers, abound, and you can even buy sweets from a 1940s' sweet shop. There's also a collection of steam engines and a reconstructed ironworks, with regular special events, street theatre and exhibitions.

ARRIVAL AND DEPARTURE BASINGSTOKE

By car Just off the M3, Basingstoke has good connections with London and the southwest. Follow signs to the central car parks.

By bus The main coach station is on Churchill Way East, in the town centre.

Destinations London (7 daily; 1hr 25min–2hr); Southampton (4 daily; 1hr); Winchester (3 daily; 35min).

By train The train station is ten minutes' walk north of the centre.

Destinations Bournemouth (every 15–30min; 1hr–1hr 25min); London (up to four hourly; 45min–1hr); Winchester (up to four hourly; 15–20min).

THE BASINGSTOKE CANAL TOWPATH

When it opened in 1794, the **Basingstoke Canal** was the longest canal in southern England, at 37 miles. Built to link the market town of Basingstoke with the River Wey, and ultimately the Thames, it provided a seventy-mile waterway to London, carrying timber and agricultural produce to the capital and bringing coal back down to northern Hampshire. However, it was never really commercially viable, and the completion of the London to Basingstoke railway in 1839 hastened its demise. In sporadic use over the next hundred years or so, the canal was derelict by the 1950s and it wasn't until the 1970s that work began to restore it to its former glory. In 1991, 31 miles of the canal were finally re-opened for leisure boats and walkers. The Basingstoke Canal **towpath** now runs the length of the canal, passing through woodland, heathland and rural villages, while the canal's clean spring waters are rich in wildlife and aquatic plants.

The pleasant Georgian town of **ODIHAM**, eight miles east of Basingstoke, is a good place to access the canal. Starting at the pleasant *Waterwitch* pub in Colt Hill, half a mile northeast of Odiham centre, it's a thirty-minute walk along the towpath to the Greywell Tunnel. En route you can visit the ruins of **Odiham Castle**, which was built by King John in the thirteenth century: it is thought that the location was chosen as it is halfway between Windsor and Winchester. The final five miles of the canal to Basingstoke have not been restored, and the **Greywell Tunnel** is its furthest navigable point, as well as being Britain's most important bat roost – some 12,500 bats of all native species live here.

John Pinkerton, a restored traditional narrow boat, leaves from Colt Hill Wharf, by the *Waterwitch*, for **boat trips** along the canal (2–2hr 30min; £10, booking recommended; see website for days and times of trips; T 01962 713564, W basingstoke-canal.org.uk).

Barley Mow The Hurst, Winchfield, RG27 8DE T 01252 617490, W barley-mow.com. Right on the canal, the *Barley Mow* is a popular spot with walkers and cyclists. It serves a good range of home-made pub dishes, as well as the popular sausage menu featuring a selection of bangers, from chorizo to pork, stilton and port, all served with mash, gravy and vegetables (£11.40). Mon–Fri noon–2.30pm & 6–11pm, Sat noon–11pm, Sun noon–4pm.

Basing House

Basing Grange, The Street, Old Basing, RG24 8AE • Free car park in Barton's Lane • March–Oct Mon–Thurs, Sat & Sun 11am–4pm • £6; under-15s £4.90 • ⓣ 01256 463965, ⓦ hampshireculturaltrust.org.uk/basing-house

Three miles east of Basingstoke, the historic town of **OLD BASING** on the River Lodden is home to **Basing House.** Now little more than a ruin, it was once the impressive palace of the Marquess of Winchester, who built what was once the country's largest private house in 1535 with a room for almost every day of the year. It was built near the site of a Norman castle, the banks of which still remain. The Marquess' impressive estate was a popular spot for visiting royals, including Henry VIII and Elizabeth I, but this approval attracted the attention of Cromwell who laid siege to the estate during the English Civil War, leaving the palace largely destroyed. Nowadays you can still enjoy the riverside walks along the River Lodden and tour the grounds that include a re-created seventeenth-century garden and the Tudor Great Barn – the only original building still standing, which was used to store agricultural goods until the 1980s.

West Green House

Thackham's Lane, near Hartley Wintney, Hook, RG27 8JB • Gardens March–Oct Wed–Sun & bank hols 11am–4.30pm • £8, under-16s £4; NT • ⓣ 01252 844611, ⓦ westgreenhouse.co.uk

Around eleven miles northeast of Basingstoke in West Green, **West Green House** is an attractive eighteenth-century house (closed to the public) surrounded by award-winning **gardens**. They're divided into a series of separate areas, including a walled kitchen garden, a "Nymphaeum" complete with a water staircase, as well as topiary, water gardens and follies. There's a pleasant tearoom, with outside seating in the summer, and the gardens also host special events including summer opera.

Wellington Country Park

Odiham Rd, Riseley, RG7 1SP • Mid-Feb to late March & late Sept to mid-Oct daily 9.30am–4.30pm • £8, under-16s £7 • Late March to late Sept & Oct half-term daily 9.30am–5.30pm • £10, under-16s £9.50 • ⓣ 01189 326444, ⓦ wellington-country-park.co.uk

Established by the eighth Duke of Wellington in 1974 for local people to enjoy outdoor pursuits, **Wellington Country Park**, eleven miles northeast of Basingstoke, is a large park with extensive woodland surrounding a central lake. Part of the Wellington Estate, it's a great place for kids, with various playgrounds and marked nature trails – some leading to the resident red deer – plus an animal park with alpaca, Shetland ponies and rabbits. There's also a café and shop, and campsite (two people and a vehicle £27.50).

Stratfield Saye

Stratfield Saye, RG7 2BT • Tours roughly hourly Easter & late July to late Aug Mon–Fri 11.30am–3.30pm, Sat, Sun & bank hols 10.30am–3.30pm; 1hr • Mon–Fri £10, children £4; Sat & Sun £12, children £5 • ⓣ 01256 882694, ⓦ stratfield-saye.co.uk

The vast estate of **Stratfield Saye**, ten miles north of Basingstoke, has been home to the dukes of Wellington since the early nineteenth century. The current duke and his family still live there, so public access is restricted to guided tours that take place for a few weeks each year. The house was bought as a country retreat for the first Duke of Wellington, Arthur Wellesley, in 1817, shortly after he received his title following the abdication of Napoleon in 1814. By then Wellesley had successfully campaigned against the French emperor in Spain and especially in Portugal, where he helped drive the occupying forces out of the country. Wellesley later entered politics, becoming prime minister in 1827.

The tour takes in an exhibition on his life – in which you can see his funeral carriage – and a look round the luxurious house, originally built in 1630 by Sir William Pitt. When it passed into Wellesley's hands, he had the property "modernized" by adding, among other things, central heating – the original radiators can be seen at the foot of the main staircase. Look out, too, for the entrance hall, which includes Roman mosaics pilfered from Silchester's Roman excavations (see below). The grounds, too, are suitably grand, though their most moving site is the ornate grave for Copenhagen – the duke's favourite horse, which he rode during the Battle of Waterloo. The duke later kept Copenhagen in his grounds for his children to ride. When the horse died in 1836 aged 28, it was buried with full military honours.

The Vyne

Vyne Rd, Sherborne St John, RG24 9HL • Admission varies; check website or phone for details • Tours sometimes available • House & grounds £13, children £6.50; grounds only £8, children £4; NT • T 01256 883858, W nationaltrust.org.uk/the-vyne

Four miles north of Basingstoke, **The Vyne** at Sherborne St John is a sumptuous, partly sixteenth-century house built for Lord Sandys, Lord Chamberlain to Henry VIII; the king was a regular visitor to the property, as was Jane Austen, who attended balls here some 250 years later. Later owned by the same family for more than three centuries, the interior is a mishmash of aristocratic opulence including statuary, paintings and ornate carpets; the Tudor chapel, with its beautiful stained-glass windows and sixteenth-century Flemish tiles, is a highlight. The family substantially adapted the building over the years, adding what is believed to be England's first classical portico on the front of the building (on the north side) in the mid-seventeenth century and constructing a walled garden in the eighteenth century. The rest of the surrounding gardens are equally impressive, set around a lake and with various woodland walks, containing one of England's oldest summerhouses, built in about 1635. There's also a pleasant café and tearoom and regular events throughout the year, including open-air theatre performances.

Silchester Roman walls and amphitheatre

Silchester • Daylight hours • Free; EH • T 08703 331181, W www.english-heritage.org.uk/visit/places/silchester-roman-city-walls-and-amphitheatre

Just eight miles north of Basingstoke, **SILCHESTER** is one of the oldest towns in England and the site of one of the country's best-preserved **Roman defensive walls**, which can be visited at a small archeological site just outside town. This was once part of the Roman town of Calleva Atrebatum. Abandoned in the fifth century, the town was then largely forgotten, giving archeologists an exciting and rare example of ruins that have not been subsequently built on or altered in some way. The walls stretch for about a mile and a half through open countryside, though little else remains – on the surface at least. Digs at the site have revealed that there was a substantial town of around 10,000 people living here up to a century before the Romans arrived; the town minted its own coins and had its own running water. This would make it a clear rival to Colchester or St Albans as England's oldest town.

Highclere Castle

Highclere Park, Newbury, RG20 9RN • Easter, first 2 weeks of April & both May bank hol weekends daily 10.30am–6pm; mid-July to mid-Sept Mon–Thurs & Sun 10.30am–6pm • Castle, exhibition and gardens £22; castle & gardens £15; exhibition & gardens £15; gardens £7 • T 01635 253210, W highclerecastle.co.uk

Known to millions of people the world over as Downton Abbey, the towers and turrets of **Highclere Castle** rise majestically above grand trees and parkland just west of the A34. Built on land originally owned by the Bishops of Winchester, most of today's castle dates from 1838, when the Earl of Carnarvon used the latest Victorian know-how to build a mansion fit to impress his guests. He employed Sir Charles Barry, architect of the Houses of Parliament – the similarity of design is noticeable. But it's the interior that's really impressive, a series of ornate state rooms, richly carpeted with sweeping staircases and soaring ceilings. The vaulted entrance hall is thoroughly Gothic, designed by George Gilbert Scott, who also designed St Pancras Station in London. Look out for the leather wall coverings in the grand Saloon, brought from Córdoba in Spain in 1631, and the library, resembling a gentleman's club and now used for weddings.

The cellars contain the **Egyptian Exhibition**, the private collection of the fifth Earl of Carnarvon, famed for his excavations of Tutankhamun in the 1920s. The collection includes his finds from other excavations in Thebes and Balamun, including embalming shrouds, jewellery and coffins, along with photos of the discovery of Tutankhamun in 1922.

However, it is to see the real-life location of TV's hugely popular **Downton Abbey** that most visitors come to Highclere – although the series has finished, you can still soak up its Edwardian atmosphere and view Lady Mary's and Lady Edith's bedrooms and the drawing rooms, which are sumptuous even without the presence of Dame Maggie Smith.

Sandham Memorial Chapel

Harts Lane, Burghclere, RG20 9JT • March & Oct Wed–Sun 11am–4pm; April–Sept Wed–Fri & bank hols 11am–4pm, Sat & Sun 11am–5pm • £10, children £5; NT • ⓣ 01635 278394, ⓦ nationaltrust.org.uk/sandham-memorial-chapel

A couple of miles north of Highclere, just east of the A34 at Burghclere, is **Sandham Memorial Chapel**, an unassuming 1920s building housing a superb display of World War I murals by **Stanley Spencer**. Spencer was already a promising artist when the war broke out, and then spent time as a medical orderly in Bristol and as a soldier in northern Greece. When he returned, wanting to record the personal experience of soldiers, he found backing from a wealthy local family who had the chapel built for him to house his paintings. He spent several years on his work, attracting a steady stream of visitors to watch him painting, including Vanessa Bell and Virginia Woolf – despite the muted colours, the vivid war scenes and portraits are extraordinarily moving and powerful, though there is no artificial lighting in the chapel so it is best to visit on a bright day. The modest red-brick chapel sits in a pretty orchard with views over **Watership Down**, best known for Richard Adams's 1972 novel about the adventures of a group of rabbits, while behind the chapel is a pretty garden of reflection.

Southampton, Portsmouth and around

MARY ROSE MUSEUM

Southampton, Portsmouth and around

Just a few miles apart facing the Solent lie the maritime powerhouses of Southampton and Portsmouth. Vast cruise liners still dock at Southampton, from where the *Titanic* departed when the port was Britain's main gateway to its empire and the Americas. Today, Southampton is more popular for its shopping than its transatlantic travel, but the town's fascinating history warrants at least a day's exploration. Nearby Portsmouth has one of the UK's main naval bases and its Historic Dockyard is the final resting place of HMS *Victory* and the *Mary Rose*, though many visitors also come here to ascend the iconic Spinnaker Tower, centrepiece of the Gunwharf Quays shopping complex.

The surrounding area is unsurprisingly rich in history too, with beautiful abbeys at Netley on **Southampton Water** and at Titchfield and **Romsey**. The legacy of the area's position on the south coast is a chain of impressive forts, including Portchester Castle, Fort Nelson and Spitbank Fort – this last on an islet a mile offshore.

Southampton

One of England's most important ports thanks to its double tides, **SOUTHAMPTON** is where King Cnut is alleged to have commanded the waves to retreat. And it was from its docks, too, that Henry V left to conquer Agincourt, the Pilgrim Fathers originally set sail for America in 1620, and the *Titanic* departed for its fateful maiden voyage in 1912. The world's largest liners still berth here, but more than half a century after World War II you feel the town is only just recovering from the dreadful pummelling it endured at the hands of the Luftwaffe, which ripped out the heart of this ancient city. Though it sits on a peninsula where the Itchen and Test rivers meet Southampton Water – an eight-mile inlet from the Solent – the **waterside** is only gradually being opened up to visitors, largely round the Ocean Village and the Civic Centre. Indeed, many people see no more than its shops or ferry terminals and do scant justice to its leafy parks, fine museums, art galleries and superb, if incomplete, set of medieval walls, all of which merit exploration.

Brief history

The **Romans** built a small settlement on the Itchen called Clausentum, but it was the **Saxons** who gave the town its name, founding a port they called Hamtun in around 700 AD. The port thrived on exporting wool and even had its own mint by the ninth century, though the town was vulnerable to attack and was frequently raided by Danes. By the twelfth century, the **Normans** had built the church of St Michael and a castle, and the port flourished on trading wool and wine, as well as on shipbuilding. In the late thirteenth century a stone wall was built to defend the town; this did not stop French raids, however, so fortifications were improved throughout the fourteenth

Passing the Test p.230
The Solent Way p.232
Spitbank Fort p.237
Hambledon: home of cricket p.242

MOTTISFONT ABBEY

Highlights

❶ **Sea City Museum, Southampton** Highlight of Southampton's Cultural Quarter, this fantastic museum is moving and informative, with its detailed accounts of the short life of the *Titanic* and her crew. **See p.224**

❷ **Kuti's, Southampton** Watch the cruise liners depart from the former gateway to America, now a sumptuous Thai restaurant in a great Art Deco building. **See p.227**

❸ **Mottisfont Abbey** This superb house is filled with works by top artists and sits in lovely grounds by the River Test. **See p.230**

❹ **Hamble-le-Rice** Take a boat trip or riverside walk from this charming riverside town, popular with the sailing set. **See p.232**

❺ **Spinnaker Tower, Portsmouth** Commanding terrific views over the town, this sleek tower is great to look at and even better inside. **See p.234**

❻ **The Historic Dockyard, Portsmouth** The heart of maritime Britain, with Nelson's HMS *Victory* as its jewel in the crown. **See p.235**

HIGHLIGHTS ARE MARKED ON THE MAP ON PP.218–219

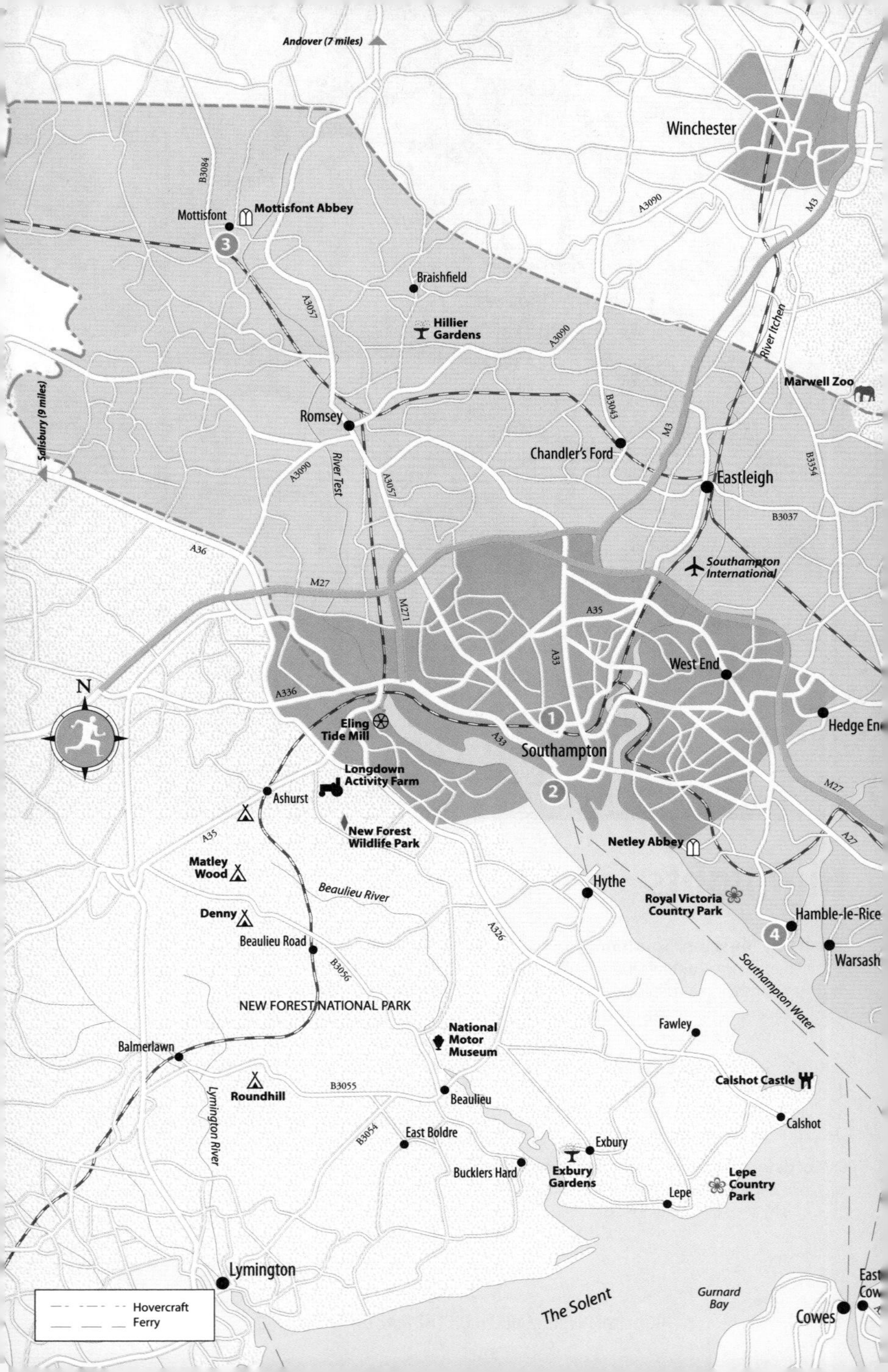

Andover (7 miles)
Winchester
B3084
Mottisfont
Mottisfont Abbey
3
A3090
M3
Braishfield
A3057
Hillier Gardens
A3090
River Itchen
Marwell Zoo
Salisbury (9 miles)
Romsey
B3043
M3
Chandler's Ford
River Test
A3090
A3057
Eastleigh
B3354
B3037
A36
Southampton International
M27
M271
A35
A33
West End
A336
Eling Tide Mill
1
A33
Southampton
Hedge End
N
Longdown Activity Farm
2
Ashurst
M27
A35
New Forest Wildlife Park
Netley Abbey
A27
Matley Wood
Hythe
Beaulieu River
Royal Victoria Country Park
Denny
A326
Hamble-le-Rice
4
Beaulieu Road
Warsash
B3056
Southampton Water
NEW FOREST NATIONAL PARK
National Motor Museum
Fawley
Balmerlawn
Calshot Castle
Roundhill
B3055
Beaulieu
Lymington River
Calshot
B3054
East Boldre
Exbury
Bucklers Hard
Exbury Gardens
Lepe
Lepe Country Park
Lymington
Hovercraft
Ferry
The Solent
Gurnard Bay
Cowes

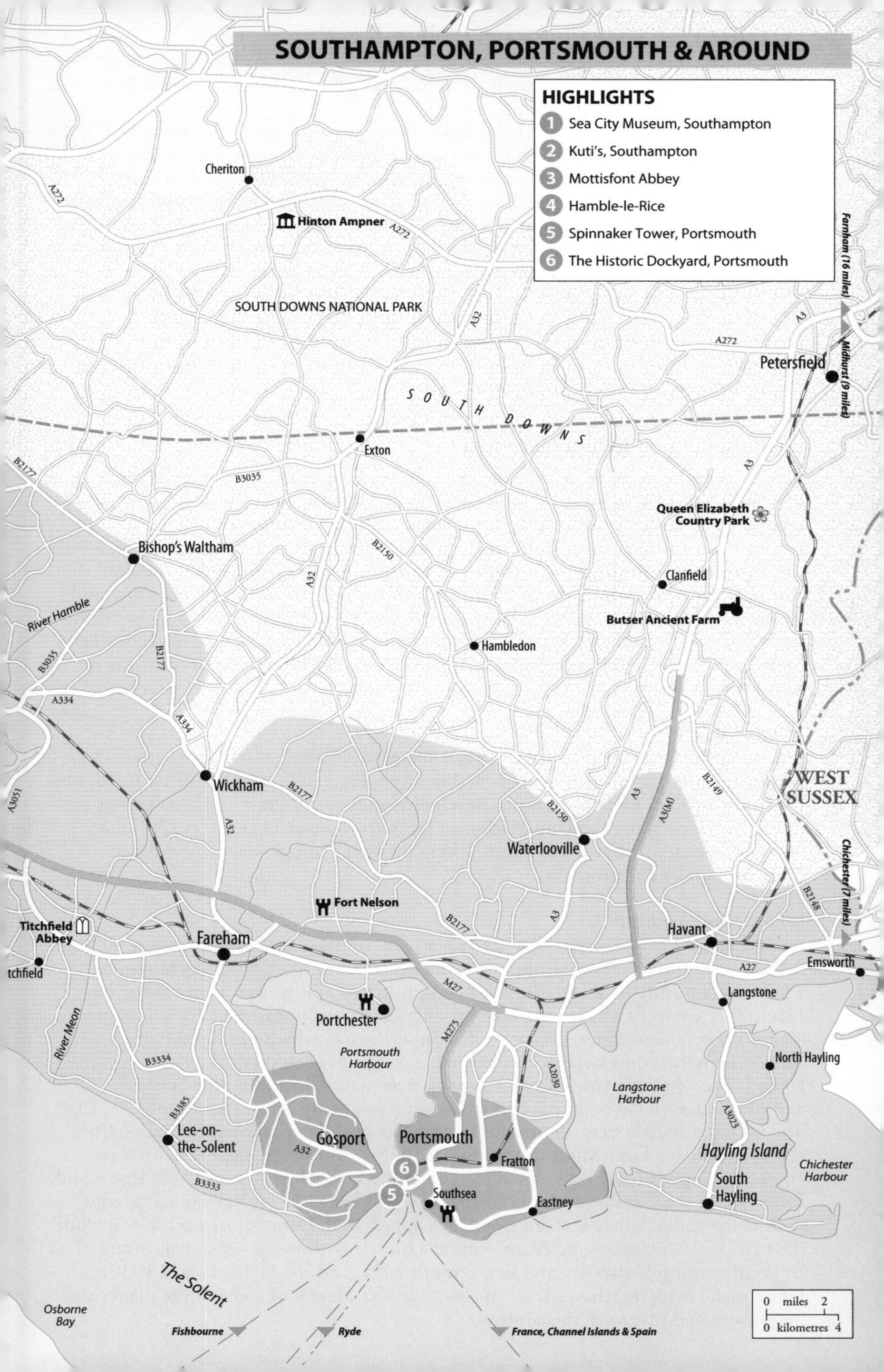

SOUTHAMPTON, PORTSMOUTH & AROUND
HIGHLIGHTS
1 Sea City Museum, Southampton
2 Kuti's, Southampton
3 Mottisfont Abbey
4 Hamble-le-Rice
5 Spinnaker Tower, Portsmouth
6 The Historic Dockyard, Portsmouth
Cheriton
Hinton Ampner
SOUTH DOWNS NATIONAL PARK
SOUTH DOWNS
Exton
Petersfield
Farnham (16 miles)
Midhurst (9 miles)
Queen Elizabeth Country Park
Clanfield
Butser Ancient Farm
Bishop's Waltham
River Hamble
Hambledon
Wickham
WEST SUSSEX
Waterlooville
Fort Nelson
Titchfield Abbey
Fareham
Havant
Chichester (7 miles)
Emsworth
tchfield
Langstone
Portchester
Portsmouth Harbour
River Meon
North Hayling
Langstone Harbour
Lee-on-the-Solent
Gosport
Portsmouth
Fratton
Hayling Island
Chichester Harbour
South Hayling
Southsea
Eastney
The Solent
Osborne Bay
Fishbourne
Ryde
France, Channel Islands & Spain
0 miles 2
0 kilometres 4

century, when most of the city walls (including Bargate) were built, along with several wealthy merchants' houses.

The first **docks** were built in the nineteenth century to handle the growing number of commercial ships and ferries. By the early twentieth century, Southampton had become the base for White Star transatlantic liners – including the ill-fated *Titanic* – and, in 1919, Cunard's services to New York. This helped Southampton thrive throughout the Depression, as did the manufacture of both flying boats and General Motors cars here in the 1930s. Historically, Southampton tended to thrive during wartime, when soldiers passed through; during World War II, however, a series of bombing raids devastated the city. The 1950s saw much rebuilding, but a combination of air travel and changes to shipping containerization saw Southampton's role as a port decline through the second half of the century. More recently, the shift has been towards commercial activity, with numerous shopping centres opening alongside the former docks.

The docks and the waterfront

Before transatlantic air travel became commonplace, Southampton was the main departure point for most liners across the Atlantic. These days its **waterfront** is rather tatty, though you do get the odd glimpse of what it must have been like in its heyday – have a look inside *Kuti's* Thai restaurant (see p.227), for example, which is the former reception terminal for Atlantic passengers. The adjacent **Mayflower Park** is the best place to view some of the 250-odd cruise ships that call annually; fireworks and events frequently celebrate ships arriving or departing. Another way to see the cruise ships and other comings and goings on Southampton Water is to take the **Hythe Ferry** from Town Quay (daily every 30min; 25min; £5.80; ⓦhytheferry.co.uk), which runs across the Solent to Hythe (see p.171).

8

Ocean Village

The waterfront area now known as **Ocean Village** is situated on what was originally Southampton's first dock, which opened in 1843. Parts of the dock wall are listed, but the entire area has undergone much development in recent years and now houses an upmarket marina, the excellent Harbour Lights arthouse cinema (see p.228), several bars and restaurants (see p.226) overlooking the water, and a new five-star hotel (currently under construction).

Solent Sky Museum

7 Albert Rd South, SO14 3FR • Tues–Sat 10am–5pm, Sun noon–5pm • £6.50 • ⓣ02380 635830, ⓦsolentskymuseum.org

A short walk from the waterfront on Albert Road South, the **Solent Sky Museum** takes an interesting look into the aviation industry in Southampton and along the Hampshire coast. In 1913, aeroplane production started in earnest in Southampton, kicked off by an aviation company called Supermarine, which produced flying boats – literally motor boats with detachable wings that could be taken off when they landed. The company continued to develop new planes, including the Spitfire in 1936 and the C-class flying boat, the first passenger plane to fly across the Atlantic, in 1938. The museum itself is in an enormous hangar-like building packed with planes, from the de Havilland Tiger Moth to an original Spitfire. The centrepiece is a vast four-engined flying boat, the only one preserved in the UK, which you can wander around. In service in the Caribbean until the 1970s, it still has some of the original interior, such as the galley, where elaborate meals were prepared. Other quirky exhibits include the first British manpowered plane – more a bicycle with wings – that was invented by Southampton University and flew 55m in 1901; and the Flying Flea, a 1930s home-made flying machine. You can also sit in the cockpit of some of the planes and helicopters and play with the controls.

The Old Town

The western extremities of Southampton's twelfth-century **town walls** are still largely intact, and are some of the best-preserved medieval walls in the country. Their sturdy structure was designed to withstand French raiders, and though much of the present structure was rebuilt after a French attack in 1338, large sections of the wall withstood the 30,000 incendiary devices deposited on the town during the last war. A well-marked circuit of the walls and towers is signed at strategic places, with the best stretch just west of Bugle Street. This street is also the most evocative of the Old Town, and home to some of the city's most historic buildings, including the **Wool House**, built around 1400 as a warehouse to store wool before it was shipped to Flanders and Italy, and now housing a popular microbrewery (see p.227). Built into the city walls in 1417, **God's House Tower** in nearby Winkle Street was Britain's first purpose-built artillery store. An amalgam of a simple gatehouse and a fifteenth-century three-storey tower and gallery, it's currently closed to the public, but there are plans to convert it into an arts and heritage centre.

Westgate Hall

Westgate St, off Bugle St, SO14 2AY • Ⓦ tudorhouseandgarden.com

Westgate Hall is a distinctive, timbered building built in about 1492 in St Michael's Square. It was used as a storage hall for woollen cloth and a fish market until 1643, when it was dismantled and moved to its current location and became a warehouse. It is also thought to be the house where the Pilgrim Fathers stayed before they set off to America on the *Mayflower*. It's hired out privately, but is not open to the public.

Medieval Merchants House

58 French St, SO1 0AT • April–Sept Sat & Sun 11am–4pm • £4.70; EH • Ⓣ 02380 221503, Ⓦ www.english-heritage.org.uk/visit/places/medieval-merchants-house

Standing in one of Southampton's busiest streets in medieval times, the **Medieval Merchants House** was built in 1290 by John Fortin, a merchant who made his money trading with Bordeaux. The house has been restored to its fourteenth-century condition, with replica furniture including an opulent canopied four-poster bed.

The Tudor House Museum and Garden

St Michael's Square, SO14 2AD • Tues–Fri 10am–3pm, Sat, Sun & bank hol Mon 10am–5pm • £5, children £4 • Ⓣ 02380 834242, Ⓦ tudorhouseandgarden.com

Like Westgate Hall, the **Tudor House** was built in 1492 by the wealthy John Dawtrey, who worked on Henry VIII's shipping fleet and embellished the house with the best glass and oak available. The house then passed on to other bigwigs, including artist George Rogers who added a new Georgian wing at the back. By the early 1800s, it sat in the middle of a district of slums and it was earmarked for demolition until saved by philanthropist and collector **William Spranger**, whose collection of Victorian curios was left when the house became a museum in 1912. Recently revamped, this excellent house museum is now an intriguing mishmash of interactive displays tracing the building's history, alongside historic paintings, artefacts including a Greek amphora, and a Victorian kitchen. You can also visit the re-created **Tudor garden** which contains a good café and the ruins of the Norman St John's Palace, built in the 1300s by a wealthy merchant when this part of town would have sat right on the quayside.

Church of St Michael's

St Michael's Square, SO14 2AD • Irregular hours but usually daily 11am–4pm • Free • Ⓣ 02380 330851

The **Church of St Michael's** is the city's oldest church and the only one to fully survive the war. It is also Southampton's oldest building still in use. It has beautiful stained-glass windows and a rare twelfth-century font made of black Tournai marble, one of six existing in England. The central Norman tower, built in around 1070, is still standing,

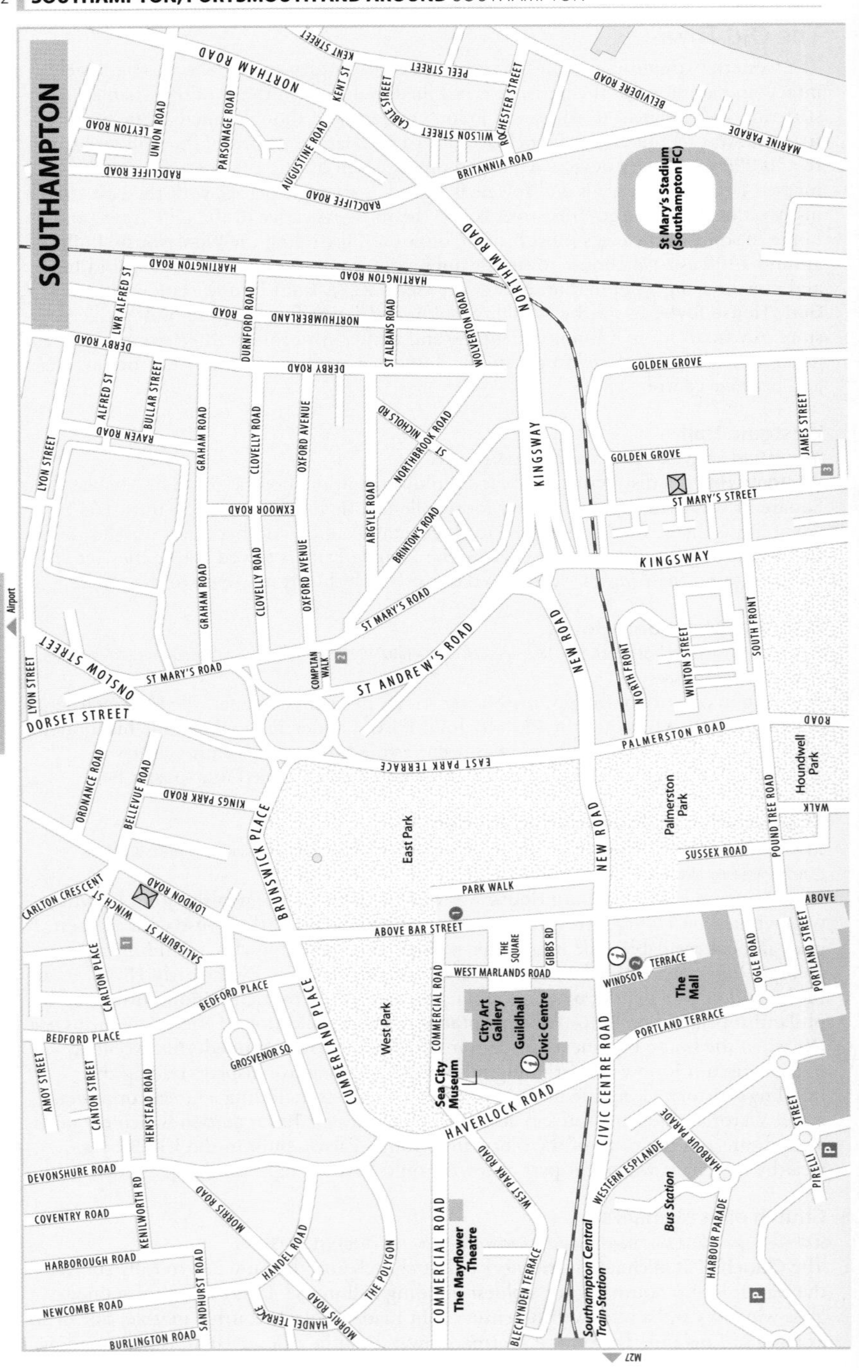
SOUTHAMPTON
8
Airport
M27
St Mary's Stadium (Southampton FC)
East Park
Palmerston Park
Houndwell Park
West Park
City Art Gallery
Guildhall
Civic Centre
Sea City Museum
The Mall
Bus Station
The Mayflower Theatre
Southampton Central Train Station
NORTHAM ROAD
KINGSWAY
NEW ROAD
CIVIC CENTRE ROAD
COMMERCIAL ROAD
HAVERLOCK ROAD
ABOVE BAR STREET
ST ANDREW'S ROAD
ST MARY'S ROAD
ST MARY'S STREET
BRUNSWICK PLACE
CUMBERLAND PLACE
LONDON ROAD
DORSET STREET
ONSLOW STREET
EAST PARK TERRACE
PALMERSTON ROAD
PORTLAND TERRACE
WESTERN ESPLANADE
HARBOUR PARADE
BRITANNIA ROAD
BELVIDERE ROAD
MARINE PARADE
HARTINGTON ROAD
DERBY ROAD
GOLDEN GROVE
MORRIS ROAD
WEST PARK ROAD
BEDFORD PLACE
DEVONSHURE ROAD
COVENTRY ROAD
HARBOROUGH ROAD
NEWCOMBE ROAD
BURLINGTON ROAD

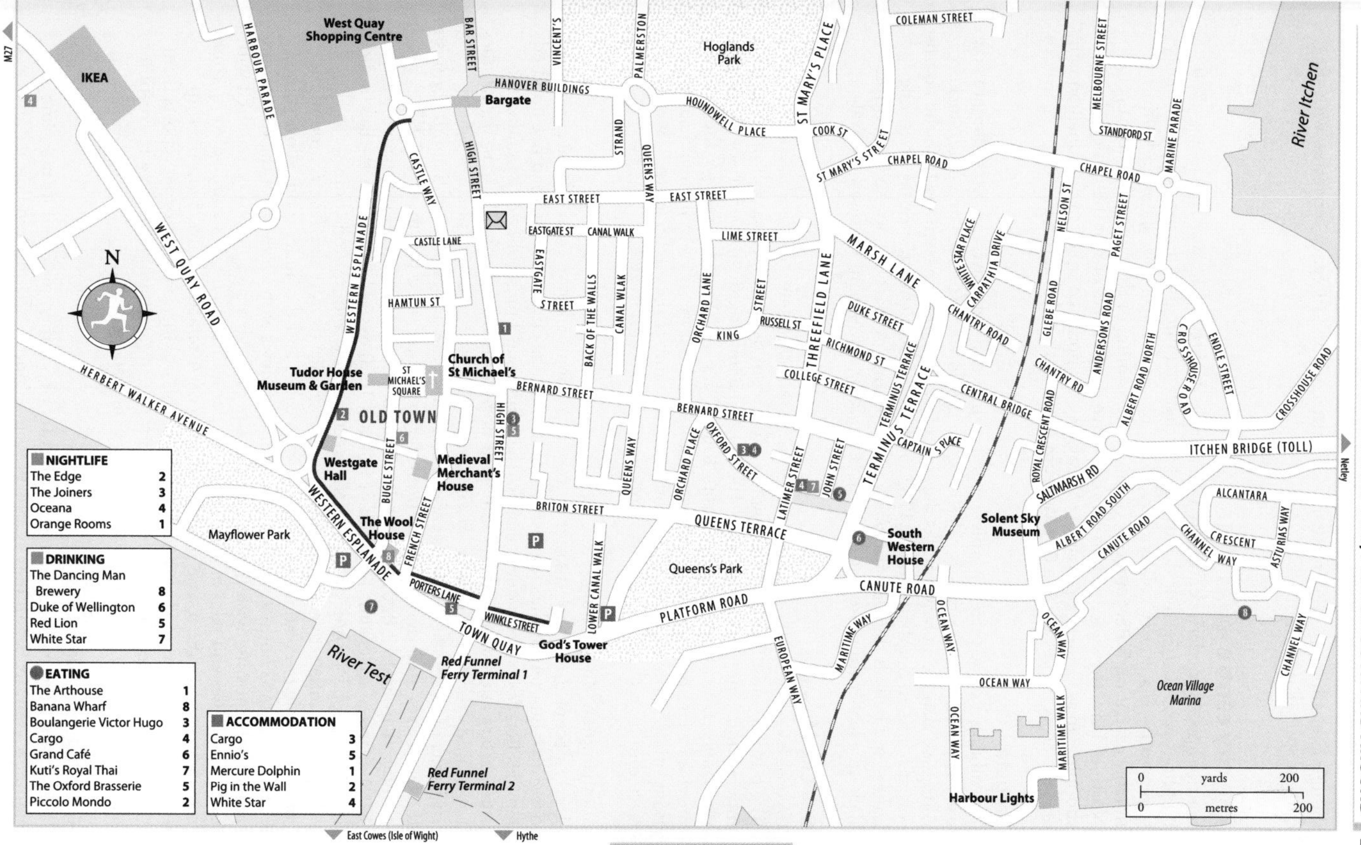
NIGHTLIFE
The Edge 2
The Joiners 3
Oceana 4
Orange Rooms 1
DRINKING
The Dancing Man Brewery 8
Duke of Wellington 6
Red Lion 5
White Star 7
EATING
The Arthouse 1
Banana Wharf 8
Boulangerie Victor Hugo 3
Cargo 4
Grand Café 6
Kuti's Royal Thai 7
The Oxford Brasserie 5
Piccolo Mondo 2
ACCOMMODATION
Cargo 3
Ennio's 5
Mercure Dolphin 1
Pig in the Wall 2
White Star 4
Netley
Hythe
East Cowes (Isle of Wight)
M27
River Itchen
River Test
Ocean Village Marina
Hoglands Park
Queens's Park
Mayflower Park
West Quay Shopping Centre
IKEA
Bargate
Church of St Michael's
Medieval Merchant's House
Tudor House Museum & Garden
Westgate Hall
The Wool House
God's Tower House
Red Funnel Ferry Terminal 1
Red Funnel Ferry Terminal 2
Solent Sky Museum
South Western House
Harbour Lights
OLD TOWN
ITCHEN BRIDGE (TOLL)
CANUTE ROAD
PLATFORM ROAD
TOWN QUAY
WESTERN ESPLANADE
WEST QUAY ROAD
HARBOUR PARADE
HERBERT WALKER AVENUE
HIGH STREET
BERNARD STREET
QUEENS TERRACE
TERMINUS TERRACE
MARSH LANE
ST MARY'S PLACE
HOUNDWELL PLACE
CHAPEL ROAD
ALBERT ROAD NORTH
ALBERT ROAD SOUTH
OCEAN WAY
MARITIME WALK
EUROPEAN WAY
yards
metres
0
200

though later additions were made in the fourteenth and fifteenth centuries, with the current spire dating from 1878.

The city centre

Southampton's modern centre fared very badly during World War II, when 45,000 buildings were damaged or destroyed. Hurriedly rebuilt after the war, most of what stands today is a motley collection of tower blocks, cheap 1960s shops and offices. A notable exception is **Bargate**, one of the last remaining of the city's seven town gates. North of here, the wide, pedestrianized **Above Bar Street** is one of the principal shopping areas, leading up past the WestQuay shopping complex to Guildhall Square and the city's impressive **Sea City Museum** in the Cultural Quarter.

Bargate

Resembling a stone turret complete with carvings and defensive apertures, **Bargate** was used as the law courts until the 1930s, while the downstairs served as a police lockup. Alongside Bargate a plaque marks the start of the **Jane Austen Heritage Trail**; the novelist was at school in Southampton in 1783, and visited frequently thereafter, attending dances and balls at the *Dolphin Hotel*, a few minutes' walk south on the High Street. Pick up a leaflet from the tourist office (see p.226) if you want to follow the walk.

Sea City Museum

Civic Centre, Havelock Rd, SO14 7FY • Daily 10am–5pm • £9.50, children £7 • T 02380 833007, W seacitymuseum.co.uk

The purpose-built **Sea City Museum** is a triumph of design that succeeds in being both moving and fun. Opened on April 10, 2012, the hundredth anniversary of the day that the *Titanic* sailed from Southampton's Town Quay on its maiden voyage, the museum provides a fascinating insight into the history of the ship, its crew, its significance to Edwardian Southampton and, of course, an account of the fateful journey, which started in high excitement to end only four days later in tragedy.

Southampton's Titanic story

The impact of the *Titanic* disaster on the city of Southampton cannot be overstated – over three-quarters of the crew lived in or around the city, and more than five hundred families here lost at least one member. The White Star Line's policy of curtailing the crew's salary at the moment any ship went down caused further hardship to the families left behind. The **Titanic gallery** upstairs starts with the names and pictures, where available, of all 897 of the ship's crew, then follows the stories of six of them. It contrasts the harsh lives of most of the crew from the city, where unemployment in 1912 numbered around 17,000, with the opulence of the ship, which set sail loaded with 1750 quarts of ice cream, 11,000lb of fish and 1000 oyster forks. The first-class breakfast menu on display includes sirloin steak, vegetable stew and mutton chops.

Impressive **interactive displays** give you the chance to steer the *Titanic* around the icebergs, while re-creations of a second-class cabin and the boiler room allow you to experience life as both crew and passenger. **Interviews with survivors** of the disaster are particularly moving, with harrowing accounts of survivors hoping to be reunited with their loved ones and tales of children being put into hessian sacks and hauled up from the lifeboats onto the rescue ship, the *Carpathia*. **Artefacts** rescued from the ship include a watch stopped at the exact time of the sinking and newspaper reports from the time, while recordings of the inquiry into the disaster are played in a re-creation of the old courtroom, complete with judge's bench and gallery.

Gateway to the World gallery

The second gallery upstairs details the history of Southampton and its **maritime heritage**, from its beginnings as a small Roman port to the modern day. Exhibits as diverse as an early log boat, found in nearby Hamble, a collection of prehistoric flints, and a giant model of the *Queen Mary* are on display. The gallery also emphasizes the importance of immigration to the city, with exhibits on the **immigrant experience** ranging from the Asian families of the 1950s to today's Polish communities.

Titanic – the legend

Downstairs, along with a temporary gallery space, is an area where children can star in their own video, dressed up as passengers or crew from the **Titanic**. *Titanic* merchandise – from the game Titanic-opoly to teddy bears, replica ship's crockery and hundreds of books about the ship – is on display, along with possible explanations for the disaster, **conspiracy theories** and a section on the **salvaging** of the ship. Screens showing various films on the subject, from the silent German melodrama *In Nacht und Eis* (1912) to a 2001 Italian animation called *The Legend of the Titanic*, via, of course, James Cameron's blockbuster (1997), are calibrated to show the same event simultaneously, portrayed cinematographically in very different ways.

City Art Gallery

Civic Centre, Commercial Rd, SO14 7LP • Mon–Fri 10am–3pm, Sat 10am–5pm • Free • ⓣ 02380 832277, ⓦ www.southampton.gov.uk/libraries-museums/art-gallery

Inside the **Civic Centre**, with its distinctive clocktower, lies Southampton's excellent **City Art Gallery**; its entrance is round the back on Commercial Road. Although only a small proportion of its collection, which is particularly strong on contemporary British art, is on show at any time, you're likely to see sculptures such as Antony Gormley's *The Diver*; paintings by Gilbert and George; and some colourful abstracts by Bridget Riley. Earlier British works include Lucian Freud's *Bananas*, a couple of Lowrys – look out for his *Floating Bridge, Southampton*, showing the ferry that crossed the Itchen River until 1977 – and some fine pieces by the Camden Town Group, including works by Augustus and Gwen John, Robert Bevan and Walter Sickert. Graham Sutherland and Stanley Spencer also make a strong showing.

The Impressionist movement is represented too, with works by Monet and Pissarro (plus forerunner Corot and Post-Impressionist Bonnard), while Sir Joshua Reynolds and Gainsborough – you can't miss his enormous portrait of *George Venables Vernon* – fly the flag for eighteenth-century British art. The remaining collection ranges from sixteenth-century Flemish and Italian paintings to Andy Goldsworthy's *Leaf Sculpture*; there are also various temporary exhibitions.

ARRIVAL AND DEPARTURE — SOUTHAMPTON

By plane Southampton's airport (ⓦ southamptonairport.com) is a short drive north of the centre along the A335 near Eastleigh, 10min by train from Southampton Central at Southampton Airport Parkway. You can also take bus #U1 from Town Quay or the train station.

By train Southampton's central train station is in Blechynden Terrace, a few minutes' walk west of the Civic Centre.

Destinations Bournemouth (4–5 hourly; 30–50min); London Waterloo (4 hourly; 1hr 20min–1hr 40min); Portsmouth (4 hourly; 50min–1hr); Weymouth (every 30min; 1hr 20min–1hr 40min); Winchester (4–5 hourly; 15–20min).

By bus National Express buses run from the bus station on Harbour Parade.

Destinations Bournemouth (10 daily; 55min–1hr); London Victoria (15 daily; 2hr–2hr 30min); Portsmouth (approx hourly; 40min–1hr); Weymouth (2 daily; 3hr); Winchester (2 hourly; 50min).

By ferry A City Link shuttle bus (every 15–30min; 10min) runs from the train station to Town Quay for ferry services to Hythe (see p.171) and the Isle of Wight (see p.246): it's free for Red Funnel (see p.246) ticket holders, £1 for everyone else.

GETTING AROUND

By bus A comprehensive network of city buses is run by Bluestar (ⓦ bluestarbus.co.uk), First (ⓦ firstgroup.com/southampton) and Unilink (ⓦ unilinkbus.co.uk).

By car Drivers should follow signs to one of the central car parks – the shops around WestQuay are well served by several multistorey car parks, though note that you may have to queue to get a spot at peak times.

By taxi There are taxi ranks at the train station and at many central points; to book a cab, try West Quay Cars (T 02380 999999, W westquaycars.com).

On foot You can easily walk round central Southampton – from Town Quay to the train station takes around 20min.

INFORMATION

Tourist office The office is in the Central Library of the Civic Centre, 9 Civic Centre Rd, SO14 7LT (Mon, Tues & Thurs 10am–7pm, Wed 10am–6pm, Fri 10am–5pm, Sat 10am–4pm; T 02380 833333, W discoversouthampton.co.uk), and can provide transport timetables, maps and details of various themed walks, including *Titanic* and Jane Austen trails.

ACCOMMODATION

Cargo 20–22 Oxford St, SO14 3DJ T 02380 829042, W cargosouthampton.com. Despite being on Southampton's liveliest street after dark, rooms in this characterful old building above a bar-restaurant (see below) are surprisingly peaceful, especially those in the attic. They are compact but modern, with flatscreen TVs and luxurious showers. **£85**

Ennio's Town Quay Rd, SO14 2AR T 02380 221159, W ennios-boutique-hotel.co.uk. Boutique-style hotel in a former warehouse right on the waterfront, opposite the Red Funnel ferry terminal. The sleek rooms – all with comfortable beds, smart bathrooms and L'Occitane toiletries – are above an excellent Italian restaurant, and the staff are friendly. **£95**

Mercure Dolphin 34–35 High St, SO14 2HN T 02380 386460, W dolphin-southampton.com. Centrally located, this fifteenth-century coaching inn is Southampton's oldest hotel and hosted Jane Austen's eighteenth birthday party. Today its rooms are a comfortable blend of historic and contemporary. **£90**

★Pig in the Wall 8 Western Esplanade, SO14 2AZ T 02380 636900, W thepighotel.com/in-the-wall. Built into the city walls, Southampton's most stylish boutique hotel has been cleverly renovated and beautifully decorated in a shabby-chic style. All the rooms have powerful showers and top-of-the-range coffee machines – the large (pricier) rooms boast glamorous roll-top baths in the rooms themselves. You can eat in the great bar/lounge/deli downstairs, or jump in one of the hotel Land Rovers which will take you to their sister hotel/restaurant in the New Forest for dinner (see p.167). **£130**

White Star 28 Oxford St, SO14 3DJ T 02380 821990, W idealcollection.co.uk/whitestartavern. Boutique-style rooms in a smart, lively hotel above a highly regarded bar-restaurant. The rooms come in various sizes – and some look out over Oxford Street – but all have comfortable beds, White Stuff toiletries and modern decor. **£105**

EATING

As you'd expect from a lively port town with two universities, there are lots of good places to eat and drink, whatever your budget. For bargain and world cuisine, head to the popular student haunts along **Bedford Place**, north of the Civic Centre; the best restaurants, however, are along **Oxford Street** or down towards the **waterfront**.

★The Arthouse 178 Above Bar St, SO14 7DW T 02380 238582, W thearthousesouthampton.co.uk. Friendly community-run café, opposite the City Art Gallery, serving delicious home-made vegan and vegetarian dishes such as bean and coconut stew (£9) and Greek meze with hummus, pitta and stuffed vine leaves (£6.45) as well as organic ciders and beers. It hosts workshops, art exhibitions, knitting circles and live music; upstairs, there's a piano, comfy sofas and plenty of board games. Tues–Sat 11am–10pm, Sun noon–5pm.

Banana Wharf Ocean Village, SO14 3JF T 02380 338866, W bananawharf.co.uk. Lively bar/restaurant with outside tables right on the waterfront overlooking the marina. Dishes include pasta (£10–13), salads and more substantial meals like nasi goreng (£17). Summer daily 8.30am–10.30pm; winter Mon–Fri 10am–10.30pm, Sat & Sun 8.30am–10.30pm.

Boulangerie Victor Hugo 50 High St SO14 2NS T 02380 632744, W boulangerievh.co.uk. With a piano, Art Deco posters on the wall and Jacques Brel playing in the background, this French boulangerie/patisserie brings a touch of Paris to Southampton. It makes all its bread, cakes and pastries on site, as well as serving good-value lunches (£4–7) such as croque monsieur, quiches, salads and baguettes. Mon–Thurs & Sun 6am–7pm, Fri & Sat 6am–11pm.

Cargo 20–22 Oxford St, SO14 3DJ T 02380 829042, W cargosouthampton.com. This fashionable lounge bar-restaurant attached to an excellent hotel (see above) is a chic spot for a drink or coffee, and also serves interesting starters such as poached duck egg with tiger prawn and chorizo (£7), plus main courses such as steak, burgers and venison pie (£12). Mon–Sat 7am–10pm, Sun 8am–10pm.

Grand Café 1 South Western House, SO14 3AS T 02380 339303, W grand-cafe.co.uk. Opened in 1872 as the *South Western Hotel* and later used by first-class passengers awaiting their journey on the *Titanic*, this is now an ornate café-restaurant. Surprisingly, the food is neither expensive nor particularly special, but it's a great place for afternoon tea (2.30–5pm) – though it is occasionally block-booked for weddings. Mon–Sat 11am–12.30am, Sun 11am–6pm.

★**Kuti's Royal Thai** The Royal Pier, Gate House, Town Quay, SO14 2AQ ⓣ02380 339211, ⓦroyalthaipier.co.uk. Chose from the a la carte menu (dishes such as sea bass wrapped in banana leaves; £17) or an excellent all-you-can-eat Thai buffet (Sun lunch £12) at this superbly ornate waterside restaurant that was once the terminal for ocean liners such the *Titanic*. There are fine views from the outside deck on summer evenings. Mon–Thurs noon–3pm & 6–10.30pm; Fri & Sat noon–2.30pm & 6–11.30pm, Sun noon–2.30pm & 6–11pm.

The Oxford Brasserie 33 Oxford St, SO14 3DS ⓣ02380 635043, ⓦtheoxfordbrasserie.co.uk. A smart restaurant specializing in contemporary cuisine largely inspired by France and Italy. Try snails in garlic butter (£7) or a tasty risotto with king prawns and rocket (£13.50). Daily noon–2pm & 6.30–10pm.

Piccolo Mondo 36 Windsor Terrace, SO14 7SL ⓣ02380 636890, ⓦpiccolo-mondo.co.uk. Small but bustling and inexpensive Italian restaurant just round the corner from the tourist office. Friendly service, filling pizzas (£7–9) and home-made pasta dishes (£7–10) along with daily specials. Mon–Wed 11am–9.30pm, Thurs–Sat 11am–10pm.

White Star 28 Oxford St, SO14 3DJ ⓣ02380 821990, ⓦidealcollection.co.uk/whitestartavern. This chic bar-restaurant has comfy sofas and evocative photos on the wall from the heyday of ocean travel. The bar menu offers tasty tapas-sized nibbles for £4.50 each (or 3 for £11), with a good wine list and tasty cocktails, or you can opt for a full meal in the restaurant, with dishes such as hake with chorizo and cockles (£16.50). Mon–Thurs 7am–11pm, Fri 7am–midnight, Sat 8.30am–midnight, Sun 8.30am–10.30pm.

DRINKING

Southampton has an extremely energetic **nightlife**, at least during term time, with many of the best bars and clubs around **Carlton Place**, five minutes' walk north of West Park.

The Dancing Man Brewery Wool House, Town Quay, SO14 2AR ⓣ02380 836666, ⓦdancingmanbrewery.co.uk. The atmospheric fourteenth-century Wool House, a medieval warehouse, now houses a lively pub and microbrewery, with the beers brewed on site in vast stills. The food is good – pies, burgers, bangers and mash (£11–16) and sandwiches at lunch (£5–7) – with waiter service upstairs and bar service downstairs. There are tables outside and dogs are welcome too. Mon–Wed & Sun noon–11pm, Thurs–Sat noon–midnight.

Duke of Wellington 36 Bugle St, SO14 2AH ⓣ02380 339222. A historic pub with a simple interior, where you can enjoy real ales and good-sized portions of pub grub (scampi, steaks and the like for £10–17) by the roaring fire, or take a seat outside on a summer's evening. Opened in the fifteenth century as the Bere House, it changed its name after the Battle of Waterloo, and despite restoration following bomb damage, its exterior looks much as it would have when it first opened. Mon–Sat 11am–midnight, Sun noon–10.30pm.

Red Lion 55 High St, SO14 2NS ⓣ02380 333595. One of the oldest and most atmospheric pubs in Southampton, dating from the twelfth century, and complete with its own minstrels' gallery plus twenty resident ghosts. The half-timbered apartment known as Henry V's "Court Room" was used for the famous trial of a group of hapless lords who had conspired to murder Henry V in 1415. Today the somewhat more peaceful pub serves fine real ales and traditional British dishes, such as lamb chops and gravy (£10) and steak and kidney pudding (£9). Mon–Sat 11am–11pm, Sun noon–10.30pm.

NIGHTLIFE

Listed magazine (ⓦlistedmagazine.com), which comes out once every two months, includes theatre, films, gigs, festivals, clubs and restaurant reviews. It can be picked up free from bars, clubs and restaurants, and can be read online.

The Edge Compton Walk, SO14 0BH ⓣ02380 366163, ⓦtheedgesouthampton.com. Southampton's main gay club: it's a friendly place with three dance floors, a large outdoor space, regular DJs and club nights. Tues, Thurs & Sun 11pm–4am, Wed, Fri & Sat 10pm–5am.

The Joiners 141 St Mary St, SO14 1NS ⓣ02381 782021, ⓦjoinerslive.co.uk. This small, gritty pub is the place to catch live bands. It has hosted some of the biggest names since the 1980s including Oasis, Coldplay and Radiohead – all booked by the late owner, Mint, just before they made it big. Check website for upcoming gigs. Most nights from 7.30pm.

Oceana West Quay Rd, SO15 1RE ⓣ08453 132588, ⓦoceanaclubs.com/southampton. One of the UK's biggest clubs, pulling in up to 4000 people at a time, this is a giant place with themed areas – a bar quarter, an alfresco courtyard, a New York disco dance floor, a shisha lounge – plus a live entertainment area and state-of-the-art sound and light systems: pretty much something for everyone. Mon, Wed & Thurs 5pm–midnight, Tues & Fri 5pm–3am, Sat 5pm–4am.

Orange Rooms 1–2 Vernon Walk, SO15 2EJ ⓣ02380 232333, ⓦorangerooms.co.uk. Popular retro-themed lounge bar with a giant fishtank, an Alpine-style lounge area, great cocktails, decent food and various events from film screenings, quizzes and live bands to guest DJs, club nights and karaoke. Daily noon–late.

ENTERTAINMENT

Harbour Lights Ocean Village, SO14 3TL ⓣ 02380 335533, ⓦ picturehouses.co.uk. Lovely cinema on the waterfront that shows arthouse and independent films.

The Mayflower Commercial Rd, SO15 1AP ⓣ 02380 711811, ⓦ mayflower.org.uk. The south of England's largest theatre, which frequently hosts West End shows.

Romsey and around

Ten miles northwest of Southampton by the River Test, **ROMSEY** is a handsome and well-to-do market town with an impressive **abbey** and the neighbouring estate of **Broadlands**. The town grew wealthy in the fourteenth century thanks to its water wheels, which supported a thriving weaving industry, together with tanning and brewing; many of its products were exported from nearby Southampton. Head up the pristine waters of the Test and you reach the impressive **Mottisfont Abbey**, while nearby lie the attractive gardens at **Hillier**.

Romsey Abbey

Romsey, SO51 8EP • Mon–Sat 7.30am–6pm, Sun 11am–6pm • Free • ⓣ 01794 513125, ⓦ romseyabbey.org.uk

The town's best-known building is the Norman **Romsey Abbey**, which dates from 1120, though the current structure is actually the third church on this site. During the Reformation, local townspeople purchased the abbey for £100 – a memorial to the Bill of Sale, signed by Henry III, can be viewed in the south choir aisle. The abbey also houses the tomb of Lord Mountbatten, great-grandson of Queen Victoria and the last Viceroy of India, who was assassinated by the IRA in 1979.

King John's House and Heritage Centre

Church St, SO51 8BT • Mon–Sat 10am–4pm • £4 • ⓣ 01794 512200, ⓦ kingjohnshouse.org.uk

Romsey retains plenty of handsome structures from its medieval heyday, most notably **King John's House and Heritage Centre**, which embraces three historic buildings and the tourist office. The Victorian museum here traces the history of the town and its links with Florence Nightingale, who lived nearby, and includes a re-creation of a Victorian shop selling guns, which was on the site in the 1870s. Of more interest is King John's House, which dates back to 1256, and was probably built as a hunting lodge; you can still see the medieval roof timbers and Tudor fittings. End up with a visit to *Miss Moody's* tearoom and a wander in the fine gardens.

Broadlands

Broadland Park, SO15 9ZD • **Tours** July to early Sept Mon–Fri 1–4pm; 1hr • £10 • ⓣ 01794 505080, ⓦ broadlandsestates.co.uk

The former home of Lord Mountbatten, the Palladian mansion of **Broadlands** is superbly sited on the River Test in expansive parkland, just south of the town centre. Most of today's structure dates from 1767, when the second Viscount Palmerston commissioned Capability Brown to redesign the gardens and oversee rebuilding work. The mansion became the country residence of former Lord Palmerston, Prime Minister from 1855–58 and 1859–65, and today still belongs to the Mountbatten family – the Queen honeymooned here in 1947, as did Prince Charles and Lady Diana in 1981.

FROM TOP SEA CITY MUSEUM (P.224); SPINNAKER TOWER (P.234); FORT NELSON (P.241) >

SEACITY
MUSEUM
THE LIVES. THE TIMES
FORT NELSON

PASSING THE TEST

You can walk the five miles to Mottisfont from Romsey as part of the 44-mile-long **Test Way**, which runs all the way from Southampton to Inkpen Hill. The **River Test** is one of the UK's cleanest rivers. Indeed, the pristine chalk stream river is rated one of the world's best for **fly-fishing**, with salmon, brown trout and grayling particularly prevalent thanks to the healthy population of shrimps and insects that breed in the waters – the area around Stockbridge (see p.202) is particularly favoured by anglers. The river is also famous for its **watercress beds**, some of which have existed since the twelfth century. In the past, this peppery plant was known as Poorman's Bread and was a healthy staple for the working classes: it is still grown alongside the river, especially around Alresford and Whitchurch (see p.204).

Mottisfont Abbey

Mottisfont, SO51 0LP • **House** March–Oct daily 11am–5pm; Nov & Dec daily 11am–4pm • **Gardens** Daily 10am–5pm • £13.60, children £6.80; NT • ⓣ 01794 340757, ⓦ nationaltrust.org.uk/mottisfont • On Sun (May–Sept), a free bus service runs between Romsey station and Mottisfont via Hillier Gardens (see below)

Around four miles north of Romsey up the Test Valley, **Mottisfont Abbey** sits in attractive grounds by the River Test. The mansion you see today largely dates from substantial rebuilding in the eighteenth century, but its origins go back to the twelfth century when it was founded as an Augustinian Priory. The estate was handed to William Lord Sandys after the Dissolution of the Monasteries, after which he converted the old abbey into a house. By the early twentieth century, the house became a popular London retreat for writers such as George Bernard Shaw. In 1934, artist Rex Whistler was employed to decorate the drawing room, whose trompe l'oeil murals give the room a rather kitsch Gothic air. In June, garden-lovers flock to the **walled gardens** when its National Collection of old-fashioned roses is in full bloom.

Inside the house, you can see works by artists such as Barbara Hepworth, Ben Nicholson, Vanessa Bell, Walter Sickert, Augustus John, Graham Sutherland and L.S. Lowry. There's also a good showing of Impressionism from Degas to Seurat.

Sir Harold Hillier Gardens

Jermyns Lane, Romsey, SO51 0QA • Daily: April–Oct 10am–6pm; Nov–March 10am–5pm • £9, under-17s £2 • ⓣ 01794 369317, ⓦ hants.gov.uk/hilliergardens • On Sun (May–Sept), a free bus service runs between Romsey station and Mottisfont via Hillier Gardens (see above)

Two miles northeast of Romsey and around three miles southeast of Mottisfont, the **Sir Harold Hillier Gardens** are most notable for their trees and shrubs – more than 40,000 of them, including rare species from around the world – covering an area of 180 acres. Spring is particularly vibrant, when the camellias, azaleas and magnolias are in bloom, but there is also an impressive Winter Garden. Look out, too, for the Nepalese garden with plants native to the Himalayas.

ARRIVAL AND INFORMATION — ROMSEY AND AROUND

By train Romsey is on the main Southampton to Salisbury train line (2–3 hourly; 10–30min).

By bus Romsey is served by Bluestar buses from Southampton (1–2 hourly; around 45min) – the bus station is just a minute's walk from the main street.

Tourist information The Visitor and Heritage Centre, opposite the Abbey at 13 Church St, SO51 8DF (April–Oct Mon–Sat 10am–5pm; Nov–March Mon–Sat 10am–4pm; ⓣ 01794 512987, ⓦ romseynet.org.uk), can give out town maps and details of the 2hr walk along the Test Way to Mottisfont (see box above).

ACCOMMODATION AND EATING

La Parisienne 21 Bell St, SO51 8GY ⓣ 01794 512067, ⓦ la-parisienne.co.uk. This old pub has been given a stylish French makeover. Choose from good-value set menus (three courses for £18–21 at lunch and £25 at dinner) or mains that usually include the likes of scallop gratin or roasted sea bass (£19–25). There is also a cheaper bar menu featuring tasty salads, steak *haché*, quiches or mussels for around £6–13, as well as cheaper baguettes. Daily 11am–2.30pm & 6–9.30pm.

The White Horse Hotel & Brasserie Market Place, SO51 8ZJ ⓣ 01794 512431, ⓦ thewhitehorseromsey.co.uk. Romsey's top hotel has boutique rooms overlooking the marketplace in a former coaching inn. Rooms at the front, in former twelfth-century guest rooms for the nearby abbey, are characterful, if small. There are others in the wonky-floored Tudor section, and more spacious modern options in the 1960s extension at the back. The brasserie here is *the* place to eat in Romsey, with a courtyard bar and a menu that features local watercress, meat, fish and cheeses. The set menu is good value at £16 for two courses (£18.50 for three), while main courses such as roast chalk-stream trout or New Forest pork cost £14–19. Daily noon–3pm & 6–10pm; kitchen close at 9pm on Sun. **£145**

Along Southampton Water

The shipping motorway of **Southampton Water** heads south into the Solent, with the fringes of the New Forest on the west side. Within easy commuting distance of Southampton, the east bank is fairly built up, but there are a couple of places that make an easy day-trip: the village of **Netley Abbey**, with its ruins of a Cistercian monastery and fine country park, and the quaint **Hamble-le-Rice**, a yachting town on the banks of the pretty River Hamble.

Netley Abbey

Abbey Hill • April–Sept daily 10am–6pm; Oct–March Sat & Sun 10am–4pm • Free • ⓣ 02392 378291, ⓦ www.english-heritage.org.uk/visit/places/netley-abbey • Southampton city bus #6 (2 hourly; 30min) or train from Southampton Central (hourly; 20min)

Around three miles east of Southampton over the toll bridge (cars 60p), **Netley Abbey** is now substantially ruined, but still the most complete Cistercian monastery remaining in the south of England. The abbey was founded in 1238 by Bishop of Winchester Peter des Roches and housed monks from the nearby Beaulieu Abbey (see p.169). Following the Dissolution, the new owner turned it into a Tudor mansion, which was abandoned in the eighteenth century; the resulting ruins were visited by various writers and artists – it was painted by Constable and thought to be the inspiration for Jane Austen's *Northanger Abbey*. Much of its appeal today is that it is open to the elements – in summer the walls of its ruined halls and rooms give shelter to families and picnickers.

Royal Victoria Country Park

Netley Abbey, SO31 5DQ • Daily: March–Oct 8am–9pm; Nov–Feb 8am–5pm • Free • **Tower tours** March–Oct Sun & bank hol Mon 2pm & 3pm; Nov–Feb Sun 2pm; 45min • £4 • **Miniature train** Sat, Sun & school hols 11am–4.30pm • £1.75 • ⓣ 02380 455157, ⓦ hants.gov.uk/rvcp

The extensive **Royal Victoria Country Park**, in the village of Netley Abbey, has numerous woodland trails, a shingle beach, playground, café and miniature train – enough to keep restless children amused for several hours. The park's most distinctive building, however, is the red-brick chapel and distinctive **tower**, all that remains of the once enormous **Royal Victoria Hospital**. You can take a guided tour up the tower's 166 steps for great views along Southampton Water and learn about the hospital's fascinating history: it was opened in 1863 to treat casualties of the Crimean War, the injured arriving on hospital ships in nearby Southampton. When built, the original hospital was England's largest building, at a quarter of a mile long with nearly one thousand beds, though Florence Nightingale – who was consulted about the design – felt that its layout was out of date before it even opened. During World War I, the hospital treated some 50,000 patients, including war poet Wilfred Owen. In World War II, the Americans used the hospital for the D-Day landings, but it was closed in the 1950s and largely demolished in the 1960s.

THE SOLENT WAY

The seven-mile walk from Southampton to Hamble-le-Rice is the first of the eastern stretch of the **Solent Way** (solentway.co.uk), a sixty-mile coastal path stretching from Milford, south of the New Forest, to Emsworth, north of Hayling Island. Waymarked with a picture of a sea bird and also known as the **Solent Coast Path**, the best stretch of the route can be picked up from Netley Abbey, from where it is an easy two-mile walk to Hamble. You can then take the ferry to Warsash for the next section, a pleasant seven-mile coastal walk to Lee-on-Solent along marshland and low cliffs.

Hamble-le-Rice

Around two and a half miles east of Netley Abbey (or slightly less if you walk the coastal path), neighbouring **HAMBLE-LE-RICE** ("rice" meaning a small hill) is an affluent yachties' village that clusters round the attractive waters of the **River Hamble**: as you'd expect, the focus of life is its sailing club and marina. It was also the location for the 1980s TV series *Howards' Way*. There are no specific sights here, though you could easily while away half a day watching the comings and goings of the sailing boats or crabbing from the jetty, or take one of the little bright-pink **ferries** across the river to Warsash. There are some great **walks** on this side of the river, especially heading north along the evocatively named Bunny Meadows.

ARRIVAL AND DEPARTURE

By bus Bus #6 from Southampton runs every 30min to Hamble-le-Rice (40min) via Netley Abbey (10min).

By ferry Ferries shuttle between Warsash and Hamble (daily, weather permitting: May–Oct 9am–6pm; Nov–May 9am–4pm; £1.50 one-way; 07720 438402, hambleferry.co.uk).

EATING

Bonne Bouche High St, SO31 4HA 01703 455771, bonne-bouche.co.uk. An inexpensive café-deli serving top-quality meats, cheeses and breads plus superb sandwiches, soups and fresh salads from around £3.50, with tables on outdoor decking. Mon–Fri 8am–4pm, Sat & Sun 8am–5pm.

The Bugle High St, SO31 4HA 02380 453000, idealcollection.co.uk/buglehamble. The best of Hamble's generous supply of pubs, with an interior of bare bricks and wood beams. It specializes in local seasonal food, with excellent main courses such as *moules frites* (£11), local trout (£15.50), or Hampshire steaks (£17). Mon–Thurs 11am–11pm, Fri–Sat 11am–midnight, Sun noon–10.30pm.

The King and Queen High St, SO31 4HA 02380 454247, thekingandqueenpub.co.uk. Known for its great collection of rums and real ales, this pub is very popular with the local yachties. There's a pretty garden outside and a log fire inside, where you can enjoy pub favourites such as fish pie or burgers (£10–14), or sandwiches at lunchtime (£5). Food served Mon–Sat noon–3.30pm & 7–9pm, Sun noon–4pm.

The River Rat Cellar and Kitchen High St, SO31 4HA 02380 457801, riverrathamble.co.uk. Fine dining and friendly service at this small restaurant with a cosy interior and a pretty garden. Starters such as lobster soup (£8) followed by fillet of wild black bream (£18) hit the spot, and there's an excellent wine list with plenty of options available by the glass. Tues–Sat 10am–6pm, Sun noon–4pm.

Portsmouth

A flourishing port, **PORTSMOUTH's** harbour swarms with naval frigates, tugs and ferries bound for the continent or the Isle of Wight. Heavily bombed during World War II, much of the city is now made up of bland tower blocks, but don't let that put you off. The substantially walled **Old Portsmouth** preserves some Georgian and Tudor character, while a little to the north, the revitalized **Gunwharf Quays** forms an attractive waterfront hub of shops, cafés and restaurants, dominated by the highly impressive **Spinnaker Tower**. It's a short stroll from here to the attractions of the **Historic Dockyard**, including HMS *Victory* and the *Mary Rose*, while half a mile beyond lies **Charles**

Dickens' Birthplace. Take time, too, to explore **Southsea**, a lively residential suburb with its own shingle beach, as well as the engrossing **D-day Museum**, **Southsea Castle** and **Royal Marines Museum.** It's also fun to hop on a ferry to the Submarine Museum and Museum of Naval Firepower in **Gosport**, while coastal defences can also be admired at nearby **Porchester Castle**, **Fort Nelson** and the offshore **Spitbank Fort**.

Brief history

PORTSMOUTH occupies the peninsula of Portsea Island, on the eastern flank of a huge harbour, a position which has enabled it to develop into Britain's foremost naval station. The Romans first raised a fortress on the northernmost edge of this inlet, but wealthy merchant Jean de Gisors is generally credited as founding the city when he

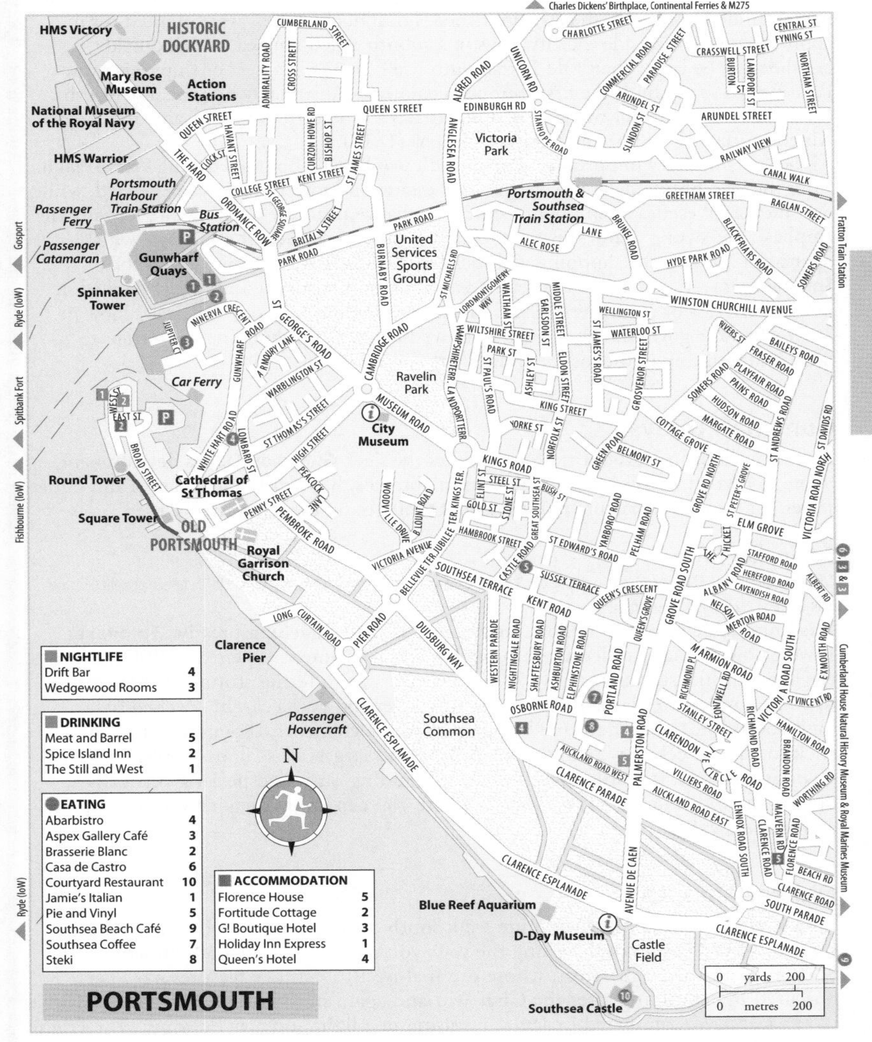

built a settlement on the island of **Portsea** in 1180 at a sheltered spot for his fleet of ships. The town was given a royal charter in 1184 and by the following century it had become a major port exporting wool and grain. The 1300s saw the port employed as a base from where the armies of Henry III and Edward I could attack France, but in the following century Portsmouth's wooden buildings were frequently torched by invading French soldiers. Henry VII improved its fortifications, established the world's first dry dock here and made Portsmouth a royal dockyard in 1495, and Henry VIII invested further, building **Southsea Castle** (1544), probably the spot from where he watched his flagship the *Mary Rose* sink in the harbour a year later. By the sixteenth century, Portsmouth's role as a port declined and it was hit heavily by the plague and bombardments during the Civil War.

By the late seventeenth century, however, Portsmouth was once again one of Europe's best-defended ports, and the city flourished. Local dockworkers were granted royal approval to build outside the city walls in a suburb called Portsea, which quickly expanded to be larger than Old Portsmouth itself. In 1787, a fleet of ships left from Portsmouth to establish the first European colony in Australia, while the nineteenth century saw the birth of two highly influential Victorians in the city, Isambard Kingdom Brunel (1806) and Charles Dickens (1812).

Due to its military importance, Portsmouth was heavily bombed during **World War II**. After the war, hundreds of prefabs, council estates and tower blocks were erected, while new industrial estates attempted to shift the reliance from the docks. More recently the emphasis has swung again, this time toward retail outlets; **Gunwharf Quays**, which opened in 2001, is the shopping and social hub of the city. Its showpiece is the **Spinnaker Tower**, which was conceived as a millennium project and finally opened in 2005 after years of controversy and budgetary wrangling. The city suffered a blow in 2013 when the government decided to move the navy's shipbuilding operations to Scotland, resulting in the loss of around a thousand jobs.

Gunwharf Quays

A short walk from Harbour train station lies the sleek **Gunwharf Quays** development, home to myriad stylish cafés, restaurants, nightclubs, high-street chain shops and outlet stores. It's also the departure point for **boat tours** round the harbour (see p.239).

Spinnaker Tower

Gunwharf Quays, P01 3TT • Daily 10am–5.30pm; check website for opening hours over Christmas hols • £9. 95, fifteen percent discount online • T 02392 857520, W spinnakertower.co.uk

It is impossible to overlook Portsmouth's iconic and hugely impressive **Spinnaker Tower**, now officially called the Emirates Spinnaker Tower. Opened in 2005, the elegant, sail-like structure rises 170m above the city, offering stunning vistas for up to twenty miles over land and sea. The three viewing decks can be reached by a high-speed lift, the highest one being open to the elements, though most people stick to View Deck 1, which has one of Europe's largest glass floors – despite its obvious strength, it is still nerve-wracking standing on it and peering vertically down. There's a café on View Deck 2, where you can enjoy the views over a cup of coffee and a cake.

Old Portsmouth

It's a well-signposted fifteen-minute walk south of the Spinnaker Tower to what remains of **Old Portsmouth**. Along the way, you pass the simple **Cathedral of St Thomas** on the High Street, whose original twelfth-century features have been obscured by rebuilding after the Civil War and again in the twentieth century. The nave was finally completed in 1991, resulting in a light and airy building. The High

Street ends at a maze of cobbled Georgian streets huddling behind an impressive fifteenth-century wall protecting the old port, where Walter Raleigh landed the first potatoes and tobacco from the New World. You can walk along the top of the walls past the Tudor **Round Tower** and neighbouring **Square Tower**, both popular vantage points for observing nautical activities. The latter details its history as the home to the town Governor in Tudor times and later its use as a gunpowder store. Also in Old Portsmouth lie the atmospheric ruins of the **Royal Garrison Church**. Dating back to 1212, when it was built as a hospice for pilgrims on their way to Winchester, it was converted into a garrison church in 1560, before being partly destroyed by a fireball in 1941.

The Historic Dockyard

Victory Gate, HM Naval Base, PO1 3LJ • Daily 10am–6pm • The all-inclusive ticket, £32 (£25.60 online), allows unlimited entry to all the attractions for a year, including harbour boat trips; see website for individual attraction prices • T 02392 839766, W historicdockyard.co.uk

Portsmouth's biggest draw is the **Historic Dockyard** in the **Royal Naval Base** at the end of Queen Street. It's made up of a series of warehouses, museums and ships that were the powerhouse of the Royal Navy for centuries. In addition to the highlights detailed below, the Dockyard houses some smaller exhibits, including **Boathouse 4** (which has activities for children, including an indoor mast for climbing), the **Historic Boat Workshop** (with its collection of historic small boats), and **Action Stations**, with interactive games and videos to simulate life on board ship.

8

HMS Victory

At the end of the long cobbled street is the Dockyard's highlight, the ornately wooden-fronted **HMS Victory**, Nelson's victorious ship against Napoleon in the Battle of Trafalgar. The ship was already forty years old when she set sail from Portsmouth for Trafalgar on September 14, 1805. A plaque on the deck marks the spot where Nelson was shot by a French musketeer off the coast of Spain, while the hold has a shrine marking the place where he finally expired. You can also see the wooden cask in which his dead body was preserved in brandy for its return to England. Arrows direct you round various decks, which get progressively more claustrophobic as you head downwards. It is hard not to contrast Nelson and Hardy's lavish polished quarters at the rear – with private bedrooms and dining rooms – with the cramped hammocks strung up for the rest of the crew in the dingy lower decks. You can still see the leg irons and cat-o'-nine tails used against those who disobeyed orders; the gallery's giant Brodie stove, the huge potential fire risk used to cook for the substantial crew; and the surprisingly airy sick bay. But above all else it is the ship's sheer size and power that are impressive – its cannons could fire shot almost a mile, while a naval army of more than 140 marines could be stationed in the middle deck, ready for battle.

Although badly damaged during the Battle of Trafalgar, the *Victory* continued in service for a further twenty years, before retiring to the dry dock where she rests today. The *Victory* has recently undergone a £2 million programme of conservation and restoration works including repainting her in the colours she wore during the Battle of Trafalgar.

National Museum of the Royal Navy

Opposite the *Victory*, various buildings house the exhaustive **National Museum of the Royal Navy**. This tells the story of the Navy from the time of Alfred the Great's fleet to today, through paintings, photos and artefacts, including a Christmas pudding dating back to 1900 which was originally sent to the Naval Brigade during the Boer War. The museum includes the **Trafalgar Experience**, which has a film re-creating the battle in vivid and noisy fashion. You can also learn about knots, scurvy and how to furl a sail, while upstairs is a fine selection of giant figureheads, rescued from various scrapped ships over the last couple of centuries. In the **Nelson Gallery**, you can see Nelson's funeral barge, which was used to parade his body down the Thames in 1806. The museum also houses a series of temporary exhibitions.

HMS Warrior

Nearest the entrance to the complex is the youngest ship, **HMS Warrior**, dating from 1860. It was Britain's first armoured (iron-clad) battleship, and was the pride of the fleet in its day. Longer and faster than any previous naval vessel – and, incidentally, the first to be fitted with washing machines – the *Warrior* was described by Napoleon III as a "black snake amongst the rabbits". The ship displays a wealth of weaponry, including rifles, pistols and sabres, though she was never challenged and fired a cannon not even once in her 22 years at sea.

Mary Rose Museum

The impressive boat-shaped **Mary Rose Museum** was purpose-built at a cost of £27 million to preserve and display Henry VIII's prize naval ship, built in 1511. The **Mary Rose** was sunk in Portsmouth Harbour while fighting invading French forces in 1545 – the king watched it sink from Southsea Castle. It lay there preserved under silt in the Solent until 1982, when archeologists not only salvaged the boat but also discovered extremely rare longbows and their arrows, some of them tipped with poison. Today, visitors view the ship through floor-to-ceiling protective windows. The museum also contains an absorbing collection of the objects retrieved from the wreck, including guns, gold coins and implements from the Barber Surgeon's cabin.

Charles Dickens' Birthplace

393 Old Commercial Rd, PO1 4QL • April–Sept Fri–Sun 10am–5.30pm • £4.20, under-18s free • ⓣ 02392 827261, ⓦ charlesdickensbirthplace.co.uk

In the north of the city, **Charles Dickens' Birthplace** is set up much as it would have looked when the famous novelist was born here on February 7, 1812. Dickens' father, John, moved to Portsmouth in 1809 to work for the Navy Pay Office before he was recalled to London in 1815. So Charles only lived here for three years, but he is said to have returned often and set parts of *Nicholas Nickleby* in the city. The modest house not only contains period furniture but a wealth of information about Dickens' life here and the influences on his novels, plus the couch on which he died. On the first Sunday of each month at 3pm, readings of Dickens' works take place in the museum (April–Sept; 45min). A new statue – the first life-sized one of the author in Britain – was erected in Portsmouth's Guildhall Square in 2014, on Dickens' 202nd birthday.

City Museum

3 Museum Rd, PO1 2LJ • Tues–Sun & bank hol Mon: April–Sept 10am–5.30pm; Oct–March 10am–5pm • Free • ⓣ 02392 834779, ⓦ portsmouthcitymuseums.co.uk

The **City Museum** has exhibits and paintings relating to the history of Portsmouth, including historical costumes, early electrical equipment, paintings, an exhibit on the city's relationship with football, and a section about Portsmouth's role in the D-Day landings. Perhaps of most interest is the *Study in Sherlock* section. Arthur Conan Doyle wrote his first Sherlock Holmes novels while working as a GP in Southsea, having moved here in 1882. His house was destroyed in the war, but fortunately a stack of Conan Doyle books and correspondence was left to the nation after the death of avid collector and Sherlock Holmes expert Richard Green in 2004.

Gosport

On the western side of Portsmouth Harbour, **GOSPORT** has traditionally shared Portsmouth's role as a major naval town but has not undergone the revitalization enjoyed by its larger neighbour over the last few decades. Nevertheless, with a couple of **museums** worth visiting, otherwise humdrum Gosport makes a decent day out, especially if you take the passenger ferry (see p.239), which departs from the Harbour train station jetty.

Royal Submarine Museum

Haslar Jetty Rd, PO12 2AS • April–Oct daily 10am–5.30pm; Nov–March Wed–Sun 10am–4.30pm; also open the same hours as rest of month on Mon & Tues in school hols; last admission 1hr before closing • £14, or included in the Historic Dockyard all-inclusive ticket (see p.235) • T 02392 510354, W submarine-museum.co.uk

The **Royal Submarine Museum** on Haslar Jetty displays six submarines, some of which you can enter. Allow a couple of hours to explore these slightly creepy vessels – a guided tour inside HMS *Alliance* gives you an insight into how cramped life was on board, and the museum elaborates evocatively on the long history of submersible craft.

Explosion! Museum of Naval Firepower

Heritage Way, Priddy's Yard, PO12 4LE • April–Oct daily 10am–5pm; Nov–March Sat & Sun 10am–4pm; last admission 1hr before closing • £10, or included in the Historic Dockyard all-inclusive ticket (see p.235) • T 02392 505600, W explosion.org.uk

Set inside a former armaments depot dating back to 1771, **Explosion! Museum of Naval Firepower** retraces the history of naval warfare from the days of gunpowder to the present. Not for pacifists, there are weapons of all descriptions here, including mines, big guns, torpedoes and even an atom bomb (fortunately not armed). You can experience vivid computer animations and interactive displays, as well as find out about the history of Gosport's docks.

Southsea

Wrapped around a broad, grassy common, **Southsea** is an appealing suburb facing a shingle beach, with some fine nineteenth-century architecture. The main tourist sights are all lined along the seafront, though the **inland streets** are also worth exploring – Osborne Road for its global restaurants; Marmion Road for quirky independent boutiques; and Albert Road for its trendy bars and cafés and antique and bric-a-brac shops.

Southsea Castle

Castle Esplanade, PO5 3PA • Easter–Oct Tues–Sun & bank hol Mon 10am–5.30pm • Free • T 02392 841625, W southseacastle.co.uk

Along the seafront, Southsea's most historic building, marked by a little lighthouse, is the squat **Southsea Castle**. It was built in 1544 from the remains of Beaulieu Abbey (see p.169) and has served as a fortress and prison. You can go inside the keep and learn about Portsmouth's military history, as well as climbing up to the

SPITBANK FORT

A mile out in Portsmouth Harbour, **Spitbank Fort** is an offshore bastion of granite, iron and brick. The circular sea fort was commissioned by Lord Palmerston in 1860 to defend Portsmouth from French attack, and was finished in 1878, actually never to be used in war. With more than fifty rooms linked by passages and steps on two floors, the complex includes a 135m-deep well, which still draws fresh water from below the sea floor. Today it's an upmarket venue, complete with outdoor hot tub, that provides luxury all-inclusive overnight stays and is rented out for private events (T 0330 333 7222, W solentforts.com/spitbank-fort).

spot from where Henry VIII is said to have watched the *Mary Rose* sink in 1545 (see p.236), though in fact you can get just as good views by climbing along the adjacent seafront ramparts.

D-Day Museum

Clarence Esplanade, PO5 3NT • Daily: April–Sept 10am–5.30pm; Oct–March 10am–5pm; last entry 30min before closing • £6.80, under-18s £4.70 • T 02392 826722, W ddaymuseum.co.uk

The **D-Day Museum** focuses on Portsmouth's role as the principal assembly point for the D-Day invasion in World War II, code-named "Operation Overlord". The museum's most striking exhibit is the 90m-long *Overlord Embroidery*, which illustrates the Normandy landings, though most moving are the reminiscences of the people who were involved.

Blue Reef Aquarium

Clarence Esplanade, PO5 3PB • Daily: April–Oct 10am–6pm; Nov–March 10am–5pm; last admission 1hr before closing • £10 (£8.50 online), under-13s £7.75 (£6.25 online) • T 02392 875222, W bluereefaquarium.co.uk/portsmouth

Next to the tourist office, the **Blue Reef Aquarium** has the usual marine life, including tropical fish, sea horses, otters, rays and sharks, and makes a good escape on a wet day. The highlight is a walk-through underwater tunnel from where you can see the fish swimming above you. There are various talks and feeding sessions throughout the day.

Cumberland House Natural History Museum

Eastern Parade, PO4 9RF • Tues–Sun & bank hol Mon: April–Oct 10am–5.30pm; Nov–March 10am–5pm; last entry 30min before closing • Free • T 02392 815276, W portsmouthnaturalhistory.co.uk

The fairly modest **Cumberland House Natural History Museum** details the wildlife that visits the area – mostly sea birds, though there is also a walk-through butterfly house (May–Sept), some fossils and geological finds, along with a small aquarium. It also hosts some interesting temporary exhibitions.

Royal Marines Museum

Eastney Rd, PO4 9PX • April–Oct daily 10am–5pm; Nov–March Wed–Sun 10am–5pm; also open the same hours as rest of month on Mon & Tues in school hols • £9, or included in the Historic Dockyard all-inclusive ticket (see p.235) • T 02392 819385, W royalmarinesmuseum.co.uk

The **Royal Marines Museum** describes the greatest campaigns of the Navy's elite fighting force from their origins in 1694 right up to recent campaigns in the Gulf. There are interactive exhibits, rifle simulators, displays of medals and military costumes and special events throughout the year. Of most interest are the details of what it takes to make a marine – which is not for the faint-hearted.

ARRIVAL AND DEPARTURE — PORTSMOUTH

By train Portsmouth's main train station is in the city centre, but the line continues to Portsmouth Harbour station, the most convenient stop for the main sights and old town.

Destinations Brighton (hourly; 1hr 20min–1hr 30min); London Waterloo (3–4 hourly; 1hr 35min–2hr 10min); Salisbury (hourly; 1hr 15min); Southampton (4 hourly; 50min–1hr); Winchester (hourly; 1hr).

By bus National Express buses run to London Victoria (approx hourly; 1hr 50min–2hr 30min) and Southampton (approx hourly; 40min–1hr).

By passenger ferry High-speed passenger ferries leave from the jetty alongside Portsmouth Harbour station for Ryde (W wightlink.co.uk) on the Isle of Wight (see p.249), and Gosport (see p.239).

By car ferry Wightlink car ferries depart from the ferry port off Gunwharf Road, just south of Gunwharf Quays, for Fishbourne on the Isle of Wight (see p.249), while hovercraft (W hovertravel.co.uk) leave from Clarence Esplanade in Southsea for Ryde (see p.249). Continental ferries depart from north of the centre, just off the M275 (W brittany-ferries.co.uk and W condorferries.co.uk).

By car As it is on a peninsula, driving into Portsmouth can be slow going at peak times, though there are plenty of central car parks.

GETTING AROUND

By bus Buses #1 and #16 run from The Hard interchange, just by Portsmouth Harbour station, via Old Portsmouth to Southsea's seafront, roughly every 15min.

By ferry Ferries run across to Gosport from Portsmouth Harbour station jetty (every 10–15min daily 5.30am–midnight; £3.30 return; Ⓦ gosportferry.co.uk).

INFORMATION AND TOURS

Tourist information There are two tourist offices in Portsmouth (both Ⓣ 02392 826722, Ⓦ visitportsmouth.co.uk), one within the City Museum on Museum Road (Tues–Sun: April–Sept 10am–5pm; Oct–March 10am–4.30pm), the other at Clarence Esplanade in the D-Day Museum on Southsea's seafront (daily: April–Sept 10am–5pm; Oct–March 10am–4.30pm).

Boat trips Various boat trips go round the harbour and Historic Dockyard, leaving from the waterfront at Gunwharf Quays: Portsmouth Boat Trips (Ⓦ portsmouth-boat-trips.co.uk) offers 40–50min tours from £8/person, or included in the Historic Dockyard all-inclusive ticket (see p.235).

ACCOMMODATION

CENTRAL PORTSMOUTH

Fortitude Cottage 51 Broad St, PO1 2JD Ⓣ 02392 823748, Ⓦ fortitudecottage.co.uk. Stylish B&B in Portsmouth Old Town overlooking the ferry terminal and Gunwharf Quays. The top-floor room has its own roof terrace with fantastic views of the water, and three others have harbour views; the least expensive rooms are on the ground floor, and lack an outlook. **£140**

Holiday Inn Express The Plaza, Gunwharf Quays, PO1 3FD Ⓣ 02392 894240, Ⓦ hiexportsmouth.co.uk. Rooms in this modern hotel are compact with the usual chain hotel decor, but its position, right on Gunwharf Quays, can't be beaten. There's a large and airy breakfast room and bar too. **£118**

SOUTHSEA

★Florence House 2 Malvern Rd, PO5 2NA Ⓣ 02392 009111, Ⓦ florencehousehotel.co.uk. Tastefully furnished boutique B&B in an Edwardian townhouse on a quiet backstreet near Southsea's waterfront, with a range of recently refurbished rooms, over three floors, all spick-and-span with flatscreen TVs. It's owned by a small local boutique hotel chain, who have renovated several of the surrounding Edwardian houses to similar standards. There's also a small garden and a pleasant on-site restaurant, *The Kitchen*. **£90**

G! Boutique Hotel 71 Festing Rd, PO4 0NQ Ⓣ 02392 822226 Ⓦ g-boutiquehotel.co.uk. Fans of kitsch will enjoy this quirky boutique guesthouse with funky decor and glamorous furniture, such as an eight-foot round bed, and a double jacuzzi. The more conventional rooms are also comfortable and stylish, and staff are friendly. **£80**

Queen's Hotel Clarence Parade, Osborne Rd, PO5 3LJ Ⓣ 02392 822466, Ⓦ queenshotelportsmouth.com. This giant Edwardian pile may be a little dated, but its location in its own grounds overlooking Southsea's common and the sea beyond is great. Communal areas are extravagantly decorated – think chandeliers and soaring painted ceilings – though the rooms are contemporary, and the best, at the front, have balconies. There's also a restaurant and champagne bar. **£105**

EATING

All the usual chains, including *Pizza Express*, *Café Rouge* and *Strada*, with outdoor tables overlooking the bustling harbour, can be found at **Gunwharf Quays**. Eating places are surprisingly scarce in **Old Portsmouth**, however, and the best place to head for food is **Southsea**, for its excellent variety of world cafés and good-value independent restaurants.

CENTRAL PORTSMOUTH

Abarbistro 58 White Hart Rd, PO1 2JA Ⓣ 02392 811585, Ⓦ abarbistro.co.uk. Vibrant bar-restaurant on the edge of Old Portsmouth, serving salads or simple dishes such as burgers and fish and chips (around £11) as well as generous mains such as fish cakes, roast pork belly, or steaks (£12–20). Or just have a drink on the outside terrace. Mon–Sat 11am–11pm, Sun noon–11pm.

Aspex Gallery Café Gunwharf Quays, PO1 3BF Ⓣ 02392 778080, Ⓦ aspex.org.uk. Portsmouth's leading centre for contemporary arts has two stylish galleries inside a former Victorian naval storehouse, while the arty bare-brick café is a great place for coffee and cakes and light lunch (daily specials £5–6). Wed–Sun 11am–4pm.

Brasserie Blanc 1 Gunwharf Quays, PO1 3FR Ⓣ 02392 891320, Ⓦ brasserieblanc.com. Large, modern brasserie with a good-value daytime set menu (until 6.30pm; £12.45 for three courses) along with tasty classic mains such as *beouf bourguignon* (£16.50), *moules marinière* (£14) and a range of steaks (£13–25). Mon–Sat 9am–11pm, Sun 9am–10pm.

Jamie's Italian S92–93 Market Square, Gunwharf Quays, PO1 3FB Ⓣ 02392 000595, Ⓦ jamieoliver.com/italian/restaurants. The decor at Jamie Oliver's Portsmouth outlet has a maritime theme, complete with reclaimed nautical winches and paraphernalia, while the food has the usual Italian twist (most dishes £10–17). The *fritto misto* is tasty, and there's a good variety of pasta dishes, as well as a few mains such as Venetian fish stew (£14). Mon–Thurs noon–10pm, Fri & Sat noon–11pm, Sun noon–9pm.

SOUTHSEA

Casa de Castro 96a Albert Rd, PO5 2SN ⓣ07507 821811, ⓦcasadecastro.co.uk. This great little café, run by a French-Brazilian couple, serves a fantastic array of cakes, buns and pastries, as well as savoury snacks such as quiche (£4.80). There's even a little garden at the back. Tues–Sat 8.30am–4pm.

Courtyard Restaurant Southsea Castle, Clarence Esplanade, PO5 3PA ⓣ02392 837370. ⓦthecourtyard southseacastle.co.uk. An interconnecting warren of rooms inside the castle walls and tables outside in the courtyard make this a great café by day and restaurant by night, serving everything from cooked breakfasts and ciabattas (£6–7) to fish or meat sharing platters (£19.50) and mains such as fish pie and steaks (£10–19). Tues–Sat 9am–11pm, Sun 9.30am–7pm.

Pie and Vinyl 61 Castle Rd, PO5 3AY ⓣ02392 753914. ⓦpieandvinyl.co.uk. Part café, part hip shop selling – as the name suggests – records and pies, plus music posters and magazines. It's a great space for browsing and chilling, with a wide range of tasty pies on offer (all pies £5.50, or £8.50 with mash, peas and gravy) – the Bombay bicycle pie is a delicious vegan option, while the all-day breakfast pie does what it says on the tin. Mon–Sat 11am–9pm, Sun 11am–5pm.

Southsea Beach Café Esplanade, PO4 0SP ⓣ02392 832854, ⓦsouthseabeachcafe.co.uk. Right on the beach, with a lovely outdoor terrace and fine views, this laidback café serves great breakfasts and lunches (£6–9) made from locally sourced ingredients – try the smoked mackerel toastie with beetroot and horseradish, or simply fish and chips. Opens later in summer for fish evenings: check website for details. Mon–Fri 9am–5pm, Sat & Sun 8am–5pm.

Southsea Coffee 63 Osborne Rd, PO5 3LS ⓣ02393 079501, ⓦsouthseacoffee.co.uk. Fantastic independent coffee shop serving fine breakfasts, such as Greek yoghurt with granola (£4.50) plus brunches and lunches with good veggie options – beetroot hummus (£4) or sharing platters (£7) – and some excellent vegan cakes. Mon–Sat 8.30am–5pm, Sun 10am–4pm.

Steki 58 Osborne Rd, PO5 3LU ⓣ02392 750200, ⓦsteki.co.uk. *Steki* brings an authentic Greek taverna feel to Southsea, with home-cooked food at reasonable prices. Greek favourites include superb souvlaki, moussaka and meatballs, but if you're hungry go for the excellent *Steki* special – a selection of grilled meats for two (£22). Mon–Thurs 5–11pm, Fri–Sun noon–11pm.

DRINKING

Meat and Barrel 112 Palmerstone Rd, Southsea PO5 3PT ⓣ02392 176291, ⓦmeatandbarrel.co.uk. A large, lively space with bare brick walls and a buzzy vibe. The craft beers are great, with a taster paddle of ales for £6, and they also do gourmet burgers (£7–9). Daily 11.30am–late.

Spice Island Inn 1 Bath Square, PO1 2JL ⓣ02392 870543, ⓦwww.spiceisland-portsmouth.co.uk. Traditional pub in the Old Town with a lovely seafront terrace, wooden floors inside and good views from the upstairs rooms. It serves decent pub grub, such as sausage and mash (£9), and has a good-value Sunday roast (£10). You can take your drinks outside to admire the view from the harbour walls in true British fashion. Daily 11am–11pm.

The Still and West 2 Bath Square, PO1 2JL ⓣ02392 821567, ⓦstillandwest.co.uk. A waterfront terrace and cosy interior with views over the harbour make this a great spot to watch the comings and goings on the water: the menu features dishes such as Asian crab cakes (£13) and chicken and ham pie (£12) – or try the fish sharing platter (£18). Mon–Thurs 9am–11pm, Fri & Sat 9am–midnight, Sun 11.30am–10.30pm.

NIGHTLIFE

Drift Bar 78 Palmerston Rd, Southsea, PO5 3PT ⓣ02392 779839. Hip lounge bar with a beer garden, serving a range of cocktails and snacks, including some very good-value lunchtime specials (around £6). DJs on Fri and Sat and live music on Sun. Mon–Wed 11–2.30am, Thurs–Sat 11–3.30am, Sun 11–1.30am.

Wedgewood Rooms 147b Albert Rd, Southsea, PO4 0JW ⓣ02392 863911, ⓦwedgewood-rooms.co.uk. Well-established venue hosting mainstream live music (including Pulp and Oasis in its time), new acts, tribute bands, comedy and club nights.

Around Portsmouth

The countryside immediately around Portsmouth is not particularly inspiring, though there are a few **castles and museums** that are worth exploring, as well as some pleasant harbourside villages. **Hayling Island**, meanwhile, is a big draw for watersports enthusiasts, with some excellent windsurfing on offer.

Titchfield Abbey

Mill Lane, Fareham, near Titchfield, PO15 5RA • Daily: April–Sept 10am–5pm; Oct–March 10am–4pm • Free; EH • Ⓦ www.english-heritage.org.uk/visit/places/titchfield-abbey

West of Portsmouth, around half a mile north of the village of Titchfield, lies **Titchfield Abbey**, the ruins of a thirteenth-century abbey that after the Dissolution was rebuilt into a Tudor mansion. Visitors entertained at the mansion, included, over the years, not only Henry VIII himself but also Edward VI, Elizabeth I, and possibly Shakespeare, who was a friend of the family and may have put on plays here. The house fell into ruin in the eighteenth century, leaving pretty much what you see today – you are free to wander round, with several panels detailing facts about the house and abbey's history.

Portchester Castle

Church Rd, Portchester, PO16 9QW • Feb half-term daily 10am–4pm; April–Sept daily 10am–6pm; Oct daily 10am–5pm; Nov to March Sat & Sun 10am–4pm • £5.80, under-16s £3.40; EH • Ⓣ 02392 378291, Ⓦ www.english-heritage.org.uk/visit/places/portchester-castle

Portchester Castle, six miles out of Portsmouth, lies just beyond the marina development at Port Solent. Built by the Romans in the third century, this fortification boasts the finest surviving example of Roman walls in northern Europe – still over 7m high and incorporating some twenty bastions. The Normans felt no need to make any substantial alterations when they moved in, but a castle was later built within Portchester's precincts by Henry II, which Richard II extended and Henry V used as his garrison when assembling the army that was to fight the Battle of Agincourt. Today its grassy enclosure makes a sheltered spot for a congenial game of cricket or a kickabout with a football.

Fort Nelson and the Royal Armouries Museum

Portsdown Hill Rd, PO17 6AN • Daily: April–Oct 10am–5pm; Nov–March 10.30am–4pm • Free • Ⓣ 01329 233734, Ⓦ royalarmouries.org

A couple of miles north of Portchester Castle, **Fort Nelson** is another highly impressive castle, one of a chain of forts along a hill facing Portsmouth and the only one open to the public. Much more extensive than you would think from the outside, it sits in nineteen acres of land on top of Portsdown Hill, with fantastic views south over the Solent and north along the Meon Valley. It was built in the 1860s to protect Portsmouth from attack by the French and subsequently used in both world wars. Inside you can visit a working blacksmith's forge, prison cells and several eerie underground tunnels.

The fort is also home to the **Royal Armouries Museum**, displaying more than 350 big guns and cannons from the national arms collection. Exhibits range from the trebuchet used in the film *Gladiator* to a wonderfully ornate Portuguese cannon from the fifteenth century, along with guns used in the two world wars to the modern-day monsters, including the Iraqi "supergun" from the first Gulf War. There are frequent demonstrations of the weapons in action, and if you are feeling generous you can even buy your loved one a voucher entitling them to fire a deafening 25-pounder gun, or similar.

Hayling Island

An anvil-shaped islet jutting into the Solent, **HAYLING ISLAND** is four miles long and the same width at its southern point. Fringed by shingle beaches, bland bungalows, run-down amusement arcades and bleak cafés, it's an unappealing spot and the only real reason to visit is for the **watersports** – its southwest corner is particularly good for **windsurfing** and hosts an annual National Watersports Festival in September (Ⓦ nationalwatersportsfestival.com). The island even lays claim to founding the sport, as local boy Peter Chilvers is credited (in some circles) with making the first windsurf board in 1958.

The island's only other claim to fame is as home to one of the UK's first holiday camps, used for the filming of the long-running TV series *Hi-de-Hi* and the film *Confessions of a Holiday Camp*.

ARRIVAL AND ACTIVITIES — HAYLING ISLAND

By bus Stagecoach bus #31 from Havant (every 30min; 12min).

Windsurfing Andy Biggs Watersports, 44 Station Rd, PO11 0EQ (T 02392 467755, W andybiggs.co.uk), can provide windsurfing and other watersports lessons, plus equipment and information on the latest conditions.

Emsworth

The pretty former fishing village of **EMSWORTH** is two miles east of the bridge to Hayling Island, on the edge of Chichester Harbour. There are some attractive waterside walks along with a diminutive **museum** at 10b North St (April–Oct Sat & bank hols 10.30am–4.30pm, Sun 2.30–4.30pm, also Fri in Aug 2.30am–4.30pm; Nov–March Tues & Thurs 2–4pm for pre-arranged visits; free; T 01243 378091, W emsworthmuseum.org.uk), which traces the town's history and includes information about author P.G. Wodehouse, who lived here for a time. Down at the waterfront, you could take a two-hour sailing trip on a traditional nineteenth-century wooden **sailing boat** (advance booking required on T 01243 377727, W oysterboatterror.org.uk; £20), originally built to support the local oyster fleet.

ACCOMMODATION AND EATING — EMSWORTH

36 on the Quay 47 South St, PO10 7EG T 01243 375592, W 36onthequay.co.uk. Comfortable, clean rooms, some overlooking the harbour, in a seventeenth-century harbourside building; you pay more for a bathroom (some have showers only). Downstairs is an upmarket foodie restaurant: it's £58 for a three-course dinner, though the delicious, exquisitely presented food is more reasonably priced at lunch (£24 for two courses). Tues–Sat noon–1.30pm & 6.30–9pm. **£110**

Fat Olives 30 High St, PO10 7EH T 01243 377914, W fatolives.co.uk. In a former fisherman's cottage, superb food is on offer at *Fat Olives*, which serves starters such as roast pigeon with red cabbage gazpacho (£7.25) and mains (around £16–22) such as sea bass with parsley gnocchi; there's also a three-course lunch menu for £21.50. Tues–Sat noon–1.45pm & 7–9.15pm.

Queen Elizabeth Country Park

Just off the A3, **Queen Elizabeth Country Park** spreads over the highest point of the South Downs and is Hampshire's largest park, passed through by a section of the South Downs Way. Once you've got your map from the visitor centre (see p.234), it's best to get clear of this area, which is blighted by traffic noise – there are various car parks dotted round the interior. The park also spreads northwest under the motorway onto

HAMBLEDON: HOME OF CRICKET

Fifteen miles north of Portsmouth, the unexceptional village of **Hambledon** is home to one of the world's oldest cricket clubs. Formed in 1750, Hambledon was England's top club for the second half of the eighteenth century and claims to have developed the modern game. The original cricket club in fact played in nearby Clanfield, where you'll find a memorial stone to the ground as well as the cosy *Bat and Ball Inn*. Once run by the club's captain, the pub was considered for a time the centre of the cricketing empire – especially after the village team soundly thrashed England in 1777. The president of Hambledon then helped form the MCC in 1787, establishing laws of the game already used by the village club and which now form the backbone of today's game.

the lower slopes of **Butser Hill** from where there are great views from alongside the radio mast (270m). This area is also a popular spot for **hang-gliding** and paragliding.

Butser Ancient Farm

Chalton Lane, Chalton, PO8 0BG • Easter–Sept daily 10am–5pm; Oct–Easter Mon–Fri 10am–4pm • £7.50, under-16s £3.50 • Ⓣ 02392 598838, Ⓦ butserancientfarm.co.uk

The **Butser Ancient Farm** is a reconstruction of an Iron Age village and a Roman villa. Several Iron Age roundhouses have been built for visitors to explore and get an insight into family life in the Iron Age. There are also demonstrations of ancient techniques, such as spinning and thatching, as well as Roman cookery, and regular workshops (book in advance) focusing on activities like bronze smelting and cave painting.

INFORMATION AND ACTIVITIES — QUEEN ELIZABETH COUNTRY PARK

Visitor centre The park visitor centre, which has a café and shop (daily: March–Oct 10am–5.30pm; Nov–Feb 10am–4.30pm), gives out maps detailing the various waymarked walking trails, cycle routes, children's play areas and barbecue areas.

Hang-gliding and paragliding Check Ⓦ skysurfingclub.co.uk for details of airborne sports in the area.

The Isle of Wight

COMPTON BAY

9

The Isle of Wight

England's smallest county – at least at high tide (at low tide, Rutland is smaller) – the Isle of Wight measures less than 23 miles at its widest point, but packs in a surprising variety of landscapes. North of the chalk ridge that runs across its centre, the terrain is low-lying woodland and pasture, deeply cut by meandering rivers, while southwards lie open chalky downs fringed by high cliffs. All this makes it a terrific place for walking and cycling, and there are waymarked trails throughout the island. With no motorways, few chain stores and a refreshingly laidback pace of life, the island seems anchored in the past, though the emergence of a lively watersports scene and some decent bars and restaurants has started to attract a younger, livelier crowd.

The island has long attracted holiday-makers, and was favoured by such eminent Victorians as Tennyson, Dickens, Swinburne, Julia Margaret Cameron and Queen Victoria, who made **Osborne House** near **Cowes** her permanent home after Albert died. This should be on anyone's itinerary, as should the sturdy remains of Carisbrooke Castle, near the island's capital, **Newport**, and the stunning landscape around the Needles at Alum Bay. Most visitors, however, are drawn by its beaches, which range from Priory Bay on the east coast to the popular sandy resort beaches at **Ryde** on the north coast and Sandown, Shanklin, Ventnor and Compton Bay on the **south coast**.

Other, less weather-reliant, attractions include a steam railway, a country park, funfairs, zoo, model village and dinosaur theme park. The National Trust is also well represented in various historic buildings around the island, while picturesque towns such as Brighstone and Yarmouth are well worth a visit. Though you can easily see much of the Isle of Wight on a day-trip, give yourself the best part of a week to do it justice and to tune in to the relaxed ambience.

ARRIVAL AND DEPARTURE — THE ISLE OF WIGHT

By ferry There are three departure points from the mainland to the Isle of Wight – Lymington, Southampton and Portsmouth. Fare structures on all routes and with all carriers are labyrinthine, varying according to the time of day of travel, how long you are staying on the island and how far in advance you book: all companies, however, offer regular special offers, so check their websites for details. Note also that many hotels offer packages with the ferry included, which can work out cheaper than booking independently.

From Lymington The most westerly and the fastest car ferry route (40min) runs from Lymington in the New Forest (see p.187) to Yarmouth. Wightlink car ferries (T 03339 997333, W wightlink.co.uk) run approx hourly 5.35am–10pm. Trains from Brockenhurst (see p.165), connecting with services from London Waterloo, run directly to the pier for the boat.

From Southampton Two routes run from Southampton (see p.225), both on Red Funnel ferries (T 08448 449988, W redfunnel.co.uk). The Red Jet Highspeed catamaran for foot passengers runs to West Cowes throughout the day (Mon–Thurs 5.45am–11pm, Fri 5.45am–11.45pm, Sat 6.15am–11.45pm, Sun 6.45am–10.45pm; every 30min–1hr; 25min). A free shuttle bus from Southampton Central station to the ferry terminal connects with train services from London Waterloo. The car ferry from Southampton to East Cowes runs every 1–2 hours (see website for seasonal details; 55min).

OSBORNE HOUSE

Highlights

❶ **Cowes** Full of fashionable boutiques and restaurants, this historic yachting town is at its liveliest during Cowes Week – though it remains one of the island's most appealing, whatever the time of year. **See p.249**

❷ **Osborne House** It's easy to see why this sumptuous house with grand gardens was Queen Victoria's favourite getaway at a time when Britain ruled half the world. **See p.251**

❸ **Bonchurch** Invigorating walks are to be had around this pretty coastal village next to Ventnor, the inspiration for several writers including Charles Dickens. **See p.266**

❹ **Royal Hotel, Ventnor** Follow in the footsteps of Queen Victoria and take afternoon tea on the hotel's wonderful garden terrace, with views over the sea. **See p.267**

❺ **Tennyson Down** Walk out to the Needles along this exhilarating clifftop path named after the famous Victorian poet who spent many hours here. **See p.271**

❻ **Tom's Eco Lodge** Stay in these fantastic upmarket tents/lodges on a farm, with great views over the north and south coasts of the island. **See p.272**

HIGHLIGHTS ARE MARKED ON THE MAP ON P.248

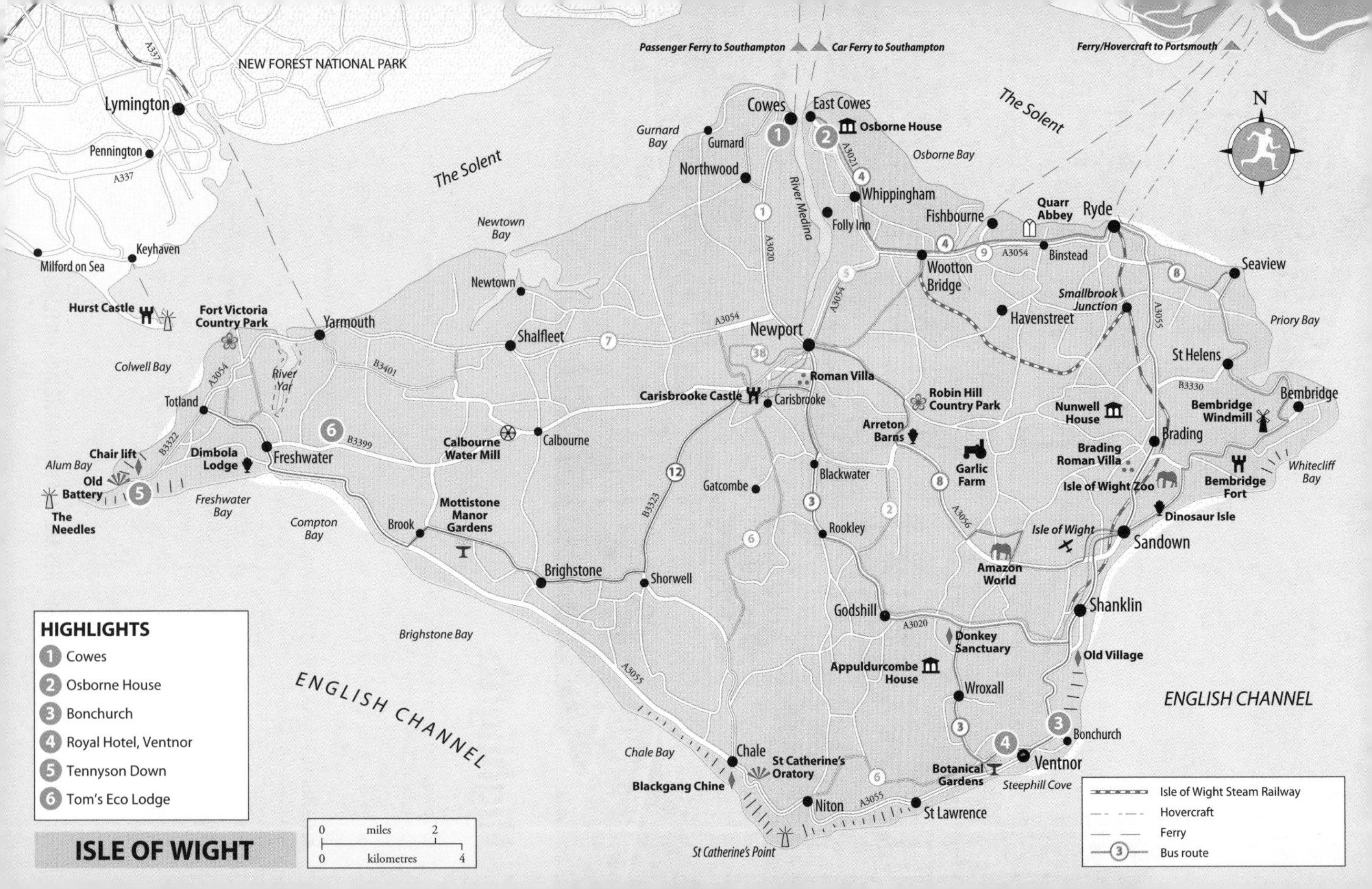

ISLE OF WIGHT
HIGHLIGHTS
1 Cowes
2 Osborne House
3 Bonchurch
4 Royal Hotel, Ventnor
5 Tennyson Down
6 Tom's Eco Lodge
Isle of Wight Steam Railway
Hovercraft
Ferry
Bus route
0 miles 2
0 kilometres 4
N
Passenger Ferry to Southampton
Car Ferry to Southampton
Ferry/Hovercraft to Portsmouth
NEW FOREST NATIONAL PARK
Lymington
Pennington
A337
Milford on Sea
Keyhaven
Hurst Castle
The Solent
ENGLISH CHANNEL
Newtown Bay
Gurnard Bay
Gurnard
Cowes
East Cowes
Osborne House
Osborne Bay
Northwood
River Medina
Whippingham
Folly Inn
Fishbourne
Quarr Abbey
Ryde
Binstead
A3054
Wootton Bridge
Seaview
Smallbrook Junction
Havenstreet
Priory Bay
St Helens
B3330
Bembridge
Bembridge Windmill
Nunwell House
Brading
Brading Roman Villa
Isle of Wight Zoo
Bembridge Fort
Whitecliff Bay
Dinosaur Isle
Sandown
Isle of Wight
Amazon World
Garlic Farm
Arreton Barns
Robin Hill Country Park
Roman Villa
Newport
Carisbrooke Castle
Carisbrooke
Blackwater
Gatcombe
Rookley
A3056
Shanklin
Godshill
A3020
Donkey Sanctuary
Old Village
Appuldurcombe House
Wroxall
Bonchurch
Ventnor
Botanical Gardens
Steephill Cove
St Lawrence
A3055
Niton
St Catherine's Point
St Catherine's Oratory
Chale
Chale Bay
Blackgang Chine
Shorwell
B3323
Brighstone
Brighstone Bay
Mottistone Manor Gardens
Brook
Compton Bay
Calbourne
Calbourne Water Mill
Newtown
Shalfleet
B3401
Yarmouth
Fort Victoria Country Park
River Yar
Colwell Bay
Totland
Freshwater
B3399
Dimbola Lodge
Freshwater Bay
B3322
Chair lift
Alum Bay
Old Battery
The Needles

From Portsmouth There are three routes from Portsmouth (see p.238). Hovertravel (T 01983 717700, W hovertravel.co.uk) runs hovercrafts from Clarence Esplanade in Southsea to Ryde for foot passengers only (every 30min Mon–Fri 6.30am–8pm, Sat 8am–10pm, Sun 9am–9pm; 10min). Wightlink (see p.238) runs high-speed catamarans for foot passengers from Portsmouth Harbour to the end of Ryde Pier (5.15am–10.45am; every 30min at peak times; hourly at quieter times; 20min). Services at Portsmouth Harbour connect with trains from London Waterloo, while at Ryde they connect with Island Line trains. Wightlink also runs a car ferry to Fishbourne from the Gunwharf Terminal in Portsmouth (1–2 hourly, 9pm–5am; 45min).

GETTING AROUND

Most places on the island are served by public transport, so it's possible to get around without a car, though the frequency of the buses is pretty patchy. You can pick up the free *Isle of Wight Public Transport Handbook* on your ferry crossing, which has detailed bus and train routes and timetables.

By bus Buses are run by Southern Vectis (T 01983 827000, W islandbuses.info), which also runs open-top tourist buses (see below). If you plan to use the bus a lot, buy a day rover ticket (£10, children £5), which gives you unlimited bus travel for 24 hours, including the open-top buses. Better value still is the weekly freedom pass (£24, children £12), which allows unlimited travel on all the island's buses.

Routes Bus #1 West Cowes to Newport (every 10–15min; 25min); bus #2 Newport to Ryde (every 30min; 1hr 20min) via Shanklin (every 30min; 30min) and Sandown (every 30min; 45min); bus #3 Newport to Ryde (every 30min; 1hr 45min) via Ventnor (every 30min; 40min), Shanklin (every 30min; 1hr), Sandown (every 30min; 1hr 15min) and Brading (every 30min; 1hr 25min); bus #4 East Cowes to Ryde (hourly; 30min); bus #6 Newport to Ventnor (5 daily; 1hr) via Carrisbrook (5 daily; 5min) and Blackgang (5 daily; 30min); bus #7 Newport to Alum Bay (1–2 hourly; 1hr) via Yarmouth (1–2 hourly; 35min), Freshwater (1–2 hourly; 45min) and Totland (1–2 hourly; 55min); bus #12 Newport to Totland (4–5 daily; 50min) via Brighstone (3–5 daily; 20min) and Freshwater (3–5 daily; 45min).

Bus tours Southern Vectis runs seasonal hop-on, hop-off open-top tourist buses with commentaries that take in most of the sights and attractions around the island. The Downs Breezer tour runs from Ryde to Quarr Abbey and Robin Hill Country Park, travelling back via Amazon World, Sandown and Brading (July & Aug; every 30min); the Island Coaster tour runs round the south coast from Ryde to Yarmouth and back (April–Sept; 1–3 daily); and the Needles Breezer runs from Yarmouth to Freshwater and back via the Needles and Totland (mid-March to Sept; every 30min).

By train There are two rail lines on the island: the eight-mile Island Line (every 20–40min; W islandlinetrains.co.uk) from Ryde Pier to Brading (15min), Sandown (20min) and Shanklin (25min), and the five-mile Isle of Wight Steam Railway from Wootton to Smallbrook Junction (5–7 daily, 30min) where it connects with the Island Line (W iwsteamrailway.co.uk).

By bike Cycling is a popular way of getting around the island, and there's a well-signed round-island route, but beware that in summer the narrow lanes can get very busy. For bike rental and guided rides contact Wight Cycle Hire (T 01983 761800, W wightcyclehire.co.uk), which has an office in Yarmouth's former railway station, but also delivers and collects bikes anywhere on the island (£12/half-day, £16/day). The tourist office in Newport (see below) also rents out electric bikes for those who are daunted by the island's steep hills for £35 a day, though discounts are often available online (Red Squirrel Bikes: W nutsnotto.co.uk).

INFORMATION

Tourist information The helpful Visit Isle of Wight is the official source of tourist information (T 01983 521555, W visitisleofwight.co.uk), and runs the island's only tourist office in The Guildhall, High Street, Newport, PO30 1TY. There are also a few seasonal information points housed in various shops and visitor attractions around the island.

Cowes and around

COWES, at the island's most northerly point, sits opposite Southampton and is the first place many people see when visiting. And a good first point of call it makes too – it's an attractive town, bisected by the River Medina. **West Cowes** is the more interesting half, though **East Cowes** boasts the biggest tourist attraction in the form of Queen Victoria's holiday home, **Osborne House**. Just south of here, the village of **Whippingham** makes a good destination for a walk or boat trip.

9

West Cowes

One of the most attractive and upmarket areas on the island, the old centre of **West Cowes** consists of a warren of narrow streets lined with smart shops, historic pubs and restaurants. The town is inextricably associated with **sailing craft** and **boat building**: Henry VIII built two "cowforts" here (hence the name) to defend the Solent's expanding naval dockyards from the French and Spanish, one on either side of the River Medina, which splits the town in two. The castle in East Cowes was demolished

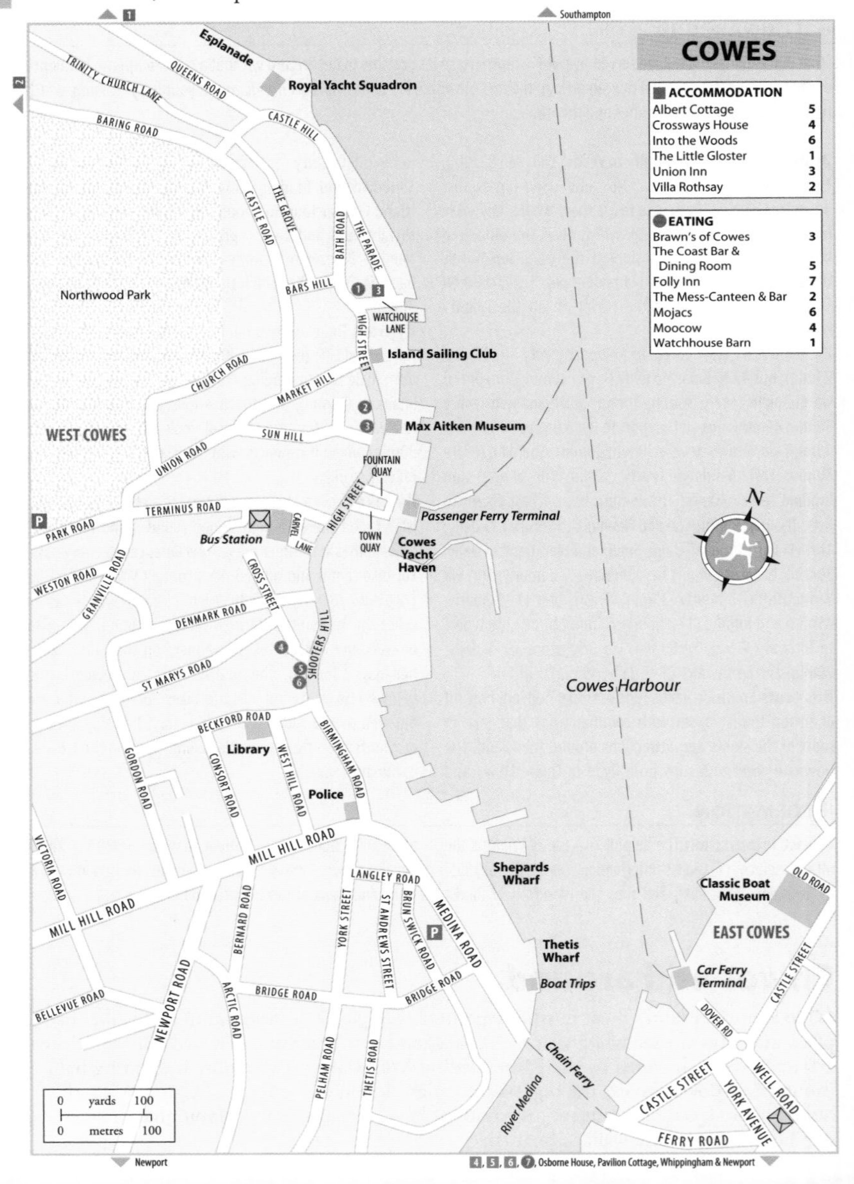

in the 1960s, but the remains of West Cowes castle now form the Royal Yacht Squadron. In 1820, the Prince Regent's patronage of the yacht club gave the port its cachet, and it's now one of the world's most exclusive sailing clubs. In the 1950s, the world's first hovercraft made its test runs here, and hovercrafts continue to be made on the island today.

Max Aitken Museum

83 High St, PO31 7AJ • May–Sept Tues–Sat 10am–4pm • Free • T 01983 293800, W sirmaxaitkenmuseum.org

To learn something about the maritime history of the town, visit the small **Max Aitken Museum**, set in a renovated eighteenth-century sailmaker's loft and containing a motley collection of maritime memorabilia such as artefacts from royal yachts, model boats, figureheads and paintings, including some original Giles cartoons.

East Cowes and around

There is not a lot to recommend East Cowes, though it is fun to take the little **chain ferry** (or the Floating Bridge) that carries cars and passengers across the 70m width of the Medina (otherwise, it's a lengthy drive). This is just one of five remaining chain ferries in England, dating from 1975, though a ferry has run this route since 1720. Although East Cowes is a fairly run-down port, around a mile uphill is one of the island's top attractions in the form of **Osborne House**.

Classic Boat Museum

Albany Rd, PO32 6AA • April–Nov Tues–Sat 10am–4pm • £4, boat museum gallery £2, combined ticket £5 • T 01983 290006, W classicboatmuseum.org

The **Classic Boat Museum** houses a large collection of vintage sailing and power boats, including a 1910 Thames river boat; the *Coweslip* (Prince Philip's boat); an Olympic gold-winning sailing boat, the *Miss Britain IV*, which set the world speedboat record in 1982; and a dinghy in which Prince Charles and Princess Anne learnt to sail. There are also photos and various maritime mementoes, including the trophy awarded to local girl Dame Ellen MacArthur, the fastest person to sail solo around the world in 2005. The **boat museum gallery** around the corner displays further boating memorabilia including several photographic collections.

Osborne House

York Ave, PO32 6JX • Daily: April–Sept 10am–6pm; Oct 10am–5pm; Nov–March pre-booked tours only • £15, under-16s £9; EH • T 01983 200022, W www.english-heritage.org.uk/visit/places/osborne • Bus #4 to Ryde or #5 to Newport from East Cowes

Queen Victoria's family home, **Osborne House**, is signposted one mile southeast of town. The house was built in the late 1840s by Prince Albert and Thomas Cubitt as an Italianate villa, with balconies and large terraces overlooking the landscaped gardens towards the Solent. The staterooms, used for entertaining visiting dignitaries, exude an unsurprising formality – the Durbar room is particularly impressive, clad almost entirely in ivory. The private apartments feel more homely, though, like the affluent family holiday residence that Osborne was – far removed from the pomp and ceremony of state affairs in London. On the top floor, the nurseries and children's bedrooms still display their toys, cradles and tiny beds, while on the middle floor, you can peer into Prince Albert's bath, hidden away in a cupboard in true Victorian fashion. Following Albert's death, the desolate Victoria spent much of her time here, and it's where she eventually died in 1901. Since then, according to her wishes, the house has remained virtually unaltered, allowing an unexpectedly intimate glimpse into the queen's family life.

The children were able to escape the confines and boredom of royal life by frolicking in the expansive grounds and in their two-storey playhouse, the **Swiss Cottage** – a fifteen-minute walk through the gardens. Inside, you can view their miniature tea sets and toys, while nearby is the remains of a barracks with its own drawbridge, built by

COWES WEEK

Early August sees the international yachting festival known as **Cowes Week** (cowesweek.co.uk), the largest sailing regatta in the world. Up to 100,000 spectators watch around a thousand boats take part, commandeered by sailors of all abilities – from enthusiastic amateurs to royalty and Olympic champions. The race first took place in 1826 (with just seven yachts) and has occurred every year since except during the world wars. Throughout the festival there's a great party atmosphere and dozens of organized events, including a spectacular fireworks display on the final Friday night. In addition to Cowes Week, most summer weekends see some form of nautical event taking place in or around town.

Note that rates for **accommodation** almost double during Cowes Week, when places need to be booked months ahead.

Prince Albert as a place where the boys could play soldiers. You can even swim off Queen Victoria's own private beach, where her original bathing machine has been restored: there's also an ice-cream parlour behind the beach with tables on the lawns overlooking the sea.

Whippingham

The small village of **WHIPPINGHAM**, a mile south of Osborne, was once part of the Osborne House estate – the area would be largely recognizable to Victoria today. There is a lovely ten-minute **trail** from the Royal Church of St Mildred down to the Medina, where you'll find the attractive waterside *Folly Inn* (see opposite).

Royal Church of St Mildred

Easter–Sept Mon–Thurs 10am–4pm • Free • Bus #4 or #5 from Osborne

Queen Victoria frequently worshipped at the Gothic Revival **Royal Church of St Mildred**, one of Albert's many architectural extravaganzas. The German Battenberg family, who later adopted the anglicized name Mountbatten, have a chapel here.

ARRIVAL AND DEPARTURE — COWES AND AROUND

By bus Buses (see p.249) pull in to the bus station on Carvel Lane, West Cowes, a short walk inland from the passenger ferry terminal.

By ferry The car ferry from Southampton arrives in East Cowes, just off Castle St.

GETTING AROUND AND TOURS

By ferry A chain ferry shuttles between East and West Cowes (every 10min or so Mon–Sat 5am–12.10am, Sun 7am–12.10am; cars £2.20 return, passengers & bikes 40p return).

Boat trips Solent & Wight Line Cruises run boat trips from Thetis Wharf, near the chain ferry, heading upriver and around the harbour (departure times vary; 25min; £4, children £2.50; 01983 564602, solentcruises.co.uk).

ACCOMMODATION

Albert Cottage York Ave, East Cowes, PO32 6BD 01983 299309, albertcottagehotel.com. Adjacent to and once part of the Osborne estate, this lovely mansion has a country-house feel to it. It's set in its own grounds and has very comfortable rooms – some with balconies and garden views – and a highly rated restaurant. **£130**

Crossways House Crossways Rd, East Cowes, PO32 6LJ 01983 298282, bedbreakfast-cowes.co.uk. This building, commissioned by Queen Victoria for the administrator of her Sea Cadets, sits right opposite Osborne House. The rooms are large and comfortable, some with four-poster beds overlooking the gardens. Breakfast includes Belgian waffles, and evening meals are also available. **£75**

★ **Into the Woods** Lower Westwood, Brocks Copse Rd, Wootton, PO33 4NP 07769 696464, isleofwighttreehouse.com. Lovely, luxury tree house (sleeps six, from £500 for 2 nights) and shepherds' huts (sleep six) to rent on a farm in a secluded wood, three miles south of East Cowes. Both are beautifully finished and ecofriendly, complete with wood-burning stoves, en-suite showers, and even wi-fi. The location is peaceful, with chickens and geese, rope swings to play on and woods to run around in – the perfect combination of nature and home comforts. Two-night minimum. **£150**

★The Little Gloster 31 Marsh Rd, Gurnard Marsh, PO31 8JQ ⓣ01983 200299, ⓦthelittlegloster.com. A couple of miles west of Cowes, right on the shore in the pretty town of Gurnard, this is a smart modern restaurant (excellent mains from £15) with three superb guest rooms furnished with Scandanavian-style decor, and all with sea views. **£160**

Union Inn Watch House Lane, West Cowes, PO31 7QH ⓣ01983 293163, ⓦunioninncowes.co.uk. The rooms above this historic pub are all large, with a boutiquey flare, and the best ones have views of the sea. As always with rooms above pubs, however, you can get noise from the bar – but you do also get a giant breakfast. **£109**

Villa Rothsay 29 Baring Rd, West Cowes, PO31 8DF ⓣ01983 295178, ⓦvilla-rothsay.co.uk. This traditional, comfortable villa has maintained its Victorian roots with period decor throughout – think drapery, ornate stairways and stained-glass windows – but with modern additions. Great views from some rooms, the grounds and the raised patio area. **£120**

EATING

Brawn's of Cowes 62 High St, PO31 7RL ⓣ01983 242144, ⓦbrawns.co.uk. This attractive restaurant, in a Georgian former butcher's with beautiful tiled walls and wooden floors, has a short menu featuring dishes made from seasonal and locally produced ingredients. Expect the likes of guinea fowl, local steaks and pan-fried cod (mains from £18). Tues–Thurs 6–10pm, Fri & Sat noon–3pm & 6–10pm, Sun noon–3pm.

The Coast Bar & Dining Room 15 Shooters Hill, West Cowes, PO31 7BG ⓣ01983 298574, ⓦthecoastbar.co.uk. Light, airy bar/restaurant with wooden floors and a lively, informal vibe. The menu features dishes such as roast venison (£16) and wild boar tortellini (£13) as well as a good selection of wood-fired pizzas (£9–12). Mon–Thurs & Sun 9am–midnight, Fri & Sat 9am–1am.

Folly Inn Folly Lane, Whippingham, PO32 6NB ⓣ01983 297171. A mile from Osborne House, this attractive waterside pub has the river lapping at its decks and is said to have replaced a French smuggler's barge that sold produce here in the 1700s. It serves decent pub food such as beef and ale pie (£11), plus tasty fajitas (£12) and a selection of steaks (£12–16). The Folly Waterbus (ⓣ07974 864627) runs a taxi service from Cowes to the jetty next to the pub. Daily 9am–11pm.

The Mess-Canteen & Bar 63 High St, PO31 7RL ⓣ01983 280083. With rustic-chic decor, this lively place serves up great burgers – try tempura soft-shell crab or halloumi – and unusual salads such as grilled peach and roquefort, plus tasty tacos such as garlic prawn and avocado, all around £7–10. There's a good range of cocktails – the Isle of Wight jam jar tea is tasty – the service is friendly and the vibe is fun. Daily 11am–11pm (shorter hours in winter).

Mojacs 10a Shooters Hill, PO31 7BG ⓣ01983 281118, ⓦmojacs.co.uk. Long-established and highly regarded restaurant serving up beautifully presented, reasonably priced dishes, such as aubergine tempura with tomato risotto (£14.50) and belly of pork with sage and onion mash (£16). Mon–Sat from 5.30pm.

Moocow 55 Cross St, PO31 7TA ⓣ01983 200750, ⓦmoocowstuff.com. It may overlook a car park, but this lively, stylish café-bar is a great place to hang out. It hosts arts and poetry evenings and serves imaginative meze dishes such as vodka-infused calamari (£8), red rice and beetroot cakes (£7) and New Forest venison on ciabatta (£9). Tues–Sat 10.30am–late.

Watchhouse Barn 31 Bath Rd, West Cowes, PO31 7RH ⓣ01983 293093, ⓦwatchhousebarn.co.uk. Small tea and coffee shop that is a big hit with children thanks to the toy train that trundles overhead. It serves a good-value all-day English breakfast (£6) or variations such as kippers with poached egg (£6.75), plus tasty home-made cakes. Daily: May–Oct 8.30am–6pm; Nov–April 9am–4pm.

Newport and around

NEWPORT, the island capital, sits at the point where the River Medina's commercial navigability ends. The town isn't particularly engaging, though it is refreshingly free of the tourist trappings of the coastal resorts and has a couple of decent museums, plus its own quaint version of Diagon Alley, Watchbell Lane. It is also the administrative centre, where you'll find most of the major supermarkets and the island's public facilities. Newport is the rather unlikely venue for one of England's best-known music festivals, the **Isle of Wight Festival** (see box, p.254), held at Seaclose Park on the northern outskirts of town.

Around Newport are some of the island's top inland attractions, including **Carisbrooke**, one of England's greatest castles, which sits alongside the remains of a fine Roman villa. Close by is **Robin Hill Country Park**, a great expanse with its own toboggan run; it's also the venue for the annual **Bestival** music festival. Families will appreciate

THE ISLE OF WIGHT FESTIVAL

The original **Isle of Wight Festival**, held in 1968, was a one-day hippy gathering near the village of Godshill – chosen because ley lines meet there – with Marc Bolan and T-Rex and Jefferson Airplane playing to a crowd of around 10,000 people. Due to its success, the following year the festival moved to Wootton near Ryde, and hosted artists such as Bob Dylan, The Who and Free, attracting an audience of around 150,000 people. However, the 1970 concert broke all records with an estimated 600,000 people swaying to performers such as Joni Mitchell, Miles Davis, Leonard Cohen, The Doors and Jimi Hendrix at East Afton Farm (clearly visible today from Tapnell Farm; see p.271). The 1970 festival remains the largest festival ever held in the UK, but it faced problems from the outset, with local residents objecting to the choice of venue – East Afton Farm was overlooked by a large hill so people could easily watch the concert from outside the site, leading to far greater numbers than predicted. Added to this, a general feeling that naked hippies taking drugs were bad for the island's reputation meant that controversy was assured. As a result, the following year the "Isle of Wight Act" was passed, preventing gatherings of more than five thousand people on the island without a licence. This put paid to the festival for 22 years, until it was revived in 2002 in its current venue near Newport. Critics argue that the current festival has lost its original rebellious spirit, with granddads of rock such as Status Quo, Billy Idol and Bruce Springsteen headlining in recent years.

the steam railway, which begins its cross-island run from Wootton, via **Havenstreet**, to Smallbrook Junction, near Ryde.

The Guildhall

High St, PO30 1TY • Mon–Fri 10am–3pm, Sat 10am–2pm • £2

The main draw in Newport is the **Guildhall** on the High Street. Designed by John Nash in 1816, the building has been used variously as a market, fire station and shop, not to mention a banqueting hall that once entertained the likes of Prince Albert and Garibaldi. Today it houses the island's tourist office (see p.249), plus the **Museum of Island History**, displaying fossils and dinosaur bones collected from round the island, together with old photographs, touch-screen displays detailing the island's history and some Anglo-Saxon jewellery, swords and axes.

Bus Museum

Newport Harbour, PO30 2EF • Easter–Oct Wed, Thurs & Sun 10am–4pm; also open bank hols and for special events – check website for details • Free • T 01983 567796, W iwbusmuseum.org.uk

Near Newport's yacht-lined harbour, in a giant warehouse, the appealing **Bus Museum** has a colourful collection of historic buses that once plied the island, including a Victorian tram, and pictures and paintings of various forms of transport over the years. Check the website for details of the Island Buses Running Day, usually in May, when some of the buses that can still work leave their warehouse for a day out.

The Roman Villa

Cypress Rd, PO30 1HA • Easter–Oct Mon–Sat 10am–4pm; July & Aug Mon–Sat 10am–4pm & Sun noon–4pm • £3 • T 01983 529720, W iwight.com/Visitors/Where-to-go/Newport-Roman-Villa

The remains of a **Roman villa** stand a well-signposted ten-minute walk south of Newport. Discovered in 1926, they date from around 280 AD and are thought to include the farmhouse of a wealthy estate. The remains of a well-preserved bathing suite with hypocaust underground heating are visible, and sections of the villa, such as the kitchen, have been reconstructed, but its sister villa in Brading (see p.262) is more impressive and gives a better idea of life in Roman times.

Carisbrooke Castle

Castle Hill, PO30 1XY • Feb half-term daily 10am–4pm; March Wed–Sun 10am–4pm; April–Sept daily 10am–6pm; Oct daily 10am–5pm; Nov to mid-Feb Sat & Sun 10am–4pm • £8.80, under-16s £5.20; EH • T 01983 522107, W www.english-heritage.org.uk/visit/places/carisbrooke-castle • Bus #7 from Newport

Just southwest of Newport lies one of the Isle of Wight's greatest attractions, the hilltop fortress of **Carisbrooke Castle**. This austere Norman keep's most famous visitor was Charles I, detained here (and caught one night ignominiously jammed between his room's bars in an attempt to escape) prior to his execution in London. The **museum** in the centre of the castle shows off many relics from his incarceration, as well as those of the last royal resident, Princess Beatrice, Queen Victoria's youngest daughter. The castle's other notable curiosity is the sixteenth-century well-house, where donkeys still trudge inside a huge treadmill in order to raise a barrel 48m up the well shaft. Visitors can also walk round the well-preserved battlements, basking in the spectacular views over the island.

Arreton Barns

Arreton Old Village, Main Rd, PO30 3AA • Free • W arretonbarns.co.uk • **Shipwreck Centre** Mid-Feb to Dec daily 10am–4/5pm • £5 • T 01983 528353, W shipwreckcentre.com • Bus #8 from Newport or Sandown

Four miles south of Newport, the **Arreton Barns** complex is a village museum that is home to a twelfth-century church, a pub, a farm shop and a selection of arts and crafts studios where you can watch glass-blowers, wood-workers, leather-workers, jewellery-makers and artists at work. It also houses the **Shipwreck Centre**, a fascinating collection of oddities salvaged from various wrecks around the island over the years. Highlights include a German submarine periscope from 1919, Dutch coins from 1627, and a narwhal tusk, found embedded in a ship's hull in 1835. At the back you'll also find old traction engines and lifeboats.

Garlic Farm

Mersley Lane, Newchurch, PO36 0NR • Daily 9am–5pm • Free • T 01983 867333, W thegarlicfarm.co.uk

Set in beautiful rolling countryside, the quirky and hugely popular **Garlic Farm** lies about four miles southeast of Newport. Here, you can learn about growing and plaiting garlic, follow the thirty-minute Garlic Farm Walk, or buy just about anything garlic-related, from garlic pesto to garlic ice cream. There's also a very good **café**, with – unsurprisingly – a large selection of garlicky dishes. There's even an annual garlic **festival** nearby each August (W garlic-festival.co.uk).

Robin Hill Country Park

Downend, PO30 2NU • March Sat–Thurs 10am–5pm; Easter to early Sept daily 10am–5/6pm; Oct half-term daily 10am–10pm • Easter hols, summer hols & half-terms £18.50; other times £14.75; toboggan ride £1.50; tickets valid for seven days unlimited visits • T 01983 527352, W robin-hill.com • Bus #8 from Newport to Sandown

Great for families, **Robin Hill Country Park** sits in 88 acres of woods and downs three miles southeast of Newport. Features include a treetop trail, falconry displays, slides, a maze and zip wires. There are many different themed play areas designed for varying age groups – the imaginative African Adventure features swings that look like giraffes – as well as some low-key rides including a swinging galleon. All the attractions are covered by the entrance fee – even the falconry displays, which are well worth catching – except for the fun **toboggan ride**, which wiggles down a steep hill. The park hosts various light displays in the woods in October (see website for details) and is closed for most of September, when it hosts the annual **Bestival** (see p.27), which attracts 30,000 wackily dressed music fans.

9

Isle of Wight Steam Railway

Havenstreet, PO33 4DS • Easter–Oct daily plus some services on Sat & Sun in Dec & Christmas hols: see website for details • £11.50, children £6; tickets valid for unlimited journeys that day • ⓣ 01983 882204, ⓦ iwsteamrailway.co.uk • Bus #9 from Newport

The **Isle of Wight Steam Railway** runs from Wootton Common, a couple of miles east of Newport, through pretty countryside for five miles to Smallbrook Junction, where it connects with the Ryde to Shanklin electric rail line. The trains are all renovated steam engines, many of which were used for scheduled services on the island in the past, and some date from as far back as 1876.

A mile and a half from Wootton, the main station is at **Havenstreet**, where there's a children's play area and a **museum** containing artefacts relating to the island's steam trains, as well as a viewing gallery where you can watch the trains being worked on in the railway workshops. Check the website for regular events such as Thomas the Tank Engine days.

ARRIVAL AND DEPARTURE

NEWPORT AND AROUND

By bus Newport is the main hub for buses on the island, with services to pretty much anywhere (see p.249). The bus station is a short walk south of the High St on Orchard St.

ACCOMMODATION

One Holyrood B&B 1 Holyrood St, PO30 5AU ⓣ 01983 521717, ⓦ oneholyrood.co.uk. Nicely furnished, comfortable rooms in a renovated Grade II-listed building with a lovely garden at the back and an excellent tearoom beneath – room 7 in the eaves is spacious, with exposed beams and a free-standing bath. **£100**

EATING

★**Bluebells Café** Bridlesford Lodge Farm, Wootton, PO33 4RY, 3 miles east of Newport ⓣ 01983 882885, ⓦ briddlesfordlodgefarm.com. Great local food from the island and the farm itself (salads, sandwiches and fish dishes £8–11) is served up at this airy café with tables outside in the courtyard. There's also a great farm shop on site and a small museum/gallery, and children can watch the cows and calves in the cowsheds. Also hosts occasional live music evenings. Daily 9am–5pm; also Sat from 7pm.

Castle Inn 91 High St, PO30 1BQ ⓣ 01983 552258, ⓦ thecastleiow.co.uk. Dating from 1684, this is the town's oldest pub, the last in England to be granted a licence for cock-fighting (in 1705) and said to be haunted. Today the fine old brick building offers decent real ales and ciders, as well as food (made from local produce where possible, from around £10). There's also a pleasant courtyard garden and live music at weekends. Kitchen Mon–Sat noon–2.30pm & 6–9pm.

Olivo 15 St Thomas Square, PO30 1SL ⓣ 01983 530001, ⓦ olivorestaurant.co.uk/newport. Fashionable Italian café-restaurant opposite the church, with appealing outdoor seats and a modern interior. Reliably tasty pasta, pizza and salads (£9.50–13) as well as grilled meats (£15–17), plus very good coffees and pastries for breakfast and lunchtime panini. Daily 8am–10pm.

★**Thompson's** 11 Town Lane, PO30 1JU ⓣ 01983 526118, ⓦ robertthompson.co.uk. Sublime cooking from Michelin-starred chef Robert Thompson at this attractive restaurant with a cosy bar area and open kitchen downstairs, plus more tables upstairs. The short menu changes regularly, but you can expect dishes such as local wild garlic risotto and roast saddle of venison – the lunch menu (two courses for £17; three for £22) is excellent value, or you can push the boat out with the £62 tasting menu. Tues–Sat noon–3pm & 6–10pm.

ENTERTAINMENT

Quay Arts 15 Sea St, PO30 5BD ⓣ 01983 822490, ⓦ quayarts.org. This excellent arts centre, set in converted riverside warehouses, puts on exhibitions, concerts, films and comedy and has its own theatre. It also has a fine café (Mon–Sat 9am–5pm) with a terrace overlooking the harbour that serves inexpensive meals, coffees and cakes.

Ryde and around

RYDE is a large, pleasantly old-fashioned Victorian resort facing a broad, sandy beach that enjoys great views over the iconic Spinnaker Tower in Portsmouth across the water. It's by no means the quaintest of places on the island, but its accessibility made it one

COWES WEEK (P.252) >

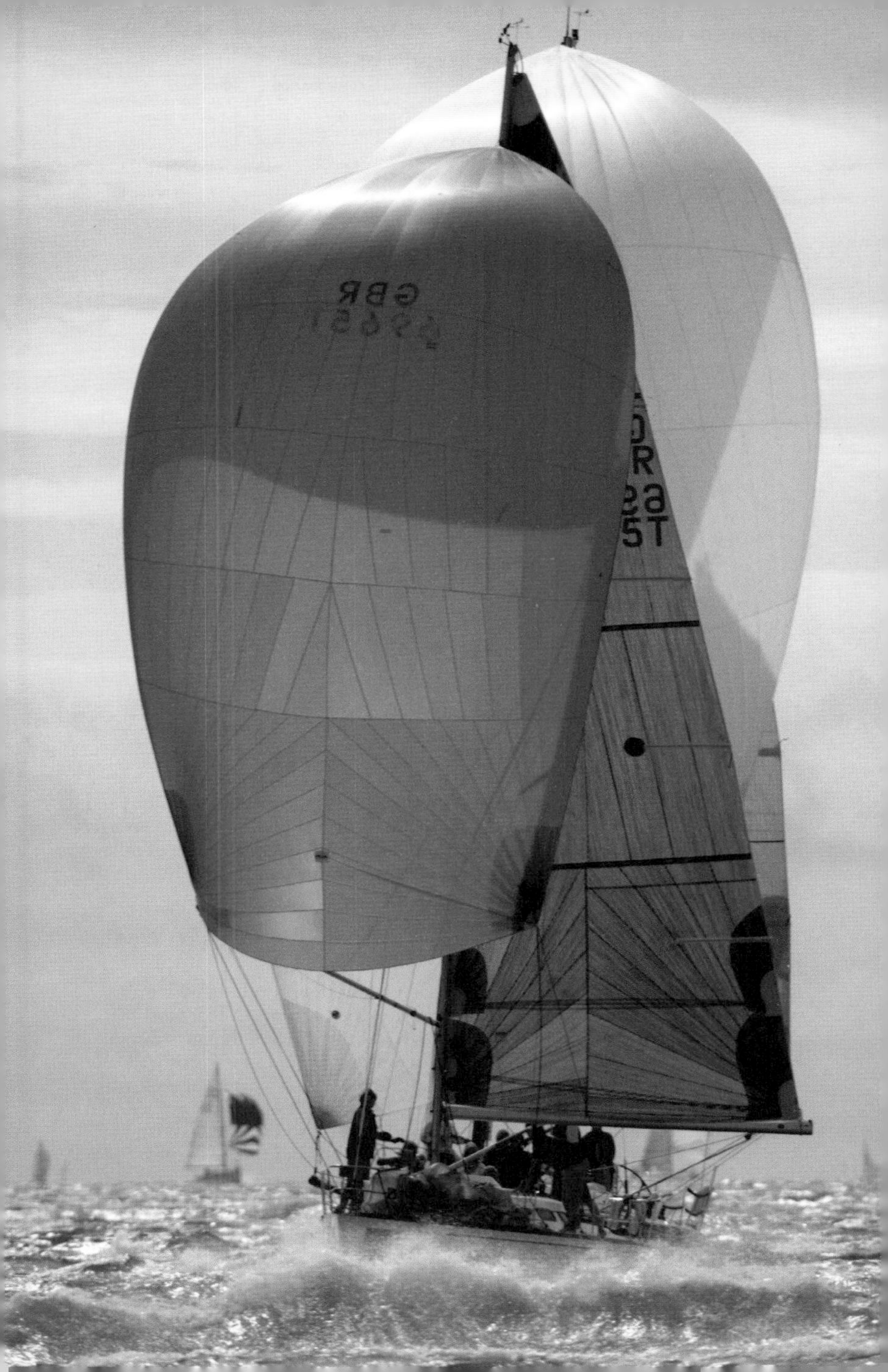

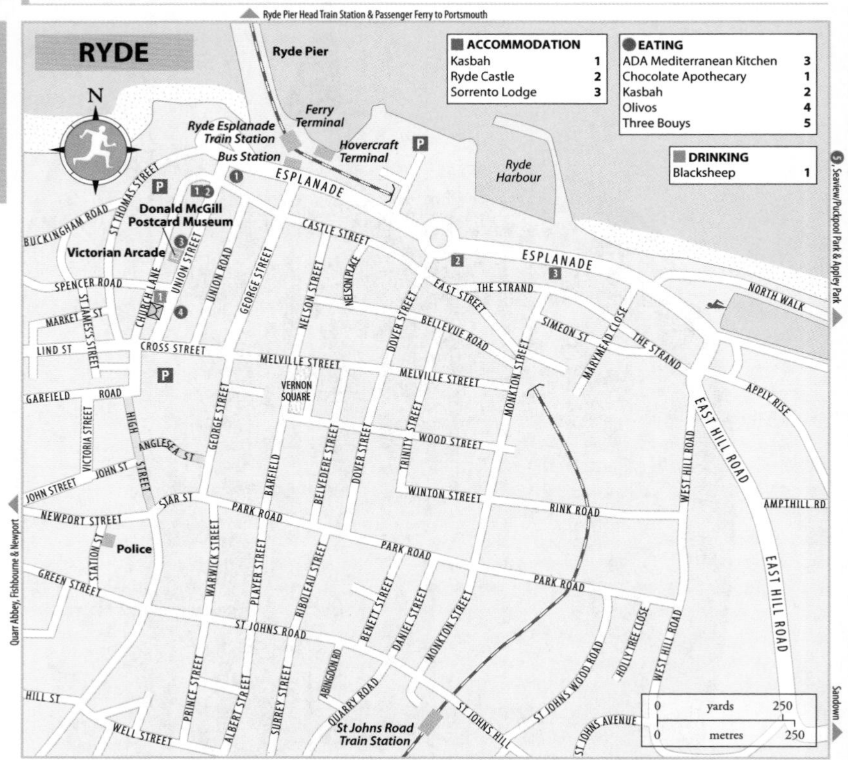

of the principal Victorian resorts and as a result it has some fine old mansions and its own small Victorian shopping arcade. It's the main arrival point for foot passengers from Portsmouth, though the car ferry from Portsmouth docks a couple of miles west at the tiny village of **Fishbourne**, which is near one of the island's most historic sites, the medieval remains of **Quarr Abbey**.

Ryde seafront

Ryde's proximity to the mainland means it is a major transport hub, with trains rumbling along the extensive **pier** that dominates the seafront. Unlike most piers, this one is essentially a giant jetty for ferries. First built in 1814 though substantially extended since, the structure is a quarter of a mile long; you can drive or walk along its wooden boards to the terminal at the end – little more than a giant car park with a café, though it offers good views back over town. But Ryde's principal attraction is its **beaches**; the best lie to the east, where the sands back onto the leafy parkland of **Appley Park**. Here you'll find **Appley Tower**, a stone folly built in 1875, now open as a shop-cum-museum filled with fossils and gemstones.

Donald McGill Postcard Museum

The Royal Victoria Arcade, Union St, PO33 2LQ • Mon–Sat 11am–4pm • £3 • T 01983 717435, W saucyseasidepostcards.com

Ryde's quirky little **Postcard Museum** crams in a good proportion of the twelve thousand saucy postcards created by artist Donald McGill, who died in 1962. The cards, produced throughout the first half of the twentieth century, reached their peak of popularity in the 1930s. Packed with daft double entendres, the collection here provides a fascinating record of the twentieth century, and shows how far things have moved since the Obscene Publications Act regularly tried to have McGill's cards banned.

Quarr Abbey

Just outside the village of Binstead, near Ryde, PO33 4ES • Gardens & tearoom Mon–Sat 10am–4/5pm, Sun 11.15am–4/5pm • Free • T 01983 882420, W quarrabbey.co.uk • Buses #4 & #9 from Ryde stop outside the abbey

Two miles west of Ryde, outside the village of Binstead, is one of the island's earliest Christian relics, **Quarr Abbey**. Founded in 1132 by Richard de Redvers, for the use of Savigny monks, the abbey was named after the quarries nearby, where stone was mined for use in the construction of Winchester and Chichester cathedrals. Only stunted ruins survived the Dissolution and the ensuing plunder of ready-cut stone, although an ivy-clad archway still hangs picturesquely over a farm track. In 1912 a new abbey was founded just west of the ruins, a striking rose-brick building with Byzantine overtones and still home to Benedictine monks: it can be visited on guided tours (check the website for times). You can wander freely around the beautiful grounds – there's an orchard, a woodland walk and pigs and chickens to admire – where you'll find a very fine tea garden with outdoor tables and a farm shop selling produce from the island and the abbey itself, including eggs, ale, cider and honey.

ARRIVAL AND INFORMATION — RYDE AND AROUND

By train Trains (see p.249) pull in at the station on the Esplanade, alongside the pier.

By bus The bus station is at the Esplanade by the train station and pier, with frequent services to Cowes, Newport, Sandown and Ventnor (see p.249).

By ferry and hovercraft Ferries dock at the end of Ryde Pier, from where connecting trains take you down to the Esplanade station, where hovercrafts dock (see p.249).

ACCOMMODATION

Kasbah 76 Union St, PO33 2LN T 01983 810088, W kasbahiw.com. Small rooms with lively decor above a funky café-bar (see p.260). They can be noisy at weekends (so it's best to be on the top floors) but they're great value, with DVD players and iPod docks plus one large family room. **£70**

Ryde Castle The Esplanade, PO33 1JA T 08456 086040, W oldenglishinns.co.uk. Victorian manor house in a great location on Ryde Esplanade right opposite the beach: the comfortable rooms are fairly standard chain-hotel fare, and probably only really worthwhile if you can bag one with a sea view. **£110**

Sorrento Lodge 11 The Strand, PO33 2LG T 01983 812813, W sorrentolodge.co.uk. Very well-kept B&B in a large townhouse with a seafront garden run by a helpful couple. Some of the rooms have sea views, all are en-suite – and the breakfasts are good. **£80**

MINGHELLAS: ICE CREAM AND MOVIES

All over the Isle of Wight, you'll find **Minghellas ice creams**, made on the island by the Minghella family since 1950. Using natural ingredients, including milk and cream from island cows, the ice creams come in a huge variety of flavours, such as gin and pink grapefruit sorbet, apple crumble ice cream, and frosted strawberry with balsamic vinegar. Italian immigrants Edward and Gloria Minghella started out making and selling the ice cream from a small café on Ryde High Street, but by 1985 it was so popular that they moved to a larger factory in Wootton, where the ice creams are still concocted today. However, it is Edward and Gloria's son, **Anthony Minghella** – director of *The English Patient*, *Truly, Madly, Deeply*, *Cold Mountain* and *The Talented Mr Ripley* – who made Minghella a household name. Born and brought up on the island, he acknowledged its enormous influence on his filmmaking, calling his nine-Oscar win for *The English Patient* "a great day for the Isle of Wight". He was awarded a CBE in 2001, but died suddenly in March 2008 at the age of 54.

EATING

ADA Mediterranean Kitchen 55 Union St, PO33 2LG ☎ 01938 564023. Friendly restaurant serving Mediterranean dishes, such as falafel, stuffed vine leaves and aubergine dip as well as hearty pizza and pasta dishes (£7–10), plus tasty lamb kebab with rice (£14). The lunch meze – a choice of three hot dishes and one cold – is great value at £9. Mon–Sat 11.30am–3pm & 5.30–10pm, Sun 5.30–9pm.

Chocolate Apothecary 7 Esplanade, PO33 2DY ☎ 01938 718292, Ⓦ chocolateapothecary.co.uk. Wonderful chocolate shop and café in a former Victorian fishmonger's with original tiles and wooden cabinets. They sell a variety of delicious home-made chocolates plus cakes and rich hot chocolate; try the chilli hot chocolate or the coffee accompanied by a chocolate of your choice – yum! Mon–Sat 10am–4.45pm, Sun 10am–4pm.

Kasbah 76 Union St, PO33 2LN ☎ 01983 810088, Ⓦ kasbahiw.com. Lively, quirky Moroccan-themed bar serving home-made pizzas, tasty cocktails and draught beers. There's a heated outdoor courtyard and live music every Thursday; you can also stay here (see p.259). Mon, Tues & Sun 11.30am–11pm, Wed 11.30am–midnight, Thurs–Sat 11.30am–2am.

Olivo 32–33 Union St, PO33 2LE ☎ 01983 611118, Ⓦ olivorestaurant.co.uk/ryde. Tasty Italian dishes in a buzzy, stylish restaurant with bare-brick walls and an open kitchen. There are decent pizzas (£9–13) and pasta dishes (£11–13), plus some less usual main courses such as swordfish with couscous (£16). Mon–Thurs & Sun 8am–10pm, Fri & Sat 8am–11pm.

★**Three Bouys** Appley Lane, PO33 2DU ☎ 01983 811212, Ⓦ threebuoys.co.uk. Excellent food in a lovely setting in this upstairs restaurant with a large balcony overlooking Ryde beach. The decor is contemporary, with wooden floors and tables and big picture windows giving fantastic views over the Solent, and the food is well cooked and presented. Dishes include seared scallops with ginger, apple and celeriac purée (£9), chickpea dhal with root vegetables (£15) and roast local duck leg (£18). Mon–Fri noon–3pm & 6–9.30pm, Sat & Sun noon–9.30pm.

DRINKING

Blacksheep 53 Union St, PO33 2LF ☎ 01983 811006, Ⓦ theblacksheepbar.co.uk. Fashionable bar, which serves good cocktails and tasty tapas-style dishes, with comfy sofas and seats outside on a patio. The Blacksheep Club Lounge under the pub has live music and DJs in a cosy space with huge sofas; check website for live music events. Mon & Tues 10am–6pm, Wed & Thurs 10am–11pm, Fri 10am–1am, Sat 10am–2am.

The east coast

Away from Ryde, the east of the island is pretty undeveloped, with relatively discreet beaches approached via small, appealing villages, such as **Seaview** and **Bembridge**, and the fine sandy beach at **Whitecliff Bay**. This is also where you will find the island's best-preserved Roman villa at **Brading**, and **Nunwell House** where Charles I spent his last night of freedom before his execution.

Seaview

The road southeast of Ryde follows the coastline, but is slightly set back in a delightful rural corner of the island. From Ryde the seafront promenade continues for two miles east along the old rampart walls to the neighbouring resort of **SEAVIEW** (bus #8 from Ryde), which is very different in feel from its larger neighbour. There is no beach as such here, but a cluster of winding streets, pretty fishermen's cottages and fine Victorian mansions abut a rocky foreshore – most with great views over the giant tankers and container ships plying the Solent.

ACCOMMODATION AND EATING — SEAVIEW

The Boathouse Springvale Rd, PO34 5AW ☎ 01983 810616, Ⓦ theboathouseiow.co.uk. Less than two miles east of Ryde (also accessible on foot along the coast), this classy gastropub has a garden with fantastic views across the Solent. A great spot for a drink, it serves baguettes, fish and chips (£8–12) and more upmarket dishes such as crab risotto (£12) and fresh fish of the day. It also has spacious en-suite rooms from £130. Daily 9am–11pm.

Northbank Hotel Circular Rd, PO34 5ET ⓣ 01983 612227, ⓦ northbankhotel.co.uk. A traditional, family-run Victorian hotel dating from 1840, in a great location with direct beach access via its gardens. It's rather old-fashioned and the rooms are not en suite, but many have sea views and it's a relaxed, child-friendly place with its own lounge and bar. **£100**

★**The Old Fort** The Esplanade, PO34 5HB ⓣ 01983 612363, ⓦ oldfortbarcafe.co.uk. Lively café-bar on the seafront, with superb views over the Solent, serving a range of fresh food including scampi and chips, curries, fish dishes, burgers (£10–11) and baguettes, along with good coffee and Sunday roasts. Summer Mon–Sat 11am–midnight, Sun 11.30am–midnight; winter Tues–Sat 11am–10pm, Sun 11am–4pm.

The Seaview The High St, PO34 5EX ⓣ 01983 612711, ⓦ seaviewhotel.co.uk. Contemporary, boutiquey rooms in a Victorian townhouse in the middle of Seaview: the rooms vary in size but all are comfortable and come with mod cons. It's good for families and has a well-regarded fish restaurant, as well as a bar serving pub meals. **£95**

Priory Bay

Beyond Seaview lies one of the best beaches along this stretch, **Priory Bay**, a long sandy strip backed by tree-lined slopes: there's direct access to the beach from *The Priory Bay Hotel* (see below), though you won't escape the crowds here as plenty of yachties descend in summer.

ACCOMMODATION AND EATING — PRIORY BAY

Dan's Kitchen Lower Green Rd, St Helens, PO33 1TS ⓣ 01983 872303 ⓦ danskitcheniow.com. Highly regarded local restaurant on the pretty St Helen's Green serving interesting and beautifully presented food at very reasonable prices for cooking of this quality. Try dishes such as crab risotto with avocado ice cream (£9), followed by sea bass with gnocchi (£21) or an open fish pie (£14). There's also an excellent choice of veggie dishes (all main courses £14), such as tomato and herb risotto, or pickled vegetables with quail egg salad. Tues & Wed 6.30–9pm, Thurs–Sat noon–1.30pm & 6.30–9pm.

Nodes Point Holiday Park Nodes Rd, St Helens, PO33 1YA ⓣ 01983 872401, ⓦ park-resorts.com. This is a large, superbly positioned campsite with great views over Bembridge Bay. It's also well equipped, with an indoor pool. There are tents and caravans to rent (3-night min stay £300), or you can pitch your own. **£30**

The Priory Bay Hotel Priory Drive, near Seaview, PO33 1YA ⓣ 01983 613146, ⓦ priorybay.com. This classy country-house hotel, in seventy acres of grounds with an outdoor pool and two restaurants, is luxurious without being stuffy. You enter through an impressive fourteenth-century stone doorway imported from France, and the rooms in the main house are plush with high ceilings. There are also self-catering cottages and yurts (April–Oct) in the superb lawned grounds, which lead down to the sands of Priory Bay. Two-night min stay in high season. **£200**

Bembridge and around

BEMBRIDGE is a well-to-do village of handsome houses and bungalows with its own deli, fishmonger's and assorted cafés and restaurants next to Bembridge Harbour, a pretty bay lined with yachts and little moored houseboats. The atmospheric **beach** of narrow shingle studded with weatherworn wooden groynes is a bit tucked away – follow signs to the coastal path or the *Crab and Lobster* pub.

Bembridge Windmill

High St, Bembridge, PO35 5SQ • Mid-March to Oct daily 10.30am–5pm • £5.80, children £2.90; NT • ⓣ 01983 873945, ⓦ nationaltrust.org.uk/bembridge-windmill • Bus #8 from Ryde, Sandown or Newport

The Grade I-listed **Bembridge Windmill** stands at the top of the High Street, just north of the village. The island's only surviving windmill, it dates from around 1700: flour ground here was sold to the Navy who sent boats ashore at Bembridge to collect it, and Bembridge flour was probably used to feed the troops during the Battle of Trafalgar. It's in a lovely position, and you can climb up the steep stepladders for great views over the nearby Culver Down.

Brading Roman Villa

Morton Old Rd, Brading, PO36 0PH • Daily 10am–5pm • £9.50, under-17s £4.75 • T 01983 406223, W bradingromanvilla.org.uk • Bus #3 from Ryde or Sandown

Just south of the ancient village of **BRADING**, about four miles west of Bembridge on the Ryde to Sandown A3055, lie the impressive remains of **Brading Roman Villa**. It's the more impressive of two such villas on the island – the other is in Newport (see p.254) – both of which were probably sites of Bacchanalian worship. The Brading site is housed in an attractive modern museum and is renowned for its superbly preserved **mosaics**, including intact images of Medusa and depictions of Orpheus. It has Roman clothes for children to dress up in and a great café with a terrace and views over the coast.

Nunwell House

Brading, PO36 0JQ • **Gardens** 1–4.30pm: late May to mid-July Mon, Tues & Thurs; late Aug & mid-Sept Wed–Fri • £4 • **House tours** Same months 1.30pm & 3pm; 1hr • £7 (includes gardens) • Hours vary from year to year so check website • T 01983 407240, W nunwellhouse.co.uk

Nunwell House, just over a mile northwest of Brading and signposted off the A3055, was where, in 1647, Charles I spent his last night of freedom before being taken to Carisbrooke Castle (see p.255) and then to his eventual execution in Whitehall. The splendid house has been in the Oglander family for nearly nine hundred years; the present building blends Jacobean, Georgian and Victorian styles. You can visit the house on a guided tour, and there are five acres of lovely gardens to explore, including a walled garden with views over the sea.

ACCOMMODATION AND EATING — BEMBRIDGE AND AROUND

Lockslane Contemporary Bistro 9 Foreland Rd, Bembridge, PO35 5XN T 01983 875233, W lockslane.co.uk. Excellent little restaurant with wooden floors and tables in a contemporary style serving fresh local fish and meat beautifully prepared and presented. The menu changes regularly, but you can expect original and innovative dishes such as local cod with a Goan coconut curry (mains £15–17) – and leave space to sample the wonderful cheese board. Wed–Sun from 6.30pm.

Pilot Boat Inn Station Rd, Bembridge, PO35 5NN T 01983 872077, W thepilotboatinn.com. The lively *Pilot Boat Inn*, down by the harbour, has portholes for windows, an open fire and a small waterfront terrace. Generous portions of pub food include lobster bisque (£7) and local crab patties with chips (£12.50), as well as Isle of Wight beers. It also has comfortable en-suite guest rooms upstairs, some with views over the harbour. Mon–Sat 11am–11pm, Sun noon–10pm. **£100**

Wonky Café Whitecliff Bay, PO35 5QB T 01983 872971, W wonkycafe.com. Laidback beach café overlooking Whitecliff Bay, a fine sandy swathe backed by cliffs, accessed via the Whitecliff Bay Holiday Park. Good breakfasts (£5), sandwiches, lunches (from around £6) and home-made flapjacks. March–Oct daily 9am–5pm; sometimes open later in high summer.

★**Xoron Floatel** Embankment Rd, Bembridge Harbour, PO35 5NS T 01983 874596, W xoronfloatel.co.uk. The *Xoron* offers unusual B&B accommodation in a converted World War II gunboat on Bembridge Harbour. The en-suite cabins are cosy and centrally heated, while the upper deck has a lounge and breakfast area with a lovely terrace at the back to watch the comings and goings in the harbour. **£70**

The south coast

The south coast of the Isle of Wight represents the island at its most varied best. Here you'll find the bucket-and-spade resorts of **Sandown**, **Ventnor** and **Shanklin** interspersed with the leafy, well-to-do villages of **Bonchurch**, **St Lawrence** and **Niton**. Families are well catered for, with the clifftop funfair at **Blackgang**, the **Isle of Wight Zoo** and **Dinosaur Isle** at Sandown. This corner is also ideal for walkers, with secluded coves and some superb coastal paths; inland, among the steep rolling downs, you'll find the splendid ruins of **Appuldurcombe House** and the idyllic thatched village of **Godshill**, proclaimed the prettiest on the island.

Sandown

The traditional seaside resort of **SANDOWN** merges with its neighbour Shanklin across Sandown Bay, and makes up the island's main holiday-making centre. Usually lively but rather worn at the edges, Sandown became a resort in Victorian times, thanks to its position on a five-mile stretch of soft golden sands, and is overlooked by the island's only surviving pleasure **pier**, which opened in 1879. There are also splendid coastal **walks**, especially heading east towards the headland of Whitecliff Point.

Isle of Wight Zoo

Yaverland Seafront, PO36 8QB • Daily, weather permitting: mid-Feb to March & Oct 10am–4pm; April–Sept 10am–5.30pm; Nov to mid-Feb 11am–3pm • Nov to mid-Feb £8, children £6.50; mid-Feb to Oct £10.50, children £8.50 • T 01983 403883, W isleofwightzoo.com

The small, low-key **Isle of Wight Zoo** displays big cats that have been rescued from circuses or private collections. Run by Charlotte Corney (partner of TV naturalist Chris Packham), the zoo is imaginatively set in the remains of a Victorian fort and has seven tigers – including a rare white tiger – plus four lions, seven species of lemurs, a jaguar, wallabies, meerkats and several species of monkeys, along with a selection of reptiles and native British animals. Throughout the day, keepers feed and give informative talks about the various animals.

Dinosaur Isle

Culver Parade, PO36 8QA • Daily: April–Aug 10am–6pm; Sept & Oct 10am–5pm; Nov–March 10am–4pm • £5, children £4 • T 01983 404344, W dinosaurisle.com

On the seafront Esplanade, near the zoo, **Dinosaur Isle** is housed in a purpose-built museum shaped like a giant pterosaur. As well as a large collection of genuine fossils, the museum's displays include robotic dinosaurs and life-size replicas of the different species once found on the island, one of Europe's richest sites for dinosaur remains and fossils.

ARRIVAL AND DEPARTURE — SANDOWN

By train The Island Line train station, served by trains from Ryde and Shanklin (see p.249), is on Station Ave, about a 10min walk inland from the pier.

By bus Services (see p.249) include buses #2 from Newport via Shanklin (every 30min; 45min), #3 from Newport via Ventnor and Ryde (every 30min; 1hr 15min), and #8 from Ryde (hourly; 1hr).

ACCOMMODATION

The Belmore 101 Station Ave, PO36 8HD T 01983 404189, W belmorebandb.com. A smart B&B in a large Victorian house in a quiet street a short walk from the beach. The comfortable rooms are newly decorated with a marine vibe and stylish furnishings. **£80**

The Lawns 72 Broadway, PO36 9AA T 01983 402549, W lawnshotelisleofwight.co.uk. This attractive Victorian guesthouse has its own gardens, bar and off-street car park. There is a range of comfortable rooms, some larger than others, with family rooms available; all have flatscreen TVs. Evening meals on request. **£90**

EATING AND DRINKING

Barnaby's 4 Pier St, PO36 8JR T 01983 403368, W barnabysrestaurant.co.uk. You can eat for under £10 a head at cheap and cheerful *Barnaby's*, which serves bargain grills, breakfasts, sandwiches and pasta dishes as well as drinks and ice creams. There are sea views on the decking; a good bet if you object to the somewhat garish interior. Daily 6am–dusk.

Beach Café 9 Pier St, PO36 8JR T 01983 719505, W beachcafeiow.co.uk. Well-priced sandwiches, ciabattas and baguettes as well as heartier meals such as fajitas (£10–13), burgers (£7–10) and pizzas (£7–9) in this light and airy café with great views over the beach. Wed–Sun 10am–4pm.

King's House 43 High St, PO36 4AB T 01983 406445. The *King's House* is a fairly average pub, but with a great terrace facing the sea, nice views and well-priced lunchtime sandwiches and snacks (from £3). Mon–Sat 11am–11pm, Sun 11am–10.30pm.

The Reef The Esplanade, PO36 8AE T 01983 403219, W thereefsandown.co.uk. A bright bar-restaurant with a large beach-facing deck, serving mid-priced dishes including stone-baked pizzas, pasta, steaks and fresh fish. Mains around £9–16. Daily 11am–11pm.

Shanklin and around

Merging with Sandown to the southwest, **SHANKLIN** is split into three parts – a scenic old town at the southern end of the functional new town and, at the bottom of the steep cliffs, a beach resort. With its leafy clifftop gardens and scenic chine (a steep gulley running down to the beach) it certainly has a more sophisticated aura than Sandown.

Shanklin's thatched **Old Village** is archetypically pretty – and mobbed with visitors for much of the year. Escape the crowds in the lovely **Rylstone Gardens** that spread along the top of the cliff, and which are a good place to spot the island's red squirrels. There are steps down from here to the broad **beach** at the foot of the cliffs, where you can hire kayaks and the like in front of a row of guesthouses and cafés.

Shanklin Chine

Chine Hill, PO37 6BW • April–Oct daily 10am–5pm; late May to early Sept 10am–10pm, depending on weather • £4.30, under-15s £2.30 • T 01983 866432, W shanklinchine.co.uk

Shanklin Chine is a twisting pathway with steps down a particularly pretty mossy gorge. There's a waterfall at the top and a series of minor attractions at the bottom of the narrow ravine including caged birds and chipmunks and a Victorian brine bath. The Chine looks particularly pretty on a summer evening, when it's illuminated, though note there is no readmission once you have exited the bottom gate. It is perhaps of most interest for its military connections. The steep slopes were used to train soldiers during World War II, and you'll see a section of PLUTO, a metal pipe that led from here under the Channel to supply troops with petrol during the Normandy Landings in France.

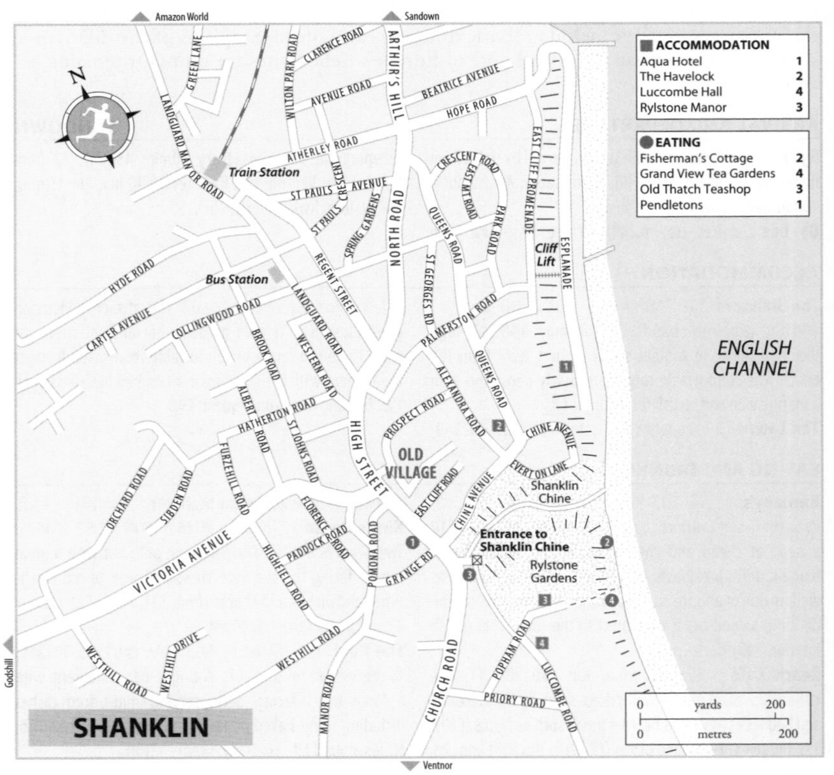

Amazon World

Four miles northwest of Shanklin at Watery Lane, PO38 0LX • April–Oct daily 10am–5pm: Nov–March opens at 10am but closing time varies: call to check • £10.50, under-15s £8.50 • ⓣ 01983 867122, ⓦ amazonworld.co.uk • Bus #8 from Sandown

For a small zoo (on the road to Newport), there is a surprisingly varied collection of small mammals, birds and reptiles at **Amazon World**, including ocelots, meerkats, lemurs, sloths and various bats, toucans, flamingos and piranha fish. Kids will enjoy the creepy-crawlies, including tarantulas and cockroaches, in the insects and spiders section; check out the times of the talks and feeding sessions throughout the day.

ARRIVAL AND DEPARTURE — SHANKLIN AND AROUND

By train The final stop on the Island Line from Ryde (see p.249), Shanklin train station is about half a mile inland at the top of Regent Street.

By bus The bus station, which has services on buses #2 & #3 from Ryde and Newport (see p.249), is a little south of the train station on Landguard Rd.

ACCOMMODATION

Aqua Hotel 17 The Esplanade, PO37 6BN ⓣ 01983 863024, ⓦ theaqua.co.uk. Small, family-run hotel in a great seafront location with its own garden and decent if unspectacular rooms. It's worth paying a bit extra for a sea-facing room with a balcony. It also has a downstairs apartment suitable for families (£140). **£90**

The Havelock 2 Queen's Rd, PO37 6AN ⓣ 01983 862747, ⓦ havelockhotel.co.uk. Lovely clifftop hotel with its own bar, heated outdoor pool and fine gardens. The best rooms have sea views and balconies and there are also family rooms. Breakfast comes with superb fresh breads. Closed Nov to mid-March. **£90**

Luccombe Hall Luccombe Rd, PO37 6RL ⓣ 01983 869000, ⓦ luccombehall.co.uk. This grand country house sits on the cliffs, with four acres of lovely gardens and splendid views over the sea. Once the summer home to the Bishop of Portsmouth, it now has superb facilities, including indoor and outdoor pools, jacuzzis, children's play area, restaurant and squash court. **£160**

Rylstone Manor Rylstone Gardens, PO37 6RG ⓣ 01983 862806, ⓦ rylstone-manor.co.uk. A superb Victorian pile, with period decor and its own bar and dining room, sitting in the middle of leafy public gardens on the top of the cliffs. No children under 16, and a 2- to 3-night min weekend stay in high season. **£145**

EATING

Fisherman's Cottage 1 Esplanade, PO37 6BN ⓣ 01983 863882, ⓦ shanklinchine.co.uk. At the southern end of the seafront at the bottom of Shanklin Chine, this atmospheric nineteenth-century thatched pub has outside tables facing the beach. The menu includes large portions of pub staples such as cottage pie or scampi and chips, as well as local fish and seafood (mains from £11), including lobster and crab when available. Mon–Sat noon–11pm, Sun noon–10.30pm.

Grand View Tea Gardens Popham Rd, PO37 6RL ⓣ 07709 087544, ⓦ luccombehall.co.uk. In the grounds of *Luccombe Hall* hotel (see above), this small hut serves teas, coffees, light lunches and delicious home-made cream teas in a lovely clifftop garden with great sea views – it also sells packed lunches to take down to the beach. Summer daily 10.30am–4pm (later in good weather); winter Mon, Tues & Fri–Sun 10.30am–4pm; all hours weather dependent.

★ **Old Thatch Teashop** 4 Church Rd, PO37 6NU ⓣ 01983 865587, ⓦ oldthatchteashop.co.uk. A warren of rooms in this friendly and efficient teahouse, with pretty gardens at the back. It serves light lunches like soup and sandwiches plus hearty main meals (from £11), and is highly regarded for its delicious home-made scones and cakes. Easter–Oct daily 10am–5pm.

Pendletons 85 High St, PO37 6NR ⓣ 01983 868727, ⓦ pendletons.org. Well-regarded restaurant serving local produce where possible, in dishes such as Ventnor Bay crab cakes (£7.50) and roast cod with garlic herb crust (£13.50). Thurs–Sat 6–11pm.

Ventnor and around

The seaside resort of **VENTNOR** and its two village suburbs of **Bonchurch** and **St Lawrence** sit at the foot of St Boniface Down, the island's highest point at 236m (787ft). The Down periodically disintegrates into landslides, creating the jumbled terraces known locally as the **Undercliff**, whose sheltered, south-facing aspect, mild winter temperatures and thick carpet of undergrowth have contributed to the

WALKS AROUND BONCHURCH

From Bonchurch's attractive, if stony, beach, there's a fine hour-long round **walk**: take the uphill path just east of the beach pottery and join the coastal path east (a short detour takes you to Bonchurch's Old Church, which dates from 1070). The coastal path crosses a field. You then follow the sign to Bonchurch Chute – the path climbs ancient woodland, home to red squirrels and the rare Glanville Fritillary butterfly. Soon you'll join a road – Bonchurch Chute – where you should turn left and head downhill to return to Bonchurch's main street, next to the ponds. Turn left here to go back down to the beach.

Alternatively, you can do the steep half-hour walk from the beach up the **Devil's Chimney**, a dramatic series of steps that wind up through the woods through a narrow crevice in the cliffs to the *Smuggler's Haven Tea Rooms* on St Boniface Downs, where you can reward your exertions with a cream tea.

former fishing village becoming a fashionable health spa. Thanks to these factors, the town possesses rather more character than the island's other resorts, its Gothic Revival buildings clinging dizzily to zigzagging bends above a small but pleasant crescent of sands.

Ventnor's frayed-at-the-edges **High Street** has an interesting mixture of smart gift shops and delis sitting next to run-down antique and bric-a-brac shops. The floral terraces of the **Cascade** curve down to the slender **Esplanade** and narrow fine shingle **beach**, which is lined with shops, cafés and restaurants. From here, it's a short walk along the seafront to the picturesque **Steephill Cove**, a tiny fishing village nestling below Ventnor's **Botanical Gardens**, while inland, there are the attractive ruins of **Appuldurcombe House** and a **Donkey Sanctuary**.

Botanical Gardens

Undercliff Drive, PO38 1UL • Daily 10am–4pm • £9.50, under-17s £5 • ⓣ 01983 855397, ⓦ botanic.co.uk

From Ventnor's Esplanade, it's a pleasant mile-long stroll along the seafront (with some steep uphill sections) to the **Botanical Gardens**, 22 landscaped acres of flourishing subtropical vegetation. The plants grow naturally because of the mild microclimate of the south-facing Undercliff. There used to be a sanatorium here for patients suffering from tuberculosis and other chest diseases, as the climate was very conducive to their recovery. It's a lovely sheltered spot for a picnic, and there's a decent café too, with a children's play area and plenty of space for running around.

Steephill Cove

A mile east of Ventnor along the seafront • There's no car access to the cove, but there's a small car park on the main Ventnor–Blackgang rd, from where it is a 5min walk down a footpath to the bay

STEEPHILL COVE is a former fishing hamlet whose whitewashed cottages tumble down the cliff to a pretty beach. There's little to it save some holiday cottages (ⓦ steephill-cove.co.uk) and a couple of places to eat, but it's a lovely spot to linger and clamber around on the rocks behind the beach.

Bonchurch

An attractive village of thatched cottages and Victorian villas, many clustered round a picturesque pond, **BONCHURCH**, a mile or so east of Ventnor, was described by Charles Dickens as "the prettiest place I ever saw in my life, at home or abroad" and was where he wrote much of *David Copperfield*. Other notable literary fans of the village include John Keats and Algernon Swinburne, who is buried in the village graveyard. The attractive seafront just below the village is **Horseshoe Bay**, from where it is a lovely twenty-minute walk along the seafront to Ventnor Esplanade.

Isle of Wight Donkey Sanctuary

Lower Winstone Farm, St Johns Rd, Wroxall, PO38 3AA • Daily 10.30am–4.30pm, weather permitting • Free; donations welcome • T 01983 852693, W iwdonkey-sanctuary.com

A couple of miles inland from Ventnor, along the B3327 and over St Boniface Down, lies the unassuming village of **WROXALL**, where you'll find a small **Donkey Sanctuary**, home to some hundred or so donkeys that have been taken into care for various reasons. It is great for kids, especially in spring when there are plenty of very cute foals.

Appuldurcombe House

Appuldurcombe Rd, Wroxall, PO38 3EW • **House** April–Sept Mon–Fri & Sun 10am–5pm • Free • **Owl and Falconry Centre** Daily displays: April–Sept 10.45am, noon & 2.30pm • £9, children £6.50 • T 01983 852484, W appuldurcombe.co.uk

Appuldurcombe House, half a mile from Wroxall, is the island's grandest pre-Victorian house sitting in picturesque, rolling countryside. From the front of the house the building looks intact, but it is in fact largely ruined. The present mansion was built in the late eighteenth century in the Palladian style, with gardens landscaped by Capability Brown. Soldiers were stationed here in both world wars – in World War II live ammunition was used for military training, exacerbating damage already caused in 1943 when a landmine was accidently dropped here. Semi-abandoned ever since, Appuldurcombe has been preserved in a scenic state of decay, the highlight being the partly renovated Great Hall, built 1701–13, and once used for banquets.

The grounds are also home to the **Owl and Falconry Centre**, which puts on regular talks and flying displays from an array of falcons including kestrels, eagles and kites – though you can't help feeling the birds don't appreciate being tethered, and you may find the similar displays at Robin Hill Park more cost-effective (see p.255). There's also a small café.

VENTNOR AND AROUND

ARRIVAL AND TOURS

By bus Ventnor is served by buses #3 from Newport and Ryde and #6 from Newport and Blackgang (see p.249): they pull in along the High Street.

Ocean Blue Adventures Hour-long boat trips leave from Ventnor Haven and run along the Undercliff in summer (£15–20; W oceanbluequay.co.uk/sea_charters), as well as lobster and fishing trips: for schedules and booking call T 07980 986232.

ACCOMMODATION

Appuldurcombe Gardens Holiday Park Wroxall, PO38 3EP T 01983 852597, W appuldurcombegardens.co.uk. Adjacent to the extensive grounds of Appuldurcombe House is this beautifully sited campsite with its own heated pool, shop (April–Oct), café and play area. There are also static caravans which you can rent (from £110). Closed Dec–Feb. **£30**

The Hambrough Hambrough Rd, Ventnor, PO38 1SQ T 01938 856333, W thehambrough.com. Smart boutique-style rooms with all mod cons including coffee machines: all except one have sea views and a couple come with their own balconies – the breakfasts are great and the staff are friendly. It also runs a couple of self-catering apartments and cottages. **£170**

★**The Leconfield** 85 Leeson Rd, Upper Bonchurch, PO38 1PU, W leconfieldhotel.com. Friendly and comfortable B&B in attractive grounds overlooking the sea. The well-kept rooms are spacious, light and airy, and many have free-standing baths and sea views – the Captain's Bridge comes with its own large sea-view terrace and a huge en-suite bathroom. The owners are very helpful, the breakfasts delicious and there's a heated pool in summer in the lovely gardens. **£90**

Royal Hotel Belgrave Rd, Ventnor, PO38 1JJ T 01938 852186, W royalhoteliow.co.uk. Built in 1832, this is one of the island's oldest hotels, successfully blending the traditional with boutique-style decor. The rooms (with flatscreen TVs and plush bathrooms) are comfortable, many with sea views, and the grounds are lovely, with a heated pool in summer, and a highly recommended restaurant (see p.268). **£210**

St Augustine Villa Esplanade, Ventnor, PO38 1TA T 01983 852285, W harbourviewhotel.co.uk. This large Victorian mansion has a great location facing the beach at Ventnor, with period fittings in the lounge. The decor may be a little dated, but most of the rooms have sea views. **£90**

9

EATING AND DRINKING

Cantina Ventnor Bonchurch Village Rd, Bonchurch, PO38 1RG 01983 855988, cantinaventnor.co.uk. Excellent café/bakery and restaurant, which makes all its bread, pastries and pizzas (£5–11) on site. It serves breakfast all day, with more substantial dishes for dinner (£10–13), such as chicken and ham pie, as well as lovely cocktails (£7–9) – Earl Grey martini or elderflower mojito, anyone? Daily 7.30am–10pm.

The Crab Shed Steephill Cove, PO38 1AF 01983 855819. Delicious home-made crab pasties and fresh mackerel ciabattas (both around £5) served from a pretty shack with outdoor seats on the seashore. Also tasty local lobster salads and daily fish specials (£9–14), which you can have with their selected wines. Noon–3pm: April–July & Sept Wed–Sun; Aug & school hols Tues–Sun; March & Oct Sat & Sun; all hours weather dependent.

El Toro Contento 2 Pier St, Ventnor, PO38 1ST 01983 857600, eltorocontento.co.uk. A cosy restaurant dishing up home-made tapas, such as chickpeas with spinach and salt cod or peppers stuffed with mushrooms and walnuts (most £5–6). Also Spanish hams and cheeses and paella (around £15 a head; min 2 people). Mon–Sat 5–10pm.

★**Fogg's of Ventnor** 11 High St, Ventnor 01983 855500, foggsofventnor.com. The interior of this attractive bay-windowed, balconied villa has wooden floors and tables and is contemporary in style, while the eclectic menu features dishes with influences from around the world, but made with local ingredients. The cooking is accomplished, with dishes ranging from a delicious Jamaican jerk chicken (£14) through local pork chops with cider and mustard sauce to the Ventnor Bay fish of the day. Service is friendly and there's a great-value set menu (two courses for £15). Tues–Sat from 6pm.

Royal Hotel Belgrave Rd, Ventnor, PO38 1JJ 01938 852186, royalhoteliow.co.uk. Wonderful food in a grand hotel dining room. I's a bit steep, at £40 for three courses, but the quality of the ingredients and cooking is high – Ventnor Bay fish soup is delicious, and the rhubarb tasting plate divine – and there's a cheaper set lunch menu (£21 for three courses) served in the conservatory or outside on the lawns on a fine day. Alternatively, try the afternoon tea – popular with Queen Victoria – a delicious tower of exquisite mini pastries, cakes, scones and sandwiches (£23). Daily noon–1.45pm, 3–5pm & 6.45–9pm.

Spyglass Inn Ventnor Esplanade, Ventnor, PO38 1JX 01983 855338, thespyglass.com. Lively pub, with a terrace, in a great location on the seafront. You can eat giant portions of pub grub, such as veggie lasagne for £11, or choose one of the home-made daily specials which often include local lobster salad (around £25). Frequent live music, too. Kitchen daily noon–9.30pm.

Godshill

Model railway Daily: March 10am–4pm; April to late July, Sept & Oct 10am–5pm; late July & Aug 10am–6pm • £4.50, children £3.50

GODSHILL bills itself as the prettiest village on the Isle of Wight. With its medley of thatched cottages, gardens and medieval church it is undeniably lovely, but sadly it is all rather commercial, full of teahouses and shops catering to tourists. Its **Old Smithy** now houses a variety of shops and cafés set in historic buildings with an attractive garden behind, while children will enjoy the **Model Village** on the High Street; along with miniature versions of Shanklin and Godshill, there's a model railway neatly laid out among shrubs and plants.

ARRIVAL AND DEPARTURE — GODSHILL

By bus Godshill is served by bus #2 from Shanklin and Newport (every 30min; 15min from both) and #3 from Newport and Ventnor (every 30min; 15–20min).

EATING AND DRINKING

The Taverners High St, PO38 3HZ 01983 840707, thetavernersgodshill.co.uk. This fine old pub, with its own vegetable garden, is famed for using fresh local produce (which it sells at its own shop) and brewing its own real ale. Food includes local ham, Isle of Wight cheeses and traditional dishes such as beef and ale pie; mains £9–14. Mon–Sat 11am–11pm, Sun 11am–5pm.

Niton and around

The western Undercliff at Ventnor begins to recede at the village of **NITON**, where a footpath continues to the most southerly tip of the island, **St Catherine's Point**, marked by a modern lighthouse; you can also walk along the cliffs to the local landmark

WALKS FROM NITON

There's a great half-hour round walk from Niton to **St Catherine's Point**, leaving from the excellent *Buddle Inn* (see below), an old smugglers' haunt. From the pub, take the signposted path opposite and follow it down the hill. Turn right and join the footpath signed off to the right, which snakes through fields to join the coast path. Here, turn right to the **lighthouse**, then cross a stile onto the lane that leads (right) back up into Niton.

Alternatively, you can take a lovely one- to two-hour clifftop walk from Niton to **St Catherine's Oratory**, a prominent landmark on the downs. Known locally as the "Pepper Pot", this was originally a lighthouse, reputedly built in 1325. Take the road uphill past the *Enchanted Manor* and pick up the coast path on the left. This climbs to a walk along the lip of dramatic cliffs all the way to Blackgang (see below). Cross the road and pick up the footpath opposite the viewpoint car park and you'll see the Oratory on the hill above you. Return the same way, or head back to Niton over the hill.

St Catherine's Oratory. On crumbling cliffs below the oratory are the rides and thrills of the **Blackgang Chine** amusement park.

Blackgang Chine

Blackgang, PO38 2HN • Daily: mid-March to mid-Sept 10am–5pm or 6pm; mid-Sept to Oct 10am–4.30pm; stays open later some nights in summer hols and Oct half-term • £17; school hols £19.50 • 01983 730330, blackgangchine.com

The delightfully old-fashioned theme park at **Blackgang Chine**, two miles west of Niton, has a great location perched right on the clifftop. Opened as a landscaped garden in 1843, it now has a series of fairly low-key attractions on themes such as the Wild West, dinosaurs, nursery rhymes and goblins, along with some museum rooms tracing the history of local crafts. Most of the rides, which are ranged down the cliff, are suited to under-12s, though older children will enjoy the roller-coaster and water chutes.

ACTIVITIES — NITON AND AROUND

Paragliding The coast around Blackgang Chine is ideal for paragliding; take a tandem flight with Butterfly Paragliding (£75 for 15–20min; 01983 731611, paraglide.uk.com).

ACCOMMODATION AND EATING

Buddle Inn St Catherine's Rd, PO38 2NE 01983 730243, buddleinn.co.uk. This great traditional pub serves a selection of real ales and good food – seafood tagliatelle, fisherman's pie, *moules frites* (most mains £11–14) – in a beamed bar with an open fire. There's a lovely garden with great views over the sea and live music most weekends. Mon–Thurs noon–11pm, Fri & Sat 11am–11.30pm, Sun noon–10.30pm.

Enchanted Manor Sandrock Rd, PO38 2NG 01983 730215, enchantedmanor.co.uk. The unusual *Enchanted Manor* is not to everyone's taste, a fairy-themed guesthouse with luxurious rooms featuring fairytale artworks. Geared up for romantic escapes, it has a Victorian billiard room and library and a hot tub in the gardens, where badgers and red squirrels can often be seen; two-night minimum stay. **£160**

Brighstone to Alum Bay

The southwest coast is largely undeveloped, with rolling countryside around **Brighstone**, a short walk from the superb gardens at **Mottistone**. Nearby are the fine bays at **Compton** and **Freshwater Bay**. The western tip of the island is fairly built up, a sprawl of development embracing **Freshwater** and **Totland**. But the big draw is the dramatic coastal formation on the westernmost tip, where the multicoloured sands of **Alum Bay** face the spectacular chalk stacks of the **Needles**. These also form the target for one of the island's greatest walks, along the clifftop **Tennyson Down** where the great poet gained much inspiration.

Brighstone and around

The village of **BRIGHSTONE** is far less visited than the much-vaunted Godshill (see p.268) but just as pretty, with an idyllic cluster of low thatched cottages a little inland from Brighstone Bay. There's a pleasant forty-minute walk round the village, which is detailed in a free leaflet that you can pick up at the village shop. The nearby stretch of coast, too, is delightfully unspoilt, with a coastal path running along a grassy clifftop.

Brighstone Museum

North St, Brighstone, PO30 4AX • Tues 9am–12.30pm, Thurs 1.30–4.30pm, Sat 10am–4pm • Free

One of the cottages on North Street has been converted into a **museum** of village life, with a re-creation of a Victorian cottage kitchen, complete with bread oven and hearth. The recordings of old villagers, reminiscing about their childhoods here, give a fascinating insight into life in a rural community.

Mottistone Manor Gardens

Mottistone, PO30 4EA • Mid-March to Oct Mon–Thurs & Sun 10.30am–5pm • £6.40, children £3.20; NT • T 01983 741302, W nationaltrust.org.uk/mottistone-gardens

You can look round the beautiful **Mottistone Manor Gardens**, a couple of miles west of Brighstone, though the manor house itself is still lived in and only open on two days a year. The house was thrust into the media spotlight when it was revealed to be the secret location of Benedict Cumberbatch and Sophie Hunter's wedding reception, after they married in the nearby twelfth-century church of St Peter and St Paul on February 14, 2015. The six acres of formal, terraced gardens form only a small part of the 650-acre estate, their beautiful displays of camellias, roses and the like giving way to wilder areas the higher you go. There's a lovely walled tea garden, which is also home to the **Shack**, designed in the 1930s by architects Seely and Paget as a country retreat, and a wonderful example of Art Deco style. Designed like a ship's galley, it was constructed to be as compact as possible, incorporating all the mod cons of the time: ladders leading up to the bunks double as heated towel rails, and the dining table fits beneath the desk.

ARRIVAL AND DEPARTURE — BRIGHSTONE AND AROUND

By bus Bus #12 runs from Newport via Brighstone to Freshwater and Totland (see p.249).

ACCOMMODATION AND EATING

Grange Farm Grange Chine, PO30 4DA T 01983 740296, W grangefarmholidays.com. This rare-breeds farm, complete with alpacas and the odd water buffalo, is a superbly located complex with its own clifftop campsite. There are also converted barns, cottages, camping pods and static caravans to rent (from around £1000 a week). Closed Nov–Feb. £19

Sun Inn Hulverstone, PO30 4EH T 01983 741124, W sunhulverstone.co.uk. An attractive thatched, dog-friendly pub with a garden with views down to the coast. It serves decent pub food, such as rare-breed pork sausages with mash and fish pie (mains £10–16). Live music most Saturdays. Mon–Fri noon–11pm, Sat noon–midnight, Sun noon–10.30pm.

Compton Bay

West of Brighstone, the coast path and road follow one of the least developed parts of the island to the superb expanse of sands at **Compton Bay**. Accessible only by foot from the car park at the top, the bay is popular with surfers and kitesurfers. The gently sloping beach backed by crumbling red rocks is also good for bathing, though at high tide it's pretty packed.

ARRIVAL AND DEPARTURE — COMPTON BAY

By bus Bus #12 runs from Newport via Compton Bay to Freshwater and Totland (see p.249).

ACCOMMODATION

Compton Farm Brook, PO30 4HF ⓣ01983 740215, ⓦcomptonfarm.co.uk. A simple, traditional campsite, around a 10min walk from the beach, in a lovely rural setting. Open Easter–Oct. £18

Freshwater and Totland

Joining both coasts of this end of the Isle of Wight, **FRESHWATER** is a sprawling community that merges with **TOTLAND** in the north and **Freshwater Bay** in the south. Totland and neighbouring Colwell Bay have a pleasant seafront promenade, though the waters on the north coast are less alluring than those on the south at Freshwater Bay.

Dimbola Lodge

Terrace Lane, Freshwater Bay, PO40 9QE • Jan Fri–Sun 10am–4pm; April–Sept daily 10am–5pm; Feb, March & Oct–Dec Tues–Sun 10am–4pm • £5 • ⓣ01983 756814, ⓦdimbola.co.uk

Just inland from Freshwater Bay, **Dimbola Lodge** was the home of pioneering Victorian photographer Julia Margaret Cameron (1815–79), who settled here after visiting Tennyson in 1860. The building now houses an eclectic collection of exhibits, including a museum of Cameron's work, with pictures of her contemporaries, such as Tennyson, Darwin, Robert Browning, the actor Ellen Terry, and Alice Liddell, the model for Lewis Carroll's *Alice's Adventures in Wonderland*. Recently there has been renewed interest in Cameron's work, with London's Victoria and Albert Museum putting on an exhibition of her photos in 2015 to commemorate Cameron's two-hundredth anniversary. The museum also has sections on the history of photography, a reconstruction of Cameron's bedroom, and a room where you can have your picture taken dressed up as a Victorian. Other exhibits include one on the history of the Isle of Wight Festival (see p.254), along with temporary exhibitions of photography, and a fine **tearoom** overlooking the sea.

Tennyson Down

Reached via the coast path from Freshwater Bay, **Tennyson Down** is a beautiful stretch of rolling downs stretching all the way to the **Needles**. It takes its name from Alfred, Lord Tennyson, who lived in Freshwater from 1852 to be "far from noise and smoke of town", and where, it is said, he had an affair with Julia Margaret Cameron (see above). He frequently walked these downs; at the top, a half-hour walk from Freshwater Bay, stands a monument to the poet. Continuing west along the well-marked path, it is another hour to the Needles – a superb walk with great views over to the New Forest on the mainland. If you're feeling energetic, you could return along the northern coast path back to Totland (around 45min).

Tapnell Farm

Tapnell Farm, Newport Rd, PO41 0YJ • Daily 10am–5pm • £7 (off-peak £5), under-17s £9 (off-peak £7) • ⓣ01983 758722, ⓦtapnellfarm.com

In a lovely location on top of a ridge with views across the site of the infamous 1970 Isle of Wight festival (see box, p.254) to the sea, **Tapnell Farm** is great for children. There are loads of farm animals to interact with, plus wallabies, meerkats and alpacas, an indoor play barn, zip-wires, a huge jumping pillow made out of the old sileage pen, a museum section with the original milking parlour, and plenty of other activities. An on-site adventure sports company (ⓦisleofwightadventureactivities.co.uk) offers climbing, zorbing, mountain-boarding, archery and clay pigeon shooting, as well as coasteering, paddle-boarding and kayaking down on the coast. The farm is also home to a variety of accommodation (see p.272), and to the great *The Cow Co* restaurant in a light and airy converted barn, serving tasty burgers and steaks and good coffee (Mon–Thurs & Sun 9am–5pm, Fri & Sat 9am–11pm).

ARRIVAL AND DEPARTURE

FRESHWATER AND TOTLAND

By bus Totland and Freshwater are served by buses #7 from Newport via Yarmouth and #12 from Newport via Brighstone (see p.249).

ACCOMMODATION AND EATING

Farringford House Bedbury Lane, Freshwater Bay, PO40 9PE ⓣ 01938 752500, ⓦ farringford.co.uk. About a mile inland, Lord Tennyson's former home sits in lovely grounds where you can rent ten comfortable, well-equipped self-catering cottages (sleep 2–8 people): there's also an outdoor solar-heated pool (May–Sept), tennis court, croquet lawn, golf course (all free to guests) and café/restaurant which serves tasty wood-fired pizzas (£8–11). Minimum two nights' stay. **£168**

The Really Green Holiday Company Afton Park, Newport Rd, Freshwater, PO40 9XR ⓣ 07802 678591, ⓦ thereallygreenholidaycompany.com. Fully furnished, eco-friendly yurts (sleeping up to 6 people) on an organic farm with great views over the countryside and river. Also has a few pitches for bring-your-own tents (£20). Around a 10min walk from Freshwater Bay. Open April to mid-Oct. Minimum two nights' stay. **£125**

★Red Lion Church Place, Freshwater, PO40 9BP ⓣ 01983 754925. This attractive traditional pub has log fires, real ales, a lovely big garden, and a good selection of home-prepared meals made with quality local ingredients – as well as pub staples (most £9–11), there's a daily-changing specials board often featuring local fish dishes. Very popular at weekends, when it's best to book. Mon–Sat 11am–11pm, Sun 11am–10.30pm.

★Tom's Eco Lodge Tapnell Farm, Newport Rd, PO41 0YJ ⓣ 07717 666346, ⓦ tomsecolodge.com. Luxury ready-erected tents, wood cabins and camping pods – plus farm cottages (sleep 8) and a beautiful manor house (sleeps 20) – can all be rented on the lovely Tapnell Farm. All the glamping accommodation is secluded and of a very high quality, with great views to the sea, fire pits and free-range chickens that you can collect eggs from. Some even come with a wood-fired hot tub. Eco-pods can be rented for a night, but tents and cabins have a two-night minimum. Eco-pods **£120**

Alum Bay

At the island's western tip, you'll find the multichrome cliffs at **Alum Bay** tumbling down to ochre-hued sands, which were used as pigments for painting local landscapes in the Victorian era. Alum Bay was also the scene of Marconi's early experiments, when he made the first telephone communications between here and Bournemouth (see box, p.39).

Needles Park

Alum Bay, PO39 0JD • Easter–Oct daily 10am–4pm, later some days in summer • Free; chairlift £6 return • ⓦ theneedles.co.uk

The **Needles Park** amusement park, at the top of the cliff, is little more than an assorted collection of rather tacky children's attractions, though the **chairlift** down the cliff to the bay is worth a ride for the stunning views. There are also a few shops and cafés on site that stay open all year, including a glass-blower's where you can watch demonstrations.

Old Battery

West High Down, PO39 0JH • Mid-March to Oct daily 10.30am–5pm • £6.85, children £3.45; NT • ⓣ 01983 754772, ⓦ nationaltrust.org.uk/needles-old-battery-and-new-battery

From the car park by Needles Park, it's a lovely twenty-minute walk to the lookout by the **Old Battery**, a Victorian fort that sits on the top of the cliffs. It was built to defend Britain from the threat of invasion by the French and was active during both world wars. You can go inside the old guardroom, from where soldiers would have watched the D-Day invasion force heading out to France, and clamber down a low tunnel to a nineteenth-century searchlight emplacement – once used to look out for night-time invasion attempts – for some of the best views of the Needles. The fort includes the remains of the original lighthouse, built in 1786 but partly obscured by the top of the cliff – hence the building of the current one, at the end of the Needles, in 1859. The small tearoom in the Old Lookout Tower has some of the best views over the headland.

THE MISSING LINK

The **Needles** are chalk stacks formed more than 60 million years ago by an upheaval in the earth's crust. They are the western end of a chalk ridge that runs across the Isle of Wight, then continues beneath the sea floor to emerge in Dorset at Ballard Down, Swanage. At one time the island was connected to mainland Britain by this chalk ridge before sea levels rose and erosion took place: by standing on top of the Needles or on Ballard Down, you can clearly see how the two land masses, now fifteen miles apart, were once linked. A fourth Needle, known as "Lot's Wife", disappeared during a storm in 1764.

New Battery

Mid-March to Oct daily 11am–4pm • Free • ⓣ 01983 754772, ⓦ nationaltrust.org.uk/needles-old-battery-and-new-battery

Just above the Old Battery lies the **New Battery**, built in 1895 as a gun emplacement. In 1956, the military started testing rockets here during the Cold War; the site became known as the High Down Test Site and once employed 200 people. Twenty-seven rockets were tested here before being launched in Australia, and the research undertaken pioneered much of the early space technology for the moon landings. Today you can explore the underground rooms where the secret testing took place; various exhibits explain what went on here.

ARRIVAL AND ACTIVITIES — ALUM BAY

By bus Bus #7 runs from Newport via Yarmouth to the Needles Park car park (see opposite), but the only bus running from there up to the Needles themselves is the open-top Needles Breezer, a hop-on, hop-off tour of the west of the island (see p.249).

Boat trips At the bottom of the chairlift, boat trips (Easter–Oct daily every 15–30min from 10.30am; 20min; £5.50, children £3.50; ⓣ 01983 761587, ⓦ needlespleasurecruises.co.uk) leave from a jetty to the Needles. The same firm also runs high-speed RIB tours (£10; 15min).

Yarmouth and around

Linked to Lymington in the New Forest by car ferry, the appealing little town of **YARMOUTH**, sitting at the mouth of the River Yar, is one of the prettiest arrival points on the island. With its good array of places to eat and drink, it also makes the best base for exploring the unspoilt northwestern tip of the island, which stretches to the ancient capital of **Newtown** and inland to the pretty village of **Calbourne**.

Bordered by the river on one side, the sea to the north and marshland to the east, Yarmouth has remained compact. One of the earliest settlements on the island – settled since at least 991, when it was known as Eremue, or "muddy estuary" – it owes its present grid system to the Normans. Yarmouth also has a Grade II-listed **pier**, England's longest wooden pier still in use.

Yarmouth Castle

Quay St, PO41 0PB • April–Oct Wed–Sun 11am–4pm • £4.90, under-16s £2.90; EH • ⓣ 01983 760678, ⓦ www.english-heritage.org.uk/visit/places/yarmouth-castle

Yarmouth, once the main port on the island, was vulnerable to attack – particularly from the French, who burnt the place down twice. Commissioned by Henry VIII as a protective fort (but only completed in 1574, long after his death), **Yarmouth Castle** was the last and most sophisticated of Henry's coastal defences, and the first to use the innovative arrowhead artillery bastion. Inside, some rooms have re-created life in a sixteenth-century castle, and there's a display on the many wrecks that floundered in the Solent here. There are superb views over the estuary from the battlements.

9

THE YAR ESTUARY AND THE FRESHWATER WAY WALK

There's a lovely four-mile round **walk** from Yarmouth that runs along one side of the River Yar, returning along the other bank. Head south from Bridge Road along the bridleway that runs behind the town car park, and follow the path for a couple of miles, through marshland and woods, looking out for red squirrels en route. Once you hit the road, turn right over the Freshwater Causeway to join the Freshwater Way with All Saints' Church on your right, and the *Red Lion* pub (see p.272) on your left. From here, you follow the Freshwater Way back up the western side of the River Yar through woods and fields to join the coast road that leads back into Yarmouth. If want to extend the walk, you can continue south along the Freshwater Way: to do this, instead of turning right at All Saints' Church, take the signed footpath on your left before you reach the church, just after crossing the stone bridge over the River Yar, the path leading a mile or so down to Freshwater Bay.

ARRIVAL AND INFORMATION — YARMOUTH AND AROUND

By bus Yarmouth is served by bus #7 from Newport (see p.249).

By ferry The ferry from Lymington (see p.246) arrives pretty much in the centre of the town.

Bike rental You can rent bikes, a great way to explore the island, from Wight Cycle Hire, Station Rd, PO41 0QU (T 01983 761800, W wightcyclehire.co.uk; £16/day).

ACCOMMODATION

The Bugle Coaching Inn The Square, PO41 0NS T 01983 760272, W buglecoachinginn.co.uk. Standard en-suite rooms, some looking over the Market Square, plus some smarter suites with four-poster beds and a family room, above a cosy pub in a great location, right in the centre of town. **£70**

The George Hotel Quay St, PO41 0PE T 01983 760331, W thegeorge.co.uk. In a good position right by the ferry dock, with a lovely garden overlooking the Solent, this seventeenth-century hotel has comfortable, elegantly furnished rooms, some with balconies overlooking the water, that have hosted the likes of Charles II. It also has two well-regarded restaurants, the fine-dining *Isla's* and the brasserie-style *Conservatory*. Minimum two-night stay at weekends. **£195**

EATING AND DRINKING

The Blue Crab High St, PO41 0PL T 01983 760014, W thebluecrab.co.uk. A simply decorated restaurant with cosy booths that offers fish and shellfish dishes such as lobster salad (£18). They also do top-quality fresh fish and chips to take away for around £7. 11am–3pm & 6–11pm: Easter–July, Sept & Oct Tues–Sun; Aug daily; Nov–Easter Tues–Sat.

Gossips Café Yarmouth Pier, PO41 0NS T 01983 760646. Cheap and cheerful café serving a huge selection of sandwiches and hot dishes (from around £5), though its main attraction is the superb view of the comings and goings of the boats. Daily 8.45am–5pm; later in summer.

Off the Rails Station Rd, PO41 0QT T 01983 761600, W offtherailsyarmouth.co.uk. In the former station on a disused railway line that is now a popular cycle path, this cosy café has train-style banquettes and a wood-burner inside with tables outside on the platform overlooking the Rive Yar. The food, and prices, are a cut above average, with breakfasts such as smoked salmon and scrambled eggs (£10.50), tasty sandwiches (£8–9) and soup, and more unusual options for dinner such as haggis risotto (£13) or Yarmouth crab penne, plus a selection of burgers (about £15). Wed, Thurs & Sun 9am–5pm, Fri & Sat 9am–10pm.

Salty's Quay St, PO41 0PB T 01938 761550, W saltysrestaurant.co.uk. In a prime location in an old warehouse next to the ferry terminal, with a bar downstairs and a nice restaurant with balcony overlooking the street upstairs. They serve local seafood (bouillabaisse, sea bass) and meat dishes, with main courses around £20. Tues–Thurs 11am–11pm, Fri 11am–11.30pm, Sat 11am–midnight, Sun 11am–6pm, though hours vary so check website: closed Christmas–Easter and Tues in low season.

The Wheatsheaf Bridge Rd, PO41 0PH T 01983 760456, W wheatsheafyarmouth.co.uk. This no-nonsense pub with a pool table and patio garden also serves some of the best-value evening meals in town (mains £9–16), including duck stir-fry, curry of the day, pizzas and a selection of tasty burgers. Mon–Sat 11am–11pm, Sun noon–10.30pm.

Newtown

Belying its history as island capital for 150 years, **NEWTOWN**, around four miles east of Yarmouth, is now little more than a peaceful village on the edge of an estuary. Founded in the thirteenth century by the Bishop of Winchester, the town grew in importance due to its location on a busy harbour that is now a peaceful **nature reserve**, one of the UK's top bird-spotting sites and home to curlews, geese and other waterfowl. The only remains of the town's prestigious past are a trace of its gridded street pattern and an incongruous Jacobean **town hall** (mid-March to mid-Oct Tues–Thurs & Sun 2–5pm; £3.80, children £1.90; NT; ⓣ01983 531785, ⓦnationaltrust.org.uk/newtown-old-town-hall), stranded in the countryside with no town. There are pleasant **walks** in the vicinity, with footpaths leading out along a jetty and over the salt marshes around the nature reserve.

ACCOMMODATION AND EATING — **NEWTOWN**

New Inn Mill Rd, Shalfleet, PO30 4NS ⓣ01983 531314, ⓦthenew-inn.co.uk. A cosy eighteenth-century pub with an inglenook fireplace, low beams and flagstone floors. It's also known for its food, which features locally caught fish and seafood – push the boat out for their Seafood Royale platter (£70 for two). There are also more affordable, good-quality pub dishes, such as the tasty home-made pie of the day (£12). Mon–Thurs & Sun 10am–10.30pm, Fri & Sat 10am–11pm.

The Orchards Holiday Park Main Rd, Newbridge, PO41 0TS ⓣ01983 531331, ⓦorchards-holiday-park.co.uk. This is a good, well-run rural campsite, about a mile inland, with eco-friendly heated showers, indoor and outdoor pools, a café and a shop. **£38**

Calbourne Water Mill

Westover, Calbourne, PO30 4JN • Easter–Oct daily 10am–5pm • £7 • ⓣ01983 531227, ⓦcalbournewatermill.co.uk

Just outside the pretty village of Calbourne, six miles southeast of Yarmouth, **Calbourne Water Mill** is the oldest working water mill on the island. You can see milling demonstrations, but the complex also includes a pottery, a café and an eclectic collection of old machinery. There are some fine woodland walks and boating on the adjacent stream.

ACCOMMODATION — **CALBOURNE WATER MILL**

Acres Westover, Calbourne, PO30 4JN ⓣ01983 531227, ⓦcalbournewatermill.co.uk. Within the mill complex, this small rural campsite has basic facilities; campers have free access to the mill's attractions and café. **£7**

DEER AT ARNE NATURE RESERVE

Contexts

History

Until Oliver Cromwell's rule in 1649, Winchester was one of England's most important cities, and the focal point for significant historical figures such as King Arthur, Alfred the Great and William the Conqueror. At one time it shared equal status with London, and many of the country's major events took place in its hinterland – today's Dorset, Hampshire and Isle of Wight. Below we give a brief account of some of the key events in the country's history, focusing on those that are most significant to this region.

Early settlers

Much of Dorset and Hampshire was inhabited in **Neolithic times** (around 3500 BC) when people first began to farm land and create defensive walls around their settlements. Their distinctive graves – long barrows – consisting of stone-chambered, turf-covered mounds, can be found throughout the area, such as at Hambledon Hill (see p.148), off the Blandford to Shaftesbury road.

Bronze Age settlers from northern Europe (around 2000 BC) also left countless barrows, along with the famous stone circles at Stonehenge in neighbouring Wiltshire, but their earthen forts were unable to withstand the invading **Celts** (around 700–600 BC). The Celts' superior iron weapons, coins and ornaments brought in the Iron Age and they are credited with giving Dorset its name, calling it Dwry Triges, which evolved into Durotriges in Roman times – meaning "tidal waters". Maiden Castle was a typical Celtic stronghold, a multiple system of ramparts enlarging a simpler and older hillfort, though it was one of the first of England's Celtic forts to fall to the next set of invaders, the **Romans**, in 43 AD, the year Claudius led his successful invasion of the country. England flourished under the Romans, who established commerce and a political structure. Winchester, then called Venta Belgarum, became the fifth-largest town in Britain.

The Saxons

From the fourth century, with the decline of the Roman Empire, the **Saxons** began to take over. The southwest of England became a stronghold of Celtic resistance, however, with semi-mythical figures such as **King Arthur** allegedly fighting to keep the invaders at bay. Some claim the wooden disc in Winchester's Great Hall to be Arthur's Round Table, and though it is unlikely to be authentic, it does suggest his activities were in this part of the country. But soon England was divided into Anglo-Saxon kingdoms – this area being the kingdom of **Wessex**. The Anglo-Saxons built stone churches, modelled on those in Rome, with round apses at their eastern end. By 664, England had adopted the **Christian faith** – the Isle of Wight was the last part of the country to be converted, in around 686. By the eighth century, a Saxon port had grown up on the River Itchen

3500 BC	700–600 BC	First century AD	686
Neolithic people begin to farm the region	Celts settle at Maiden Castle near Dorchester	Winchester becomes Britain's fifth-largest town	The Isle of Wight finally succumbs to Christianity – the last place in England to adopt the faith

known as Hamtun – later Southampton – which gave the county the name Hampshire. By 825, with the death of King Offa, Wessex became the dominant Anglo-Saxon kingdom and a fortress was built at Wareham to protect against marauding Vikings – its protective walls, later strengthened by the Normans, can still be seen today.

Vikings and the Norman Conquest

By 865, the **Viking** army had conquered much of England. They soon turned their attentions to **Alfred the Great**'s Wessex but, despite having inferior forces, Alfred stubbornly resisted the attacks, forcing the Vikings to sign a truce, agreeing to fix a border between Wessex and the Danelaw – the Viking territories to the north. Alfred made Winchester his capital, and for the next two centuries, the town was equal to London in importance.

After King Alfred died in 899, his successor, Edward the Elder, continued to build on Alfred's achievements and soon established himself as the de facto ruler of the country. His grandson Edgar's achievement was to gain the allegiance of Scotland and Wales, and Edgar's son, Edward the Martyr, was crowned next. In 978, aged just 16, Edward was murdered at Corfe Castle, it is thought by his stepmother – who was anxious to get her own son, Ethelred the Unready, on the throne. Edward's tomb now lies in Lady St Mary's Church in Wareham.

King Cnut ruled 1016–35, and it is in Southampton that he allegedly commanded the waves to retreat – probably not from a misguided sense of his powers, but as a rebuke to his obsequious courtiers. The king's bones now lie in Winchester Cathedral. By 1042, Edward the Confessor was king, but he allowed power to be wielded by Godwin, Earl of Wessex, and his son Harold. When Edward died, Harold took over, only to be defeated at the Battle of Hastings in 1066, an event that quickly ushered in the Normans.

Norman rule

The **Normans** set about building various castles under **William the Conqueror**, who constructed abbeys and churches in the style of mainland Europe such as the cathedral in

THE JURASSIC ERA

Dorset's Jurassic Coast is over 200 million years old, and has been much eroded by the sea, leaving it one of the best places in the country for finding fossils, especially around **Lyme Regis** and **Charmouth**. The **Isle of Wight**, too, shares the Jurassic Coast's geology, and over twenty species of dinosaur have been identified on the island: many of their bones can be seen in Dinosaur Isle in Sandown (see p.263).

Much of Dorset is made up of the hard Portland and Purbeck stone, which formed in Jurassic times when the Purbeck sea was shallow and warm. **Portland stone** has been quarried since Roman times, and has been used in such iconic buildings as St Paul's Cathedral and the Bank of England. The dramatic Portland headland is still heavily quarried today, with former disused quarries and spectacular cliffs making it ideal for climbers, while you can also visit the atmospheric, disused **Purbeck stone** mines around Tilly Whim Caves, Dancing Ledge and Winspit, which supplied the stone for Lulworth and Durlston castles.

825	827	978	1087
Wessex, including Dorset and Hampshire, becomes Britain's dominant kingdom	Egbert, the first king of all England, is crowned at Winchester	Edward the Martyr is murdered at Corfe Castle by his stepmother	William Rufus is shot by a crossbow while hunting in the New Forest

ENGLAND'S FIRST GRAND DESIGN

One result of the Hundred Years' War was the development of the **Perpendicular** style of architecture, which was characterized by a rectilinear design to draw your gaze upwards, towards God. It was the first major architectural genre unique to England – before the Hundred Years' War, the predominant design was Gothic, which was copied from the French. One of the main driving forces behind the Perpendicular style was master mason **William Wynford**, who was responsible for the chantry tombs in **Winchester Cathedral**, a fine example of the genre.

Winchester (begun in 1079), with its cruciform ground plans and huge cylindrical columns topped by semicircular arches. Appropriately, William the Conqueror's double coronation took place in both London and Winchester. William also used Winchester's monks to prepare the **Domesday Book** (1085–86), which recorded land ownership and the population of the country for the first time, providing the framework for taxation and feudal obligations. In 1079, William requisitioned the **New Forest** as his own private game reserve. It was the Normans, too, who gave the Isle of Wight its first ever lord, William Fitz Osbern, in 1066, though actually he ruled very little – the Domesday Book records that at this time the island had just 126 properties, 24 water mills and 10 churches.

In 1087, William the Conqueror's son, **William Rufus**, became king, but was shot by an arrow while hunting in the New Forest at a spot now marked by the Rufus Stone (see p.180). There are plenty of theories surrounding his death – although officially it was a hunting accident, he was such an unpopular king that murder is a perfectly feasible explanation. His mortuary chest lies in Winchester Cathedral alongside the remains of England's early leaders. In 1100, William Rufus' successor, Henry I, gave the Isle of Wight to Richard de Redvers, who founded Newport in 1118. In 1292, the Isle of Wight became Crown property and the island's defences were improved.

The Hundred Years' War

In 1337, the **Hundred Years' War** with France began, with the French sacking Portsmouth and attempting to invade St Helens on the Isle of Wight. Six years later, King Edward III set sail from St Helens to invade Normandy, but the French returned later that century to attack Carisbrooke Castle and ransack Newport.

As frontline ports, Portsmouth and Southampton suffered numerous French attacks but were also the bases from which the English launched counteroffensives across the Channel. Henry V's famous victory against the French at **Agincourt** began when his troops departed from Southampton, and largely secured the safety of the Isle of Wight.

The Tudors

The start of the **Tudor period** in the fifteenth century saw England begin to develop as a major European power. With England's overseas expansion, Portsmouth was made the royal dockyard in 1495 and the world's first dry docks were built here.

Under Henry VIII, the English Church was forced to secede from the Roman Catholic Church and instead recognize the king as Supreme Head of the Church of England, which was followed by the **Dissolution of the Monasteries**. This allowed the

1495	**1594**	**1620**	**1640s**
Portsmouth is made Royal Dockyard and home to the world's first dry docks	Sir Walter Raleigh retires to Sherborne Castle to smoke and to eat potatoes, after a stint in the Tower of London	The Pilgrim Fathers set sail in the *Mayflower* for the New World from Southampton, stopping to fix a leak in Plymouth	Cromwell's thugs riot in the streets of Winchester, destroying both its castle and Corfe Castle

king and his nobles to take over monastic property, including the enormous estate of Beaulieu (see p.168), formerly one of England's most influential monasteries, and St Peter's monastery, now part of the Abbotsbury estate (see p.122).

When **Elizabeth I** became queen in 1558, England was divided on religious grounds, following the reign of her predecessor – her Catholic half-sister, Mary. Though threatened by Spain under the powerful Philip II, Elizabeth (a Protestant herself) governed wisely, steering a more conciliatory path on religion and allowing the merchant classes to flourish. Seafarers also were successful, with the likes of Walter Raleigh, who had long lived in Dorset (see box, p.103), prospering from his raids on Spain's American colonies. Eventually, Philip II sent his Armada to attack in 1588, but after it was defeated, England became a major **maritime power**.

The early Stuarts and Cromwell

Though a Catholic was in power again in the early 1600s – James I – for those ardent believers who had suffered under previous reigns, the Stuart king didn't do enough for their cause, nor attempt to satisfy their demands. A small group, including a young and fervent **Guy Fawkes**, decided that enough was enough and conceived a plan to blow up Parliament in the **Gunpowder Plot** of 1605.

Life under James I was tricky for many Protestants, too: some turned to Puritanism and looked to move away from their turbulent island, keen to establish a "New Jerusalem" in North America. In 1620, the **Pilgrim Fathers** set sail from Southampton to establish a colony in New England, but their boat began to leak so they stopped at Plymouth before continuing in the *Mayflower* – a journey that would encourage thousands of Puritan emigrants to follow over the next few decades.

In 1645, **Oliver Cromwell**'s Roundhead troops effectively ended Winchester's position as a major player in English politics during the English Civil War, largely destroying its castle (now the Great Hall), breaking up the mortuary chests of previous kings and smashing the stained glass in the cathedral. Cromwell's troops were even more destructive in their siege of Corfe Castle, which lasted for six weeks thanks to the steadfastness of Lady Bankes (see p.69), before the Roundheads finally achieved victory, blowing the castle into its current ruinous state. In 1647, Charles I fled to Nunwell House on the Isle of Wight, but he was soon captured and executed in London two years later.

The Restoration and the Hanoverians

In 1685, another Catholic, James II, became king. The Protestant Duke of Monmouth, an illegitimate son of James' brother, Charles II, raised a rebellion, landing at Lyme Regis in an attempt to overthrow James, but he failed and was beheaded. His followers were brutally dealt with by Judge George Jeffreys' **Bloody Assizes** in Dorchester, where the rebels were tried before a series of executions took place throughout the area – eighty were put to death in Dorchester, twelve in Lyme Regis and Weymouth and several others in Sherborne, Poole, Bridport and Wareham.

A certain stability was restored to the region under **Hanoverian** King George I, who came to the throne in 1714, when England's first de facto prime minister, Robert Walpole, governed over a brief period of growth. The wealthy spent huge sums of

1647	1685	1789
Charles I flees to Nunwell House on the Isle of Wight, but is found and later executed in London	Judge Jeffreys' "Bloody Assizes" imposes its merciless rule on Dorset, sentencing nearly 300 men to death	Mad King George discovers the joys of Weymouth, drinking sea water and eating earwigs there for the good of his health

CAPABILITY BROWN

"Capability" Brown (1716–83) – real name the only slightly more prosaic Lancelot Brown – was so-called because he assessed the "capabilities of landscapes". He modified the estates of the gentry into ornate landscapes, complete with romantic ruins or pagodas, a scale and natural style of gardening unprecedented at the time. His work was hugely popular among the contemporary nobility, and his garden designs and influence can still can be seen throughout the country – most especially, in this region, at **Appuldurcombe House** on the Isle of Wight, as well as at **Sherborne** and **Highcliffe castles** and **Milton Abbas**, among others.

money on lavish buildings and their grounds, employing the likes of "Capability" Brown (see box above) to landscape them, and many of the region's grand country houses date from this period.

Napoleon and Nelson

Under George III, England was engaged in the American War of Independence and, busying itself with affairs across the pond, neglected France's woes over the Channel. In the bloody aftermath of the Revolution, **Napoleon Bonaparte** rose to fame but his military progress was interrupted by Nelson's victory at the **Battle of Trafalgar** in 1805 – you can see his victorious ship (and ultimate deathbed) HMS *Victory* in Portsmouth (see p.253). Napoleon was finally defeated at Waterloo a decade later by the first **Duke of Wellington** – who lived in Hampshire's Stratfield Saye House, which has been home to the Dukes of Wellington since 1817, and still contains the original Duke's funeral carriage.

The Industrial Revolution and Victorian times

The late eighteenth century ushered in the **Industrial Revolution**, which accelerated after James Watt patented the steam engine in 1781. As industry flourished, so did the population, with towns and cities expanding rapidly. Much of rural England, however, was bypassed by the new technologies – Dorset was largely owned by just three major landowners, who refused to let train lines be built on their estates, leaving the county isolated and the people impoverished. The suffering of the rural poor inspired the pastoral yearnings of the **Romantic writers** such as Keats, who wrote many of his poems on the Isle of Wight, and Percy Bysshe Shelley, who was buried in Bournemouth (see p.43). Later, Thomas Hardy's novels traced the changing lifestyles of "Wessex" (see p.97), most notably in *The Mayor of Casterbridge*.

The great architect of the time was **John Nash** (1752–1835), who is associated with the Regency period of the Prince of Wales (later George IV). His stucco and decorous styles are evident today throughout Weymouth and at East Cowes Castle, Whippingham Church and Ryde Town Hall on the Isle of Wight. Under George IV, workers' associations were legalized and a civil police force was created. This, however, did not stop the **Tolpuddle Martyrs** from being transported to Australia for founding an agricultural trade union in 1834 (see p.98). Poverty and injustice became the key political battlegrounds under **Queen Victoria**, a theme picked up in the novels of **Charles Dickens**, who grew up in Portsmouth (see p.236). This was also the age of the railway,

1805	**1834**	**1872–95**	**1901**
Nelson sets sail from Portsmouth for the Battle of Trafalgar in his ship HMS *Victory* – and is victorious	The Tolpuddle Martyrs found England's first agricultural trade union	Thomas Hardy chronicles the harsh life of Dorset's rural underclass	Queen Victoria dies in her favourite home, Osborne House on the Isle of Wight, where she spent most of her holidays

with rail services opening up many of the south coast's resorts such as Bournemouth and the Isle of Wight to tourists – and royalty, with Victoria frequently holidaying at her family home at Osborne House (see p.251).

The twentieth century

In common with much of the country, World War I decimated the young male adult population throughout the region, though the area itself played a larger part in **World War II.** Several places were requisitioned in the war – Blandford Camp, employed for training in World War I, was again put to use as a US hospital after the Normandy landings in 1944, while the whole village of Tyneham and its surroundings were evacuated so it could be utilized for army training – the land around Tyneham belongs to the army to this day and the village stands eerily deserted (see p.80). US troops were based at Bridport and Poole, while Studland was used for tank training exercises – famously viewed by Churchill, George VI and Eisenhower. **D-day landing** troops set off from several ports along the coast, including Portsmouth, Southampton, Poole and Weymouth, to Omaha beach in France, while in 1943, the Fleet Lagoon near Portland was used to test Barnes Wallis's famous Bouncing Bomb, as depicted in *The Dam Busters.* The German Luftwaffe caused massive destruction, damaging or destroying one in three properties in the three counties, with the ports of Portsmouth and particularly Southampton severely blitzed. Postwar, there was an extensive rebuilding programme with an emphasis on office buildings and shopping centres to serve the hurriedly erected tower blocks and cheap housing – resulting in the bland cityscape of Southampton. Ironically, however, the land taken over by the army since the war has left much of the Isle of Purbeck wonderfully undeveloped – this area has escaped the explosion of bungalows and retirement homes that now blights much of the south coast.

The twenty-first century

With **tourism** such an important source of revenue throughout the region, large areas have received protection from future development thanks to the awarding of World Heritage status to the Jurassic Coast in 2001, plus the creation of the New Forest National Park in 2005 and South Downs National Park in 2010. The new millennium has also seen huge **investment** in the revitalization of Southampton, with its new cultural quarter, and Portsmouth's old dockland area, where the successful Gunwharf Quays complex goes from strength to strength. Weymouth's hosting of the sailing events in the 2012 Olympics led to improved roads and infrastructure for the town and the previously depressed Isle of Portland. Bournemouth, too, invested in the creation of Europe's first artificial surf reef in 2009 (see p.43) which, although ultimately unsuccessful, led to the **regeneration** of the previously rather run-down suburb of Boscombe. Bournemouth has also become a growing centre for the **digital economy**, and in 2015 it was declared the UK's fastest-growing area for tech start-ups over the past few years.

Ironically, however, it was the country's economic crisis that led to the real resurgence of tourism in the area. With people looking to cheaper, simpler holidays, the joys of camping (and glamping, for those wanting extra comfort), cycling and traditional British beach resorts less than three hours' drive from the capital are increasingly appealing.

1943–44	**2005**	**2012**	**2016**
The beach at Studland is used for World War II tank exercises	The New Forest National Park is created, followed by the South Downs National Park in 2010	Weymouth and Portland host Olympic sailing events	South Downs National Park becomes England's second Dark Sky Reserve, an area valued for being free of light pollution

Wildlife

The counties of Dorset, Hampshire and the Isle of Wight cover a relatively small area but offer an extremely varied range of natural habitats, including deciduous woodland, tidal estuaries and jagged coastal cliffs. Chalk ridges make up the Dorset and South Downs, Cranborne Chase, the Purbeck hills, and Tennyson Down on the Isle of Wight, while clay is the dominant soil in the Frome and Stour valleys and the Hampshire basin. The New Forest and the area around Bournemouth consist largely of heathlands that survive on shallow sand, clay and gravel. Much of the coast is made up of hard Portland and Purbeck stone, which causes the spectacular sheer cliffs, while other sections of the coast – such as around Old Harry – are made of soft chalk.

The Solent – once a river before sea levels rose, separating the Isle of Wight from the mainland some seven thousand years ago – itself creates a unique habitat thanks to its unusual double tides (caused by the irregular depth of the channel between Cherbourg and the Isle of Wight, which gives additional tidal oscillation), while warm currents feed much of the Dorset coast, encouraging occasionally exotic foreign visitors to its waters.

Mammals

In common with much of England, mammals such as foxes, hedgehogs, badgers, roe deer, stoats and weasels are relatively common in this part of the country. The Isle of Purbeck has large colonies of various types of **deer**, many of which thrive on Ministry of Defence land, which – the odd rocket aside – provides a safe haven for local wildlife. Sika deer in particular thrive on Purbeck, to the extent that they are creating a certain amount of damage to the protected wetlands at Arne. These deer – native to Japan – escaped from captivity in the nineteenth century and have been breeding here ever since. The New Forest, too, has a healthy deer population, though is best known for its **ponies**. These are not wild but belong to commoners, as do the pigs let loose to feed on acorns in autumn (see p.164). Grey squirrels, hailing from America, can be seen pretty much anywhere. These aggressive incomers have driven out the native **red squirrel** from most of England; however, the Isle of Wight and Brownsea Island have resisted the grey invasion and on both islands red squirrels thrive.

The area's rivers – mostly extremely clean – support a good array of mammals including **otters** and water voles, though the latter are threatened by the introduced American mink.

The Isle of Wight and parts of southern Dorset and Hampshire are home to the very rare Bechstein's **bat**, which likes dense woodland and can reach twenty years of age. Even rarer is the greater horseshoe bat, which can live up to thirty years; there are around two hundred breeding females in Dorset, where they are being encouraged to reproduce in some of the former stone quarries around Purbeck. The Greywell Tunnel on the Basingstoke Canal is Britain's largest bat roost, with all the country's native species living here.

Insects, amphibians and reptiles

Hampshire and Purbeck's chalky terrain provides a ready habitat for some beautiful and unusual **butterflies**, including the Lulworth skipper – Purbeck is the only place where it flourishes – and the chalkhill blue, while the scarce Glanville fritillary butterfly can be seen on the Isle of Wight. Durlston Head is also home to dingy and grizzled skippers, chalkhill and small blue butterflies. The heath **grasshopper** can only be found in Dorset and the New Forest, while Dorset's heathlands also support endangered reptiles such as the **smooth snake** and **sand lizard**. Rare **natterjack toads** can be found in some coastal dune areas such as on Hengistbury Head. Prevalent throughout the regions are the harmless **grass snake** and the mildly venomous **adder**, often found basking on warm rocks in sunny weather. They are brown with a lozenge pattern down their back – they will flee if they sense you coming and only attack if they feel threatened. In the unlikely event that you are bitten, seek medical attention at once. Other summer nuisances are **mosquitoes** – anywhere near damp ground will see them flourish, while care should also be taken with **ticks**, which lurk in bracken.

Birds

The south of England is a rich habitat for a diverse range of birds including giant **buzzards** – usually seen swooping in pairs, often above the warm thermals created by hot tarmac roads in summer – kites, kestrels, nightjars and kingfishers. Dorset's heathlands support rare birds such as the Dartford warbler, while the increasingly endangered **skylark** is thankfully still present on coastal grasslands such as on Hengistbury Head (Dorset) and Tennyson Down (Isle of Wight).

The cliff ledges west of Portland Bill are home to some of the largest **sea-bird colonies** on the south coast and you can usually see guillemots, razorbills and kittiwakes. Similar bird colonies can be seen on the cliffs around Durlston in Purbeck, which also support the manx shearwater, European storm petrel, pomarine skua, little tern, puffins, common guillemot and ring-necked parakeet.

There are also some great **wetland areas** for very different birds. Particularly good for bird spotting are the marshy wetlands around Lymington, Stanpit (Christchurch) and Arne (near Wareham), where you can see species such as marsh and hen harriers, peregrine falcons, lesser spotted woodpeckers and waders such as the avocet, little egret, whimbrel, sandwich tern, spoonbill and heron. The Fleet Lagoon by Chesil Beach, though, is *the* spot for birdwatchers, attracting thousands of summer and winter migrant birds as well as being home to England's largest population of mute swans (see p.122).

Marine life

The Swanage coast supports a diverse array of peripatetic sea life including **dolphins**, **porpoises**, the odd whale and occasionally giant leatherback turtles, which can be over 2m in length and drift along a migration route from their tropical breeding grounds usually in late summer, often on the trail of **jellyfish**. The latter can provide an occasional hazard, especially when the venomous (but thankfully rare) Portuguese man-of-war drift into UK waters. Stings are extremely painful for up to three days. Also to be avoided is the weever fish, which lurks in the sands of shallow tidal waters. If you tread on the spines of their venomous dorsal fins, it can be excruciating – the best treatment is to immerse the affected part in water as hot as you can bear for around twenty minutes. Another exotic but harmless marine lifeform native to these shores is the spiny **sea horse**, which is relatively common around Shell Bay – Britain's largest colony of the beautiful creatures lives off South Beach, though they are increasingly threatened by boats anchoring on their breeding grounds. Environmentalists have been campaigning to have the bay declared a Marine Conservation Zone to protect the sea horses.

The clear waters of the rivers Test, Itchen and Avon are world famous for their **fish**, especially for trout and salmon. The tidal areas, meanwhile, are rich in shellfish including crayfish, oysters, lobster and crab – a fact enjoyed by many of the pubs and restaurants around the Fleet Lagoon and the Isle of Wight, which regularly serve fresh seafood.

Books

We have highlighted a selection of books below that will give you a flavour of the area, or which were influenced by the region. Books marked ★ are particularly recommended.

FICTION

Richard Adams *Watership Down*. This classic children's story tells the tale of rabbits forced to move from Sandleford Warren in Berkshire to Watership Down in Hampshire – the locations are all based on the area where Adams grew up, south of Newbury.

★Jane Austen *Pride and Prejudice*. The classic tale of love, intrigue and misunderstanding, partly set in "Meryton", based on Basingstoke. Austen's *Persuasion*, set partly in Lyme Regis, is the tale of Anne Elliot's growing self-awareness of love and self-interest. Will she be persuaded to marry for money, or opt for the first love of her life, the once socially inferior Captain Wentworth?

Julian Barnes *England, England*. Barnes uses the Isle of Wight as the location for a witty novel about duplicating tourist sights at a theme park containing copies of, among others, Big Ben, Stonehenge and Princess Diana's grave.

Enid Blyton *Five on Kirrin Island Again, Five Have a Mystery to Solve, Five go to Mystery Moor*. Enid Blyton set many of her classic *Famous Five* children's stories in and around Purbeck (see p.70); Kirrin Island is based on Corfe Castle, while Mystery Moor is based on the area around Stoborough. Wonderfully dated, the books about the adventures of four children and their dog nevertheless are still hugely popular with children today, their plots regularly recycled in cartoons such as *Scooby-Doo*.

Tracy Chevalier *Remarkable Creatures*. A readable romp set in Lyme Regis, this fictionalized account is based on the story of Mary Anning, her discovery of the ichthyosaur and her friendship with Elizabeth Philpot.

Arthur Conan Doyle *The White Company*. Best known for his Sherlock Holmes stories, Doyle also wrote this well-received historical novel about the Hundred Years' War. It relates the tale of a couple of monks – the headstrong Hordle John and the brave Alleyne Edricson – who leave the sanctuary of the monastery in Beaulieu to join The White Company, a team of archers who set off for the war in France.

★John Meade Falkner *Moonfleet*. The late Victorian novelist and poet lived for a time in Weymouth. His most famous work is a gripping tale of an orphan who unwittingly becomes involved in smuggling, with the action taking place around Chesil Beach, Portland Bill (which he calls The Snout) and Purbeck.

★John Fowles *The French Lieutenant's Woman*. Fowles, a keen fan of Thomas Hardy, wrote this classic tale in 1969 and it was later made into a successful film starring Meryl Streep. Set in Lyme Regis, it relates the tale of the mysterious Sarah Woodruff, a manipulated or manipulating woman – the book is given three alternative endings to help you decide.

Thomas Hardy *Under the Greenwood Tree, The Mayor of Casterbridge, Tess of the D'Urbervilles, The Return of the Native, Far from the Madding Crowd*. All of Hardy's novels depict the harsh conditions of rural life in nineteenth-century Dorset. *Under the Greenwood Tree*, based on his childhood experiences near Dorchester, is perhaps the most cheerful, telling the tale of church musician Dick Dewy's awkward wooing of a new, beautiful school teacher, Fancy Day. His other novels all describe places recognizable today (see box, p.92). ★ *The Mayor of Casterbridge* traces the rise and fall of Mayor Michael Henchard in a fast-changing society, who seems forever cursed by his decision to auction his wife. *Tess of the D'Urbervilles* is perhaps his most famous novel: a bleak tragedy, it relates the tale of Tess, a poor girl who tries to better her lot by seeking out the wealthy D'Urbervilles who she believes are distantly related. Alec D'Urberville takes a shine to Tess, which eventually brings about Tess's tragic end in Wintoncester prison – based on Winchester.

P.D. James *The Black Tower*. Scotland Yard's Adam Dalgliesh, recuperating in Dorset after an illness, finds himself caught up in a murder mystery in which the tower – influenced by Clavell Tower in Kimmeridge Bay – plays a key part.

Ian McEwan *On Chesil Beach*. Virtually a short story and not perhaps his greatest book, but a highly evocative account of a newly married couple's disastrous sexual experience while honeymooning on Dorset's famous pebble beach.

Edward Rutherford *The Forest*. A detailed and comprehensive, if rather lengthy, history of the New Forest, from the death of William Rufus to the twentieth century, told through the adventures of fictional and real characters.

Alfred, Lord Tennyson *The Complete Works*. The works of the great Victorian Poet Laureate – who coined expressions such as "*Tis better to have loved and lost, Than never to have loved at all*" – include many poems composed while strolling on the eastern extremities of the Isle of Wight, now named Tennyson Down. His best-known works are *The Lady of Shalott* and *The Charge of the Light Brigade*.

Damien Wilkings *Max Gate*. An interesting, well-written tale about the last days of Thomas Hardy and the wranglings leading up to his burial, as told from the viewpoint of his maid Nellie Titterington.

Virgina Woolf *Freshwater*. This was Virginia Woolf's only play, a comedy of manners set in Freshwater on the Isle of Wight and centring on the excesses of Alfred, Lord Tennyson and Woolf's great aunt, the pioneering photographer Julia Margaret Cameron. It was resurrected on Broadway in New York a few years ago.

HISTORY AND BACKGROUND

Bill Bryson *Notes From a Small Island.* American writer and anglophile Bryson's tour of Britain, mostly using public transport, includes his wry account of Bournemouth and much of the south coast. It and its follow-up – *The Road to Little Dribbling*, written twenty years later – are both witty and enlightening to Americans and Britons alike.

Mike Clement and Ted Gosling *Dorset Railways*. A photograph-based look at the steam trains and stations that once dotted the county, many of them now defunct.

John Leete *In Time of War: Hampshire*. A vivid account of the extraordinary activity that took place in Hampshire during World War II, including photographs and first-hand accounts.

Richard Ollard *Dorset*. A fascinating round-up of the county's history, culture, folklore and buildings by a renowned historian.

Nikolaus Pevsner and John Newman/David Lloyd *The Buildings of England: Dorset/Hampshire and the Isle of Wight.* Part of a series covering facts about virtually every building of note in the country. Though not updated for many years, the books' background information is still relevant today.

Nicola Sly *Dorset Murders/Hampshire Murders*. A look back in time at various evil deeds committed in the two counties, including unsolved mysteries and the real-life murder that inspired Thomas Hardy's *Tess of the D'Urbervilles*.

Claire Tomalin *The Time-Torn Man.* Biographer Tomalin turns her skilled and insightful gaze onto the life of Thomas Hardy. Starting with the death of his wife Emma, she examines his troubled first marriage, the influences of his childhood, and his eventual contentment with his second wife Florence.

Peta Whaley *West Country History: Dorset*. A comprehensive account of key moments and figures in the history of the county, by a Shaftesbury-based author.

NATURE GUIDES

Martin Cade and George Green *Where to Watch Birds in Dorset, Hampshire and the Isle of Wight*. A comprehensive guide to the best sites for birdwatching throughout the year, including places with disabled access.

Dorset Wildlife Trust *The Natural History of Dorset.* Slightly dated but comprehensive round-up of the county's natural history, including detailed illustrations and photographs.

Barry Goater *The Butterflies and Moths of Hampshire and the Isle of Wight.* A scholarly look at the rich diversity of these insects, which flourish in this part of the country.

Gilbert White *The Natural History of Selborne*. This eighteenth-century account of the area's flora and fauna was written by a man who preceded Darwin by a century but who made many of the same observations. It also includes letters to explorers and fellow naturalists.

WALKS AND OUTDOOR PURSUITS

AA *50 Walks in Dorset/50 Walks in Hampshire and the Isle of Wight*. A good range of walks with interesting introductions to each, though the maps are somewhat sketchy and not all routes are easy to follow.

Collins *Short Walks in Dorset*. Details of twenty walks of five miles or under with good OS maps and attractive photos.

David Foster (ed) *Pathfinder Hampshire*. Details of walks of varying lengths throughout the region, including the New Forest and South Downs National Parks.

Mike Power and John Roland Quarendon *More Pub Walks in Dorset*. Manageable walks for those who like a pint or two at the end of a ramble. The maps are a bit sketchy so you'll need an OS map to help with some of them. Last updated in 2009, but the walks still hold good for the main part.

Martin Simon *Walk! The Isle of Wight*. Excellent, detailed descriptions of forty walks, most with public transport access, throughout the island.

Ben Searle *New Forest Cycling Guide*. A waterproof map showing a selection of the best rides in the southern half of the New Forest.

Daniel Start and Lucy Grewcock *Wild Guide Southern and Eastern England*. Where to go for "wild" weekends, including wild swimming and camping spots and walks to lost ruins, with sections on the New Forest and the Isle of Wight.

Roland Tarr *South West Coast Path: Exmouth to Poole*. The most comprehensive guide to the section of the South West Coast Path that passes through the Jurassic Coast and Dorset.

Robert Wood *Walks into History: Hampshire*. Sixteen circular walks in and around places such as Winchester, Southsea Castle and the New Forest, though not updated for several years.

Small print and index

A ROUGH GUIDE TO ROUGH GUIDES

Published in 1982, the first Rough Guide – to Greece – was a student scheme that became a publishing phenomenon. Mark Ellingham, a recent graduate in English from Bristol University, had been travelling in Greece the previous summer and couldn't find the right guidebook. With a small group of friends he wrote his own guide, combining a contemporary, journalistic style with a thoroughly practical approach to travellers' needs.

The immediate success of the book spawned a series that rapidly covered dozens of destinations. And, in addition to impecunious backpackers, Rough Guides soon acquired a much broader readership that relished the guides' wit and inquisitiveness as much as their enthusiastic, critical approach and value-for-money ethos. These days, Rough Guides include recommendations from budget to luxury and cover more than 120 destinations around the globe, from Amsterdam to Zanzibar, all regularly updated by our team of roaming writers.

Visit **roughguides.com** to find all our latest books, read articles and get inspired.

Rough Guide credits

Editor: Rebecca Hallett
Layout: Nikhil Agarwal
Cartography: Ashutosh Bharti
Picture editor: Michelle Bhatia
Proofreader: Jan McCann
Managing editor: Natasha Foges
Assistant editor: Divya Grace Mathew
Production: Jimmy Lao
Cover photo research: Sarah Stewart-Richardson
Editorial assistant: Freya Godfrey
Indexer: Helen Peters
Senior DTP coordinator: Dan May
Programme manager: Gareth Lowe
Publishing director: Georgina Dee

Publishing information

This third edition published January 2017 by
Rough Guides Ltd,
80 Strand, London WC2R 0RL
11, Community Centre, Panchsheel Park,
New Delhi 110017, India
Distributed by Penguin Random House
Penguin Books Ltd, 80 Strand, London WC2R 0RL
Penguin Group (USA), 345 Hudson Street, NY 10014, USA
Penguin Group (Australia), 250 Camberwell Road, Camberwell, Victoria 3124, Australia
Penguin Group (NZ), 67 Apollo Drive, Mairangi Bay, Auckland 1310, New Zealand
Penguin Group (South Africa), Block D, Rosebank Office Park, 181 Jan Smuts Avenue, Parktown North, Gauteng, South Africa 2193
Rough Guides is represented in Canada by DK Canada, 320 Front Street West, Suite 1400, Toronto, Ontario M5V 3B6
Printed in Singapore

296pp includes index
A catalogue record for this book is available from the British Library
ISBN: 978-0-24125-393-9

1 3 5 7 9 8 6 4 2

Help us update

We've gone to a lot of effort to ensure that the third edition of **The Rough Guide to Dorset, Hampshire and the Isle of Wight** is accurate and up-to-date. However, things change – places get "discovered", opening hours are notoriously fickle, restaurants and rooms raise prices or lower standards. If you feel we've got it wrong or left something out, we'd like to know, and if you can remember the address, the price, the hours, the phone number, so much the better.

Please send your comments with the subject line "**Rough Guide Dorset, Hampshire and the Isle of Wight Update**" to mail@uk.roughguides.com. We'll credit all contributions and send a copy of the next edition (or any other Rough Guide if you prefer) for the very best emails.

Find travel information, read inspiring features and book your trip at roughguides.com.

ABOUT THE AUTHORS

Matthew Hancock is a freelance journalist and editor based in Bournemouth and spends most weekends cycling round the Dorset coast and the New Forest. He is also author of the Rough Guides to Lisbon, Algarve and Madeira and co-author of the *Rough Guide to Portugal*.

Amanda Tomlin grew up on the northern Hampshire borders and has worked for Rough Guides since the 1990s. She now lives in Dorset and spends her spare time walking the local countryside with her two children and her dog.

Acknowledgements

Thanks to everyone who helped with our research, especially Sue Emerson at the Isle of Wight tourist office, Wightlink ferries, David Tucker, Camilla Colley and *The Alexandra*, Charles Lotter at *Summer Lodge*, the *Leconfield*, the Bournemouth *Hilton* and the members of the Gentleman's Cycling Club of Southbourne. Huge thanks to Elise Barton for her invaluable inside info on Portland, and to Alex and Olivia Hancock-Tomlin for their help and support. Also thanks to everyone at Rough Guides, especially Rebecca Hallett for her dedicated editing, and Ashutosh for the new maps.

Readers' updates

Thanks to all the readers who have taken the time to write in with comments and suggestions (and apologies if we've inadvertently omitted or misspelt anyone's name):

Mary Birch, Georgina Chapman, Ann Hirst, Jo Hudson-Cook, Alice Lowe, Jessica Lowther, Marilyn Meaker, Dave Moon, Jan Voisey.

Photo credits

All photos © Rough Guides, except the following:
(Key: t-top; c-centre; b-bottom; l-left; r-right)

1 AWL Images: Mark Hannaford
2 AWL Images: Alan Copson
7 Getty Images: Julian Elliott (t)
9 Alamy Stock Photo: Dom Greves (t); Ken Leslie (c)
10 Getty Images: Chris Hepburn
11 Alamy Stock Photo: Martin Bennett (c); Extremevisuals (t). **Corbis:** Adam Burton (b)
12 Alamy Stock Photo: Banana Pancake (t). **Getty Images:** Danita Delimont (b)
13 Alamy Stock Photo: Jeff Gilbert (b). **Corbis:** Michael Jenner (t)
14 Alamy Stock Photo: M Stansfast (t). **Getty Images:** Travel Ink (b)
15 Alamy Stock Photo: amc (b). **Dreamstime.com:** Acceleratorhams (t). Square and Compass (cl)
34 Alamy Stock Photo: Ian Badley
63 Dreamstime.com: Ian Woolcock
87 Corbis: Latitude
95 Alamy Stock Photo: Graham Hunt (b)
109 Alamy Stock Photo: Ian Dagnall
123 4Corners: SIME/Alessandra Albanese
139 Getty Images: Peter Lewis
147 Corbis: Julian Elliott (b)
158 Alamy Stock Photo: Robin Weaver
161 Alamy Stock Photo: Geoff A Howard
177 Corbis: Adam Burton (t)
190 Alamy Stock Photo: Simon Tranter Photography
193 Alamy Stock Photo: Lebrecht Music and Arts Photo Library
205 Corbis: John Miller (b)
214 Alamy Stock Photo: VIEW Pictures Ltd
229 Alamy Stock Photo: Gregory Davies (t). **Corbis:** Edmund Sumner (b)
247 Alamy Stock Photo: Patrick Eden
257 Corbis: Leo Mason

Front cover, spine and back: *Swanage beach huts*
4Corners: Jordan Banks

Index

Maps are marked in **grey**

E

F

G

H

I

J

K

Q

R

S

Map symbols

The symbols below are used on maps throughout the book

Listings key

- Accommodation
- Eating
- Drinking/nightlife

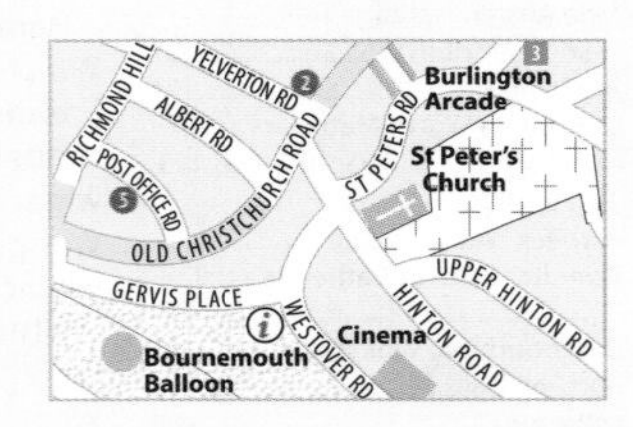